ILLUSIONS OF CONTROL

COLUMBIA STUDIES IN TERRORISM
AND IRREGULAR WARFARE

COLUMBIA STUDIES IN TERRORISM AND IRREGULAR WARFARE

Bruce Hoffman, Series Editor

This series seeks to fill a conspicuous gap in the burgeoning literature on terrorism, guerrilla warfare, and insurgency. The series adheres to the highest standards of scholarship and discourse and publishes books that elucidate the strategy, operations, means, motivations, and effects posed by terrorist, guerrilla, and insurgent organizations and movements. It thereby provides a solid and increasingly expanding foundation of knowledge on these subjects for students, established scholars, and informed reading audiences alike.

Andreas E. Feldmann, *Repertoires of Terrorism: Organizational Identity and Violence in Colombia's Civil War*

John Horgan, *Terrorist Minds: The Psychology of Violent Extremism from Al-Qaeda to the Far Right*

Harrison Akins, *The Terrorism Trap: The War on Terror Inside America's Partner States*

Rita Katz, *Saints and Soldiers: Inside Internet-Age Terrorism, From Syria to the Capitol Siege*

Tricia L. Bacon and Elizabeth Grimm, *Terror in Transition: Leadership and Succession in Terrorist Organizations*

Daveed Gartenstein-Ross and Thomas Joscelyn, *Enemies Near and Far: How Jihadist Groups Strategize, Plot, and Learn*

Boaz Ganor, *Israel's Counterterrorism Strategy: Origins to the Present*

Joseph M. Brown, *Force of Words: The Logic of Terrorist Threats*

Arie Perliger, *American Zealots: Inside Right-Wing Domestic Terrorism*

Erin M. Kearns and Joseph K. Young, *Tortured Logic: Why Some Americans Support the Use of Torture in Counterterrorism*

Lorenzo Vidino, *The Closed Circle: Joining and Leaving the Muslim Brotherhood in the West*

Aaron Y. Zelin, *Your Sons Are at Your Service: Tunisia's Missionaries of Jihad*

Mariya Y. Omelicheva and Lawrence P. Markowitz, *Webs of Corruption: Trafficking and Terrorism in Central Asia*

Bryan C. Price, *Targeting Top Terrorists: Understanding Leadership Removal in Counterterrorism Strategy*

Wendy Pearlman and Boaz Atzili, *Triadic Coercion: Israel's Targeting of States That Host Nonstate Actors*

For a complete list of books in the series, please see the Columbia University Press website.

ILLUSIONS OF CONTROL

DILEMMAS IN MANAGING
U.S. PROXY FORCES
in
AFGHANISTAN, IRAQ,
AND SYRIA

ERICA L. GASTON

Columbia University Press
New York

Columbia University Press
Publishers Since 1893
New York   Chichester, West Sussex
cup.columbia.edu
Copyright © 2024 Columbia University Press
All rights reserved

Library of Congress Cataloging-in-Publication Data
Names: Gaston, E. L., author.
Title: Illusions of control : dilemmas in managing U.S. proxy forces in Afghanistan, Iraq, and Syria / Erica L. Gaston.
Other titles: Dilemmas in managing U.S. proxy forces in Afghanistan, Iraq, and Syria
Description: New York : Columbia University Press, [2024] | Series: Columbia studies in terrorism and irregular warfare | Includes bibliographical references and index.
Identifiers: LCCN 2023057164 (print) | LCCN 2023057165 (ebook) | ISBN 9780231210126 (hardback) | ISBN 9780231210133 (trade paperback) | ISBN 9780231558280 (ebook)
Subjects: LCSH: Paramilitary forces—Iraq. | Paramilitary forces—Afghanistan. | Paramilitary forces—Syria. | United States—Armed Forces—Management. | Special operations (Military science)—United States—History—21st century. | Proxy war—United States. | Terrorism—Prevention. | Counterinsurgency.
Classification: LCC UA13 .G37 2024 (print) | LCC UA13 (ebook) | DDC 322.4/2—dc23/eng/20240206
LC record available at https://lccn.loc.gov/2023057164
LC ebook record available at https://lccn.loc.gov/2023057165

Printed and bound by CPI Group (UK) Ltd, Croydon, CR0 4YY

Cover design: Milenda Nan Ok Lee
Cover photo: Jake Simkin

CONTENTS

Preface: On the Heels of Militia Mobilization   vii
List of Abbreviations   xv

INTRODUCTION   1

1. THEORETICAL FRAMEWORK: AGENCY THEORY VERSUS FOREIGN POLICY ANALYSIS   41

2. BARGAINING MOMENTS AND STRUCTURES: COMPARING THE SONS OF IRAQ AND THE AFGHAN LOCAL POLICE   65

3. SEARCHING FOR UNICORNS: RISK MITIGATION IN THE INTERNAL AND EXTERNAL POLICY DELIBERATIONS OVER SYRIAN ARMED GROUPS   102

4. STANDARD OPERATING PROCEDURES AND EXCEPTIONS TO THE RULE: ORGANIZATIONAL LENSES AND BUREAUCRATIC TRANSFER, FROM LOCAL FORCE INITIATIVES TO COUNTERTERRORISM AUXILIARIES   154

5. CHANGE OVER TIME: TRANSNATIONAL NETWORKS, THE LEAHY LAW, AND HUMAN RIGHTS CHECKS FOR LOCAL AND SUBSTATE FORCES 195

6. FOREIGN PLAYERS IN THE MIX: DIRECT AND INDIRECT BARGAINING AND INFLUENCE STRATEGIES BY NON-U.S. GOVERNMENTS 218

CONCLUSION 239

Acknowledgments 279
Notes 281
Bibliography 365
Index 401

PREFACE

On the Heels of Militia Mobilization

On July 22, 2010, I, along with about a dozen other representatives from civil society groups and international organizations, crowded into the hot, airless boardroom of an NGO office in Kabul, a five-minute walk from the concrete jungle of embassies, international bases, and Afghan ministerial compounds that served as the nerve center of Afghan policy. We were there to hear a presentation by a brigadier general named "Scottie" Miller, supported by other representatives of the NATO mission in Afghanistan, the International Security Assistance Force. Years later, Miller would serve as the last American commanding general in Afghanistan, overseeing the end of the twenty-year-long engagement in Afghanistan in July 2021. But at the time he was heading up one of the U.S. Special Operations commands, known as Task Force Alpha.

I had been acting as a human rights researcher and advocate in Kabul for well over a year at that point, focused on documenting civilian casualties and other conflict-related abuses. The idea that U.S. Special Operations Forces (SOF) were reaching out to NGOs and civil society groups to answer questions about a new security initiative was notable. Among international forces, SOF and their activities were the most opaque. They were not in the business of responding to NGO or press queries about their operations or practices, much less consulting with such organizations about new initiatives.

But this briefing was to be different. Rather than the night raids and stealth operations that SOF at the time were known for,[1] it concerned a more public-facing counterinsurgency effort to mobilize community and tribal militias against the Taliban insurgency. The military presenters shied away from the term "militias," referring to the groups they planned to mobilize as community self-defense units, "village defense forces," or *arbakai*—a traditional Afghan term for tribal self-defense forces.[2] "Community watch[es] with AK-47s" was the way that General David Petraeus, the commanding general of U.S. and NATO forces in Afghanistan from 2010 to 2011, would later frame the initiative.[3]

The assembled NGOs and civil society representatives received the news of militia mobilization (however they were named) with reactions ranging from suspicion to outrage. If there is one country whose history might make you think twice about mobilizing militias, it is Afghanistan's. Looking back only to the last few decades, in the 1980s, Afghan resistance fighters known as the mujahideen turned the Soviet occupation of Afghanistan into a bloody quagmire.[4] Some of those militias then set their sights on the United States, with former mujahideen joining Osama bin Laden to form al-Qaeda, the terrorist organization whose presumed threat would dominate global security dynamics for the next two decades.

Throughout the 1990s, militias continued to roil the Afghan state and to prey upon the population. During the 1980s, the Afghan state—then controlled by a left-leaning Marxist-Leninist party known as the People's Democratic Party of Afghanistan (PDPA)—began mobilizing its own pro-government militias to counter the mujahideen. These militias, known as the Regional Guard Brigades, were known for their lawless behavior and corruption, and over time the PDPA's overreliance on such groups contributed to the Afghan state's collapse in 1992.[5] What ensued at that point was a bloody, internecine civil war between all of these competing factions and their associated militias, decimating cities like Kabul and ravaging the Afghan population.[6] Many outlying provinces and regions were awash with banditry and infighting between a range of competing militias and ethno-political or tribal factions.[7] As scholar Ashley Jackson observed of dynamics in eastern Nangrahar Province, "At one point, the roughly 80 km road from Jalalabad to the Torkham border crossing into Pakistan was controlled by five different commanders, each demanding their own taxes and occasionally going to war with one another."[8] The level of violence, atrocities, and disorder across Afghanistan was so extreme that much of the population initially welcomed the Taliban's promises of harsh order and its subsequent assumption of control in 1996.

Nor were the cautions about militia mobilization a matter of historical record alone. Since 2001, the international community had embraced a neo-Weberian vision for the new Afghan state. International interventions aimed to reinforce (or create) the Afghan state's "monopoly on force," by countering the latent Taliban threats, but also by disbanding or taming all the other warlords, militias, and commander networks that had accrued in the prior two decades. However, in reality, those same warlords and militias who had torn the country apart in the 1990s still thrived—with leading warlords embedded in key positions within the new Afghan state.[9] Rather than cooperating with international disarmament plans, the warlords-cum-government avoided disarmament by appointing their militias to the new Afghan police, army, and other security positions.[10] This patronage-based system, together with overall weak rule of law in the post-2001 period, meant that Afghan security forces and pro-government militias were rarely held to account, even for egregious abuses.[11] They predated upon the population and engaged in other abuses that were seen as a driving source of resentment, contributing to the Taliban's resurgence from 2005 onward.

International actors had a mixed record on these "militias in uniform." Parts of the international community put substantial effort behind disarmament and demobilization efforts, security sector reform, or other initiatives designed to clean out the corrupted and abusive Afghan security forces. However, many of these commanders and militias were treated as "trusted" allies, whom international military forces counted on to pursue al-Qaeda targets and Taliban insurgents. As a result, while some parts of the international community were dedicated to disarmament and institutionalized security force developments, others, in particular the U.S. military, helped sponsor a range of militia mobilization efforts, or directly partnered with militias and commanders with nefarious records.[12]

All of these risks and consequences were front and center in the minds of the assembled NGO and civil society audience as the idea of further militia mobilization was proposed. In more than an hour of questions and answers, civil society representatives and NGOs warned that the program would be hijacked by the same warlords and commanders who had exploited past quasi-statutory mobilization initiatives;[13] that it would undo past disarmament efforts and unleash a new round of abusive militias on the population; and that there would be no way to unwind the initiative at the end of it. One longtime Afghanistan researcher characterized the initiative as a Pandora's box, and argued that once mobilized, these forces would be hard to demobilize and stand down. Community mobilization would open new divisions and old wounds; once awakened, once cleaved, these would not be so easily put back together.

For each objection and critique, Miller and the other members of his team had a response and corresponding measure. To the fears about warlord co-option, the presenters responded that there would be close consideration of which communities might participate, and both SOF and community oversight of the forces mobilized. To fears about abuses and accountability, the presenters responded that these forces would be vetted for their past human rights records, and then given training in human rights and the laws of war. When one advocate raised the potential for detention abuses, Miller or one of his aides responded that they would consider an amendment to the program rules that would prohibit the local forces from taking part in detention operations. Reflecting the atmosphere in the meeting, Human Rights Watch researcher Rachel Reid later reported that in creating these local defense forces, "the US say they have learned the lessons of the past and that this time things will be different. Supporters point in particular to what they describe as more rigorous measures to involve the local community in selecting and vetting recruits, as well as efforts to avoid empowering pre-existing militias and heavy oversight by US special operations forces for most of the new forces."[14]

Although these responses were not fully persuasive to the audience assembled that July afternoon, the initiative was nonetheless authorized soon after in the form of the Afghan Local Police (ALP) (discussed further in chapter 2). All of the various safeguards, checks, and controls that had been proposed to counter objections to the program—human rights vetting and training, careful selection and monitoring to limit warlord intervention, rules against the ALP taking part in offensive or detention operations, etc.—were fully incorporated into the program guidance, and these continued to be part of the formal rules and model for these forces throughout the ten years that the program was authorized and funded.

The sensitivity to civil society concerns over the ALP, and the way these were encoded in these preventive mechanisms or restraints—which this book will refer to as "control mechanisms"—might be viewed as simply the product of a particular ideational moment in Afghanistan. The ALP was created at the height of a counterinsurgency push in Afghanistan. At the time, military strategies and foreign assistance were substantially animated by the idea that "population protection," tackling corruption, empowering "community-based strategies," and "bottom-up state building" would be key to reversing the spiraling situation in Afghanistan.[15] NGO voices had greater traction in this environment, both because their concerns about human rights abuses and corruption tapped into what were viewed as the largest strategic threats, and because of their perceived ability to connect with the Afghan population, and to shape the narrative in Afghanistan.

However, as I began to work on similar issues in other country contexts, I saw that this greater attention to risks and controls was not singular to that Afghan moment. In 2016, I began to work more in Iraq, as a conflict analyst and researcher, mapping the mobilization of non-state and substate forces as part of the efforts to counter the Islamic State of Iraq and the Levant. Though very different conflicts and with very different U.S. strategies involved, many of the same control mechanisms and checks on local forces appeared to be manifesting with U.S.-supported local forces in Iraq and Syria.

These same mechanisms of control and risk mitigation manifested not just with the counterinsurgency-themed local forces in Iraq (which were similar to the ALP), but with forces and programs nurtured under a very different model and over whom there were few prospects of control. The Syrian rebels who received arms and equipment from the Central Intelligence Agency (CIA) through a covert assistance program authorized in 2013 (discussed further in chapter 3) went through even more hoops and hurdles than ALP forces did. There was extensive vetting, which appeared to include scrutiny of the ideology and affiliation of the groups in question as well as of their past records of conduct. CIA-supported fighters submitted payroll stubs, filed video or written after-action reports, and returned spent missile casings to receive more.[16] Some remembered a sort of human rights or laws of war protocol, and groups being cut from funding or subject to retraining on best practices where their strikes caused collateral damage. To borrow a Shakespearean metaphor, it was as if the United States had "let slip the dogs of war," but in this case it would take steps to regulate and tame them.[17]

I recall my own trajectory here to be transparent about my background vis-à-vis the research questions, and to introduce some of the larger questions that intrigued me about this practice. As a human rights lawyer and rule-of-law practitioner, I was initially interested in these risk-mitigation practices for their potential to address misconduct and limit civilian harm by militias or other irregular forces. There are due diligence obligations under international humanitarian law (IHL), under which warring parties have an obligation to ensure that IHL is respected and "not to encourage" violations.[18] This has been interpreted as implying some degree of affirmative or proactive duty where states arm, support, and (especially) direct non-state armed groups in another state.[19] However, the extent of this duty is ambiguous, under-implemented, and under-enforced. It presents an exceedingly weak legal stick, and one that the United States might easily override where such due diligence measures proved difficult to apply or costly, as one might expect with these groups and in these environments.

Instead, the more I studied the use of these control mechanisms, the more I was struck by the political nature and context surrounding them. With the ALP, the motivation for these forces, as well as the objections to them, strongly played into the surrounding counterinsurgency and bottom-up state-building dynamics. In Syria, the heavy emphasis on control mechanisms smacked strongly of the overall fixation on risks and risk aversion that pervaded the Syria policy environment. Even more intriguing, in many cases, those who were demanding controls and using them to constrain U.S. military initiatives were not even U.S. government actors, but other foreign state officials or the sort of NGO or civil society actors who featured in the 2010 meeting described above.

Although it was my past exposure that sparked my interest in these questions, this book is not a personal narrative; rather, it is an academic inquiry into how international relations or conflict studies might explain some of the dynamics I observed. Are these the sort of checks or levers of control that we might expect in any sort of proxy relationship? Should we view these controls, at least the human rights–related ones, as the result of "activists without borders"—the sort of transnational activists and NGOs described above in the ALP meeting?[20] Were there other domestic political factors within the policy environment in Washington, DC, or in the countries in question that either contributed to, or limited the emergence of, such control mechanisms?

Exploring these research questions offers insights into a much larger and highly relevant policy question: Is it possible to regulate irregular forces—to work with actors known to come with a host of policy risks and costs while maintaining the ability to constrain or mitigate those risks, even in environments least disposed to control? And if it is not—as many of the case studies suggest—what are the larger costs for policy making? In the ALP authorization debate previewed above, control mechanisms played a central role (at least rhetorically) in the question of whether to authorize these forces. Are policy makers more willing to engage with these "risky" forces where they think that they can somewhat mitigate or constrain the associated risks? And if so, what are the consequences when those expectations prove to be false? Again and again in the policy situations examined in these pages, there appeared to be a fallacy that it was possible to "have your cake and eat it (too)," so to speak—to work with risky actors in some of the most perilous environments, but without the costs of doing so. This book considers how this policy conceit impacted policy makers' decision making, and the moral hazard of doing so.

ABBREVIATIONS

ABM	anti-ballistic missile
ALP	Afghan Local Police
ANA	Afghan National Army
ANAP	Afghan National Auxiliary Police
ANA-TF	Afghan National Army Territorial Force
ANP	Afghan National Police
AP3	Afghan Public Protection Program
AQI	al-Qaeda in Iraq
BPA	bureaucratic policy analysis
CENTCOM	United States Central Command
CERP	Commander's Emergency Response Program
CFSOCC-A	Combined Forces Special Operations Component Command—Afghanistan
CIA	Central Intelligence Agency (United States)
COIN	counterinsurgency
CSO	Bureau of Conflict and Stabilization Operations (United States)
CT	counterterrorism
DoD	Department of Defense (United States)
DRL	Bureau of Democracy, Human Rights, and Labor (United States)

DTO	Designated Terrorist Organization
EU	European Union
FPA	foreign policy analysis
FSA	Free Syrian Army
FY	fiscal year
GIROA	Government of the Islamic Republic of Afghanistan
GVHR	gross violations of human rights
HRW	Human Rights Watch
ICRC	International Committee of the Red Cross
IEDs	improvised explosive devices
IHL	international humanitarian law
ISAF	International Security Assistance Force
ISIL	Islamic State of Iraq and the Levant
KDP	Kurdistan Democratic Party
LDI	Local Defense Initiatives
LHSF	local, hybrid, and substate forces
MOC	Military Operation Center
MoD	Ministry of Defense (Afghanistan)
MoI	Ministry of Interior (Afghanistan)
MOM	Müşterek Operasyon Merkezi (Joint Operation Center)
NATO	North Atlantic Treaty Organization
NDAA	National Defense Authorization Act (United States)
NDS	National Directorate of Security (Afghanistan)
NEA	Bureau of Near Eastern Affairs (United States)
NGO	nongovernmental organization
NSC	National Security Council (United States)
PDPA	People's Democratic Party of Afghanistan
PKK	Partîya Karkerên Kurdistanê (Kurdistan Workers' Party)
PMF	Popular Mobilization Force (Iraq)
RS	Operation Resolute Support
SDC	Syrian Democratic Council
SDF	Syrian Democratic Forces
SIGAR	Special Inspector General for Afghanistan Reconstruction (United States)
SOF	Special Operations Forces
SOPs	standard operating procedures
TMF	Tribal Mobilization Force (Iraq)

TOW	tube-launched, optically tracked, wireless-guided
UNAMA	United Nations Assistance Mission in Afghanistan
VSO	Village Stability Operations
YPG	Yekîneyên Parastina Gel (People's Protection Units)

INTRODUCTION

States have long used proxies, including irregular forces, to advance security interests in areas beyond their control.[1] Nonetheless, changing international dynamics after the end of the Cold War fed increasing interest in "new warfare" and the role of militias, rebels, proxies, mercenaries, and other non-state armed groups within it.[2] The 2001 al-Qaeda attacks on New York and Washington, DC, and the U.S. response to those attacks was a further prod, spawning a two-decade focus on asymmetric threats and the terrorist and insurgent groups producing them.

And yet, though irregular forces figured as major U.S. security targets, they also came to be the United States' key allies or necessary bedfellows as they sought to counter those asymmetric threats. When U.S. forces needed ground partners to help overthrow the Taliban in 2001 and 2002, they turned to a loose coalition of warlords and factional militias known as the Northern Alliance.[3] The United States and its NATO partners then continued to support many of these warlords and their militias, or cultivated other non-state or quasi-statutory forces to stand in for or supplement gaps in Afghan security forces for the next two decades.[4] From 2006 to 2008 in Iraq, and then from 2009 to 2013 in Afghanistan, the United States mobilized and supported some 120,000 tribal and community militias as part of its counterinsurgency strategies in both countries.[5]

The Syrian Civil War that devolved out of initially peaceful Arab Spring protests in 2011 opened a new arena for U.S. non-state partnerships. The United States—alongside many other regional partners and international allies—provided arms, tactical equipment, intelligence advice, and a range of other nonlethal equipment and support to Syrian rebels opposed to President Bashar al-Assad. With the rise of the Islamic State of Iraq and the Levant (ISIL) and its takeover of substantial parts of Syria and Iraq in late 2013 and early 2014, U.S. support to irregular or community-based forces in both countries became much more substantial, leading to the overt "training and equipping" of a range of Syrian armed groups against ISIL and U.S. sponsorship of a second tribal mobilization initiative in Iraq.[6]

Of course, such irregular partnerships have not been confined to Iraq, Afghanistan, and Syria (the three countries of focus in this book). Since 2001, U.S. Special Operations Forces (SOF), often operating with U.S. intelligence agents, have worked alongside or provided support to a range of non-state armed groups, including clan militias in Somalia, community self-defense groups in Nigeria, and a range of Libyan militias, from Misrata to Benghazi.[7]

Outsourcing war fighting to non-state, privatized, or other irregular forces is certainly not new to the American way of war. The United States relied on mercenaries, naval privateers, and other privatized or irregular forces in nearly every major conflict from the American War of Independence through to the Second World War, and any number of "small wars" along the way.[8] During the Cold War, the United States backed a range of guerrillas, rebels, self-defense forces, and mercenaries in countries including Afghanistan, Nicaragua, Colombia, El Salvador, Angola, Laos, and Peru.[9]

Yet while not new, proxy warfare and support to irregular forces has taken on a different tenor in the post-2001 years. In an era that witnessed the increasing embrace of remote war-fighting strategies like drone strikes or special operations missions, addressing security threats via proxies or other security forces became a much more prominent part of the U.S. security strategy.[10] By the end of the Obama administration, working via other partners had cohered into the "by, with, and through" approach, the predominant operational paradigm for U.S. forces globally.[11] The preference was still to work "by, with, and through" the forces of other state partners.[12] However, in many cases, security threats have emerged in areas where the sovereign state lacks full control or is unwilling to pursue U.S. security objectives. In such contexts, the United States has frequently sought alternative partners in the form of irregular, non-state, or, at best, quasi-official forces.

As these irregular partnerships have emerged more frequently, they have come out of the shadows, and become a much more openly acknowledged and embraced part of U.S. security responses. In country after country, crisis after crisis, partnerships with non-state forces have risen from ad hoc, expedient initiatives to central and highly visible parts of the U.S. strategy. The "Sons of Iraq," or *sahwa* forces (a focus of chapter 2)—Iraqi tribal militias who joined the United States to counter al-Qaeda in Iraq—were treated as one of the key ingredients of the U.S. counterinsurgency success.[13] In part because of that inspiration from the *sahwa* in Iraq, a 2009 tribal mobilization initiative in Afghanistan (also discussed in chapter 2) was promoted as the lynchpin of the counter-Taliban strategy at the time. It quickly blossomed from a few dozen Special Forces test initiatives to a thirty-thousand-strong community guard force that was fronted as the way the Afghan state would reach out to and enable service delivery and security in rural Afghanistan.

This sort of open acknowledgment and normalization has not been limited to the more frontal, counterinsurgency-linked forces, nor to the three countries of focus in this book. The billion-dollar, multi-year CIA program to arm and support parts of the Free Syrian Army (FSA)—which funded, armed, and trained rebel forces who were mobilized against another sovereign state—was technically a covert operation, but it functioned as an open secret. Details of it were well-known and published concurrently with operations. Then secretary of defense Chuck Hagel even testified openly to its existence in 2014.[14] Even the proxies attached to covert Special Operations missions or intelligence agency counterterrorism operations are no longer a guarded secret. Rather, they are an open practice, supported by a regular defense appropriations line, known as the 127e or "127echo" funds.[15]

The normalization of these proxies and irregular partnerships has happened in part due to frequency—the perceived need to have such partners in Iraq, Afghanistan, Syria, Libya, and the dozens of other sites of global counterterrorism operations since 2001. In 2017 alone, U.S. SOF were reported to be active in over 130 countries annually, with ongoing operations "across 80-plus countries" on a daily basis.[16] With each of these missions comprising only a limited number of forces or agents, U.S. forces or intelligence agents relied on whatever state or non-state forces were available.

Beyond expediency and frequency, there were also significant ideational shifts happening at this time that helped to legitimize the use of local or irregular forces, at least from the point of view of some policy makers. Since the 1990s a large part of both the academic and policy communities saw major threats to international peace and security in "failed states"—weak states that were incapable of addressing citizen needs or grievances, and of maintaining order effectively and preventing conflict eruption or spillover.[17] The common "liberal peace" remedy called for erecting strong states with a "monopoly on force" and robust institutions able to provide public goods and services, maintain law and order, regulate disputes, and sustain a functioning market economy.[18] But this experiment in liberal peace building proved challenging from the start. Across any number of contexts, building strong states in conflict-torn societies proved exceedingly challenging, with a mismatch between the scale and ambitions of the peace-building agenda and the resources and timeline of would-be intervenors.[19] Even worse, evidence suggested that in many cases the "failed state" prognosis became a self-fulfilling prophecy, and that the state-strengthening agenda prescribed as the remedy reinforced sources of conflict and tension rather than addressing them.[20]

Critics of this liberal peace mode of intervention questioned not only the "state-building" remedies imposed, but also the underlying premise that weak states were the root problem. Historical and cross-case analysis suggested that situations of "limited," "mediated," or contested statehood are not a deviant or exceptional situation, but are much more the norm in terms of state-societal relations than the neo-Weberian idea of a state with a monopoly on violence and coercive power.[21] As Volker Boege and his colleagues observed, in a great number of countries, "'The state' is only one actor among others, and 'state order' is only one of a number of orders claiming to provide security, frameworks for conflict regulation and social services."[22] In these so-called hybrid political or security orders, state actors share power and legitimacy with a range of customary, traditional, alternative, "non-statutory," or informal actors or frameworks.[23]

Academics and practitioners alike documented how territorial control, governance, or other "state-like" functions devolved in situations where the formal state had long been absent or played only a marginal role. As one 2019 Chatham House report observed, across the Middle East, "governance vacuums are filled by alternative actors that perform state-like functions in place of, or alongside, weakened official institutions. This results in hybrid orders where the distinction between formal and informal actors in the state is blurred, as too are the lines between the formal, informal and illicit economies."[24] A plethora of studies explored the nature of "governance without government" and service delivery and governance dynamics in so-called ungoverned spaces.[25] Rather than a "security vacuum" emerging in pockets of weak or failing states, militias, rebels, warlords, and other armed groups were stepping in to provide security and order.[26] Where there were little to no state-administered services, a host of other local, community-based, tribal, or "traditional" actors—some armed and some not—did the business of substate governance, dispute resolution, or providing other core services.[27]

International policy makers who were frustrated with decades of state-building failures quickly latched on to these ideas of alternative state builders and service providers. They offered a potentially more effective, and expedient, route for addressing lingering security or governance challenges. What are sometimes called "second generation" approaches to peace building or state building sought to better incorporate non-state, "traditional," or "customary" actors and mechanisms, and to achieve security, governance, or justice-related goals through "community-based" or "bottom-up" approaches.[28] At a programmatic level, international donors channeled money into community-based governance and development bodies or, in the justice sector, into customary, traditional, or alternative dispute-resolution mechanisms.[29]

This book is not focused on evaluating such second-generation state building. Nonetheless, this context is important given that many of the security partnerships in this book were animated by a theory of "bottom-up" state building and security sector development. Turning to militias or community forces was frequently framed as a way of recognizing alternative service providers beyond state institutions, or of empowering local communities to provide for their own protection. In Iraq and Afghanistan, where such theories of "bottom-up" state building cross-pollinated with counterinsurgency theories, leading U.S. officials posited that these local force initiatives were not only crucial to the strategy—providing immediate manpower and local know-how in hard-to-reach areas—but were also more legitimate than supporting the state forces attached to corrupt and discredited national governments.[30] In essence, this narrative functioned as a legitimating factor, helping to normalize these irregular partnerships within U.S. policy making.

Such rationalizations were important given the greater spotlight on these controversial partners. Whatever their immediate value or contribution to the security demands in question, many of these groups were former insurgents or criminals, with spotty reputations and spurious connections. Partnering with such forces came with the potential for substantial reputational costs, as well as possible consequences or risks for other key policy priorities. Militias, rebel or insurgent forces, and other irregular armed groups come with a reputation for war crimes, atrocities, and high levels of violence.[31] Irregular forces may also generate substantial political and security risks. As one former U.S. Special Forces member quipped, "The problem with irregular forces is that they act irregularly. You can't predict what they do, which can create a dangerous political situation."[32] Many of the forces the United States has partnered with had connections with terrorist or insurgent groups, warlords, or criminal networks.[33] U.S. officials feared that supported groups would sell U.S.-provided weapons and equipment to other insurgent or terrorist groups, or "go rogue"—becoming the next al-Qaeda, as parts of the U.S.-supported Afghan mujahideen did in the 1990s.[34]

As a result, although recurrent security crises pushed U.S. policy makers toward a more open embrace of irregular partnerships, there was increasing pressure to do something about the range of risks and potential adverse consequences associated with them. In response to such concerns, U.S. policy makers over the last two decades have increasingly applied measures to try to limit or mitigate some of these risks—the sort of checks and safeguards described in the preface for some of the Afghan and Syrian forces. They have taken steps to screen fighters or commanders for past human rights abuses, affiliation with hostile groups, or other questionable behavior. Those who pass screening were often provided with a code of conduct and training, or asked to pledge to adhere to certain standards, including abiding by key IHL provisions. There was then a panoply of monitoring and reporting requirements to help ensure compliance or detect defaults. Groups that crossed these redlines—for example, by affiliating with banned groups or perpetrating war crimes—have been penalized or have seen their U.S. funding completely cut.

This book focuses on the emergence of these risk-mitigation efforts—or "control mechanisms," as they will generally be referred to—in the context of U.S. partnerships with a range of non-state or irregular forces. These will be explored in nine case studies centering on Syria, Iraq, and Afghanistan from 2004 to 2020. Each considers why control mechanisms manifested, and their interrelationship with other political dynamics.

One might well ask, why focus on these risk mitigation measures, which often manifest as relatively minor technical features of these partnerships? The answer is that, though minor programmatic elements, these controls tend to sit at the crux of what is controversial or challenging about these programs. They are explicitly designed to try to address or mitigate risks that make these relatively unknown, unknowable, and hard-to-control actors so objectionable as partners, at least for democratic states. Because these risk-mitigation features are often designed in response to various stakeholders' concerns, they signify the compromise or political bargain struck over these forces. They represent the blend of concessions, safeguards, and compromises that allows the larger policy sphere to be reconciled to these risky initiatives. As such, they tell an important story about policy accommodation and rationalization where security imperatives clash with other policy preferences.

In addition, as the case studies will illustrate, these control mechanisms do not emerge in a U.S. bubble. They are as likely to be demanded, advanced, jettisoned, or modified by a range of other non-U.S. stakeholders—from foreign diplomats to civil society or nongovernmental constituencies, and ultimately to the irregular forces themselves. Focusing on these mechanisms thus offers a window into the layered interactions and subnational to transnational bargaining and deliberations that tend to emerge within these hybrid policy arenas.

THEORETICAL FRAMEWORK

Before discussing the theoretical framework and premise, a few definitional clarifications are in order. The forces that are the subject of the case studies span the full range of categories and armed group typologies discussed within conflict studies.[35] Some are pro-government in their alignment, while others are clearly "rebel" or opposition forces. Many still had links to insurgent or terrorist groups. Some chapters are focused on organically developed local or community-based self-defense forces, while others focus on well-trained paramilitary forces who work in close cooperation with U.S. military or intelligence units. Some of the armed groups in the case studies represent very localized and operationally limited forces, while others demonstrate a level of autonomy and coercive power that make them more akin to warlords,[36] or what have been described as "hybrid" or "near-state" actors.[37] The latter set of terms has been used to describe armed actors that enjoy a level of coercive or territorial control of a state but lack the full legal recognition of a sovereign state or one of its subsidiary parts.

Ambiguity and flux in the exact legal status of these forces is a common phenomenon in hybrid political environments. Militias or other localized forces may at times be given a degree of legal recognition—at which point they are sometimes referred to as "state-parallel," paramilitary, or quasi-statutory forces.[38] But this link with the state does not always change their de facto command structure, behavior, or objectives, and it may be only temporary and its legal status questionable. On the flip side, in many "limited" or mediated states, parts of state forces—the army or police—may behave more like militias or non-state actors in practice.[39] They may effectively be controlled and guided not by state institutions, but by patronage lines or their own affiliated political party or leader, who uses these state-funded forces to advance independent political agendas. For that reason, clinging to terms like "non-state" or even "quasi-statutory," which hinge on a legal status definition, may be inexact. "Substate" forces will be used at times to denote this broad spectrum of actors operating below the level of a national state force. In addition, because the groups in the case studies traverse any number of categories or typologies, this book will refer to them generically as "local, hybrid, or substate forces" (LHSFs).

A large body of literature has explored why states outsource security functions to substate or non-state forces. Domestic regimes may turn to such forces as a means of patronage or political coercion, as a way to shore up regime stability or "coup-proof" the state, or as a means of outsourcing transgressive violence or evading accountability.[40] In hybrid political orders or so-called mediated states, where the state is not a monopolist but merely one player among others, cooperating with other non-state, traditional, or alternative brokers may be a reality of governing.[41] In the context of proxy warfare, supporting militias, rebels, or other substate forces may offer external powers a way to project force or pursue their interests with fewer resources, less domestic blowback, more plausible deniability, and lower international reputational costs than deploying their own forces.[42]

There may be particular reasons for states, or other external actors, to turn to local forces—which might include ethnic, sectarian, or other community-based forces. They tend to be cheap to mobilize and readily available. They know local areas and security dynamics better than external actors, and they may have more legitimacy with a given community or constituency than the government.[43] Those writing on counterinsurgency themes or on civil war dynamics have argued that the local know-how, credibility, and staying power of local or community-based forces can make them more effective at countering insurgents than those from other areas.[44] External states may be particularly tempted to rely on local forces for their know-how and connections when countering domestic insurgencies.[45]

The reasons that the United States embraced community or tribal mobilization in Iraq and Afghanistan mirrored the common reasons espoused in the literature on the advantages of local forces: these forces were cheap, readily available, and came with greater knowledge of the local community, local insurgents, and the local terrain.[46] They relieved the burden of deploying additional U.S. troops and offered tactical advantages that foreign or even non-local Iraqi or Afghan forces would have been unable to provide.[47] U.S. reliance on a range of non-state armed groups in Syria, and the more clandestine use of various statutory, non-state, or quasi-statutory paramilitary groups for counterterrorism missions in all three countries, tend to reflect expectations in the literature surrounding proxy warfare and reasons for delegating certain types of violence.[48]

At the same time, while there may be many advantages or benefits to delegating security tasks to LHSFs, there are also frequently trade-offs. Extensive scholarship has documented high rates of violence, transgressive behavior, and atrocities or war crimes linked to militias or other non-state armed groups.[49] Mobilizing militias and other irregular forces has been shown to extend the duration of civil wars and seed local cycles of violence, potentially fomenting instability and new security threats.[50] In addition, patrons may fear that armed groups will pursue their own interests rather than those of their patrons and either unintentionally or intentionally be the generator of security or political risks.[51] In such situations, relying on proxies can lead to unwanted conflict escalation or result in the patron being more deeply entrenched in the local conflict.[52]

To capture how patrons might weigh these different costs and benefits, or other dynamics within proxy relationships, many of those writing on U.S. security assistance to external armed groups (state and non-state) have applied concepts from principal-agent theory.[53] Principal-agent theory offers a useful paradigm for capturing why states might delegate or outsource security functions to other actors, the sort of problems or dilemmas likely to arise within that delegation, and certain measures, or control mechanisms, that principals might take to mitigate or limit the risks or potential consequences of agents' actions.[54] This includes a typology of control mechanisms that patrons might use to try to limit or mitigate the risk of agents slacking on the job or otherwise engaging in counterproductive or undesirable behavior. This includes *selection mechanisms* to identify less risky agents; establishing *rules and standards* of conduct; conducting *monitoring and oversight* to ensure those standards are met; and creating *sanctions or rewards* that punish slacking or incentivize the desired behavior.[55] The extent to which patrons or principals will resort to these controls tends to be portrayed as a sort of cost-benefit analysis, with patrons weighing the relative benefits of imposing controls (including the likelihood that they will be effective) against the costs of imposing them.

Given this core premise, principal-agent theory would not expect patrons in a conflict situation to rely heavily on control mechanisms. This is because the dynamics within conflict zones make it extremely costly to impose controls, with little promise that such controls will be effective. Limited access to territory in conflict zones due to insecurity or political barriers creates high information asymmetries and limits the prospects for effective monitoring and enforcement. The volatility within conflict environments can further heighten information asymmetries and increase the costs of managing and controlling agents. There are also frequently substantial political and time pressures in crisis situations, and limited options for finding a "like-minded" partner whose similar interests might limit the risk of deviant behavior. The "good-enough" or like-minded-enough agent may be all that is available. Moreover, in many contested areas, there are multiple competing patrons, which can make it easier for agents to switch allegiance and ignore directives and sanctions. For all these reasons, conflict environments tend to lie on the extreme end of the spectrum in terms of high costs of controls, and minimal dividends from them. As a result, while some of the analysis applying principal-agent theory to security delegation have introduced the theoretical premise of control mechanisms, they have tended to stop with the conclusion that controls would be extremely costly and minimally effective in conflict environments—with the implication that they therefore would not be applied.[56]

This truism leaves something of a puzzle given the evidence in this book. Despite the fact that there were substantial barriers to control, and that they would be costly—and likely impossible—to overcome in the three environments in question, the United States repeatedly applied a range of conditions or mechanisms to try to limit the risks associated with substate forces in Iraq, Afghanistan, and Syria. Not only were control mechanisms applied in situations in which doing so was costly, but the evidence suggests that the use of control mechanisms increased over time and across different national and conflict contexts. They have persisted even when they have outlived their usefulness, failed to limit risks, or proven costly to implement, even to the point of neutering the overall objectives of support.

To explore these questions requires a different set of analytical tools, those that might offer explanations for how surrounding political dynamics, contexts, or policy structures can potentially affect some of the assumptions of principal-agent theory and explain why U.S. policy makers might adopt control mechanisms even where doing so was costly and unlikely to work. Given this, a second explanatory lens considered will be that of foreign policy analysis, also described as bureaucratic policy analysis (BPA). BPA views foreign policy outcomes as the product of bargaining between different actors or "players" in the foreign policy process, or, alternately, as the result of tendencies or scripts within the bureaucracy and the organizational units that make it up.[57] In this view, the surrounding policy structures, the lenses or interests of the key policy makers in question, and the organizational processes and routines invoked often determine the foreign policy outcome, notwithstanding the objective costs or merits of the proposed policy direction.[58]

On first glance, BPA might not appear the most obvious lens for analyzing these relationships. BPA originated as a tool for understanding how the domestic political dynamics or the psychosocial environment surrounding policy makers could influence foreign policy outputs.[59] As a result, it has more commonly been used to explain predominantly domestic interactions, deliberations, and bargaining surrounding a foreign policy crisis or issue.[60] A quintessential example of BPA analysis is Graham Allison's 1971 study of the Kennedy administration's internal deliberations surrounding the Cuban Missile Crisis.[61] Allison and his coauthor, Mort Halperin, also used BPA to dissect other U.S. security decision making during the Cold War, such as White House deliberations over whether to deploy more troops or a missile defense system over Europe, and how these were affected by inter-bureaucratic bargaining, tendencies, and interests.[62] In line with this tradition, most BPA literature concerns domestic debates, bargaining, and organizational processes—for example, the deliberations or organizational scripts within an executive branch, or bargaining between legislative and executive actors.[63]

Those involved in policy considerations surrounding the LHSFs in question have tended to invoke a much wider circle of players than U.S. government actors alone. It might include a range of nongovernmental actors within the U.S. policy sphere, including Congress, NGOs, transnational interest groups, private-sector actors, and the media. Situations in which LHSFs are supported also tend to invoke the interests and intervention of foreign leaders and parts of their bureaucracy, other international or transnational organizations, and, in some situations, even the LHSFs themselves. While this wider cast of characters has not typically figured in BPA analysis, this book takes the perspective that they are a reason to turn to BPA, not a reason to discount it. BPA has always held the promise of being applied to more transnational policy-making situations.[64] One of its virtues has been the ability to get into the "black box" of domestic politics, and to identify the way that domestic influences or micro-political considerations that are well beyond grand foreign policy strategy could affect policy decision making.[65] While past BPA analysis has focused more on domestic insiders, the same tools might easily extend to a range of unconventional players and sources of influence. Rainer Baumann and Frank Stengel argue that, with its emphasis on going beyond the unitary state, BPA would be well suited to exploring the role of nonstate actors—from international organizations to private security companies to transnational NGOs—as increasingly important global "policy generators."[66]

Moreover, BPA appears particularly apt for the subject matter in question. As illustrated in the Allison and Halperin studies cited above, a core terrain for BPA has been U.S. security decision making. In a world in which war fighting is increasingly done through remote-operated drones, Special Forces, and proxies, the question of whether to support a militia or rebel group may be the twenty-first-century equivalent of the Cold War decision of whether to deploy ballistic missiles or a missile defense system. Updating BPA to include a more expansive circle of players may well be a necessary way of capturing how such security decision making devolves in the twenty-first century.

Extending BPA's tool kit to these more transnational policy-making situations and unconventional policy generators offers a potential solution to the puzzle noted above. BPA's view of policy outputs as the result of different actors' preferences and agendas would suggest that rather than control mechanisms appearing as the result of rational calculations about the relative costs and benefits of those controls, they served other political agendas and bargaining demands. Instead, they more often reflect deliberations between competing policy stakeholders about the risks invoked by the policy choices in question. On this explanation, the control mechanisms that manifested would more strongly correlate with the degree of bargaining and contention, and the structure of the bargaining environment, than the costs and benefits involved in imposing controls. In addition, many of the controls manifest as technical, programmatic features. As such, BPA might also see them through the lens of BPA's organizational precepts, with controls manifesting as the product of standard operating procedures (SOPs) and bureaucratic repertoires commonly applied in such scenarios.

The case studies and chapters will use these two frameworks of principal-agent theory and BPA to ask a series of interrelated questions:

What factors or dynamics drove the manifestation of control mechanisms? How did control mechanisms relate to internal decision making over whether to support a given security partner, or the bargaining dynamics with other external actors and partners? What explains the persistence of controls over time, even where they failed to limit risks, proved costly to implement, or neutered much of the potential impact of the initiatives in question? Do control mechanisms factor into explanations of why states might be more likely to delegate to LHSFs?

The resulting analysis contributes theoretical insights to a number of fields. As noted, the depth of case study research and examples of armed group dynamics—some of it with previously under-discussed or under-documented groups—may substantially contribute to the conflict studies literature on armed group typologies and dynamics. However, the larger contribution relates to the two main theoretical frameworks explored. Overall, the case evidence more strongly correlates with BPA explanations, yet the dividends of exploring this counterhypothesis in many ways contributes to and enriches the principal-agent and proxy warfare frameworks that they challenge. Many of the case studies do in fact bear out the expectations of principal-agent theory—anticipating the friction or slack that will almost certainly arise in these situations and the futility and costliness of control mechanisms in trying to mitigate that. But rather than pursuing the logical expectations of principal-agent theory—that the controls will therefore not be deployed—the case analysis suggests that in certain situations political contestation or engagement or other organizational processes intervened to disrupt what we might characterize as the more natural rhythm of principal-agent dynamics. The resulting analysis offers a more nuanced framework for considering how patron or proxy dynamics perform in practice.

Meanwhile, applying BPA to this less-trod territory of armed group controls and hybrid political situations significantly extends the remit and tool kit of BPA itself. In addition to extending BPA to situations that have so far been largely unconsidered in the BPA literature, the application of BPA to these hybrid political situations requires identifying pathways for unconventional policy "players" to take part in BPA processes. This enables BPA to be used to explain a much wider array of twenty-first-century decision-making contexts. Finally, by combining traditional BPA analysis with insights from literature on transnational advocacy networks and normative change, the chapters offer a theory of change over time within BPA—an element that has long been missing from its theoretical premises.

METHODOLOGY, CASE SELECTION, AND ARMED GROUP TYPOLOGIES

The subsequent chapters will use case studies of control mechanisms in U.S. relationships with LHSFs to explain how and why control mechanisms manifest in practice, and to test the expectations of principal-agent and BPA theories against this empirical evidence. The case studies seek to provide a more nuanced, qualitative account of how both principal-agent and BPA expectations might manifest in substate security politics, and in relation to more transnational policy-making situations. To do so requires some degree of process tracing to establish causality, and to adapt or extrapolate from existing hypotheses. The method used within each case study is to approach the question of causality by tracing the sequence of events, decisions, and organizational, political, or situational dynamics that appeared to lead to the outcomes in question. This process tracing then seeks to establish what causal factors or drivers of control mechanisms are relevant to decision-making processes across different contexts and situations.

The case studies and countries chosen were not selected with a view toward creating a structured comparison. Instead, the case studies are used to qualitatively illustrate how external actors (in this case the United States) engage with substate security politics and issues of risk and risk mitigation in these hybrid political environments. The intent is to be able to consider how these issues manifest in a wide range of conflict environments, and involving the full spectrum of actors who might be found within them.

Focusing on Iraq, Afghanistan, and Syria advanced this approach because across these three countries there were (1) a significant number and range of U.S.-sponsored LHSF initiatives; (2) differing intervention contexts and environments, which would appear to predispose for different outcomes for control; and (3) evidence of policy transfer between the initiatives. Programs designed to support, but control, irregular forces have been tested in Afghanistan repeatedly, with continuous examples of such initiatives stretching back to the U.S. invasion and continuing to the complete withdrawal of U.S. forces in 2021. There has been a similar volume of LHSF initiatives in Iraq. However, the surrounding security context, the levels of U.S. manpower on the ground, and the U.S. strategy have not remained constant in either country. These different contextual factors might influence the program evolution and control dynamics over time.

Syria completes this picture, with control policies and approaches that had matured as part of the U.S. engagement in Afghanistan and Iraq then applied in Syria, despite the markedly different ground dynamics and more limited potential for U.S. control. The substantially different intervention context in Syria, where U.S. support of non-state armed groups was in opposition to the sovereign state, rather than in support of it, was also important. This allowed some consideration for whether control mechanisms were affected by the nature of the relationship with the sovereign state in question. One might expect the risks to be higher in a situation of hostile intervention, but also that the prospects for control would be more limited, either because of more limited access to territory, greater liability concerns, or inability to rely on the institutions and resources of the sovereign state in question as a proxy control strategy.

Examining U.S.-backed forces in other countries (for example, in Libya, Yemen, or Somalia) was considered, and would no doubt offer important additional perspectives. However, a greater number of case study countries would have limited the degree of attention given to interrogating political bargaining and intervention dynamics in each case study. Given the theoretical framework adopted, such qualitative case consideration was important. Iraq, Afghanistan, and Syria appeared to offer more examples of LHSFs, particularly those that were large and long-standing enough to generate sufficient data and attention. There also appeared to be interconnections between the dynamics in these three countries, which might allow some basis for observing policy transfer as well as potentially some synergies in the research and contextual learning on each country. For example, the United States adopted similar counterinsurgency and state-building approaches in Iraq and Afghanistan, and many of the same personnel rotated between both countries. Because the ISIL threat crossed both Iraq and Syria over the same period, there were common security concerns and contextual elements across both of those countries for several of the case studies. Given this, the choice of these three countries offered contrasting dynamics, but also common points for comparison.

The cases chosen capture the major U.S. LHSF initiatives in each country in the period in question; however, they are not exhaustive. For example, not every U.S.-supported LHSF initiative in Syria is detailed here, but the ones selected include the most prominent initiatives in Syria, and were also selected to include some variance in terms of the type of program and the U.S. institutional actor involved (the CIA, the State Department, the Department of Defense, etc.). In Iraq and Afghanistan, the major initiatives in the time period are well covered, but not all at the same depth. A more detailed and distinct treatment might have been given to each of the 2009–2012 pilot local defense forces in Afghanistan, or to the many different initiatives that are generically grouped under the terms *sahwa* or "Sons of Iraq." The counterterrorism auxiliaries are analyzed as a whole but typically were mobilized as distinct, ad hoc, and often quite short-term initiatives.

The groups examined span the full range of nomenclature and typologies within conflict studies literature. The armed groups in the chapters discussing Iraq and Afghanistan would all be described as "pro-government forces," but with varying degrees of connection with the Iraqi and Afghan governments. Both of the case studies introduced in chapter 2—the 2005–2008 Sons of Iraq or "Awakening" groups (hereafter referred to by way of the commonly used term *sahwa*), and the groups that would become the Afghan Local Police (2010–2020)—were examples of U.S. efforts to build local "counterinsurgents" or local defense forces.[67] Such local defense forces—also sometimes referred to as community watches, home guards, self-defense forces, or civil defense groups—might be defined as a "defensive form of pro-government militia that incumbents often use to harness the participation of civilians during a counterinsurgency campaign."[68] Two later forces discussed in chapter 4, the 2015–2019 Tribal Mobilization Force (TMF) in Iraq and the 2018–2021 Afghan National Army Territorial Force, were formed in the image of the *sahwa* and the ALP, but were smaller in size and substantially more integrated into host institutions from the onset. These features made them less like the prototypical homegrown counterinsurgent force, and more like a local recruitment model or guard force for the regular army.

Chapter 4 will also include a smaller discussion of Iraqi and Afghan tribal forces and militias who acted as auxiliaries or surrogate forces for covert CIA- or SOF-led counterterrorism operations. Though nominally pro-government forces, these counterterrorism auxiliaries (as they will be generically discussed) typify the image of a proxy or paramilitary force, or even of "death squads," and tend to have little to no legal association with the host states.[69] As compared to larger counterinsurgency forces like the ALP or the *sahwa*, these counterterrorism auxiliaries tend to be smaller, more mobile, and much more militarily competent. They may number in the dozens. By contrast each of the four cases of local forces in Iraq and Afghanistan mobilized more than 20,000 forces, with the largest example, the *sahwa*, exceeding 100,000 by some estimates.

The Syrian groups discussed in chapter 3 are all squarely non-state forces, and those affiliated with the FSA have almost without exception been categorized as rebel or opposition forces. Two of the forces discussed in northern Syria are often associated with discussions of proxy forces in Syria, a group of Syrian Arab fighters sponsored by Turkey (also with U.S. support briefly), and the Syrian Democratic Forces (SDF), who would become the United States' most prominent partner in Syria.[70] The SDF blend the characteristics of a number of different typologies. Their core leadership drew from a Kurdish resistance group, the Partîya Karkerên Kurdistanê (or Kurdistan Workers' Party), which has been designated as a terrorist group by a number of countries. But the SDF developed into a much larger organization, with a parallel political arm that was able to govern substantial territory autonomously—making it most similar to discussions of "hybrid" actors. Its command structure and military hierarchy was in many ways closer to that of a regular state force, but the SDF also included subsidiary "self-defense" units formed from local Arab tribes in areas formerly controlled by the ISIL. The SDF were neither squarely for nor against the Assad regime, but were aligned with the U.S. because of their staunch anti-ISIL position. Jentzsch, Kalyvas, and Schubiger make the point that opposition to (or support for) the government may not be as defining a characteristic as whether a group is opposed to insurgent or rebel forces in the territory.[71] The SDF would appear to be a prime example of this.

Having this range of armed group typologies and characteristics might pose an issue if the intent of this book was to further discussion of a particular typology or armed group dynamic. However, although the level of detail and case examination will certainly contribute to the literature on armed group typologies, the major aim of the case studies is not to further the classification of these armed groups. Nor, despite the focus on control mechanisms, is the major goal to interrogate how these different group characteristics might affect the degree to which the risks can be controlled. Instead, in many ways, the main actor under examination here is the United States, and how its political decision makers and bureaucratic organs respond to the challenge of working with armed groups not under full state control, whatever their form, function, degree of allegiance, or categorization.

A last important characteristic to discuss is the degree to which each of the case study groups constitute irregular or non-state actors, which boils down essentially to their legal status. After an initial U.S.-led mobilization period, both the *sahwa* and the ALP initiatives were brought under Afghan and Iraqi state institutions formally. The two later iterations of local forces in both countries, the Iraqi TMF and the Afghan National Army Territorial Force (ANA-TF), were mobilized in conjunction with state institutions almost from their inception. They were embedded in state structures, nominally took orders from state actors (albeit in practice this was often not the case), sported uniforms, and received formal training.

Given the focus on analyzing U.S. relationships with forces outside of state control, it might seem natural to exclude groups that reached a level of state recognition or integration. However, to characterize these groups as regular state forces would also be inexact. Despite their formal titles, many remained closer to irregular or local forces than full state actors in terms of their connection and subservience to state control, their degree of organization and command and control, and the political and community dynamics surrounding them. For example, although under the Afghan Ministry of Interior for well over a decade, at its closure, the ALP still acted and was treated more as a collection of state-linked militias than as a regular state force. The vast majority of forces in these four different initiatives remained very localized in their recruitment and writ (albeit with some greater exceptions for the ANA-TF).[72] Each individual unit's connection to Afghan or Iraqi state officials (if any) was brought about more through informal patronage networks and linkages than through any official integration or command and control.

Even more significant for the focus of this book, legalization or partial institutionalization of these forces tends to be part of the risk-mitigation strategy. The quasi-institutionalization of these forces within state structures is often demanded by the United States as a way to address state responsibility concerns (i.e., to allay legal or reputational risks on the part of the United States), or as an additional oversight or monitoring mechanism, in effect borrowing the disciplinary and oversight structures of the host state as an added control mechanism. Thus, excluding groups from this book once this institutionalization or quasi-official designation takes place would be to exclude much of the action in a story about how states try to control these forces and mitigate the risks surrounding them.

It is important to recognize that many of the risks and risk-mitigation strategies that will be discussed below would also apply to state forces. However, there are several reasons for the greater focus on irregular forces. Although state and non-state forces may share many of the same drawbacks or risks, the risk calculations may differ slightly with non-state or quasi-official forces. Irregular forces are more likely to lack the sort of command-and-control structures, or disciplinary processes that might constrain ultra vires acts or abuses.[73] The lack of such institutional constraints might not only make abuses more likely, but also—given that institutions take time to build—can be harder to rapidly substitute for through ad hoc control mechanisms.

Another reason to distinguish non-state forces is that they introduce different responsibility and liability issues not present when dealing with the forces of another state. From a legal standpoint, even where another state's institutional and military command structures do not actually fulfill their role of restraining or punishing misconduct or abuses, they at least absorb the legal responsibility for doing so. In addition, whether merited or not, non-state forces come with the stigma of being unaccountable, abusive, or pernicious forces,[74] and so may appear more costly for Western states worried about domestic public opinion or international reputational costs. These same risks also extend to non-state forces that have only recently been granted some degree of state status or are only quasi-institutionalized. They still tend to behave like militias, with lower levels of discipline and forces that are less subject to state control. Such groups may also still be perceived as militias, engendering the same reputational costs and potentially a greater degree of external state responsibility when foreign forces are directly engaged.

A last rationale for focusing on irregular forces, or at best on only newly institutionalized, quasi-statutory forces, is that they offer a more open terrain for analysis. Many control mechanisms and risk-mitigation strategies have already been built into U.S. regulatory mechanisms and laws governing state security assistance. As such, it is a much less dynamic space for examining how bargaining demands and country or political conditions might influence control mechanisms, and vice versa, than in the less established terrain of security sector assistance to non-state forces.

Table 0.1 summarizes some of the terms or typologies that would commonly be applied to the case study groups.

This criteria for selecting groups creates a slight bias toward focusing on larger LHSF initiatives rather than small, ad hoc efforts. This is to some extent inevitable both because the larger and longer-running programs are more likely to have triggered risk-mitigation discussions, and because there is more data available on them. Nonetheless, some smaller and previously unexamined or under-documented initiatives are also included as a point of comparison, in particular in chapter 4. The contrast drawn between the larger and more long-standing LHSFs and the more covert and smaller "counterterrorism auxiliary" forces introduced in chapter 4 also helps to nuance and reinforce the bargaining and organizational theories introduced in this book. Larger and more politically prominent initiatives are "too big to hide" and thus are more likely to generate the sort of "bargaining moment" that can lead to controls. The larger forces have also frequently been associated with counterinsurgency-focused strategies and thus tend to be approached through organizational lenses and assumptions that presume benefits from better-controlled (and better-behaving) forces.

TABLE 0.1 Common terms or categories applicable to case study groups

Group, period examined in case study	Common terms applied	Discussion in book
Sahwa* or Sons of Iraq, mid-2006–2009	Local or self-defense forces, counterinsurgents, "anti-insurgent" forces; some subgroups connected to/identified as warlords or criminal gangs	Chapter 2
Afghan Local Police,* 2010–2020/precursor local defense forces, 2009–2012	Local or self-defense forces, counterinsurgents, pro-government militias; some subgroups connected to/ identified as warlords or criminal gangs	Chapter 2, chapter 5
Free Syrian Army, late 2012–2014 for nonlethal support; late 2012–2017 for CIA covert support	Local forces or militias in level of organization, but rebel or opposition groups in alignment	Chapter 3
New Syrian Force, summer 2014–Oct. 2015	Local forces opposition or counter-terrorist (against ISIL) groups, proxies or surrogates (for United States)	Chapter 3
Other northern Syrian Arab groups, Oct. 2015–late 2016	Rebels, opposition forces, counter-terrorist forces (against ISIL), proxies (for Turkey)	Chapter 3
Syrian Democratic Forces, 2015–2019	Near-state or hybrid armed actor; counter-terrorist (against ISIL); proxies or auxiliaries (for United States); includes subsidiary or affiliated forces (a) designated as terrorist groups (PKK); (b) acting as local, self-defense forces (self-defense units)	Chapter 3
Tribal Mobilization Force* (Iraq), 2015–2019	Local forces, self-defense forces, counterinsurgents	Chapter 4
Afghan National Army Territorial Force,* 2018–2021	Local forces, paramilitary forces, pro-government forces	Chapter 4

(Continued)

Group, period examined in case study	Common terms applied	Discussion in book
Sahwa* or Sons of Iraq, mid-2006–2009	Local or self-defense forces, counterinsurgents, "anti-insurgent" forces; some subgroups connected to/identified as warlords or criminal gangs	Chapter 2
Counterterrorism Pursuit Teams or "campaign forces" (Afghanistan), 2002–2021	Militias, paramilitary, or auxiliary forces; pro-government forces; death squads; surrogates or proxies (for U.S. counterterrorism missions)	Chapter 4
Tribal counterterrorism auxiliaries (Iraq), late 2014–2019	Militias, paramilitary, or auxiliary forces; pro-government forces; surrogates or proxies (for U.S. counterterrorism missions)	Chapter 4

Note: The dates indicated roughly correspond with the duration of the force or of U.S. support to it. The start date generally includes the period of deliberation immediately prior to formal authorization or actual delivery of assistance. Additional temporal information is included in the case studies when relevant. Initiatives or forces designated with an * indicates those that were granted some degree of state title, status, or recognition.

RESEARCH SOURCES, TOOLS, AND ETHICAL CONSIDERATIONS

The analysis draws from a range of sources, including academic articles and books, governmental or nongovernmental studies and assessments, media reports, congressional testimony, relevant legislation, government program documents or press briefings, and other written accounts of the case study groups or decision-making moments. The research also substantially draws from 226 in-depth, qualitative interviews conducted primarily from 2016 to 2021, with a select number of follow-up interviews between 2022 and 2024. Those interviewed include U.S. civilian and military officers; representatives of partner governments and militaries; Iraqi and Afghan officials and forces; Turkish diplomats working on Syria policy; representatives of the military and political bodies of the Autonomous Administration of North and East Syria (Rojava); members or commanders of the LHSFs; United Nations officials and representatives in these countries; representatives of NGOs and civil society groups; and other experts, journalists, academics, or observers.

Much of the research for this book was developed in the course of pursuing a PhD with the University of Cambridge from 2017 to 2021, and then in follow-up interviews as the material was developed into a book. Fieldwork from 2016 to 2019 included multiple one- to three-week trips to Afghanistan, Iraq, and Turkey, an extended period interviewing policy officials in the Washington, DC, and a one-week trip to northeast Syria. The field research in Turkey primarily focused on interviews with Syrian groups or analysts. Interviews and research conducted from 2020 to 2023 were primarily conducted remotely, but for a brief trip to Afghanistan in 2023 during the course of this book's finalization. Nearly all of the interviews, field research, and analysis on Afghanistan were developed during the period when the previous Government of the Islamic Republic of Afghanistan was in control, before the Taliban's assumption of power in August 2021. The case studies focus on U.S.-supported initiatives with the pre–August 2021 regime, and so it was not necessary to update them to reflect the power dynamics as of the time of writing.

Although the bulk of the research was conducted from 2016 on, before beginning this project, I had previously worked for more than a decade in human rights documentation, conflict analysis, and rule-of-law development in a variety of countries, including Afghanistan and Iraq. In particular, I had pursued a policy-focused research project on the groups in question, as well as other substate forces in Iraq and Afghanistan, with the Global Public Policy Institute prior to beginning this research. As a result, I had baseline information on many of these programs prior to the start of this study, which was useful for generating interviews and contributing to the literature review.

These past research positions, the preexisting network of contacts they generated, and my reputation as a credible researcher on sensitive security and rights issues helped me to identify research subjects and facilitated interview requests. I would not have been able to capture as wide a range of views, across three different country contexts, without prior research experience and networks in these areas. Many interviewees were only comfortable discussing these issues because they were aware of my prior background and knowledge or because they had interacted with me on prior research projects.

Nonetheless, there is always a risk that prior experiences and lenses can affect the objectivity of the analysis, either contributing to preexisting perceptions for the researcher or influencing the way that interview subjects react to the researcher. Although I have never worked for or been part of the U.S. government or U.S. military, my research and programming have frequently been part of the policy dialogue and sometimes directly aimed at shaping U.S. policy in the countries in question. In Iraq, and in certain contexts or with certain interlocutors in Syria and Afghanistan, the fact that I am American by nationality might create perceptions or assumptions of me as an "insider." In addition, although my lens set was not influenced by any experience serving in a U.S. government position, the factors that I identified and gave weight to may well have been influenced by my past work as a human rights advocate, or as a conflict researcher in these areas. My overall take on the influence of these factors on the research would largely reflect the conclusions of Rachel Ormston and her colleagues that "all research will be influenced by the researcher and there is no completely 'neutral' or 'objective' knowledge," but that we nonetheless can—and must—strive to "avoid obvious, conscious, or systematic bias and to be as neutral as possible in the collection, interpretation, and presentation of data."[75] To do so, it was important to take into account not only my own positionality, but also the potential for bias or misrepresentation (intentional or not) among interlocuters. This made it all the more important to interview those whose backgrounds, positions, or viewpoints were different from mine, and also to have a variation in the types of sources, enabling a more robust cross-checking of accounts.

Where specific claims were made about the program design or the control mechanisms developed, supporting documents or evidence were requested and frequently available, in the form of internal memos, policy documents or summaries, briefings or presentations, or other concurrent accounts. In some cases, it was possible to document exchanges or "bargaining" between different actors from copies of email correspondence at the time. Across all of the case studies, accounts of control mechanisms, bargaining positions, and the nature of government approaches were cross-verified and triangulated across interviews. If an interviewee mentioned a particular feature as part of a common approach, this point was then raised with other policy officials serving in roughly the same, or immediately subsequent, time period as a means of cross-verification or to seek further information. For example, within the Syria case study, U.S. officials' observations that there was "double" or "triple" vetting, that vetting criteria included the concern that the groups were "too Islamic," or that there were concerns about "marbling," were then cross-checked across multiple interviewees.

In some cases, accounts by interviewees who came from different sides of the bargaining debate or different sides of the U.S.-LHSF relationships were cross-checked against each other. For example, accounts from FSA commanders and members were useful in comparing how control mechanisms were used by different U.S. agencies and initiatives, given that many had experience across multiple iterations of U.S. support. This also helped in corroborating U.S. government officials' accounts of the control mechanisms applied. Where a specific control mechanism was enforced—for example, a group was cut from U.S. funding due to misconduct—the account was verified by both U.S. official sources and the groups in question, or else was not explicitly provided as an example. Beyond checking factual points or examples, corroboration or cross-comparison was also used to evaluate perceptions of the most significant issues or turning points within bargaining dynamics. For example, it was helpful to compare U.S. and NATO officials' accounts of the ALP debate with those of NGOs, UN representatives, or other external actors; the similarity in their recollections about how the debate devolved, what sort of bargaining took place, and the key issue sets helped to confirm the reliability beyond any one individual's account.

An additional reliability check was that no case study account depended on interview reflections alone. Evidence in media, governmental, or nongovernmental reports written concurrently with the initiative in question helped corroborate the interview testimony. This additional literature and reporting, along with prior academic articles on these groups or periods of time, helped to further expand the sources of information and analysis beyond what would have been possible through interview outreach alone. Although the majority of interviewees were only interviewed once, it was also possible to interview some sources over the course of several interviews. This was additionally useful as a way to cross-check information received from other interlocuters.

Most interviewees preferred to remain anonymous. Given that, and to further protect identities, the default preference is to quote all interviewees anonymously unless permission to do otherwise was explicitly granted by the interviewee. Some interviewees chose to only speak on background and are thus not cited—even anonymously—in the text of this book. Given that some of these programs, or program details within, them might involve sensitive or classified material, former or current government officials interviewed were encouraged to use their discretion and not respond to any questions that might invoke confidential information.

Interviewees were identified through a process of snowball sampling. Past experience and work in the three case study countries furnished an initial list of interview subjects. Each person interviewed was then asked for recommendations for further interviews. Additional interviewees were identified through the literature review. For each of the case studies, it was important to identify individuals who had been involved at different levels of engagement, both those involved in authorization decisions and bargaining, and those concerned with implementing control mechanisms or working with the forces in question. This resulted in some interviews with senior policy makers and officials. For example, interviews included those with former U.S. National Security Adviser H.R. McMaster, retired general (and former CIA director) David Petraeus, retired ambassador Karl Eikenberry, former senior advisers to President Barack Obama, former Afghan President Hamid Karzai, several acting or former ministers of defense and interior from Afghanistan, senior Turkish officials, and senior advisers in the prime minister's office and the National Security Council from Iraq and Afghanistan, respectively. These were extremely important in understanding concerns and back-and-forth over particular LHSF initiatives at particular moments of deliberation, especially where they were able to be compared with concurrent written accounts of these debates (for example, in leaked policy cables, or in other written accounts). Equally important, though, were the inferences of mid- to lower-level policy staff, who often had a more granular account of the way that controls and risk mitigation came into the policy choices and implementation.

The same general inquiries or questions arose with each case study, but whether certain question sets were relevant or not for a given interview depended most strongly on the position of the individual in question. In most cases, interviewees only had insight or perspectives into one country, one particular case study initiative within that country, or only one aspect of that U.S.-LHSF relationship or control mechanism. For example, in an interview with a high-level U.S. decision maker, it might be more important to focus on the most critical issues in deciding whether to partner with a given LHSF, or the most salient aspects or points of tension in debates with other foreign leaders or with Congress over the LHSF initiative in question. By contrast, a lower-level State Department or Defense official might have more technical information about the nature of the control mechanism in question, how it was developed, when, and what other inputs or factors affected its implementation. This made it crucial to spend the first few minutes of every interview identifying with greater precision how the individual was connected to the programs in question, over what period of time, and then adopting an interview approach and set of questions that would accord with their level of knowledge.

A last important point to address concerns the general challenges and methodological issues that arise with regard to research in conflict zones. A wide body of literature has considered the ethical and practical challenges of research in conflict zones, from issues of security and access to concerns about greater risk of politicization and of generating harm to interview subjects.[76] As Wood aptly summarizes, "the ethical imperative of research ('do no harm') is intensified in conflict zones by political polarization, the presence of armed actors, the precarious security of most residents, the general unpredictability of events, and the traumatization through violence of combatants and civilians alike."[77]

Some of the same approaches that are generally endorsed as ways to respond to bias, positionality, or dissimulation in qualitative research are all the more important in the highly fraught context of conflict zones. This includes some of the methods discussed above related to diversity and variation in sources, seeking a range of views that is as wide is possible (and safe), flexibility and adaptability in research methods (as needed for both safety concerns and variation), and an even greater sensitivity to issues of confidentiality.[78]

Navigating these issues and mitigating some of the surrounding risks was significantly aided by my prior research exposure, and the length of time that I have engaged with the subject matter in question. To conduct field research in conflict zones, researchers should have a deep understanding of the patterns of violence and conflict, surrounding power dynamics, potential political or safety implications for fellow researchers, interview subjects, or the wider community, and modes of operating that might address these risks. My more than a decade of experience in and out of these conflict environments was thus a crucial asset in developing and conducting the research. It also contributed insights and points of information that would likely have been lost in a purely historical or desk-based review of these programs. Being present in Afghanistan as the ALP was created, conducting research around Mosul as the TMF were being deployed, or in Washington, DC, during the period of fervent policy debates about how to support the FSA in Syria made me aware of certain contextual dynamics, micro-policy developments or exchanges (i.e., meetings or junctions at which these issues were considered), and relevant interlocuters that I might have missed without these experiences.

While my presence in these environments, often at the same time as these programs were being developed, lent insights and observations that would not have been available through desk research or historical research alone, most of the academic research and interviews were conducted after these programs had closed. This decreased some of the potential sensitivities and risks that might have been triggered by concurrent research. For example, it was much less sensitive to be asking about CIA or State Department support to select FSA groups in 2018 than it would have been in 2013. The latter would have presented substantial roadblocks, dissimulation of information, and, in certain locations, safety risks; it also would have been more susceptible to politicization in the context of the 2013 "information economy"—a high point for deliberation over further U.S. intervention. The fact that most of these initiatives had already ended also decreased the potential that my asking questions about them would create false expectations, or be seen as legitimizing these groups, which are also important risk factors to be aware of in conflict research.

Notwithstanding the risks and additional methodological challenges of research in conflict zones, qualitative and detailed research in these areas is absolutely crucial for the larger field of conflict studies, and for any policy or practitioner decision making that draws from it. As Jonathan Goodhand has written, "If researchers and analysts are not prepared to engage until the guns fall silent, knowledge and understanding tend to be stuck at the pre-war level."[79] This has the risk of leading to analytical conclusions that do not reflect the reality on the ground, and as Goodhand notes, to policy responses that "are likely to be in appropriate."[80] A significant contribution of the subsequent case studies is the degree to which they test theoretical assumptions about proxy warfare dynamics or about interstate relations in these hybrid environments against empirical evidence. The findings significantly correct or further nuance assumptions premised purely on data that is removed from these field-based perspectives. Empirical data and interview-based evidence, of the sort collected in this book, also have their limitations and do not represent the sole truth, but they are an important part of the puzzle. Thus, while additional care needs to be taken, field research in conflict situations is a crucial part of the overall ecosystem of knowledge within international relations.

CHAPTER OUTLINE

Building from this introductory chapter, chapter 1 will elaborate on some of the theoretical expectations and assumptions that will guide the subsequent analysis and argument. The chapter will first introduce the core premises and expectations of principal-agent theory and BPA, considering how they might apply to U.S.-LHSF relationships and to the controls in question. Because principal-agent theory has frequently been applied to security assistance delegations, existing literature can be used to extrapolate a series of expectations for these U.S.-LHSF delegations. While many of these expectations appear to hold true based on the existing evidence, the U.S. decision to apply control mechanisms even where highly costly and unlikely to work does not. The chapter then introduces the bargaining model and the organizational perspectives of BPA as an alternative counterhypothesis. However, to apply BPA to these heterogeneous, transnational policy situations, what is needed is a more expansive conception of the sort of "players" that might be involved in a bargaining moment—from members of foreign governments or bureaucracies, to transnational networks or NGOs, to the LHSFs themselves. To advance this, chapter 1 introduces some of the theories and bodies of literature that might be explored in order to extend BPA to the wider circle of actors and organizations likely involved in the LHSF initiatives and decision making.

The subsequent three chapters introduce the core case studies. They are presented in roughly chronological order but are clustered together in ways that draw out key themes and theoretical insights. Chapter 2 offers a contrast between the two earliest LHSF case studies examined: U.S. support to tribal militias in Iraq from 2005 to 2009, known popularly as the Sons of Iraq or *sahwa* initiative; and to tribal militias in Afghanistan from 2009 to 2012, initially framed as local defense forces and later formalized as the ALP. The contrast between these two initiatives helps to evaluate the strength of either principal-agent or BPA expectations in explaining the control mechanisms and dynamics that resulted. Grouping these two case studies together also begins to demonstrate the larger themes surrounding how control mechanisms play into bargaining debates and establish common bargaining tropes.

Chapter 3 uses five mini-cases of U.S. support initiatives for Syrian LHSFs to broaden the analysis across a range of bargaining scenarios, both between U.S. actors and with other foreign actors. U.S. partner choices and intervention pressures in Syria were a world away from the counterinsurgency and state-building goals that had motivated U.S. support to LHSFs in Iraq and Afghanistan. Despite this, some of the same control mechanisms and bargaining tactics that appeared in Iraq and Afghanistan manifested in U.S. support to Syrian LHSFs. This was even more surprising in the Syria context, where most of the controls were not legally required, and the lack of access to territory, the overall political dynamics, and the nature of the conflict would make control mechanisms extremely costly to impose and very unlikely to work.

Each of the five mini-case studies introduces different bargaining situations and players, as well as armed groups and political stages within the Syria conflict. These range from bargaining situations that resemble those traditionally considered within BPA analysis, like high-level bargaining surrounding the U.S. president (over CIA support to the FSA) or between Congress and the executive branch (as in in the first overt, train-and-equip program for Syrian rebels), as well as more unconventional bargaining dynamics, between U.S. officials and those of foreign governments or even the LHSFs themselves (with two LHSF initiatives in northern Syria). The way that controls manifested across these different bargaining situations and environments helps affirm the counterhypothesis that controls emerge as the product of competing preferences and bargaining, rather than (as principal-agent theory would have it) because the benefits outweigh the costs of imposing them. The chapter concludes by questioning whether these various controls ultimately helped to mitigate the risks in question, or whether they may have actually increased them by masking or rationalizing risks that could not ultimately be controlled.

Chapter 4 pivots from the prior two chapters' focus on bargaining to instead offer a deeper exploration of organizational theory, as well as policy transfer and change. It picks up with some of the Syria examples introduced in chapter 3, exploring how BPA organizational tendencies interacted with bargaining dynamics in the Syria case studies. It then considers both legacy effects and some of these organizational dynamics in two new post-2015 LHSF initiatives in Iraq and Afghanistan—the 2015 TMF and the 2018 Afghan ANA-TF. Across all of these examples (the revisited Syria examples, and the TMF and ANA-TF), organizational tendencies help explain some of the controls that manifested, but usually in interaction with, or as triggered by, other bargaining dynamics and prompts.

Collectively, these examples from Syria, Iraq, and Afghanistan offer a portrait of a set of common controls emerging as something like a default or standard menu of risk mitigation over time. This idea of a "common approach" to risk mitigation is then contrasted with a final case study of LHSFs that represent decided exceptions to the rule. Auxiliary militias engaged with U.S. Special Forces or intelligence operations on counterterrorism missions in Iraq and Afghanistan appeared subject to much fewer (or substantively different) controls. Considering bargaining triggers and dynamics—or the absence of them—in these counterterrorism auxiliaries helps test the generalizability of the bargaining theory, and to further nuance the explanation of how bureaucratic or organizational frames and images can shape the policy dynamics and outcomes.

The final three chapters collate and pull together the conclusions from the case studies into larger thematic or theoretical insights. Chapter 5 builds from chapter 4's assertion of an emerging "common approach" to risk mitigation by exploring what processes or interactions might have contributed to that cohering approach—seeking, essentially, to provide an account of change over time within bureaucratic and organizational processes. It does so by looking at two different junctures of change over time, both focused on examples of human rights–related control mechanisms. Human rights organizations and transnational networks frequently advocated for human rights control mechanisms within specific authorization moments, for example, during the ALP authorization debate, but also pressed to institutionalize them as global standards, and to encourage their implementation in practice. The first case study will revisit the ALP, examining the repeated call for stronger human rights–related control mechanisms over the entire ten-year lifetime of the initiative. The second case study considers a related advocacy push to strengthen a globally applicable human rights–related control mechanism, the Leahy Law. Both examples help to explore the role of practice in internalizing and institutionalizing control mechanism as an emerging SOP or common approach. The focus on transnational advocacy networks and human rights NGOs within this chapter also helps to concretize chapter 1's call for considering how unconventional actors—in this chapter, external, nongovernmental actors—might take part in policy decision making and development.

Taking up chapter 1's call for a more expansive conception of BPA bargaining, chapter 6 collates and assesses the evidence of foreign governments influencing or taking part in U.S. policy decision making from across all of the case studies. It draws a contrast between foreign leaders or officials having a more indirect influence on U.S. decision making and those situations in which foreign leaders are directly participating in bargaining and decision making. The former relies on pathways of influence already identified in the literature on alliance theory, on transnational networks and normative change, and on foreign policy implementation. The latter situation of foreign leaders as full players or co-participants in bargaining and decision making requires some theory building and extrapolation from literature on compromised or shared sovereignty. In both Iraq and Afghanistan, situations of compromised or shared sovereignty created regular patterns of de facto coadministration and governance. This allowed BPA bargaining dynamics that usually occur within an administration to manifest transnationally, across two governments. Two cases from Syria provide an even more provocative extension of this idea of transnational bargaining by illustrating how external actors who are not even the titular sovereign—Turkey and the SDF—could figure as players and co-deliberators in U.S. bargaining and decision making by virtue of their de facto territorial control, access, and coercive capacity in Syrian territory. As a whole this chapter widens the circle of which actors might be presumed to be players in BPA bargaining, or to otherwise have an influence on foreign policy outputs.

The conclusion responds to the overarching question of why control mechanisms manifest, and their relationship to U.S. decision making regarding LHSFs. Reflecting on how control mechanisms were used in the case studies, it suggests that control mechanisms facilitated a compromise between the competing interests of bargaining players and bureaucratic actors. By facilitating this compromise, it allowed controversial LHSF initiatives to go forward notwithstanding concerns about their risks. As such, control mechanisms might be viewed as an enabling device, allowing a wider practice of engagement with LHSFs, even when the costs and benefits of doing so did not necessarily add up. This had broader ramifications for U.S. policy concerns and interests. While controls did little to address the risks presented by LHSFs, they could distort the policy decision-making process in ways that might have enabled riskier security choices. In addition to reflecting on the costs of such policy rationalization, the final chapter will discuss the implications for policy making related to LHSFs, and also the implications for future research.

APPLICABILITY OF FINDINGS

In many ways this is a book about U.S. foreign policy within a specific era of security policy. With substantial empirical detail (in some cases related to previously undisclosed or under-discussed initiatives) and close analysis of key internal policy debates, the subsequent chapters offer an abbreviated history of some of the most significant arenas of U.S. foreign security policy in the post-2001 period. However, although the United

States is in many ways the singular focus, the policy and theoretical implications are much broader.

On the policy front, while the case studies draw from U.S. practice there are direct analogues and lessons learned from these U.S. experiences to dilemmas that other peer countries, or even international institutions, face in similar hybrid political environments. Indeed, French and British Special Forces or intelligence operatives have worked in some of the same global counterterrorism hot spots since 2001, and often with the same range of state and non-state partners and proxies within them.[81] A number of European countries supported non-state armed groups during the conflict in Syria, including British, Dutch, and German nonlethal assistance to parts of the FSA, and French and British intelligence and tactical support to the SDF.[82] In Afghanistan and Iraq, countries who were part of the NATO coalition, including the United Kingdom, Denmark, the Netherlands, and even Sweden, provided training or other in-kind support to some of the substate or semi-state local forces mobilized under U.S. initiatives. Those countries engaged in stabilization or peacekeeping operations in Somalia and Libya (among other countries) have faced the recurrent dilemma of whether to support local militias or quasi-statutory armed groups in order to provide security or retrench the state government.[83]

Nor has the instinct to try to balance or mitigate the risks of these endeavors been singular to the United States. When faced by the policy dilemmas of pursuing security demands via these forces, countries like the United Kingdom, the Netherlands, and other European states have also considered different forms of risk mitigation.[84] The United Nations has adopted a system-wide due diligence policy that also mirrors some of the vetting and sanctioning criteria discussed in this book. These trends suggest that while other actors may not adopt precisely the same tools and approaches as the United States, the question of risk mitigation in these sorts of environments is relevant to a much broader policy audience.

A larger question that might be asked is why we should focus on these non-state and substate partnerships at all, as the era in which international security policy was dominated by asymmetric conflict appears to be giving way to one with a renewed focus on geopolitical competition. As this book was going to press, the central international security dynamics revolved around Russia's invasion of Ukraine and increasing competition and Cold War–esque tensions between the United States and China.

State-on-state conflict is back, many would argue, making threats posed by non-state or substate actors less of a priority.

While it is true that the focus on irregular warfare is not as fervent as it was at the time these forces were mobilized, they are far from out of use. U.S.-LHSF partnerships in Afghanistan ended with the U.S. withdrawal and collapse of the previous regime in August 2021. In Iraq, they had largely drawn down already by 2019. However, as of the time of writing U.S. proxy sponsorship in Syria continued. In addition, there was ample evidence of foreign sponsorships of militias, community defense forces, or other non-state or substate forces in other countries, including in Mali, Burkina Faso, and a number of countries confronting the threat of Boko Haram or other extremist groups.[85] Over the course of 2022 and 2023, new reports of local militias rising up against the Islamist extremist group Al-Shabaab in Somali were creating policy responses that mimicked those documented in Afghanistan and other "counterinsurgency" locales.[86] "It's groundhog day all over again," reflected researcher Ashley Jackson, drawing parallels between the enthusiasm for local mobilization in Somalia with what she witnessed in prior research during the height of the surge in Afghanistan.[87]

Even though higher-level policy attention may be more focused on state-on-state competition, crisis situations and security threats in any number of countries will continue to demand some form of intervention or response, creating a persistent temptation to address these perceived threats through substate or irregular partners. "You have to be able to do both. . . . These missions still exist—so you have to ask how you can conduct these missions better," explained retired general and former CIA director David Petraeus—who played a significant role in many of the LHSF initiatives analyzed in this book.[88] "This kind of activity may be more important than it ever was because we will [be] carrying out missions without substantial forces on the ground," he added.[89]

Such dynamics may even be relevant within state-on-state competition. Academics studying proxy warfare have suggested that rather than the issue going away, increased geopolitical tensions and a more multipolar system might actually increase states' interest in working through proxies.[90] During the Cold War, while the overall political discourse was dominated by competition between the two superpowers, much of the actual activity and action was conducted via proxies in a number of hot conflicts.[91] While not yet quite at that level, there has already has been evidence of popularly mobilized or local forces making an appearance in ongoing sites of geopolitical tension. Civil defense forces have played a significant role in the Russia-Ukraine conflict and have been contemplated as an additional deterrent against a much-feared Chinese invasion of Taiwan.[92]

What this suggests is that the temptation for states to resort to irregular or quasi-state partnerships are not going away anytime soon. The time is still ripe for lessons learned about risk mitigation in proxy partnerships, and some of the unintended side effects or limitations of trying to do so.

The second reason that this book is more broadly applicable is that in many ways it is less about the narrow practice of risk mitigation with LHSFs than it is about developing tools for analyzing foreign policy decision making in and surrounding these hybrid political environments. One larger insight that has emerged from literature reconceptualizing "new warfare" and state sovereignty dynamics in the last two decades is the need for both states and the field of international relations to go beyond state-based assumptions and frameworks—the need to engage more with the range of non-state or, at best, quasi-statutory actors who hold sway in many of these "hybrid" security systems and "ungoverned" environments.[93] In a review of three books focused on state-sponsored militias, governance in ungoverned spaces, and foreign policy in an era of softened sovereignty, Arie Kacowicz concluded that "States have to learn how to live—and even coexist, cooperate, and prosper—with alternative forms and spaces of governance, including actors that use power and violence, sometimes in connivance with states but sometimes in collusion and conflict with them."[94]

This book responds to that larger call in two ways. First, the case studies offer concrete examples of state engagement within these hybrid environments and with a variety of non-state and substate actors. The focus is primarily on U.S. engagement, but also considers engagement by a number of other peer states, particularly in the Syria cases. By exploring the mechanisms of state engagement and attempted regulation or control of these irregular forces, the case studies offer insights into how states go about adjusting the regular tools of statecraft—including tools of engagement, conditionality, and assistance—to non-state or substate actors and policy dynamics.

Second, by combining insights and tools from fields of international relations that incorporate a more diverse set of international and transnational players and actors with domestic bargaining and organizational theory, this book helps to expand the theoretical tool kit for exploring transnational foreign policy generation. As the subsequent case studies will illustrate, to initiate and manage these relationships the United States had to work with, or around, foreign leaders, diplomats, and bureaucrats, international and nongovernmental organizations, local community stakeholders, and even non-state armed groups themselves. To mobilize and maintain these forces they had to get into the messy underworld of substate security politics in some of the most complex and challenging policy arenas in the world. By incorporating perspectives from the literature on transnational networks and normative change, together with what tend to be domestically focused bargaining and organizational dynamics, the analysis broadens existing paradigms for understanding foreign policy decision making in these more transnational or hybrid policy arenas.

What results is an updated set of tools for analyzing an important swath of current policy situations. While grand meta-theories like realism or institutionalism still hold, they lack the sort of mid-level tools of analysis that might allow us to unpack and explain dynamics and interactions at a street level of international relations—the everyday of national and international security policies. Nor are these sufficiently supplemented by the hyperrationalized logic of micro-behavioral theories like principal-agent theory or proxy warfare, which—as the subsequent chapters illustrate—may not account for the range of intervening political, institutional, and psychosocial factors at play. What is needed is a set of mid-level tools for exploring how subnational or transnational bargaining and other organizational or bureaucratic factors can affect policy debates and the outcomes that result from them.

One might well ask how a book squarely focused on the bureaucratic machinery and political touch points of one very singular foreign policy actor, the United States, might do that. Yet foreign policy analysis, and BPA within it, has a long history of using single-case analysis to extrapolate larger explanations of organizational or individual behavior. BPA has tended to produce hyper-detailed and contextualized analysis into the interactions or processes specific to one country, or even one set of policy processes, and to use these to explore broader theoretical contentions or premises. Yet this has not so far limited the inferences being drawn, and the same tools adopted to understand other, unrelated foreign policy dynamics and systems in very different decision-making scenarios. For example, Allison's signature book kick-starting BPA was an in-depth treatment of the Cuban Missile Crisis. Yet the tools and analytical frameworks he developed proved highly relevant in analyzing other decision-making contexts, even if the other situations analyzed bore little to no similarity to the dynamics within the Cuban Missile Crisis (itself a unique foreign policy event), or to the U.S. executive branch dynamics that were Allison's focus. Looking further into the broader field of foreign policy analysis, much of that writing has taken on an almost sociological, psychosocial or historiographical approach. The case studies typically focus on one particular foreign policy actor, state, or subject matter, yet the tools, or the concept that the analysis has come to stand for, has been much more far-reaching. For example, Michael Brecher's almost sociologic tome on the national security culture in Israel allowed the extension of FPA tools and analysis to give greater attention to metapsychosocial issues related to national identity and culture.[95]

This book makes a similar ask. It focuses on the particular practices and pathologies of the U.S. foreign policy machinery as they relate to risk mitigation, to non-state and substate armed groups, and to its engagement in hybrid security environments. Yet the theoretical tools developed could be applied to diverse situations—whether those related to irregular or substate partnerships or in any number of other situations of policy engagement where transnational bargaining or sub-state policy implementation is at issue. This might include a wide range of international assistance—well beyond security assistance—in so-called fragile states. It might also include the range of transnational and interinstitutional bargaining that shapes foreign policy decisions well beyond conflict arenas. As the penultimate chapter will show, while so far limited, FPA concepts have been applied to some intergovernmental institutions or transnational policy situations, including within institutions such as the European Union or in situations where states have delegated authority to multilateral organizations. The analytical tools developed would also advance understanding of policy making in these environments, which are very different from the settings described in this book.

Finally, because this book focuses on capturing decision-making lenses and dynamics in a particular era of U.S. security policy, it in many ways responds to a much larger policy question: how one of the world's leading democracies reconciled itself with an open policy of supporting irregular forces with a reputation for violence and questionable political affiliations and motivations. Ultimately this is a story about risk taking and risk mitigation, about policy leaps and innovation, as well as the crutches that policy makers fall back on. It is about how the U.S. bureaucracy dealt with high-risk situations and actors at the "tip of the spear" of its transnational security policy, and what this suggests about decision making in the hybrid, fluid, and mediated world of twenty-first-century policy making.

1

THEORETICAL FRAMEWORK

Agency Theory Versus Foreign Policy Analysis

This chapter will introduce some theoretical expectations for why control mechanisms might arise, borrowing primarily from two conceptual frameworks: principal-agent theory and bureaucratic policy analysis. A substantial body of literature has relied on principal-agent theory to explain why states delegate security tasks to external actors, the risks that arise as a result of such delegation, and the control mechanisms that principals deploy to address these risks. Preliminary analysis suggests that many of the expectations of principal-agent theory bear out in the security partnerships and situations that are of primary interest in this book. However, they appear to fall short in explaining why the United States as principal might adopt control mechanisms in situations where they show little promise of working and are costly to deploy.

To respond to this puzzle, this chapter will introduce a counterhypothesis grounded in bureaucratic policy analysis. BPA has been used less commonly in situations like that of LHSF support, but its premise that foreign policy decisions are driven by intra-bureaucratic deliberations and organizational frameworks offers an alternate explanation and potential driver of controls. The second half of this chapter will introduce the primary bargaining and organizational paradigms that might be used to explain manifestation of control mechanisms in many of the case studies. It will also explore how BPA tools, which tend to be grounded in analysis of domestic actors, might be expanded to consider the broader range of non-U.S.-government actors who took part in or shaped deliberations about LHSFs.

PRINCIPAL-AGENT THEORY

Agency or principal-agent theory emerged within academic economic literature in the 1970s as a way to understand relationships within complex organizations, and the consequences of differing interests within such relationships.[1] Principal-agent theory gained greater prominence in political science with the rise of rational choice theory.[2] Most political science discussions of principal-agent theory have focused on the delegation of power and authority within political organizations and bureaucracies—for example, that between the legislative body and the government bureaucracy.[3] However, principal-agent theory has also been applied in the international relations and conflict studies literature. It has been used to understand the delegation of authority by states to international organizations or with intergovernmental bodies, such as the European Union.[4] It has been a prominent framework used to discuss proxy warfare relationships and dynamics,[5] and to explain dilemmas surrounding state delegation of security tasks, both to other states[6] and to non-state forces.[7]

The overall construct of principal-agent theory is to analogize relationships to a contract in which one party, the principal, delegates a task to another party, the agent.[8] Delegation allows for division of labor and time and/or cost savings for the principal.[9] Delegation will be particularly attractive where the agents have specific expertise, knowledge, or technical competency, or where the task would be particularly costly for the principal to perform.[10] However, agents tend to have their own interests and preferences. As Oliver Williamson described them, agents are "self-interest seeking with guile."[11] They may shirk the task they are given, or act in other ways that are adverse to the principal's interests, what is referred to as policy "slack."[12] To limit such slack, principals will try to pick agents whose interests align most closely with their own. However, principals frequently lack information about the agents and their interests, and such *information asymmetries* can lead the principal to choose an agent ill-suited to the task, or whose interests, profile, or objectives pose greater risks than are acceptable.[13] This is known generally as *adverse selection*.[14] Choosing an agent without full knowledge of the risks involved can increase the overall *moral hazard* of the relationship.[15]

Principal-agent theory predicts that principals might try to minimize shirking or slack by developing mechanisms of control.[16] In addition to developing *selection mechanisms* to try to choose the best agent or filter out those with conflicts of interest, the principal might establish *rules and standards* of conduct for the agent, or set out parameters for carrying out the task. Establishing *monitoring and oversight* or reporting mechanisms can determine whether those rules and parameters are being followed, while *incentives or sanctions* can be used to enforce compliance. In some delegation situations, the principal might create *checks and balances* by vesting other institutions or agents with overlapping or competing mandates, so that various agents check each other without the principal having to be involved.[17] In addition, a classic construct in principal-agent theory is that control mechanisms might be enforced through either "police patrols" or "fire alarms."[18] In the former, the principal expends effort (or details agents) to actively monitor for slack or transgressions, while in the latter, the principal does no active patrolling but assumes that interested parties—for example, the media, interested citizen groups or NGOs, or other stakeholders—will alert the principal where something goes wrong.

Of these different control mechanisms, the selection controls, and overall constraints on effective selection, tend to be the most significant. Finding a like-minded agent decreases the likelihood of significant slack or adverse behavior without the need to deploy costly control mechanisms.[19] In addition, where selection is limited or misplaced, it can have knock-on effects or correlate with the weakness of other control mechanisms. Information asymmetry and/or lack of principal knowledge of a situation (or at least less relative to the agents) can both impair agent selection, and make any subsequent monitoring or enforcement more difficult. Somewhat relatedly, situations where there is only a limited selection pool can create a higher risk of slack or undesirable behavior. With fewer options, the likelihood of finding the right agent is lower. In addition, in a limited selection pool, "agents know that principals have few other options," and so sanctions are less likely to be credible, note Hawkins and Jacoby.[20]

While control mechanisms might sound attractive in theory, there may be many reasons that principals decide not to introduce them, or to do so only minimally. A core assumption of principal-agent theory is that control mechanisms are costly, and that in many situations they may not bring substantial dividends or work at all.[21] The resources and time spent trying to enact them may outweigh the benefits of the delegation. In some situations, introducing cumbersome control mechanisms might impede the ability of the agent to carry out the task effectively. For all of these reasons, principal-agent theory presumes that principals will not pursue control mechanisms where the costs of imposing them outweigh the benefits, and that as a rule, principals will pursue the least costly control mechanisms available.[22] Because we assume that principals will only impose control mechanisms where the benefits outweigh the costs, we would not expect heavy use of controls in cases where they are unlikely to work.

Principal-agent theory offers a number of factors that might make control mechanisms too costly. Control mechanisms significantly depend on knowledge of what the agent is doing, whether it has carried out the assigned tasks, stuck to the standards in questions, or engaged in undesirable behavior or slack. High information symmetries—which might be due to the nature of the environment, the knowledge base of the principal, or the relative specialization of the agent—will make it difficult for the principal to obtain that information. The degree of physical observability (or how costly that would be) may also be important. As Erica Gould summarizes, monitoring "will be more costly if that activity is less observable, less measurable, and more dependent on agent expertise."[23] Control mechanisms would also be considered too costly where they undermine agents' efficiency and the value of delegation. As Darren Hawkins and his coauthors note, "If the principal must learn everything that the agent knows and observe everything the agent does, the gains from specialization diminish accordingly. At the extreme, with perfect knowledge and monitoring, it is almost as if the principal has performed the task herself."[24]

Other qualities or characteristics of the delegation might also impair control mechanisms. Where the task delegated represents a high policy priority, and there are no credible alternatives (for example, by the patron directly taking on the task itself), then principals may be more willing to tolerate slack.[25] In addition, because sanctions are less credible where agents know that the principal has limited alternatives, we would expect weaker results from control mechanisms in these high-priority delegations.[26] Control mechanisms might also be weaker, or less likely to succeed, due to the nature of the principal, or of the agent in question. For example, "complex patrons"—principals with more than one actor or entity within it, as with a bureaucracy—may face higher coordination costs in trying to exert controls, and because agents can play the multiple parts off against each other, complex principals may be less effective in enforcing standards and conditions.[27] In situations where there are multiple, competing principals vying for agents, agents are less reliant on any one patron, and threats or sanctions may be less effective. Last, where the delegation is highly dependent on or motivated by agent expertise, we might expect monitoring or other control efforts to be less effective because in such scenarios the agent likely has more knowledge or access to information than the principal, and could thus easily evade attempts at control.

Applying these general theories to situations in which states delegate tasks to outside agents generates the following expectations:

- Expectation 1: States will delegate where it allows them cost savings, division of labor, and specialization.
- Expectation 2: However, such delegations will frequently result in side effects or costs for the patron because of dissimilar interests between the principal and the agent. Information asymmetry and a limited selection pool will tend to increase such adverse selection and the accompanying agency slack.
- Expectation 3: Principals are likely to try to address slack by erecting control mechanisms, such as selection, monitoring, enforcement, and sanctions, but these are costly and frequently weak, particularly in environments with high information asymmetry, a limited selection pool, and high principal dependence on the delegation.
- Expectation 4: Where monitoring and enforcement would prove costly or ineffective, where delegation is a high priority, and/or where there are limited delegation options (the agent is indispensable), principals are likely to have a high tolerance for slack and exert minimal effort at control mechanisms.

PRINCIPAL-AGENT THEORY EXPECTATIONS FOR LHSF DELEGATIONS

To explore how these expectations might help explain the dynamics surrounding LHSF delegations, it is helpful to briefly examine what the available literature suggests about these principal-agent theories in the sort of conflict environments and security assistance delegations at issue in the case studies.

Expectation 1: States will delegate where it allows them cost savings, division of labor, and specialization.

A wide body of literature supports the idea that states will delegate to foreign forces where doing so saves them from deploying their own forces, not only to the forces of other partner states but also to irregular forces and LHSFs.[28] Such proxies enable "warfare on the cheap," saving both financial and political costs of greater troop deployments.[29] Local forces may offer additional cost savings because they are already present in the target locations, and may have few other employment options, meaning they can be mobilized more cheaply and quickly than either external states or even those of the third-party state.[30] In addition to such cost savings, local forces are valued for bringing substantial local know-how, relationships, and intelligence.[31] Framed in principal-agent terms, they might be viewed as specialists in the local conflict or geographic area.[32]

Such arguments have been applied specifically to LHSFs in Iraq, Afghanistan, and Syria. Supporting Syrian forces was much less politically costly than the idea of deploying U.S. ground forces.[33] In Iraq and Afghanistan, supporting local tribal counterinsurgents did not prevent substantial U.S. deployments, but it reduced the number that would have been needed for the proposed "surge" strategies to succeed. In addition, in both contexts, local forces were presumed to offer division of labor and specialization benefits—they knew the local fighters, insurgent networks, and communities much better than either U.S. or other Iraqi or Afghan state forces.[34]

Expectation 2: However, such delegations will frequently result in side effects or costs for the patron because of dissimilar interests between the

principal and the agent. Information asymmetry and a limited selection pool will tend to increase such adverse selection and the accompanying agency slack.

Existing literature also readily supports the second proposition, with examples of adverse selection and agent slack across U.S. security assistance relationships in Iraq, Afghanistan, and Syria. Where the United States has sought to delegate counterterrorism or counterinsurgency tasks, the third-party states or non-state forces in question have frequently shirked the desired tasks, or have only pursued security tasks as it suited their own interests.[35]

In some cases, substantial information asymmetry—particularly in environments where the United States had less means for overcoming information barriers—generated a greater degree of slack. This would particularly be the case in Syria, where both the high level of flux and complexity in the environment and the lack of U.S. presence (which reduced observability) led to extreme information asymmetries. One policy study that applied a principal-agent lens to U.S. proxy dynamics in Syria concluded that "information deficiencies" and "lack of knowledge by sponsors, including the US, was so extreme as to not just cause problems inside one sponsor-proxy relationship," but to skew the "entire reading of the conflict environment."[36]

In some situations, it is less that the United States is blind to agent slack than that a limited selection pool leaves few other alternatives. Taking the example of U.S. counterinsurgency goals in Iraq and Afghanistan, Stephen Biddle and colleagues noted that, in such situations, "the US is rarely free to choose some better qualified local ally than the threatened regime, as the point of the war is to preserve the regime."[37] The selection pool of non-state actors is often equally limited. Where the United States has partnered with non-state actors, it is often as a last resort, because no state partners are able or willing to address the security threats in that territory. Within these conflict contexts, there is usually a limited subset of armed actors that know the local context, are militarily capable, and are willing to partner with the United States (or vice versa). In a remote Afghan village, there might only be one local tribal leader with both the capability and the will to raise a force that would fight with the United States. In Syria, hundreds of armed groups formed after 2011, but only one fighting coalition, the Kurdish-led Syrian Democratic Forces (discussed further in chapter 3), proved to have sufficient military capacity and enough common interest in defeating ISIL.[38]

Expectation 3: Principals are likely to try to address slack by erecting control mechanisms, such as selection, monitoring, enforcement, and sanctions, but these are costly and frequently weak, particularly in environments with high information asymmetry, a limited selection pool, and high principal dependence on the delegation.

A survey of news reports and publicly available policy documents provides clear evidence that the United States has tried to address slack and other risks in its partners by introducing control mechanisms like vetting, monitoring, and sanctions in LHSF relationships.[39] As the subsequent three chapters will establish in greater detail, the United States has adopted a range of control mechanisms with its LHSF partners in Afghanistan, Iraq, and Syria. These include formal and complex vetting processes and criteria, as well as informal selection processes.[40] In many cases, the United States developed formal codes of conduct or rules, which were then inculcated through training or through U.S. forces' advising and mentoring.[41] There also tended be a variety of monitoring and reporting mechanisms, designed to detect noncompliance, and, in many of the programs, sanctions to reduce pay or equipment for forces who did not comply.[42]

Principal-agent theory would suggest heavy costs and limitations when control mechanisms are applied in conflict environments.[43] Principal-agent theory expects that controls will be more costly or harder to enforce where the information is less observable or depends on agent expertise. Conflict zones represent such limitations to an extreme degree because the security or political dynamics therein frequently limit direct observation by the patron (at least not without costly deployment of further troops or staff), as well as the prospect of other, nongovernmental observers who might otherwise act as a watchdog or free monitoring device for the patron. The sort of NGO or media "fire alarms" envisioned in some principal-agent literature could be equally limited by security concerns in such environments. The complexity and frequent fluctuations in conflict dynamics might also make it more time-consuming and costly for the patron to obtain up-to-date and accurate information, such as would be necessary for effective monitoring. In addition, the United States would often be delegating to these local forces because they are local conflict specialists, and as such, the agent would have a better grasp of the fast-changing and fluctuating dynamics than would be possible for any outside actor, reinforcing information asymmetries.[44]

In addition to the challenges of the environment, U.S. dependence on these crucial security partners, and the nature of both the LHSFs and of the United States as a principal, would also tend to result in weak or underenforced controls. The situations in which the United States resorts to partnering with LHSFs tend to be those where other alternatives have been exhausted, and also where the delegation itself enables a high policy priority—for example, the ability to pursue terrorist or insurgent threats without putting U.S. forces at greater risk. Principal-agent theory suggests that in such situations, the United States would have a fair amount of tolerance for slack. The United States is also a classic "complex principal," with different parts of the bureaucracy and Congress collectively taking part in managing security assistance. In addition, the United States would also not be the only potential patron in these environments, given the range of external and domestic stakeholders in Iraq, Afghanistan, and Syria.[45] These two factors would make it more difficult for the United States to exert control mechanisms consistently, and would create opportunities for LHSFs to ignore or evade them.

Last, some of the literature also suggests that even with effectively supported control mechanisms, they might not work well with the groups in question. Neil Mitchell, Sabine Carey, and Christopher Butler argue that there will be more adverse behavior by militias because they lack institutional screening, training, and inculcation of professional values (what might be described as institutionalized control mechanisms).[46] A core focus of the book is how the United States as a principal might try to address this issue by inserting control mechanisms for these more thinly institutionalized forces. However, Mitchell and colleagues suggest that even if these are introduced, they will be less effective with irregular forces than similar mechanisms would with state forces because militias or other irregular actors are "less likely to have internalized systems of ethics, less likely to value their positions, and are less likely to have Arrow's 'reputational enforcements.'"[47]

Expectation 4: Where monitoring and enforcement would prove costly or ineffective, where delegation is a high priority, and/or where there are limited delegation options (the agent is indispensable), principals are likely to have a high tolerance for slack and exert minimal effort at control mechanisms.

If the third proposition is found to hold up, it then raises a puzzle with regard to the fourth and final one. The forgoing discussion would suggest that in conflict environments, and especially with regard to these LHSF delegations, there would be a high likelihood of adverse selection, information asymmetry, agent slack, and ineffective control mechanisms. In addition, in these complex and fluid conflict environments, with limited access due to security issues and other conflict sensitivities, one would expect any attempt at control mechanisms to be highly costly. Exerting high costs to try to rein in LHSF agents would likely be even less desirable given the high priority given to these delegations, and the likely limited results of those controls. Principal-agent theory expects that, where such mechanisms are likely to be both costly and ineffective, principals will not pursue them, or will only do so minimally.

However, this is not what happened with regard to U.S. delegations to LHSFs. As chapters 2 through 5 will show, this expectation from principal-agent theory is not adequately borne out in practice. Despite the fact that most of these control mechanisms delivered minimal benefits, and were known to be costly, they were introduced and sustained, even where not formally required. Moreover, despite their record of ineffectiveness and high costs, the overall trajectory has been not only to sustain these control mechanisms within individual LHSF support programs, but to increasingly apply them as new LHSF relationships emerged.

This book will approach this puzzle by supplementing these principal-agent expectations with those of another theoretical framework, that of foreign policy analysis or bureaucratic policy analysis. Even those considering these security delegations according to a principal-agent lens frequently note that other political considerations may influence the decision to delegate or control.[48] Given this, the political bargaining and bureaucratic management frames within BPA might provide an alternate answer for why control mechanisms emerged in so many cases.

BUREAUCRATIC POLICY ANALYSIS

Foreign policy analysis emerged in response to calls in the 1950s and 1960s to look beyond the state level of analysis, and to understand foreign policy decision making in terms of not only external but also internal or domestic factors.[49] Jean Garrison describes FPA as an attempt to "open the black box of domestic politics and policymaking in an effort to understand actors' choices in global politics."[50] Rather than viewing foreign policy outcomes or actions as the product of organized, rational responses to systemic factors or other stimuli, early FPA theorists argued that foreign policy decision making had much more to do with the subjective and highly irrational range of factors that lay within the heads of decision makers, the "psycho-social milieu" in which they operate, and the larger sausage factories and bureaucratic environments that produce foreign policy for a state.[51]

While a full review of FPA theories is beyond the scope of this book, it is worth noting a few of the different approaches, if only to illustrate the diversity within FPA.[52] A substantial focus has been on the psychological factors affecting foreign policy decision makers, including group or leader predispositions, profiles, and typologies, as well as the way that foreign policy leaders take in and interpret information, which is inevitably impaired by cognitive limitations, and framed or shaped by cognitive lenses, biases, and misperceptions.[53] Others have focused on how group dynamics (including "groupthink"), role conceptions, or social practices can take over, resulting in foreign policy outcomes that appear against the individual or national interests of the actors involved.[54] Scholars like Michael Barnett and Peter Katzenstein explored how not just individual or group ideas and beliefs, but national identity, culture, and social practices within a society or within the foreign policy–making apparatus, shaped state positions.[55]

Graham Allison's seminal 1971 book *The Essence of Decision-Making* sparked a new subfield within FPA, which tends to be referred to as bureaucratic politics analysis, and which will be the primary theoretical focus of this book.[56] Allison challenged the rational policy approach, arguing that "attempts to understand happenings as the more or less purposive acts of unified national governments" leave out a crucial part of what is driving foreign policy, namely what is happening among the political players and institutions that make up the foreign policy bureaucracy.[57] Allison offers two other "models" or accounts that instead view foreign policy decisions or outputs as the products of competitive, discursive, or organizational tendencies within the policy-making apparatus.[58] Writing with Morton Halperin (his frequent coauthor on BPA), Allison argued that, "the 'maker' of government policy is not one calculating decision-maker, but rather a conglomerate of large organizations and political actors who differ substantially about what their government should do on any particular issue and who compete in attempting to affect both governmental decisions and the actions of their government."[59]

Allison coined the idea of the "stand-sit" position—the proposition that "where you stand depends on where you sit."[60] Essentially, the position taken by any given stakeholder or player substantially reflects the organizational position or interests of the part of the bureaucracy they represent, as well as potentially their personal background, experiences, or commitments.[61] The ultimate policy outcome is the result of bargaining between these different stakeholders, and should be considered a compromise of these competing views and stand-sit positions, rather than any given player's preference.[62]

Most of Allison and Halperin's writing, as with subsequent BPA studies, has focused on high-level debates surrounding the executive, frequently in crisis moments (the sort of deliberations invoked in the Cuban Missile Crisis debates). However, Allison and Halperin, among others, also recognize that other parts of the bureaucracy are engaged in lower-level decision making and bargaining.[63] There is frequently a lot of leeway in how to implement a top-level decision, and implementation choices might be determined by the same sort of stand-sit positioning and bargaining as the high-level decision making.[64] A separate body of "implementation" literature argues that bargaining and decision making in the course of implementation can be even more significant in determining foreign policy outputs than what happens at key decision moments.[65] As Schroeder and Friesendorf argue, "Implementation is not a technical process of simply translating political decisions into practices. Instead, implementation is a game of political bargaining that crucially depends on the interests of the implementing actors."[66]

BPA also tends to include a slightly distinct but complementary approach: the organizational process model. Organizational process theory considers how foreign policy outputs are shaped by the routines, processes, and ordering tendencies of the organizations and subparts of the bureaucracy involved. Like the metaphor of a person holding a hammer seeing a nail in everything, organizations tend to see foreign policy problems through their own mission set, policy approach, and tool kit. From this lens, organizations have their own interests—they compete for roles, missions, and resources that advance those interests or their own survival.[67] As Christopher Hill summarizes, a large bureaucracy or organization has a tendency to "socialize its staff into a particular set of values ... over and above apparently superordinate value-systems such as 'national interest.'"[68]

Organizational process theories also place a heavy emphasis on the way that standard operating procedures, protocols, and lenses shape the way information is received, what policy alternatives or options are developed, and how decisions are implemented. As Allison offered, "At any given time, a government consists of existing organizations, each with a fixed set of standard operating procedures and programs. The behavior of these organizations—and consequently of the government—relevant to an issue in any particular instance is, therefore, determined primarily by routines established in these organizations prior to that instance."[69] On this view, organizational routines or patterns may queue a certain lens or approach to a given foreign policy problem, somewhat predetermining a solution, or at least the logic by which it is decided. SOPs or other common "programs or repertoires" of response may also be triggered by the nature of an issue or by the foreign policy decision in question, which leaves much of the content or output of the foreign policy issue in question to be determined by bureaucratic routine rather than, arguably, by rational decision making.[70]

Although BPA has been used to analyze many crisis and security situations, it has been invoked less often than principal-agent theory to analyze security assistance partnerships. Thus, there is not a readily available body of literature applying these concepts to the sort of situations explored in this book. However, from the above principles of BPA we might extrapolate several expectations for the subsequent cases. First, we would expect that the proposal or idea of supporting a given LHSF would generate bureaucratic debate and bargaining in many (if not all) scenarios. In the classic BPA examples of bargaining, a crisis moment like the emergence of the Cuban Missile Crisis,[71] or a policy decision point like whether to withdraw American troops from Europe during the Cold War,[72] would trigger a "decision" or "action" game within the bureaucracy. Different policy principals or agency or department figures would bargain and maneuver to try to persuade the president to take their preferred course of action, or to prevail in securing the policy proposal or budgetary allocation they deemed best. They might do so by leveraging their own authority on an issue, or their relationship with the president, or use other tactics of persuasion to build a coalition of co-supporters or to marginalize or limit opposing viewpoints.[73] "Control of implementation, control over information that enables one to define the problem and identify the available options, persuasiveness with other players (including players outside the bureaucracy) and the ability to affect other players' objectives" were among the bargaining advantages that Allison and Halperin identified.[74]

The question of U.S. support for a given LHSF might trigger a similar action game or bargaining moment. In a climate in which the national security strategy is increasingly operationalized "by, with, and through" local partners,[75] the decision to mobilize LHSF units might be viewed as the twenty-first-century equivalent of whether to deploy or counter intercontinental ballistic missiles. LHSFs may also win adherents or spark internal debates because they represent unique bureaucratic opportunities: such proposals often come with substantial funding and manpower, or they may offer particular U.S. agencies or institutions greater influence or prominence in critical foreign policy situations. Some subsets of the U.S. government—for example, so-called white SOF, who specialize in supporting indigenous forces—may see such initiatives as part of their mission set and tool kit, and thus more readily support them.[76] Meanwhile, given all the risks associated with LHSFs, other bureaus or departments may see such initiatives as threatening their core mission sets, values, or interests, negatively triggering their respective "stand-sit" positions. For all these reasons, the question of whether to mobilize local forces or expand an existing LHSF initiative is very likely to trigger an internal bargaining scenario, with the fate of that initiative, and the funding, mandate, and rules surrounding the forces in question, strongly shaped by the parameters and outcome of that bargaining debate.

Within such a bargaining process, BPA expects that different actors or parts of the bureaucracy will try to persuade or coerce others to accept their view. One might expect risk-mitigation and responding control mechanisms to play a prominent role in such persuasion and bargaining tactics. LHSFs present a range of countervailing policy considerations, and a host of legal, reputational, or consequential security risks. As a result, policy debates surrounding such forces tend to consider not only whether the benefits outweigh the costs, but whether those costs can be mitigated or contained to some degree. The sort of control mechanisms that were introduced in the discussion of principal-agent theory—selection mechanisms that might vet for more like-minded, better-behaving, or otherwise less risky forces; restrictions on the supported LHSFs to ensure that they did not transgress policy redlines; and monitoring and sanctions to enforce those redlines—might be central in such a debate. For proponents, adjusting an LHSF proposal by including control mechanisms might be a way to persuade senior policy makers that the risks were manageable, or of blunting the critiques of those opposing the initiative. Opponents or skeptics might insist on such measures as a way to address the risks that concerned them most. According to BPA expectations, the ultimate program design or parameters adopted for LHSFs, including the control mechanisms, might not resemble any one party's preferred model, but would represent a compromise between different stakeholders in the bargaining process.

A last important application of BPA theory and expectation for control mechanisms is that there may be entrenchment effects once these are adopted. Much of the writing on the organizational attributes of bureaucracies concerns the claim that they adopt internal rules, norms, and operating procedures or scripts, which then determine how they approach policy decisions, and the options available for responding to a given dilemma or policy choice. The presumption of organizational theory is that these organizational processes and rules structure policy outcomes in ways that are difficult for any single policy maker to change or diverge from.[77] Allison described a sort of bureaucratic or organizational inertia that could allow for incremental change, but would also limit dramatic splits from existing organizational scripts or processes: "Organizational procedures and repertoires change incrementally.... A program once undertaken is not dropped at the point where objective costs outweigh benefits. Organizational momentum carries it easily beyond the loss point."[78]

This inertial quality of organizational rules and processes allows us to explore a counter-hypothetical for why control mechanisms might be proposed or endure even when their costs would seem to outweigh their benefits, challenging the principal-agent explanations. Control mechanisms typically take the form of contract rules, monitoring mechanisms, or fixed penalties, mechanisms that feature as standard procedures and elements within bureaucratic management. Particular programs or repertoires of these policy-management tools will become part of the SOPs or rules for a given area of programming or type of U.S. government activity. As a result, one might hypothesize that, once certain controls or risk-mitigation strategies become relatively routine, and are absorbed into organizational SOPs or practices, they then would continue to be performed out of habit, regardless of the costs or benefits, or the particular bargaining interests invoked by a given situation. The conservative tendencies of bureaucracies would protect or sustain these rules and approaches even where other players' interests did not demand them, and even where imposing them might be costly.

A WIDER RANGE OF PLAYERS IN LHSF BARGAINING

All of the above conjectures suggest that BPA theory might offer useful insights into how risk-mitigation mechanisms emerge and how they connect to political decision making and organizational dynamics surrounding LHSFs. However, one challenge of applying the BPA framework to the case studies in question is that BPA has tended to focus on bargaining and organizational effects within the state policy-making apparatus alone, to the exclusion of external stakeholders.[79] By contrast, a prima facie examination of the case studies suggests a much wider range of actors have been involved in bargaining around LHSF authorization and program design, including foreign government leaders and bureaucrats, Congress, civil society or nongovernment organizations, and potentially even the LHSFs themselves. While this does not rule out applying BPA principles and theories to these cases, it does require a degree of theorization and extrapolation of how external players might take part in U.S. bureaucratic bargaining.

In much of BPA writing, the focus is on the most central or prominent decision-making structures—those within formal positions of power officially mandated to decide and develop policy, and often those at the higher echelons of such structures. Allison and Halperin, for example, focus much of their discussion on the inner circle surrounding the U.S. president. They discuss Congress and other actors such as the media and interest groups, but only as "ad hoc players" in the "wider government game," with little seeming actual role or influence charted in the examples and case studies given.[80] Foreign leaders received even shorter shrift. The influence of foreign leaders and other external actors were treated primarily as stimuli, indirectly sparking the foreign policy issue that must be dealt with or shaping the crisis parameters. As Allison and Halperin wrote, "Since actions by other nations can affect the stands players take, and thereby affect decisions and actions, we must consider how actions of other nations enter into the process of decision bargaining and how they affect actions."[81] They gave the example of how Soviet deployment of an anti-ballistic missile (ABM) triggered the question of whether the United States should do the same to avoid an "ABM gap."[82]

Much of the BPA analysis since Allison and Halperin's early writing has followed this approach, focusing on the key principals and bureaucratic institutions within the executive, and in particular the U.S. executive branch. This has led to a number of critiques that BPA is too state-centric, and that it has not given enough attention to the legislative branch or other external stakeholders.[83]

Some authors have sought to fill this gap through a deeper examination of the role of the legislature vis-à-vis the executive branch in policy decision making,[84] or by mapping the interactions between Congress, the executive, and interest groups.[85] Although much less numerous, some studies have applied BPA's precepts to organizations or bureaucracies that operate transnationally, like the European Union,[86] or to international organizations that administer foreign policy on behalf of multiple states.[87]

Yet although application of BPA to transnational settings or to bargaining involving foreign or nongovernmental actors remains the minority approach, BPA has long held the promise of being applied in such situations. In Michael Brecher's classic 1972 study of the role national culture and identity as a factor within FPA, he observed, "The presence of externally based foreign policy interest groups is widespread in an age of 'penetrating political systems': no state is totally immune from group pressures stemming from beyond its territorial bounds."[88] In a 1995 article surveying the first few decades of FPA, Valerie Hudson argued that FPA's potential to explore more diverse sources of foreign policy creation and influence—including the personal characteristics of even minor foreign leaders, "legislative politics, opposition groups, domestic political imperatives," and other factors—was even more needed in post–Cold War political dynamics.[89] Writing more recently, Rainer Baumann and Frank Stengel argued that FPA, with its emphasis on going beyond the unitary state, would be well suited to exploring how a range of non-state actors— from international organizations to private security companies to transnational NGOs—are increasingly acting as "policy generators," directly involved in decision making and policy implementation.[90]

The subfield of foreign policy implementation, which considers the implementation of a decision as equally crucial to the content of foreign policy as the initial decision making, has also tended to include a wider range of actors.[91] Discussions of how a policy is shaped in the course of implementation have tended to include not only the executive branch bureaucrats in question, but also representatives of foreign states, international organizations, and even non-state actors.[92] For example, Ursula Schroeder and Cornelius Friesendorf explored how bargaining and negotiations between representatives of international missions, aid agencies, Bosnian political institutions, and the field offices of international organizations influenced the implementation of international law enforcement policies in postwar Bosnia.[93]

Such literature offers a starting point for applying BPA in bargaining scenarios that significantly involve actors outside of the U.S. government. However, a degree of theory building is needed to apply these starting conceptions, and to identify pathways by which nongovernmental or external actors might play a role in policy bargains and bureaucratic decision making. Three categories of players are likely to be important for the LHSF scenarios in question: Congress, transnational or nongovernmental actors and organizations, and foreign leaders or members of foreign government bureaucracies.

Congress has not been completely absent from past treatments of BPA. In their early writing, Allison and Halperin tended to conceptualize it as one of the less directly involved "concentric" circles of influence surrounding the president, alongside other lobbyists and the media.[94] Subsequent writing has offered a slight correction to this narrow view of Congress's role. Jonathan Bendor and Terry Moe offered a three-way model of U.S. foreign policy making, with constant bargaining and indirect influence strategies between the executive branch, Congress, and outside interest groups shaping the ultimate policy outcomes.[95] In a later book, Halperin devoted a chapter to the role of Congress, noting that Congress can influence foreign policy outputs by shaping shared images of national interest or by changing the "rules of the game" and mandating specific roles, functions, or bureaucratic structures within the executive branch.[96] Although not within the field of BPA, other political scientists have expanded the tools by which Congress might influence executive policy making by examining the scope of delegation, means of oversight, and how other congressional functions outside the formal legislative arena might shape bureaucratic deliberations and outcomes.[97]

These legislative functions can have a direct bearing on controls, either by creating parts of the bureaucracy that would become in-house constituencies for human rights controls (further illustrated in chapter 5), or by directly mandating certain control mechanisms—for example, vetting, reporting, or monitoring structures—within funding legislation (further illustrated in some of the Iraq and Syria case studies).[98] In addition to being able to directly mandate certain controls, congressional actors play an important shaping role on executive branch decision making through their oversight and accountability functions. Congressional actors may spotlight risks or concerns related to LHSFs through their power to call public hearings, or in their regular questioning and monitoring functions. They may also threaten to withhold or block funding if their concerns are not sufficiently responded to or addressed, which in some cases could generate pressure for the adoption or strengthening of controls. In some situations, these regular congressional oversight and reporting functions enable a continuing participatory role for Congress throughout the implementation of LHSF programs, including that of any control mechanisms.

Congress is also an important actor to explore as a conduit of influence for other external stakeholders, such as domestic or transnational interest groups and networks, the media, public interest constituencies, and even other foreign officials. In theorization of FPA processes as well as in certain treatments of principal-agent theory, the relationship between Congress and external interest groups or the media has sometimes been framed as a symbiotic one.[99] Under-resourced congressional staff and representatives rely on outside groups to provide information and generate policy ideas of relevance to particular issue areas, which enables more active congressional monitoring and policy generation. On the flip side, these outside groups depend on Congress's voice and funding strings to exert a powerful influence on the executive branch.[100] A wide range of literature has explored how—similar to domestic interest groups—transnational actors and networks may work through or with Congress to influence outcomes in U.S. foreign policy.[101] Such transnational networks or epistemic communities may be comprised of nongovernmental advocacy groups or civil society organizations, but they might equally be made of up representatives of foreign governments acting in their personal capacity.[102] Foreign governments may also utilize contacts in Congress—as well as other pressure points or relationships with members of the executive branch and bureaucracy—to try to exert influence on foreign policy processes in ways that align with their state interests and formal policy positions.[103]

Transnational actors and networks, and other domestic civil society bodies or NGOs, may also influence foreign policy decision making through a number of other persuasion and pressure strategies outside of congressional connections. A broad range of literature has considered how transnational networks, civil society, nongovernmental organizations, and social movements can work to shift or ingrain norms, or to elicit changes in foreign policy positions and rules over time. They might use information, evidence, and documentation to shed light on an issue, to frame the debate, and to generate credible policy solutions; or they might engage those in power in regular dialogue and argumentation to persuade them to implement a particular policy, reform, or position.[104] Those operating in a transnational sphere can use their position to advance an issue "from above" and also "from below"—leveraging opportunities in both international and local policy spaces—while also looking for both short- and long-term opportunities to nudge an issue forward.[105]

There is every reason to anticipate some success in these influencing strategies as concerns the key themes in this book. International human rights is one of the key areas that scholars have suggested is more accessible and susceptible to transnational advocacy.[106] Transnational human rights actors have frequently focused their advocacy campaigns on many of the armed groups and policy situations at the center of this book, with some significant success in introducing constraints where U.S. military strategies and support appear likely to result in further human rights abuses.[107] Media reporting and public evidence suggests that control mechanisms related to preventing or responding to such abuses have been one of the major issues of contention across the case studies. Thus, while transnational networks and NGOs have not so far been the focus of much of the BPA literature, it will be worth exploring their role within the case studies.

A final category of potential players to consider would be the leaders, bureaucracies, and forces of foreign states, or those de facto holding territory in their place. As noted, in some cases, foreign officials might exert influence through indirect strategies, similar to those used by transnational actors or NGOs highlighted above. They might take part in coordinated campaigns of persuasion (often in conjunction with Congress, or other transnational networks), or leverage their informal exchanges and relationships with U.S. officials or interest groups to influence U.S. decision-making processes.[108] In some scenarios, foreign states may have an additional leverage point via institutionalized co-decision-making norms or structures. Thomas Risse-Kappen has argued that the "collective identity" of NATO member states and "norms committing allies to timely consultation" gave less powerful states in the alliance a conduit to shape the decisions of their most powerful ally, the United States.[109] Other studies of military coalitions have found similar institutional leverage points.[110] Such dynamics might be particularly important in environments like Afghanistan, Iraq, and Syria, where U.S. officials and policy makers frequently made security decisions in the framework of multilateral coalitions. In these situations, regular protocols of consensus and co–decision making might offer junior partners an influence over, if not a full vote on, U.S. security assistance prerogatives.

The literature on foreign policy implementation referenced above suggests another avenue for indirect influence, where foreign states are engaged alongside the United States in the implementation of policies surrounding LHSFs. The implementation literature suggests that the high-level decision (for example, to engage with a given LHSF) is not as important as the scores of minor choices of how to implement that decision. As applied to international assistance, this would offer avenues for the range of actors (members of non-U.S. governments, international organizations, civil society groups, or others) also taking part in the implementation of programming to shape the policy outcomes. For example, Schroeder and Friesendorf used this implementation lens to explain how a range of international and domestic actors—including the NATO stabilization force, many of its individual members, and those in organizations or domestic institutions charged with overseeing or carrying out the work in question—collectively shaped the counter-crime agenda and policies in post-Dayton Bosnia-Herzegovina.[111] International assistance to LHSFs in Afghanistan, Iraq, and Syria would offer similar international practice situations. These initiatives tended to be situated within larger international security or governance projects, implemented by and shaped by a range of both domestic (Iraqi, Afghan, or Syrian) and international actors. A foreign policy implementation perspective might identify the collaboration between foreign donors, NGOs, civil society groups, and other for-profit contractors during the implementation of assistance to LHSFs as of equal significance to bargaining back in Washington, DC, in terms of shaping foreign policy outcomes.

In addition to these established pathways for foreign influence, one hypothesis explored in greater detail in the case studies is that there may be some situations in which foreign leaders find themselves directly at the bargaining table with U.S. decision makers, in a more co-decisional position. FPA and some of the related organizational process concepts have been applied to analyze co–decision making within European Union institutions, or in cases where more than one government has delegated a degree of decision making to international organizations.[112] Both scenarios involve situations in which the delegation for or institutional decision-making arrangement has resulted in some pooling or ceding of sovereign authority.[113] Situations like those presented by the U.S.-led interventions in Iraq and Afghanistan present an even more provocative test case for transnational bargaining because of the compromised or shared sovereignty invoked by these situations.[114]

U.S. dealings with the Iraqi and Afghan governments would likely offer the most obvious examples of how situations of shared sovereignty might lead to a transnational BPA bargaining phenomenon. However, other situations of de facto territorial control by external actors or even non-state armed groups might also invoke a shared or mixed administration, which might give way to similar transnational BPA dynamics. A significant body of literature has explored the "limited" or "partial" nature of sovereignty in countries under transition or facing security turmoil. In such "ungoverned" spaces, as Anne Clunan and Harold Trinkunas have described them, non-state actors or armed groups, substate or regional forces with loose links to the sovereign state, or groups acting at the behest of neighboring states or international actors may hold sway, asserting a degree of territorial control and governance usually associated with sovereign states.[115] Such dynamics frequently arise in the very situations where the United States seeks to mobilize LHSFs; indeed, the United States seeks these partnerships precisely because the titular sovereign is weak or lacks full control in these areas. In such "ungoverned" or contested spaces, another external state, or even a non-state actor, may have such substantial territorial control that they become relevant co-deliberators with the United States. The discussion of LHSFs in Syria provides examples of this, given that large parts of Syrian territory were administered or de facto controlled by forces not aligned with the Syrian state.

In conclusion, while external players' engagement is not a regular feature of classic BPA analysis, the forgoing discussion suggests a number of pathways by which a range of actors outside the U.S. government might play a role in decision making around LHSFs, including Congress, transnational networks or interest groups, foreign leaders or bureaucracies, or the LHSFs themselves. The subsequent case studies will further identify how these external actors—meaning those outside formal U.S. government positions—play into the debates and policy formulation surrounding LHSFs. Chapter 6 will use these examples to build out the theorization of how these external actors might influence foreign policy decision making, identifying the pathways by which they become "players" within bargaining processes, or are otherwise able to influence them.

TWO FRAMEWORKS FOR ASSESSING LHSF CONTROLS

This chapter has introduced two different theoretical frameworks for considering the subsequent case studies, and a series of expectations for each. Principal-agent theory offers a starting point for understanding why states might delegate to LHSFs and also a typology of control mechanisms that we might expect to manifest as ways to constrain or mitigate some of the risks they pose. However, based on these principal-agent expectations, the environments in Iraq, Afghanistan, and Syria, and the LHSF relationships in question, appear least predisposed toward control mechanisms, raising a puzzle as to why they appeared to manifest.

The subsequent case studies will thus consider what BPA theories about bargaining and organizational dynamics offer to explain this puzzle. The counterhypothesis explored in each of the case studies is that the control mechanisms introduced were driven more by some of the tactics and strategies linked to different stakeholders' bargaining interests and tactics, or by other organizational scripts, processes, or dynamics within the relevant bureaucratic entity. As the case studies will show, this counterhypothesis does not necessarily disprove or discount principal-agent theory. Many of the expectations do appear relevant to these scenarios, and they offer helpful constructs for explaining control dynamics in these environments. However, this additional lens of bargaining and organizational theory helps to explain where other intervening political factors or dynamics might disrupt some of the regularly anticipated principal-agent dynamics.

In exploring this counterhypothesis, the case study chapters will also offer illustrations of a more expansive version of BPA, one that includes a range of external actors—representatives of non-U.S. governments, nongovernmental or civil society organizations, and non-state armed groups—as potential players or participants in the bargaining. After exploring evidence of this more expansive BPA in the case study chapters (chapters 2–4), I seek in chapter 6 to contribute to theory building in this domain by reflecting on the pathways by which external actors take part in or influence bureaucratic bargaining and foreign policy decision making.

2

BARGAINING MOMENTS AND STRUCTURES

Comparing the Sons of Iraq and the Afghan Local Police

Both 2005 in Iraq and 2009 in Afghanistan were viewed as crucial turning points by U.S. military leaders and officials. Escalating insurgent threats and violence in both countries not only endangered communities and the larger stabilization efforts, but posed a direct risk to the 150,000 U.S. forces deployed in Iraq, and some tens of thousands in Afghanistan.[1] Outside of this larger security exigency, the nature of the insurgencies in each country, their respective terrains, and their domestic political dynamics differed enormously. Nonetheless, the strategies developed in both were quite similar: a surge in international forces, and initiatives to raise tribal and community forces against the insurgent threat. This parallel was not accidental. U.S. military leaders and policy makers saw the Sons of Iraq or "Awakening" forces (the *sahwa* in Arabic)[2] as so transformative in Iraq that they would try to replicate that success in Afghanistan by way of an initiative that would become known as the Afghan Local Police.

Yet though the inspiration may have been similar, the two programs were different in one important respect. The *sahwa* program featured very few "control mechanisms," while the ALP program was studded with them. Why did these two programs, otherwise very close to each other in time, ambition, and intent, have such different pathways in terms of the number and type of controls that manifested? This chapter will use the contrast between these two programs to illustrate the role of bargaining and political deliberations in introducing control mechanisms and in influencing which controls are deployed and when. It concludes that while some of the principal-agent expectations introduced in the prior two chapters certainly hold true, they fall short of fully explaining why control mechanisms manifested, particularly in Afghanistan. Revisiting the sequence of events surrounding these programs' authorization and expansion helps to illustrate how differences in the bargaining environment and players contributed to different outcomes in control mechanisms, while also beginning to illustrate the transnational bureaucratic policy making dynamics involved.

THE SAHWA OR SONS OF IRAQ (MID-2006-2008)

After the U.S. invasion and overthrow of Saddam Hussein in April 2003, the Coalition Provisional Authority's De-Baathification orders 1 and 2 in May 2003 dismantled the Iraqi military apparatus.[3] An estimated 500,000 former Iraqi service members were unemployed overnight. This generated a yawning security vacuum and a flood of disgruntled fighters, further stoking armed opposition and general unrest. The U.S. plan for restoring order and addressing these burgeoning security threats was to build a new Iraqi Army and security forces, initially planned for a force size of 40,000 and later one of 350,000.[4] However, the actual development of Iraqi security forces stuttered, and the nascent security force that had been put in place by 2004 was no match for the growing security crisis.

Political and security dynamics deteriorated rapidly over the course of 2004. Violent uprisings broke out in Najaf, Falluja, on the outskirts of Baghdad, and in other cities. Across the country, the rate of extrajudicial killings, abductions, and other violent attacks soared. Iraqi security forces were of little use in quelling the violence. When faced with organized, armed uprisings Iraqi police stayed in their stations, at least until their stations became direct targets—as happened in Sadr City and Najaf—at which point they simply fled.[5] In response to the escalating violence, Iraqi security forces hemorrhaged manpower. In the Iraq Civil Defense Corps alone, desertion rates in April 2004 were estimated at 49 percent in Baghdad and 82 percent in western Iraq.[6]

Worse, in many areas, Iraqi security forces were part of the problem.[7] By 2005, there was an increasingly sectarian bent to the Iraqi security forces, particularly those under the control of the Ministry of Interior.[8] The Iraqi police had become a revolving door for Shi'a militias, many of them armed and trained by Iran to foment violence or attack U.S. forces.[9] Iraqi police not only stood by as sectarian violence raged, but in fact were often directly or indirectly implicated in attacks on Sunni communities.[10]

By January 2006, the number of civilians killed per month had doubled, going from 610 the previous January to 1,222.[11] Then in February 2006, what were presumed to be al-Qaeda fighters attacked and blew up the golden dome of the Al-Askari Mosque in Samarra, one of the most sacred Shi'a sites. Whether it was a bellwether or a trigger, the bombing in Samarra marked a turning point in the conflict toward all-out sectarian warfare.[12] On the same day Shi'a militias retaliated by attacking twenty-seven Sunni mosques in the capital alone.[13] Throughout mid-2006, bombs and large-scale attacks manifested on a nearly daily basis. Sectarian kill squads roved Iraqi cities and towns engaging in extrajudicial killings and other retaliatory violence. In mixed cities like Baghdad, the bodies piled up in the streets, often with signs of gruesome torture.[14] Under intense pressure from both Shi'a militias and Maliki's increasingly sectarian government, Sunni areas of Baghdad became ghost towns, in what diplomats and historians have described as no less than the "ethnic cleansing" of Baghdad.[15]

Civilians bore the brunt of this violence—at its peak, between roughly mid-2006 to mid-2007, the civilian death toll ranged from 2,100 to 3,300 each month.[16] By August 2007, some 4.2 million Iraqis had fled their homes, either displaced internally or outside Iraq.[17] But U.S. and coalition casualties were also climbing, in large part due to the growing threat of improvised explosive devices (IEDs). Over the course of 2004, the rate of IED incidents tripled, and in 2006, there were an average of 2,008 IED incidents per month.[18] By 2007, IEDs would be responsible for 70 percent of U.S. casualties in Iraq.[19]

The perception that Iraq was spinning out of control—effectively that the U.S. was losing—was slow to sink in among Bush administration officials. One former congressional staff member remembered his visit to Baghdad in late 2006 as follows: "Bombs are going off everywhere. No one is in the streets. It was like coming into the apocalypse... and yet military advisers were still insisting that we were winning."[20] But by late 2006, Bush's approval ratings had fallen to 36 percent, and in November 2006, Republicans lost a significant number of congressional seats in that year's midterm elections.[21] In response, Bush overhauled his national security team, replacing his secretary of defense, the chairman of Joint Chiefs of Staff, the commanding general in Iraq, and the U.S. ambassador. He replaced them with a team that was fully cohered behind a new vision for Iraq, led by General David H. Petraeus and inspired by the principles embedded in the U.S. counterinsurgency manual Petraeus had just coauthored, *Field Manual 3-24*.[22]

The Iraq counterinsurgency strategy was widely known for its rhetoric of "winning hearts and minds" and for the decision to "surge" troop numbers to support it, which Bush authorized in January 2007. But an equally significant part of the strategy involved the effort to flip former insurgents and Sunni tribes to the U.S. side. However, unlike the "surge," the *sahwa* initiative was not a top-down decision; rather, it emerged from the bottom up, through ground contacts between U.S. commanders and Iraqi community or tribal leaders who were fed up with the violence and chaos generated by al-Qaeda in Iraq (AQI).

AQI recruited heavily from among Sunni tribal communities in provinces including Salah ad-Din, Ninewa, Baghdad, and Anbar (an area sometimes referred to as the Sunni Triangle),[23] but they did not enjoy universal support. AQI assassinated or threatened tribal leaders who opposed them, which sapped many tribal leaders' initial willingness to fight back, but would ultimately feed a strong counter-AQI constituency.[24] AQI expansion along the border areas also threatened the lucrative smuggling and illicit trade routes that many border tribes controlled and profited from.[25]

In mid-2006, one such disgruntled smuggler and tribal leader named Abu Sattar al-Rishawi approached the U.S. commander in Ramadi, in Anbar Province, Colonel Sean MacFarland, and proposed to join forces against AQI.[26] In exchange for security guarantees, he promised to contribute men to the struggling police force and to share intelligence on AQI networks and activities with U.S. forces.[27] MacFarland agreed, and in September 2006, Sattar announced the creation of a tribal coalition against AQI.[28]

Although this tribal coalition was not as broad-based as Sattar first implied, the men he brought in knew enough about the insurgent networks around Ramadi to provide valuable intelligence for U.S. targeting operations.[29] Sattar's willingness to cooperate with the Americans, and MacFarland's demonstration that he would follow through on security promises, created a reverse domino effect, and more tribes began to reach out to U.S. forces. As MacFarland recounted to journalist Stephen Ricks, "Whenever a tribe flipped and joined the Awakening, all the attacks on coalition forces in that area would stop, and all the caches of ammunition would come up out of the ground. If there was ever an attack on us, the sheikh would basically take responsibility for it and find whoever was responsible, and this happened time and again. So it was incredibly effective and they were as good as their word."[30]

Over the course of a few months, violence levels decreased dramatically in Ramadi. With encouragement from Petraeus and his second-in-command, General Raymond Odierno, U.S. commanders across Iraq began reaching out to conclude similar "cease-fires" with tribal leaders and local armed groups.[31] These were then formed into local auxiliary forces or local watch units, carrying out functions like manning checkpoints, patrolling streets, or simply being paid to pass on information and assist U.S. forces in tracking down assailants. Although they were given benign names—"neighborhood watches," "desert protectors," "emergency response units," and even "Concerned Local Citizen" groups—these were substantially (if not mostly) made of former insurgent groups.[32] Converting former insurgents to the U.S. or Iraqi government side was key to the strategy. The idea was to "flip" tribes and communities from supporting insurgents, gaining intelligence sources and reducing potential insurgent recruits in the process.

With ample discretionary funds available to pay these forces, via each individual unit's Commander's Emergency Response Program, the *sahwa* or Sons of Iraq initiative quickly spread across Anbar, Ninewa, and Salah ad-Din, and then into other more mixed provinces like Baghdad and Diyala.[33] By January 2008, the program had spread to some two-thirds of Iraqi governorates, with 95,000 tribal or local forces on the U.S. payroll.[34] At its height it was estimated to have reached 103,000 members, with the United States was paying some $30 million a month in *sahwa* salaries.[35]

COUNTERINSURGENCY SUCCESS, BUT WITHOUT ANY COUNTERINSURGENCY CONTROLS

The *sahwa* was held up as the ultimate counterinsurgency success, but it lacked much of the emphasis on good conduct that later came to be rhetorically associated with "winning hearts and minds" in the U.S. counterinsurgency strategy.[36] Like Sattar, many of those recruited were described as thugs and racketeers who could be abusive or predatory.[37] Some of the tribal militias that emerged early on in Anbar bore the trappings of "death squads," according to a U.S. adviser at the time, Carter Malkasian.[38] Public accounts of the Ameriya Knights—one of the early Concerned Local Citizens groups in Baghdad—suggest they were tactically effective and quickly shut down the AQI cell in the area, but they were also accused of brutality, corruption, and murder.[39]

Because of concerns about these groups' conduct or affiliations, some U.S. military commanders tried to limit the type or pace of U.S. support early on.[40] However, the evidence suggests that across most of the *sahwa* mobilization, there was virtually no selection criteria or other controls at the beginning.[41] It was a "walk-in affair," remembered one policy maker who monitored the *sahwa* developments at the time.[42] At most, in some areas, there was a form of tribal guarantee or safeguard. Scholar Kimberley Marten offers this account from a U.S. colonel who observed such "tribal vetting" in Anbar and Diyala: "Anytime we went in to recruit, the lists would go to the tribal leadership for vetting. There's no database that you can turn to, to do background checks on these guys. You have to rely on the integrity of the tribal system and the word of the sheik, which carries a lot of weight."[43]

Such loose controls and lack of selection criteria might be seen as largely in line with the initiative's perceived strategic value. While some of the community forces took part in local policing and sentinel duties—where good relations and behavior might presumably be important—the *sahwa*'s primary value was as a vehicle to bring former and potential insurgents onside. As a result, the *sahwa* were "explicitly not about vetting," one former U.S. intelligence officer offered. "Baked into the idea was that they were terrible, that they were insurgents."[44] In addition, at the point when most of the *sahwa* emerged, the level of threat was so high that it obviated significant consideration of future risks or drawbacks. As one former U.S. commander offered, "the exigency of the AQI threat and the pressure from the White House was so great that the near-term concern of getting this mess under control" was prioritized above any future consequences.[45]

By the second year of the program, as security pressures receded, some minimal control mechanisms were introduced in the form of greater tracking of *sahwa* forces, and of any weapons and equipment provided to them. By the end of 2007, U.S. forces were regularly collecting basic identification and biometric information, tracking the serial numbers of weapons provided, and overseeing more regularized pay processes.[46] In theory, if *sahwa* forces went rogue, and returned to supporting the insurgency, they might more easily be tracked down with this information. However, there is no indication that this greater data collection and tracking was used to monitor or control the *sahwa* forces' behavior in any significant way.[47] For example, U.S. forces did not use the personal information to follow up on allegations of misconduct, track down perpetrators, or penalize them by docking salary payments, suspending them, or seeking criminal punishment.[48]

While even these late-stage controls were still quite de minimis, it is important to understand how and why they emerged. In part, these tracking and biometric registration efforts were motivated by U.S. forces' own interest in mitigating the risks of working with unknown forces, as well as the greater time available to do so once the situation began to stabilize.[49] Interviewees and other literature suggest that the collection of such data began with the *sahwa* units formed from former detainees—those presumably presenting higher security risks—and only later expanded to other *sahwa* units.[50]

There was also a certain sensitivity to the potential public, and congressional, perception that the U.S. was funding violent militias. Toby Dodge, an Iraq historian who at the time was an adviser to the U.S. commanding general, David Petraeus, noted that Petraeus and his advisers worried they would be perceived as mobilizing militias and bankrolling criminals and insurgents.[51] While Petraeus and his team were concerned about this negative perception, it did not outweigh the immediate security needs of the moment, including the need for greater intelligence and force protection from local allies. However, once the violence had ebbed, there was greater bandwidth to address such concerns by introducing some controls and tracking that might make the *sahwa* appear closer to regular forces. Principal-agent theory would explain this as a higher U.S. tolerance for slack in the early period due to the exigency of the threat, which made *sahwa* mobilization more important and any controls that might slow or limit its spread more costly. Once threat levels had diminished, the costs were more tolerable.

However, the more significant narrative that emerges from the interviews and documentation of the program is that these late-stage control mechanisms were primarily driven by U.S.-Iraqi deliberations over the program. The degree of Iraqi government opposition to the program, at least once it moved out of tribal Anbar Province, cannot be overemphasized.[52] Many Iraqi politicians viewed the *sahwa* forces as terrorists, thieves, and criminals—a perception that was not entirely untrue.[53] There was also a political aspect to this opposition. Prime Minister Nouri al-Maliki saw U.S. empowerment of Sunni political leaders and constituencies (the main demographic in the *sahwa*) as a threat to his Shi'a political base.

U.S. military and political leadership were well aware that Maliki would oppose the program. Wishing to avoid the perception that they were funding militias and insurgents, and worried about Maliki's outrage, U.S. military officials initially downplayed the level and nature of the *sahwa* support. As Dodge described it, "The Americans lowballed the process . . . [they] tried to hide it." However, as soon as Maliki realized the scope of the program, "he moved heaven and earth to stop it, and to find ways to present opposition to it," Dodge remembered.[54] Another lead Petraeus adviser, journalist Emma Sky, offered a similar account in public reporting: "In the initial months, we weren't even telling them [Iraqi government officials], we were just doing it." When the Maliki government did learn of the full nature of the practice of paying former insurgents to come onside, it "accused us of creating a Sunni army that could lead to warlordism and possibly to a civil war," she continued.[55]

It was at this point that the sort of tracking and de minimis controls entered the conversation. Dodge describes these efforts to demonstrate accountability as "instrumental" to trying to appease Maliki: "When that [hiding the program] became impossible to sustain—because they're on the payroll and very present around the country—then they [the U.S. military] start taking their data, to show that they're accountable."[56] The need to win Iraqi approval and buy-in became even more acute as the

United States moved toward withdrawal. U.S. forces and policy makers wanted the Iraqi government to adopt the *sahwa* as an institutionalized force, as an Iraqi National Guard.[57] The need for Iraqi government approval and cooperation gave Maliki greater leverage, and he used it to bargain for Iraqi institutional control over the *sahwa*.

When the issue was first introduced, Maliki's position was weak. The United States was the preponderant military power in the country and could influence whether Maliki would stay on as prime minister following the planned (but subsequently delayed) 2008 elections.[58] Maliki's first move was a classic bureaucratic stalling technique—creating a committee to consider the future of the *sahwa*.[59] The committee would take a year to release its findings, which ultimately argued for the institution of more control mechanisms. The lead representative of the committee, Safa Rasul al-Sheikh, said the report detailed the risks of these forces, and proposed tighter institutional accountability—formal background checks and registration procedures, oversight through regular Iraqi security forces, and the potential to exert discipline or eject members who engaged in criminal activity.[60]

Such demands generated American pushback, but then ultimately some concessions. The initial American response to Iraqi demands was that the *sahwa* already had sufficient controls. The Americans would argue, "We have checked them. We have vetted them. They are good people . . . with honorable tribes and backgrounds and so on," according to former Iraqi minister Hoshyar Zebari.[61] A former U.S. Army colonel who helped manage the tracking data remembers that whenever the issue came up, U.S. officials would redouble their efforts to collect information on the *sahwa*.[62] By the time the program closed, he said they had "file cabinets full of information" on these forces.[63] He also remembered other concessions—for example, a conference in 2007 in which the United States agreed to put the *sahwa* forces under the authority of the local chief of police in their respective areas, although it is not clear whether this ever happened on a systematic basis.[64]

There was never a conclusive result from this back-and-forth; ultimately, U.S. resistance reached a dead end with the security transition and withdrawal. Responsibility for the *sahwa* forces was handed over to the Iraqi government in October 2008 as part of a larger security transition process.[65] Once under full Iraqi authority, the *sahwa* were subject to mechanisms that on paper typified controls. These included formal background checks and screening, Iraqi government institutional oversight and regulations, and sanctions—lots of them. The Iraqi government removed *sahwa* members deemed ineligible and arrested and detained many for alleged misconduct or legal violations.[66] However, although these mechanisms took the form of control mechanisms, or general institutional checks, they were ultimately more about political control than about any monitoring or disciplining of the *sahwa* force. Rather than being used to shift the behavior of potentially unruly or risky forces (or agents, in principal-agent language), the control mechanisms were used as a way for the Maliki government to wrest control back from the Americans and to dissolve a political force that it had never liked or trusted.[67] In this context, the late-stage controls that the United States had introduced substantially to appease or reassure Maliki became something of a Trojan horse. As Dodge notes, "The collection of biometric data from former insurgents in return for payment made . . . [*sahwa* forces] simultaneously visible and vulnerable to whatever organisation had access to that information."[68]

In reflecting on the overall *sahwa* trajectory and experience, in many ways the initial period of development followed the expectations of principal-agent theory. Even if former insurgents or those affiliated with them presented some risks, they were the agents with the greatest capacity or specialization for the task at hand, with local knowledge of insurgent networks and routes that gave them the ability to detect local threats and increase actionable intelligence. Those who reached out to the United States also arguably had the closest fit with U.S. interests on at least one crucial level—they viewed AQI as the most important threat. Moreover, although the forces presented risks, given the security exigencies, exerting the time and resources to assert more control would have proved too costly, and so they were not pursued. U.S. control mechanisms in the form of greater registration and tracking only came once the security situation relaxed, making it less costly to exert time and resources to implement them.

The emergence of a bargaining moment and conditions by the Iraqi government interrupted this more natural principal-agent equilibrium. A limited number of control mechanisms were instituted by the end of the *sahwa* initiative, but the motivation behind them—on both sides—had less to do with controlling the risks posed by the *sahwa* forces than with the political bargaining surrounding them. On the U.S. side, efforts to increase registration and tracking and to regularize these forces were designed to help rebut accusations that these were unaccountable, risky, or militia-like forces, and to persuade Maliki and other skeptical Iraqi officials to accept them. On the Iraqi government side, controls proved to be less about constraining or regulating the behavior of the *sahwa* forces than identifying a means of exerting political control, ultimately with a view to ending the program.

Because controls were such a minimal part of the *sahwa* experience, this case study provides only a limited example of the political bargaining dynamics surrounding them. Nonetheless, it offers an important baseline for how control mechanisms were viewed early on, a point revisited in later chapters. In addition, as the following case study will illustrate, the same tactics that came to the fore in bargaining over the *sahwa*—proponents' use of control and accountability mechanisms as a means to defend the initiative from its critics, versus opponents' use of them to try to limit the program—also manifest more fully in other, more robust bargaining scenarios.

AFGHAN LOCAL DEFENSE FORCES AND THE AFGHAN LOCAL POLICE (2009-2020)

In 2008, it was not obvious that arming tribal and community actors would become the new zeitgeist in Afghanistan. The international community had spent the previous six years investing in the Afghan Army and police and trying to demobilize all other forces that were not part of these state entities. The Afghan government had just announced a new effort to reign in armed groups outside of state control by disbanding or better regulating private security companies, which had often served as a legal cloak for warlords to keep their militias.[69] Moreover the military counterinsurgency strategy embraced at the time was premised on protecting the population and supporting the Afghan state. Where international forces or the Afghan government had experimented with LHSF initiatives in the past, it had resulted in the opposite—with militias or other privatized or semi-state forces preying on the population, fueling criminality, and contributing to greater grievances against international forces and the Afghan government.[70]

Yet despite this, practical demands and some ideational trends pushed for an embrace of tribal or community-based militias. International forces had been steadily expanding their force presence via provincially based development and military hubs known as Provincial Reconstruction Teams since 2005. As they did so, they were frequently confronted with the large gaps in Afghan security forces and state control. Across vast stretches of Afghanistan, the only security actors who might help international forces to repel increasing Taliban attacks were a motley crew of warlords, local strongmen, tribal forces, and militias.[71] Thus, even though the top-line state-building ethos was to create a sort of neo-Weberian "monopoly on force" for the Afghan state, and in accordance with this, to rely only on state partners, the security dynamics and resource constraints made a turn to alternative, non-state or community actors a recurrent temptation.[72]

Such practical demands dovetailed with a larger donor reappraisal of state-building strategies in Afghanistan, and a turn toward local or "bottom-up" initiatives.[73] Since 2002, the international intervention in Afghanistan had followed the orthodoxy of so-called liberal peace interventions, focused on strengthening state institutions, developing laws, holding elections, and fostering a liberal market economy.[74] However, by the late 2000s, Afghanistan appeared to be a prime example of larger critiques of liberal peace state-building modalities.[75] An overly formalistic, top-down approach—one focused on building national institutions, promulgating laws, hosting elections, and other Kabul-centered reforms—had resulted not in a strong state, but in hollow institutions that served the interests of the elite, at the expense of any services or protections for the large majority of the Afghan population.[76] The Afghan government's underwhelming performance and reputation for venality led to greater interest among donors in "alternatives to the state," and for aid or funding modalities that would provide governance, development, or other services from the "bottom up," in partnership with local, community-based, or other "informal" or "traditional" service providers.[77]

In essence, the dry wood for a large-scale non-state and community mobilization strategy was already there; a renewed strategic push toward counterinsurgency, premised on what (in the U.S. view) had proved so successful in Iraq, became the activating match. With the incoming Obama administration's renewed focus on Afghanistan, many of the same generals and military officers who had pioneered the *sahwa* and the counterinsurgency strategy in Iraq rotated back to Afghanistan from 2009 onward. One of Obama's first steps in 2009, was to replace the commanding general of U.S. forces and the International Security Assistance Force (ISAF) in Afghanistan with General Stanley McChrystal, a former Special Forces officer who had made his career in Iraq. He was succeeded within a year by General Petraeus. Both would try to turn the situation around using a strategy similar to that employed in Iraq: a "surge" of international forces, and an emphasis on mobilizing tribes and communities against Taliban insurgents.

Yet while the tribal mobilization efforts were similar in inspiration, there were also important differences in how they were implemented in the two countries. The push for local and community defense forces progressed much more slowly in Afghanistan. It took a year for the Afghan Local Police (as the initiative came to be known) to emerge, and even after four years, the ALP would not reach a third of the numbers of the *sahwa* forces.[78] There was also a much greater emphasis on accountability and control, at least rhetorically. From the earliest pilot efforts to support the ALP, the Afghan local defense forces were subject to a much more robust menu of controls, including multi-stakeholder vetting, codes of conduct and training, and a web of oversight mechanisms, monitoring, and sanctioning devices. Box 2.1 below summarizes the control mechanisms applicable in the first year of the program's inception; these are also analyzed further below.

Principal-agent theory might explain the difference in control mechanisms by looking to factors like whether the controls were less costly in Afghanistan, whether the benefits were assumed to be higher, or whether there was simply a higher degree of tolerance for slack in Iraq because of the necessity of delegation or a lack of alternatives. On the last, certainly, interviewees working on Iraq policy in 2005 and 2006 stressed the exigency and extreme violence of the situation in a way that was not reflected in interviews with Afghanistan policy makers and forces serving in 2009. Thus, there may well have been a higher tolerance for deviant behavior from the *sahwa* forces. Nonetheless, while perhaps slightly

BOX 2.1. SUMMARY OF CONTROL MECHANISMS FOR THE ALP

As authorized, the ALP program included the following control mechanisms, according to principal-agent typologies:[79]

Vetting and selection

- Site selection—selecting for strategic area, community buy-in, as well absence of harmful elements (i.e., warlord capture)
- Vetting through village elders, as well as by the National Directorate of Security and district police chiefs, with information provided to provincial governors and district officials
- Biometric data and screening for criminal records or links with Taliban or other terrorist groups

Standards, rules, and their reinforcement (i.e., training)

- Comply with all Ministry of Interior (MoI) regulations and Afghan laws
- ALP code of conduct (including general good conduct, restrictions on poppy growth or narcotics use, and operations no further than 1 km from village)
- Oath of loyalty to the Afghan government
- No support or assistance to Taliban and no "tie to tribal militias" allowed
- Twenty-one-day training (including on human rights, laws of war, and the ALP code of conduct)
- SOF mentoring new forces

Monitoring and oversight

- Community *shura* oversight
- Command and local oversight from local chiefs of the Afghan National Police and governors
- Institutional oversight from MoI, and accompanying chain of command
- Oversight from SOF/other international military
- Biometric registration, identification cards, and weapon licenses

Sanctions and incentives

- Development funding for communities that participated
- Informal sanctions from community elders (stigma/social pressure)
- MoI disciplinary procedures or prosecution
- Potential for withdrawn U.S. funding, support or mentorship (later formalized into a specific protocol)

less exigent, the idea of mobilizing local defense forces was viewed as no less indispensable to the counterinsurgency strategy adopted for Afghanistan than it had been in Iraq.[80] In some ways, the idea of prevailing via what were supposed to be trusted local actors was even more important for the Afghanistan strategy, given the emphasis on winning over rural Afghan communities through "bottom-up" service provision and governance.

On the other side of the ledger, the Afghanistan environment would likely have presented much higher costs and more barriers to effective control. Effective monitoring or oversight—the key means of enacting controls—depends substantially on observability,[81] which is more realistic when the principal has ample staff or resources on the ground. This was there in spades in Iraq. As noted, the *sahwa* initiative sprang up so quickly in large part because there were already over 150,000 U.S. forces deployed across the country, working side by side with, or at least in the same communities as, the emerging *sahwa* forces. By contrast, in Afghanistan in 2009, there were not even half as many U.S. forces, staff, and contractors, and they were spread across a much larger, mountainous terrain. Differences in the tribal organization, cohesion, and affiliation patterns might also have made Afghanistan a more difficult case for control. Military officers working across the two initiatives observed that Afghan tribal connections and networks were less hierarchical and consolidated than in Iraq, with no connection and vast differences between sub-tribes from one mountain valley to the next.[82] This required an even more granular approach for any degree of direction or control to be achieved, requiring even more personnel and time.

However, while control mechanisms might have been more costly to impose in Afghanistan, there were also greater perceived benefits in that country. Given Afghanistan's problematic history with militias (as referenced in the preface), and the substantial issues surrounding warlord abuses and failed disarmament since 2002, the Afghanistan policy environment was highly sensitized to the pitfalls of militia mobilization.[83] In addition, although the counterinsurgency strategy in Afghanistan was inspired by that in Iraq, there were subtle differences. McChrystal's Afghanistan counterinsurgency strategy was much more focused on winning back the Afghan population to the government side.[84] The sort of risks frequently posed by uncontrolled militias—including civilian harm, collusion with corrupt power brokers, or harassment and predation of the population—would run counter to these goals. These risks were arguably just as material in Iraq, but they were overshadowed there by the extreme levels of immediate violence. Translated into principal-agent theory, the risks of misbehaving militias might have been weighted more heavily by US policy makers in the Afghan than in the Iraq case, making greater regulation and risk mitigation worth the cost of enacting controls.

All of these background conditions would certainly have generated greater sensitivity to the risks of supporting unruly militias in Afghanistan; however, they ultimately are not a sufficient explanation in themselves for the greater controls placed on the ALP. These background conditions had been present at increasing levels since 2001 and did not generate substantially greater efforts toward accountability with other forces, particularly the category of other internationally backed militias or LHSF partnerships. As chapter 4 will discuss, counterterrorism auxiliary forces faced little scrutiny or controls throughout the entire period of engagement in Afghanistan. Instead, a closer examination of how control mechanisms emerged within the initial local defense force pilot initiatives and then the ALP suggests that the more important difference between Iraq and Afghanistan was the nature of the surrounding policy environment, and the way that the decision to authorize the ALP triggered a bargaining moment.

TESTING LOCAL DEFENSE FORCES AND EARLY BARGAINING OVER THE FUTURE ALP

One of McChrystal's first steps upon assuming command was to introduce a strategic review. The strategy adopted had echoes of the surge and local force strategies in Iraq, albeit adjusted to the Afghan context: it also called for a surge in international forces, but with an even greater emphasis on winning over communities through a "bottom-up" or community-based counterinsurgency strategy. The counterinsurgency strategy adopted was to focus on bringing communities back to the government's side by offering protection and addressing prominent grievances, ranging from lack of service delivery and corruption to civilian casualties and misconduct by international and Afghan forces.[85] Local defense forces were a linchpin of this new strategy. They were to fill immediate gaps in the security forces and provide protection in rural communities through a mode that (it was argued) was more in keeping with Pashtun tribal traditions of self-governance and defense.[86]

Beginning in 2009, U.S. forces began a number of pilot initiatives to test different models of local or community mobilization. The two most prominent were the Afghan Public Protection Program (AP3), which began in early 2009 in central Wardak Province, and the Community Defense Initiatives, later rebranded the Local Defense Initiatives (LDI), which were initiated shortly thereafter in a dozen mostly southern and southeastern districts.[87] The AP3 was organized in cooperation with the Afghan Ministry of Interior, but the LDI were organized without any Afghan buy-in or consent. This was in part because SOF feared that involving Afghan institutions—which had a reputation for corruption and links with predatory warlords—might undermine the initiatives' ability to win over communities.[88] Both were small initiatives—mobilizing a few thousand forces in a dozen communities—and kept very quiet initially, with little to no public awareness or debate.[89] The core model for both was roughly the same. SOF embedded in what were viewed as strategic locations for a few weeks, working with tribal elders to raise a local force that could help win over communities and "hold" territory against the Taliban.[90]

There were a limited number of control mechanisms even in these early experiments with community defense forces. In both the Wardak pilot and the LDI, there was a heavy emphasis on what might be framed as "community controls."[91] SOF were to embed in these communities for weeks before establishing a local force to ensure that the communities selected for these forces were willing to turn against the Taliban and were not otherwise under the control of warlords or other hostile actors (essentially a SOF-overseen "selection" mechanism for identifying appropriate communities, and monitoring mechanism to identify any risks or slack that emerged). Within each community, community elders would be given responsibility for vetting members of the tribal forces—ensuring that they were of good character and not linked to the Taliban (a community-based selection mechanism). Elders, or by extension the community at large, would then be responsible for overseeing the community force once mobilized (a community-based oversight mechanism).

These early controls come closest to realizing principal-agent assumptions about why control mechanisms might emerge. SOF commanders and advisers who designed this initiative genuinely thought these community checks would do a better job of producing accountable and effective counterinsurgents.[92] Quite in keeping with principal-agent expectations about selection mechanisms in such environments, they argued that those local to an area would be better at knowing the local forces and selecting those who were most respected by the community and most likely to protect them. It was also presumed that community actors would do better at oversight and accountability—that their "kinship and familial ties" would be a more effective control than any outsiders' efforts.[93]

However, even in these early controls, there is some foreshadowing of the bargaining to come, and of the role that control mechanisms would play within that bargaining. During the initial pilot stages, SOF and their advisers already knew that the proposed local defense forces would be controversial. A similar local force initiative premised on seconding tribal militias to Afghan police forces (the Afghan National Auxiliary Police, or ANAP) had ended disastrously only a year before.[94] Even more recently, in 2008, the United Kingdom had proposed a NATO policy of cooperating with tribal *arbakai* (an Afghan term describing tribal self-defense forces) – only to have the idea roundly rejected, including by the leading U.S. general at the time.[95] Proponents knew that parallels would be drawn between the new pilot initiatives and the failed ANAP initiative in particular, and appeared to develop many of the control mechanisms as a way to counter such critiques. For example, those working on the community and tribal defense forces would argue that one of the reasons the ANAP had failed was because it lacked "mentoring of local forces in the field," or because they were not "integrated into local tribal structures"—issues that would in theory be addressed by the SOF mentorship and community controls established in the pilot programs.[96] Additional checks designed to distinguish these initiatives from the failed ANAP initiative included a longer training time, and in the Wardak pilot, more integrated institutional controls and oversight.[97] What this illustrates is that before a full debate had even arisen over these new community defense forces, control mechanisms were positioned as a way to defend these initiatives from critics and overcome objections to their full authorization.

By the end of 2009—roughly half a year into most of the pilot initiatives—McChrystal had decided that they were a success, particularly the more community-based LDI model.[98] But broader buy-in and support was needed to expand them. One initial estimate suggested that SOF hoped to earmark $1.8 billion for the initiative.[99] Afghan policing programs to that point had been supported through a multi-donor trust fund managed by the United Nations. There was an additional pool of U.S. funding available, but it required approval from the U.S. ambassador, who at the time was (retired) Lieutenant General Karl Eikenberry. In addition to these financial resources, SOF had argued that for the initiative to succeed it would have to be accompanied by parallel local governance, development, and stabilization initiatives—referred to as Village Stability Operations.[100] To fully succeed, these would require the cooperation and support of a range of international security and development actors, as well as the Afghan government.

To win this broader support and funding, in the fall of 2009, U.S. military officials began briefing other parts of the U.S. and Afghan governments—touting not only the initiatives' promise but also the control mechanisms that had already been put in place to address concerns about mobilizing militias. The reactions of the different U.S. and Afghan stakeholders, though, ultimately appeared to be linked more to their "stand-sit" positions than to the persuasiveness of any controls. BPA assumes that any given player's position within a bargaining debate depends on where the individual or institution "sits," and thus that their position will strongly reflect their organizational equities, mission sets or capacities, or possibly the personal lenses and commitments of stakeholders involved.[101] These "stand-sit" positions were on full display in the reactions for and against expanding the community defense forces, particularly the LDI model championed by SOF.[102] On the side of proponents, the so-called white SOF—those who specialize in building up local partnerships and counterinsurgency efforts—saw these initiatives as a way to get back to their core mission, and were therefore fully supportive.[103] They were supported by the DoD as a whole, which saw the initiative as a way to have "hold" forces supporting U.S. troops who were surging into the country. Two minor Afghan ministries that were to be given a role in the initiative, and thus had institutional incentives at play, were also in favor of the LDI going forward.[104]

However, these "stand-sit" positions or interests also placed some significant U.S. and Afghan stakeholders in the camp of opponents. The Afghan Ministry of Defense was opposed to these community defense forces because it saw them as little more than militias, the mobilization of which went against the ministry's more strongly rooted ethos of building professional security forces.[105] The influential minister of interior, Hanif Atmar, also staunchly opposed the initiative, arguing that mobilizing local forces in the way that the LDI had been—outside of Afghan state control—would weaken state authority and institutions.[106] Atmar had long expressed a vision of strengthening the state by bringing other non-state armed groups under its institutional control; thus, many observers have linked his opposition to this round of LHSFs with the MoI's exclusion from the LDI (by contrast Atmar had supported the parallel AP3 initiative, in which the MoI was given a designated role).[107]

One of the most critical opponents was Ambassador Eikenberry himself. He and other counterparts in the State Department viewed the proposal negatively in part because the skirting of Afghan institutions in the LDI model, and Afghan opposition to it, clashed with the State Department's institutional commitments to state building and to Afghan-owned governance. However, Eikenberry also noted that he could not help but view these initiatives through the lens of his prior experiences in Afghanistan.[108] A career army officer, he had served multiple tours in Afghanistan before being appointed U.S. ambassador. In his first tour, he became known as the "father of the Afghan National Army" for helping create the ANA, and on a later tour he was tasked with reforming the broken Afghan police.[109] His last posting, beginning in 2005, was as the lead commander of U.S. forces in Afghanistan, effectively one of McChrystal's predecessors. Those experiences made him mistrustful of "quick fixes" for gaps in Afghan security forces, and of anything that smacked of shortcuts to long-term institutional investment.[110] They also meant that he had greater personal credibility to question military strategies than perhaps any other sitting ambassador.

In a November 2009 State Department cable, Eikenberry opposed expansion of these initiatives, at least without a number of checks and accountability measures, essentially an array of control mechanisms. He argued that "local solutions are permissible only as a closely monitored and tightly controlled stop-gap measure tied to ANSF. . . . Otherwise, U.S. support for unconventional forces (particularly if they prove prone to manipulation by local power-brokers) could . . . reinforce a traditional 'worst practice'—the arming of ethnic or sub-tribal militias."[111]

Beyond simply warning of the risks, Eikenberry used his authority as chief of mission to block Special Forces from relying on a key funding mechanism needed for expansion, and to restrict any U.S. personnel from engaging with the local defense forces until his concerns were addressed, and until there was formal Afghan agreement to the program.[112] With this, none of the funds necessary for expansion, nor any accompanying State Department development support, would be available without formal Afghan buy-in, and greater evidence that the local defense forces would be "monitored" and "tightly-controlled" by both the Afghan government and the international community.[113]

Eikenberry's cable back to Washington, DC, made this the subject of an inter-bureaucratic debate within the State Department (as not all within the department took Eikenberry's view), and between the State Department and other U.S. government agencies. Because Eikenberry made clear that he disfavored authorization without full support and buy-in from Afghan president Hamid Karzai, it also opened another bargaining front to try to win support from the Afghan government. Then in early 2010, the idea that the U.S. military was set to mobilize tens of thousands of militias leaked publicly, sparking objections from a much wider range of stakeholders and opening a much broader and much more public bargaining debate. In short, in a situation that was quite different from the trajectory of the *sahwa*, proponents' need for more funding and broader support, coupled with Eikenberry's cable, opened a bargaining moment quite early in the ALP development process. From Eikenberry's initial insistence on some checks on these forces, to Afghan demands for institutional integration, to civil society calls for human rights safeguards, control mechanisms were a central demand across all of these bargaining arenas. The following section illustrates how these debates unrolled and how each of the control mechanisms lined up with different bargaining tactics or stakeholder demands.

CHECKS, CONTROLS, AND BARGAINING TACTICS

In January 2010, the *Washington Post* leaked the story of U.S. military plans to mobilize tribal militias, and of Eikenberry's cable halting it.[114] The news sparked an immediate firestorm. Non-U.S. ISAF member countries—who at this point contributed just under half of international troops and a substantial swath of the development and stabilization funding—were not eager to fund unregulated militias. In addition, other international stakeholders who had been vested in past state-building efforts—to include other donor countries, UN officials, and other international organizations and civil society organizations—argued that the initiative would undo the prior decade of disarmament and state-building work, to the benefit of warlords and other non-state power brokers.[115] Leading Afghan government figures, Afghan civil society, and a range of international human rights organizations and advocates objected that this initiative would only replicate past cycles of militia abuse and violence.[116] One editorial in the Afghan paper *Hasht-e Sobh* argued, "The fact that these forces may become new warlords is not mere speculation. It is an irrefutable truth."[117]

Both in behind-the-scenes negotiations and in the public debate, proponents countered such critiques by stressing that measures like close SOF supervision and vesting these forces within their communities (essentially the community controls) would limit warlord co-option of these forces and prevent unruly behavior. Yet for a range of critics, this was insufficient, leading to a six-month period in which new controls were added to respond to the full range of different stakeholder demands.

Eikenberry's cable had effectively given the Afghan government a veto on the program, making the Afghan institutional concerns the top priority. Although many Afghan officials, including Karzai, also raised concerns about the risk of war crimes, the primary demand was that the LDI would come under Afghan control, specifically under Atmar's MOI.[118] "We were against local militias from the beginning. We thought they were going to hurt the population and the country.... The key for us was having Afghan institutions involved," Karzai said, arguing that having legally regulated and accountable local police (not militias) was what would ensure that they would act "in the interest of the Afghan people."[119]

McChrystal was removed in July 2010 and replaced with Petraeus, who reportedly placed such emphasis on getting the initiative authorized that he raised the issue in his first meeting with Karzai.[120] According to a former adviser to the Afghan president privy to the initial negotiations, Petraeus's first proposed model of local defense forces already included more explicit and robust controls than even the pilot programs, with more rigorous vetting and selection to prevent warlords and militias from hijacking it, and safeguards to restrain forces from abusive or unruly behavior.[121] Karzai remembered such proposals, and that they were unpersuasive from the Afghan government perspective: "No matter how strong the vetting or controlling or disciplinary measures, we were against the very fact of raising militia forces. We were against the very principle of the idea."[122] Karzai insisted that unless the forces were put under Afghan authority—under Afghan ministries, wearing state uniforms, and selected by Afghan government stakeholders rather than international vetting schemas—he would not approve their formation.

Though Karzai eventually agreed, he only did so once his primary condition of Afghan institutionalization under the MoI had been met. This demand would introduce a panoply of institutional controls for the Afghan government: the ability for MoI to have input or control selection (rather than the selection of particular groups determined by community preferences or at SOF's discretion); background checks and vetting by Afghan security institutions; rules and codes of conduct in accordance with MoI processes; oversight by chiefs of police and provincial governors; and the authority to sanction or dismiss.

Karzai's governing coalition also had another demand, although it was more about taking away existing controls than adding new ones. In the early development of the local defense force model, U.S. SOF had developed criteria for site selection, including that it be located in areas of strategic importance, and that it be a location that appeared likely to bolster the presence of community-supported counterinsurgents, rather than power broker–linked militias. This ruled out much of northern Afghanistan, where at the time there were both lower security concerns and Taliban infiltration, and also a much higher risk of warlord or power broker domination of the force.[123] Northern power brokers within Karzai's coalition objected, decrying this as a "Pashtun handout" program.[124] They won the concession that the program would be expanded nationwide.[125]

Acceding to these Afghan demands thus introduced controls, but it also undid some of those aimed at constraining the agents and containing program risks. The changes ultimately pushed the program to become yet another vehicle for patronage and power broker control.[126] Ultimately, despite a heavy emphasis on risks in the language of the ALP debate, control mechanisms were less motivated by a desire to control the agents in question and address the risks identified than by institutional or personal agendas on the part of key stakeholders.

With the agreement to institutionalize the force under the ALP, the main objections of other diplomats and international actors focused on state building were also satisfied. It also was sufficient to win Karzai's approval, and thereby Eikenberry's. Although no European country would ever help fund the ALP, other major donor countries also relaxed their opposition once it was agreed that the force would come under Afghan institutional control. Vygaudas Usackas, the European Union's special representative in Afghanistan at the time, offered tentative support for the idea of raising community protection forces but only if accompanied by Afghan government buy-in and control: "The concern which we had as the European Union is to see a clear chain of command [within the Interior Ministry] so it doesn't become a separate militia."[128] One UN official characterized the European position as one of resignation: "The

---

BOX 2.2. EXCERPT FROM JANUARY 2010 BRIEFING ON LOCAL DEFENSE INITIATIVE

- Village Shura and Local Defense Force members sign Compact with GIRoA
- Vetting through village elders and Shura, as well as NDS [National Directorate of Security], district police chief, district and information provided to provincial governors
- Loyalty oaths for all members
- Administrative and Biometric Registration of Local Defense Forces
- Pay through banking system to individual, not through commanders [. . .]
- Identification Cards, Weapon licenses
- No Poppy growth or Narcotics usage allowed in village
- No tie to tribal militias allowed [. . .]
- No authority for Local Defense Force outside home village area (area approved by district)[127]

Americans wanted to have this project: they would fund it; they would staff it; it would be their baby ... as long as it's formally under the MoI and you [the Americans] take care of it, then it's fine."[129]

Throughout this bargaining period, additional minor controls were added that made the program even more palatable to different international and Afghan institutional stakeholders.[130] It was made explicit that the forces would not have any link to the Taliban and would not engage in poppy growing or "narcotics usage" (a prominent issue among past ANAP forces and a particular concern among those working on antinarcotics issues; see box 2.2).[131] The Afghanistan COIN strategy was partly premised on strengthening Afghan government institutions and improving their legitimacy in the eyes of the public through greater government service provision and Afghan-led governance. The final program rules for the ALP gave a nod to this strategy (and the stakeholders that supported it) by creating linkages and oversight mechanisms with a range of district and provincial officials.[132]

The more intransigent opposition came from an unexpected quarter—the officially powerless but highly vocal contingent of international representatives, NGOs, and civil society groups who were concerned about the human rights implications. Every SOF adviser or U.S. or NATO military official interviewed for this book who was involved in the deliberations at the time remembers the UN Assistance Mission to Afghanistan (UNAMA) and various NGO and civil society being influential at this time, and that their objections influenced the ALP debate.[133] More than one interviewee remarked that this was an ISAF leadership that included Sarah Chayes, a former journalist who had been running an NGO and soap factory in Kandahar for a decade, as a key ISAF adviser.[134] Human rights NGOs and the UNAMA human rights unit were regularly invited to ISAF's command headquarters to raise issues with or provide feedback on command initiatives.[135] This was in part because the ideas underlying the COIN strategy were framed around addressing good governance, corruption, and protection issues—areas in which NGO and civil society representatives had a degree of specialization and an ability to press their influence. Shortfalls in services and governance were so great that international organizations and NGOs together acted as an almost parallel civil service, such that their support and participation—or objection—to an initiative could determine its success or failure.[136] Because of more stable security conditions overall, there was also a fairly strong degree of access, freedom of movement, and media and civil society coverage of what was happening across Afghanistan. This created stronger public leverage points that NGOs and civil society actors could use to strategic effect. NGO advocacy on civilian casualties and detention abuses, for example, had helped elevate these human rights issues to what were viewed by the ISAF command at the time as serious strategic issues that merited attention.[137] For all of these reasons, while NGO and civil society actors might not be described as true players, they had the potential to act as spoilers, and so ALP proponents paid attention to their critiques.

Marc Jacobson, a senior NATO political adviser who worked with SOF and those in the ISAF leadership who wished to promote the ALP initiative, remembered proponents' greatest concern being how to reconcile the UN, NGOs, and other civil society members to the initiative, both because they thought the "hardest questions" would come from this contingent, and because of fears that NGO or UN opposition could derail approval.[138] At a minimum, NGO advocacy could become a useful tool in the hands of other players. In the past, Karzai had frequently been the most vocal advocate on civilian casualty and detention issues—a sort of informal ally of human rights groups on these points. As a result, proponents of the local defense forces feared that public NGO opposition or private UN objections might harden Karzai's resistance or give him additional leverage in bargaining with the U.S. military. In addition, Eikenberry was sympathetic to the concerns raised by civil society advocates and sensitive to their opposition to the initiative. Jacobson also remembered that part of why he and other proponents of the ALP were trying to win NGO and UN approval was the sense that Eikenberry would absolutely not support the initiative if the UN and NGOs were openly opposed to it.[139]

None of this is to suggest that these nongovernmental and civil society voices were the preeminent influence on the ALP authorization debate, but these levers appeared to be sufficient for these voices to be heard, and their concerns at least somewhat taken on board in the form of control mechanisms. In meetings between NGO or civil society representatives (like the one described in the preface), a range of objections to and potential risks stemming from the ALP were presented as reasons not to go ahead with the proposal.[140] For every objection or critique, proponents—whether the SOF commander, Lieutenant General Miller, or other officials—would try to rebut them by identifying measures designed to mitigate or address those risks—essentially the array of proposed control mechanisms. To the critique that this would empower "roving militias," SOF and NATO advisers pointed to a rule that the forces were not to operate more than a kilometer from their village and that "Local Defense Forces cannot form or support militias."[141] In response to repeated concerns about supporting abusive forces and past cycles of impunity, SOF advisers promised that there would be vetting and scrutiny of the forces' past records, the goal being to prevent hiring abusive forces (although initially the form and type of vetting beyond SOF scrutiny and community controls was left vague). In response to NGO and civil society concerns, training explicitly on human rights and international legal standards, and of a longer duration than that for past auxiliary forces, was made mandatory. Although only added once the force was finally approved, NGOs were also the first to raise, and were ultimately successful in obtaining, restrictions on ALP forces' engagement in detention operations.[142]

As a result of this back-and-forth, the ultimate outcome—or "resultant," in the language of Allison's BPA—was an ALP policy replete with checks and controls, each seeming to tick off or respond to different stakeholders' concerns and objections. The summary in table 2.1 offers an amended list of the control mechanisms introduced at the start of the chapter, indicating on the right the connection with different stakeholder interests or motivations.

ANALYSIS OF CONTROL MECHANISMS AND BARGAINING FOR THE ALP

The development and authorization of the ALP suggests several ways that control mechanisms were used. Control mechanisms nominally reflected the terms of the debate and the need to mitigate the risks of militias, but more often they appeared to represent maneuvers or tactics for winning over skeptics and prevailing over other players within the bargaining arena. BPA expects that players in the game will evaluate the ways in which they can advance their interests. Part of that is building coalitions within the "action game" in question, and converting or overcoming adversaries.[143] In one article, Allison and Halperin offer a checklist of

TABLE 2.1 Summary of control mechanisms for the ALP

Control mechanism	Use or connection vis-à-vis bargaining positions or actors
Vetting and selection	
Site selection—community approval plus SOF confirm the site meets criteria	Aimed at controlling agent; plus some anticipatory/preemptive bargaining motivations
MoI *tashkil* selection process—national and local elites allowed input into which sites are chosen	Advanced by Afghan government stakeholders for patronage-based motivations
Vetting through village elders and community members	Aimed at controlling agent; plus some anticipatory/preemptive bargaining motivations
Vetting by MoI and NDS	Advancing Afghan institutional control
Standards, rules, and their reinforcement (i.e., training)	
Comply with all MoI regulations and Afghan laws	Advanced by Afghan government stakeholders to enable institutional control; also meeting international representatives' state-building and accountability demands
ALP code of conduct (including general good conduct, restrictions on poppy growth or narcotics usage, and operations no further than 1km from village)	Individual provisions within code of conduct demanded in response to range of stakeholder concerns (i.e., those related to counter-narcotics, risk of human rights abuses, threat to state building, etc.)
Oath of loyalty to the Afghan government and restrictions on any ties to Taliban	Exact origin unknown, but likely proposed to satisfy public concerns about using this as a reconciliation vehicle or U.S. (DC-based) concerns about Taliban infiltration; see chapter 2, note 131 for additional discussion
No "tie to tribal militias" allowed	Response to concerns that this would fuel unruly militias
Twenty-one-day training (including on human rights, laws of war, and the ALP code of conduct)	In pilot stages, some extended training used as preemptive/anticipatory defense against critiques; human rights training later expanded in response to demands from human rights advocates

(*Continued*)

Control mechanism	Use or connection vis-à-vis bargaining positions or actors
SOF mentoring of forces	Aimed at controlling agent; plus some anticipatory/preemptive bargaining motivations

Monitoring and oversight

Community *shura* oversight	Aimed at controlling agent; plus some anticipatory/preemptive bargaining motivations
Command and local oversight from local chief of ANP and governor	Advancing Afghan institutional control and Afghan stakeholder patronage interests; also responding to state-building and governance concerns
Institutional oversight from MoI and accompanying chain of command	Advancing Afghan institutional control
Oversight from SOF, other international military	Aimed at controlling agent, but also reinforced to respond to international stakeholders' demands for checks and accountability
Biometric registration, identification cards, and weapon licenses	Exact origin unknown, but likely part of other measures to demonstrate accountability and that forces would not go rogue

Sanctions and incentives

Development funding for communities that participated (proposed during LDI pilot program, in lieu of full payment)	Aimed at controlling agent, incentivizing community participation as agent checks and controls
Informal sanctions from community elders (stigma/social pressure)	Aimed at controlling agent
MoI disciplinary procedures or prosecution	Advancing Afghan institutional control; also satisfying international demands for accountability checks

considerations for bureaucratic players, including an analysis of "who are natural allies, unappeasable opponents, neutrals who might be converted to support, or opponents who might be converted to neutrality," and the arguments or maneuvers that would be necessary to achieve that.[144]

For proponents of local forces—U.S. military leadership, SOF, and their advisers—control mechanisms were a way to prevail in these bargaining debates. Acceding to Afghan oversight, vetting, and controls was a compromise from their vision of what would produce strong counterinsurgent forces,[145] but it transformed the Afghan government from a staunch opponent to a supporter. It also neutralized the critiques of state building–minded diplomats—both U.S. State Department officials and those of other NATO partners.

It would be hard to argue that the human rights vetting and training persuaded human rights NGOs to support the remobilization of militias. They represented the sort of "unappeasable opponents" noted in the quote from Allison and Halperin above. However, reinforcing such controls muted or quieted opposition at least, and was a way to demonstrate to other key decision makers—like Eikenberry—that NGO concerns were being addressed. These "unappeasable opponents" became more isolated once other key stakeholders and players had been neutralized or brought onside.

Controls were also used by others in the bargaining arena. For the Afghan government, control mechanisms were in fact about control, but control in the sense of their ownership of the program, not control in the sense of constraining the ALP (agents). Afghan government arguments for institutionalization were as much about ensuring that Afghan officials could allocate the benefits of the program as about an inherent belief that institutionalization was necessary. It was a tactic that allowed Afghan officials to switch the locus of control from international forces to the country's own government, and for their organizations and personal networks to benefit from the resources and influence of the program.

For some players, controls appeared to function as what we will call a "limiting device," a last-resort tactic to at least constrain the riskiest or most problematic elements of a program they could not halt entirely. European allies could not stop the United States from going forward with the program, but at least urging Afghan institutionalization and more oversight curbed some of the riskiest elements from a state-building perspective. One UN official said that while other European partners in ISAF were not enthusiastic about the ALP, if the program was to go forward, it was viewed as better to have these militias under the Afghan police, rather than mobilized and reporting only to U.S. Special Forces, because it offered a potential pathway for regularization.[146]

Last-resort or limiting device tactics can also be seen among the human rights and civil society players. Most NGOs did not believe that they could stop a program that already appeared to be a fait accompli.[147] Given this, while many would have preferred to halt the program altogether, they could at least limit the worst risks, through human rights–based vetting requirements, by urging some greater training, and insisting on rules that might reduce situations known to lead to abuses in the past (e.g., limitations on offensive operations and detention).

Even Eikenberry's opposition might be seen as something of a limiting device. His own recollection of the bargaining dynamics was that there was little that he as ambassador could do to stop the U.S. military leadership—the "800-pound gorilla" in the Afghan policy space—from getting approval for this program.[148] However, he argued that his insistence on some modifications at least slowed down what otherwise might have been a much more rapid, widespread, and unilateral U.S. mobilization of militias: "We slowed it down from 100 miles per hour to 50 miles per hour."[149]

Comparing this account with the expectations of principal-agent theory discussed in chapter 1, this bargaining perspective appears to offer a much closer fit with the evidence and offers a stronger explanation of which control mechanisms manifested and why. Principal-agent theory presumes that control mechanisms will manifest where it is deemed necessary to limit agency conduct, and that they will not manifest where doing so would prove costly. However, in the ALP case, the manifestation of control mechanisms appeared to be contingent not on any such cost-benefit analysis, but rather on the bargaining interests involved. It was not that a policy decision was made that mitigating risks was highly important, and then control mechanisms selected that would best mitigate those risks. Instead, controls were proposed as the result of bargaining, and represented explicit compromises or concessions between those promoting local defense forces and those more concerned about the risks of raising such forces. The adoption of control mechanisms that would respond to the concerns of Karzai and Atmar, of Eikenberry, of other international diplomats, and of the UN and human rights NGOs were mechanisms that ultimately facilitated a compromise between these competing views and allowed the program to go forward.

COMPARING THE *SAHWA* AND THE ALP: CONTROLS AS A BARGAINING DEVICE

Although the *sahwa* and the ALP were different types of forces within very different contexts, in both situations, the emergence of a bargaining moment appeared crucial to whether control mechanisms manifested or not. Once such moments did emerge, control mechanisms aligned with different players' bargaining tactics in quite similar ways.

First and foremost, control mechanisms appeared to emerge predominantly as a political tactic, not as a means of agent control. In both the *sahwa* and ALP examples, most control mechanisms manifested after a bargaining moment was triggered, as they proved useful to the interests of players in the bargaining arena. Proponents used them to defend the proposals against particular criticisms or counterarguments. In Iraq, late-stage controls were an attempted response (if ultimately an unconvincing one) to critiques that the United States was funding unaccountable militias who posed a threat to the Iraqi regime. In Afghanistan, control mechanisms were used to rebut or assuage concerns that the initiative would threaten the authority of the state, energize warlords and militias, and/or enable violence and human rights abuses.

Opponents also used control mechanisms to advance their agendas. Both Maliki and Karzai, and their supporting regimes, sought greater ownership of the programs, and used control mechanisms to help facilitate institutional takeover of the programs. Unlikely to persuade the United States to end the program he detested, Maliki demanded a series of institutional control mechanisms that would ultimately provide his government with the means to simply decommission the *sahwa*, one by one. Karzai and the factional leaders and politicians in his government also sought to wrest control of the program—and specifically the selection mechanisms for it—from U.S. forces and used arguments about Afghan institutionalization to do so. In both cases, Afghan and Iraqi leaders demanded a greater number of institutional control mechanisms, but less for the purpose of actually controlling and constraining the forces in question than to use these institutional mechanisms as a sort of *takeover device*.

The ALP case study also introduced another common motive or tactic: demanding a control mechanism, not as a way to prevail in the debate, nor to "take over" the program, but simply to put some outer limits or constraints on it. Critics of the idea of mobilizing irregular forces—whether Ambassador Eikenberry, human rights NGOs, or other international diplomats and representatives—used control mechanisms as *limiting devices*. Although these parties presumed that they would not succeed in blocking the initiative altogether, the safeguards and controls they proposed might at least limit or mitigate the worst risks or tendencies of the program.

This account suggests that control mechanisms manifested less as a mechanism of principal control than as the result of bargaining dynamics. At least in the Afghan case, controls became a mechanism of compromise, allowing competing views on the costs and benefits of the program to be harmonized, and enabling the program to go forward. The Iraq case represents more of a failed compromise: despite U.S. efforts, control mechanisms could not overcome Maliki's hostility to the program. In addition, changing dynamics and the U.S. withdrawal collapsed the bargaining moment and obviated any need to compromise with U.S. demands almost as soon as Iraqi institutional control was assumed.

The contrast between the two cases also offers insights into *when* we might expect controls to be triggered—notably in response to the emergence of a bargaining moment. No real bargaining moment emerged with the *sahwa* until it was already substantially in existence. This was in part due to the fast-paced, bottom-up manner of mobilization. The *sahwa* expanded almost overnight—with close to 100,000 members within a year—generating fewer opportunities for potential critics to try to impose limits or controls. By contrast, the ALP was a much slower-moving process, with almost a year of deliberations, allowing any number of stakeholders to weigh in.

The nature of the surrounding policy arena may make it more or less likely that bargaining will emerge. Afghanistan was a more diffuse and multilateral policy environment, with a more dispersed distribution of resources and decision-making authorities. This more readily lent itself to a contested bargaining environment. By contrast, in Iraq, the number of U.S. troops, the level of funding, and even the degree of active control over territory and resources on the ground, dwarfed the military and civilian resources of almost any other policy actor. To offer a comparison, over the course of 2005 U.S. forces represented 86 percent of coalition troop numbers in Iraq, while at the start of 2009 U.S. forces amounted to only 49 percent of international forces in Afghanistan.[150] One senior U.S. military official observed that because of the high violence levels in Iraq in 2005 and 2006, in many parts of the country local Iraqi officials were not regularly present. Because of both U.S. funding and the substantial ground presence of U.S. troops, "in a way, we were the Iraqi government in certain parts of the country," the same official observed.[151] In such an environment, U.S. troops had the resources to mobilize 100,000 *sahwa* members without needing buy-in from anyone else—at least at the start.

U.S. decision-making authorities and patterns were also more consolidated in Iraq. After Bush reorganized his Iraq policy team in 2005, General Petraeus had virtually unquestioned support and backing from all key U.S. principals—from the White House to the U.S. ambassador in Iraq.[152] "Petraeus's power was unparalleled—it was huge," Dodge offered, both in terms of the general's ability to advance U.S. policy and vis-à-vis other non-U.S. stakeholders in Iraq.[153] Because of the preponderance of U.S. resources and manpower in Iraq, U.S. military leadership did not typically consult with coalition partners on key security prerogatives. Iraqi buy-in would become important later on, but at least at the start, "Iraqi permission didn't matter," one DoD adviser offered.[154] Or, as one senior Iraqi official more colorfully put it, "The Americans began the program without any consultation with the Iraqis. When it began to succeed they tried to engage the Iraqi government. It was like the baby was already born, and handed to the Iraqis."[155]

Combined, all of these factors meant that at least in the first year, there was no "bargaining moment" in Iraq. It is not that there was an absence of concerns about the *sahwa*—they presented the same panoply of risks as any other irregular force, and many stakeholders in Iraq were concerned about those risks. However, the United States did not need to obtain approval or buy-in from other stakeholders, and so there was no bargaining moment to provide critics the opportunity to litigate these concerns and force concessions, including control mechanisms. Only once Iraqi participation was needed did a limited bargaining moment emerge, and along with it, control mechanisms.

By contrast, in Afghanistan, the idea of local defense forces was introduced into a much more diffuse, multipolar, and competitive policy environment, and one that was much more seized with taming militias and warlords and preventing abuse by government-aligned forces. Even after two U.S. troop surges, by early 2010, U.S. forces still provided a little more than half (55 percent) of international forces in Afghanistan.[156] The United Kingdom, Canada, Germany, the Netherlands, Italy, and France took charge of key regional commands or some of the twenty-six Provincial Reconstruction Teams and generally led on development, humanitarian, and governance support in those areas. Other key donors—the EU, Japan, other Scandinavian countries—were crucial stakeholders in supporting a range of other related activities like police reform, disarmament and demobilization, or other development and humanitarian support. There were also more significant stakeholders outside of government—from the UN to more vocal, and influential, NGOs and civil society bodies.

All of these factors meant that a much wider range of stakeholders was generally consulted or had the necessary leverage to weigh in on key security initiatives in Afghanistan. The dual-hatted U.S. general in charge of the U.S. and ISAF missions had significant command authority, but he tended to consult on key security initiatives with at least the most substantial troop contributors within the forty-one-nation coalition, as well as with other key donors and the range of stakeholders within the Afghan government. Even within the U.S. government, Afghanistan policy was less cohesive and more contentious. The U.S. embassy alone had five ambassadors, led by Eikenberry. Obama had also appointed Ambassador Richard Holbrooke as the special representative for Afghanistan and Pakistan, and his office intervened on many key security debates. Overall civil-military relations between Obama and his key generals was more fraught—a fact best illustrated by Obama's firing of McChrystal within a year of his appointment.[157] As a result, far from the virtual monopoly on decision making that Petraeus enjoyed in Iraq, the commanding general in Afghanistan had a far more diverse, and contentious, policy environment to deal with.

There were also more significant resource needs and constraints for the ALP in Afghanistan. Although the ALP was inspired by the *sahwa* experience, the proposal for local forces in Afghanistan operated along a different model. It was less about flipping former insurgents and their affiliates, in the hopes of draining insurgent recruitment and gaining intelligence about them, than about using a bottom-up model of security and governance to persuade communities to support the Afghan government, and to gradually extend the legitimacy and reach of the state. The former could work with the sort of short-term incentives (cash via discretionary funds) and security guarantees (U.S. manpower) readily available to U.S. forces in Iraq. The latter could only succeed, SOF argued, if it was adequately supported over a number of years, and with levels of governance and development support that were equal to the amount of military support.[158] To achieve that across a wide swath of Afghanistan's territory, the program would need the support and buy-in of the U.S. government as a whole, other ISAF partners in charge of Provincial Reconstruction Teams, a wide range of international development actors, NGOs and civil society, and, most crucially, the Afghan government.

All of this generated an environment in which ALP proponents needed the approval, support, or some degree of buy-in from a range of different official and informal stakeholders. This made it much more likely that controls would emerge as concessions to different stakeholders than in the largely bilateral—at times almost unilateral—decision-making environment in Iraq. The difference between the ALP and the *sahwa* program suggests that controls appear as a by-product of a competitive bargaining moment. The more contentious the issue, and the greater number of players, the more likely that controls will be generated as part of the policy compromises and concessions.

The above insights about control mechanisms in the *sahwa* and ALP are broadly consistent with BPA's view of policy outcomes as the result of stakeholder competition. However, one prominent element in the case studies that differs from traditional BPA analysis is the significant role played by those outside the U.S. government apparatus—from Karzai and Maliki to NGOs, civil society, and UNAMA. The way that these external stakeholders participated in the bargaining moment in each country offers a concrete example of chapter 1's call for an expanded conception of the players in BPA. Subsequent chapters will draw from these examples, and also those subsequently introduced in Syria, to further theorize how these external actors came to play a role in U.S. deliberations.

A last, important point for the subsequent discussion concerns the legacy effects of the *sahwa* and the ALP. The perceived tremendous success of the *sahwa* program came to stand as proof that reliance on LHSFs could work and should be embraced, while the abrupt end of the program when Maliki took over would later serve as a note of caution about mobilizing such forces without full local buy-in. The ALP was motivated in part by the perceived success of the *sahwa*, but it was adapted to accommodate critiques and concerns that were more potent in the Afghan political environment. The ALP would come to stand for the idea that leveraging irregular forces was acceptable so long as it was accompanied with a degree of accountability and tight control. Subsequent chapters and LHSF case studies will revisit some of these legacy effects, including in later iterations of local force development in Afghanistan and Iraq.

3

SEARCHING FOR UNICORNS

Risk Mitigation in the Internal and External Policy Deliberations Over Syrian Armed Groups

In August 2011, after months of escalating violence against civilian protestors and opposition groups and increasing potential for regional spillover, President Barack Obama called for Syrian president Bashar al-Assad, to step down. But Security Council authorization for any form of direct intervention, or even harsh sanctions, was blocked due to Russian and Chinese vetoes, and a divided Congress was unwilling to authorize unilateral American intervention. Wary of committing the United States to another war in the Middle East, Obama quickly took direct military action off the table. Even after Obama's "red line" had been crossed, with the Assad regime's clear use of chemical weapons in August 2013, Obama balked at direct action.[1]

Despite this unwillingness to support direct military intervention, the United States ultimately provided billions in other military and nonmilitary support to Syrian armed groups and opposition figures. From 2012 to 2022, the United States provided more than $1.3 billion in stabilization assistance, which included efforts to support rebel governance enclaves, as well as at least $400 million in nonlethal assistance to armed Syrian rebels (the second case study in this chapter).[2] Separate from this there was a $1 billion covert program to arm, train, and equip anti-Assad rebels (the first case study). After the rise of ISIL, an expansive, multiyear "Train and Equip" initiative was created for Syrian forces willing to fight against ISIL, three iterations of which are explored below. This chapter will use case studies of five of these initiatives or periods of support to further test some of the principal control and bargaining expectations introduced in prior chapters.

While the focus of analysis across these case studies is on U.S. practice, it is important to remember that the United States was not alone in providing this sort of assistance. A number of Gulf countries, as well as Turkey, Jordan, the United Kingdom and France, among other allies, collaborated with the CIA in the provision of covert, lethal assistance to the Free Syrian Army. In many ways, Saudi Arabia, Qatar, and Turkey played a far more material role in supporting the Syrian rebels than the United States, bankrolling or servicing U.S. arms and equipment going to the FSA, in addition to their own bilateral efforts. The United Kingdom and France provided trainers to several of the "Train and Equip" programs for anti-ISIL forces, and deployed Special Forces within Syrian territory on advisory missions in support of the Kurdish-led Syrian Democratic Forces.[3] The United States, as well as the United Kingdom, France, and the Netherlands, all provided "nonlethal" assistance to parts of the FSA,[4] while Germany provided limited humanitarian supplies.[5] A much wider circle of countries, including Canada, Denmark, Germany, the Netherlands, and the United Kingdom, joined the United States to support *unarmed* police, local councils, and emergency and medical brigades, and to otherwise reinforce opposition governance and control in parts of Syria.

Across all five of the case studies, risks and risk mitigation appear front and center. Indeed, one former White House adviser framed President Obama's concerns on arming the Syrian opposition in the following terms:

> Look at the situation in Syria: You have Syria, a state sponsor of terrorism armed by Iran, also a state sponsor of terrorism, fighting alongside Russia, an adversary of the U.S., and also fighting alongside Hezbollah, another terrorist organization. We are also fighting against ISIL, a terrorist organization. And the best we could find as a [U.S.] partner is the PKK [Partîya Karkerên Kurdistanê, or Kurdistan Workers' Party], a Designated Terrorist Organization. Take that situation [in which you have] seven malign actors: from the perspective of the United States, sending weapons into the country is a problem.[6]

From the onset, there were concerns about assistance to the Syrian opposition being construed as contravening international norms of nonintervention in the affairs of other states, essentially a violation of Syria's sovereignty. When the United Kingdom and France lobbied for lifting the EU arms embargo on Syria to enable them to arm Syrian rebels, fellow EU members accused them of breaching international law on these grounds, and of aiding and abetting human rights violations.[7] Although the United States and other countries did ultimately provide lethal assistance to some parts of the FSA, it is notable that they chose to do so covertly, largely out of sensitivity to these norms of nonintervention. The United States ultimately only provided lethal assistance *overtly* under the banner of countering ISIL, which it justified under its theory of sovereign and collective self-defense.[8]

Nor was the controversy only limited to lethal assistance. By some interpretations, even nonlethal assistance to groups working counter to the Syrian regime could constitute a violation of sovereignty—particularly where that "nonlethal" assistance included equipment of military or tactical value, such as trucks, body armor, night vision goggles, other defensive equipment, and even communications gear.[9] Even fairly standard donor-funded activities—for example, support to local councils, community-based development, and service delivery—were fraught in the opposition context in Syria.

In addition to these security risks, there were also profound moral and political concerns. It was an increasingly bloody, internecine conflict, with war crimes on all sides and hostile actors in abundance. Any arms or equipment provided might go to groups or individuals engaged in atrocities, potentially even directly enabling the commission of such acts. Many of the supported LHSFs also used whatever fighters were available, including underage recruits whose involvement might contravene international legal norms on child soldiers.

The complex and chaotic armed group environment exacerbated both the legal and security risks associated with providing assistance to these groups. There were hundreds of armed groups in Syria, with new ones constantly forming or rebranding and affiliations between these groups constantly in flux. U.S. policy makers tended to describe the Syrian opposition groups as "marbled," meaning that they were so intermixed that policy makers could not distinguish those who were "moderate" or secular (and thus acceptable partners in the U.S. view) from those viewed as too close to Islamic extremist organizations, several of which had been designated as terrorist organizations under U.S. law.[10] This was a major problem. In addition to the consequences of passing weapons or equipment to hostile actors, under U.S. law, provision of support to "Designated Terrorist Organizations" (DTOs) is a criminal offense, regardless of whether that support was intended or inadvertent.[11]

Amid the complex and shifting armed group dynamics in Syria, it was impossible to be sure that arms and equipment would not fall into the wrong hands. Even if a group was not known to affiliate or identify with Islamic extremist groups, it would be impossible to ensure that foreign assistance stayed out of the hands of DTOs once delivered into Syria. By late 2012, Islamic extremist groups like Jabhat al-Nusra (the Nusra Front)[12] had become dominant among the opposition and seized territory and supplies from smaller groups frequently. As the conflict went on, even the more ideologically moderate FSA groups would tacitly or openly cooperate with these more powerful groups in order to survive. This was a major factor for why most European countries balked at providing any "lethal" assistance. As one European diplomat framed such calculations, "if a food basket ends up in Nusra's hands, it's not a big deal," but weapons ending up in the wrong hands would be "politically intolerable."[13]

A last major set of concerns were the mid- to long-term risks of what would happen with these groups once supported and enabled by the United States. U.S. officials worried that, if not already a security threat, these groups could become one in the future. In the 1980s, the CIA provided covert support to anti-Soviet mujahideen fighters in Afghanistan, some of whom, including Osama bin Laden, would go on to form al-Qaeda. As Secretary of State Hillary Clinton would later note in her account of debates over Syrian assistance, "the story of the *mujahideen* in Afghanistan remained a powerful cautionary tale never far from anyone's mind."[14] Alternately, while Syrian rebels might not become the next major terrorist threat, they might prove weak in containing it. Some within the U.S. establishment feared that if Syrian rebels prevailed, they would prove worse than the Assad regime at keeping Jabhat al-Nusra, ISIL, or other terrorist groups in check. Other regional partners had their own qualms about the direction of U.S. support. As will be prominent in discussions of the last two initiatives, Turkey had no tolerance for U.S.

support to the SDF, which it viewed as a front for the PKK, which it had fought for decades. Turkish officials feared that any arms or training given to the SDF would later be used against Turkey, and U.S. support to these groups created major political risks for its relationship with Turkey and for regional stability.

The United States ultimately ended up tolerating these risks, but it did so only with an elaborate web of checks and controls on each level and type of assistance. All five initiatives noted above involved multipronged vetting protocols, codes of conduct or redlines, and extensive oversight and reporting mechanisms. Where redlines were crossed, sanctions in the form of funding cuts were frequently applied, at least with the early FSA initiatives. The CIA covert program, as well as the later DoD-managed programs, also involved training on the laws of war and other international legal standards.

Security risks were front and center, but these extensive checks and controls were also aimed at preventing human rights abuses or other political consequences. A standing provision of U.S. law known as the Leahy Law prohibits DoD or State Department funds from going to foreign forces against whom there is credible information of gross violations of human rights. Although it was not formally applicable to any of the assistance to Syrian armed groups,[15] it was such a well-established and long-running provision of U.S. assistance that it nonetheless cast a shadow over any hint of providing support to those with a record of abuse. In addition, given the prevalence of underage fighters there was a real risk that all Syria assistance might be halted under the Child Soldiers Prevention Act.[16]

Such a robust menu of controls might appear to be a natural response to the number of risks involved. An administration dominated by lawyers was taking steps toward intervention that were increasingly risky both legally and politically.[17] Moreover, they were doing so under a global magnifying glass, with high levels of public attention on Syria and ample documentation of abuses and issues that arose. However, principal-agent theory does not assume that where the risks are higher, so follows the number of control mechanisms. Instead, principal-agent theory frames the decision to use control mechanisms as a cost-benefit analysis, weighing how likely they are to work and bring benefits versus how costly they will be to apply. In the case of Syria, no policy maker thought that these controls were likely to entirely, or even perhaps significantly, mitigate the risks in question. As one senior State Department official observed, "there is no such thing as perfect vetting in that environment."[18] Given limited direct access to Syrian territory, the unknown nature of the armed groups in question, the number of competing (and often hostile) parties and patrons involved, and the multiplicity of risks, Syria presented something approaching a worst-case prospect for agent control and fidelity.

These high costs and limited benefits played out in a manner that was to be expected: the panoply of control mechanisms introduced generated significant costs, in many cases proving so cumbersome, or introducing selection and cut-off criteria that were so significant, that they prevented the program from achieving its overall goals. One former State Department official observed that an approach heavily tilted toward risk mitigation was ill-suited to the reality of partner choices in Syria. "In a situation like Syria, a multiyear civil war in which actors on the ground face no good choices, you will not get anyone who meets all the perfect standards."[19] What stands out from the Syria examples is that while principal-agent theory predicted the costs of controls, it does a poor job of explaining why policy makers chose to impose them.

Instead, what emerges from close case examination is that these controls and risk-mitigation mechanisms were largely generated in the course of bargaining debates between different political stakeholders—either principals within the U.S. government, those working inside or with the U.S. bureaucracy in the course of implementation, or even foreign actors with a stake in the programs in question.

Although there were many different permutations of U.S. assistance to non-state armed groups in Syria, five case studies or periods of support will be examined. The time period examined in each is indicated in parentheses, with further information provided in the respective case studies.

- CIA covert, lethal support to FSA groups (September 2012–January 2017)
- Early State Department nonlethal assistance to the FSA (fall 2012–end of 2014)
- The first congressionally authorized program to "Train and Equip" Syrian rebels against ISIL, called the New Syrian Forces (summer 2014–October 2015)

- A revised version of the anti-ISIL "Train and Equip" program, partnering with Turkey to support groups in northern Syria (October 2015–end of 2016)
- Use of "Train and Equip" funds to support forces that would become known as the SDF (October 2014–December 2019).[20]

The first three case studies explore the earliest iterations of U.S. assistance to Syrian armed groups largely from the perspective of internal U.S. bargaining. As such, they reflect several classic BPA bargaining paradigms, from an example of a high-level "decision-game" with the internal White House debate over CIA covert support to an illustration of lower-level and incremental bargaining within State Department deliberation and implementation of nonlethal assistance to the FSA. The third case study more strongly introduces the role of Congress, whose approval and funding were necessary to create the overt Train and Equip program (the New Syrian Forces). The last two case studies will explore control mechanisms in two later iterations of the Train and Equip program, but with a greater focus on the input provided by two foreign actors: Turkey and the LHSF in question, the SDF.

CASE 1: HIGH-LEVEL BARGAINING AND THE CIA LETHAL SUPPORT PROGRAM (SEPTEMBER 2012–JANUARY 2017)

In 2012, U.S. policy makers saw few good options in Syria.[21] The initially peaceful Arab Spring protests had escalated into a bloody and complex civil war. Assad's brutal response—from starvation-inducing siege tactics on opposition strongholds, to indiscriminate bombardment, to hunting down and torturing suspected opposition members—were resulting in rates of civilian death and destruction that exceeded even the Iraqi civil war.[22] But in February 2012, Russia and China vetoed a Security Council resolution that would have condemned the Assad regime and called for a cessation of hostilities. Violence only escalated after UN mediation led by former UN secretary-general Kofi Annan collapsed in June 2012. By the end of that year, the death toll exceeded fifty thousand; and by March 2013, the number of Syrian refugees had reached one million.[23]

Within the State Department, there was a fervor to do something. Journalist Mark Landler describes Secretary of State Hillary Clinton's internal advocacy on Syria in this period as "casting about for solutions, however far-fetched,"[24] while another former State Department official remembered Foggy Bottom's feverish focus on Syria at the time as akin to a "passion project."[25] The initial response of the State Department had been to ramp up humanitarian aid and other in-kind support to protestors and civil society groups, while quietly working to "peel back" support for Assad among regional and Arab partners.[26] After Obama's August 2011 announcement that it was time for Assad to step aside, and the seeming dead end of UN diplomacy over the course of 2012, there was increasing internal and external pressure for direct military intervention.[27] Liberal interventionists within the Obama administration, close foreign allies like France and the United Kingdom, and prominent civil society groups had successfully argued for military intervention in Libya in March 2011, and many now argued for the same in Syria.

But the U.S. intervention in Libya cut both ways. As former Obama official Mona Yacoubian notes, while outside observers questioned why the United States was not more "forward-leaning" on Syria, as it had been in other Arab Spring contexts like Egypt and Libya, the lessons learned from Libya was that intervention was unlikely to work.[28] One former senior Obama adviser noted that President Obama "came off the intervention in Libya with the sense that it had not been the right choice, and he had opened a Pandora's box."[29] Thus, while some hawks and liberal interventionists argued for, at a minimum, targeted strikes on Assad regime air assets or a no-fly zone to protect civilians, the U.S. military establishment warned that any engagement would be a slippery slope toward full-blown intervention, and one that would require substantially more blood and treasure than the engagement in Libya.[30] A president who had campaigned on withdrawing U.S. forces from multiyear engagements in the Middle East would not so soon seek to generate another Iraq- or Afghanistan-style commitment.

But there was still continued pressure to do something, both given the dire situation of the Syrian population and the ample regional and transnational security risks that were brewing in Syria. As the Assad regime lost its grip on Syrian territory, the vacuum was filled not only by Syrian civil society and pro-democracy advocates, but by a number of Islamist extremist groups, several linked to al-Qaeda. More secular or non-extremist groups existed among the opposition; in July 2011, for example, a group of former Syrian Army officers had announced the formation of the Free Syrian Army, which presented itself as the more secular and moderate front for the opposition. However, particularly in this early period, most of the support being provided was by Saudi Arabia and Qatar, and transmitted via Turkey, each of which favored groups that ideologically identified as Islamist, notwithstanding these forces' many links with extremists.[31] Better organized, better supplied, and more cohesive than the FSA, these Islamist groups quickly became the strongest forces on the ground. In particular, the group known as Jabhat al-Nusra, an al-Qaeda affiliate that later split with them, was becoming increasingly dominant. CIA operatives had been quietly providing advice and working to channel Gulf funding and arms to more moderate FSA groups.[32] But internally, a range of senior Obama officials worried that unless the United States got more "skin in the game"—through directly supporting rebels—it would not be able to control who was funded and how assistance was provided by other U.S. allies.[33]

In addition, in April 2012, Arab members of the Friends of Syria group pledged $100 million in salaries for armed Syrian rebels, creating even more pressure for the United States and other Western donors to increase their level and type of support.[34] The United States and other Western members of the Friends of Syria group pledged to provide communication equipment and other nonlethal support to armed opposition groups, the starting point for much of the State Department's nonlethal assistance program (discussed in the second case study).[35]

While deliberately eschewing a commitment to *overtly* arm Syrian rebels, this commitment to nonlethal assistance—and pressure to do more by key regional allies—lent fuel to the internal U.S. debate about whether to provide arms to parts of the FSA covertly.[36] The plan that was ultimately developed was one that Obama never liked. It came with a high level of risk and few prospects of making any strategic difference in Syria. However, with military strikes or intervention foreclosed, and facing continued pressure to do something, the administration chose to provide support to Syrian rebels and armed groups—a decision that appeared the "least bad option among many even worse alternatives," in Clinton's recollection.[37]

RISKS AND CONTROLS IN THE CIA COVERT ASSISTANCE

The CIA program to covertly arm, train, and support Syrian rebels was authorized in April 2013, with the rollout beginning in the fall of 2013. It was provided in conjunction with other international partners through two intelligence hubs, the Joint Operation Center (Müşterek Operasyon Merkezi, or MOM) in Turkey and the Military Operation Center (MOC) in Jordan.[38] These two hubs included intelligence representatives from Saudi Arabia, Qatar, the United Arab Emirates, the United Kingdom, France, briefly Italy, and the two host countries of Jordan and Turkey.[39]

U.S. lethal assistance to the FSA featured a degree of control mechanisms that is perhaps surprising given that covert assistance enjoys fewer formal constraints than DoD or State Department support.[40] Many of the control mechanisms embedded in law—from the Leahy Law to conditions related to Syrian sanctions or other congressional restrictions—would not apply to CIA support. Nonetheless, although in theory less constrained, the control mechanisms adopted for the CIA program appeared in some ways more extensive than those that would manifest in other overt security assistance in Syria. This was particularly true for those individuals or groups given antitank munitions known as TOW (i.e., tube-launched, optically tracked, wireless-guided) missiles, the most advanced weaponry provided. FSA members interviewed described the vetting process as like a "job interview" or a "visa process," in contrast to the primarily name-based, unit-level database check used for other U.S. support programs.[41] It took months, not weeks.

Once vetted, oversight and scrutiny that was in some ways more extensive than the overt assistance continued. Journalist Adam Entous writes that "Those who made the cut, earning the label 'trusted commanders,' signed written agreements, submitted payroll information about their fighters and detailed their battlefield strategy."[42] FSA factions who received TOW missiles were required to track each use, and to bring back spent casings in order to receive new ones.[43] They were regularly (often monthly) required to report to the two joint intelligence centers in Turkey and Jordan—the MOM and the MOC—for debriefings and questioning. This frequently involved providing an assessment of the situation in a given area, or after-action reports on operations that had been supported, including specific reporting requirements, such as providing additional video or written evidence of how TOW missiles were launched.[44]

There appeared to be oversight, redlines, and controls related not just to the supported fighters' performance or potential security concerns, which might be expected given the CIA's intelligence-gathering mandate, but also to their conduct. FSA commanders and others privy to the process said that when FSA members were called before the MOM and MOC, the intelligence representatives assembled would raise human rights and conduct issues. In at least one case, with an Aleppo-based FSA faction known colloquially as the al-Zenki group,[45] support was cut in part because the group in question had violated these human rights standards.[46] One commander whose group received TOW missiles even remembered a human rights protocol or code of conduct that they had to affirm in training. When another of the groups he worked with struck a civilian target, the MOM recalled the offenders' rockets and launchers, and forced them to reaffirm the code of conduct and receive additional training on avoiding civilian harm, the FSA commander said.[47]

Expectations of good conduct also extended beyond questions of civilian harm. One example given concerned a commander in northern Syria named Jamal Maahrouf who, while effective and secular, was passed over for U.S. covert funding because he had "established a reputation as a warlord," and engaged in smuggling, extortion, and other questionable behavior.[48] As Syria analyst Nick Heras argued, "Here's a guy who would have fit the 1980s playbook [of U.S. covert support], but he didn't make it in this iteration" because of greater concern under the Obama administration over who was being funded.[49]

One might well wonder why this CIA approach was seemingly so different from the past, so laden with controls. For a start, some of the program features were not so distinct from the agency's overall approach to partner management. While agency training and vetting protocols are classified, former intelligence officials interviewed argued that, generally speaking, more extensive background checks are built into the CIA's DNA as an intelligence agency.[50] This would have been particularly germane to those FSA members physically appearing at the MOM and MOC, or receiving training on TOW missiles in Qatar.[51] In addition, certainly some of the robust scrutiny and oversight—for example, in the review panels at the MOM and MOC—would have the side benefit of offering greater situational awareness and intelligence gains.

Yet even this explanation is somewhat unsatisfying given how costly these controls proved to be. For an average $1 billion annual operating cost, the program accomplished very few of its goals, with the supported FSA groups regularly losing territory both to pro-Assad forces and to other extremist groups.[52] While tight controls were not the sole cause of these setbacks, they were a big part of it. Tight vetting and weapons tracking, coupled with the highly bureaucratic approach, slowed the overall volume and pace of assistance, to the point where it significantly undermined the fighting capacity and potential impact of the supported FSA.[53] As one former senior White House official interviewed by analyst Mona Yacoubian observed, "When the decision was finally made to provide lethal assistance, the pace at which it was pursued was glacial. There was no real commitment. There was a great deal of caution and the whole focus was on the cost of action."[54]

In an interview with the *Wall Street Journal*, one FSA fighter claimed that it might take two weeks for the approving committees in the MOM or MOC to approve a given weapon request, at which point the opportunity for the operation in question had passed.[55] FSA commanders said that even when they got the weapons, ammunition, or other material requested, it would often fall far short of what was needed to supply their forces, hold the position, or otherwise execute the strategy proposed.[56] The CIA program ultimately included none of the sophisticated weapons—such as surface-to-air missiles—or levels of support that would have been game changing.[57] One former senior military leader engaged in the support recollected that the FSA members couldn't even keep the weapons they trained on.[58]

There were also opportunity costs in terms of whom the United States could partner with. In a context in which a large share of the opposition self-identified as Islamic resistance to some degree, the tight vetting and stigma against cooperation with any "Islamist" group eliminated many potentially productive partners.[59] The additional criteria related to good conduct might have further winnowed down the number of potential partners. One Syria analyst, Charles Lister, argued that these concerns about risk shifted the selection analysis from one that might have analyzed which groups were most capable within the context of the realities on the ground—and thus might have enabled the program to have a strategic impact—to one that gave greater primacy to ticking off select risk criteria. He observed, "If we want a big impact, then very strict criteria isn't going to work in our favor. We'll either get cheated, or we won't get the best players."[60]

Nor could it be argued that these tremendous costs could be justified by the presumed benefits, in terms of controls reducing the sort of agent slack or adverse consequences likely to result from it. Extensive weapons tracking and missile casing collection perhaps kept some greater hold over U.S.-provided arms, but as one White House adviser observed, in the Syria environment, "inevitably weapons would go astray—and they did. [It is] impossible to say how many."[61] All of the extensive vetting, interviews, and other reporting and intelligence gathering provided a greater degree of information, but not enough to enforce redlines credibly and consistently. One adviser who was familiar with the deliberations in the MOC observed that they would get information that a group had cooperated with a banned group, passed weapons on, or committed other infractions, but given the still largely remote management of the force, it was "hard to vet whether the allegation had occurred."[62] In addition, he noted that "in Syria, where you had such a great number of local actors, and such a wide spread of potential backers," it became "much messier" and harder to manage these relationships effectively.[63] Such observations recall the expectations of principal-agent theory—it was an environment where the complexity of principal-agent dynamics and the lack of physical presence made information harder to come by, and one in which Syrian groups had multiple patrons they could turn to.

In essence, all the costs and barriers that principal-agent theory expects would deter principals from imposing controls were there, but extensive control mechanisms still manifested. At least based on the preliminary evidence, principal-agent theory provides an unconvincing account of why so many control mechanisms were present. The following section will turn to the internal debate surrounding the CIA covert assistance in order to evaluate the significance of controls for those deliberations, and what this record suggests about what motivated the introduction of these controls.

HIGH-LEVEL BARGAINING IN CIA LETHAL SUPPORT TO THE FSA

In the classic examples of high-level bargaining or policy "decision games"—for example, Allison's analysis of the Cuban Missile Crisis, or Halperin's discussion of decisions surrounding the deployment of intercontinental ballistic missiles—policy principals try to persuade the president to take their preferred course of action by leveraging their own authority or their relationship with the president, or by building a coalition of support among other players in the game.[64] Each player's likelihood of succeeding depends on their bargaining advantages and position—for example, their relationship with the president or their institutional or personal authority on the issue.[65] As a result, the substantive outcome may have more to do with the bargaining tactics and positions than the merits of the issue in question.

The debate over the authorization of CIA covert support to FSA groups presented a similar bargaining scenario, with different agency or department principals vying for President Obama's support for arming Syrian rebels. Control mechanisms became a key tactic in that debate, used to redefine the problem and the solutions to it and to overcome the reluctance of a president who overall thought the plan would not work.

The proponents of a plan to arm Syrian rebels were the unlikely bedfellows of the State Department and the CIA. Many members of the State Department had already been internally lobbying for greater U.S. engagement in Syria, due to both their own personal commitments on the issue and to the mounting diplomatic pressure from European and regional allies.[66] However, given the sensitivities in Syria, overt intervention was not politically tolerable, making covert support via the CIA the only tractable avenue for arming Syrian rebels at the time.

While the CIA as an institution had reengaged in paramilitary operations since 2001, most of these operations involved supporting forces in the dozens, not in the thousands or tens of thousands, as might be involved in a full-fledged FSA support program.[67] It was thus a strange twist of fate that at that moment, the man most responsible for nurturing the U.S. mobilization of 100,000 local forces in Iraq, and then 30,000 in Afghanistan, was now heading the CIA. In September 2011, General David Petraeus retired from the army and was subsequently appointed CIA director. When lead State Department officers sought to get support to moderate Syrian rebels, Petraeus was an obvious potential ally. According to journalist Mark Landler, in February 2012, Robert Ford, then U.S. ambassador to Syria, reached out to Petraeus, a former colleague from their time in Iraq.[68] Alarmed at the growing strength of Jabhat al-Nusra, Ford was looking for ways to get "weapons in the hands of more moderate rebels, chiefly the Free Syrian Army."[69] Clinton's account suggests she had the same impulse: "As it became clear that the Geneva effort was stalemated, I and others on the Obama national security team began exploring what it would take to stand up a carefully vetted and trained force of moderate Syrian rebels who could be trusted with American weapons."[70] Given his experience working with local forces in Iraq and Afghanistan, she reached out to Petraeus to discuss "whether it was possible to vet, train, and equip moderate opposition fighters."[71]

Petraeus, seconded by Clinton, first proposed the plan for covert CIA lethal assistance to the FSA at a September 2012 meeting of the National Security Council (NSC).[72] The first reaction to what became known as the "Clinton-Petraeus plan" was not overwhelmingly positive. Over that summer, Obama had commissioned a study from the CIA analyzing past efforts to covertly arm and train rebel groups in places like Angola, Nicaragua, and Cuba, among others.[73] It found that past efforts had only a limited impact, especially when not accompanied by U.S. forces on the ground, as would be the case in Syria.[74] In short, the CIA study suggested that the plan would not work. In addition, it would incur the full range of risks or costs discussed in the introduction. U.S. assistance could be diverted to groups like Jabhat al-Nusra, used to further war crimes, or inadvertently enable the next al-Qaeda.

Some of the most serious objections to the plan—that arming rebels would be insufficient to achieve the strategic objectives—could not be countered, at least not without direct U.S. intervention. So instead, proponents opted for a bargaining tactic that thrives well beyond the realm of political science: they changed the subject. They focused on how means of implementing the program, and specifically a number of control mechanisms, might mitigate some of the downstream risks. Even the first version of the plan presented included a number of control mechanisms—some of the same vetting measures and other monitoring and oversight controls that had been used in Iraq and Afghanistan, as well as in the State Department's nonlethal assistance up to that time (discussed as the next case study).[75] Relying on these, Clinton argued that what she and Petraeus were proposing—"responsibly training and equipping a nonextremist rebel force"—was different from simply dumping weapons into a volatile environment.[76] Proponents argued that the very "real risks," including that of funding future extremists, could be mitigated "if rebels could be vetted and trained effectively."[77]

This tactic was at least partly successful. An account of the meeting from a senior White House official whom Landler interviewed suggests that the overall debate went from questions about the overall efficacy or wisdom of arming rebels to an almost technical, lower-level discussion about controls and program management. The debate came to center on the following questions: "What would be the chain of custody the weapons would have? Who trains the people to use the weapons? Is there a command-and-control structure around these people? Or are we just dumping the weapons in?"[78] Obama did not accept the plan at the time, according to the same White House official quoted by Landler, because there were insufficient answers to these questions, making the proposal appear "half-cooked."[79] Other key principals also remained unconvinced, including Vice President Biden, National Security Adviser Susan Rice, and several other prominent NSC staff members.[80] But in the language of BPA theory, what proponents had accomplished even in that first round was to redefine the agenda and the problem, as well as the menu of solutions deemed appropriate to respond to it. A rejection based significantly on poor program design opened the possibility of winning the debate by putting forward a plan with more robust controls.

In December 2012, proponents tried again in another NSC meeting. Petraeus had resigned by that point, but Landler notes that Petraeus's successor "had retooled the Petraeus plan to address Obama's skepticism, sharpening U.S. control over the weapons."[81] Although this reportedly won over a few more White House skeptics, Obama still was not convinced. He was worried about the slippery slope, and specifically about the strength of controls. As Landler reports, he "still wasn't satisfied with the level of vetting for the rebels."[82]

Obama would later approve the same plan in April 2013. The description of how Obama eventually agreed to the program suggests that control mechanisms were not fully persuasive in themselves: it took additional months of internal pressure, pressure from regional allies, and then finally the tipping factor of the need to do something following evidence of Assad's use of chemical weapons.[83] However, while the control mechanisms were not in themselves sufficient to overcome Obama's doubts, the significant focus on these mechanisms in the prior debates suggest that the program likely would not have been authorized without them. They helped defray some of Obama's concerns about the downstream risks and brought on board a wider range of allies within the administration.

Controls also played into a second, shorter round of debate with congressional intelligence committees. Although covert action is authorized by an executive order, it has become standard practice for the Senate and House Intelligence Committees to be informed of any covert action and to then be able to exercise an informal veto. In addition, although the president could authorize the program, the funds for FSA support had to be diverted from other programming that the intelligence committees had already approved.[84] Thus, in the summer of 2013, the administration floated the proposed plan to the House and Senate committees. Press reports suggest that the congressional committees raised some of the same concerns as in the earlier White House debate, including the ideological bent of many of the Syrian groups, the difficulty of knowing who would receive U.S. weapons and support, and then preventing their transmission to extremist groups like Jabhat al-Nusra.[85] Administration officials rebutted these concerns with many of the same counterarguments that were used in the internal debates. In addition to arguing for the plan on its merits—for example, that it would allow the United States "skin in the game," or it was the best option available for countering extremist groups—they pointed to the panoply of control mechanisms that would allow for careful vetting and accountability over the weapons and materiel provided.[86] Such arguments appear to have won out, as the intelligence committees ultimately gave their support to the plan in July 2013.

The foregoing account of the authorization debate suggests that control mechanisms were introduced and added on in the course of bargaining as a way to address internal critics' concerns about the program. Similar to the tactics and strategies introduced in the ALP and *sahwa* debate, they were a way for proponents to prevail in the bargaining, bringing additional supporters on board or trying to neutralize critics' objections. One might also see some limiting devices in some of the controls—a way for internal critics (including Obama himself) to at least put some outer guardrails on the program in an attempt to mitigate or limit the worst outcomes from manifesting.

One might counter that even though these took the form of arguments within the bargaining debate, they do not resolve the question of why the control mechanisms continued to be applied in practice, even as the costliness of this control-heavy approach became apparent. After all, if not bound by law to take into account concerns over the conduct of supported FSA groups, one might imagine the CIA simply dispensing with these bargaining demands over time. However, interviewees suggested that, contrary to public perceptions, this is not how CIA political directives work.[87] When asked about these conduct-based restrictions, interviewees who would have been familiar with the program (but would not discuss a classified program directly) noted that when the CIA is given requirements and restrictions as part of its political directives, these are strictly followed.[88] Public comments and interview observations support the idea of a link between the political directives or tone set in the authorizing debate and controls that were subsequently adopted. In reporting on how tight weapons tracking hampered the program, Entous quotes a senior administration official's rebuttal that such strictness was necessary: "This was consistent with the administration's legal responsibilities and strongly held views in Congress."[89] Given this, it seems likely that these controls were mandated in the executive order, or that CIA officials simply internalized these as the expectations for the program.

Interviewees familiar with CIA operations and protocols also emphasized that, far from the public image of an agency that operates above the law, the CIA and its operations are subject to internal accountability mechanisms and congressional oversight. These can lead to changes in practice or in parameters of operating, either due to changes in the administration or because of congressional dictates. It is worth bearing in mind that this debate was unrolling under an administration that had early on (in 2009) established new standards for covert action, including the requirement that such action should not undermine "the development of stable, non-corrupt, and representative governments that respect the human rights of their citizens."[90] In addition, congressional oversight and rules like the Leahy Law might still guide agency standards informally, even if they would not technically be applicable to activities supported under "Title 50" of U.S. law, which funds and legislatively authorizes covert activities. For example, although no official interviewed confirmed (or denied) what appeared to be a Leahy Law–like vetting criteria within the covert FSA assistance, some of those interviewed observed that congressional expectations developed in relation to overt activities, which are supported under Title 10, can bleed over into covert practice, including those related to human rights standards. Discussing whether a Leahy Law–like standard might ever manifest in covert assistance, one senior agency official observed that, "Perhaps legally you could make a Title 50 argument [that it is not applicable], but in practice you're going to run afoul. If you get fancy with this stuff... and split hairs about Title 50 versus Title 10 distinctions... it's gonna backfire."[91] Given that failing to take reports of abuses by partner forces into consideration in covert operations would potentially compromise the strategy and contravene important U.S. principles, this sort of legal hairsplitting would likely not hold up under congressional scrutiny, he said.[92] It might also create complications for the Title 10 (DoD) forces operating alongside agency officials.

Overall, this case study highlights several inferences that we might add to those introduced in prior chapters. The examination of the bargaining surrounding the CIA's covert support suggests an important facilitating role for control mechanisms—while not the sole tipping factor that persuaded a reluctant president to authorize the program, they softened objections, brought more of the internal players on board, and made authorization more likely. In addition, the close attention to risks and controls in the authorization debate helps fill in the blanks in terms of how and why control mechanisms manifested and were carried on in practice, even when the cost-benefit analysis and the legal constraints would have made them unlikely. The evidence suggests a sort of trickle-down effect—with the heavy emphasis on controls appearing to flow from the heightened attention to risk mitigation from the authorization debate onward. These inferences from the CIA program add further evidence to the overall hypothesis that control mechanisms manifest less as a mechanism of agent control than as a product of political calculations and bargaining. While the controls applied to the FSA were not disconnected from concerns about their behavior, they were primarily introduced in response to bargaining dynamics, not because they appeared likely to limit the risk of adverse behavior by the agent in question.

CASE 2: LOWER-LEVEL AND ITERATIVE BARGAINING OVER STATE DEPARTMENT NONLETHAL ASSISTANCE (FALL 2012–END 2014)

A similar sort of political bargaining preceded the CIA debate, but at a lower level and with a different part of the bureaucracy.[93] Before the CIA was authorized to provide lethal support, the State Department was providing nonlethal assistance to select FSA groups. While much BPA analysis has focused on higher-level bargaining between policy principals, there is also recognition that other parts of the bureaucracy are engaged in similar bargaining games, either at a lower-level of decision making or in the course of implementation.[94] There is frequently a lot of leeway in how to implement a top-level decision, and implementation choices might be determined by the same sort of "stand-sit" positioning and bargaining as the high-level decision making. A separate body of "implementation" literature argues that because of this substantial leeway, bargaining and decision making in the course of implementation can be even more significant in determining foreign policy outputs than what happens at key decision moments.[95] Internal and interagency deliberations over State Department nonlethal assistance provides an illustration of this lower-level bargaining. As this case study will discuss, the controversial nature of the program generated ample cause for control mechanisms to be generated within those internal debates; meanwhile the continuous and more iterative nature of bargaining within implementation created ample opportunities to do so.

U.S. public commitments in the April 2012 Friends of Syria meeting raised the question of expanding nonlethal assistance to a wider swath of the opposition, including both unarmed police and the FSA. This triggered substantial internal objections and debate, much of it in line with what BPA might frame as the stand-sit positions of different State Department stakeholders.[96] The Bureau of Conflict and Stabilization Operations (CSO) was a strong proponent of expanding nonlethal assistance in Syria. CSO had only been recently created, and many in the bureau saw in these Syria initiatives an opportunity to clarify and expand their still-new mandate. After an internal competition, CSO won approval to lead the nonlethal assistance within the State Department; however, it would still have to contend with the many reservations and concerns of other State Department bureaus.[97] The Office of Legal Affairs at the State Department (the chief legal adviser's office) emphasized the legal risks and liabilities of providing assistance to Syrian opposition; the Bureau of Democracy, Human Rights, and Labor (DRL), which has primary responsibility for overseeing the Leahy Law, highlighted the risk of abuses by supported groups or individuals; the department's Syria desk and the Bureau of Near Eastern Affairs (NEA) raised the risk that the assistance might fall into the hands of groups like Jabhat al-Nusra and ISIL, further enabling their expansion.[98]

There were also objections from outside the State Department. White House staff and congressional committees both brought a skeptical view to any Syria assistance, but this was particularly pronounced for something as controversial as aid to Syrian rebels. Through congressional and executive oversight, they would regularly interrogate State Department officials about the range of risks involved and what was being done to manage or mitigate them.

Both at the inception of the program and with each stage of its expansion or evolution, CSO needed to win or maintain the buy-in of these different bureaucratic actors. Because so many of these objections invoked a particular set of risks, CSO frequently relied on control mechanisms to do so. At the start there was a risk-assessment document outlining a range of oversight and risk-mitigation measures designed to respond to the concerns raised by different stakeholders.[99] This included controls like tracking or accounting for assistance, which was designed to reduce the risk of any assistance being transferred to banned or dangerous groups; vetting, oversight, and sanctions designed to deter or stop funding to those who engaged in abuses or atrocities; as well as monitoring and reporting designed to safeguard against or detect corruption or other misuse of funds.[100] Outlining and proposing such measures was a way of rebutting the critique that this type of assistance could not be implemented with any accountability. Given that the key stakeholders outlined above had to sign off on this risk assessment, it was a crucial process step, enabling CSO to demonstrate that risks were addressed, consolidate internal buy-in, and move forward with programming.

Another important early decision (which would influence subsequent Syrian armed group support) was the idea of developing a "Leahy Law–like" human rights–based vetting criteria and process. As noted, the Leahy Law prevents State Department funds from going to foreign forces deemed to have committed gross violations of human rights. To do so, individuals or units set to receive State Department or DoD funding must be vetted against a global database of abuses maintained by DRL; where derogatory information is found and deemed "credible," the individual or units are "blocked" from funding. This can happen either in the initial vetting process or after it, if credible allegations are subsequently found.

The Leahy Law obligations did not formally apply to Syrian opposition forces. In part this was because the type of emergency and contingency funding used for nonlethal assistance relied on presidential emergency authority and could be used notwithstanding other standing provisions of law, including the Leahy Law.[101] In addition, since the Leahy Law applies to forces of a foreign country, it was deemed inapplicable to non-state actors working in opposition to the foreign state in question (Syria in this case).[102]

The fact that the State Department decided to develop its own Leahy Law–like process of vetting and blocks even though it was not required to do so is notable. Application of the Leahy Law is normally a time-consuming process, and the law has a proven track record of ineffectiveness, in part due to under-implementation but also because of the difficulty of capturing and preventing human rights abuses through a name check against a database managed in Washington, DC.[103] Thus, from a principal-agent standpoint, this was already a control mechanism that was known to be highly costly and minimally effective at preventing the slack in question.

These costs and challenges would be even higher in the Syria context because CSO would not even be able to rely on the existing DRL database, and would instead have to build one from scratch. There also was almost no information on any of the Syrian groups, so CSO would have to expend significant staff time and resources gathering information for vetting purposes. Staff spent weeks scouring old newspaper accounts and social media and calling other grantees and interlocuters in Syria to try to get more information about these groups, all in an effort to populate their new database.[104] They then had to triangulate any potential information with sources on the ground or other donors.[105] In a rapidly changing environment like Syria, it was a virtually constant cycle of commissioning research and weighing and cross-checking evidence. Vetting was initially estimated to take ten days, but this eventually stretched to several weeks as the process went on. Given short funding cycles, groups and recipients had to be re-vetted every few months, whereupon the process would have to be repeated.

It would be very hard to justify such significant monitoring costs from a principal-agent perspective, but from an internal bargaining and public management perspective, these processes were invaluable. The promise to do Leahy Law–like vetting provided a response to the internal skeptics, particularly in DRL and the Office of Legal Affairs, who were concerned about U.S. funds going to those who had perpetrated human rights abuses. While CSO reiterated that no vetting was perfect, this at least was a due diligence measure that the State Department broadly deemed acceptable for responding to such risks. It also was a way to forestall or satisfy congressional objections: one staff noted that since Congress had ratified and even expanded the Leahy Law for more than a decade, it demonstrated a clear "congressional intent" that this was the sort of due diligence approach to security assistance that they expected, even when not required by law.[106]

The vetting process, and the general information-gathering, monitoring, and oversight that surrounded it, were also part of CSO's strategy for building credibility, which would give them leverage in future intrabureaucratic debates. CSO staff said they started with less controversial types of programming assistance—for example, humanitarian supplies to civil society—and used the evidence that they could account for any assistance provided and track whom they were funding within these less controversial initiatives in order to "build trust" with other players in the State Department.[107] It was a proof-of-concept exercise to demonstrate to others within the bureaucracy that the risks in Syria assistance could be managed. When CSO proposed expanding nonlethal assistance to *armed* actors, it provoked another internal standoff, but CSO was able to prevail in large part by pointing to the existing processes and record of controls.[108]

The effort to build trust and anticipate the next round of bargaining or bureaucratic contestation was important because the nonlethal assistance was part of an iterative and continuous bargaining process. The bargaining that took place in the implementation phase could be reopened with each program development or expansion. This was particularly likely in the case of the nonlethal assistance due both to the structure of funding and the nature of the Syria policy environment. The emergency and contingency funding came in spurts, with the possibility of more questions, countered by more risk mitigation, each time more funding was sought. In general, the Syria funds were also subject to congressional notification, creating a regular cycle of reporting to Congress with each significant step in implementation.[109] CSO staff frequently relied on the control and accountability mechanisms that existed, or promises to reinforce or more stringently apply them, to forestall the threat of congressional "holds" or blocks on funding through these notification processes.[110]

This sort of iterative bargaining, in such a high-profile and controversial program, led to a ratcheting up of control mechanisms over time. Whenever a report surfaced of assistance going astray, or of FSA affiliating with blocked groups or engaging in misconduct—which was frequently the case—it could spark a new round of internal debate.[111] When this happened, staff would often soothe objections or threats to cut the program by redoubling efforts to demonstrate accountability. Vetting went from an informal, ten-day vetting process to what State Department staff internally referred to as "double" or even "triple" vetting, lasting multiple weeks and involving rechecking and re-vetting persons even if no derogatory information was found.[112] At DRL's request, the Leahy Law–like vetting was codified, thereby changing it from a regular but informal process into a formal protocol.[113] The application of sanctions also increased. There was such a degree of attention to any reports of misconduct or transgression of redlines that staff involved said that it was easier to enforce sanctions and cut the questionable group from funding than to fight the certain bureaucratic opposition to continuing to support them.[114]

In sum, bargaining was not only very much present in the nonlethal assistance but was also conducted in ways that would increase and reinforce controls over time. As with the forgoing account of bargaining in the lethal assistance program, control mechanisms were established to counter critics' fears about support to Syrian opposition, to build trust, and to persuade a reluctant bureaucracy that the risks could be mitigated and managed. Those involved in the program argued that nonlethal assistance would absolutely not have gone forward without this elaborate web of risk-mitigation measures.[115] However, unlike with the high-level decision-making moment, it was not a one-off debate. Each time there was a new request for funding, an expansion of assistance, or news reports of assistance going awry or of a supported group's alleged transgression, it prompted renewed debate over the riskiness of the endeavor, which led to the imposition of ever more stringent controls. Controls were crucial to the assistance being authorized, and increasing levels of controls were necessary to keep it from being cut off.

Similar to the conclusions drawn from the CIA support, it is not that the controls were completely divorced from the idea of controlling the agent behavior—the role that principal-agent theory would envision for them. Those developing and applying these controls certainly hoped that vetting and oversight would prevent U.S. assistance from going to bad actors or being used to perpetrate crimes. At the same time, none imagined that the controls were fail-safe, and many thought that they did not justify the amount of staff time and costs involved. One State Department policy adviser observed that the vetting protocols and checks he saw "bore no relation with the reality on the ground," and fundamentally obstructed any chance of the assistance doing something meaningful. "In situations like Syria, you can have accountability, or you can have programming—but not both," he said.[116]

While other State Department staff were more positive about the vetting protocols and other controls, they frequently focused on the benefits in terms of enabling policy processes or addressing personal or institutional risk exposure, rather than on the benefits derived from greater agent control.[117] Fears of "owning bad behavior" were ever-present for those managing these programs.[118] One senior policy maker observed, "If anything went wrong—if something negative got out in the media, there was no way to undo or explain it. Those managing the programs knew that in such a scenario it would be their jobs or their careers sacrificed, or, worst case, going to jail."[119] One senior policy maker noted that though she was comfortable that the vetting lowered the risks of funds going to bad actors, she was careful to warn congressional staff or representatives that there were no guarantees in an environment like Syria.[120] In essence, even if they were only a minimal check against misconduct or other "agent slack," controls operated as a substantial bureaucratic safeguard.

The trajectory of control mechanisms within the State Department nonlethal assistance—the ratcheting up of controls in response to any bureaucratic objections, threats to funding, or even risk of professional liabilities—illustrates yet again the strong linkage between control mechanisms and bargaining demands. Control mechanisms were increasingly applied and maintained less because of their likely effect on the FSA than because they responded to various internal players' concerns or agendas. They increased in proportion to the degree to which they advanced bargaining tactics, regardless of the increasingly high costs of imposing them, and the effect this would have on the overall programming.

CASE 3: INTERBRANCH BARGAINING AND CONTROLS IN CRAFTING THE NEW SYRIAN FORCES (SUMMER 2014-OCTOBER 2015)

In September 2014, Congress more fully entered the bargaining arena over Syria assistance with its decision to authorize training and overt lethal assistance for Syrian fighters.[121] DoD was to recruit "moderate" members of the Syrian opposition, and form these "vetted" fighters into a new entity, the "New Syrian Forces" (the program's official name, used hereafter).[122] Due to restrictions against U.S. personnel operating in Syria, the New Syrian Forces were to be trained and equipped in Jordan and Turkey, and then redeployed into Syria to counter ISIL. Within a year, the effort had completely failed. It struggled to recruit the three thousand fighters set as a target for the first year, and most of those who were trained decamped or were attacked upon reentry into Syria.[123] After almost a year of effort, and with at least half of the $500 million expended, Pentagon leaders testified that only "four or five" trained fighters remained in the fight.[124] Importantly for this study, one of the reasons that the program failed—if not the largest reason—was the hefty amount of control mechanisms placed on it. "Vetting killed this program" was the blunt assessment of one former State Department official, reflecting the sentiments of most officials and experts interviewed.[125]

The role of Congress—particularly in generating and insisting on certain controls—is more significant here than in the prior two case studies. In the first, congressional intelligence committees weighed in on the decision to arm Syrian rebels, reinforcing the control mechanisms and outer parameters generated in the high-level White House debate. Through its regular monitoring and reporting demands, Congress was also a continuous pressure point on the State Department nonlethal assistance, contributing to the ratcheting up and reinforcement of controls. However, with this first Train and Equip program, Congress came more fully into the bargaining because in being asked to create a new line of funding, it had the opportunity to legislate formal constraints.

What triggered this greater congressional role was first and foremost a shift in the nature of the conflict in Syria and the U.S. response to it.[126] Similar to Obama's inclinations, many members of Congress had long opposed overt support for the Syrian opposition. But when ISIL seized Mosul and much of northern and central Iraq in June 2014, the pressure for a ground partner in both countries suddenly became a much more significant political imperative. In June 2014, President Obama requested funding for *overt* military training and support to "vetted" Syrian opposition forces, alongside congressional authority to train and equip Iraqi forces.[127] Shortly thereafter, in August 2014, a video of ISIL militants beheading the kidnapped American journalist James Foley appeared on YouTube—further focusing White House and congressional attention on the need to do something. Yet, still without any political tolerance for U.S. forces on the ground, or even substantial air operations, all that was left for the administration was to fund Syrian fighters to counter ISIL.

Although the program was in many respects the boldest and most ambitious U.S. intervention yet in Syria, it was accompanied by an extreme level of risk avoidance and aversion. Even once authorized in September 2014, the choice to arm Syrian rebels remained so controversial and unpopular that there was almost no tolerance for the possible costs or consequences. As Lieutenant General Mike Nagata, who was charged with leading the New Syrian Forces program, later said of the U.S. position, "We appeared to be seeking maximalist results for minimalist investments. Our policy goal was to defeat an ISIS army that was orders of magnitude more capable, proficient, and much better armed and led than AQI ever was, but with considerable restraints."[128]

This filtered down into an even wider panoply of control mechanisms. The Train and Equip programs inherited many of the control mechanisms generated in prior debates and program decisions. As with the nonlethal assistance program and (judging by the evidence) the CIA covert support, the Train and Equip programs adopted a Leahy Law–like vetting process, screening recruits for allegations of gross human rights abuses and cutting those for whom there were credible allegations of such abuse. Also similar to the prior lethal and nonlethal assistance programs, they scrutinized recruits for any connection with other banned groups or those whose ideology was deemed too "Islamist."[129]

In addition to these legacy vetting requirements, DoD adopted control mechanisms that reflected its own standard approaches for scrutinizing and constraining partner forces. It provided a full "law of land warfare" curriculum to recruits, which included material on human rights obligations, prohibitions against using child soldiers, and other standard elements of DoD practice in partner security assistance.[130] Because the recruits would be trained by U.S. and allied states' trainers, vetting also screened for personal security risks.[131] There was a plan to adopt additional remote monitoring and oversight controls, including regular call-ins, video or photographic reporting, or other remote reporting procedures to keep account of U.S.-provided weapons, communication devices, and other equipment once fighters were redeployed into

Syria.[132] However, the program was so short-lived that these were never realized in practice.

Some of these controls arguably reflected standard bureaucratic behaviors and instincts, a point that will be discussed in the next chapter. However, many more appeared to be driven by bargaining considerations, both deliberations within the administration and between the executive branch and Congress. During the congressional deliberations and inquiry leading up to the program's authorization, Nagata remembered being pressed by members of Congress on how the program would prevent Syrian fighters from engaging in atrocities or abuses, and how to ensure that U.S. weapons would not fall into the hands of Jabhat al-Nusra or ISIL.[133] Although he argued that it was no substitute for having troops co-deployed into Syria with the recruited and trained forces, the next best risk-mitigation approach was that they would be given formal "law of land warfare" training, and that there would be some kind of monitoring and oversight to track both "behavior and accountability of weapons and material provided to these forces" at a distance.[134]

The congressional testimony of senior officials during the debate over program authorization reflects this back-and-forth bargaining between the executive branch and Congress.[135] In a September 2014 Senate Armed Services Committee hearing, Secretary of Defense Chuck Hagel responded to concerns about the risks of arming Syrian rebels as follows: "A rigorous vetting process will be critical to the success of this program. DoD will work closely with the State Department, the intelligence community, and our partners in the region to screen and vet the forces we train and equip. We will monitor them closely to ensure that weapons do not fall into the hands of radical elements of the opposition, ISIL, the Syrian regime, or other extremist groups."[136] In other testimony, senior officials further reinforced these rebuttals by noting past experience with such risk mitigation and controls, both in the prior Syrian assistance programs and in other countries like Afghanistan.[137]

Congress ultimately accepted these reassurances to some degree, but it also embedded many of the promised control mechanisms in the authorizing legislation, to a degree that is unusual for security assistance programming. The authorizing legislation within the National

Defense Authorization Act (NDAA) for FY2015 stipulated that all supported Syrian opposition groups were to be screened for affiliation with terrorist groups, those affiliated with Iran, Shi'a militias, or the Assad regime.[138] "Appropriate vetting" was explicitly defined in the law as requiring "a commitment from such elements, groups, and individuals to promoting the respect for human rights and the rule of law."[139]

In addition to the vetting and human rights requirements, Congress imposed additional constraints related to some of its "big picture" concerns with the initiative. From the congressional perspective, this was the first major use of force authorization since the 2002 vote to authorize the Iraq War—a vote that many still regretted.[140] This vote would again bring U.S. troops into Iraq, as well as authorizing military engagement in Syria, which the majority of Congress opposed. While clearly most congressional representatives felt compelled to do something to counter ISIL—the ultimate vote tally was 273 to 156 in favor—there were serious misgivings about giving the Obama administration a "blank check" to start another war in the Middle East.[141]

The language in the administration's initial request for funding in June 2014 was broad enough to allow the Train and Equip money to be used for both anti-ISIL and anti-Assad efforts.[142] Congress firmly rejected that approach, dropping the language that might have allowed more flexibility to go beyond a strict anti-ISIL mandate.[143] In addition, congressional representatives made clear in their interrogatories and deliberations with the administration that the funds should only go to support armed groups engaged in fighting ISIL and not Assad.

As a result of this congressional directive, in implementing the new program, candidates for the New Syrian Forces would be required to pledge that they would only fight ISIL, and those who "expressed a desire to fight Assad" were sent home before completing the training.[144] In deference to both this restriction and the other legislative clauses requiring commitments related to human rights and the rule of law, DoD required members of the New Syrian Forces to swear a pledge. The text of this pledge (see box 3.1), which reads as a distilled version of international humanitarian law, represents a quite novel form of control mechanism—a commitment device explicitly codifying the "codes of conduct" in question.[145]

> **BOX 3.1. EXCERPT FROM PLEDGE OF THE NEW SYRIAN FORCES**
>
> I swear by my God, as a member of the Syrian Revolution and the New Syrian Forces, to defend the Syrian people from Dai'ish [ISIL]. . . . I announce my unconditional commitment to the rule of law and following rules of the law of armed conflict:
>
> I will fight only combatants. I will not harm civilians who are not directly participating in the fight, the wounded and sick, detainees, and parachutists of disabled aircraft, people performing medical duties, relief workers, chaplains, or journalists.
>
> I will treat humanely all who surrender or are captured. I understand all detainees must receive medical treatment, food, water, shelter, basic hygiene, basic clothing, and adequate conditions. I will treat women and children with respect.
>
> I will not kill or torture detained personnel. . . . Collective punishment is strictly forbidden.
>
> I will collect and care for the wounded, including those who have fought against us.
>
> I will not attack protected persons or protected places. . . . I will facilitate relief efforts and humanitarian work. . . .
>
> I will destroy no more than the mission requires.
>
> I will treat all civilians humanely. I understand that attacks against civilians are strictly forbidden, as is terrorizing or otherwise compelling civilians to abandon their homelands. I will not harm anyone on the basis of their religion, political affiliation, or gender. . . .
>
> I will prevent violations. I understand that every fighter must know and follow the rules and help ensure that his fellow fighters follow the rules. . . .
>
> I will report violations to my chain of command. If in command, I will investigate all credible complaints regarding violations and take all necessary measures to prevent violations and to discipline those responsible for any violations.
>
> I understand that I am duty bound to protect the principles and the responsibilities noted above and that failure to do so will subject me to discipline and possible expulsion form the New Syrian Forces.

The choice to support only those who would commit to fight ISIL rather than Assad proved to be the most significant hurdle to the program's success.[146] Most Syrian fighters had only taken up arms to defend their communities and/or to fight against the Assad regime. While they may have been willing to also fight against the threat posed by ISIL, the more dedicated of them were not willing to pledge to refrain from fighting the Syrian government. Other recruits were weeded out by the other vetting and criteria noted above, from the Leahy Law–like vetting criteria to screening related to ideology.[147] The numbers recruited and trained were in the dozens, not the thousands initially hoped for. In addition, given the restriction against fighting Assad, those recruited tended toward the more mercenary elements of the force rather than the sort of "moderate" forces that the program hoped to attract. Within a year, the program was considered such a resounding failure that the Obama administration requested to repurpose the funds, which would then be used for the subsequent Train and Equip programs described in subsequent sections.

It is hard to rationalize such extensive and costly controls through a principal-agent lens alone, even taking into account the additional coordination and mis-coordination costs introduced by greater congressional engagement (a classic "complex principal" situation). Instead, these multiple layers of controls are better understood as stemming from a snowballing of multiple institutions' risk profiles and demands. The New Syrian Forces program inherited the legacies of the prior nonlethal assistance and covert assistance debates, and the control mechanisms and risk-mitigation measures that came with them. Layered onto those were the controls generated in response to congressional concerns and demands, both those generated in the course of congressional debates, which were adopted as an understanding of congressional intent, and those written into the legislation. Summarizing all of these various sources of controls, one senior congressional staff member involved in the drafting process characterized the resulting New Syrian Forces program as follows:

> There was the broader policy dynamic of the administration not willing to fund more decisive efforts against Assad, and we [Congress] were only willing to fund [against] ISIS. Then, within the legislative branch, you had the sausage-making of Congress, so they [congressional representatives] keep adding additional conditions. . . . Then you had traditional executive branch restrictions and requirements, [and] congressional restrictions on when you can use these authorities.[148]

In essence, once this very controversial idea of arming opposition forces made it to an open public debate, the only way it could survive authorization was by nodding to the concerns of every key player in the policy process, whether big picture strategic concerns or concerns about downstream risks. These collective caveats and constraints, which tended to manifest as control mechanisms, facilitated the compromise that was necessary for the program to be authorized, but functionally they limited the program to the point of uselessness.

A last point to consider for this case study is the range of tactics and motivations on display with the various controls. The administration used control mechanisms as a way to rebut critiques and encourage a greater number congressional representatives to support the initiative. Congress accepted these control mechanisms and encoded many of them in legislation. However, it also proposed its own control mechanisms, which it used to address what it saw as the larger concerns with the program—that it would be used to pursue further action against the Assad regime. The choice to use control mechanisms in this way is yet another example of controls as a limiting device, setting outer limits on the program. It is notable that this restriction—which would have the most significant consequences for program effectiveness—had little to do with controlling the Syrian forces in question, and instead was focused on constraining the executive branch. Given the pressure to confront ISIL and the consensus against extensive U.S. ground forces, the support for Syrian forces enjoyed a virtually unstoppable level of policy momentum. For those who thought it was ill-advised, they could not stop it, but they could insert control mechanisms that would prevent funding from being used in ways that they thought were most dangerous.

In addition, there is a bit of dual agenda going on with the New Syrian Forces, with some officials interviewed suggesting it was not just the nominal opponents and critics (Congress) using controls to limit the program, but also the administration itself. There was a "deep ambivalence" within the administration about funding opposition forces, given both the risks surrounding these forces and the fear that even if they succeeded, their victory might produce even worse outcomes.[149] As RAND analyst Jeff Martini described it, "There was a fear of 'catastrophic success': What if you roll back ISIS too quickly with no one to hold . . . [the group's territory] after they leave? Or what if Assad is toppled but what comes after is worse?"[150] One former State Department official said that in his personal view the "Train and Equip [program] was a ruse for inaction—the people who backed the Train and Equip lawyered it up to the point of oblivion . . .

and teed it up to fail. It was a way to stop it. You can blame it [failure in Syria] on the un-vettable entities instead of blaming our own inertia or lack of action."[151] The policy momentum had prodded a reluctant Obama and the other skeptics in his administration to support ground action in Syria, but they ensured that it had enough limitations and controls on it that the biggest risks—of catastrophic success—would not materialize.

CASE 4: BARGAINING WITH TURKEY OVER TRAIN AND EQUIP FORCES: A FAILED PERSUASION CAMPAIGN (OCTOBER 2015–END OF 2016)

The discussion of Syrian armed group support so far has focused on intra-U.S. bargaining; however, as the Iraq and Afghanistan case studies illustrated, a range of external, non-U.S.-government actors may also influence U.S. decision making surrounding LHSFs. The two subsequent U.S. Train and Equip initiatives, which took place from 2015 onward in northwest and then northeast Syria, involved bargaining dynamics that involved foreign actors to a more significant degree—Turkey and, to some extent with the LHSF in question, the SDF (discussed in the final case study). Because of the substantial influence of foreign stakeholders, these are different bargaining dynamics than those classically examined in BPA theory. However, they also lead to similar conclusions, in that the control mechanisms adopted appeared as much about mediating key stakeholder concerns as about controlling the agents in question.

With the apparent failure of the New Syrian Forces, in October 2015 the Obama administration requested that Congress repurpose the Train and Equip funds; rather than forming, training, and equipping a new anti-ISIL force, the funds would help train and support existing groups fighting ISIL inside Syria.[152] This diversion did not appear to trigger substantial conceptual rethinking or bargaining with Congress. It was not about initiating a new program, or even substantially revisiting the assumptions and bargains struck only the year before in terms of controls and authorization. It was simply finding a different delivery mechanism for the existing program: a different set of fighters, facilitated and trained through different means.

Given that a substantial hurdle had been the challenge of recruiting and mobilizing a de novo force outside of the country, the program would now try to find a way to support groups already fighting in ISIL-dominated areas in Syria. Turkey was an obvious choice to facilitate this new modality, at least for forces in northern Syria.[153] It not only had the territorial proximity to supply and train the fighters, but it also claimed that it had ties with enough northern Syrian groups to raise a substantial force.[154] Moreover, Turkey had already played a role in implementing the first Train and Equip program, hosting some of the training sessions and helping to redeploy some few dozen fighters of the New Syrian Forces into Syria.[155] In keeping with this new plan, already by December 2015, Turkey had agreed to allow some 2,000 fighters to be trained in Turkey, and then to support their reentry into Syria.[156]

However, Turkey's interests were substantially different from those of the United States. Turkey had long argued for greater U.S. support to Syrian rebels, and even for some form of military intervention, including frequent calls for a buffer or no-fly zone as far south as Aleppo.[157] Accordingly, while not opposed to fighting ISIL per se, it would not prioritize it above other objectives in Syria.

Even more significant, Turkey's engagement in the Train and Equip program was less about facilitating U.S. aims against ISIL than preventing the United States from supporting Kurdish forces. In the fall of 2014, Kurdish fighters in northeast Syria, together with some allied Arab forces, mounted the most significant resistance to ISIL expansion to that point. They halted ISIL advances on the Kurdish-majority border town of Kobane and then succeeded in retaking the town and much of the territory surrounding it. The United States supported these efforts through limited air strikes and air-dropping weapons and equipment, and it appeared poised to shift more of the Train and Equip funds and support to these northeastern groups.[158] This was anathema to Turkey. A number of local Arab groups took part in this resistance, and these were nominally the groups that would receive support.[159] However, the core military forces and direction came from the People's Protection Units (Yekîneyên Parastina Gel, or YPG), a paramilitary force linked to the PKK. The PKK had waged a multi-decade insurgency campaign against the Turkish state, for which the United States had designated it a foreign terrorist organization in 1997. While the United States may have been willing to overlook this terrorist affiliation, Turkey was not.

Turkish officials would use whatever arguments or tactics were available to prevent U.S. support from going to what they considered to be their archenemy. Turkish officials' arguments that they could mobilize northern Syrian opposition groups to fight ISIL, and that support to YPG-affiliated groups was thus unnecessary, should largely be viewed in this light.

In terms of applicable control mechanisms, this initiative was still subject to the same Train and Equip legislation, meaning that many of the same DoD regulations and controls that had been developed for the New Syrian Forces applied to these fighters. Some of the rules had been slightly relaxed—for example, there would be no pledge committing fighters to pursue only ISIL and to fight according to the strictures of international humanitarian law. However, the broad program restrictions and redlines remained the same.[160] Per the NDAA provisions, U.S.-supported fighters would be screened for affiliation with terrorist groups, Iran, Shi'a militias, or the Assad regime, and would have to commit to respecting "human rights and the rule of law."[161] As noted, DoD had developed a Leahy Law–like vetting process, in addition to other vetting protocols against potential terrorist or extremist group affiliations. In the previous Train and Equip program, DoD had also developed a standard law of armed conflict curriculum as part of training. Although in this round of the Train and Equip programming, the training was to be less extensive, it still involved some of these components.[162] Syrian commanders and fighters who went through the process remembered these restrictions—for example, the stipulations against passing on any weapons to other groups, the extreme sensitivities about potential extremist connections or their own ideological background, and prohibitions on abuses or misconduct. As one Syrian fighter remembered, "This is very important in talking with the Pentagon—to have a clear CV. It's written in all the Pentagon reports and rules."[163] In terms of other controls, like follow-on monitoring or sanctions, these were presumably the same as were planned for other Train and Equip programming. However, there is little evidence of them being applied because the initiative ended so quickly.

What was novel in this iteration was that Turkey's role in identifying and managing the groups that would receive U.S. support created a sort of dual selection and control process, albeit not a frictionless one.[164] "The ideal for this program was to have forces that were mutually accepted by both Turkey and the United States, but . . . that proved hard to come by," one former State Department officer noted.[165] Turkish officials were primarily responsible for identifying and nominating the selected groups, and they tended to nominate Syrian groups with more Islamist ideological leanings, whether because of similar political alignment or because that was who was most available in northeast Syria. This clashed with U.S. vetting standards, which would have excluded many of the more ideologically Islamist groups that Turkey favored. This split in preferences generated rancor on both sides. One senior Turkish official recounted the U.S. reaction to groups they nominated as being almost prejudicial in tone, and out of step with the reality of the Syrian armed group landscape: "They did not like them because they are religious.... As soon as the Americans see an Islamic group, they think it's the Taliban or al-Qaeda.... They think they are fanatical religious groups and that if they support them against Daesh [ISIL], at the end of the day they will become too powerful."[166]

U.S. officials also said that they were worried that Turkey was more interested in cultivating proxies they could control than strong self-defense forces who could mount a challenge against ISIL. One State Department officer said that the United States would go to Turkey to get sign-off on groups and forces, but they "rarely green-lighted" the stronger groups that the United States wanted, which left only "really ineffective fighters... truly abysmal. They just took the hiluxes [trucks] we gave them and abandoned them in the field for ISIL," she remembered.[167] U.S. officials said that after many months they began to suspect that Turkey did not have substantial enough contacts with Syrian armed groups to feed the demand for field partners, and was simply using the initiative to forestall other support. As one former White House official remembered, "we continued to negotiate with Turkey for alternatives [to arming Kurdish forces]. Turkey would say, 'You don't need to work with them... there are other fighters you can work with,' but when we would ask them about these fighters, they never materialized."[168] Internally, some in the State Department began to refer to these forces as the "unicorn forces" because this ideal of strong, law-abiding, anti-ISIL forces appeared to be a policy fantasy, one former U.S. official noted.[169]

Syrian fighters who observed or went through the process said the diplomatic friction was evident even from their level of operations. One Syrian commander noted that the speed of vetting depended on the "political situation between the United States and Turkey. If the situation was good, it went through quickly. If their relations were bad, then it took much longer."[170] Other analysts observed that the Turkish approach clashed with the requirements of the Train and Equip program, and that with lighter or differently managed U.S. training modalities, they might have gotten more recruits (albeit not necessarily more competent ones).[171]

Whether because of Turkish foot-dragging, or simply too disparate selection preferences, the initiative resulted in far fewer forces for the program than was needed to gain any traction against ISIL. The numbers provided were ultimately so small, and the fighters produced so ineffective, that the United States increasingly shifted its support behind Kurdish-led forces. Turkey still managed Arab militias in northwestern Syria for many years, but the degree of U.S. engagement or support going to them appeared scant from late 2015 on.[172] Many of these groups continued to fight as Turkish-backed militias or proxies, but in campaigns that were either not coordinated with the United States or that the United States openly opposed.

The U.S.-Turkish endeavor provides another example of a failed bargaining scenario, one in which control mechanisms, among other tools of persuasion, failed to broker a compromise. In most of the previous bargaining examples, control mechanisms were used by different parties to achieve their interests—to assuage or overcome critics, or to limit the proposed initiative. In this way, the control mechanisms helped to facilitate a compromise between different players, allowing the program to go forward. In the case of this U.S.-Turkish cooperation, the control mechanisms failed to bring this about, and may even have obstructed cooperation. Rather than addressing the concerns of either side and allowing opposing positions to be nudged or appeased, the control mechanisms were tightly wedded to each country's interests and objectives, which were so oppositional that no compromise was possible.

CASE 5: INTERNAL AND EXTERNAL BARGAINING OVER THE SDF (OCTOBER 2014–DECEMBER 2019)

The bargaining did not cease with the failed effort to create a Turkish-managed anti-ISIL force.[173] If anything, control mechanisms became a more important—if still failing—tactic within U.S.-Turkish negotiations over the SDF.

The 2014 battle for Kobane would later be considered a turning point in the war—both because it was the first time that local Syrian forces successfully ousted ISIL from territory it held and because of how that success would transform U.S. assistance. After years of struggling with disorganized and "Islamist"-leaning FSA groups—many of whom had little interest in taking on ISIL—the SDF (as it came to be known) appeared not only to be the last available option, but also for many U.S. policymakers, the best one.[174] They had a level of command and control akin to many state forces in the region. They could plan operations and seize and hold territory on their own, they maintained discipline within their own ranks, and they even came equipped with the language of democratic institutions and women's empowerment. Moreover, they possessed a dedication to protecting their homeland from ISIL that was equal to the United States' desire to pursue the extremist group.

Yet, though to many U.S. officials, the SDF appeared the best (or only) option for pursuing ISIL, there was still substantial deliberation about shifting support to them. "Risks were definitely part of the policy debate," one former State Department officer remembered.[175] Chief among these was the cost to the relationship with Turkey, a major NATO ally who played a crucial role in maintaining any Syrian and anti-ISIL operations. The second main concern, according to a senior U.S. official privy to the debate, was the "legal ability of the United States to work with an organization so closely connected to a DTO."[176] Although the forces in the northeast comprised a range of different Kurdish and Arab groups and constituencies, the core military leadership came from the Syrian paramilitary force the YPG, which had long been linked to the PKK, itself a DTO.

U.S. officials would try to nuance the issue for years, both legally and diplomatically, through the rebranding of the coalition under the name of the SDF, and through continued insistence that the YPG were not the same as the PKK. But it was an uncomfortable facade. Even if the YPG were not a direct subsidiary of the PKK (which some argued was the more correct characterization), there was certainly a connection, as even senior defense officials publicly recognized.[177] Some flow of weapons to the PKK would be inevitable. As noted in the introduction to this chapter, the U.S. legal standards on "material support" are quite strict and hinge not on *intent* to support DTOs, but simply on any support falling into such groups' hands. Additional risks and concerns raised were the effects on overall dynamics in Syria, and fears about potential human rights abuses by Kurdish forces.[178] Arab communities and civil society voiced a sense of betrayal at the shift in U.S. support, and argued that empowering the Kurds would lead to Arab marginalization, and possibly even ethnic cleansing.[179]

In the internal U.S. deliberations after the battle for Kobane, proponents, including the CENTCOM leadership and the White House special envoy Brett McGurk, argued that Kurdish forces were the only way to pursue the established priority of defeating ISIL.[180] The NSC and DoD political leadership were divided on the issue. Some leading White House officials and policy people within the Office for the Secretary of Defense still harbored misgivings about the strategic costs of going against the wishes of a major NATO ally, Turkey. The State Department, particularly NEA, presented some of the most vocal opposition.

The split in opinions might be viewed as a classic representation of institutional stand-sit positions. The institution chiefly in charge of U.S. diplomacy, the State Department, was seized above all with the nearly certain diplomatic consequences for the U.S. relationship with Turkey, as well as potential ripple effects for regional policy. Meanwhile, military leaders who had been given the task of pursuing ISIL militarily without substantial "boots on the ground" prized the one Syrian force that appeared most capable of fighting ISIL.

Other U.S. officials also observed a degree of personal commitment and attachment in these stand-sit positions, as is also anticipated by BPA.[181] One State Department officer characterized the idea of shifting support from the FSA in any degree as a "third rail"—a "very emotional issue within the policy debate" that could not be broached.[182] Another State Department officer observed a degree of "clientitis" in both State and DoD officials' positions.[183] She noted that by that point, the State Department officials had become very attached to the Syrian Arab partners who had been their chief interlocuters for years, and saw the shift in support—to those whom some Arab communities feared and mistrusted—as something edging toward betrayal.[184] On the other side, DoD and U.S. military officials would become equally attached to the Kurdish forces—so much so that when President Trump (first) announced in

December 2018 that he would end SDF support, it prompted a level of bureaucratic outcry that included a letter of resignation from the secretary of defense.

Ultimately, the proponents of SDF support had necessity on their side. Unless the White House was willing to either forgo the commitment to pursue ISIL in Syria or deploy substantial U.S. troops to directly facilitate such an effort, the SDF was the way forward, whatever the costs.[185] However, as with the prior Syria support programs, the Obama administration tried to soften the perceived risks and consequences of that choice through some of the same, and some new, control mechanisms.

Attempts to defray Turkish concerns that the United States was arming the PKK can be seen throughout the different iterations of support, through control mechanisms and other political guarantees and means of persuasion. During the early Kobane operations in 2015 and 2016, as the United States airdropped arms, heavy weapons, and other advanced equipment to the Kurdish coalition, U.S. officials argued that support was only being provided to the Arab contingents fighting within the larger coalition, not the PKK elements.[186] At certain stages, there were also direct calls to Turkish president Tayyip Erdogan in advance of any material provided in an effort to reassure him that Turkish concerns were being heeded.[187] Later, as the United States appeared poised to enter into a more regular and direct relationship with Kurdish parts of the coalition, U.S. officials tried to create further distance between the PKK and the forces it wanted to work with by asking the YPG-led force to rename itself. The group rebranded as the "Syrian Democratic Forces" in October 2015.[188]

This rebranding did nothing to assuage Turkish concerns, so U.S. officials redoubled their efforts to use a combination of controls and diplomatic assurances to persuade Turkey that its support to the SDF was not a threat. The United States established a series of checks and safeguards on any U.S. weapons or equipment provided to the SDF. These were kept under tight inventory and periodically verified to demonstrate that weapons, arms, or other materiel transferred was still accounted for, and was not being siphoned off to the PKK. "Everything is written and archived. Like when they give the salary for 300 fighters, they'll come and check that they are all there. . . . Even if it's a cigarette, we have to sign our name for it," one senior commander from Manbij recounted.[189] Some of this information—for example, rosters of equipment provided—was then shared with Turkey to demonstrate that it was all accounted for and that weapons or equipment would not later be used in a conflict against Turkey.[190] As one SDF adviser explained, "There is a type of document that the SDF sign for getting support.... It is like an itemized list—this many vehicles, weapons, including serial numbers, and everything. Turkey gets a copy of the list ... that way if the weapons appear on the black market or are captured by criminals, Turkey can know where they came from."[191]

One senior official said that part of the reason that more U.S. forces were co-deployed in SDF areas was to "reassure them [Turkey] that we were watching closely and that there wasn't material going north [i.e., to the PKK in Turkey] to be used against them."[192] Some weapons—notably anti-aircraft weapons—were not provided out of deference to Turkish concerns.

There was also a substantial screening and vetting process, at least on paper. Those who underwent training with U.S. forces (some 11,000 fighters by early 2018),[193] or who were responsible for receiving material or in significant contact with U.S. forces on the ground, underwent a vetting process.[194] The structure of this process was largely the same as prior Train and Equip iterations, and was still governed by the congressional authorizing legislation detailing "appropriate vetting," including screening for any links to terrorist groups, Iranian or Shi'a militias, or the Assad regime.[195] This screening would have been viewed as required not only because of the NDAA language but also to be in compliance with the no "material support" prohibitions in other legislation. SDF forces who received training from the United States remembered having their background and biometric information taken at the onset of any new training, and they presumed that some basic scrutiny or vetting process had been applied.[196]

Beyond these formalistic controls, there was also an ongoing conversation with the SDF that was designed to shape their behavior, in ways that would either respond to Turkish objections or satisfy other stakeholders. For example, the United States would take Turkish sensitivities into account in developing the battlefield strategy, specifically in relation to which parts of northern Syria the SDF might advance upon. This does not mean that the United States and its SDF partners kept to a territorial zone of Turkey's liking—as perhaps best illustrated by U.S. support to Kurdish and Arab fighters in Manbij from the summer of 2015 onward. Turkey had drawn a line against Kurdish expansion west of the Euphrates River, and Manbij is located just along its western bank.[197] Nonetheless, at multiple steps in the campaign against ISIL, efforts were made to coordinate or inform Turkish officials of the upcoming SDF advances, and to negotiate agreement on lines of control and expansion.[198]

None of these efforts were ever persuasive. Turkey would continually lobby for the United States to break ties with the SDF. If anything, the attempt to massage the issue through demonstration of tight checks and controls only added insult to injury. As one senior Turkish official recounted, "From the beginning we are saying that we are categorically against this [support to the SDF]. And then at the same time we are receiving lists of things they're giving [them]. It's ridiculous."[199] The damage to the U.S.-Turkish relationship was all the worse, he noted, because (in the Turkish view) the United States did not even stick to its commitments on checks and controls much of the time. He said that agreements to verify and remove weapons after an operation had ceased, to ensure that Kurdish troops did not enter certain territorial zones, or other commitments made in response to Turkish concerns about the SDF, were routinely ignored throughout the multiyear engagement.[200]

Most officials and commentators interviewed deemed the damage to the U.S.-Turkish relationship over the SDF to be significant and lasting—on some counts, among the most damaging outcomes of the Syrian conflict in terms of U.S. interests. The United States' unsuccessful efforts to use control mechanisms to assuage Turkish concerns recalls the equally unsuccessful efforts to use controls to persuade Maliki that the *sahwa* were not a threat. Turkey viewed the YPG-led forces with as much hostility as Maliki viewed a potential "Sunni army" being mobilized without his consent. No amount of vetting, registration of arms, or other accountability mechanisms would mitigate this fundamental distrust.

BARGAINING WITH THE SDF

Deliberations with Turkey were not the only type of bargaining afoot, nor the only type that would influence the development and application of controls. Interestingly, the other main negotiations relevant to this case study concerned those with the SDF itself. These dynamics differ from the previous case studies, both because they involve the LHSF itself and because the more harmonious relationship between the United States and the SDF raised fewer contentious issues, and if anything, relaxed the resulting controls and/or their application.

As noted in the introduction, there were several concerns with regard to the SDF, beyond stoking Turkey's ire. Arab communities' concerns about their exclusion, and potentially of direct abuses at the hands of Kurdish forces, were raised even during the earliest discussions about shifting U.S. support to Kurdish forces. There were also more serious allegations, including a report from Amnesty International in late 2015 that the SDF were indiscriminately razing Arab villages and forcing displacement in the course of their operations against ISIL.[201]

There were already some conduct-based standards and checks and controls built into the SDF support. Because it was funded through the same Train and Equip funding legislation, it inherited control mechanisms from prior Train and Equip iterations. This included the provision in the Train and Equip funding legislation that supported forces respect "human rights," a degree of Leahy Law-like scrutiny, and some of the training standards developed for prior Train and Equip programming (but not the pledge that featured with the New Syrian Forces).[202]

However, the U.S. approach to applying these formalistic controls was looser, or at least more informally negotiated, with the SDF than with prior groups funded under the same legislation. Whereas the prior versions of the Train and Equip programs and FSA support were rife with stories of lengthy and extensive vetting procedures, and of sanctions leading groups to being cut from funding, there was no evidence of SDF forces failing such vetting or later being subject to sanctions. On the concerns about abusive or indiscriminate conduct, as typified in the Amnesty report noted above, these were put directly to SDF leadership in order to urge them to take more caution. No accounts suggested that they provoked the sort of retraining, cut-offs, or other control-mechanism enforcement that were reported in the prior FSA support programs.

Taking an informal approach and raising issues with Kurdish leadership, and allowing them to take measures, was true even with what might have been the most sensitive issue—integrating Arab fighters from former ISIL-held areas into the force. In contrast with the extensive deliberations about "marbling" and which fighters were too close to extremist groups in the prior FSA support programs, when it came to the SDF, this issue was largely left to the SDF's discretion.[203] One senior official's observations suggested a low level of vetting or scrutiny: "We were mostly taking groups that already existed. If the commander said our guys are OK, then we took his word for it."[204] Other observers and SDF interlocutors also remembered very little emphasis on vetting or other checks in actual practice with the SDF.[205]

Some conduct issues did arise with the SDF, but they tended to be dealt with through high-level political discussions, rather than by exercising cut-offs of particular groups. For example, in the summer of 2015, a Human Rights Watch report alleged that Kurdish forces were using or recruiting child soldiers.[206] Such allegations were to be taken seriously. In addition to the moral implications, evidence of use of child soldiers could trip the 2008 Child Soldiers Prevention Act and end all Syria funding (unless an exception was granted).[207] Unlike in the past Syria programs, the response to this, though, was not to generate stricter formal controls—for example, new vetting or monitoring mechanisms. Instead, U.S. officials raised the issue with SDF leadership directly, and received assurances that the SDF would tighten its screening to prevent underage recruitment.[208]

This approach was also taken to respond to concerns about the SDF and Kurdish administration excluding Arab groups. Such concerns had always been part of the dialogue, but they only increased as the SDF successively expanded its territorial reach, and especially as it retook Arab-majority areas from ISIL like Raqqa and Deir ez-Zor. As the then Syria director in Obama's National Security Council, Alexander Bick, observed, "There is animosity towards the Kurds in some Arab areas for what is perceived as heavy-handed governance or the inequitable sharing of power and resources."[209] The response was not to tighten formalistic controls but to urge Kurdish leadership to take steps that demonstrated inclusivity. As Bick himself suggested, "the Defense Department is well aware of [this issue], and has tried to address [it] by pushing the SDF to be more inclusive."[210] Some of the responses included creating a federalist structure within the autonomous region, with Arab-majority areas following their own local governance and laws, under the direction of locally appointed councils that included Arab representatives.[211] Local Arab fighters tended to be incorporated into local self-defense units (once they were deemed not to be in league with ISIL) rather than into the broader SDF body.[212]

What stands out from this case study is that while on paper the SDF support was subject to ample control mechanisms—those developed to try to mitigate Turkish objections, those inherited from the prior Train and Equip programming, and some de novo demands specific to conduct vis-à-vis non-Kurdish communities—in practice there was a much looser application of control mechanisms and scrutiny as compared to many of the prior Syrian groups. This was in part due to the different modalities of the partnership. Because of the higher levels of command and control within the SDF (more akin to that of state forces), the United States left much of the recruitment, vetting, and training to the SDF itself. It then applied security-assistance controls in much the way it does with state forces—establishing the rules and controls applicable to the SDF as a whole but not necessarily overseeing the application of them for each unit in question. As a result, vetting or other checks tended to be applied only to the top leadership, rather than to each subunit or fighter that received support.

The looser scrutiny was also in part because on the two main criteria of past vetting—affiliation with Islamist extremist groups and human rights concerns—SDF fighters generally enjoyed a much better reputation than previously supported groups. ISIL posed a far greater threat to Kurdish communities than to the United States, and so there was not the same issue of "marbling" as with the FSA. In addition, Noah Bonsey, a leading Syria researcher, observed that, while not perfect, "The SDF is better behaved in terms of human rights than almost any other armed actor in Syria."[213]

Last, the more professionally structured force and the SDF behavior overtime appeared to instill a greater degree of trust. Most U.S. military and government officials said that U.S. oversight was looser with the SDF because the SDF demonstrated that they took discipline and control of their fighters seriously, appearing to hold members to account for misconduct and to respond to concerns or requests (i.e., concerning inclusion or conduct issues) by instilling discipline and enforcing directives down the line.[214] As Bonsey also observed, "The SDF might be more autocratic in its tendencies but it is better organized than all the rest of them. They have command and control. When there were really flagrant problems, they have been responsive to concerns."[215]

Overall, the U.S. support to the SDF suggests a slightly different relationship than some of the other local force partnerships described so far. In nearly all of the other case studies, there was bargaining with foreign, external actors over the forces in question, but less evidence of direct negotiation with the LHSF itself. The SDF appears almost as a player in its own right, deliberating with the United States in the same way that other foreign state leaders and officials did. State Department and U.S. military officials who worked with the SDF tended to characterize the relationship as a cross between mentorship and close state partnership, with competing interests and viewpoints negotiated by both sides, rather than the SDF directed by U.S. decision makers.[216] By virtue of the SDF's autonomous governing position, they were more akin to the position of Afghan or Iraqi officials, and the U.S. relationship with them more analogous to the co-deliberation and coadministration described in chapter 2.

However, unlike the U.S. bargaining with Iraqi, Afghan, or Turkish leaders, there was much less friction in the U.S.-SDF relationship. This helps connect the observation of a lower incidence of controls—at least outside of those designed to appease Turkey—in the SDF relationship to the overall theory of controls manifesting as a result of contentious bargaining; here, where that was absent, tight application of controls did not manifest.

MITIGATING OR MASKING RISKS? THE MORAL HAZARDS OF INCREASING CONTROL MECHANISMS IN SYRIA

Across the case studies of Syrian armed groups, there were a range of U.S. government and congressional actors involved; a variety of Syrian groups, with differing profiles and motivations; and significant differences in the types of assistance. What was consistent across all of the initiatives was the plethora of controls. This, despite an environment that was not conducive to accountability, widespread policy expectations that controls were not achievable, and in many cases an absence of any legal obligation to enact them.

With this greater share of empirical examples, it is worth revisiting some of the conjectures and expectations set out in chapter 1. Chapter 1 offered a preliminary suggestion that many of the expectations of principal-agent theory did not hold with the empirical evidence. The Syria examples help add color to that contention. In Syria, the lack of access to territory and the overall political dynamics created such significant barriers that any attempt to increase control would prove extremely costly. Principal-agent theory would suggest that in such an environment, controls would not be pursued because the costs of doing so would not justify the benefits. Instead, control mechanisms did manifest—across all initiatives examined.

Nor did this tendency shift as the costs began to manifest. Developing these vetting and control processes proved extremely time-consuming and demanded significant compromises in terms of program implementation and effectiveness. Yet rather than being dropped, control mechanisms were strengthened, with a tendency toward more being added all the time. This happened both within particular programs (for example, over the course of the nonlethal assistance program) and across programs, as illustrated in the full panoply of controls that had accrued by the time the Train and Equip programs began.

The evidence suggests that this increasing level of control was due to the contentious nature of Syria policy, particularly with regard to supporting Syrian rebels, and the many different players with a stake in the policy outcomes. There were strongly held and opposing views on whether and how the United States should intervene in Syria within the executive branch, within Congress, and within the wider U.S. foreign policy establishment. These starkly divergent and strongly held views generated significant competition among different organizations and players within and across U.S. policy making when any Syria policy issue arose. Proposals to support opposition groups served as a lightning rod, generating bureaucratic and policy resistance and competition with each new iteration or type of support.

The premise that control mechanisms were generated in relation to the level of political contention and bargaining also held true in the latter two case studies, which focused more on deliberations with external actors. In the latter two Train and Equip programs examined, new control mechanisms arose primarily as a way to try to respond to Turkish concerns and demands. By contrast, the relatively harmonious partner relationship with the SDF did not produce a panoply of new control mechanisms (other than those demanded by Turkey). In many ways, but for the Turkish element, the SDF relationship might have followed normal principal-agent expectations, with the controls appearing, or not, depending on the costs and benefits of imposing them.

As such, all five of the case studies reinforce the view of control mechanisms as a function or product of political deliberations more than a means of agent control. Although many of the controls were not unrelated to security or conduct concerns vis-à-vis the Syrian armed groups, the manifestation of controls, and the nature and content of the controls in question, appeared to be better explained by the surrounding political dynamics. They tended to map onto the interests and risk perceptions of different stakeholders involved, and the way that bargaining devolved surrounding these programs.

Each of the case studies illustrated different types of bargaining scenarios or configurations, from high-level "decision games" within the executive branch, to lower-level bargaining within the bureaucracy, to bargaining with Congress. Across these different types of bargaining situations, there were common threads in the way that control mechanisms were used, similar to what was observed in the *sahwa* and ALP case studies. Whether in trying to persuade a skeptical president to support covert action, appease State Department lawyers, or reduce potential opposition from rights-protective congressional staffers, control mechanisms were frequently introduced by proponents to try to counter or win over critics. Control mechanisms helped neutralize concerns about these risky endeavors, making it easier for proponents to build successful coalitions and to receive authorization to go forward. Opponents of these programs used control mechanisms too, primarily as a limiting device. Where there appeared no other policy alternative and/or the momentum behind supporting these groups appeared unstoppable, control mechanisms offered a way to limit the worst aspects of these programs. Within the first three case studies, control mechanisms were proposed to exclude the riskiest elements or actors, or to constrain what other branches of government or the implementing departments in question could do with a particular program. In the latter two case studies, control mechanisms offered Turkey the chance to influence or limit U.S. policy choices—or at least that was the intent behind many of their demands (whether ultimately successful or not).

Focusing on the bargaining dynamics within these cases offers additional insights into the role of control mechanisms and their political import. Both the case studies involving bargaining with Turkey represented a failed compromise—no control mechanisms or risk mitigation at a tactical level could bridge the fundamental differences in U.S. and Turkish positions on the Syrian groups in question. However, for each of the U.S. cases, control mechanisms facilitated a compromise. Because of this, control mechanisms proved to be crucial in the authorization of each of these programs, and in some cases in continuing that support. They were certainly not the only tools of persuasion and argument that facilitated agreement, but given how central risk and risk mitigation were to debates about such partnerships, control mechanisms played a significant part. They enabled these risky partnerships by appearing to address policy concerns, making it more feasible that a compromise would be erected.

This insight raises an important question, which is whether these risk-mitigation devices generated a degree of moral hazard. As seen in several of the authorization debates, control mechanisms could enable authorization by appearing to minimize the costs or risks involved, even though the prospects for actually controlling the forces in question was extremely slim. As such they may have enabled riskier intervention strategies and proxy arrangements through what was effectively the false conceit of control.

Because control mechanisms more often masked rather than mitigated risks, they had the potential to forestall tough decision making on competing policy goals. In interviews, policy makers working on Syria frequently framed their choices as between having accountable programming and effective programming; between working with militarily strong partners or those with the right background or conduct; or between advancing immediate tactical goals versus protecting long-term interests and commitments. The bevy of control mechanisms papered over what were in practice irreconcilable goals and tough trade-offs implicit in partner choices. As one former State Department official put it, "There always was this cohort of what I would call Syria true believers who wanted to pretend that we could find groups who could fight for us in Syria . . . that would be amazing fighters, from the right [ethnic or ideological] background, and abide by international law to the hilt."[217] Elaborate vetting criteria, program rules, training, and codes of conduct were developed in pursuit of that "idealized" force, but these never bore much relation to the reality on the ground in Syria, he observed.[218]

Another consequence of this risk "masking" function was that control mechanisms could inadvertently enable poor choices by offering a false "middle ground," as best illustrated in the SDF case study. Rather than choosing to prioritize the relationship with Turkey, or the immediate ability to pursue ISIL via the SDF, the United States adopted control mechanisms that nominally allowed it to do both—to work with the SDF, but with weapons tracking and accounting designed to reassure Turkey. In reality, weapons tracking did nothing to address Turkey's anger over U.S. support to a group it viewed as an existential threat. The fallout in terms of deteriorating relations with Turkey—which many interviewees framed as one of the most significant long-term costs of the Syrian war—was predictable. As one former U.S. official involved in the discourse reflected, "We should have come into it with clear eyes that you can either satisfy a NATO partner (Turkey) or you can have effective guys on the ground (YPG). There is no middle ground."[219]

Some former officials or observers interviewed saw such false "middle ground" choices as a reflection of larger lenses or tendencies within U.S. foreign policy. "We want to have it all and believe we can do it if we just put our minds to it," one former State Department officer observed, likening this optimism in the ability to achieve competing objectives to something of a "pathology" in the American policy-maker psyche.[220] In practice, the reality often proved to be quite different, she observed.[221] Other U.S. officials and implementing partners framed this as political buck-passing, pushing difficult political choices down to lower levels of the bureaucracy. Elaborate criteria and control mechanisms developed to satisfy a range of policy concerns and objections in Washington bore "no relation with what was going on" in Syria, another State Department political adviser offered.[222] But they were nonetheless adopted, and it was left to middle- and lower-level State Department officials and military officers, as well as their implementing partners and the Syrian forces themselves, to try to marry irreconcilable goals and positions at the level of implementation.

These observations underline the fact that beyond questions of agent control and due diligence, control mechanisms can have a significant impact on the success of the initiative and on the overall policy deliberations. Their emergence may contribute to blind spots within U.S. foreign policy making, masking rather than mitigating the risks involved. The concluding chapter will revisit this concern about how control mechanisms introduce moral hazard and might have enabled resort to LHSFs more often. The intervening chapters will pick up on some of the tactics and bargaining dynamics illustrated so far in Syria, Iraq, and Afghanistan, and will delve further into what they signify about the evolution of control mechanisms over time.

4

STANDARD OPERATING PROCEDURES AND EXCEPTIONS TO THE RULE

Organizational Lenses and Bureaucratic Transfer, from Local Force Initiatives to Counterterrorism Auxiliaries

The prior chapters and case studies focused on BPA bargaining dynamics in the case studies. But BPA places an equal emphasis on organizational theory and the ways that bureaucratic structures, norms, and tendencies drive or shape policy outputs. As illustrated in the last chapter, bargaining was an important driver of controls in each of the Syrian armed group assistance initiatives; however, bargaining demands were also shaped by and interacted with other organizational dynamics. Bargaining moments prompted or triggered the need for control mechanisms, but standard operating procedures (SOPs), routines, and organizational scripts helped queue the content of controls.

Two further case studies will then explore some of these organizational dynamics in later iterations of LHSFs—a 2015 anti-ISIL Sunni tribal-mobilization initiative in Iraq that was modeled after the *sahwa*, and a new ALP-like force created in early 2018 in Afghanistan. Both programs were in many ways an echo of their predecessors, inheriting most of the control mechanisms generated in the prior debates over the *sahwa* and the ALP. These legacy effects, plus additional evidence of organizational scripts emanating from the Washington, DC, bureaucracy, had a powerful shaping effect on the control mechanisms, in many ways stronger than the immediate bargaining dynamics.

Evidence from the Syria cases, coupled with these two post-2014 Iraq and Afghanistan initiatives, begin to suggest a larger trend of increasing—and increasingly standardized—control mechanisms across LHSF initiatives. While perhaps not so formalized as to constitute an "SOP" on LHSFs, what appeared to be emerging was a "common approach" toward risk mitigation in LHSFs, constituting some degree of human rights and counterterrorism vetting, codes of conduct or training that also reflected these and other risks, and several layers of oversight or monitoring to enable the application of sanctions or cut-offs where redlines were crossed.

The final section considers a counterview to this idea of a common approach emerging, or at least one with a high number of controls. LHSFs acting as auxiliary forces on covert counterterrorism or intelligence missions in Iraq and Afghanistan (among other countries) have not appeared to be subject to the same panoply of control mechanisms. Does this contradict the idea that there is a trend toward greater reliance on control mechanisms over time? Or is there something about these types of forces that would make them an exception to the rule? This final section will explore these propositions by considering evidence of the absence of control mechanisms for these counterterrorism auxiliaries (the term used generically below, regardless of whether they are attached to Special Forces or intelligence units). Analysis of the differing operating and funding patterns for these counterterrorism auxiliaries, and the different institutional lenses and masters associated with them, suggests that bargaining and organizational theories are just as relevant for explaining the absence of control mechanisms with this group as they were for understanding the emergence of controls in prior case studies. Analyzing the contrast between these two types of LHSFs helps further nuance the theories explored so far by identifying particular characteristics and organizational dynamics that are either more or less likely to trigger bargaining and the insertion of greater control mechanisms.

ORGANIZATIONAL TENDENCIES AND SOPs INFLUENCING CONTROL MECHANISMS IN SYRIA PROGRAMS

Chapter 1 briefly introduced the concept of organizational tendencies or paradigms within BPA. BPA theories on bargaining and decision games conceptualize foreign policy outputs as the resultant of different players' interests, positions, and tactics. By contrast, the organizational side of BPA tends to portray government as the composite of different organizational units, with the competing organizational tendencies, lenses, and protocols collectively determining the foreign policy result. As a starting point, organizational theory assumes that each organizational unit will pursue its own interests, even where these are not aligned with the overall national interest.[1] "The organization will jealously guard and seek to increase its turf and strength, as well as to preserve undiluted what it feels to be its 'essence' or 'mission,'" observed scholar Valerie Hudson.[2]

Bureaucratic mission sets or lenses may also then influence foreign policy decision making by structuring the way that a foreign policy issue is perceived and the logic by which it is managed. Common mission beliefs, attitudes, or "shared images" can influence how a particular foreign policy crisis or issue is understood and the range of responses that are typically used in response.[3] Bureaucratic structures or protocols may determine which route—or which part of the bureaucracy—will take an issue forward, which can influence which tools or approaches are used to respond to the problem. Bureaucracies tend to develop policy scripts and repertoires of standard approaches and practices derived from their organizational tendencies, outlook, and mandate. These are triggered when it comes to implementing or carrying forward a policy decision and may furnish the content of the bureaucratic response.[4]

The Syria case studies provide apt illustrations of these dynamics, with organizational dynamics, protocols, and profiles strongly shaping bargaining debates and the control mechanisms that emerged from them. Although the Syria crisis and the programming that emerged in response were quite singular, the ways that the bureaucracy responded to demands for accountability and risk response were in many ways not. SOPs, policy repertoires, and scripts drove, contributed to, or otherwise shaped the control mechanisms that manifested.

The State Department's nonlethal assistance offers a starting point for examining these organizational tendencies. As the last chapter illustrated, CSO was prompted to establish a series of control mechanisms as part of bargaining and policy deliberations. However, the control mechanisms CSO developed tended to be based on already well-developed bureaucratic processes, SOPs, and approaches. In summer 2012, when first confronted with how to implement nonlethal assistance in an environment replete with human rights risks, State Department officials' first response was to retool the same human rights screening mechanisms it had been charged with overseeing for nearly two decades, those associated with the Leahy Law. This included replicating the conduct standard that exists within the Leahy Law (the interpretation of "gross violations of human rights"), and creating a new database modeled on the existing one.[5] Similarly, things like third-party or "end-use" monitoring, extensive reporting requirements, or vetting based on potential affiliation with DTOs were already de rigueur parts of State Department programming in any conflict environment at the time.[6]

This is not to suggest that what was ultimately adopted was merely boilerplate. Because the Syria context was so different from many others (where the U.S. assistance has typically been in support of a sitting government), the standard practices had to be modified. And given the heightened security and political concerns, it was often modified in ways that increased the rigor of the control mechanisms. For example, third-party monitoring was supplemented by more time-intensive remote monitoring, with State Department staff calling recipients or third parties on the ground by phone or bringing armed group leaders or recipients to Turkey to meet with State Department staff. The "Leahy Law–like" vetting process developed for Syria was much more proactive than in most contexts in which the Leahy Law is applied. State Department staff actively sought information about the Syrian actors involved and interrogated allegations of abuse throughout the course of the program implementation, often down to lower levels of a force or recipient organization. By contrast, in most countries, the Leahy Law functions as an almost perfunctory name-check of the senior commander or unit name against the database in DC, with little active searching for derogatory information (if at all). In sum, the accountability mechanisms were modified or innovated to respond to the Syria context and pressure points, but the approaches themselves very much drew from the State Department's standard repertoire of accountability mechanisms.

The same tendency to reach for existing practices could be observed in other agencies' control mechanisms. When DoD took on Syria support with the first Train and Equip program in 2014, it applied training standards and criteria that reflected DoD standard practices in security assistance. It developed "law of land warfare" training for the Train and Equip program and applied monitoring and training protocols related to compliance with the 2008 Child Soldiers Prevention Act, which had become standard in other DoD partner security assistance. The latter recurred in all of the subsequent DoD-implemented LHSFs. Some evidence of standard responses or SOPs can even be seen with covert CIA assistance. While it might have seemed a novel approach for the CIA to demand that FSA groups bring back spent missile casings as a way to verify their use, this was not entirely new. Albeit not stringently enforced, CIA support to the Afghan mujahideen in the 1980s also included this requirement.[7]

These different examples suggest an interdependent relationship between these organizational routines and the bargaining process. Bargaining generated a demand for a risk-mitigation response; the existing protocols and practices then queued a particular pathway for demonstrating risk mitigation and accountability. For example, in the initial Syria Train and Equip program debate, Congress pressured administration officials about how they would limit the prospect of abuses or security risks. The response (on Nagata's account, shared in chapter 3) was to apply standard protocols developed for ensuring accountability in partner forces—laws of war training, common conduct restrictions, and monitoring and reporting measures on weapons tracking among other things. Congress triggered a need for an accountability response; the DoD response was to reappropriate SOPs and routines already common in security assistance.

Another example of the link between standard protocols and bargaining can be seen in the multiagency adoption of Leahy Law–like standards. Those in charge of developing the State Department nonlethal assistance, the DoD Train and Equip programming, and the covert CIA support, proposed a Leahy Law–like process as a way to win over unconvinced players in the bureaucracy—signaling that human rights accountability would be taken into consideration—and also to forestall congressional concerns.[8] As such, although this was an SOP in many ways—the Leahy Law had existed and been operating for over a decade—it was an SOP that was not legally applicable for the Syrian groups. Accordingly, what prompted its application in Syria was neither legal obligation nor bureaucratic automation, but its usefulness in the bargaining arena. Bureaucratic routines and scripts certainly shaped the nature of the control that resulted, but it was the bargaining demands in that moment that triggered the bureaucratic response.

These examples suggest a tendency to reach for approaches that have already been internalized or deployed when called to respond to a bargaining demand. There are several reasons why that might be the case. First, the fact that these practices or routines are already available and known makes it easier for the bureaucracy to immediately apply them in the midst of a crisis. Second, there is a "logic of appropriateness" element to already established practices.[9] Once such practices have been internalized as an organizational norm, they begin to be applied because they are deemed appropriate rather than because of any situation-specific rationale. Many of the interviews with State Department personnel and military officers involved in these programs suggest a similar "logic of appropriateness" underlying many of the controls proposed and adopted. For example, one State Department official offered that the sort of initial "risk assessment" that was conducted at the onset of nonlethal assistance (in early summer 2012, during internal debates over nonlethal assistance programming) and the vetting requirements that accompanied it had become "relatively commonplace" for any country that invoked conflict or terrorism risks.[10] He assumed that vetting—whether human rights–related vetting or that connected to security risks—had been introduced at the start of the nonlethal assistance simply because it was common practice to do so on both fronts.[11] A certain logic of appropriateness can also be seen in the CSO officer's comments that establishing a Leahy Law–like vetting process was in part viewed as "intuiting Congressional intent."[12] Such observations suggest that these sort of human rights controls had simply become internalized as the appropriate, de minimus response within the bureaucracy, and that they would be applied even when not legally required.

Lastly, a strong motivation for applying these already accepted tools is that established practices may have an additional legitimizing or persuasive effect. Where a bargaining demand has triggered a need for accountability, turning to practices that have already been internalized as a legitimate response might be more convincing to other players within the bargaining game. The Leahy Law was not just an expected and standardized part of the State Department tool kit; it was a more convincing response to those concerned about human rights abuses, specifically because it had already been accepted for more than a decade as an appropriate human rights due diligence response.

This additional legitimating function where already existing practices are concerned helps explain why there was cross-agency adoption, and a sort of "instant SOP" aspect to certain controls, even within the narrow band of time of Syria programming. BPA expectations with regard to organizational lenses presume them to be quite specific or parochial to the department, ministry, agency, or other unit in question. They are presented as stemming from the given organizational unit's vision or mandate, their particular institutional expertise or tool kit, their organizational needs or ambitions, or simply the institutional practices that have uniquely developed and become encoded within their SOPs and organizational routines over time. One would thus not necessarily expect something that reflected a standard State Department operating procedure to be picked up by a DoD program dealing with the same groups, much less by the CIA. However, this is precisely what appeared to happen with control mechanisms in Syria. The same control mechanisms developed within State Department nonlethal assistance programming were subsequently picked up by other parts of the U.S. government when they sought to demonstrate accountability in Syria armed group support. For example, every subsequent Syrian assistance program adopted a form of Leahy Law–like vetting, some doing so with explicit claim that they were borrowing the CSO's prior approaches and experience.[13] Landler's account of how the initial proposal for arming Syrian rebels was developed notes collaboration between State Department and CIA officers, drawing from some of the accountability mechanisms and approaches the State Department was developing in its early assistance; this suggests a similar borrowing and adoption of preexisting approaches.[14]

In these cases, what was likely attractive about these control mechanisms was not just that they had already been applied to the groups in question and so appeared fit for purpose for the policy dilemma at hand, but also that they had successfully diffused critiques and countered skeptics in prior bargaining debates. As these practices are picked up from one part of the bureaucracy to another, to address one problem set or program challenge after another, they are further reinforced as part of the repertoire of responses that are appropriate for these situations.

This evidence of how control mechanisms were appropriated from one program to another suggests a means of policy transfer, not just across agencies or other distinct organizational units of the bureaucracy, but also across different country contexts and LHSF experiences. In responding to congressional questions about the first Train and Equip program, the chairman of the Joint Chiefs of Staff, General Martin Dempsey, pointed not only to the experience of control mechanisms in the nonlethal assistance program, but also to prior experience with vetting and monitoring in Iraq and Afghanistan.[15] In essence, these were persuasive solutions to demands to demonstrate accountability because they had already been accepted as such in other, equally risk-sensitive contexts. They had already been normalized to some degree as the sort of due diligence measures that were appropriate for this type of situation or this type of risk.

Adopting this additional organizational lens offers a more nuanced view of the factors behind control mechanisms, both at discrete moments and as an evolving process over time. These examples suggest an interaction between bargaining demands and organizational lenses or routines: with the first three Syria case studies, bargaining queued a need for risk-mitigation devices and controls; where it did so, SOPs, organizational protocols, and past approaches furnished the ready content for these control mechanisms. The continuance and replication of some of the control mechanisms—across the different Syria initiatives, and also in reference to LHSFs in other countries—suggests that organizational tendencies and approaches can act as mechanisms of policy transfer from one LHSF initiative to the next.

Presented in this light, organizational tendencies help explain how repertoires of accountability and control might be ingested by the bureaucracy as the result of a particular experience and then appropriated and used for other programs, either within the same country context or in other country contexts presenting similar dilemmas. Over time, repeated appropriation, coupled with use of the same control mechanisms across different LHSFs and countries, might themselves congeal into a sort of standardized approach. By 2014, this had not cohered to the degree that one might consider it to be a fully internalized SOP, but there was certainly evidence in the Syrian cases of an emerging common approach to responding to LHSF risks. The following two case studies will explore this idea of a common approach by examining the origin of control mechanisms in two post-2014 initiatives in Iraq and Afghanistan.

LEGACY EFFECTS AND ORGANIZATIONAL LENSES IN THE IRAQI TRIBAL MOBILIZATION FORCE (2014-2019)

The influence of these organizational tendencies also manifested in local force mobilization happening on the other side of the Syria-Iraq border—in an anti-ISIL tribal force in Iraq that was funded through the same legislative authority as the first Syria Train and Equip program. Although the local force initiatives in Iraq and Syria were driven by the same crisis, the controls that emerged for the Iraqi TMF were shaped by very different factors.[16] While the Syria Train and Equip initiatives were strongly influenced both by the crisis situation in Syria and bargaining over how to respond to these risks back in Washington, DC, the Iraqi TMF appeared to be shaped to a much greater extent by events and bargaining in Iraq that took place almost a decade before. The legacy of the *sahwa* experience and the points of contention and bargaining of a decade before strongly shaped how policy proposals were viewed and the solutions sought to respond to them, including control mechanisms. Analyzing these legacy effects, together with evidence of other organizational routines at play in the TMF, helps to deepen the discussion of how bargaining and organizational triggers interact, and how these might offer a means of policy transfer and SOP development and reinforcement over time.

During the period of the "surge," al-Qaeda in Iraq's operating space had been dramatically reduced and the group had been forced underground due to a combination of U.S. operations and the *sahwa* movement. But the group had not completely gone away. After the abrupt U.S. withdrawal from Iraq in 2011, the Maliki government's increasingly sectarian and heavy-handed policies nurtured grievances that would create an opening for AQI's resurgence. With the collapse of state control in large parts of Syria, AQI and other Islamic extremist groups had substantial operating space and an ample source of new recruits. They regrouped into an even more organized insurgent movement, the Islamic State of Iraq and the

Levant), taking Raqqa in Syria as their capital in 2013. By early January 2014, ISIL had gained a foothold in western Anbar Province. Then, in the span of a little over a week in June 2014, it assumed control of much of northern and central Iraq, including Iraq's second-largest city, Mosul, the Sunni heartland from Tikrit to the Syrian border, and the many diverse, multiethnic communities in between.

In the face of this lightning advance, Iraqi forces crumbled and retreated, and a range of substate groups, local actors, and militias mounted the most substantial immediate resistance. Following a call to arms by Iraq's most prominent Shi'a cleric, Ali al-Sistani, Shi'a militias calling themselves the Hashd ash-Shaabi, or the Popular Mobilization Forces, helicoptered into the shrine city of Samarra and other parts of Salah ad-Din Governorate to halt ISIL's advance onto Baghdad.[17] On the northern front, Kurdish Peshmerga, the forces of Iraq's Kurdistan Regional Government (KRG), mostly held the line against ISIL along the border with the KRG. The PKK, together with its local affiliates, saved thousands of Yazidis (an ethnoreligious Iraqi minority group targeted by ISIL) in northwestern Iraq by opening an escape corridor to Syria in August 2014.

The United States, along with other international allies, responded by sending support to the Iraqi state forces and by mounting a limited campaign of air strikes. But it also backed some of these local and substate forces. The United States provided training and weapons to the KRG's Peshmerga forces, which, though constitutionally sanctioned, had challenged the government in Baghdad for decades.[18] The U.S. strategy also heavily backed a new local force initiative designed to mobilize Sunni tribal forces and other local communities against ISIL. As one of the most senior SOF commanders involved in the anti-ISIL fight, Major General Pat Roberson, observed, "I was here in 2016, and at that time, in DC and in the embassy, tribal forces were treated like a silver bullet because of the past experience with the *sahwa*."[19] It was such a high priority that Secretary of State John Kerry raised the idea of a second Sunni tribal force in his first meeting with Prime Minister Haider al-Abadi in the fall of 2014.[20]

Such high-level pressure was essential. The Iraqi government also saw the proposed second tribal mobilization through the lens of the *sahwa*—and was as jaded by the comparison as the United States was enthusiastic. It was as suspicious of the United States mobilizing Sunni forces in 2014 as it had been in 2007. As one U.S. official remembered, "The crux of the issue for us ended up being getting Iraqi government, which was

Shi'a, approval of a second paramilitary tribal operations done by Sunnis."[21] Many Iraqi officials and leaders also believed that ISIL was partly made up of former *sahwa* members, in their view proving the point that these Sunni tribal actors were not to be trusted.

In addition, there were a number of other substate contenders to deal with. ISIL's mass takeover of territory had temporarily upended political dynamics and control lines in Iraq. This triggered a sort of zero-sum competition, with political parties, sects, ethnicities, leaders, and even local stakeholders competing to ensure that their constituencies were armed, protected, and would have a territorial and political stake in the future.[22] In this context, the United States' proclaimed aim of helping "Sunni communities secure their own freedom from ISIL's control" (as Obama framed it in his first speech on the ISIL strategy) was viewed not as a neutral act, but as one that could potentially tip the scale toward one group over others in highly sensitive areas.

There were particular tensions with the PMF, which in November 2016 had been legalized as a parallel force alongside the Iraqi Security Forces, subsequently becoming a major political force within Iraqi politics.[23] The PMF's roughly 125,000-strong membership drew from a range of tribal, ethnic, and sectarian backgrounds. But the core of the PMF were sectarian Shi'a militias and leaders who had cut their teeth fighting as anti-U.S. insurgent groups during the Iraqi civil war.[24] Several of these groups or their leaders had been designated as terrorist organizations or global terrorists or by the U.S. Treasury Department.[25] These leading PMF forces also raised and supported their own local Sunni tribal units as they expanded into parts of Salah ad-Din, Kirkuk, Diyala, and Ninewa, but they were not in favor of the United States doing so.[26]

All of these different political dynamics, together with the substantial domestic debate over authorizing the expanded use of force in Iraq and Syria (discussed in the previous chapter), created an environment that was rich with competing stakeholders and players. It was just the sort of policy context that might lead to contentious bargaining and produce a bevy of controls. Certainly, the Tribal Mobilization Force was studded with a range of control mechanism almost from its inception. Yet, digging deeper into the dynamics that produced those controls, bargaining appeared to be a much smaller driver than in the previous case studies in Iraq and Syria. Instead, the control mechanisms appeared much more reflective of an echo effect vis-à-vis the previous debate, as well as some of the organizational tendencies introduced in the prior section. Before getting into those factors, however, it is helpful to introduce the controls in question.

CONTROL MECHANISMS IN THE TRIBAL MOBILIZATION FORCE

After approval by the Iraqi government, the TMF began to be mobilized in the fall of 2015. Although U.S. forces and officials were involved in the initial mobilization, which began in Anbar Province, the TMF was structured as a subsidiary force of the Iraqi Security Forces. The funding was provided through the same NDAA legislation that supported Syrian Train and Equip forces on the other side of the border, but all funding and equipment was channeled through the Iraqi government rather than provided directly to the TMF units (as had been the case with the *sahwa*).

The TMF evolved from a somewhat ad hoc, partly volunteer force of as many as 60,000 fighters during the main operations in Anbar, to a smaller but more formalized force consisting of some 32,000 members by the time it expanded to support operations in Ninewa Governorate in late 2016.[27] From the outset, the TMF were subject to a broad range of checks and control mechanisms, imposed by either the Iraqi government or the United States. In addition, similar to the trajectory of controls in the Syria nonlethal assistance, those control mechanisms increased and were formalized over time, as they were demanded either formally or informally by a range of different stakeholders.

Vetting and selection mechanisms: There were multiple layers of vetting by the U.S. and Iraqi governments as well as other local stakeholders. The NDAA provisions supporting the TMF contained vetting standards that mirrored those of Syrian Train and Equip forces. As such, U.S. officials screened for "associations with terrorist groups or with groups associated with the Iranian government."[28] This counterterrorism or "CT" vetting (as it was known among U.S. officials) was applied alongside the Leahy Law human rights standards.[29] The TMF had no formal legal grounding under Iraqi law before the November 2016 PMF law.[30] Nonetheless, because the United States treated the TMF as part of the Iraqi state forces, it formally applied the Leahy Law to the TMF from the start.[31]

TMF members were also subject to vetting by the Iraqi government, which was enabled by background checks conducted by the Iraqi National Security Service.[32] When the program expanded to Ninewa Province in 2016, a new selection process via a multi-stakeholder selection committee was introduced. Each tribal leader proposed for the Ninewa TMF had to be approved by a committee including Iraqi and Kurdish national security officials, representatives of the governor's office, and coalition representatives. Vetting input from Kurdish officials was in theory to be based on background checks overseen by the Regional Security Council (a collective body that functioned as the national security office for the KRG); in practice, the vetting appeared to be more political than technical in nature and was used to exclude Sunni political forces that were mistrusted by Kurdish political stakeholders.[33]

In addition to all these formal vetting steps, at least during the initial Anbar mobilization, key PMF leaders like the late Abu Mehdi al-Muhandis (killed by a U.S. drone strike in January 2020) and Hadi al-Amri had an unofficial vetting role. They had a say in which tribal leaders were approved for a TMF unit, any requests for additional men per unit, or any provision of heavy weapons or significant equipment.[34] This was usually accomplished through informal shuttle diplomacy, with Iraqi officials serving as the formal go-betweens but with U.S. officials' full awareness. Giving the example of whether the United States would provide heavy weapons to a given TMF contingent, one of the U.S. officials involved remembered, "It depended on where, the type of forces, name of the people. . . . It was a decision we had to balance on a case-by-case basis, to balance between what we could accept them [the TMF unit] having, what was necessary to keep forces on the ground in the fight, and what Iraqi Shi'a leadership were willing to tolerate."[35]

Codes of conduct, rules, and restrictions: There were restrictions on where and how the TMF could operate, as well as specific rules and codes of conduct. The TMF formally operated under the Iraqi Security Forces, and so were technically subject to any of the forces' regulations or disciplinary rules, as well as to any other provisions of Iraqi law. U.S. and other international coalition forces (to include Spanish, British, Danish, and Dutch trainers) provided an optional ten-day training to the TMF, which included a basic primer on human rights and the laws of war.[36]

Forces were only to be provided with personal weapons, with the exceptions, noted above, of explicitly negotiated more advanced equipment.

Whether due to political limitations or program restrictions, the size of each unit was kept small—between one and two hundred members on average.[37] There were also restrictions on where the TMF units could be created, with such units ultimately receiving authorization only in Anbar and Ninewa Governorates.

Oversight, monitoring, and sanctions: Both Iraqi and U.S. institutional actors had a part in overseeing and monitoring the TMF, as well as any cut-offs or disciplinary sanctions imposed on them. The TMF initially came under the authority of an Iraqi three-star army general, and later was brought under the PMF command structure.[38] In the course of operations (for example, the retaking of Ninewa and Mosul), TMF were overseen by the Federal Police or Iraqi Security Force command center in their area.[39] Where issues arose, TMF members might be dismissed from the program or subject to disciplinary sanctions by Iraqi Security Forces. In at least one case, feuding TMF members in Ninewa were referred to local law enforcement.[40]

While the TMF formally came under Iraqi authority, U.S. officials at the embassy in Baghdad and the consulate in Erbil were actively involved

TABLE 4.1 Summary of control mechanisms for Iraqi Tribal Mobilization Forces

Selection mechanisms (vetting)	• Background checks and selection by Iraqi forces • Background checks and selection input by KRG and Ninewa governor's office (Ninewa only) • U.S. vetting for terrorist or Iranian links (NDAA requirements) and Leahy Law vetting • Informal political vetting by key Baghdad stakeholders (PMF)
Rules and guidelines	• Establishment of mandate of local protection and self-defense • Prohibitions on certain actions—use of heavy weapons • Ten days training, including instruction on human rights and laws of war • Regular Iraqi Security Force guidelines and codes of conduct
Monitoring and oversight	• Regular monitoring by U.S. officials • Units subordinated to Iraqi security forces and officials in day-to-day command (mostly Federal Police) • Oversight and management by PMF (~2018 on)
Sanctions	• Some units blocked or dismissed for violations of GVHR • Some units blocked due to allegations of child soldiers • Prosecutions or arrest by Iraqi law enforcement for misconduct

in oversight.[41] This included continued monitoring to ensure compliance with U.S. law—for example, investigating allegations of gross violations of human rights per the Leahy Law or use of child soldiers. In some cases, where such evidence was found credible TMF units were cut from the program.[42] For example, a Sunni Arab TMF unit in southern Ninewa was blocked from the program after evidence emerged that it had tortured suspected ISIL members whom it had detained.[43]

LEGACY EFFECTS QUEUING BARGAINING AND CONTROLS IN THE TMF

As the diversity of controls might suggest, there were a range of factors and stakeholder interests behind these control mechanisms, but two key factors stand out: the legacy of the bargaining and dissention over the *sahwa*, and institutional lenses or repertoires emanating from Washington, DC. On the first, it was hard for the TMF to escape the shadow of the *sahwa*. Even on a purely personnel level, those involved in the TMF on both the U.S. and the Iraqi sides had past experience with the *sahwa*. Former or active U.S. military who had worked with the *sahwa* in the early 2000s helped kick-start the TMF by reaching out to former tribal contacts.[44] Once the force was established, those involved in monitoring and supporting it were also largely those with prior *sahwa* experience. There was a similar level of institutional memory on the Iraqi side. Maliki was still the prime minister when the idea was first raised. Although he had stepped down already by August 2014, many of his key advisers, including those responsible for the first *sahwa* review and deliberations, remained in the Prime Minister's Office (under newly selected Prime Minister Abadi).[45]

Whether due to this institutional memory or the parallels in the different situations, both sides tended to view the TMF through the prism of the past *sahwa* experience. When the question of mobilizing a new force first emerged, the bargaining assumed the same lines of contention that had emerged in the prior *sahwa* debate. Still suspicious of a U.S.-mobilized Sunni force, Iraqi officials demanded the same institutional control mechanisms they had lobbied for in the *sahwa*—that it be an Iraqi force, under the command authority of an Iraqi general, with Iraqi officials in charge of screening, recruiting, and determining which forces would be accepted.[46] Iraqi officials also raised similar concerns about the geographic scope. In both the *sahwa* and TMF experiences, Iraqi officials were relatively sanguine about the prospects of additional local support in Anbar, which Iraqi forces from other parts of the country struggled to control, but they raised more objections when the United States proposed expanding the initiative to more areas.[47] In the TMF, the Iraqi government did not allow the U.S.-sponsored program to expand to the more politically sensitive governorates of Salah ad-Din and Kirkuk, despite requests to do so.[48]

The United States for its part acceded to Iraqi demands more readily in the TMF case, in part because of the changed bargaining dynamics but also because of U.S. officials' own takeaways from the *sahwa* experience. The United States did not have the same political autonomy in Iraq in 2014 as it did in 2007, and it certainly had nowhere near the troop levels. As such, U.S. officials needed Iraqi buy-in and support to mobilize the TMF, and would need to concede to more demands to win that. However, equally important were the lessons the United States learned from the *sahwa* experience. U.S. officials viewed the quick dissolution of the *sahwa* after the U.S. withdrawal as a lost investment, with the Iraqi government throwing away what—in the U.S. view—had proved to be one of the most important stabilizing elements in the country. They also saw the *sahwa*'s dissolution as a symptom of the sort of sectarian behavior that had contributed to the rise of ISIL. In their view, the Iraqi Security Forces would ultimately have to be more reflective of Iraq's diverse ethnic and sectarian make-up, including Sunni tribal fighters, whose recruitment had now twice fueled a virulent Islamic insurgency in Iraq.[49] This time around, U.S. officials wanted the tribal forces to be preserved once the immediate security crisis was over. If getting greater Iraqi ownership, institutionalization, and buy-in might help accomplish that, then U.S. officials were willing to accede to Iraqi demands.[50] In essence, the Iraqi institutional controls that the United States accepted had as much to with preventing past issues with the *sahwa* from recurring as it did with addressing either the perceived risks of the TMF units or de novo bargaining demands.

The most significant "new" element was the intervention of Shi'a PMF leaders and the KRG parties, and their ability to influence the selection of TMF members. This is a notable example of unconventional stakeholders acting as players by virtue of their de facto political weight and influence in the policy sphere at the time. Shi'a PMF leaders were too significant a political force to be ignored. As one U.S. official involved in the early program management argued, "If you're sending money, resources, and equipment to Sunni tribal fighters, there have to be commensurate control mechanisms for Shi'a government officials and those with power behind them (and that could include Hadi al-Amri or al-Muhandis [leading PMF officials]). . . . They have to feel they have some control, and that these forces will not threaten your government."[51] As for the KRG, the United States needed the buy-in of KRG officials in order to support Ninewa operations (including TMF support) from Kurdish territory. Once given a say, PMF and KRG vetoes prevented tribal leaders whom they perceived as political threats from receiving key resources from the United States. It is another example of using control mechanisms as a "limiting device," albeit this time not even from foreign state actors, but rather from substate and non-state powerbrokers linked to the Iraqi state.

Notwithstanding these new players and the say they had in controls, the overall dynamics surrounding the TMF suggest that while there was nominal bargaining over the TMF control mechanisms, this was much more of an echo of the previous debate than an example of de novo bargaining. When this new debate over mobilizing Sunni forces emerged in 2014, it queued the same lines of contention, as well as the same response or solution, that had developed in the prior *sahwa* case, in the form of a series of Iraqi institutional controls. In that sense, the *sahwa* legacy appears to have contributed to a more ready compromise in the TMF case. In contrast to the nearly two years of foot-dragging, stalling, and bargaining over the *sahwa*, the U.S. and Iraqi sides reached a compromise on the TMF within six months. It was easier to come to a solution on what institutional parameters or redlines would make the TMF palatable on both sides because the blueprint for doing so had already been charted through the *sahwa* debates. In a way, the bargain had already been struck and simply had to be revived—a much easier lift at this demanding crisis moment.

Yet, though a compromise was more readily reached in the case of the TMF, this did not prevent the force from being politically sabotaged and ultimately dissolved, in much the same way that the *sahwa* had been. Already a minor force by 2017, it was fast on its way to complete dissolution or absorption into the larger PMF by 2019.[52] This was partly because of the security dynamics involved and the U.S. response to them. ISIL proved a different type of insurgent threat than AQI had been, and ousting it would ultimately require larger force operations and air power than localized tribal groups could muster. However, the TMF also failed to take off in part because the Iraqi controls played the same role as they had in the *sahwa*—as a limiting device intended to constrain the impact of this U.S. initiative. Vetting scrutiny—whether in the hands of the prime minister's office, the PMF leaders, or Kurdish leaders—was used to exclude those tribal leaders who were viewed as a political threat. Iraqi control and prerogatives on where the program could be developed, the size of units, and the level of U.S. support also kept it to a very marginal force. Overall, Iraqi institutional controls, as well as the informal political controls, were used by Iraqi players as limiting devices aimed more at undermining the initiative than as mechanisms for constraining TMF fighters and their associated risks.

INSTITUTIONAL LENSES AND ORGANIZATIONAL TENDENCIES BEHIND TMF CONTROLS

While these legacy effects were notable, there was also another strong element shaping the TMF controls, in particular those imposed by the United States. Many of the U.S.-managed controls—counterterrorism and human rights vetting, basic conduct standards, other constraints designed to minimize concerns related to "militia empowerment"—reflect many of the rationales and practices already seen in the prior Syria and Afghanistan case studies. And yet what is different about the TMF case is that these controls appeared to be applied almost reflexively, without being prompted by internal or external bargaining demands.

Unlike with the Syria Train and Equip forces created from the same legislation, there was no significant opposition to or deliberations over the TMF within the U.S. government or between Congress and the executive branch. While the congressional record of the debate over Syria is studded with references to fears of Syrian forces perpetrating human rights abuses or passing weapons on to hostile groups, such objections and fears were absent from congressional deliberations over Iraqi Train and Equip support. To the contrary, because of the legacy of the *sahwa*, remembered as a huge success, congressional representatives had already been calling for a second "Sons of Iraq" for some six months before the Obama administration's request.[53] They ratified it without really questioning the logic of the initiative or the potential risks involved.

Nor was there significant hand-wringing within the executive branch about the potential risks of the TMF, despite arguably some of the same risks of "marbling" with ISIL or of Iranian interference. No officials interviewed remembered the sort of internal U.S. bargaining, deliberations, and standoffs documented in the prior chapter on Syria for the Iraqi TMF. Those involved in the TMF remembered very few questions about whether TMF forces had passed vetting, crossed redlines, or were affiliating with the wrong groups—the sort of continuing questioning that prompted a ratcheting up of controls within the Syria programming. Given this fact, it would be hard to argue that bargaining pressures were what led to the numerous controls on the U.S. side.

One potential factor was simply a sort or crossover or seepage from the parallel Syria debate, which was funded through the same legislation. The applicable language on vetting and controls for Train and Equip forces in Syria and Iraq is strikingly similar, down to the same key phrases about what constituted "appropriately vetted" forces, the same provisions on "association with terrorist groups . . . or groups associated with the government of Iran," and the same "commitment . . . to promote respect for human rights and the rule of law.[54] However, congressional staff involved in drafting the legislation suggested that it was less that the Syria conditions were transposed onto Iraqi forces than that these sorts of conditions and requirements were considered appropriate for forces like the TMF. When asked about these control mechanisms, one of the congressional staff involved noted that the vetting and controls in the TMF legislation were the sort of accountability measure that was "important with a local hold force" or counterinsurgency force like the TMF.[55] There was a presumption that ensuring better conduct by these local forces might help them to "win hearts and minds" and to maintain credible governing authority with the local community.

U.S. government officials involved in the TMF offered similar explanations or reactions to the control mechanisms—offering that "CT" or counterterrorism vetting and some sort of human rights criteria were standard practices for forces of this type.[56] Some of the controls, like basic training on laws of war, or monitoring to check against potential use of child soldiers, had become a regular part of DoD partner assistance, and appeared to be applied as a sort of SOP for partner forces. To some extent, DoD officials also appeared to be applying the range of practices and approaches embodied in the ALP as if it were itself an SOP with forces of this kind. Similar to the language used in the ALP debate, U.S. government or military officials who managed or worked with the TMF hoped that training and oversight would reinforce good conduct and "good governance" approaches—as befitted a local counterinsurgency force.[57] Program guidelines intended to keep the force small and defensive in nature were in keeping with all that was necessary for a hold or "local watch" force without incurring further risks.[58]

Taking stock of all the different U.S. mechanisms and restrictions applied, what stands out is that the TMF in many ways reflected the model of layered controls developed in the ALP. There was an evolving idea about the sort of counterinsurgency forces that might be nurtured in these environments, and within that same institutional mold, the control mechanisms or accountability measures deemed appropriate for that type of force. This offers further evidence of an evolving common approach in effect. By this point, the U.S. bureaucracy was several years into the ALP experience, had gone through multiple rounds of deliberations over Syrian armed forces, and had witnessed similar LHSF support debates in other countries not covered in this book. Building from these collective experiences, this particular blend of security and conduct-based controls had begun to gather bureaucratic momentum (or arguably inertia) as the sort of due diligence and risk-mitigation checks that were appropriate for forces in these sorts of hybrid security environments. The standard menu of control mechanisms for LHSFs was being applied out of a "logic of appropriateness" more than due to any explicit demands for them.

Collectively, the case study of the TMF offers examples of several different types of organizational or institutional lenses and how these might interact with bargaining to produce the controls in question. The United States saw the emergence of ISIL through the lens of the prior experience with a virulent Islamist insurgency in Iraq, mounted by AQI, and reached for the same policy response. This not only queued a similar sort of policy solution—a force inspired by the *sahwa*—but also triggered a redux of the same type of bargaining demands (between U.S. and Iraqi officials) and the same responsive controls that were developed for the prior force. In addition to being guided by these legacy effects, the TMF controls were also shaped by common U.S. legislative and administrative protocols and accountability mechanisms, some of which were reflective of an emerging common approach toward risk mitigation in LHSFs. The evidence of this emerging common approach in yet another LHSF and in a different country context further illustrates the fact that the bureaucratic internalization and repurposing of common mechanisms and practices can be a means of policy transfer from one area to another.

THE AFGHAN NATIONAL ARMY-TERRITORIAL FORCE (2018-AUGUST 2021): A REFORMED ALP

Over what would prove to be the last four years of U.S. military engagement in Afghanistan, U.S. officials and those of the Government of the Islamic Republic of Afghanistan worked to mobilize a new LHSF, the Afghan National Army-Territorial Force. There was a similar echo effect on display here, with the ANA-TF very much created in the image of the ALP, or at least as a modified version of what the ALP should have been. Both the controls introduced for and language surrounding the ANA-TF also suggest further evidence of bureaucratic absorption of LHSF controls, in particular given that the common or standard menu of controls were introduced under a different administration than the prior LHSF cases. Despite the fact that the Trump and Obama administrations had very different outlooks on issues like human rights accountability and use of force regulations, the control mechanisms developed for the ANA-TF replicated those identified as part of the common approach in the prior case studies.

The idea of a new local force initiative was first floated in the fall of 2017, in conversations between Afghan president Ashraf Ghani and the U.S.-led military command in Afghanistan, at that point operating under mission Resolute Support (RS).[59] Since the drawdown of major international combat operations in 2014, the Taliban (at that point still a nonstate insurgent movement) had been steadily gaining ground. In addition, beginning in 2016, a new Islamic State affiliate, the Islamic State in Khorasan, emerged in eastern Afghanistan. However, while the threats were increasing, international willingness and commitments to respond to them were on the decline. There was a need to strengthen the Afghan Army, but on an increasingly lean international support budget. To do so, the Afghan and U.S. leaderships turned again to the idea of local forces, which were cheaper to mobilize and sustain.[60]

Similar to the links between the *sahwa* and the TMF, the link between the ALP and the ANA-TF was in some measure due to the individuals and institutional memory involved. All of the U.S. forces and advisers behind the ANA-TF had also helped develop and build the ALP. The commander of RS at the time—Brigadier General "Scottie" Miller had been the head of the Special Forces command that supported the early local defense pilots and the ALP in its initial years. The supporting policy unit for the ANA-TF even included some of the same civilian RAND Corporation advisers who had helped develop the ALP model. Moreover, given that the ALP had been going for seven years (eight if the preceding pilots are considered), all of the Afghan leaders and ministerial officials had ample experience with this sort of force. When it came to developing the ANA-TF, these same U.S. and Afghan officials reached for the ALP blueprint they had initially developed, including its multilayered control mechanisms, but with some lessons learned and corrections built into it.

While many in the U.S. military argued that ALP forces had proven to be crucial local stalwarts, many (if not most) ALP units were problematic, preying upon the local population, spurring local conflict, or enabling warlords and criminal networks—the same consequences that opponents of the ALP had warned about in 2009.[61] Many of those designing the ANA-TF—the vast majority (if not all) of whom had been involved in the ALP—tended to argue that the issue was less that the original idea was bad than that it had not been implemented as it was designed to be, and certainly not with sufficient levels of accountability. Due to security pressures, the ALP had been forced to grow by more than double its original size in its first three years. The force ballooned from a couple thousand forces at the end of the initial pilots in 2010 to just under thirty thousand by 2013.[62] This created pressure to mobilize each unit as quickly as possible and limited the time and resources available to apply most of the controls, including those involving careful site selection, force recruitment, community consent, training, mentorship, and oversight.[63] For example, in some cases, SOF personnel had no more than a week in a community to identify and mobilize a force, which made it virtually impossible to ensure the sort of careful site selection, community engagement, and vetting and mentorship processes originally envisioned.[64] Finally, rather than acting as an institutional oversight mechanism, the Ministry of Interior had proven to be a conduit for corruption, and power brokers and politicians easily used the ALP program to fund their own parochial militias and patronage networks.[65]

As a result, when it came time to craft the ANA-TF, the same U.S. and Afghan advisers largely kept the same controls but put renewed attention to actually enforcing them.

Vetting and selection: There was the same tri-party vetting or scrutiny—by the Afghan government, by U.S. institutions, and (at least in theory) by communities—that had existed with the ALP.[66] This included, on the U.S. side, vetting both for terrorist affiliations and for past gross violations of human rights (the Leahy Law standard). There were also the same criteria for site selection designed to avoid warlord or militia empowerment, local conflict or other risks, and community checks and controls. The difference with the ANA-TF could be seen in greater attention to ensuring that these criteria were implemented (with the exception of the community controls, which were only rhetorically emphasized in the ANA-TF).[67] This was done through slow expansion and mobilization, and by allowing greater deliberation over site selection and recruitment.[68]

Codes of conduct, rules, and restrictions: There were similar codes of conduct and operating limits on ANA-TF forces to those imposed on the ALP, including the commitment that they would only operate as defensive "hold" forces, limited to their home areas. As with the ALP, ANA-TF members received training on these rules and on human rights and laws of war. However, the lessons learned from the ALP was that more needed to be done to promote "institutionalization and accountability"—in essence to establish mechanisms that would enforce these rules.[69] Part of the reason the Afghan Ministry of Defense (MoD) was preferred over the Ministry of Interior as the host institution for the ANA-TF was because of the former's stronger reputation for accountability and command and control. There were also additional measures designed to strengthen the military command's ability to restrain or control behavior—including having a regular ANA commissioned officer in charge of each unit (the ALP had been under their own local commanders); a longer training time (from three to four weeks with the ALP to twelve with the ANA-TF); and co-locating ANA-TF in ANA barracks (members of the ALP had lived at home).[70] Where divergence from these established training or indoctrination measures manifested, there was a greater emphasis on correcting them. For example, over the summer of 2019, due to further Taliban advances, the Afghan government accelerated ANA-TF mobilization, resulting in the deployment of some companies that had only been half filled or that had received insufficient training, equipment, or tactical support. In part due to pressure from RS and other international advisers, several of these companies were later pulled back and re-vetted or retrained.[71]

Monitoring, oversight, and sanctions: These enhanced ANA and MoD control mechanisms also strengthened the overall monitoring and oversight of the ANA-TF. In addition, as with the ALP, there was a degree of monitoring and oversight by U.S. or RS officials and also by local communities (the latter, again, more rhetorically). Where this monitoring detected issues, ANA-TF might be sanctioned through some of the same mechanisms as the ALP—including cut-offs obligated by the Leahy Law where gross human rights violations manifested, and Afghan disciplinary procedures or criminal prosecution. Once again, the main difference appeared to be a greater commitment to designing institutions that would actually apply these sanctions.

Overall, the controls within the ANA-TF largely replicated the same control mechanisms that had been generated in the previous bargaining over the ALP. Even the elements that were different—for example, the enhanced institutional controls—stemmed largely from the lessons learned from the ALP experience than in response to fault lines within the bargaining arena. One of the few signs of resistance and internal (intra-bureaucratic) bargaining came from the MoD. MoD leaders initially resisted the creation of the ANA-TF. In keeping with BPA theories of "stand-sit" positions, MoD leadership viewed the proposal through their organizational lens, mission set, and self-image as a professional military force. They did not want their professional ranks polluted by uncontrolled "militias."[72] After months of discussion, MoD officials agreed to host the ANA-TF, but only if there were greater institutional controls that would bring the ANA-TF closer to a professional force than the ALP had been—the additional training, command authority, and other measures discussed above.[73] These MoD demands might be considered a bargaining request; however, since MoD concerns about preventing militias and unprofessionalism in its ranks dovetailed with U.S. officials' own desire to avoid the ALP's missteps, it was bargaining without much resistance. Both sides readily embraced the idea of a more institutionalized force, such that the outcome was less the result of a compromise on differing bargaining positions than an expression of largely concordant views.

What of other potential bargaining actors or points of division? The same coterie of actors that had raised concerns about human rights and militia empowerment in the ALP reacted similarly to the news of a new LHSF program. The first news story to leak of the planned force was headlined "U.S. Plan for New Afghan Force Revives Fears of Militia Abuses," while immediate NGO reactions and commentary disparaged the idea as "militia déjà vu."[74] NGO and UNAMA representatives (who incidentally included many of the same individuals involved in the ALP authorization debate) followed a similar course as they had with the ALP, raising objections and concerns either publicly or through private meetings with the officials and forces involved.[75] In response to such critiques, proponents of the ANA-TF followed a similar script to that of the ALP bargaining, defraying concerns by pointing to the existing controls and the efforts to reinforce them.

This is not to suggest that the dialogue between those developing the program and outside critics was insignificant. NGO and civil society critiques appeared to reinforce the perception that checks and controls needed to be kept. However, they were much less generative of new controls or program modifications than in the initial ALP debate. The control mechanisms that were generated in the bargaining over the ALP—demands for training on human rights or laws of war, vetting based on past human rights abuses, or program limits intended to decrease the risk of the different ALP units becoming mobile militias—were already built into the model before outside opponents raised a single objection. In a way, the dialogue between RS or Afghan officials and outside NGO or civil society voices fell along the same pathways as the prior debate, illustrating yet another legacy effect of the ALP debate. At this point the objections to and potential risks of this type of initiative were well-known, as were the control mechanisms deemed appropriate to respond to those critiques. When NGOs *called* for more accountability for local forces or objected to the record of misconduct in the ALP, the *response* was to redouble the existing conduct-based and accountability controls. (The following chapter will expand on this idea of a "call and response" between officials and external critics.)

The ANA-TF also illustrates some of the organizational tendencies and SOPs introduced in chapter 3 and offers further evidence of an emerging common response. As noted in the TMF example, by this point, measures like vetting for terrorist affiliation or gross violations of human rights had come to be seen by a large swath of the U.S. bureaucracy as the sort of due diligence or risk-mitigation mechanisms that were appropriate for local forces. U.S. officials working on the ANA-TF appeared to be applying this organizational lens or preset when they crafted the control mechanisms. For example, when asked what kind of constraints would be placed on the ANA-TF given the risks associated with local forces, a DoD official at the U.S. embassy at the time responded that there would be standard precautions like Leahy Law vetting and counterterrorism or "CT" vetting, in addition to the other Afghan institutional checks.[76] This particular individual had not had prior experience with the ALP and was new to the assignment in Afghanistan, suggesting that what was informing his reaction was less a legacy effect than the fact that he viewed such measures as the default for these sorts of programs. Even the language used indicates a hardening of these due diligence prescriptions, as terms like "CT vetting" became a standard part of the bureaucratic lexicon for State and Defense Department officials. While security concerns were part of the ALP background checks, the original ALP debate described them as screening for Taliban or warlord connections, with no references to the "CT vetting" that had also manifested as standard in U.S. vetting in Iraq and Syria.[77] While only one example, this illustrates the extent to which these sorts of measures had become almost rote by this point in LHSF development, applied as much for the "logic of appropriateness" as for the likelihood that the controls would effectively address the risks in the case in point.

A final notable point is that these assumptions and SOPs carried over despite the change in administrations. Most of the case studies discussed so far emerged under the Obama administration, whose more lawyerly approach and greater concern for accountability may have contributed to a more focused attention on control mechanisms. The Trump administration was not marked by the same characteristics. However, the ANA-TF—the most heavily institutionalized and control-metered LHSF of those examined so far—emerged fully under the Trump White House, at a time when the administration was simultaneously drawing down other human rights–protective rules within its Afghanistan policy.[78] The fact that the change in administrations appeared to make little difference in the control mechanism deployed suggests that, to some extent, this "common approach" had already started to be ingrained within bureaucratic practices, applied by rote rather than governed by political pressures or directives.

The overall description of the ANA-TF suggests a force whose parameters and control mechanisms were largely already part of an accepted, existing model, with some slight tailoring to institutional partner requests and force requirements in Afghanistan. As one of the international advisers to the force recalled, the model for the ANA-TF was fairly "intuitive": "We spent more time thinking about 'don't do this' than the 'do's,'" she noted.[79] While bargaining was not completely absent, it was substantially overshadowed by the legacy effects of the ALP and institutional scripts surrounding what was expected when mobilizing local forces. At this point in the cycle of LHSF partnerships, consistent demands from the DC bureaucracy on things like the Leahy Law and CT vetting had cohered into part of a common menu of controls.

EXCEPTIONS TO THE RULE: COVERT PARTNERSHIPS AND COUNTERTERRORISM MODALITIES

The previous case studies have suggested the emergence of a common bureaucratic lens or approach to LHSFs, particularly in Iraq and Afghanistan. Nonetheless, there have also been some glaring exceptions to this emerging rule in the same countries—with LHSFs attached to U.S. Special Forces or intelligence units conducting counterterrorism raids seeming to be unconstrained by the panoply of checks and controls introduced in prior chapters. This last section explores what might be different about these LHSFs compared to other LHSF partnerships, and what that suggests about when (or whether) bargaining or organizational pressures might queue risk-mitigation controls.

From the initial invasion of Afghanistan up to the withdrawal of U.S. forces in August 2021, CIA agents and U.S. SOF frequently turned to Afghan militias and irregular forces, relying on them as auxiliary forces on counterterrorism and intelligence missions.[80] From 2002 through 2012, there were common reports of nighttime raids and detention operations carried out by nonuniform or irregular Afghan militias in the company of a small number of U.S. agents or forces. Afghans tended to refer to such forces as "campaign forces," but internal accounts have referred to them as "Counterterrorism Pursuit Teams."[81]

Distinct subunits or forces of these Counterterrorism Pursuit Teams were deployed in specific geographic areas. Examples include the Kandahar Strike Force in Kandahar Province, the Afghan Security Guards in Paktika Province, and the Khost Protection Force in Khost Province.[82] Reports suggest that these units were directly selected and controlled by U.S. Special Forces and CIA officers.[83] Many were co-located on U.S. bases, where they received substantial training and instruction.[84] These Counterterrorism Pursuit Teams were active at least until 2013, when President Karzai called for forces outside the Afghan chain of command to be demobilized.[85] Although these forces likely never entirely went away, reports of their activities decreased for a few years.

In 2015, the emergence of the Islamic State in Khorasan increased the demand for U.S. counterterrorism missions in Afghanistan. With these came a new group of auxiliary militias, known as "01" and "02" forces for the military code assigned to the regions in which they operated. Similar to the prior "campaign forces," these clandestine militias engaged in nighttime raids that deployed high levels of violence and frequently resulted in the killing (rather than the detention) of presumed targets. Public reporting and interviews suggest that the units themselves as well as the target-selection process were directed by CIA or "black ops" Special Forces, outside of the regular Afghan chain of command or RS targeting processes.[86] Media accounts suggested that some 01 and 02 units were directly accompanied by U.S. personnel, and that they enjoyed a level of coordination and confidence to be authorized to call in U.S. air strikes.[87]

The recurrent pattern of counterterrorism auxiliaries in Afghanistan suggests enduring and quite close relationships between U.S. forces or intelligence agents and these paramilitary auxiliary groups. The same commanders, group names, and local mobilization patterns recurred for nearly two decades. That length of time, plus the reports of co-location with U.S. forces and direct training by U.S. personnel, suggests that there have been ample opportunities to develop and exert control mechanisms of the sort discussed in prior case studies.

However, while training may have been provided to improve these units' tactical and operating efficiency, their conduct suggests that there was not the same focus on conduct-based or human rights controls as in the overt LHSF initiatives in Afghanistan. Substantial reports of war crimes and human rights violations accompanied each iteration of these forces, including reports of extrajudicial killings and detention, torture and ill-treatment of those detained, and indiscriminate or unruly behavior vis-à-vis civilians, including raids or operating patterns that smacked of collective punishment.[88] The reports of misconduct and abuse continued up to the last iteration of counterterrorism auxiliaries in Afghanistan. Media accounts and civil society activists frequently denounced the so-called 01 and 02 forces as "death squads" due to their record of extreme violence.[89] Those tracking them have found no indication that these counterterrorism auxiliary forces had ever been held to account, despite often very unit-specific evidence provided to U.S. officials.[90] Far from seeking more controlled and rights-compliant behavior, such a record suggests that the United States used these forces in ways that mirrored standard assumptions about why states outsource to paramilitary forces and militias in the first place—as a way to distance themselves from such "dirty work" and defray accountability or reputational costs for abusive behavior.[91]

A different standard also appeared applicable for counterterrorism-related auxiliary forces mobilized concurrently with the TMF in the campaign against ISIL. Amid the tribal mobilization happening through the TMF, U.S. Special Forces also identified those whose tribal affiliations and territory crossed the border into Syria, grooming them as auxiliary forces for cross-border counterterrorism operations.[92]

The exact patterns and control mechanisms applied to these tribal auxiliaries can be difficult to identify because the same forces also took part in TMF-organized operations, and received material and salary payments alongside other TMF units who were not operating in this counterterrorism auxiliary capacity. However, the counterterrorism auxiliaries appeared to be treated as a distinct subset, with different partnering modalities, rules, and equipment and training. U.S. officials working on the TMF program noted that the overall program restraints and conditions (including those we might frame as control mechanisms) applicable to the broader TMF did not appear to apply to this subset of cross-border tribal auxiliary forces.[93] For example, these forces were not subject to the same Iraqi government–imposed selection, and they appeared immune to Iraqi-administered command and control or oversight. In addition, they seemed to have a different source of funding. When some of the sources for weapons and salaries for the TMF diminished after the Anbar campaign, these forces continued to receive support. Similarly, when training for the TMF had all but stopped, these select groups continued to receive training, not only by U.S. forces but also by Danish forces (who also had special forces operating on both sides of the border).[94]

They also did not appear to be automatically subject to the same U.S. vetting and oversight applicable to the rest of the TMF.[95] Congressional officials noted that the Leahy Law or other legislative proscriptions like those attached to the broader Train and Equip funding would not apply to forces funded through the so-called 127e fund, which is the most likely source of funding for these Iraqi counterterrorism auxiliaries.[96] Even though not formally required, it is possible that SOF imposed additional constraints—for example, Leahy Law–like human rights vetting—on a policy basis (as happened in Syria). This is difficult to verify one way or another given the secrecy surrounding these forces. Further, the scant public reporting from these border areas, and the fact that these cross-border auxiliary forces were intermixed with other TMF, makes it hard to draw inferences based on distinct conduct patterns. However, given the overall tone taken in counterterrorism operations in Iraq, a stronger assumption would be that where they were not required, conduct-based control mechanisms were not applied to these counterterrorism auxiliaries.[97]

In sum, while knowledge of the control mechanisms deployed with these covert auxiliary forces is inevitably limited, the available information suggests that they were not subject to the same panoply of risk-mitigation measures discussed in the other LHSF examples, particularly those related to laws of war or human rights obligations. It is particularly notable that there was such a sustained exception in Afghanistan, a country that has otherwise provided some of the strongest evidence of trends toward greater restraints and controls.

UNDERSTANDING COUNTERTERRORISM AUXILIARIES' EXCEPTIONALITY: A DELIBERATE CARVE-OUT OR THE BY-PRODUCT OF OPERATING MODALITIES?

The forgoing description of counterterrorism auxiliaries somewhat challenges the overall trajectory described in this chapter of an evolving "common approach" replete with ever-increasing controls and risk-mitigation devices. It is therefore important to examine what distinguishes these LHSF partnerships, and why some of the bargaining or other organizational factors that appeared to trigger controls in other LHSFs might not have generated the same response in these forces.

As a starting point, the lack of extensive conditions and risk-mitigation measures for counterterrorism auxiliaries appears to have been in part a deliberate policy choice. The length of the partnerships and close cooperation in evidence with the Counterterrorism Pursuit Teams in Afghanistan (and their successors, the 01 and 02 forces) suggests that the level of controls or regulation were not the product of short-term expediency or lack of manpower or leverage to develop and apply controls as much as the result of deliberate choices.

A degree of intentionality can also be read in the "no strings attached" tenor of 127e funding, which up until 2021 had enjoyed minimal reporting requirements and none of the congressional strings seen in other regular Train and Equip funding lines. This might change in the future—in 2020, congressional staff mooted additional conditions on 127e funding, including some variant of the Leahy Law or other additional reporting requirements.[98] The FY2021 NDAA, which passed in December 2020, for the first time introduced a human rights–related condition on the 127e funds, requiring DoD to report on "steps taken to ensure that the recipients of support have not engaged in human rights violations."[99] However, prior to 2021, there were very few constraints attached to these counterterrorism funds.

Both principal-agent theory and the larger literature on why states delegate to paramilitary groups offer several reasons as to why the United States might deliberately maintain a less restrictive "gloves off" approach for covert counterterrorism partners. States frequently delegate security tasks to paramilitary or irregular forces as a way to outsource the "dirty work" of violence.[100] The more covert or clandestine the partnership, the greater the degree of plausible deniability, which allows states that care about human rights norms, reputational costs, or the likely geopolitical repercussions of such interventions to avoid or mitigate these consequences.[101] These more covert and shadowy counterterrorism auxiliaries would seem to typify such expectations, particularly the Afghan paramilitaries, whose operations were closer to the pattern of "death squads" than those of other LHSFs in the country. In addition to potentially creating a stronger linkage with the forces in question, thereby eroding plausible deniability on the part of the client, efforts to rigorously regulate the conduct of such forces would also undermine the purpose of delegation where the goal is to outsource unacceptable means of violence.

An explanation grounded in principal-agent theory might view such unsavory violence not as the objective of the delegation (the "outsourcing the dirty work" hypothesis), but as an unavoidable side effect. Principal-agent theory expects a lesser emphasis on control mechanisms in high-priority delegations, or where there is a more limited selection pool, both of which apply in this situation. These auxiliary and surrogate partnerships are accorded extremely high priority because they allow the United States to pursue global counterterrorism objectives with few costs—that is, few U.S. forces on the ground, much less public attention, and correspondingly fewer political constraints. In addition, fielding highly competent militias capable of maintaining operational secrecy is an incredibly specialized task, and as such would draw from an even more limited selection pool than other LHSFs. On this view, the fact that these forces come with higher rates of abuse or other costs and consequences is tolerated because of what they deliver, and the limited options for otherwise pursuing these highly valued counterterrorism objectives.

However, if we adopt this principal-agent explanation—that slack was tolerated and controls not pursued because of the costs and benefits inherent in the situation—this then begs a second question, which is why the same factors that derailed the expectations of principal-agent theory in the other LHSF case studies did not do the same with these counterterrorism auxiliaries. Many of the other LHSFs were also indispensable partners, enabling less U.S. troop exposure in high-priority security situations that were equally limited in terms of choice of viable partner forces. However, as the prior examples illustrated, in case after case, bargaining dynamics and institutional demands and expectations for risk mitigation led to the adoption of control mechanisms.

Instead, the more significant explanation is that the level of secrecy these forces maintain and the areas and contexts in which they operate limit both public and official awareness of their actions, foreclosing potential bargaining moments and the sort of broad-based public pressure that might lead to demands for accountability.

The more limited exposure to bargaining triggers stems from several factors. First, there is limited information, even among a wide range of internal policy makers, about these forces, and a much lower chance of public exposure. Most of these counterterrorism forces operate in areas where insecurity prevents outside access; that plus the covert or classified nature of these operations limits the level of media coverage or reporting. With this limited level of public and even internal U.S. government knowledge about these forces, the sort of stakeholders who were successful in raising objections and bargaining for controls in other LHSF situations would have fewer opportunities to do so here. The secrecy surrounding these groups might also neuter the potential for bargaining with the host country, where government leaders were not informed of the full scope of operations or where the partnership was so small or secret that it failed to generate domestic pressure to rein these forces in.[102]

Limited prospects of public disclosure might also foreclose the need to adopt controls in anticipation of future objections or issues. For example, in the Syria cases, most of the control mechanisms were not required but were adopted voluntarily since those responsible feared being held to public account should risks manifest. One U.S. official observed that even if the forces in Syria were not technically subject to the Leahy Law, the program still had to "pass the *Washington Post* test."[103] By this he meant that there was enough of a risk that war crimes or other misconduct by U.S.-supported forces might be exposed (in the *Washington Post* or other such media outlets). In that event, having some form of due diligence would provide at least a degree of political coverage. However, for forces—like the counterterrorism auxiliaries—whose actions are less likely to face public exposure (because of their size, greater access to covert means of support, and tendency to operate in zones where reporting is less robust), there would be less pressure to adopt preemptive due diligence measures.

The way that counterterrorism auxiliary forces have been buried within larger "by, with, and through" operating patterns further limits the sort of attention that might generate objections or constraints from other players. As noted in the introduction, since 2001, SOF and intelligence agents have pursued counterterrorism targets and objectives in myriad countries worldwide—130 by 2017, according to one public estimate.[104] They frequently do so with the sort of auxiliary forces discussed above acting as force multipliers or surrogate forces.[105] Because there is such a volume of these small auxiliary support partnerships happening on a global basis, not all of them receive congressional attention or trigger substantial internal debate. For example, after U.S. Special Forces were killed alongside partner forces in Niger in October 2017, one news headline aptly summarized the degree of public and congressional awareness, asking, "Why were US soldiers even in Niger?"[106] As one congressional staff member offered, "12 guys in a desert in Niger gets less attention than 30,000 guys in Syria."[107]

This notion of "12 guys in a desert" points to another key point: that the size of these forces matters. The degree to which such secrecy and low attention can be maintained depends not only on the covert or overt nature of these operations, but also on the scale of operations and size of the force. During the early days of the *sahwa*, Petraeus and other commanders tried to dissimulate or hide the significance of the initiative so as not to spark public criticism or Maliki's ire; similarly, SOF in Afghanistan kept a close hold on the early local defense force pilots in 2009 to prevent their being blocked. However, at a certain point, these forces became too big to hide, and too large to be sustained without greater buy-in and approval. Emphasizing this point, one congressional staffer underlined that it was important to think about the "different scale" involved, because the size of the force changes the profile and awareness of the initiative, and in turn the "risk calculus" surrounding it: "say you have Special Forces working with nontraditional units. If they're building one unit—50 to 100 guys—it's different than working with 100,000 people."[108] The latter requires much more support, and funding, he noted, and, "as the dollar amount goes up, then the restrictions go up. From working with one unit to working with tens of thousands of forces, the scrutiny can go from basic due diligence to a bevy of hurdles."[109] Once prominent enough to attract public scrutiny or large enough to trigger an authorization or expansion debate, these initiatives are more susceptible to accountability pressures and the sort of bargaining situations that can lead to control mechanisms.

Reexamining the one covert program discussed so far, the CIA support to the FSA, helps reinforce these distinctions between the sort of smaller counterterrorism auxiliaries discussed above and larger and more prominent LHSFs. Although technically covert, the CIA support to the FSA was too large to keep quiet, with some 20,000 forces eventually provided weapons or equipment by the time of its closure.[110] It became the "worst-kept secret covert action program in history," in one security expert's reckoning.[111] There were ample media reports of the program's mechanics, the type of aid, and which groups were supported.[112] Cabinet officials referenced it in public testimony.[113] There were even administration responses to allegations of abuse by supported partner forces.[114] As such, it was exposed to some of the same public accountability pressures as other overt LHSFs discussed. In addition, the greater knowledge and attention to the program, even within the administration, generated a substantial bargaining moment. As documented in chapter 3, there was a nearly year-long authorization debate during which objectors, first within the higher levels of the Obama administration and then within Congress, had ample opportunities to force concessions and controls.[115]

By contrast, counterterrorism auxiliaries are generally small enough to be funded out of CIA and SOF funds (like the 127e funds) without the need for a larger, force-specific appropriation. SOF do not need to seek congressional permission or higher-level authorization each time they pursue a target or engage in such auxiliary force partnerships. The U.S. interpretation of sovereign self-defense would permit its forces and agents to pursue threats to U.S. national security wherever they manifest, and the open-ended congressional authorization introduced with the 2001 Authorization for Military Force covers the domestic legal basis for most operations without needing further congressional approval.[116] Although there is annual and monthly reporting to Congress on these operations, such reporting tends to be at the level of general operating profiles and missions, and does not tend to trigger a specific authorization debate and questioning of the risks involved in any given auxiliary force.

Relatedly, because in many of these countries, SOF may partner with auxiliary forces only for a one-off mission or short period of time, the operation may not even trigger the congressional notification requirements for the funds in question.[117] Even if there were congressional awareness, Congress is not well positioned to consider the risk dynamics in each of these missions in a way that might result in conditions or controls. As one congressional staffer (the same person who noted the lack of attention to the events in Niger) observed, neither Congress nor the public has the capacity to keep track of so many global operating spaces in a way that might result in meaningful controls. "Surrogate and proxy wars are very gray areas. Most folks on the Hill don't have enough time to understand the situation and dynamics" to an extent that would allow them to develop "tailored conditions," he said.[118]

As a result of all of these factors, most of the smaller counterterrorism auxiliaries have not generated an authorization debate, limiting opportunities for critics in the executive branch or in Congress to demand additional controls. The imposition of constraints on the 127e fund under FY2021 funding, which also created additional reporting requirements, may lead to a shift in such bargaining dynamics.[119] It may lead to greater congressional awareness of specific operations and partnerships and the sort of authorizing moments or bargaining triggers that open the possibility for more conditions and constraints.

A third important distinguishing element relates to the institutional lenses and intentions attached to these forces. A strong theme of BPA is the way that foreign policy images or lenses can influence the way that decision makers react. Such lenses might also influence how a particular LHSF is viewed, how its costs, benefits, and risks are assessed, and the tools or policy prescriptions deemed appropriate for that force. For example, the larger and more overt LHSF initiatives like the ALP or the TMF tended to be mobilized as "hold" or local "counterinsurgency" forces, or to some degree even viewed as an exercise in "bottom-up" state building. By contrast, counterterrorism auxiliary forces tend to be used purely as surrogate forces, "force multipliers," or intelligence assets, without a larger governance or political role.

Such ascriptions or lenses (whether accurate or not) matter because the bureaucracy will weigh the potential benefits of the force, as well as the costs and consequences, through these lenses. Enforcing conduct standards may be perceived as more important for a counterinsurgency force, in line with mission goals of "population protection" or "winning hearts and minds." Similarly, the risk that a given force will seed local conflict, or that it will be seen to hold significant coercive power outside of state control, might be given greater weight for a force that is imbued with a governance or state-building role. The prior evidence suggests that such distinctions and lenses became even more important over time, as distinct expectations arose surrounding a particular type of force. As the TMF case study illustrated, by 2014 there was a set of expectations surrounding what were appropriate restrictions for "hold" forces, which in turn led to differences in the way these groups were treated compared to the cross-border counterterrorism auxiliaries operating in their midst.

These lenses might also influence the likelihood that controls will be imposed by invoking either a wider or narrower circle of players. The wider the mandate ascribed to the force, the more likely that other parts of the bureaucracy or other stakeholders' interests would be invoked, which might make bargaining dynamics more likely. For example, a LHSF force that was seen as either a complement or a potential competitor to other state-building goals and initiatives might be more likely to trigger objections from civilian quarters of the U.S. government than one whose contribution was more narrowly focused on tactical military gains. This offers another example of how organizational lenses can influence the controls brought to bear, with the lenses attached to these forces then largely determining the breadth and composition of the bargaining arena.

The discussion of counterterrorism auxiliaries provides additional nuance to our evolving expectations of where control mechanisms might manifest with LHSFs. Previous case studies have suggested that more contentious bargaining situations are more likely to lead to a range of controls. This analysis builds on that claim by suggesting that these bargaining opportunities are more likely to arise in forces of a certain size and duration, because they are harder to keep quiet and need more support and buy-in across a range of U.S. stakeholders, or with the host government in question. Similarly, for larger and more widely known forces, officials have to be more attentive to public demands for accountability and the risks of domestic political constraints or reputation costs. This does not fully contradict the idea of there being an emerging common approach, but it does suggest an important limitation—that this approach has evolved to apply only to LHSFs that rise to a certain size and level of public attention and funding.

What emerges from the forgoing discussion is a bifurcated approach, with two clear typologies or categories of LHSFs, and differing levels and types of controls associated with each:

1) counterterrorism partnerships—usually short-term, covert or secret, and small in size; they are used as auxiliary or surrogate forces in support of discrete intelligence goals or kinetic operations; and
2) counterinsurgent or local defense forces—typically overt, larger, less specialized, and community-based forces; they may be mobilized to advance both security and other state-building, governance, or political goals.

The differing intentions regarding these forces, the differing institutional masters they tend to be managed by, and the covert or overt status set up different parameters for how such forces are treated and different SOPs or scripts for regulating them. For the latter category of counterinsurgency or local defense forces, the applicable SOP or regulatory framework would be the common approach outlined in previous case studies. It includes a relatively high number of controls, including those related to human rights and restraining misconduct. By contrast, the differing operating profile and lens or purpose ascribed to counterterrorism auxiliaries allowed them to fly under the radar of common bargaining prompts and triggers, creating a built-in exception to this common approach.

Finally, although counterterrorism auxiliaries have so far been exempted from the common risk-mitigation approach, the recent amendment to the 127e funds suggests that they are not completely immune from this larger trend toward control mechanisms. It may simply be that, for all the reasons noted so far, it has taken longer for them to attract the sort of bargaining demands and momentum that would lead to such constraints. With the passage of time, and with a greater degree of public and congressional attention to the practice as a whole, this might cumulatively lead to some demands for controls, of which the FY2021 changes are the first piece of evidence. Such an interpretation, while necessarily preliminarily given the recentness of these developments, might further strengthen the claim that there is a growing trend toward imposing these sorts of controls on partner operations over time, even in the most clandestine relationships.

STANDARDS, AND EXCEPTIONS, WITHIN AN EMERGING COMMON APPROACH

The first section of this chapter used material from some of the Syria case studies to identify how organizational dynamics might interact with bargaining demands to jointly generate control mechanisms. With the first three Syria case studies, bargaining queued a need for risk-mitigation devices and controls; but where it did so, SOPs, organizational protocols, and past approaches supplied the ready content for these control mechanisms.

The subsequent two case studies on the TMF and the ANA-TF introduced the idea of legacy effects as another institutional lens and an important means of both policy transfer and reinforcement. The legacies of the *sahwa* and ALP initiatives affected the tactics, demands, and scripts within the deliberations over whether to authorize the TMF and the ANA-TF. Policy makers saw the challenges in their respective country environments, as well as potential solutions, through the lens of past experience. When faced with exigent security challenges, they repurposed existing models of LHSFs in those countries, including their control mechanisms. These legacy effects and the reflection on past experiences largely determined the parameters of the debate, and also queued the control mechanisms that would be deemed appropriate for resolving any issues.

Bargaining effects were not absent with regard to the TMF and ANA-TF, but the bargaining demands and triggers tended to be interpreted through the lens of prior debates, past LHSF experiences, and controls. As such, bargaining was less significant in explaining the majority of control mechanisms that emerged in these latter LHSFs. There was an important interaction, though, between these bargaining dynamics and the legacy effects. By providing a more ready pathway for resolving differences in positions vis-à-vis these forces, these legacy effects may have made it more likely that a compromise would be reached and the forces authorized.

The interaction between such bargaining and legacy effects explains many of the controls that arose in the TMF and the ANA-TF, but not all of them. There was also evidence within the TMF and the ANA-TF of the same controls seen in earlier LHSFs being applied almost by rote or as a default practice for these sorts of forces. Together with the organizational reflections on the Syria cases, this contributes to the idea of an evolving common approach to risk mitigation. Although it would be hard to argue it was standardized to the point of being a fixed policy or template, the following risk-mitigation measures were part of the standard menu for responding to perceived risk and accountability issues with LHSFs:

- human rights and counterterrorism-related vetting;
- provision of standards via training, codes of conduct, or other established redlines; standards including some basic awareness of key human rights and laws of armed conflict obligations;
- oversight and monitoring, including remote monitoring and tracking, co-location and U.S. force mentoring, or institutionalization in the host state; and
- enforcement measures, most often to be blocked from U.S. funding and support, but sometimes also other checks and balances or incentives.

The final set of examples surrounding CIA and SOF auxiliary or surrogate forces in Afghanistan and Iraq introduced cases that did not appear to follow this pattern. However, rather than contradicting the importance of bargaining or organizational tendencies in explaining controls, a closer examination suggests that the differing contexts in which counterterrorism auxiliary forces are used, and the differing operating modalities surrounding them, have simply been less likely to trigger bargaining demands or institutional constraints. Their profile, size, and the way they are usually deployed tends to regularly circumvent bargaining pressures, limiting the opportunities for objections to be raised and then countered via control mechanisms. As such, rather than detracting from the idea of an emerging approach, this analysis of the exceptions reinforces the significance of bargaining and institutional lenses or niches in explaining the manifestation of control mechanisms.

Cumulatively, the different case studies point to more of a rule-but-exception framework. They suggest that there has been a trend toward a greater number of control mechanisms for LHSFs, the "common approach" or menu outlined above. However, the operating modalities and lenses attached to counterterrorism auxiliaries create an exception to this rule. The next chapter will build on this idea of an emerging common approach by exploring what mechanisms or processes might have led to the bureaucratic internalization of that common menu of controls. This requires greater consideration of which processes result in change over time, and of the socialization of such ad hoc practices into a standing bureaucratic repertoire of controls.

5

CHANGE OVER TIME

Transnational Networks, the Leahy Law, and
Human Rights Checks for Local and Substate Forces

The prior chapter considered means of policy transfer and evidence of an emerging common approach to LHSF risk mitigation. But this evidence then begs another question: By what mechanisms or processes might such controls become internalized as SOPs within the bureaucracy? One of the long-standing critiques of BPA, and in particular its organizational theories, is that bureaucratic practices and SOPs are assumed to be so fixed that it is hard to derive an account of change in a given policy over time—something that would allow for the emergence of a new SOP or norm.[1] This chapter responds to that question by examining the development and adoption of human rights controls over time, and the transnational advocacy networks that consistently pushed for their erection and development.

Exploring this particular group of actors is helpful for responding to this question because the literature surrounding transnational networks already has a theory of how normative, bureaucratic, and policy changes happen over time in response to transnational advocacy. The way that these nongovernmental or transnational actors and networks influence foreign policy decisions tends to be portrayed as a multistep or incremental process.[2] These outside actors may capitalize on particular opportunities or moments for change—for example, to press for a commitment to a certain standard through a new treaty or piece of legislation, or to change the "rules of the game" by creating rules or procedures that might shape future policy outcomes in a way that advances their agenda. However, they will also work to gradually nudge forward behavior and advance incremental policy changes by socializing desired norms and practices, or by attempting to influence the way policies or rules are implemented in practice.[3]

This chapter will explore these processes of bureaucratic change and adoption by considering two key junctures or stages in the development of human rights controls. First, it will dive back into examples of how human rights advocates and networks pushed for human rights controls and constraints on the ALP, not just in the authorization debate but over the entire ten-year lifetime of the ALP. Examples from this more extended persuasion and pressure campaign illustrate how pushes for incremental change, and for realizing commitments in practice, can gradually socialize certain standards and processes. Contrary to expectations, this resulted in additional human rights controls over the life of the ALP, and also helped to reinforce evolving SOPs of human rights controls for LHSFs.

Second, the chapter will analyze a particular juncture where collaboration between U.S. (domestic) civil society, transnational human rights networks, congressional actors, and internal Obama administration advocates resulted in a major change in the "rules of the game" concerning human rights controls—a series of legislative and administrative rule changes surrounding the Leahy Law. Exploring the particular "policy assemblage"[4] that contributed to these changes offers an example of transnational actors contributing to changes to the rules of the game, while also providing a key link to the overall narrative described in this chapter—of how human rights controls became embedded in U.S. bureaucratic approaches.

These two campaigns or international advocacy projects interacted; in large part because of the degree of advocacy and attention to human rights abuses by Afghan forces, Afghanistan became a test case and important site of practice for the newly revamped Leahy Law. Examining these two examples together thus helps to illustrate the multistep and incremental processes that might over time generate new repertoires of control and risk-mitigation mechanisms. The combination of rule changes at key moments, repeat pressure to accept and apply these controls, and then reinforcement through regular practice, helped establish these human rights controls firmly within the U.S. bureaucracy's repertoire of accountability mechanisms.

This chapter focuses on NGOs and transnational actors and their role in cementing human rights controls as part of a "common approach" to LHSF mitigation. However, this is not intended to suggest that human rights advocates were the only mechanisms of change and bureaucratic normalization over time, nor that this sort of internalization was confined only to human rights–related control mechanisms. Instead, the case studies or perspectives included in this chapter should be taken as select examples that illustrate the dynamics of policy transfer, as well as SOP evolution and development. These are intended to illustrate why and how common approaches toward risk mitigation with LHSFs might emerge, but not necessarily to suggest that these were the sole actors or dynamics driving practice across the range of control mechanism described in this book.

NORM AND PRACTICE REINFORCEMENT OVER TIME IN THE ALP

Chapter 2 introduced the idea that NGOs and other human rights advocates played a role during the authorization debate for the ALP, even if they might not be described as full players. Human rights NGOs, civil society members, and UN actors pushed first and foremost for U.S. forces to abandon the idea of mobilizing new militias. Failing that, they argued for at least placing strong human rights controls and checks on any forces that were created. As chapter 2 discussed, they succeeded to some degree. For example, the creation of human rights–related controls in the ALP (background checks and screening on the basis of past evidence of abuses, explicit training on human rights, other mechanisms of oversight and accountability) appeared linked to efforts to win over or neutralize this contingent. However, human rights advocacy on these issues did not stop with ALP authorization. It continued throughout the life of the ALP and, unlike many of the other control mechanisms (which were dropped almost as soon as the program devolved), resulted in additional or strengthened human rights controls over time.[5]

To better examine this longer trajectory of ALP engagement, it is helpful to first reflect on what the literature on transnational networks and normative change suggests about tools of persuasion and influence. In their seminal account of how advocacy networks influence international politics, Margaret Keck and Kathryn Sikkink offer four key tools or tactics of influence, what they call information politics, symbolic politics, leverage politics, and accountability politics.[6] With information politics, NGOs or other transnational actors can use information, evidence, and documentation to shed light on an issue, to frame the debate, and to generate credible policy solutions. Through "accountability politics," NGOs or other transnational networks may also call for powerful actors to be held to account for existing policy commitments or to a certain set of international standards, a strategy also sometimes more popularly framed as "naming and shaming" governments into action.[7] They might undertake these strategies more effectively in combination with "leverage politics," which could refer to strategies of associating an issue with other material, monetary, or other strategic goals, or of simply leveraging relationships with other, more powerful actors.[8] More simply put, "finding a sympathetic ear in high places" can be one of the most effective influence strategies, according to Ann Florini.[9]

Such strategies are even more effective where transnational networks are able to advance an issue from multiple policy loci or positions. Thomas Risse identifies transnational networks' ability to exert pressure both "from above" and also "from below"—at a local, decision-maker level and with other international or transnational audiences and pressure points—as a key advantage.[10]

The activity preceding and surrounding the ALP reads as a textbook example of such strategies and tactics. Years of documentation, "naming and shaming," and public advocacy helped shape the agenda and policy discourse in Afghanistan, such that by the time the ALP was proposed, concerns about unruly militias and prevention of civilian harm were already built into the parameters of the debate.[11] Once the local defense forces had begun operating and the proposal to authorize and expand them was initiated, transnational advocates also used the tactics of documentation, public "naming and shaming," and dialogue with key military and policy officials—both in Afghanistan and back in Washington, DC—to further frame the debate and the policy responses to it, including those to do with controls. Already while the pilot programs were underway, national and international human rights advocates and international organizations, including Human Rights Watch, the International Committee of the Red Cross (ICRC), the Afghanistan Independent Human Rights Commission, and the UNAMA human rights unit, began documenting abuses by the local defense forces, as well as other issues in the programs.[12] Evidence of abuses by past pro-government militias, or by the pilot local defense forces themselves, were used demonstrate to policy makers the issues with these forces, to show the gap between pledged promises about the program and actual conduct, and to propose policy recommendations.[13] Among these were policy proposals for further checks and controls—for specific training on human rights, stronger vetting mechanisms to exclude those who had committed past violations, tighter accountability and oversight mechanisms, and restrictions on certain operating modalities or duties that might run a higher risk of civilian harm.[14]

While NGOs or other advocates will certainly seek to promote policy change at discrete junctures (as in the ALP authorization debate), the literature on social movements, normative change, and transnational advocacy in many ways anticipates an even greater impact over time. The key assets and tools that NGOs, civil society, and transnational networks might have—developing clear documentation and evidence, using it to influence public opinion and pressure points, or building a campaign of internal and external advocates with collective leverage over key policy questions—are likely to take longer to come to fruition. Strategies of engagement and persuasion campaigns are presumed to be more effective as a repeat process because the repetition is a central part of socialization.[15] As scholars Thomas Risse and Stephen Ropp argue, "involving and entangling norm violating governments in an argumentative process which then becomes self-sustained, constitutes an extremely powerful socializing tool."[16]

Martha Finnemore and Kathryn Sikkink offer another way to think about how such continued engagement results in behavior change over time. They frame socialization and norm adoption as a multistep process, with international organizations or NGOs first pushing for a policy or standard to be erected, "teaching" how it should be interpreted and applied, and then pushing for further enforcement, application, and practice over time.[17] They offer the example of the ICRC as a "socializing agent." The ICRC first pressures states to ratify treaties or otherwise comply with the standards of international humanitarian law, and then follows up by teaching state forces or policy makers about the rules they have committed to, and collecting information and monitoring compliance as a way to "pressure violators to conform."[18] Such practices might be seen both as a form of accountability politics, used to nudge better compliance and change over time, and as ways of socializing or contributing to the internalization of a norm. Richard Price argues that this sort of "teaching" results in states not only learning the appropriate response or practice, but also learning to identify the behavior in question as problematic: "Both the problem and the solution are taught to governments, who come to see new practices as appropriate for themselves as members of international society."[19] In sum, transnational advocates or networks can use long-term engagement strategies to nudge forward incremental policy changes, while gradually socializing ideas or norms in ways that might lead to shifts in policy positions over time.

A last important concept in thinking through norm or rule socialization and change over time concerns the role of practice. Keck and Sikkink argue that where NGOs or other transnational actors are able to pressure or persuade those in power to translate commitments into practice—which they define as "the act of doing something repeatedly"—and where that practice becomes so routinized that it gains a "taken-for-granted quality," it can signal a deeper and self-reinforcing normative shift.[20] When powerful actors not only commit to certain standards, but the bureaucracy is then regularly reminded of those standards and pressured to apply them routinely, those principles or practices can become internalized and take on this self-reinforcing or "SOP" quality.

All of these strategies can be seen in the nearly ten-year campaign surrounding the ALP. International and national human rights organizations, the UNAMA human rights unit, and other transnational research or advocacy organizations regularly documented evidence of human rights abuses or other issues by ALP members, clear gaps between what the ALP rules and regulations required and actual practice.[21] This happened not just during the buildup to the ALP and the authorization debate, but throughout the life of the ALP. In keeping with transnational advocacy theory, there were efforts to increase pressure "from below," within the Afghanistan policy space, and also "from above." Human rights advocates met with U.S. DoD and State Department officials in DC and with U.S. congressional representatives, or with policy makers in the capitals of other NATO states, to raise key points about human rights concerns and deficits with controls.[22] Afghan officials or SOF advisers in Afghanistan might not directly be persuaded by NGO engagement. But they might be forced to respond to Pentagon officials' orders to do so, which were themselves often driven by congressional threats to cut funding for the program (a near annual threat according to staffers).[23]

Illustrating the role of documentation in driving pressure from above and below, in 2011 Human Rights Watch (HRW) published a scathing report on the ALP and the predecessor local defense forces. It documented numerous abuses, warlord connections, and ways that the program fell far short of the promises of accountable and controlled forces.[24] The report generated such significant public and ultimately congressional attention that DoD was forced to launch a formal inquiry into the allegations, a process that lasted over a year and resulted in a thousand-page follow-up report.[25] The DoD investigation was largely aimed at rebutting the initial claims, but it nonetheless helped spur some policy reforms. It revealed that many of the early pilot programs or ad hoc initiatives had not applied the Leahy Law to Afghan local forces. Although not formally announced as a policy, from this point on, the Leahy Law became firmly attached to the ALP vetting processes. Moreover, some immediate measures were taken to address issues in vetting. In mid-2012, ISAF and the MoI tightened procedures for vetting, re-vetted more than half of the then 18,000 members, and pledged a "more pro-active approach" to investigating misconduct and addressing abuses.[26] Also following the HRW report (with the change attributed to that report), CFSOCC-A (Combined Forces Special Operations Component Command—Afghanistan) issued several new directives, including one stipulating that SOF partnering with the ALP must report any allegations of abuses, and where such abuses were significant enough, cease working with those forces.[27] The HRW report and other continuing documentation also contributed to other changes in oversight and in ALP conduct restrictions, including longer training (from three to four weeks) and with greater specificity on human rights and ethics. A 2014 DoD report to Congress attributed the change to "ethical concerns about the ALP cited by international organizations."[28]

In addition to public pressure campaigns, human rights advocates had regular meetings with members of the ISAF command, members of the MoI charged with overseeing the ALP, or members of the U.S. SOF advisory cell for the ALP, either to push for policy or rule changes, or to "teach" the content of those rules. For example, almost from the inception of the program, UNAMA's human rights unit called for "putting in place accountability structures/personnel to investigate complaints of [Afghan Local] police abuse within the Ministry of the Interior."[29] After the MoI created the ALP Monitoring and Investigation unit in mid-2012 (which in itself might be described as a new control mechanism), it began working with this unit to strengthen how it was applying MoI rules and procedures.[30] UNAMA officials met monthly with this new unit, referred cases of ALP abuses to it, and used such evidence to show gaps between the unit's oversight mandate and its actual record of investigations and prosecutions. Over time, the number of ALP members investigated and referred for disciplinary action or prosecution increased.[31] In essence, human rights advocates first pushed for the principle of a regular accountability process for the ALP, and then once the unit was created, worked with its members to "teach" them about investigatory practices and regular accountability processes, and to both enable and increase pressure for enforcement.

As a result of such efforts, the number and strength of human rights–related or conduct-based controls increased over time to include longer and more detailed training on human rights and international humanitarian law; more specific program rules that prohibited engagement in activities that human rights advocates worried about (notably restriction from detention activities); more elaborate and more frequently applied oversight mechanisms; and additional vetting and sanctioning requirements based on human rights conduct. Table 5.1 briefly summarizes the most important of these additional human rights–related or conduct-based controls.

The increase in human rights controls is all the more notable given that other promised control mechanisms were allowed to lapse almost as soon as the program was initiated. Those that SOF had fronted in the pilot programs as the strongest means of control—careful site selection, SOF embedding within and mentoring the forces, and community engagement and controls—gave way to implementation pressures almost

TABLE 5.1 Developments in human rights–related controls for the ALP over time

Initial human rights– and conduct-based controls at ALP authorization (August 2010)	Controls added or strengthened after authorization
Training that includes basic concepts in human rights and international humanitarian law	Longer training, including greater specificity in human rights and IHL
Program rules and codes of conduct restricting offensive operations, reinforcing good conduct	Additional restrictions, such as prohibiting ALP engagement in detention operations (by March 2011)
MoI oversight and enforcement (authority to enforce MoI regulations and Afghan law; command oversight through chief of police)	Creation of ALP Monitoring and Investigation unit within MoI (mid-2012); gradual increase in investigations and prosecutions over time
SOF engagement and mentorship (implicitly would reinforce good conduct principles)	2012 rule for SOF reporting on human rights abuses and cut-off of abusive forces
Community vetting (presumed to select against abusive or predatory individuals/militias); Afghan government background checks (filtering for criminality and drug abuse)	Leahy Law vetting (and potential for blocks) applied to the ALP, at least from 2014; 2012 changes in the vetting process to better capture a record of abuse or corruption; and re-vetting of over half of the force for such issues*

* UNAMA, *Protection of Civilians in Armed Conflict Annual Report 2012* (Kabul: Office of the High Commission for Human Rights, 2013), 43.

immediately.[32] These and other control mechanisms that were dropped had been useful for prevailing in the authorization debate, but as soon as the debate was over, the real costs of applying these mechanisms materialized. By contrast, the pressure and persuasion tactics from NGOs, civil society, and other human rights allies made attention to human rights concerns a continuing bargaining issue, reinforcing the need for human rights control mechanisms throughout the life of the ALP.

An additional point to draw from the trajectory of increased human rights controls is an understanding of how success at changing "rules of the game" at discrete moments, together with repeated pressure and reinforcement spurring the actual enactment or practice of these rules, might contribute to rule internalization. The specific example of NGO pressure over the Leahy Law in Afghanistan helps to illustrate this.

THE LEAHY LAW MEETS ALP ADVOCACY: CALLS TO RESPOND AND TO PRACTICE

As discussed in prior chapters, the so-called Leahy Law prohibits U.S. assistance from going to security forces of a foreign country who have committed gross human rights abuses. It does this by requiring that any unit or individual set to receive State Department or DoD assistance (save for some exceptions) must be vetted against a database of known human rights abuses maintained by the State Department's Bureau of Democracy, Rights, and Labor, or DRL.[33] Where there is "credible information implicating that unit in the commission of gross violations of human rights," the offending individual(s) and their wider unit will be "blocked" from funding, unless steps are taken by the host government to hold them to account, known as "remediation."[34] Remediation could be satisfied through formal charges and prosecution for the individuals involved, or by vaguer processes, such as disciplinary measures, retraining, or reorganization of the unit in cases where only some individuals within it are implicated.[35] Importantly for this book, the Leahy Law functions as both a vetting mechanism and a sanction. U.S. officials' efforts to apply it may also force a degree of monitoring and oversight.

Among the various human rights controls that NGOs pressured for in the ALP, applying the Leahy Law vetting and sanctions was a key priority. NGO reports and public rebukes on the ALP called out the lack of vetting on the basis of past misconduct from the very first pilot programs, throughout the life of the ALP. Advocates pushed for human rights scrutiny to be an explicit standard in the vetting of the force and then, once it was clear that the Leahy Law was considered to be applicable to the ALP, called out examples of abusive commanders who had not been blocked.[36] As noted above, continued attention drove some changes and improvements in human rights vetting policies or practice for the ALP, including explicit vetting provisions built into the initial ALP model, a commitment to strengthen vetting and to re-vet existing members following the 2011 HRW report, and a shift to formally require Leahy Law vetting for the ALP.

Because this was a repeat process carried out over a ten-year span, it gained a sort of rote or routine quality, calcifying expectations that human rights vetting was an appropriate way to demonstrate accountability. Throughout the lifetime of the ALP, and then continuing with the ANA-TF, whenever public criticisms reached a head, DoD officials or those working on the issue at the U.S. embassy in Kabul or in the U.S. military command within ISAF would respond by committing to apply the Leahy Law more fully. This was the case with the 2011 HRW report. It also happened after several different iterations of UNAMA annual reporting that provided substantial evidence of ALP abuses, as well as after several scathing reports from the Special Inspector General for Afghanistan Reconstruction about loopholes in Leahy Law application in Afghanistan.[37] After such public callouts (often accompanied by further congressional pressure), U.S. officials responded by committing to improve processes or mechanisms for stronger implementation, issuing additional guidance to U.S. forces and personnel, or (as in 2012) re-vetting parts of the Afghan force. As identified in the prior chapter, by the time the new ALP-like ANA-TF was established, calls to apply the Leahy Law human rights vetting and blocks to these forces was so well ingrained that it became an almost automatic response to concerns of human rights risks. NGO calls for accountability triggered a response in the form of a commitment to apply the Leahy Law and other human rights standards. It was an internalization of this mechanism as an appropriate policy response to demands for accountability.

In addition, in keeping with the theory of NGOs and transnational networks working "from above" and "from below," many of the same NGOs and human rights advocates who were pressing for stronger human rights enforcement or controls on the ground in Afghanistan were also involved in pushing for improvements in the Leahy Law back in Washington, DC. Afghanistan was not the sole focus of this advocacy, but it would come to play a significant role in testing improvements to the law.

The Leahy Law had been passed as a regular (annual) provision of the U.S. Foreign Appropriations Act since 1998. However, for the first decade of its existence, the Leahy Law was largely under-implemented.[38] The earlier versions of the law included more exceptions and a narrower definition of what constituted "assistance," meaning that it was not applied to many categories of U.S. support and programming. There were also numerous implementation challenges—from how vetting might be applied on a systemic basis, to inadequate staff resources devoted to fully applying it, to a lack of political will on the part of U.S. embassies, which are the first point of response in initiating Leahy Law scrutiny and vetting.[39]

Beginning with FY2010 funding, Congress appropriated more funds and support to allow DRL to operationalize Leahy vetting more robustly, including by building a new global database against which all prospective fundees would be vetted. Congress also broadened the scope of activities for which the Leahy Law was applicable and clarified some of the ambiguities that had enabled loose enforcement.[40] DoD and the State Department responded with a series of memorandums or implementing regulations that would improve coordination and implementation of the Leahy Law.[41] Among the most significant of these, in 2012 the State Department's Office of Legal Affairs revisited the interpretation of "assistance" in the Leahy Law, and determined that it applied to virtually any form of funding or programming—meaning that it would include support for conferences, dialogues, or other nonmaterial "assistance." This was a much more expansive reading of "assistance" than in prior practice, and it would mean that the Leahy Law applied to a much wider swath of U.S. assistance, particularly of State Department assistance. Empowered with this renewed congressional mandate and led by appointees who were dedicated to pushing it, DRL became much more active in pressing other parts of the State Department and DoD to implement the law.

What factors drove such reforms? To frame the post-2009 reforms, it is useful to look back to the context and actors surrounding the original creation of the Leahy Law. Winifred Tate offers the concept of a "policy assemblage" to capture how NGO and congressional collaboration, happening at a particular moment of policy opening, led to the creation of the Leahy Law.[42] Starting in the early 1970s, Congress began attaching human rights conditions to U.S. military and economic assistance bills for countries with a long track record of abuses, including Colombia, Argentina, Chile, and Uruguay.[43] Congressional efforts to highlight such abuses and generate restrictions were significantly enabled by the increasing professionalism and transnational activity in the NGO field, Tate argues.

Transnational NGOs linked to grassroots networks and individual activists in these countries furnished credible documentation of abuses, driving public attention and pressure toward these issues. Moreover, the crucial element of this "policy assemblage" was that these transnational NGOs, with their grassroots counterparts, worked in concert with those who had policy-making authority and an interest in policy change. Congressional staff, such as Tim Rieser on Senator Leahy's powerful Appropriations Committee staff, invited NGOs to help develop public hearings, and even to review legislative funding provisions before they were introduced. In addition, Tate notes, such NGO and congressional collaboration was happening at a moment that was more favorable to human rights expression in U.S. foreign policy.[44] It was all of these factors and elements—the alliance between well-positioned congressional aides and activist NGOs, acting jointly at the right ideational flex point for change on this issue—that generated a policy assemblage behind greater human rights constraints on U.S. security assistance and that made the creation of the Leahy Law possible.

A similar range of congruent factors might be identified in the post-2009 reforms to the Leahy Law. Barack Obama's 2008 win, together with a Democratic majority in the Senate from 2007 to 2015, strengthened the hands of advocates for stronger human rights accountability. Senator Leahy, a Democrat, had greater seniority on committees than he had enjoyed in the 1980s and 1990s; that plus the Democrats' majority position gave him even more power over appropriations bills and processes. In addition, the composition of the Obama administration and the people brought within it made for an executive branch that was much more open to the idea of greater Leahy Law enforcement and to encoding greater accountability measures within the rules of the bureaucracy. This was an administration with Samantha Power—a long-standing human rights and accountability advocate—in a senior White House position. The chief State Department lawyer was Harold Koh, a law professor who had written extensively and sympathetically on human rights norms and promotion. The former Washington, DC, office directors for both HRW and the Open Society Foundations—organizations that had long championed the Leahy Law—were appointed to prominent positions in DRL.[45]

There were also developments and activities on the nongovernmental side of this policy assemblage. NGOs and civil society organizations had for many years documented failings in the Leahy Law—for example, foreign officials or forces who continued to receive assistance despite flagrant human rights abuses.[46] They commissioned research to identify issues in implementing the law and then framed this information in specific requests for reform, raising such concerns with either Senator Leahy's staff or executive branch officials.[47] Such long-standing evidence showing the gaps in the U.S. government's implementation of its own standards created external pressure for reforms, and also helped set the agenda and inform the proposals for how to adjust Leahy Law practices. Similar to NGO input into proposed human rights riders and legislation in the 1980s and 1990s, this was not simply a matter of external pressure—it was also an example of active collaboration. NGOs continued to work with Senator Leahy's staff (still through the same chief of staff, Tim Rieser), with NGOs reviewing proposed legislative amendments or internal rule changes before they were passed to provide feedback, actively given a role in public hearings, and other joint pressure strategies.[48]

All of this describes the particular ingredients of the policy assemblage that would enable passage of Leahy Law reforms from 2009 onward. However, what is arguably even more important for the focus of this chapter is the policy assemblage that contributed to greater efforts to apply these new rules in practice. Afghanistan played a particular role within the Leahy Law expansion, similar to that played by Colombia and other Latin American countries in the earlier period of Leahy development. Afghanistan offered a prominent example of abusive forces continuing to receive support. NGO documentation and advocacy of abuses by Afghan forces together generated the pressure to apply the law as well as the fuel to do so. The well-documented examples of abusive Afghan forces provided key test cases for the newly expanded Leahy Law mechanisms. No sooner had the new reforms been passed than NGOs and journalists began forwarding evidence of Afghan units and commanders implicated in gross violations to DRL in an effort to help populate the newly created database.[49] This provided the "credible evidence" that would in theory create the trip wire for the United States to cut abusive forces under the Leahy Law.

If greater evidence of abuses by Afghan forces was the spur to a more focused application of the law in practice, greater bureaucratic experience and resources in-country furnished the means to do so. The degree of U.S. resources, knowledge, and personnel in-country can matter a good deal in terms of how robustly the Leahy Law is implemented. The initial starting point for vetting under the Leahy Law is the U.S. embassy in the country in question, and so the likelihood that vetting will be applied, and applied appropriately, depends to some extent on the personnel in each country and their knowledge of the forces in question. Staff typically have information about the overall organizational structure of the force and some understanding of patterns of concern, as identified through media or NGO reporting or the State Department's annual human rights report for that country. But this usually does not amount to the sort of granular detail—which specific units or commanders were known to be involved in abuses—that would be necessary to block individuals under the Leahy Law. Nor are most embassies staffed in ways that would allow for proactive investigations or inquiry into more accurate vetting. In most embassies, one or at most two staff members oversee a large, multimillion-dollar portfolio of security assistance. They are not equipped with the sort of investigatory resources that would be needed to go beyond the organizational chart-level of detail.

In addition, the Leahy Law process requires that prospective recipients of U.S. security assistance are cross-checked against the database of known offenders (based on the "credible evidence" standard) maintained by DRL back in Washington, DC. A drawback of this process is that the vetting is only as good as the database itself. In countries for which the U.S. government has less data, or where there is less public documentation and reporting available (for example, due to restraints on media, limitations in access due to security, or a less active civil society presence), the record would likely be incomplete, and vetting would fail to capture many of those with past records of abuse.

These practical limitations on vetting were not present in Afghanistan, at least not up until the major troop withdrawals took place in 2014. By 2012 and 2013, when the legislative and administrative reforms to the Leahy Law began to take effect, the United States had spent more than a decade in Afghanistan, with military or civilian staff deployed across Afghan ministries, and even down to the district level in areas across Afghanistan. As a result, the U.S. government was the "holder of information, not just following up on reports," one former DoD official said.[50] It had more capacity to investigate allegations of abuse, greater knowledge of the Afghan systems and institutional organizations, and more longstanding relationships with Afghan officials, which would help in wielding the carrot-and-stick approach built into the Leahy Law. The U.S. bureaucracy was arguably better positioned to apply the Leahy Law in Afghanistan than anywhere else.

As a result, when Congress indicated further steps to tighten the Leahy Law in 2013 and 2014, DoD decided to develop a more proactive system of pursuing Leahy investigations in Afghanistan.[51] DoD staff actively looked for allegations of gross violations of human rights by Afghan forces (including but not limited to the ALP) by scanning news media, internal intelligence reports, or other sources.[52] DoD and State Department officials would then meet monthly to review any potential allegations and decide whether to block or clear an accused force based on the credibility of the allegations.[53] This more proactive system of investigating and seeking out potential derogatory information that might trip the Leahy Law was not formally put in place in any other country.[54] To borrow a classic principal-agent construct, in most places in the world, the Leahy Law depends on "fire alarms"—alerts from the media, NGOs, citizen groups or other regular reporting processes—to alert the bureaucracy to "credible information" of human rights abuses.[55] It is all the more notable that in Afghanistan, they chose to create "police patrols"—essentially to exert bureaucratic effort to monitor and enforce the Leahy Law controls themselves.

While there are no public statistics available, State Department officials interviewed said that as a result of these processes there were a higher number of Leahy Law investigations in Afghanistan than in other countries, as well as more cases of "remediation."[56] This might be credited to both the greater availability of information (much of it furnished by NGOs and other advocates) and greater governmental resources to follow up on cases. All of this generated a much more substantial discussion and practice of applying the Leahy Law in Afghanistan.

Reflecting on the forgoing evidence, the way that the newly reformed Leahy Law interacted with prompts for accountability for Afghan forces helps illustrate how the different pathways anticipated within transnational advocacy and social movement theory interacted with each other. These might be seen as forming a multistep process that overall contributed to the development of a screening and sanctioning SOP. In the first step, NGO pressure together with collaboration with internal advocates (those in Congress and in successive administrations) since the 1980s helped to socialize the principles underlying the Leahy Law as appropriate de minimis accountability measures. A post-2009 policy assemblage contributed to further legislative and administrative reforms to the law. However, the content of these principles and legislative change then had to be "taught" and reinforced in practice. Each time abusive reports manifested, NGOs or other civil society advocates (often working in concert with other congressional allies) would question why U.S. funding was (still) going to perpetrators of war crimes or human rights abuses and why vetting had not taken place or had not been robust enough to screen out such forces. This regular pattern of submitting evidence, demonstrating gaps between the policy and the practice, created the sort of pressure that might force the bureaucracy to more regularly apply and develop the tools that had been created.

This regular pressure contributed to internalization in two ways. First, in the decade and more of calling for these risky forces to be constrained, NGOs and their institutional allies regularized human rights complaints as an accepted basis for appeal—something that policy makers could be called to account for. Within this "call and response" pattern, control mechanisms like the Leahy Law came to be seen as appropriate measures for responding to such critiques. This reinforced vetting and threats of cut-offs for gross violations of human rights as a necessary due diligence step and part of the "repertoire" of government accountability responses.[57] Second, human rights NGOs and transnational actors repeatedly pushed policy makers and institutions to engage in the *practice* of human rights accountability and controls. With the successive and regular practice of applying and implementing these rules, these vetting and sanctioning practices became more entrenched as standard operating procedures—the sort that would be applied by routine, out of force of habit, even when they were not explicitly called for or required.

Although not solely attributable to advocacy around the ALP, attention to the institution played an important part in socializing this emerging practice. The ALP was a lightning rod for attention over some ten years, garnering both greater NGO and media attention and greater policy-maker energies than its relatively small size might have suggested. As a result, there were specific efforts to capture and document abuses by the ALP and continuing pressure to do something about them. What emerged was a nearly ten-year-long continuous pressure campaign, with all the right ingredients to contribute to a larger socializing effect. It is of further significance that all of these prompts to practice and the reinforcement of risk-mitigation norms were happening in Afghanistan—a high-profile U.S. foreign policy priority for nearly two decades. The Afghanistan experience was formative for an entire generation of DoD and State Department bureaucrats, as well as other U.S. forces and officials. Greater attention to human rights accountability and the practice of enacting controls in Afghanistan compared to other countries would be more significant for mainstreaming similar policies across the bureaucracy.

This is not intended as an argument that the Leahy Law was effective in preventing or addressing human rights abuses, or even that it significantly advanced accountability in Afghanistan. Although U.S. officials pursued a more proactive, police-patrol model for the Leahy Law overall in Afghanistan, they still used exceptions to protect important security partners in ways that undermined accountability. At the same time that Congress was tightening the Leahy Law rules, it agreed to leave a carve-out for Afghanistan forces only permitting a waiver of the Leahy Law where the secretary of defense deemed a member of such forces to be necessary. This was frequently applied, including to senior commanders with long and prominent records of abuse.[58] In addition, many of those interviewed argued that at no point in the Afghanistan experience did U.S. officials or commanders prioritize human rights accountability over security demands. Pointedly noting the lack of accountability for the ALP, former Afghan minister of interior Ali Jalali observed that "the idea of U.S. policy was not primarily to go after corrupt officials—it was to go after terrorists. This meant in some cases [U.S. officials] closing their eyes to those doing drug trafficking or engaged in corruption, as long as they could fight the Taliban."[59] One former U.S. Marine commander with multiple tours in Afghanistan offered a similar perspective: "from what I've seen, U.S. forces have never cut off Afghan forces on misconduct grounds. They have occasionally been under such pressure that they were forced to let some commanders go—but only when under such pressure that there was no wiggle room. . . . In Afghanistan, the argument of operational expediency has always trumped."[60]

As a result, advocates and journalists often expressed frustration that promises of human rights accountability and greater technical mechanisms were all that was achieved. Tate observed a similar issue in her analysis of the early development of the Leahy Law, noting that the focus on the Leahy documentation drew attention away from broader accountability issues or restraints on military forces, undercutting a lot of what advocates intended for these measures.[61] She observed that "the law shifted US policy, but not in the ways that the activists and policymakers who designed the law originally intended."[62] The evidence in these case studies suggests a similar story.

At the same time, there were signs that the full internalization of the Leahy Law and its underlying human rights considerations achieved a level of indoctrination that went far beyond the letter of the law, in ways that its advocates might not have anticipated. One senior military leader characterized the Leahy Law amendment as a "huge sword of Damocles hanging over all these [local partner] operations.... If they run afoul from the standards set in the Leahy amendment, you have to walk away from these groups."[63] He and other U.S. officials interviewed argued that the deterrent effect of the Leahy Law, coupled with its role as a forcing element—forcing U.S. officials to take human rights risks into consideration—had more of an effect on U.S. policy makers' behavior and choice of partners than the simple record of blocks or cuts of forces might imply.[64]

Further evidencing the degree of internalization was the fact that the Leahy Law standards became an implicit deterrent even for programs not technically subject to it. As noted in chapter 3, a particularly curious element of the Syria examples was the CIA's decision to adopt a human rights standard within its vetting and management of the covert support program—replicating some of the Leahy Law standards in practice. This is surprising given the general presumptions about CIA covert support, the impossibility of fully vetting for and monitoring against such standards in Syria, and the fact that the Leahy Law has never been contemplated for CIA-furnished assistance. Thus, while one might imagine the general practice and mainstreaming of the Leahy Law standards to influence State Department and DoD programming, the CIA would appear divorced from these larger socialization processes. However, those who worked within the agency as well as alongside it in partnering operations in Iraq, Afghanistan, and Syria said in interviews that this was not the case. One former senior official within the CIA observed that in his experience, even though the agency was not technically subject to the Leahy Law, "We operated [in many cases] as if it did."[65] Congressional expectations and reinforcement of such standards through informal monitoring and oversight role of covert operations partly explain this. In addition, what the interviews and examples suggest is that, contrary to popular perceptions, the CIA is not divorced from the larger ecosystem of U.S. government norms and organizational expectations. Its actions and policy tools are also influenced by the internalized political logic and associated routines or scripts of the larger bureaucracy as a whole. Its adoption of Leahy Law standards in many situations thus signifies the broader internalization and adoption of this standard within the U.S. bureaucracy.

In summary, the post-2009 development of the Leahy Law offers a strong example of how bureaucratic practices or SOPs might evolve. Opportunities to change the rules of the game and to shift policy standards at key junctures—as with the changes to the Leahy Law early in the Obama administration—were important. But equally important were the calls to practice and the bureaucracy's repeated adoption and application of those standards. These appeared to have broader socializing effects that could result in an internalization of norms and practices in ways that led them to be applied by rote, even absent legal or political prods to do so.

REFLECTING ON DRIVERS OF BUREAUCRATIC CHANGE OVER TIME

This chapter, and the different examples of pressure for human rights controls and the development of the Leahy Law, offered tools for analyzing what factors or processes might help to develop and encode new SOPs within a bureaucracy. Borrowing some of the theorization of how norms are introduced and inculcated within state policies, the final case study suggested a multistep process by which SOPs might become ingrained. A rule or standard might first emerge and be adopted in discrete moments of change, as was the case with the initial ALP rules and policies, or the reforms to the Leahy Law and the accompanying changes in administrative rules. However, for this to become internalized as a standard or default operating practice requires reinforcement of that rule or standard and its repeated application in practice. The former might emerge where large parts of the bureaucracy are regularly forced to account for compliance with that standard. In the case of the Leahy Law, this happened through Congress's repeated questioning of the administration's application of the Leahy Law, as well as the emphasis on Leahy Law application as part of the regular "call and response" between external critics and members of the bureaucracy in theaters like Afghanistan. This "call and response" contributes to the socialization and internalization of these measures as the appropriate response. However, equally important is the element of practice—of being forced to regularly apply the principles until they became somewhat routine. Afghanistan functioned as a crucial site of practice for the revamped Leahy Law.

This account of change and internalization over time allows us to modify the tools within our BPA analysis and understand not only how organizational and bureaucratic practices and lenses might influence policy outputs, but how they might evolve or change over time. The overriding image provided by the organizational side of BPA theory is that of machinery proceeding like clockwork, with even leading policy makers constrained by existing scripts, routines, and SOPs. As Allison wrote in one early article, "Government leaders can trim the edges of this output and exercise some choice in combining outputs. But the mass of behavior is determined by previously established procedures."[66] Further, he continued, "Since procedures are 'standard' they do not change quickly or easily.... When properly triggered ... programs cannot be substantially changed in a particular situation."[67] Such perspectives have led to the critique that BPA offers a weak account of change.[68]

However, as this chapter has illustrated, the lenses, SOPs, and scripts within a bureaucracy need not be viewed as immovable. While rapid or instant change may be unlikely, incremental changes and gradual socialization can over time shift the rules of the game, as well as the way that policy makers and the bureaucratic organizations as a whole view the foreign policy issue and the appropriate response to it. Examples like those provided in this chapter suggest that long-term, back-and-forth exchanges and pushes toward practice might contribute to new SOPs or the modification of existing ones over time.

The foregoing examples from Afghanistan suggest that we might be more likely to see socialization under three particular conditions: (1) where there is a body of evidence and a push by external actors for officials and bureaucrats to apply the principles, policies, or laws in question, such that it is possible for practice to be generated; (2) when this happens over some extended period of time, allowing for the regularization of practice; and (3) where the group or issue in question is given high priority or a high profile, because in these cases, it might be more likely to invoke a larger share of either the bureaucracy or U.S. policy makers' bandwidth, thereby creating a wider footprint for socialization. The Afghanistan experience, and specifically the ALP, was formative in helping to solidify LHSF controls because it combined all of these factors.

However, while the Afghanistan case was significant, the evolution of a set of practices in only one country would be unlikely to entrench and render globally applicable a specific rule, no matter how significant the foreign policy arena in which it was incubated. It would take a much larger body of practice, across a wider range of countries and scenarios, to fully ingrain these varied checks and controls as part of the standard repertoire of accountability responses. All of the LHSF initiatives documented in prior chapters functioned as sites of practice and drivers of socialization, as did other places where security assistance was repeatedly put to the test vis-à-vis the Leahy Law, as well as other types of control mechanisms in this book.

This chapter has focused on the Leahy Law and other related human rights controls in order to illustrate processes of change and bureaucratic rule adoption. The assumption is that similar processes—pushed by a different set of stakeholders, driving events, and dynamics—would have been responsible for helping to prompt internalization for some of the other controls discussed in this book. For example, we might expect a similar sort of "call and response" pattern explaining adoption of "CT vetting" and security-related controls. Although there were additional regulations and heightened sensitivity to inadvertent "material support" to terrorists since shortly after the 2001 attacks, these did not immediately invoke a set of prescribed control mechanisms for working with LHSFs (or other security actors). Continued public attention to security incidents and blowback in environments with a high reliance on LHSF partnerships have over time reinforced the need to adopt risk-mitigation strategies and control mechanisms. In the subsequent two decades, each time U.S. materiel was passed on to terrorist groups directly or via another partner, this created an external pressure point that drove a need to respond with greater due diligence measures. Each incident or situation would prompt the bureaucracy to develop a response or precautionary measure for such risks, cohering over time into its own "call and response" cycle and reinforcing certain risk-mitigation practices or controls. Gradually, this would include "CT vetting," an amorphous term that usually refers to the cross-checking of a series of U.S. intelligence databases for any known affiliations with banned groups.[69]

A last important point to highlight is how the evidence in this chapter helps to advance one of the larger subthemes of this book—that of understanding the levers or pathways for non-U.S.-government actors to influence U.S. government bargaining and decision making. This chapter has helped provide concrete examples and a greater theoretical exploration of how one set of non-U.S.-government actors might do so. The evidence suggests that while NGOs and transnational actors were certainly not the only drivers within the "policy assemblage" that helped mainstream and institutionalize the Leahy Law, they played an important role. Further, the analysis suggests that NGOs and transnational advocates might be seen as a more significant player when viewed over a longer span of time.[70] By continuing to press for many years and across different policy spaces (in Afghanistan and internationally), human rights NGOs and civil society advocates could exploit policy openings and opportunities wherever and whenever they arise, gradually nudging forward commitments or practice. This flexibility to exploit openings for influence wherever and whenever they occurred suggests that NGOs, transnational networks, or other nongovernmental actors may play a more significant role when viewed over a longer span of time than in any single bargaining moment, where they are likely to have less power and influence than official stakeholders.

6

FOREIGN PLAYERS IN THE MIX

Direct and Indirect Bargaining and Influence Strategies by Non-U.S. Governments

Within Allison and Halperin's initial studies, and in much other subsequent BPA analyses, the actions of foreign leaders or their bureaucracies tended to be treated as external stimuli, sparking the crisis decision making or in some cases affecting the "stand" that internal players would take within internal policy making, but they are not really part of the foreign policy decision.[1] While the degree of influence varied, across nearly all of the case studies, a range of foreign interlocutors and government actors functioned as more than purely "stimuli." Foreign leaders like Prime Minister Maliki in Iraq and President Karzai in Afghanistan were key stakeholders in negotiations over the *sahwa* and the ALP, respectively, with control mechanisms designed to respond to their demands. In other case studies, foreign leaders or bureaucrats did not appear to act as direct "players," but they still wielded some influence over how LHSFs or their risks were perceived, the parameters of the debate, or how LHSF initiatives or the control mechanisms attached to them were implemented. Such examples run counter to what we might expect from traditional BPA analysis.

This chapter will explore some of the pathways by which members of non-U.S. governments or bureaucracies, or in at least one case, an armed group standing in for the state, came to play a role in U.S. decision making. The first section considers situations in which representatives of non--U.S. governments have played a more indirect or shaping role, borrowing from theorization within alliance theory, foreign policy implementation, and some of the same transnational network theories introduced in the last chapter. The second section considers situations in which foreign leaders or bureaucrats appear more like direct players or co-deliberators in the bargaining and decision making. In the latter, theory building from literature on shared or compromised sovereignty helps to understand when and how a transnational decision-making situation might emerge, and how foreign leaders might come to find themselves at the figurative bargaining table.

INDIRECT PATHWAYS FOR SHAPING LHSF DECISION MAKING

Existing international relations literature already identifies at least three pathways by which foreign leaders or members of foreign bureaucracies might indirectly or informally influence U.S. decision making: via some of the same transnational advocacy strategies identified in the prior chapter; through established co-decisional routines or procedures within alliance or coalition situations; or through the greater number of access points (direct and indirect) available in foreign policy implementation.

As a first take, the literature on transnational networks that was the focus of chapter 5 suggests that foreign diplomats or bureaucrats acting beyond their official roles might also take part in the persuasion and advocacy campaigns advanced by transnational networks.[2] In the examples discussed in that chapter, NGOs were certainly at the forefront of ALP pressure campaigns, but many foreign diplomats and government officials also played a role through their internal advocacy. A willing ear is part of how NGOs and civil society came to have such a prominent voice in the ALP authorization debate—through EU diplomats as well as some U.S. diplomats (Eikenberry) giving heed to their human rights concerns. NGOs and civil society were further enabled in their pressure campaigns throughout the ALP's duration by a number of sympathetic government officials (U.S. and European) who were also personally committed to improving accountability in Afghanistan.[3]

There were similar dynamics in the Syria case studies. NGOs, Syrian civil society actors, the media, and other transnational human rights activists helped shape the U.S. foreign policy agenda on Syria, including, at certain points, by encouraging further U.S. intervention, advocating what type of assistance to provide, and spotlighting the risks or public sensitivities that would help drive control mechanisms.[4] However, foreign diplomats from both European countries and regional allies also played a quiet role in some of these transnational advocacy campaigns. Individual diplomats pressed at different points for a no-fly zone or other forms of greater U.S. engagement, and later played what might be considered an internal advocacy role in determining which groups to support or not (i.e., within the SDF).[5]

The transnational advocacy literature focuses more on government officials or foreign diplomats who take part in pressure campaigns and advocacy networks by virtue of their own personal commitments. By contrast, studies unpacking cooperation and power dynamics within alliances identify ways that foreign governments use indirect pathways and personal relationships to influence the decisions of more powerful allies as part of achieving their foreign policy objectives.[6] Robert Keohane argued that foreign allies leverage contacts and relationships within American society—for example, with those in regional bureaus in the U.S. State Department, in congressional offices, or within the defense industry or other active U.S. domestic constituencies and lobby groups—to shape U.S. foreign policy decision making.[7]

There was evidence of this sort of informal advocacy or lobbying in several of the case studies examined thus far. In the case of Syria, a number of European and Gulf states, as well as Turkey and other regional allies, were pressing for greater U.S. involvement, including increasing levels of support to Syrian armed opposition.[8] Such pressure manifested through official channels—for example, private diplomatic exchanges or foreign allies' public statements (before the UN, say, or other Friends of Syria meetings)—but also indirectly, by supporting vocal external advocates to try to shape international options or through informal pressure through personal contacts and private relationships within the U.S. government. This happened not just in the Syria cases, but also with regard to LHSFs in Iraq. U.S. officials interviewed observed cases of foreign governments or constituencies working through congressional relationships to ensure additional resources or protection for particular LHSF groups.[9] Protection for these groups even extended in some cases to congressional officials intervening to argue against the application of certain control mechanisms (like the Leahy Law exclusions) to their preferred actors.[10]

In some scenarios, foreign states may have additional leverage points via institutionalized co-decision-making norms or structures. Thomas Risse-Kappen has argued that the "collective identity" of NATO member states and "norms committing allies to timely consultation" gave less powerful states in the alliance a conduit to shape the decisions of their most powerful ally, the United States.[11] Studies have found that junior partners in an international military coalition might constrain the decision making of more powerful states through their participation in institutionalized joint decision-making mechanisms.[12] On these theories, the United States might make concessions either out of deference to the established institutional norms and routines of consultation, or because larger partners need to make concessions to keep the participation of other coalition members. It is worth flagging the similarity between the causal mechanisms in these alliance theories and those of BPA organizational theories. In essence, the argument is that institutional norms and scripts (in this case of co–decision making) queue processes that shape foreign policy outcomes in ways not anticipated by an analysis based on competing state interests or internal power dynamics alone.

In all three of the countries under study, Afghanistan, Iraq, and Syria, U.S. officials made or enacted security decisions as part of multilateral coalitions or partnerships, although the degree of influence via these co-decisional frameworks varied. As chapter 2 highlighted, greater burden sharing among ISAF partners and what was overall a more multilateral and diffuse policy environment meant that in Afghanistan the United States consulted with other members of ISAF to a greater degree than it did its coalition partners in Iraq.[13] It was relatively common for the U.S. commanding general in Afghanistan to consult at least with major troop-contributing nations and donors on major security initiatives. As a result, when the ALP was proposed, the ambassadors or senior military officials of other major ISAF countries or major donors in Afghanistan were consulted. While they did not have a full veto, their concerns—about undermining other state-building priorities or empowering warlords and enabling abuses—helped shape the parameters of debate and the impetus to adopt several of the control mechanisms.

In the two case studies on assistance to the FSA (both the State Department nonlethal assistance and the covert CIA assistance) we see evidence of these institutionalized consultation processes, and also of some of the processes anticipated within foreign policy implementation. On the first, CIA support was delivered via two operational hubs, the MOM in Turkey and the MOC in Jordan. These hubs coordinated not only U.S. assistance to the FSA but also any weapons, salaries, equipment, or tactical support or intelligence contributed by other members, including Saudi Arabia, Qatar, the United Arab Emirates, the United Kingdom, France, and the host countries of Turkey and Jordan.[14] Those who participated in or observed the MOM and MOC described a collective information-gathering and decision-making process, with FSA commanders called before a sounding board made up of the different member states' representatives and jointly questioned about developments in Syria, needs for further weapons, salaries, or materials, and allegations of misconduct or abuse.[15] There was then a collective decision-making process for when FSA had crossed redlines and should be blocked from funding.[16] Although the degree of secrecy surrounding the MOM and MOC processes makes it difficult to ascertain how formalized such processes were, what is described suggests some degree of consultation and joint decision making among those countries that had agreed to participate in the provision of covert assistance.

One might counter that, although these other countries sat at the literal (not just figurative) table with U.S. intelligence representatives, the United States would still have decisive influence on the collective decisions. This certainly was the case. For example, one FSA representative said that once the United States decided not to fund a particular group, all other funding also stopped out of fear of U.S. retaliation if one partner was perceived as supporting a blocked group: "Even though 70 percent of the money for weapons, if not more, comes out of Saudi Arabia, Qatar, the UAE, and Turkey, the decision of who to fund and whether to keep funding largely tracks U.S. [decisions]."[17] However, one might find a more decisive U.S. role and still see an influence for other states sitting within this sort of collaborative structure.

In the studies noted above examining how junior partners influence more powerful states via coalition dynamics, the assumption is not that the more powerful state lacks an ability to set the agenda or to exert decisive influence. Instead, the key question is how junior partners may nonetheless exert an influence on U.S. decisions even when the formal balance of power and decision making is unequal.[18] The descriptions of what transpired in the MOM and MOC suggest that other countries were consulted and able to take part in the decision making, even if their views were not controlling in each instance. They might, for example, contribute to the determination of whether a redline was crossed, which groups should be brought in for questioning, or other choices that affected the way that control mechanisms were applied, at least as much as any top-down political decisions in Washington, DC. In addition to the descriptions of how decisions were made, those who took part in or otherwise observed or interacted with the MOM and MOC noticed distinct differences in the type of groups funded and the way they were managed, which they attributed to the differing attitudes and influence of the host states, Turkey and Jordan.[19] This also implies the particular influence of Turkey and Jordan over the ultimate outcome, despite arguably being themselves junior partners.

These examples of collaboration within the MOM and MOC reflect not just the idea of institutionalized decision making but also the ability of other countries to exert influence in the implementation of foreign policy decisions. The literature on foreign policy implementation holds that choices made in the course of implementing a policy are as important as the initial bargaining moment, and that these implementation decisions can involve bargaining from a wider ambit of external actors and partners, from other states, to international organizations, to nongovernmental or private-sector actors involved in the actual implementation.[20] Existing literature has already applied such implementation theories to understand external actor influence in comparable conflict or transition situations. For example, Schroeder and Friesendorf adopted this implementation framework to explore how a range of international and domestic actors—to include representatives of foreign donors, the UN mission, the EU police mission, and domestic regulatory agencies and elites—collectively shaped the counter-crime agenda and policies in post-Dayton Bosnia-Herzegovina.[21] They note that "Implementation is not a technical process of simply translating political decisions into practices. Instead, implementation is a game of political bargaining that crucially depends on the interests of the implementing actors."[22] The counter-crime policy was not determined by a top-level decision-making process alone. Instead, it was shaped by the various national and international stakeholders who were engaged in deciding how a policy would actually be implemented.

What was happening within the MOM and MOC was effectively the implementation phase for FSA lethal assistance. The decision to offer lethal assistance, and to do so with certain parameters and controls, had already been made at higher levels (in Washington, DC, as well as in other capitals also offering such support). It was then up to the range of states represented in the MOM and MOC to collectively decide how this decision would be implemented in terms of which groups were funded, which were cut, how risks were contained, and any number of other implementation choices. For each of the countries involved, weighing in on how rules and standards were applied in implementation was a pathway of influence on how U.S. (among other countries') assistance was provided. Each country's institutional or political lenses—where their redlines or preferences lay in terms of the ideology or profile of particular FSA groups, how seriously to weigh allegations of war crimes or other transgressions—could affect the micro-choices of who was funded or not, and with what means.[23]

These theories about routines of institutionalized cooperation and policy influence via implementation also offer insights into how foreign states influence foreign policy outcomes in the State Department's non-lethal assistance. The State Department managed its Syria assistance writ large (including but not limited to the assistance going to armed opposition groups) alongside other Western donors, including the United Kingdom, the Netherlands, Canada, Denmark, and Germany. At least for certain elements of the assistance, the degree of cooperation was close enough to resemble co-decision making. One prominent example was coordination over the Free Syria Police, the unarmed counterparts of the FSA. Through a steering committee in Istanbul these six donors triangulated and pooled information, including that used as a basis for vetting recipients, and also developed common positions and redlines that would determine when sanctions were applied and which groups would be cut.[24] The

State Department nonlethal assistance to the FSA was managed outside this collaborative steering committee process because, except for the United Kingdom and the Netherlands, the other countries would not provide overt nonlethal assistance to *armed* Syrian opposition. Nonetheless, because the Free Syria Police and community council support programs were much larger and more long-lasting than the FSA support, many of the standards generated for these larger programs were then later applied to other forms of U.S. assistance, including FSA nonlethal assistance.[25] This included the standards and protocols for vetting recipients, decisions or criteria on when groups should be blocked from funding, the degree of monitoring and verification required, and the understanding of risk factors in particular locations and how control mechanisms were applied to deal with them. It is another example of how other countries' input at the implementation phase indirectly shaped how control mechanisms were applied for the U.S. nonlethal assistance to the FSA. These countries (and their contracted implementing partners) were not at the bargaining table, but they were at the implementing table, so to speak.

All of these examples reinforce the premise mooted in the introductory chapters—that non-U.S. governmental representatives often go beyond the role of pure "stimuli" in influencing U.S. bargaining. In the first pathway identified, foreign diplomats or officials could influence U.S. decision making over LHSF controls in much the same way that other NGOs and transnational advocates did—by highlighting key risks, or in some cases their preferred policy options, and using indirect public or private persuasion strategies to shape the debate over these initiatives. In the second pathway identified, foreign allies might leverage norms of consultation or processes of joint decision making within alliance structures to indirectly influence U.S. decisions about LHSFs. In the third pathway identified, foreign representatives (as well as nongovernmental partners) might exert influence through the implementation of policy decisions, in this case by helping determine the standards for and application of control mechanisms. In the situations considered so far, the non-U.S.-government actors identified were not so influential as to be considered "players" in the bargaining game afoot, but the case studies have already suggested that this might indeed be possible in certain scenarios. The following section will consider the more provocative case of foreign leaders directly co-participating in U.S. decision-making.

FOREIGN LEADERS AS PLAYERS IN SITUATIONS OF COMPROMISED OR SHARED SOVEREIGNTY

The case studies of the *sahwa* and the ALP were notable in many respects, but one of the most interesting dynamics was the prominent role played by Prime Minister Maliki in Iraq and President Karzai in Afghanistan. Each was directly involved in the most significant bargaining surrounding the initiatives in their respective countries, actions that determined the ultimate formal authorization of these initiatives. Several of what would amount to the most crucial control mechanisms (or arguably all of them, in the Iraq case) were created to try to win over their support and to prevent them from vetoing the initiatives. They also demanded their own preferred control mechanisms, or relaxation of others.

Nor were they the only Afghan or Iraqi participants involved. Maliki's and Karzai's respective ministries and bureaucracies were also involved in these authorization debates, albeit not always in agreement with each other. As described in chapter 2, Afghan institutional actors were split on their support of the ALP—the minister of interior, Atmar, initially opposing the initiative, while other ministerial leaders with more to gain from the ALP were supportive. Such inter-bureaucratic wrangling and positioning based on organizational interests and positions typified the "stand-sit" positions that are such a central concept in interagency BPA bargaining.

What the forgoing describes is a situation in which non-U.S. leaders, and their bureaucracies behind them, were neither merely stimuli nor—as the previous section covered—engaged in exerting indirect influence. Instead, they appeared to be full co-participants or players within the bargaining games afoot in what we might describe as a sort of intergovernmental or transnational application of BPA.

Because BPA has focused mostly on deliberations within the executive branch, there are no ready pathways for understanding how a transnational BPA situation might arise. However, examining the nature of the relationship between the Afghan and U.S. or Iraqi and U.S. governments in this period offers a ready explanation for how transnational or shared decision making might arise. During the periods in question, both Afghanistan and Iraq were in a situation of compromised and/or shared sovereignty, with U.S. officials—alongside their Afghan and

Iraqi counterparts—involved in the de facto administration and governing of large parts of the state.

One reason to look to the literature on compromised or shared sovereignty is simply the nature of the policy issue being deliberated, as well as both sides' degree of involvement or authority within that decision's outcome. The most common frameworks for considering interstate deliberations within international relations studies tend to depict states as competing against each other, bargaining for their own distinct governing interests and positions vis-à-vis an international issue.[26] However, in the scenarios described in chapter 2, both the United States and the Afghan or Iraqi governments were not deliberating about competing positions vis-à-vis a crisis situation—for example, whether one side or the other will position intercontinental ballistic missiles to counter the other, or whether one side will adopt a particular trade policy or tariff either as a means of cooperating with or challenging the other's economic interest. Rather, they were deliberating to resolve a mutual policy challenge—how to jointly address gaps in their security forces and constrain insurgent operating space, recruitment, and influence in territories that they both de facto partly controlled. Each government, and the various subparts and players within them, brought a different answer to that challenge, in line with their own "stand-sit" positions and interests. But such differences might be described as reflecting BPA expectations that the range of bureaucratic players involved in internal bargaining will bring to the table "differing conceptions" of the right way forward, rather than descriptions of competing foreign policy positions.[27] Notwithstanding differing policy solutions or positions, the problem they sought to resolve was a common one.

In addition, although still largely under-theorized, where authors have considered FPA or related organizational theories in the context of transnational governance situations, the underlying situations have involved some compromised or shared sovereignty dynamics. A few authors have considered whether FPA dynamics might better explain the intergovernmental decision-making and organizational tendencies of EU institutions, particularly in fields or on issue sets where EU institutions have exerted primacy of jurisdiction.[28] The manifestation of organizational tendencies and interests have also been considered in situations in which states delegate authority to international organizations. For example, scholars Michael Barnett and Martha Finnemore found that similar to the organizational theories within BPA, the decisions and outputs of international organizations are as much influenced by organizational pathologies and "behavioural proclivities" as by any imputed delegated tasks or authorities delegated to them by their state patrons.[29]

The common thread connecting these two dynamics is a degree of shared or delegated sovereignty, which then generates a situation in which representatives from a range of governments—or potentially standing bureaucracies or organizations they have created to represent them—are put in a position to mutually decide and develop common policies. While the context was very different in Iraq and Afghanistan, in both countries a situation of compromised and de facto shared sovereignty generated a regular pattern of co-decision making and co-administration between members of more than one government—the sort of situation where transnational BPA-style dynamics might arise.

There is a large body of literature on how international interventions can lead to situations of compromised or shared sovereignty—whether due to coercive military intervention and occupation, or to so-called consensual intervention in sovereign decision making—for example, as part of international funding and conditionality.[30] In these situations, although the government in question retains formal legal or juridical sovereignty, its ability to decide matters within its own territory is not fully independent or autonomous. External states or international organizations might demand a particular policy outcome—for example, the appointment of key domestic officials, the creation or adjustment of domestic institutions (i.e., creation of a central bank), or measures determining how the juridically sovereign state should respond to internal security threats.[31] In many post-conflict scenarios where there is a substantial peacekeeping force, a degree of international administration, or other marks of significant external intervention, representatives of the international community may even directly take over aspects of domestic governance for a period of time.[32]

Afghanistan and Iraq after the U.S. invasions offer classic examples of such compromised or shared sovereignty, both "coercive" and "consensual" in nature. Many definitions of Westphalian or Weberian sovereignty start with the presumption that the state possesses territorial control, a monopoly on the means of violence, and an administrative infrastructure that would help it enforce rules, levy taxes, or provide services.[33] In post-2003 Iraq and post-2001 Afghanistan, juridically sovereign governments were established, but external actors, in particular the United States, held preponderant influence or direct control over many of these expected "state" functions. High international troop numbers gave the United States and other coalition partners substantial control over coercive force and the means of violence in these countries. There were technically more Afghan and Iraqi forces throughout this period.[34] However, there was a high proportion of ghost forces in the Iraqi and Afghan armies, and substantial deficiencies in equipment, military capacity, and in overall institutional coherence and loyalty.[35] The result was that the military power that leaders in both countries largely depended on to sustain their regimes (including vis-à-vis other domestic competitors), control territory, and combat insurgent groups was that of international forces. As scholar Astri Suhrke aptly notes, "ISAF was in a sense Karzai's army," with the ability to check other regional warlords and strongmen in ways that were otherwise beyond either his personal power or the state's capacity.[36] Arguably, this most fundamental function or pillar of state coercion and sovereignty—control over the means of violence—lay more significantly with international rather than domestic forces.

In addition, throughout this period, conditionality attached to foreign assistance facilitated significant intrusion into domestic institutions and decision making. Astri Suhrke estimates that approximately 90 percent of the Afghan budget was supported by international assistance for at least the first decade after 2001.[37] Such large aid flows, Suhrke argues, meant that donors had "a more important voice" than parliament or other domestic constituencies. Donors erected "a thick network of controls, through oversight in administrative and fiduciary matters and political appointments; joint rules for reconstruction and statebuilding . . . and funding a 'second civil service' (and topping up salaries), including 105 positions in the Office of the President."[38] Through such controls or direct conditionality and intervention, external donors intervened regularly in appointment powers at all levels of government.[39]

There were similar issues of economic dependence and donor incursions on Iraqi sovereignty and internal governance. In post-2003 Iraq, the United States undertook a complete overhaul of the country's governing institutions, structures, and mandates—using its occupation authority to craft or re-craft nearly all government ministries, financial institutions, and rules of federal governance. Even at a lower level, it often sidelined Iraqi authorities and undermined independent decision making. Describing the early post-2003 period, Eric Herring and Glen Rangwala note that despite Iraqi officials being portrayed as having increased responsibility for governance, "in cases of dispute the Coalition tended to overrule and marginalise officials who sought to act as autonomous decision-makers."[40] Some of this direct supervision and subversion of institutional power decreased after the initial occupation period, but the United States continued to wield significant influence over many ministries, for example, still significantly influencing or dictating appointments as well as key institutional priorities and policies in many security institutions.[41] This was in significant part because Iraq, despite its substantial oil wealth, still depended heavily on international assistance to support the huge reconstruction and stabilization needs. By the end of 2006, the United States alone had spent $16 billion on Iraq's reconstruction, with another $18 billion appropriated.[42] Other coalition member countries, or international institutions like the World Bank and International Monetary Fund also contributed support, and each came with their own conditionality and demands for institutional or policy change.[43]

It was not just that foreign actors could substantially influence or direct key sovereign decision making and prerogatives, but that the scale of in-country personnel, resources, and activities brought these foreign actors into a regular co-participation in governance, alongside Iraqi and Afghan bureaucrats and institutions.[44] The United States and other foreign actors and their agents (be they contractors, international organizations, or NGOs) administered significant development funds, engaged in governance activities, and directly provided services typically associated with a sovereign state in both Afghanistan and Iraq. Astri Suhrke describes the emergence of "parallel structures of administration on virtually all levels of government" in Afghanistan.[45] This ranged from civilian and military personnel based in Provincial Reconstruction Teams (PRTs), to the assistance implemented by donor-funded NGOs, contractors, and international organizations on everything from justice and governance support, to key infrastructure, health, and educational services. One senior U.S. official who served multiple tours in Afghanistan observed, "We talked the language of it being an Afghan sovereign state.... [But] you have PRTs everywhere. U.S. officials are dealing directly with cabinet officials on high-level issues. It's a parallel government.... With 100,000 troops and [a] big development budget, our presence transforms everything. You can say he [Karzai] is the president, but he's not fully sovereign."[46]

Similar trends transpired in Iraq, with a large share of U.S. and other international assistance administered either by U.S. forces and personnel or by a network of contractors, international organizations, and NGOs.[47] One senior U.S. military official observed that because of the high violence levels in Iraq in 2005 and 2006, in many parts of the country there was not even a regularly present local official involved in decision making. "In a way we were the Iraqi government in certain parts of the country," he observed.[48]

However, although foreign personnel were often directly involved in administering parts of the Afghan and Iraqi states, they were not doing so alone. Across all of these sectors there tended to be a high degree of joint decision making and collaborative implementation. For example, in the security sector, while there were many operations carried out independently by either international or Afghan or Iraqi forces, many operations were planned and executed jointly between international and domestic forces. In both Iraq and Afghanistan, international advisers were embedded in key ministries, from those covering security to the central bank.[49] The sort of functions that these international advisers exercised daily—from drawing up long-term strategic plans and proposed policy initiatives or laws, to advising on responses to key crises or decision points—were central to the execution of that ministry's or unit's institutional mandate. However, such decision making was a collaborative affair, exercised jointly with the other Afghan or Iraqi officials in those ministries or units. The same was true at a local level, with Afghan or Iraqi representatives often collaborating with those delegated to handle donor funds—representatives of foreign donors, or NGOs, or civil society actors contracted by them—in joint decision making about local governance, rule of law, or development initiatives.

This shared sovereignty was undergirded by both sides' mutual dependence. As much as the Afghan and Iraqi governments depended on international actors, international actors depended on the host governments to accomplish their objectives in these countries. Despite capacity issues and political dysfunctionalities, the Afghan and Iraqi governments and their associated forces brought manpower, a degree of local know-how, and arguably a greater sense of "symbolic power" or legitimacy than those perceived as foreign or occupying powers.[50] On the military side, the sheer number of forces required, and the expense of deploying international forces alone to meet those needs, meant that Afghan and Iraqi forces still had an important contribution to make in defraying international troop numbers. The same was true for the Afghan and Iraqi ministerial bureaucracies in terms of administering the state.

Moreover, the logic of both liberal peace interventions and counterinsurgency strategy—the two critical frames influencing international engagement in Afghanistan and Iraq at the time—depended on the host governments reforming themselves. As Suhrke writes, "The fact of mutual dependence buttressed [Afghan elites'] autonomy. Afghanistan's political and strategic significance to NATO created bargaining power. With so much invested in the country, the US-led coalition could not credibly threaten to withdraw support unless the government fully cooperated."[51] This kept Afghan and Iraqi prerogatives at play even in areas where donors supplied most of the funding or where their forces or representatives were directly involved in administering security or services.

As a result of these dynamics, there tended to be a high degree of joint decision making and collaboration between Afghan and Iraqi leaders or bureaucrats and their foreign counterparts across a range of sectors. On a regular basis, U.S. and Afghan or U.S. and Iraqi policy makers found themselves at the same bargaining table, whether bargaining surrounding high-level decision making (which might include a decision to authorize and expand LHSFs) or the lower-level, iterative bargaining that took place in the course of implementation. When an issue like the ALP or *sahwa* debate arose, it did so within this contentious but ultimately shared model of co-administration. Although both sides had their own positions, the policy in question was designed to resolve a security issue in territory that was (at least as far as security matters were concerned) jointly administered and controlled. This helps explain how in many situations, U.S. and Afghan or U.S. and Iraqi officials might find themselves in situations that were closer to the internal deliberations of a single government—administering services or engaging in state decision making for the same territory—than the sort of oppositional bargaining usually invoked to describe the interactions of representatives of opposing states.

This de facto co-administration created an arena in which BPA tools that typically might be applied domestically within a single administration are relevant for a bargaining situation between two or more governments. As could be seen in the case study of the ALP, when the initial proposal for local defense forces emerged, different principals or agencies within both the U.S. and Afghan governments took their own "stand-sit" positions, derived from their internal organizational interests, missions, or applicable tool kits, or in some cases personal lenses and experiences vis-à-vis local forces. These were then litigated and negotiated in part via interagency interaction from one part of the bureaucracy to another, albeit in this case such "interagency" deliberations were occurring transnationally between the actors of two governments—from the U.S. government's military command (McChrystal and other SOF representatives) to the Afghan government's MoD, MoI, and other relevant ministries.

The issue then escalated to a high-level decision game, of the sort typified by Allison's analysis of the deliberations surrounding President Kennedy during the Cuban Missile Crisis. However, in this transnational BPA situation, the high-level decision game involved the top principals of two governments, that of Afghanistan and the United States. Because of the way that bargaining devolved, Karzai held the ultimate veto or decision point. As a result, what was created was very like the sort of classic BPA scenario in which different principals or agencies are vying for presidential authority, but the president in this case was the Afghan one, while the subordinate persuaders involved principals from both the Afghan and U.S. governments.[52] A similar transnational BPA analogy could be applied to the interactions between the prime minister's office and parts of the U.S. military in Iraq (in terms of lower-level games) and between Maliki and Petraeus (in terms of higher-level decision games) in the Iraq case study.

This analysis suggests that we might find what are typically internal BPA dynamics spread across two governments in situations of compromised sovereignty and de facto administration of territory. When bargaining commenced in both Iraq and Afghanistan, the dynamics between different U.S. and Iraqi or U.S. and Afghan players or ministries were more akin to the sort of intra-bureaucratic or intra-branch deliberations described in classic BPA texts. Different players or principals advance "differing conceptions" of what would be the best way forward on a mutually governed or administered issue.[53] While not lacking in hostility (especially in Maliki's case), it was a different sort of bargaining situating than the sort of conflictual or oppositional dynamics usually used to characterize deliberations with opposing states.

The ALP and *sahwa* case studies illustrated these dynamics between the sovereign government and a significant foreign intervenor. However, a further question is whether such transnational bargaining need be limited only to situations in which, however compromised, at least one of the key players is the titular sovereign. The Syria examples suggest this might not be the case. Throughout the period under examination, large parts of Syrian territory were administered or de facto controlled by forces not aligned with the Syrian state. Such dynamics recall the broader literature on situations of "limited" or "partial" sovereignty and de facto governance dynamics in such spaces. Across such "ungoverned" spaces, non-state actors or armed groups, substate or regional forces with loose links to the sovereign state, or groups acting at the behest of neighboring states or international actors may hold sway, asserting a degree of territorial control and governance usually associated with sovereign states.[54] Such dynamics frequently arise in the very situations where the United States seeks to mobilize LHSFs. The United States has sought irregular partners in these areas precisely because the titular sovereign is weak or lacks full control there. In such "ungoverned" or contested spaces, another external state, or even a non-state actor, may have such substantial territorial control that they become relevant co-deliberators with the United States.

The two latter case studies focusing on Syria illustrated these dynamics with two foreign interlocutors. As the case studies in the Syria chapter illustrated, many of the most significant controls both for the Train and Equip groups in northwestern Syria (case study 4 of chapter 3) and with the SDF (case study 5 of chapter 3) were the focus of substantial bargaining with Turkey. Moreover, the nature of those bargaining dynamics appeared to be much closer to those typified in the U.S.-Karzai and U.S.-Maliki relationship than some of the other indirect pathways sketched in the early part of the chapter. In the SDF case study, the United States was using control mechanisms as a bargaining tactic in its negotiations with Turkey, similar to the way that it proposed control mechanisms to try to appease Maliki over the *sahwa*. Controls on which weapons the SDF could have, the weapons' verification, and other controls on where SDF could go or on the vetting of their membership were enacted to try to address some of Turkey's concerns and soften that country's opposition to the initiative. While these did not actually alter such opposition, Turkish officials were happy to see control mechanisms that might hamstring or constrain the program, preventing the SDF and its affiliates from receiving heavy weapons or advancing on territory closer to Turkey's strategic interests.

Ultimately the positions were so irreconcilable that, as with the *sahwa* case, the Turkish-U.S. bargaining over the SDF did not result in a compromise. Nonetheless, it is an important example of transnational BPA bargaining because it is contingent on de facto territorial control or influence rather than a situation of compromised sovereignty. Turkey did not directly control the territory in question during the periods covered in the case study (although later it did come to exercise direct control over parts of northern Syria). But its geographic proximity and ability to support LHSFs or other groups in that territory gave it almost equivalent levers of control to those enjoyed by Maliki or Karzai. It was the indispensable partner whom the U.S. government needed either to mobilize the forces in question or, in the case of the SDF, prevent their efforts being sabotaged.

U.S. negotiations with the SDF offers an even more provocative example of transnational bargaining, in this case with a non-state armed group that formally lacked sovereignty but in practice arguably exercised more territorial control and was more responsible for "state-like" service provision than the Afghan government during the period of the ALP debate. The SDF and the Syrian Democratic Council (SDC) exercised de facto but full territorial control and governing authority in northeastern Syria. Their consent and participation were as crucial to U.S. security objectives in northeastern Syria as the governments in Afghanistan and Iraq were in the prior case studies.

As a result, although from one perspective the SDF featured as an agent, with control mechanisms applied to them, other dynamics of the relationship put them in a position closer to a player or co-participant in U.S. decision making. Unlike with all of the other LHSFs discussed, when concerns arose about SDF members' conduct or about the need to impose more limitations to satisfy Turkey, these tended to be brought to SDF leadership, or their SDC counterparts, to enable them to take forward appropriate policies or offer their own views or counterviews. The SDF and SDC decided on how vetting and scrutiny for ISIL affiliation would be taken up in places like Raqqa, as well as how other concerns about inclusion of non-Kurdish groups or the means of addressing the potential use of child soldiers might be addressed. These decisions were taken at the encouragement of U.S. officials but exercised in a way that involved mutual consultation and decision making, rather than the risks or concerns being addressed through U.S.-imposed controls. It was not quite the same level of joint participation in policy making as in the ALP and *sahwa* cases—but as much because the United States was not there on the ground in northeastern Syria.[55] Nonetheless, U.S. officials did tend to describe their efforts to influence the SDF or SDC as more akin to that of its relations with other state partners and officials than that of a subsidiary proxy force.[56]

The other key difference with the SDF was that it was an overall harmonious relationship, with less dissonance between the United States and SDF positions and interests, at least over the period in question. Although both sides might be characterized as "players," no similarly contentious bargaining moment emerged of the sort that might generate controls. This can make it difficult to compare with some of the other LHSF bargaining situations considered because it was not generative of controls. Nonetheless, the overall position of the LHSF and its relations with the United States illustrate that these sorts of co-deliberative or transnational bargaining dynamics might well emerge not just with third party states but also with non-state actors, provided they have sufficient de facto territorial control or governance capacity.

TOWARD A MORE EXPANSIVE BPA ANALYSIS

This chapter has built on chapter 1's call for a more expansive BPA analysis. Beyond simply adducing that other stakeholders might be relevant to BPA bargaining debates or other implementation paradigms, it identified the pathways by which they might shape U.S. bargaining, decision making, and implementation of assistance.

In the first set of examples, representatives of non-U.S. governments (diplomats or members of the bureaucracy) interacted with U.S. decision making indirectly, in ways that were not that dissimilar to that of the transnational networks described in the prior chapter. When in coalition environments, they might rely on shared norms and co-decisional structures to offer another lever over U.S. decision making. Alternatively, where other state partners were coordinating or co-implementing assistance (whether having to do directly with the LHSFs or on related assistance portfolios), they could influence the outcome of U.S. policy in implementation, through models of interaction and micro-level decision making anticipated by the literature on foreign policy implementation. Across all of these examples, while the foreign diplomats or bureaucrats in question did not hold a direct veto, they had a more significant ability to influence and shape U.S. foreign policy decision making and outputs than has been recognized by BPA's domestic-focused bargaining models.

The second half of the chapter analyzed situations in which foreign leaders and their bureaucracies played an even more significant role, as well as the application of BPA to transnational bargaining or policy making situations. By virtue of shared sovereignty dynamics in both Iraq and Afghanistan following U.S. intervention, U.S. and Iraqi and Afghan officials regularly engaged in joint deliberation and implementation of crucial security initiatives, co-administering parts of the Iraqi and Afghan state. As a result, when deliberations over the *sahwa* and the ALP emerged, Karzai and Maliki, and their bureaucracies behind them, were very much at the same table with U.S. officials. They were necessary participants with as much ability to demand or enact control mechanisms as the U.S. government itself.

The last two Syria cases offer even more provocative examples of BPA transnational bargaining by virtue of shared sovereignty because in these cases the titular sovereign was not even involved. Turkey and to a lesser degree the SDF acted as co-participants in bargaining and deliberations with the United States, placing them in a position similar to that of the Iraqi and Afghan governments in chapter 2. In these cases, de facto territorial control or access and the degree to which these external actors governed Syrian territory or were able to implement initiatives within Syria (including LHSF initiatives) provided the sufficient hook for them to take part in direct bargaining with the U.S. as co-players. As such, the examples of bargaining with Turkey and the SDF help reinforce the earlier distinctions on direct versus indirect bargaining, while also extending inferences on *which* foreign actors might figure as players.

Cumulatively, these examples suggest that in considering BPA bargaining deliberations, one might look not just at the interior circle around the president, the surrounding bureaucracy, or even its deliberations with Congress, but that other states or non-state actors might also be understood as significant players at the bargaining table.

CONCLUSION

This book has traced the trajectory of U.S. engagement with non-state and substate forces since 2001 in three countries. However, unlike many treatments of militias and proxies, the focus of analysis has not been on the groups themselves, nor on their use as proxies. Instead, these examples were used to explore a much larger issue, which is the nature of bargaining and policy evolution in the murky and fluid policy arenas of substate and transnational politics.

The main actors in this drama have first and foremost been the U.S. policy officials involved in promoting, overseeing, and in some cases attempting to restrain or end these LHSF partnerships. But a host of other actors were also involved. To initiate and manage these relationships, U.S. officials had to work with or around foreign leaders, diplomats, and bureaucrats, international and nongovernmental organizations, local community stakeholders, and even non-state armed groups themselves. It is a much more diverse cast of characters than is typically considered in either principal-agent analysis of proxy situations or BPA treatments of decision-making moments.

Because risk mitigation was a central issue across nearly all of the bargaining debates surrounding LHSFs, examining control mechanisms offered a novel testing ground for exploring tensions between these different stakeholders and across competing U.S. foreign policy objectives. Control mechanisms frequently arose as a way to reconcile those opposed to these initiatives and to win approval. The control mechanisms that were ultimately adopted tended to represent the compromises struck between competing stakeholders and between competing preferences or objectives for the policy arena in question. As such, they tell an important story about processes of policy accommodation and rationalization in situations where security imperatives clash with other policy preferences.

Examining these situations has helped us to nuance expectations of principal-agent theory, to expand BPA analysis to a wider range of participants and situations, and to better understand the possibilities and pathways for bureaucratic change and absorption over time. In addition, the focus on control mechanisms allowed greater interrogation of the temptation in these situations to "have your cake and eat it" so to speak—to work with risky actors in some of the most fraught security situations while mitigating the risks of doing so. While the case studies have not suggested specific ways to achieve this, they have offered important insights into the pitfalls of this approach, and what these suggest for future policy development in this area. This final chapter will reprise some of the key lessons learned and tools developed. It will also offer suggestions for further research and ways that policy makers might use the findings from the case studies.

A CASE OF CONTROL OR BUREAUCRATIC POLITICS?

This book has sought to explain the puzzle of why the U.S. would impose control mechanisms on the proxy forces it supports in conflict contexts, despite the high costs in terms of staff time, resources, and policy priorities and the minimal prospect of success. The preliminary framework was that of principal-agent theory, which has frequently been applied to U.S. security assistance relationships and to proxy or surrogate partnerships. Principal-agent theory also offers a typology of control mechanisms that strongly matches those that emerged in practice: selection or vetting mechanisms; codes of conduct, standards, and other rules or restrictions regarding the scope of activities; monitoring and oversight; and enforcement or commitment devices, including sanctions or incentives. However, principal-agent theory expects that patrons will not adopt extensive control mechanisms where the costs of exerting them are higher than the benefits. They are even more likely to be dispensed with where the delegation supports a high policy priority, or where a limited number of agents or a high number of competing patrons leaves the patron with few options and correspondingly lower leverage over behavior.

The situations where the United States sought to delegate to LHSFs tended to present a worst-case scenario in terms of the prospects for successfully controlling and mitigating risks: extreme and insurmountable information asymmetries, limited access to territory or means of conducting oversight, and a limited choice in agents.

- In Afghanistan, U.S. forces seeking to mobilize local counterinsurgents in villages under Taliban control often only had a selection pool of one group in that local area. Once mobilized, the remote location of these forces in areas beyond state control made it extremely costly (and unlikely) for either U.S. officials or partner forces and institutions to regularly monitor their behavior or impose conditions on them. Certain vetting conditions, for example, for past human rights abuses, would have ruled out significant numbers of forces if they had been fully applied.
- In Syria, the shakier legal foundation for U.S. intervention and the hostile relationship with the Assad government made territorial access and oversight an even greater challenge. The complexity of the situation, the volume of armed groups, and the fast-changing nature of conflict dynamics made it difficult for the United States to know with whom it was dealing (extreme adverse selection), and even more difficult to monitor their behavior after the fact.
- In Iraq, for the TMF program, staff had scant monitoring resources and substantial access limitations, which created similar barriers to exercising and enforcing controls. The Iraq examples also illustrate how controls might compromise the potential benefits of delegation and specialization: too much scrutiny in selection of agents in the early *sahwa* period would have reduced the ability to recruit former insurgents or those with knowledge of them, and thus would have undermined the point of delegation.

In addition to these selection and monitoring challenges, in many of these environments, the United States faced competition from other patrons, a situation that, according to principal-agent expectations, would significantly limit the prospects of enforcement and increase the costliness of controls. U.S. efforts to control LHSFs as agents would also face the handicap of a classic complex patron. Across all the case studies, a range of U.S. institutions, officials, and forces, as well as Congress and other U.S. interlocuters, were involved in managing the LHSFs. This made it more costly to enact controls and easy for the agent to play one part of the bureaucracy against another, thereby evading controls.

These were not hidden costs: U.S. policy makers demonstrated a high degree of awareness that the control mechanisms they developed would offer "imperfect" results and invoke significant trade-offs. The costs became increasingly apparent over time. In Syria, applying control mechanisms took significant U.S. staff time and resources to implement and limited the number of potential partners, often to a degree that neutered the value of the program. Rigorous and time-consuming selection processes, tracking, and post hoc reporting slowed the volume and type of CIA assistance to the point where it was tactically of little use to the FSA groups, and nowhere near the level of resources needed to accomplish the purported strategic goals of the program. With the State Department nonlethal assistance, vetting and micromanagement of "redlines" and sanctions took up substantial staff time and a significant proportion of the funds involved. One State Department officer estimated that to fully vet 1,000 fighters to be eligible for nonlethal assistance might have cost $1 million, a process that had to be repeated every few months.[1] When an issue arose, "everything would grind to a halt," another State Department adviser remembered of the program, leading him to conclude that in Syria, "you can have programming, or you can have accountability, but not both."[2] Across nearly all of the programs, the broad selection criteria that ruled out partners deemed "too Islamist" or those with other stains on their record meant that the United States would not work with the dominant or most tactically effective partners in a given area. In the first Train and Equip iteration, the New Syrian Forces program, vetting and other program restrictions were so tight that the program failed to field more than a few dozen fighters. In the brief Train and Equip partnership with

Turkey, U.S. criteria was so tight and so mismatched with Turkey's preferences that the recruits who might have fit both were referred to as imaginary "unicorn" forces.[3]

Despite policy makers' awareness of the high costs and limited benefits of such controls, numerous control mechanisms were enacted, not only in the Syria cases but across nearly all of the LHSF partnerships examined. They were sustained throughout the life of these programs, even as the diminishing returns and high costs manifested. Moreover, they were repeatedly applied to new iterations of LHSFs. Use of control mechanisms became such a default reaction that policy makers interviewed in 2018 and 2019 referred to such controls as the common or standard approach to working with LHSF partners in areas like Syria, Iraq, or Afghanistan.

Such evidence contradicts principal-agent expectations about the factors or structural dynamics likely to lead to control mechanisms. In addition, the evidence within each case study tended to go against principal-agent assumptions about *why* principals enact controls. Principal-agent theory assumes that control mechanisms are enacted as a way to control or constrain the behavior of the agent, in this case the LHSFs in question. However, in examining each case, the evidence that control mechanisms were designed to control or constrain the LHSFs in question was minimal. Instead, most control mechanisms appeared designed to constrain other policy stakeholders (for example, congressional controls used to constrain the executive branch in the New Syrian Forces case study), or to prevail in the given bargaining debate. The case studies offered ample evidence of ways different stakeholders used controls to advance their agendas.

- Prevailing in authorization debates: Control mechanisms were frequently introduced by proponents of these LHSF partnerships as a way to counter objections and defray criticisms that might have prevented the initiative from going forward. In scenarios like the authorization of the ALP or covert support to the FSA (among others), proponents of initiatives within the U.S. government used the promise of rigorous controls to respond to critics, win over undecided players, or at least mute the objections of irreconcilable opponents. As such, control mechanisms helped proponents to build winning coalitions

within the different bargaining scenarios, and as often as not, contributed to LHSFs being approved or sustained.
- Shifting the locus of control: When LHSFs were proposed in Iraq and Afghanistan, both Maliki and Karzai, respectively, saw these forces through the lens of what they might mean for their own patronage networks and sources of power within the neo-patrimonial systems that predominated in each country at that time. Theirs was a takeover maneuver, using control mechanisms as a means for wresting greater institutional, and ultimately personal, control over the resources. While not completely divorced from agent control (Karzai and Maliki cared very much about selecting "like-minded" or loyal agents while dismissing the rest), the underlying rationale for introducing controls was more about curbing U.S. authority and wresting control over these forces. In a way, these foreign leaders used the United States' own tools against it, using the language of accountability, oversight, and state authority to subvert U.S. intentions for the program.
- Limiting devices: Opponents or skeptics of these initiatives also sometimes proposed control mechanisms as a way to try to limit the worst risks of the initiative should it go forward. In the first Train and Equip program, the political momentum behind supporting an anti-ISIL ground force was virtually unstoppable, leading Congress to authorize the initiative despite substantial misgivings. Congress instead used control mechanisms to at least protect major political interests or prevent risks, limiting the ability of the administration to use the force for broader (anti-Assad) intervention aims in Syria, and providing political cover for downstream risks like weapons going to terrorist groups or enabling atrocities. Those worried about the risks of the ALP—ranging from human rights advocates to diplomats vested in the state-building project—saw U.S. support to local defense forces as inevitable, given the surrounding context and frequent resort to such quasi-official forces. They used their bargaining leverage to at least demand controls that might curtail the biggest threats to civilian protection or state-building objectives.

These various control mechanisms (whether used by proponents or skeptics) were of course not completely removed from the idea of constraining the behavior or activities of LHSFs (the agents). Nominally, this was the goal of each proposed measure. However, what tended to drive the proposal of each of these measures was the political debate and deliberations over the initiative in question, rather than the level of risk or the degree to which control mechanisms had any prospect of mitigating them.

This evidence of the motivations that drove specific control mechanisms points to a different explanatory framework. BPA sees foreign policy outcomes as the product of competing views between different policy stakeholders, which are negotiated through a process of bargaining and persuasion. The policy outcome that results will represent a compromise of these different viewpoints, rather than the preferences of any one player or bureaucratic constituency within the bargaining debate or the conclusions of a rational cost-benefit analysis by any of these players. Applying a political bargaining lens to these situations helps to better explain both what drove the enactment of control mechanisms in each LHSF case study and why control mechanisms arose when the costs and benefits did not add up.

Building from this, the evidence from the case studies, in addition to the analysis of the bargaining patterns within each, further suggests that the structure of the bargaining environment was more predictive of whether control mechanisms would emerge than elements such as the costliness of control mechanisms. Typically, it was only once a bargaining moment emerged that numerous and hefty controls came into play. Such bargaining moments had a greater likelihood of being triggered in more open, diffuse, and multiplayer bargaining arenas. In other scenarios—for example, in a more unilateral decision-making environment like the early *sahwa* period in Iraq, or in situations with a smaller level of force mobilization that did not require broader funding or buy-in (like the covert auxiliaries discussed in chapter 4)—a bargaining moment was less likely to be spurred, and very few control mechanisms were in fact generated. It was not that these forces were any less risky, but rather that the political dynamics did not force the sort of bargaining deliberations that would lead to the proposal of risk-mitigation measures and responses. This suggests that rather than predicating the emergence of controls on the costs and benefits of exerting them (as principal-agent theory would expect), we should look to the structure of the bargaining arena and moment to anticipate whether substantial control mechanisms would emerge.

THE INTERACTION BETWEEN BARGAINING AND ORGANIZATIONAL THEORY

BPA theories were also important in understanding the growing influence of organizational processes and tendencies and their ability to explain the growth in control mechanisms over time. Bargaining dynamics manifested across all of the case studies, up to the most recent case of the ANA-TF's creation in 2018. However, over time such bargaining interacted with a growing number of institutional standards and expectations for dealing with these situations. BPA theory considers not only the effects of bargaining on foreign policy outputs, but also the influence of other ideational, organizational, or institutional elements. Across the case studies, these were in evidence: organizational preferences, missions, and routines determined how LHSF proposals were viewed by different bureaucratic actors or players, as well as the set of risk parameters and accountability repertoires deemed appropriate for these situations. They also then queued the appropriate responses, often in the form of particular control mechanisms.

The relationship between these organizational tendencies and bargaining dynamics tended to be interactive, with a particular bargaining moment over LHSFs queuing the need for risk-mitigation measures or controls and the established SOPs and routines furnishing the content. When DoD was tasked with implementing congressional conditions that Syrian and Iraqi Train and Equip forces demonstrate "respect for human rights and the rule of law,"[4] they reached for their standard protocols for partner security assistance—training on the "law of land warfare" or instituting safeguards with regard to child soldiers. When called on to demonstrate some form of accountability in its assistance to Syrian opposition, State Department bureaucrats repurposed and modified existing vetting, monitoring, and other risk-mitigation practices and protocols. Although such processes were not legally required in many cases, and were arguably inapt for Syrian conflict dynamics, they provided a ready—indeed, almost automatic—route for responding to accountability demands. Moreover, they enjoyed greater credibility during the rounds of internal bargaining precisely because these were already accepted modes of responding to risks.

Chapter 4 considered an additional type of institutional or organizational lens—that produced by the legacy effects of prior LHSFs. When two new LHSFs were proposed in Iraq and Afghanistan after 2014, the prior experiences of the *sahwa* and the ALP queued similar bargaining trajectories, resulting in control mechanisms that were more of an echo of their predecessors than the result of any de novo political demands. While bargaining was not absent, it was in many ways pro forma. The pathway for compromise between the U.S. and Iraqi and U.S. and Afghan governments had already been established in the *sahwa* and the ALP experiences, and the same controls proposed in those prior initiatives were repurposed or adapted for their post-2014 successors. Over time, continued experience with counterinsurgency-themed LHSFs in Iraq, Afghanistan, Syria, and other locales nurtured their own set of images of LHSFs, and the policy tools deemed appropriate for constraining the risks associated with those forces. Chapter 4 also observed that differing lenses or images of the more overt, counterinsurgency-themed forces versus the paramilitary auxiliary forces attached to counterterrorism teams generated different standards, with the former aligning overall with a greater number of control mechanisms.

BPA's organizational theory would assume that once internalized and adopted by the bureaucracy as appropriate measures, control mechanisms might be generated even without bargaining triggers, and in situations where the costs and benefits of doing so did not add up. However, the gap in prior BPA theorization concerns how those organizational protocols emerge and are internalized, such that they achieve this application-by-rote standard. The analysis of bargaining and other dynamics within some of the more recent LHSF initiatives in chapter 4, and of processes of change over time in chapter 5, suggested some pathways to explain how these control mechanisms might become entrenched. Repeated "calls and responses" to apply control mechanisms, as well as pressure to put them to regular practice, helped to socialize and ingrain these practices within the U.S. bureaucracy. They became a part of the routine or program activated when concerns about LHSF risks manifested. Over time they cohered into a regular part of the U.S. government's repertoire of accountability responses—something that might be applied by default, even when not called for by the surrounding political dynamics.

What the case studies in chapter 4 suggested was that while perhaps not yet at the level of a full SOP for LHSFs, a common approach or organizational tendency toward risk mitigation with LHSFs had emerged by the end of the Obama administration—at least the more overt and counterinsurgency-framed ones. Over time there appeared to be a tendency to apply a standard menu of control mechanisms whenever LHSFs were proposed, even if not queued by the bargaining demands in the case at issue.

Perhaps the best test of how ingrained these processes had become as organizational SOPs, or something close to it, was their continuance across administrations with very different policy preferences. Although many of the control mechanisms were developed under the Obama administration, the same approaches continued under the Trump administration, even though the latter demonstrated substantially different policy sensitivities to questions of risk and accountability. By the end of the Trump administration, there was no substantial retrenchment of existing control mechanisms. Instead, there was further expansion, with human rights controls even added to the counterterrorism auxiliary partners supported by the 127e fund. BPA suggests that once adopted, SOPs and scripts can be difficult to reverse or change. The fact that these mechanisms lived on, and were even expanded under the Trump administration, suggests that while they may not have achieved the internalization of full SOPs, there was already a degree of stickiness, such that a change of administration—even one with substantially different policy positions—could not undo them.

These two processes, bargaining pressure and the internalization of control practices over time, help explain the first puzzle: why control mechanisms were adopted even in cases where doing so would be costly and counterproductive to the aim of the initiative. They also explain why control mechanisms were increasingly adopted and expanded over time, despite repeated evidence of their failures and trade-offs. Once control mechanisms were established as the rules or SOPs of dealing with LHSFs, and socialized as such, the bureaucracy would revert to these mechanisms, even where the costs and benefits of doing so did not add up.

A MORE EXPANSIVE BPA FRAMEWORK

While the case study evidence suggested greater alignment with BPA theories than with principal-agent expectations, this required some modification of standard BPA approaches and analysis. This was most notable in the exploration of a much more significant role for a range of non-U.S.-government actors in U.S. policy deliberations. Most traditional BPA bargaining treatments focus on intra-bureaucratic bargaining and deliberations, often limited to the president or executive's inner circle. But across the case studies, a range of non-U.S.-government actors stepped in to either directly or indirectly shape the debate, in many cases directly volunteering or necessitating the application of control mechanisms.

Congress directly mandated a number of control mechanisms (and the criteria for their use) in the funding legislation that applied to the post-2014 Train and Equip programs in Syria and Iraq. Congress's indirect or informal pressure also contributed to the stronger application or interpretation of controls in other cases—for example, by continuing to exert pressure on the ALP throughout its life span, and through its insistence on supporting only anti-ISIL fighters in the New Syrian Forces initiative, the vetting criteria most associated with its failure.

There were also a range of other actors able to exert indirect or informal influence on U.S. internal bargaining debates. NGOs and other transnational networks advocated for human rights–related controls across nearly all of the programs in question. They created significant pressure, and thus the demand, for control mechanisms in the ALP authorization debate. Their ability to influence the agenda and the parameters of the debate through garnering public attention, accountability politics, and other means of advocacy indirectly but significantly influenced the controls developed. They also featured as prominent long-term actors in the development and reinforcement of human rights controls both over the course of the ALP and with regard to strengthening the framework and application of the Leahy Law globally.

Diplomats and bureaucrats of foreign countries also sometimes collaborated with U.S. congressional actors or transnational advocates to try to shape U.S. decision making on these initiatives indirectly. Where foreign allies were working closely with U.S. officials in implementing security or governance assistance in the countries in question, they were able to play an even more significant role. For example, in the debate over the ALP, as well as both the State Department and CIA assistance to the FSA, the diplomats of allied countries were able to indirectly shape U.S. decision making about LHSF programs and policies through co-decisional structures and routines, or through joint participation in the implementation of LHSF initiatives or related programs.

Most provocatively, in several cases, foreign leaders and their bureaucracies appeared closer to direct players or co-participants in the bargaining over what were ultimately U.S. policy choices. Chapter 6 argued that situations of compromised or shared sovereignty generated situations in which two or more governments (or in the case of the SDF, a non-state governing actor) served as co-participants in policy decisions for that territory. This included decisions about supporting LHSFs, such that where U.S. initiatives were proposed, these non-U.S.-government actors found themselves with a seat at the bargaining table and thus a direct role in the outcome of U.S. decision making. In bargaining over the *sahwa* and ALP, Iraqi prime minister Maliki and Afghan president Karzai had arguably the strongest influence on the outcome of bargaining and on which of the proposed control mechanisms were adopted.

A more limited example of this foreign bargaining dynamic was observed in deliberations with Turkey over jointly managed LHSFs in northwestern Syria and attempts to address Turkey's concerns over the SDF. Such transnational bargaining also appeared to manifest to some degree with the SDF. U.S. deliberations with the SDF, a non-state armed group, were more akin to coadministration and internal bargaining than subsidiary principal-agent dynamics. This goes beyond the idea of a situation of shared sovereignty and suggests an important lever of influence by virtue of de facto governing authority.

The different pathways of influence identified, along with the range of actors who appeared to play a role in the U.S. decision making, offer a much more expansive view of BPA bargaining and analysis, one more suited to the hybrid political systems and the overall heterogeneity that characterize many foreign policy situations.

CONTROLS AS AN ENABLING DEVICE

A starting point for this book was the observation that the United States has appeared to be more open to LHSF partnerships in the last two decades compared with other peer states. As we have seen, the United States has worked with a range of LHSFs since 2001, much more frequently than other Western states, and at least more overtly and expansively (if not more frequently) than it had prior to 2001. Many factors have influenced this trend, but control mechanisms also appear to have played their part.

First, control mechanisms frequently contributed to the authorization and initiative of these LHSFs. They facilitated policy compromises by bridging differences in various stakeholders' risk preferences and concerns. Such compromises facilitated LHSF support in situations where it otherwise would have been too controversial or where the initiative lacked sufficient internal bureaucratic or external partner support to be sustained. The ALP would not have been authorized without adopting some control mechanisms, in deference both to Karzai's objections and to the range of other concerns raised by State Department officials, other diplomatic partners, NGOs, and UN representatives. A second *sahwa*, the TMF program, would not have been permitted by Iraqi authorities if the United States had not acceded to their demands for institutional control. Likewise, the controversial lethal and nonlethal support for the FSA would not have survived the onslaught of internal critiques and objections without offering some concessions in the form of risk mitigation.

Second, part of what enabled such compromises to be struck was the fact that control mechanisms could shift the perceived costs or likely consequences of these programs. U.S. policy makers' decision about whether to support LHSFs or not might be framed as a cost-benefit analysis. They saw the benefits of such initiatives—for example, reducing the exposure of U.S. forces, or the advantages gained in terms of the intelligence or tactical assets of local partners. However, they also saw the costs, including the public, reputational, or legal repercussions of being seen to enable abusive militias or Islamic extremist groups, or the long-term risks of contributing to another al-Qaeda spin-off or of seeding local conflicts. Control mechanisms could facilitate authorization or expansion of these forces by appearing to mitigate or reduce at least some of these costs, making it more likely that a cost-benefit analysis would tip in favor of going ahead with the force. Some examples of how control mechanisms might sway the decisions:

- Efforts to set standards, increase awareness of existing standards through training or other communication of redlines, or induce compliance, either through precommitment mechanisms (e.g., the "pledge" for New Syrian Forces) or through the threat of sanctions, represent attempts to prevent these costs from materializing, at least in part.
- Institutionalizing LHSFs within host institutions—as with the ALP, the TMF, or the ANA-TF—could in theory mitigate concerns about misconduct by LHSF forces, including human rights abuses, by using institutional mechanisms to inculcate and enforce appropriate standards of behavior. For concerns that further arming and empowering LHSFs might contribute to an erosion in state authority or the "monopoly on force" (a common state-building objective), vesting these forces in state institutions might offer the prospect of gradual integration and state control.
- Institutionalization also helped defray U.S. public or legal liability, because the Afghan or Iraqi states would bear a greater share of state responsibility for any consequences that followed. If LHSFs were affiliated with the forces of the host state, then any misconduct by the LHSFs might be attributed to that state, rather than its international backers.
- Given that no one assumed that the above measures would entirely prevent certain issues with these forces, vetting or cut-offs promised to at least limit the public or reputational costs by ensuring that there was a mechanism to prevent U.S. funds from going to the most problematic units or forces. Even if this was not entirely successful, having such vetting at least demonstrated some attention to the problem, which might defray public criticism, legal liability, or reputational costs to a degree.

- Weapons tracking, or measures like requiring FSA fighters to return spent missile casings, might limit the number of weapons that go astray. However, as with the vetting, this was also a signaling device, at least demonstrating to internal or external critics that something was being done to try to address these unpalatable risks, thus mitigating some of the public blowback.

The degree to which each of these control mechanisms actually reduced the risks they sought to address is an open question. But the promise of being able to mitigate risks could nonetheless shift U.S. policy makers' calculations. Even if they did not fully change skeptics' overall view that these were risky forces or risky initiatives to support, they might minimize the perceived costs in ways that would allow the initiative to go forward. For example, in the case of arming and supplying FSA groups with lethal assistance (covertly), it is not clear that Obama ever thought this was a sound way forward, but he at least acceded to the pressure from his cabinet and regional allies, so long as some of the risks could be mitigated or reduced.

A third, related way that control mechanisms might enable LHSF partnerships is by rationalizing them despite their potential to undermine other U.S. policy commitments or goals. The decision to partner with an LHSF usually presents trade-offs as regards other policy goals or principles. Co-opting militias may appear the most immediate way to satisfy a need for local manpower and intelligence, but it can also present the risk of undermining other self-identified governance or state-building objectives in the same country, for example, by increasing the prevalence of forces outside state control or their ability to hold and govern territory. Supporting forces that may have the best chance of countering insurgent or terrorist groups in a given environment could lead to enabling or endorsing groups that do not uphold secular democratic values or that have engaged in war crimes or other misconduct. There is not always a way to reconcile these competing goals, at least not within the limited options available in a given country context. But control mechanisms became a powerful rationalizing device because they offered the promise, or the pretense, that this might be possible.

The LHSF dilemmas in Syria presented perhaps the starkest example of such challenges. Each of the LHSF initiatives working with

FSA-associated Arab groups were layered with a panoply of criteria for supported fighters and other controls that, if fully implemented, would have ruled out the large majority of fighting groups and individuals. Some former State Department and DoD officials or officers interviewed framed these unrealistic controls as either "wishful thinking" or a form of self-delusion that enabled support to go forward even though it contradicted U.S. policy principles.[5] As one former State Department official said, "There always was this cohort of what I would call Syria true believers who wanted to pretend that we could find groups who could fight for us in Syria . . . [and who] would be amazing fighters, from the right [ethnic or ideological] background, and abide by international law to the hilt."[6] Those fighters did not exist in Syria (or possibly anywhere), he noted, but the elaborate vetting and training criteria, discussions of redlines, and other program features and controls were pursued as if doing so would result in all of the concerns and commitments being addressed.

Another former State Department officer offered similar reflections about what she framed as the inherent trade-off between security expediency and human rights priorities, at least insofar as the partners in Syria were concerned: "There is a certain pathology of U.S. foreign policy that democracy is always part of the mission . . . [but] in many situations there is a direct trade-off between effectiveness and human rights. . . . We want to have it all and believe we can do it if we just put our minds to it, but it's not clear we can."[7]

From this perspective, control mechanisms offer a way to reconcile (at least on the surface) competing commitments—for example, to pursue LHSF partnerships that presented a risk of enabling war crimes without making the choice to abandon the U.S. commitment to human rights. When asked why U.S. bureaucrats might continue to pursue this course even after the costs and consequences had manifested, the same former State Department officer simply responded, "The system starts to believe its own rhetoric."[8]

Control mechanisms could also be seen as playing a rationalizing role in the trade-off between working with the SDF at the cost of relations with Turkey. Control mechanisms like weapons tracking and limitations (as well as the renaming of the SDF) were the sort of compromise that the U.S. bureaucracy identified as the middle ground that would allow it to work with the highly valued SDF while also addressing Turkey's concerns with the partnership. In reality, it was always a false middle ground, given that such tactical controls would never have addressed Turkey's objections to the arming of PKK-linked forces. The same former State Department officer who had discussed the pathology of U.S. foreign policy saw it as an attempt to paper over the failure to make tough decisions between competing priorities: "There was no decision to abandon Turkey and its preferences, and no decision to abandon the fight against ISIL."[9] Control mechanisms allowed a reluctant bureaucracy to rationalize an extremely difficult and unpalatable choice, but they never had much potential to address the underlying policy dilemma.

BPA's organizational theory offers an important perspective on such rationalizing properties. Organizational theory presumes that bureaucratic organizations (and the decision makers and bureaucrats within them) will interpret information and adopt positions or policies that accord with their larger mission sets, images, and values. In some scenarios they might do this by rejecting propositions that run counter to their mission set and values. This certainly manifested in many of the LHSF bargaining debates, wherein those parts of the bureaucracy whose interests or mission was not served or aligned with the LHSF initiative in question would raise objections or try to block its authorization. However, failing that, the bureaucracy might seek to reconcile or rationalize unavoidable policy decisions with their internal mission sets and values.

Here it is important to reflect on the trajectory and normalization of LHSFs discussed in the introduction. As LHSFs have come out of the shadows and become a more overt and regular part of U.S. operating modalities and security strategies, the risks surrounding these forces have to be more openly reconciled with other U.S. commitments and interests, whether those related to promoting human rights or the preference for working through state institutions. To be sustained on a systemic basis, these required some degree of rationalization and bureaucratic adjustment. Considering (per BPA expectations) the United States less as a unitary actor and more as a policy arena made up of competing institutions, each with its own foreign policy tendencies, values, and guiding mission sets, helps to understand why this might be important. While parts of the U.S. security or defense establishment might find the costs or side effects of LHSFs to be acceptable given the need for immediate security partners, other parts of the U.S. bureaucracy might weigh the costs to other priorities or to long-term U.S. interests more heavily. For example, parts of the State Department might find it difficult to reconcile such partners with their state-building goals or their concerns about legal consequences or human rights commitments. As these partnerships became more regular, these other parts of the bureaucracy would have to find a way to reconcile regular support to LHSFs with their core values and mission sets. Control mechanisms facilitated this by presenting a regulatory facade that helped to reconcile uncomfortable policy decisions with the larger organizational values and principles. The rationalizing properties of control mechanisms allowed an administration like Obama's—filled with lawyers and human rights champions—to support partnerships that inevitably compromised their personal or institutional values and commitments. They did so by allowing policy makers to proceed as if the risks had been appropriately regulated and mitigated to the greatest extent possible.

In this light, control mechanisms might be viewed as a regulatory accoutrement to or by-product of the larger trend of working through LHSF partners—a policy self-justification that allows LHSFs to be rationalized, notwithstanding their likely cost to other U.S. commitments and foreign policy images. In doing so they act as a larger enabling device for the "by, with, and through" paradigm and for these types of partnerships.

It is important to emphasize that control mechanisms did not facilitate this practice on their own. Threat perceptions, security demands, and limitations in what the U.S. policy arena or public would tolerate in terms of U.S. troop exposure were important drivers of this expansive LHSF practice. Legal theories and innovations developed since 2001—pushing the envelope on legal interpretations of executive power under U.S. law and sovereign self-defense rights within international law—have provided the legal pretense for using LHSFs more regularly as counterterrorism auxiliaries and surrogates in other countries. The larger ideational trends discussed in the introduction, of embracing alternative non-state or hybrid security governance and "bottom-up" state building, also helped facilitate bureaucratic acceptance of this practice. However, control mechanisms would also play their part by quieting dissent and rationalizing the practice vis-à-vis larger U.S. commitments and risk preferences.

Overall, the analysis suggests that control mechanisms may have contributed to the United States' more frequent resort to LHSFs through these various enabling and rationalizing properties. All three of the above enabling functions are interrelated, and as such might contribute to LHSF use or authorization at any time. In any given authorization moment or decision, control mechanisms might enable a compromise, appear to diminish the costs and tip the balance toward authorization, or help sustain an unpalatable partnership by rationalizing the trade-offs involved. Assuming that these different enabling functions happen across any number of countries and any number of potential LHSF partnerships, we might expect more situations in which U.S. policy makers are persuaded to go forward with LHSF engagement, as well as a more frequent turn to LHSFs partnerships more generally.

CONTRIBUTIONS TO THE LITERATURE AND FUTURE RESEARCH

The forgoing case studies and analyses have significantly advanced the theorization and application of two major frameworks within international studies, nuancing the expectations of principal-agent theory while also expanding the use of BPA and its related tool kit to novel situations and actors. In addition, though, the theoretical tools and approaches developed have a potentially far wider remit. They could yield useful insights for a number of parallel policy scenarios—for example, risk mitigation in other proxy or irregular force contexts. In addition, the focus on political bargaining and bureaucratic dynamics throughout this book has offered insights far beyond the narrow question of risk mitigation. It offers the potential to develop a series of mid-level tools that would be useful for unpacking and exploring a range of policy- and decision-making dynamics in hybrid and transnational policy settings.

The counterhypothesis explored in this book was that control mechanisms were less a reflection of a calculated decision to balance the costs and risks of engaging in these controversial partnerships—the standard explanation within principal-agent theory or proxy warfare accounts—and instead tended to reflect deliberations between competing policy stakeholders or, alternately, the organizational tendencies and pathologies built into the bureaucratic apparatus administering them. Collectively, the trajectory of control mechanisms in each of the case studies, how they either mapped onto bargaining dynamics or strongly reflected organizational tendencies and SOPs, suggests a closer fit with BPA theory than with principal-agent control.

Nonetheless, principal-agent theory was still valuable in understanding some of the dynamics and considerations at play in these relationships. The case studies provided further evidence of the importance of agent selection and the challenges of controlling slack or divergent behavior in conflict settings, confirming principal-agent expectations on these points. Principal-agent theory was not as useful in predicting or explaining whether and which control mechanisms manifested, but this was in large part because it did not have a way to integrate or consider the range of intervening political and organizational considerations that in effect derailed standard principal-agent expectations. Given this, the case studies and additional bargaining and political analysis in this book might be seen less as disproving principal-agent theory as providing supplementary explanations that help nuance its tools and allow us to better understand how these relationships devolve in practice.

The analysis has provided equally significant contributions to BPA. Writing within foreign policy analysis, and specifically BPA, has long been appreciated for its ability to unpack the "black box" of domestic influences on foreign policy decision making.[10] And yet that contribution is limited where it *only* considers domestic influences, given the wide range of actors and sources of influence in the current international system. The case study evidence illustrated how a range of non-state and non-U.S.-government actors played a major role in the case studies and analyses—to include foreign leaders, diplomats and bureaucrats, international and nongovernmental organizations, and even non-state armed groups themselves. By broadening the frame of analysis to include this more diverse range of actors and sources of influence, this book updates BPA theory and applies it to a wider range of foreign policy scenarios. This extended theorization of how standard protocols and organizational features may form and change over time, drawing from the literature on transnational networks and normative change, also supplements the existing BPA framework, both in more traditional (domestic focused) settings and in this broader range of hybrid and transnational arenas.

The analysis also offers important material for consideration beyond the two frameworks of principal-agent theory and BPA. In several chapters, literature on transnational advocacy networks and normative change was useful in drawing out and supplementing BPA theories, both in terms of understanding the role and contributions of a broader number of players and in advancing a theory of change over time within BPA's bargaining and organizational theory. However, the contributions could be seen as going both ways. Chapters 5 and 6 offered further case applications of how transnational advocacy networks are able to intervene to shape agendas, socialize ideas, and otherwise influence policy positions. The focus on illustrating changes over time in chapter 5 offers an important illustration of the step-by-step process through which NGOs might collaborate to change the "rules of the game" and embed them in practice. While the literature on transnational networks and normative change anticipates such processes, there have been limited cases of application and illustration of these tactics to the groups and environments discussed in this book.

Lastly, the analytical approach adopted here has allowed for consideration not only of how and why control mechanisms evolve, but also what these tell us about the dynamics and disjunctures that arise when highly advanced administrative states try to engage in hybrid or mediated political environments. U.S. efforts to work with LHSFs or other substate political actors might be seen as an effort to embrace a more fluid approach to managing international relations—going beyond the typical state-based logic of diplomacy and state engagement. But they still did so using the tools and approaches of the administrative state, attempting to regulate and manage the relationship with the same bureaucratic processes and machinery that governed other matters of state policy. The case studies do not suggest tremendous results from this approach. While this panoply of controls appealed to technocrats in Washington, DC, they held little traction with those whose behavior they were (nominally) intended to change.

Such findings are largely in keeping with the broader literature on international engagement in these hybrid or mediated spaces. In such environments, the governing order or logic tends to be a patrimonial- or relationship-based governing order, regardless of the outward trappings of an institutional state.[11] An institutionalized rule or standard that could be very powerful in shaping U.S. policy makers' risk preferences and policy responses would have at best only a temporary weight or meaning in these environments. In many ways, it was as if both systems were speaking different languages, with much lost in translation. These observations reinforce the call to go beyond existing dichotomies within international relations—for example, the construct of state versus non-state actors or formal or informal systems and structures. However, it offers the caution that these binaries are deeply embedded not only in the way we think about and analyze international relations, but also in the ways that states or other actors make their moves within the international system.

Overall, this book has offered a set of mid-level tools for analyzing and understanding transnational foreign policy making, both as it devolves in conflict spaces like Afghanistan, Iraq, and Syria in the periods in question, and back in the bureaucratic corridors of Washington, DC. The processes of policy rationalization discussed in this book, and the bureaucratic maneuvers accompanying them, are not as exciting as the sort of grand strategic machinations that tend to be associated with proxy warfare analysis and theorization. Their ad hoc and case-specific nature make them less satisfying than the more rational and regular cost-benefit-based theories of delegation. However, these sorts of internal to transnational bargaining dynamics, and the bureaucracy's efforts to absorb and rationalize the outputs stemming from them, are the reality of governance and policy decision making in these sorts of mixed transnational and subnational policy environments.

These theoretical insights and modified tools would apply in many more situations than those that feature in this book. In terms of further research and analysis, the most direct extension would be to apply these tools to other LHSF support scenarios. As noted in the introduction, application of this framework to U.S.-supported LHSFs in other arenas, such as Libya or Somalia, or to the more ad hoc support taking place in a number of locations in West Africa, was considered, but was thought to be beyond the scope and time frame of this research project. LHSF relationships in these contexts would likely be closer to the counterterrorism auxiliary relationships described in chapter 4, but with some variation. The differing geographic base and U.S. strategic interests in these other locations would also likely trip different domestic interests and foreign policy lenses. As a result, extending this framework of analysis to these differing situations might test the bargaining and organizational premises developed in this book, thereby helping to further nuance the tools and insights gained from them.

Consideration of risk-mitigation tendencies and policy development among other states or multilateral institutions could also be fruitful, beginning with like-minded countries or institutions that have engaged with substate actors, including the United Kingdom, France, Denmark, the Netherlands, Germany, or even the UN, with its due diligence policy.[12] Although these countries share common normative and institutional instincts with the United States on many levels, these other governments and entities would no doubt approach issues of substate partner risks and risk mitigation differently from the United States. Examining such alternate case studies might lend greater insight into risk-mitigation policies and dynamics. In addition, just as examining risk mitigation in U.S. practice offered broader insights into U.S. policy making, examining how other states or institutions approached these questions would garner insights into how these other states approach dilemmas within hybrid political situations, and the processes of bureaucratic accommodation and rationalization that follow.

An even further extension would be to consider issues of control and risk mitigation with states that are not so like-minded. The United States is somewhat of an outlier among Western states, having engaged in proxy support to LHSFs in far more situations, and with deeper levels of proxy support and engagement. But it is far from alone in terms of the general practice of nurturing proxy forces among substate or local actors in other countries. In the three countries examined alone, LHSFs have also been supported by Iran, Turkey, the UAE, Saudi Arabia, Qatar, Russia, and Pakistan.

Based on existing descriptions of some of these proxy relationships, we might expect to find very little in the way of human rights controls, and likely less of the bureaucratization of controls than was seen in the U.S. examples. But as was illustrated in the brief case study of U.S.-Turkish collaboration in supporting Syrian forces in northwestern Turkey, Turkey certainly demonstrated its own preferences in terms of selection (with its like-minded agents selected in part based on ideological affinities) and took steps to control what these forces did once deployed in Syria.[13] To offer another example, other literature on Iran's proxy relationships suggests a less institutionalized approach, with little evidence of the sort of technical, administrative, or regulatory checks seen in U.S. practice.[14] Yet, there were clear efforts to exert influence over proxies and to control for certain risks or issues, often through the levers of long-standing personal relationships and behavioral incentives, as well as a more flexible, pluralistic approach to proxy cultivation.[15]

Though the nature and means of deploying controls would be different, these controls would likely be no less affected by a blend of domestic and international considerations than they were in the U.S. case. They may also have been mediated and developed under the influence of complex, internal to transnational bargaining processes. Such studies would be more methodologically difficult given the relative lack of public information about decision making within the sponsoring regimes in question, as well as the greater risks of obtaining nonpublic information. Yet if feasible, approaching these proxy relationships through this political bargaining lens may fill a gap in the existing literature, which has so far tended to analyze such relationships through the arms-length approach of power balancing and proxy stratagems alone.

More broadly, this sort of application of bargaining or organizational insights to other proxy relationships might contribute to a richer and more nuanced analysis of proxy warfare. As noted, one of the major insights of this book is that expectations of principal-agent theory or proxy warfare, while not exactly misplaced, nonetheless offer only a starting point for understanding how the proxy relationship would devolve in practice. Going forward, the more interesting question to explore in many proxy situations is not where principal-agent expectations follow through, but where they do not, and why. This could include greater attention to the way that other bargaining or political dynamics intervene to disrupt principal-agent expectations, as happened in the case studies or as may be the case in some of the other proxy contexts identified above. Taking more of a foreign policy–implementation lens and exploring how a broader range of players and influences affected the micro-political decisions and deliberations within proxy relationships could yield greater insights into the ways that proxy warfare is manifesting, and potentially evolving, in the twenty-first century. Doing so would also respond to repeated calls for greater attention to the degree of agency enjoyed by the agents in these proxy relationships, as well as that enjoyed by other intervening actors.[16]

Beyond proxy relationships and armed groups, the larger question interrogated by the case studies was to consider how modern administrative states—like the United States—engage at the substate and transnational level of international policy. The case studies identified situations of transnational bargaining in the sphere of foreign security assistance, but this same sort of analysis would also be applicable to a range of other fields of foreign policy assistance—including substate governance, rule of law or justice promotion, or other peace-building endeavors. In considering how these approaches might explain decisions in a broader range of foreign policy assistance, the concept of transnational bargaining and co-decision making in situations of compromised and shared sovereignty merits particular attention. Theories of transnational bargaining and co-participation in policy deliberations or implementation need not be limited to cases where the key authorities in question are exercised in an almost fully joint manner—the shared sovereignty dynamic identified at certain points in Iraq and Afghanistan. While U.S. officials or other international actors might not become so intimately involved in administering territory and domestic policies in other countries as they were at the height of interventions in Afghanistan and Iraq, international donor assistance, conditionality, and situations of compromised sovereignty are certainly not rare. Transnational bargaining and a more porous donor-state decision-making process would also manifest in a range of situations in which donor assistance and conditionality is invoked, including those that fall short of a full compromise of sovereignty.

Nor, as many of the case studies suggested, should we expect transnational bargaining or sources of influence to be limited only to policy-making environments like those in Iraq, Afghanistan, and Syria. Certainly, some of the unconventional actors shaping U.S. policy were Afghan, Iraqi, and Syrian actors—whether the sovereign leaders of those countries or other non-state interlocuters or partners. But there were also examples of transnational bargaining and mediation happening in Washington, DC, with intervention in and influence over U.S. decision making coming from a range of interlocuters beyond these three countries. European partners, regional allies, and transnational advocacy organizations played a part in U.S. decision making, and presumably would also do so on a range of foreign policy scenarios well beyond questions of LHSFs or U.S. security policy in conflict-affected regions. As such, although the theorization helped explore state engagement within hybrid political environments, we should not conclude that U.S. decision making is more porous *only* when dealing with these hybrid political situations and non-state actors. This more expansive view of BPA bargaining and theorization might be applied to a wide range of policy issues in order to better explain institutional decision making in this globalized era of foreign policy making. This would, for example, align with other emerging research that has begun to explore the role of non-state or transnational actors in shaping policy decision making within EU institutions, or in other policy environments completely removed from conflict situations.[17]

EFFECTIVENESS OF MILITIA SUPPORT AND CONTROL

While this book has not focused on the effectiveness of supporting irregular forces in these contexts, interviewees frequently volunteered their perspectives on this question. Many (particularly military personnel) espoused the view that turning to militias, local fighters, or other irregular forces could be a way to address security threats, and even to provide a measure of protection to local populations. However, even proponents of LHSF support tended to argue that the way that the United States has deployed its support for these actors has made it difficult to achieve either goal. The reasons for this were not solely due to the risk-mitigation efforts and control mechanisms, although in many ways these reflected the larger shortcomings in the U.S. approach.

The objectives for the LHSFs discussed in this book varied—ranging from those whose main value to the United States was pursuing a particular security threat or target (e.g., the anti-ISIL forces in Syria) to those who were also seen as being able to contribute to "bottom-up" state building, local community protection, and governance (e.g., the ALP and the TMF). However, regardless of their objectives, the effectiveness of these strategies tended to depend on the number of resources invested in the initiatives in question, interviewees said. The notion of resources here goes beyond provision of small arms and material goods to include whether these initiatives were backed by much more substantial security and political resources—whether local forces were accompanied, overseen, and supported by larger and more significant force deployments (by U.S. forces or other national actors), or whether there was sufficient political will to provide broader and more long-term support. Because LHSFs tended to be treated as a "quick fix" solution, they tended not to be accompanied by either. As a result, almost axiomatically, the United States turned to LHSFs in precisely the situations where it was unwilling to provide the level of support needed for them to succeed.

Those who worked with or observed these LHSFs tended to argue that local or irregular forces needed to be accompanied by a larger infrastructure of support—embedded within a larger troop-mobilization strategy or at least mentored and supported by better-trained professional forces—to succeed in their tactical or security goals.[18] In the debate over the CIA support to the FSA, the internal CIA study concluded that using militias or rebels as proxies was rarely successful in achieving the desired security or strategic goals unless accompanied and supported by substantial U.S. forces and efforts.[19] Those who observed the ALP in Afghanistan argued that they had a degree of success when and where they were accompanied and closely mentored by international forces, or at least embedded within a larger troop deployment and operational strategy in the area.[20] But when international or other Afghan state forces withdrew, the ALP were much less successful in holding their own in an area.[21] Those involved in the initial Syria Train and Equip programs thought their prospects of achieving tactical success, as well as their ability to prevent the risk of misappropriation of weapons or war crimes, was very limited without co-deploying U.S. forces alongside the New Syrian Forces.[22] As one retired Special Forces officer who had been involved in the Syria initiative observed, "The only way you can really know what's going on is when you're out there.... This approach works when we're willing to put [U.S. forces] next to them—to help achieve tactical success ... [and also] to influence events as they're happening from an ethical perspective."[23] Yet in each of these cases, the larger motivation for turning to these LHSFs was that of cost avoidance—the desire to avoid deploying U.S. forces into sensitive situations (in the Syria cases) or at numbers greater than were already being deployed (in Afghanistan and Iraq). As a result, from the view of those working with these initiatives, they were set up to fail almost from the onset.

Where the LHSFs in question were linked to broader governance or political goals, the essential resource missing tended to be a sufficient political commitment—either in terms of its duration or its prioritization vis-à-vis other policy objectives. Those developing the initial ALP model saw it primarily as a local governance and community redevelopment strategy—enabling communities to take charge of their own security while also helping advance overall community development, governance, and revitalization.[24] They argued that it would only work if supported and seen through over a much larger time horizon than even the decade given it.[25] As one of the Special Forces officers involved in the original local defense pilots, Scott Mann noted, "When you are building capacity in an informal society, it is a multi-decade endeavor.... It took forty years to break informal mechanisms in rural Afghanistan; it will take at least that long before you can restore it and create a level of local capacity that can stand on its own."[26] While Mann and others argued for a more organic and cautiously developed model of community governance and security, U.S. military leaders at the time saw a more urgent need for local manpower in hard-to-reach Taliban areas, and the sort of "quick wins" that might enable a reversal of Taliban momentum before Obama reversed the "surge" in U.S. forces.[27] They prioritized using the ALP more as a quick stopgap over a model of long-term community development—to the initiative's detriment, Mann and others argued.

There were similar tendencies to view LHSFs as a short-term or expedient solution rather than part of a long-term strategy in both Iraq and Syria. With the SDF, it was a question of both timing and prioritization vis-à-vis other partnerships and objectives. Given Turkey's continued opposition, most SDF and SDC officials interviewed felt it was only a matter of time before U.S. political support for their position collapsed, and with it their ability to maintain the de facto governing authority and semi-autonomous standing they had achieved.[28] Lack of political capital and commitment was also an issue in Iraq. In addition to seeking to support additional manpower to counter ISIL, there was a deeper political strategy or rationale behind U.S. support for Sunni forces in the TMF. U.S. officials argued that greater inclusion of Sunni constituencies in the Iraqi government, and particularly the security forces, would prevent the sort of marginalization-based grievances that had twice contributed to the rise of extremist insurgencies.[29] Yet a relative gain in the political power of Sunni tribal actors ran counter to the goals of many other Iraqi political stakeholders.[30] Ultimately, the U.S. commitment to the idea of rebalancing Iraqi security institutions was low, and U.S. officials did not extend the amount of political resources and pressure that would have been required to protect this minority force. Within a short period of time, most of the units that had been mobilized had either been de facto demobilized or were brought under the control of more politically connected Shi'a PMF units.

This question of the degree of political commitment connects to a larger critique of the U.S. approach to proxy partnerships, and to a deficit in its underlying strategy of control. Again and again, a critique that surfaced among U.S. government officials, U.S. military officers, and outside experts (U.S. and otherwise) was that the United States' approach to managing its local partners was too short-term and "transactional," and that this created very weak incentives and levers of control among the proxies in question.[31] For example, a common sentiment expressed during interviews in Iraq was that the United States had less influence over Iraqi partners vis-à-vis Iran because it was only interested in cultivating short-term partners, and only when there was an immediate political or security crisis.[32] As one Iraqi commentator offered, while U.S. interest in Iraqi support waxed and waned with the political moment, "Iran will never change its position based on one election. Its short-term, midterm, and long-term goal is to influence Iraq and other countries in the region."[33] This perception was driven in large part by U.S. on-and-off support for some of the LHSFs featured in this book: Sunni forces fought for the *sahwa*, only to be abandoned by the United States and left to Maliki's persecution; many of those that survived then rallied for the TMF, only to later be dissolved or have to make amends with Shi'a-led PMF. Kurdish officials expressed a similar tale of waxing-and-waning support and abandonment—with the United States sometimes strongly supporting KRG interests, but then, from the Kurdish view, abandoning them to side with Baghdad.[34] In short, across a range of stakeholders in Iraq, the United States was perceived as an unreliable partner. Faced with such a partner, "the lesson learned would be 'don't put your eggs in one basket,'" quipped

Safa Rasoul Al-Sheikh, who served as deputy national security adviser for Iraq for several years.[35]

The heavy reliance on technical control mechanisms to achieve risk mitigation both reflected and exacerbated the shortcomings of this approach. U.S. forces interviewed who had decades of experience in developing and mentoring forces tended to argue that the most powerful constraints or incentives for shaping behavior were only available in long-term relationships.[36] On this view, a longer time span allows a level of trust to develop at an interpersonal level, which in turn allows for the reinforcement of standards and expectations in a way that can contribute to the gradual socialization of normative rules and a stronger performance on the tactical or operational levels over time. In addition, where partner forces know that they would be protected, not just in the immediate threat environment, but tomorrow and thereafter, they in theory would be more willing to accept U.S. conditions or constraints on behavior. Instead, the short-term approach that the United States adopted left these more substantive control mechanisms unavailable. As a result, all that was left was to try to accomplish the same objectives via technical or contractual controls—running a database check to screen for problematic past behavior, providing training on human-rights compliance, or technical reporting and tracking on weapons possession (often remotely). Most of those engaged with these LHSFs argued that these technical controls and the immediate transactional incentives that reinforced them (primarily the risk of having funding cut) were weak substitutes compared to the more interpersonal and long-term levers of influence over behavior.[37]

Such reflections suggest some inherent limitations on trying to achieve a greater degree of accountability and control with the sort of operating profile that typically accompanies "by, with, and through" arrangements. Choosing to operate at arms-length limits personal risks to U.S. officials or forces, and may defray some domestic costs, but it inevitably comes with a loss of control. As one former Special Operations commander framed this trade-off in risks, "It's an understandable temptation—especially if you're viewing the conflict from DC—to want to try to control things. But if you wanted maximum control, you would send the U.S. military.... When you go the indigenous route, you have ceded some control in order to put less of your own forces at risk.... I've lowered risk to my soldiers but increased the risk to the mission itself."[38] That arms-length operating profile, combined with a tendency to view these non-state or substate partners in a more short-term, expedient, and transactional light, impedes the ability to exert control or leverage over the groups in question.

HUMAN RIGHTS–RELATED CONSTRAINTS AND CONTROLS

As noted in the preface, what animated my initial interest in this question was whether efforts to address human rights risks and misconduct by these forces proved effective. Control mechanisms related to LHSFs' potential to carry out war crimes, abuses, or other misconduct were present in nearly all of the cases examined—from vetting prospective commanders based on allegations of past abuses to providing explicit training on laws of war or human rights abuses in the country in question.

Although these measures are still very new, there was only limited evidence of them changing the behavior of the fighters in question. In each case study, there were multiple examples of LHSFs engaged in war crimes and other abuses—this despite the fact that many of them had been vetted under the Leahy Law or, in Syria, "Leahy Law–like" vetting procedures, and that in many cases they had received some form of human rights training or "redlines" against engaging in abuses. It is difficult to measure the counterfactual—the levels of abuse had no controls been in place. Nonetheless, with the exception of some of the FSA commanders who had been supported through multiple U.S. initiatives, few of those at the unit or commander levels even seemed to be aware that human rights abuses were a redline when it came to U.S. cooperation.[39]

There are multiple reasons why these human rights checks had only a limited effect. Rules and regulations—for example, the ALP codes of conduct, the New Syrian Forces pledge, or any training on human rights and laws of war—tend to be viewed as more effective when they are reinforced by broader institutional structures and norms.[40] While advocates pushed for program features like training and indoctrination on human rights, most military officers interviewed offered that a ten-day training—or even longer—would do little unless continually reinforced by commanding officers and other institutional pressure.

On the effectiveness of the Leahy Law or similarly inspired vetting and sanctioning mechanisms, implementation challenges abounded. One former State Department officer who worked on the Leahy Law implementation offered a summary of some of the key challenges in these sorts of environments: "A lot of it depends on what you can scrape from sourceable material. The vetting is only as good as the database and there are limits to what the database can give you."[41] Many abuses take place in locations where access is difficult, and there is no documentation of it, he said. In addition, he offered that, "while journalists and human rights organizations do good documentation, it's selective. It doesn't represent the full scope of abuses going on out there. There is lots of dark matter out there.... There's no way a database is comprehensive enough to make vetting meaningful."[42]

In addition, the Leahy Law's deterrent effect is contingent in part on the linkage with state institutions. For state-based forces, the Leahy Law is designed to provoke a larger conversation about human rights accountability with host governments. This is why the law requires that governments be notified where particular units are blocked. However, LHSFs tend to have a tenuous link with state institutions and accountability structures—or in some cases no link at all. As such, institutional deterrence and accountability tends to be ineffective with more irregular or devolved forces. In some LHSF scenarios, there may be insufficient command and control and institutional organization to even have any kind of a deterrent effect, even with more direct commander-level engagement.

In addition, even where some state institutional linkage was present—as with the ALP and the TMF—it was undercut by what might be framed as "security exceptionality." In both Afghanistan and Iraq, the Afghan National Security Forces and Iraqi Security Forces were the most prominent U.S. security partners. There were well-documented and more numerous abuses by prominent commanders within these forces. Yet, in part because of evidentiary challenges, and in part (at least in Afghanistan) due to deliberate loopholes and exceptions for key partners, leading state forces or commanders implicated in gross abuses were not blocked from U.S. funding.[43] To the extent that any message trickled down to subordinate units and LHSF partners, it was that human rights obligations were fungible.

This is not to suggest that U.S. standards of conduct established for partner forces had zero impact. Senior Afghan officials interviewed in 2021, as the United States was preparing to withdraw from Afghanistan, suggested that U.S. insistence on standards of conduct as a condition of assistance had created (positive) institutional constraints, even if not to the level that U.S. officials or human rights advocates might desire. For example, one senior Afghan security official cautioned that the first thing to go out the window with the U.S. withdrawal would be any semblance of restraints on conduct. "Where you have forced international standards . . . they don't let you take the shortcut," he said. "But if you have this constant fighting and security pressures [due to Taliban advances], but you no longer have international pressure on the other side, you will continue to lower the quality of Afghan forces. It will continually force these short-term choices. . . . If the United States leaves and there's no peace deal [with the Taliban] . . . it will just be a fight for survival."[44]

Such comments, alongside those of other senior U.S. military and security sector specialists, suggest a more nuanced takeaway. It was not that creating standards of conduct in line with international law was necessarily ineffective, but the degree to which they were heeded and institutionally absorbed depended on the prioritization given to them, how consistently they were reinforced, and over what length of time. One senior U.S. military commander offered that the problem was that the United States had often not been consistent in enforcing any standards or conditions with partner forces; this led to lack of compliance even among state partner forces, but it became even worse "when we get to these smaller groups, guys on a mountain top."[45] "We are not very good about putting our foot down and saying [to U.S. local partners], 'You must meet this requirement,'" he observed. "When we go into these relationships, we need to be very firm on what the standards are, what conditions are demanded, and hold the forces to it."[46] The inconsistent approach taken to implementing the Leahy Law—in certain arenas due to a lack of political will, though in many cases due to a host of implementation challenges—meant that it delivered only a weak message. Particularly with LHSF forces, which tend to be more removed from institutional constraints and pressures, this would have very limited effect, if any at all.

There is another way to consider the effects of human rights controls: in terms of the degree to which they shaped U.S. policy makers' behavior and choices. As seen in many of the case studies in the book, often the goal of some of these controls was not actually to constrain the forces in question, but to limit U.S. policy makers from partnering with the worst actors or to otherwise constrain risky LHSF initiatives. The evidence of how such human rights controls shaped U.S. policy makers' choices was mixed. On the one hand, there was some evidence of these human rights checks having either a negligible or even a potentially damaging effect on U.S. decision making. Several U.S. officials as well as other non-U.S. partners who had observed the implementation of the Leahy Law in practice said it often veered toward a "box-ticking" exercise. The same State Department official who highlighted the implementation challenges above also noted that because the Leahy Law (or similar standards) does offer this sense of having "checked the box," it could be detrimental to human rights scrutiny. He said that based on what he had observed, "Having procedures in place debilitated a larger discussion of how to mitigate the risks. . . . It creates a sort of 'artificial confidence' about the groups you're working with, and stops the degree of policy consideration of whether working with these groups is good."[47]

On the other hand, some of those working within the U.S. government offered the counterview that, while in some cases it was applied too formulaically and with insufficient rigor, the Leahy Law still acted as an important forcing agent compelling the bureaucracy to take human rights risks into consideration systematically across potential partner choices. As one U.S. official who served in the U.S. embassy and in other senior policy positions observed, "At the embassy level, I saw a great deal of attention going to the Leahy Law and a great deal of concern about the behavior of militias and units. . . . It created top-down pressure to pay attention to extrajudicial killings and other abuses."[48] His view was that while the U.S. record on human rights was not perfect in Afghanistan—or in the other countries discussed in this book, for that matter—it would have been far worse without application of the Leahy Law.[49]

Some of the evidence discussed in chapter 5 is also relevant for considering the Leahy Law's broader effects. As cited in that discussion, one senior military leader characterized the Leahy Law amendment as a "huge sword of Damocles hanging over all these [local partner] operations. . . .

If they run afoul from the standards set in the Leahy amendment, you have to walk away from these groups."[50] There was also the evidence of Leahy Law human rights standards seeping into the calculations of the CIA, as observed with the FSA in Syria. This suggested a degree of inculcation of Leahy Law standards—or at least the principle that some degree of human rights scrutiny was expected—well beyond the letter of the law, and even when it comes to irregular force partners. Such observations suggest effects that are larger than might be indicated by Leahy Law investigations and blocks alone.

The overall findings on how well the Leahy Law addressed human rights risks are in many ways similar to critiques of the overall approach toward LHSFs discussed in the previous section, suggesting real limits of using technical- or tactical-level controls to shape or curb militia forces' behavior. Such findings also recall the earlier observation that U.S. regulatory approaches can almost be seen as "lost in translation" when applied to LHSFs in these hybrid environments. It is not that the Leahy Law was ineffective per se, but it appeared to have a much stronger effect on U.S. policy makers than it did on the conduct of the LHSF groups in question.

ILLUSIONS OF CONTROL: THE LIMITS OF A RISK-MITIGATION APPROACH TO LARGER FOREIGN POLICY DILEMMAS

The case studies in this book have traversed some of the most complex and fraught arenas of U.S. foreign and security policy of the last two decades, and within them, some of the most controversial security relationships. For many, these partnerships represent some of the worst tendencies of U.S. security policy—a willingness to partner with those with blood on their hands and questionable motives and linkages in order to pursue the security threat of the moment. For others, the willingness to partner with non-state or substate forces where they are the relevant players represents a form of foreign policy pragmatism, a willingness to get beyond the too-limited state-based framework. Control mechanisms sat at the intersection of these competing views, responding to demands for control and accountability and offering a middle ground that might square the circle between immediate security interests and long-term normative commitments.

Yet, that middle ground proved to be a false one. Technical, bureaucratic mechanisms were hard to apply in conflict situations, and were largely misaligned to the sort of incentives and disincentives that would actually change the calculus of armed groups in these environments. These controls proved to be more effective at shaping U.S. policy makers' decisions than at shifting the behavior of the LHSFs in question. As a result, the reliance on such controls introduced a degree of moral hazard. By shifting U.S. policy makers' perceptions of the costs, they helped justify LHSF partnerships whose outcomes would inevitably produce trade-offs for U.S. policies and principles, thereby masking rather than mitigating the strategic risks or consequences of such partnerships.

Much of principal-agent theory's consideration of such proxy or surrogate relationships focuses on the ways that structural factors, information asymmetries, or other agent or principal characteristics make it difficult to constrain costly behavior. However, as viewed through this larger lens, the real challenge presented by such control mechanisms might not be the degree to which they fail to constrain risks, but the fact that they worked all too well in terms of enabling risky choices in larger political decision making.

In the summer of 2023, I returned to Afghanistan—this time with a very different purpose, and in many ways to a different country. In August 2021, as U.S. forces were near to completing their withdrawal from Afghanistan, the Government of the Islamic Republic of Afghanistan collapsed. The Taliban insurgent movement had been rapidly seizing control of Afghan territory since President Biden announced the full withdrawal of the United States in April 2021. When they reached the gates of Kabul in mid-August, they found a capital city undefended and theirs for the taking. Hours after former president Ashraf Ghani had fled the country, the Taliban occupied the presidential palace, restoring the government of the Islamic Emirate of Afghanistan to power.

By 2023, life in the Islamic Emirate appeared much the same as it had under the Islamic Republic (the shorthand already used to refer to the regime of the previous two decades)—at least on the surface. There was the same gaggle of street life and traffic in Kabul. Women still went about their business around the capital despite a spate of restrictions on women's dress and basic freedoms. There were even some of the same bureaucrats in government offices, going through the same official procedures and practices developed under the previous regime, albeit now under a Taliban flag.

Yet beneath the sameness there were dramatic changes, as much in terms of what was not there as what was—first and foremost, in the absence of women and girls in many areas of public life. Through a spate of restrictive edicts,[51] girls were banned from secondary schools and universities; female government officials were kept on the payroll but prohibited from showing up to work in person; women were banned from working for the UN or leading NGOs and were prohibited from taking part in a host of other sectors. There were additional restrictions on women's ability to travel, to go to parks, recreation spaces, even national monuments.

Gone, too, were the more than 1.6 million Afghans who had fled since the Taliban took power.[52] For those who stayed behind, a new panoply of moral codes and restrictions were gradually silencing aspects of public life. Imagery and billboards deemed un-Islamic were painted over or replaced. With bans on music, wedding halls no longer blared out tinny regional standards—a nightly reprieve for many residents. But Taliban restrictions had also closed the space for open dialogue and dissent. Crackdowns on protestors, intimidation of journalists, and other social restrictions had quickly choked off media and civil society—once arguably the freest in the region.[53]

Not all changes or absences were bad. The near pervasive conflict and fighting that had dominated the past decade and a half was significantly diminished. For the first time since 2004, the number of attacks had fallen so low that one international conflict tracker deemed that Afghanistan no longer met the definitional threshold of armed conflict.[54] Though sound statistics were sparse, reports of crime and corruption were also down.

Because of this, some Afghans welcomed the Taliban's approach—far better, they argued, than the perpetual conflict and the rampant abuses of the prior government. But for many Afghans I spoke to, there was a tremendous sense of loss at the rollback of a generation of hard-fought gains and investment. "It's like Afghanistan has been taken back a hundred years," one Afghan nurse in a remote district of the Central Highlands observed.[55] Even those who might not endorse Western values—conservative religious figures, those from the Taliban heartland who had little access to the benefits and reforms of the prior decades—often objected to the Taliban's restrictive policies. I spoke with a group of women from rural areas of southern Afghanistan who were not opposed to the Taliban's return to power. Steeped in conservative values, they had never enjoyed, or even contemplated, a full education. But they nonetheless said that they thought girls' education was important, that services for all were a fundamental right, and that they should have a voice.[56]

Would the outcome have been different in Afghanistan had the United States taken a different approach on some of the partnerships and policy dilemmas discussed in this book? In some ways, no. The success or failure of the intervention in Afghanistan hinged on much larger strategic choices and missteps. The many different militia or community mobilization initiatives proposed throughout the two decades of engagement never proved to be as "game-changing" as they were promised to be.

And yet, some of the instincts behind the United States' turn to these LHSFs, in addition to its particular way of managing those relationships, certainly links back to some of the larger failings of the U.S. engagement. I was reminded of one Turkish official's critique of the U.S. approach to local partners. In his conversations with them, U.S. officials would always frame the United States' partnership with the Kurdish SDF as "transactional, temporary, and tactical"—even if, in his view, it was anything but.[57] The same mantra of "transactional, temporary, and tactical" could be applied to the U.S. approach to the ALP in Afghanistan, and indeed to the United States' engagement in Afghanistan as a whole. Yet the change that the United States hoped to produce in Afghanistan was supposed to be the opposite. The objectives required investments and change that would be strategic, long-standing, and political in nature. Such effects could not be achieved by tactical-level innovations like LHSFs, or by technical approaches to larger partner and political choices alone. The tools that the United States was willing to adopt were fundamentally mismatched to the larger objectives.

The approach to risk mitigation—the focus of this book—has in many ways been symptomatic of this larger disjuncture. Too often U.S. policy makers have responded to significant international policy challenges through the adoption of technical- or tactical-level tools in ways that effectively shaped the trajectory of these signature foreign policy initiatives. These tools increased in number and sophistication, but they never added up to a strategic response—either to the political or security dynamics that the United States sought to alter or to the human rights and accountability challenges that abounded. As a result, the strategies adopted largely tweaked around the margins of unpalatable policy choices rather than fundamentally altering their direction. Risk-mitigation devices—among other foreign policy tools and crutches—created the illusion of control, without doing anything to address the foreign policy dilemmas in question.

ACKNOWLEDGMENTS

The author would like to thank the many colleagues, fellow scholars, policy makers, and friends who offered their time and their insights for this book. Special thanks are due to Glen Rangwala for supporting this work all along, from the research concept through to the final draft. I would also like to thank the many colleagues and friends who offered their feedback throughout the research and writing process, including David Talbot, Sophie Rosenberg, Rachel Reid, Frances Brown, Ashley Jackson, Steven Tankel, Geoffrey Swenson, Florian Weigand, Fiona Mangan, Jasmine Bhatia, Devon Curtis, Rebecca Wright, and many others. The field research would not have happened without the insights, suggestions, and on-the-ground camaraderie of a number of fellow researchers, including Philipp Rotmann, András Derzsi-Horváth, Kate Clark, Deedee Derksen, Renad Mansour, Mac Skelton, Douglas Ollivant, Candace Rondeaux, and a number of Afghan, Iraqi, and Syrian researchers (who wish not to be named). Last, but certainly not least, my deepest gratitude to my parents for supporting me emotionally and materially throughout this process (down to proofreading chapters!). And also to Marshall.

NOTES

PREFACE

1. Erica Gaston and Jonathan Horowitz, *The Cost of Kill/Capture: Impact of the Night Raid Surge on Afghan Civilians* (New York: Open Society Foundations, 2011); Mark Mazzetti, *The Way of the Knife: The CIA, a Secret Army, and a War at the Ends of the Earth* (New York: Penguin Books, 2014).
2. The term *arbakai* is associated with a tradition of tribal self-defense and collective enforcement originally native to the southeast area of Loya Paktia. Mohammed Osman Tariq, *Tribal Security System (Arbakai) in Southeast Afghanistan* (London: Crisis States Research Center, London School of Economics, 2008). Its appropriation and use by both international forces and Afghan powerbrokers to rebrand local security initiatives in the 2001–2021 period led to it having many of the same pejorative connotations for Dari- and Pashtu-speakers as the term "militia" has for many global audiences.
3. *Developments in Afghanistan: Hearing Before the Committee on Armed Services*, 112th Cong., 1st Sess. (March 16, 2011), https://www.govinfo.gov/content/pkg/CHRG-112hhrg65591/html/CHRG-112hhrg65591.htm.
4. Barnett R. Rubin, *The Fragmentation of Afghanistan* (New Haven, CT: Yale University Press, 2002), 201–225; Olivier Roy, *Islam and Resistance in Afghanistan* (Cambridge: Cambridge University Press, 1986), 13–14.
5. Antonio Giustozzi, "Auxiliary Irregular Forces in Afghanistan: 1978–2008," in *Making Sense of Proxy Wars: States, Surrogates & the Use of Force*, ed. Michael A. Innes (Washington, DC: Potomac Books, 2012), 89–107; Rubin, *The Fragmentation of Afghanistan*, 158.
6. Thomas Barfield, *Afghanistan: A Cultural and Political History* (Princeton, NJ: Princeton University Press, 2010), 135–136; Afghanistan Justice Project, "Casting Shadows:

War Crimes and Crimes against Humanity: 1978–2001" (working paper, Afghanistan Independent Human Rights Commission, 2005).
7. Barfield, *Afghanistan*, 252–254; Rubin, *The Fragmentation of Afghanistan*, 258–263, 274–278.
8. Ashley Jackson, *Politics and Governance in Afghanistan: The Case of Nangarhar Province* (Kabul: Afghanistan Research and Evaluation Unit, 2014), 13.
9. Roger Mac Ginty, "Warlords and the Liberal Peace: State-Building in Afghanistan," *Conflict, Security & Development* 10, no. 4 (2010): 578–592, https://doi.org/10.1080/14678802.2010.500548; Mark Peceny and Yury Bosin, "Winning with Warlords in Afghanistan," *Small Wars & Insurgencies* 22, no. 4 (2011): 603–618, https://doi.org/10.1080/09592318.2011.599166.
10. Deedee Derksen, "Commanders in Control: Disarmament, Demobilization and Reintegration in Afghanistan Under the Karzai Administration" (PhD diss., King's College London, 2016); International Crisis Group, *A Force in Fragments: Reconstituting the Afghan National Army*, Asia Report No. 190 (Brussels: International Crisis Group, 2010); Antonio Giustozzi, "Bureaucratic Façade and Political Realities of Disarmament and Demobilisation in Afghanistan," *Conflict, Security & Development* 8, no. 2 (2008): 169–192, https://doi.org/10.1080/14678800802095369.
11. Carl Forsberg and Tim Sullivan, "Criminal Patronage Networks and the Struggle to Rebuild the Afghan State," *Prism: A Journal of the Center for Complex Operations* 4, no. 4 (2013): 157–173; Erica L. Gaston, "Afghanistan Case Study," in *Elite Capture in US Security Assistance* (Washington, DC: United States Institute of Peace, 2022); William Maley, "Statebuilding in Afghanistan: Challenges and Pathologies," *Central Asian Survey* 32, no. 3 (2013): 255–270, https://doi.org/10.1080/02634937.2013.834719.
12. Human Rights Watch, *Today We Shall All Die: Afghanistan's Strongmen and the Legacy of Impunity* (New York: Human Rights Watch, 2015); Matthieu Aikins, "Our Man in Kandahar," *The Atlantic*, November 2011, https://www.theatlantic.com/magazine/archive/2011/11/our-man-in-kandahar/308653/.
13. As will be discussed in chapter 2, prior to this 2009 initiative, there had been various efforts to mobilize irregular forces or tribal militias into quasi-statutory bodies in support of the state. These and other private-sector support trends are discussed at greater length in Erica Gaston and Kate Clark, *Backgrounder: Literature Review of Local, Community or Sub-state Forces in Afghanistan* (Berlin: Global Public Policy Institute, 2017).
14. Rachel Reid, *"Just Don't Call It a Militia": Impunity, Militias, and the "Afghan Local Police"* (New York: Human Rights Watch, 2011), 2.
15. Astri Suhrke, "The Long Decade of State-Building in Afghanistan," in *Managing Conflict in a World Adrift*, ed. Chester A. Crocker, Fen Osler Hampson, and Pamela Aall (Washington, DC: United States Institute of Peace, 2015), 555–570; Jonathan Goodhand and Aziz Hakimi, *Counterinsurgency, Local Militias, and Statebuilding in Afghanistan* (Washington, DC: United States Institute of Peace, 2013), https://www.usip.org/publications/2013/12/counterinsurgency-local-militias-and-statebuilding-afghanistan.

16. Adam Entous, "Covert CIA Mission to Arm Syrian Rebels Goes Awry," *Wall Street Journal*, January 26, 2015; Adam Entous, "U.S. Readies 'Plan B' to Arm Syria Rebels," *Wall Street Journal*, April 12, 2016.
17. William Shakespeare, *Julius Caesar*, act 3, scene 1.
18. Legal discussions surrounding such obligations gravitate around the influential (if controversial) International Court of Justice 1986 judgment in the case Military and Paramilitary Activities (Nicaragua v. United States), Judgment, 1986 I.C.J. Rep. 14, §220. See also International Committee for the Red Cross, "Rule 149. Responsibility for Violations of International Humanitarian Law," Customary IHL Database, accessed November 7, 2023, https://ihl-databases.icrc.org/customary-ihl/eng/docs/v1_rul_rule149.
19. International Committee of the Red Cross, "Rule 149"; Knut Dörmann and Jose Serralvo, "Common Article 1 to the Geneva Conventions and the Obligation to Prevent International Humanitarian Law Violations," *International Review of the Red Cross* 96, nos. 895–896 (2014): 707–736, https://doi.org/10.1017/S181638311400037X; International Committee of the Red Cross, *Allies, Partners, and Proxies: Managing Support Relationships in Armed Conflict to Reduce the Human Cost of War* (Geneva: International Committee of the Red Cross, 2021); Erica L. Gaston, *Regulating Irregular Actors: Can Due Diligence Checks Mitigate the Risks of Working with Non-state and Substate forces?* (London: Overseas Development Institute; Berlin: Global Public Policy Institute, 2021), https://gppi.net/2021/06/02/regulating-irregular-actors.
20. Margaret E. Keck and Kathryn Sikkink, *Activists Beyond Borders: Advocacy Networks in International Politics* (Ithaca, NY: Cornell University Press, 2014); Winifred Tate, *Counting the Dead: The Culture and Politics of Human Rights Activism in Colombia* (Berkeley: University of California Press, 2007); Julie A. Mertus, *Bait and Switch: Human Rights and U.S. Foreign Policy* (New York: Routledge, 2008).

INTRODUCTION

1. Andrew Mumford, *Proxy Warfare* (Cambridge: Polity Press, 2013); Alex Marshall, "From Civil War to Proxy War: Past History and Current Dilemmas," *Small Wars & Insurgencies* 27, no. 2 (2016): 183–195, https://doi.org/10.1080/09592318.2015.1129172; Alejandro Colás and Bryan Mabee, eds., *Mercenaries, Pirates, Bandits and Empires: Private Violence in Historical Context* (New York: Columbia University Press, 2010); Karl W. Deutsch, "External Involvement in Internal War," in *Internal War*, ed. Harry Eckstein (New York: Free Press of Glencoe, 1964), 98–110.
2. Mary Kaldor, *New and Old Wars: Organised Violence in a Global Era* (Stanford, CA: Stanford University Press, 2010); Herfried Munkler, *The New Wars* (Cambridge: Polity Press, 2004); David Keen, *Complex Emergencies* (Cambridge: Polity Press, 2008).
3. Richard B. Andres, Craig Wills, and Thomas E. Griffith, "Winning with Allies: The Strategic Value of the Afghan Model," *International Security* 30, no. 3 (2005): 124–160, https://doi.org/10.1162/0162288057759695913; Stephen Biddle, "Allies, Airpower, and

Modern Warfare: The Afghan Model in Afghanistan and Iraq," *International Security* 30, no. 3 (2005): 161–176, https://doi.org/10.1162/016228805775969555.
4. Giustozzi, "Auxiliary Irregular Forces in Afghanistan"; Deedee Derksen, *Non-state Security Providers and Political Formation in Afghanistan* (Waterloo, ON: Centre for Security Governance, 2016), https://reliefweb.int/report/afghanistan/non-state-security-providers-and-political-formation-afghanistan; Kate Clark et al., *Ghosts of the Past: Lessons from Local Force Mobilisation in Afghanistan and Prospects for the Future* (Kabul: Afghanistan Analysts Network; Berlin: Global Public Policy Institute, 2020).
5. In Iraq, there were an estimated 95,000 forces mobilized into the Sons of Iraq by early 2007. Statement of Stephen Biddle, senior fellow, Council on Foreign Relations, *Stabilizing Iraq from the Bottom Up: Testimony Before the Committee on Foreign Relations*, 110th Cong., 2d Sess. (April 2, 2008), 3, https://www.cfr.org/report/stabilizing-iraq-bottom. Tracking by the UN mission in Afghanistan documented just over 25,000 tribal and community members mobilized into the Afghan Local Police by the end of 2013. Clark et al., *Ghosts of the Past*, 75n3.
6. Aaron Stein, *Partner Operations in Syria: Lessons Learned and the Way Forward* (Washington, DC: Atlantic Council, 2017); Rod Thornton, "Problems with the Kurds as Proxies Against Islamic State: Insights from the Siege of Kobane," *Small Wars & Insurgencies* 26, no. 6 (2015): 865–885, https://doi.org/10.1080/09592318.2015.1095844.
7. Shawn T. Cochran, "Security Assistance, Surrogate Armies, and the Pursuit of US Interests in Sub-Saharan Africa," *Strategic Studies Quarterly* 4, no. 1 (2010): 111–152; Thijs Jeursen and Chris van der Borgh, "Security Provision After Regime Change: Local Militias and Political Entities in Post-Qaddafi Tripoli," *Journal of Intervention and Statebuilding* 8, no. 2–3 (2014): 173–191, https://doi.org/10.1080/17502977.2014.925249; Craig Whitlock, "U.S. Intensifies Its Proxy Fight Against al-Shabab in Somalia," *Washington Post*, November 24, 2011, https://www.washingtonpost.com/world/national-security/us-intensifies-its-proxy-fight-against-al-shabab-in-somalia/2011/11/21/gIQAVLyNtN_story.html; Emadeddin Badi, *Exploring Armed Groups in Libya: Perspectives on Security Sector Reform in a Hybrid Environment* (Geneva: Geneva Centre for Security Sector Governance, 2020), https://www.dcaf.ch/exploring-armed-groups-libya-perspectives-ssr-hybrid-environment; Adam Day, Vanda Felbab-Brown, and Fanar Haddad, *Hybrid Conflict, Hybrid Peace: How Militias and Paramilitary Groups Shape Post-conflict Transitions* (New York: United Nations University Centre for Policy Research, 2020); Ken Menkhaus, *Non-state Security Providers and Political Formation in Somalia* (Geneva: Center for Security Governance, 2016).
8. Max Boot, *The Savage Wars Of Peace: Small Wars and the Rise of American Power* (New York: Basic Books, 2014); Alan Axelrod, "Mercenaries of the Air (1861–Present)," in *Mercenaries: A Guide to Private Armies and Private Military Companies* (Thousand Oaks, CA: CQ Press, 2014), 123–148; Jonathan Phillips, "Mercenaries, Private Military Contractors, and Non-traditional Forces," in *Blackwell Companions to American History: A Companion to American Military History*, ed. James C. Bradford (Oxford: Blackwell Publishers, 2010), 507–516.

9. William Blum, *Killing Hope: US Military and CIA Interventions Since World War II* (London: Zed Books, 2014); Michael McClintock, *Instruments of Statecraft: U.S. Guerrilla Warfare, Counter-Insurgency, and Counter-Terrorism, 1940–1990* (New York: Pantheon Books, 1992); William Rosenau and Zack Gold, *The Cheapest Insurance in the World? The United States and Proxy Warfare* (Washington, DC: Center for Naval Affairs, 2019).

10. Andreas Krieg, "Externalizing the Burden of War: The Obama Doctrine and US Foreign Policy in the Middle East," *International Affairs* 92, no. 1 (2016): 97–113, https://doi.org/10.1111/1468-2346.12506; Nick Terse, *The Changing Face of Empire: Special Ops, Drones, Spies, Proxy Fighters, Secret Bases and Cyber Warfare* (Chicago: Haymarket, 2012); Thomas Waldman, "Strategic Narratives and US Surrogate Warfare," *Survival* 61, no. 1 (2019): 161–178, https://doi.org/10.1080/00396338.2019.1568049; Mazzetti, *The Way of the Knife*.

11. Joseph L. Votel and Eero R. Keravuori, "The By-With-Through Operational Approach," *Joint Force Quarterly* 89, no. 2 (2018): 40–47; Department of Defense, *Summary of the 2018 National Defense Strategy of the United States of America* (Washington, DC: U.S. Department of Defense, 2018).

12. Cochran, "Security Assistance"; Votel and Keravuori, "The By-With-Through Operational Approach."

13. David Romano, Brian Calfano, and Robert Phelps, "Successful and Less Successful Interventions: Stabilizing Iraq and Afghanistan," *International Studies Perspectives* 16, no. 4 (2015): 388–405; Biddle statement, *Stabilizing Iraq from the Bottom Up*; Linda Robinson, *Tell Me How This Ends: General David Petraeus and the Search for a Way Out of Iraq* (Washington, DC: PublicAffairs, 2008).

14. *The Authorization of the Use of Force in Syria: Hearings Before the Committee on Foreign Relations*, 113th Cong., 1st Sess. (September 3, 2013), https://www.foreign.senate.gov/imo/media/doc/090313_Transcript_The Authorization of the Use of Force in Syria.pdf.

15. See, e.g., National Defense Authorization Act for Fiscal Year 2018, Pub. L. No. 115-91, 131 Stat. 1283 (2017), sec. 127. Congressional staff interviewed described it as a fund designed to enable proxy relationships, and one that was deliberately agnostic on whether it supported state or non-state forces. Senate Armed Services Committee staff, interview by author, Washington, DC, May 31, 2018, interview 89; House staffer involved in foreign operations oversight and accountability issues, interview by author, Washington, DC, June 6, 2019, interview 93; Senate Armed Services Committee staff, interview by author, Washington, DC, September 24, 2019, interview 99. For illustrations of its use see, Wesley Morgan, "Behind the Secret U.S. War in Africa," *Politico*, July 2, 2018, https://www.politico.com/story/2018/07/02/secret-war-africa-pentagon-664005; Nick Terse, "Special Operations Forces Continue to Expand Across the World—Without Congressional Oversight," *The Nation*, July 17, 2018, https://www.thenation.com/article/archive/special-operations-forces-continue-expand-across-world-without-congressional-oversight/.

16. See statement of General Raymond A. Thomas III, U.S. Army commander, United States Special Operations Command, *Three Decades Later: A Review and Assessment*

of Our Special Operations Forces 30 Years After the Creation of U.S. Special Operations Command: Hearing Before the Subcommittee on Emerging Threats and Capabilities of the Committee on Armed Services, 115th Cong., 1st Sess. (May 2, 2017), https://docs.house.gov/meetings/AS/AS26/20170502/105926/HHRG-115-AS26-Wstate-ThomasR-20170502.PDF; Terse, "Special Operations Forces Continue to Expand Across the World."

17. Robert I. Rotberg, *When States Fail: Causes and Consequences* (Princeton, NJ: Princeton University Press, 2010); Francis Fukuyama, *State-Building: Governance and World Order in the 21st Century* (Ithaca, NY: Cornell University Press, 2004); Stephen D. Krasner and Carlos Pascual, "Addressing State Failure," *Foreign Affairs* 84, no. 4 (2005): 153–163; Robert I. Rotberg, *State Failure and State Weakness in a Time of Terror* (Washington, DC: Brookings Institution Press, 2003).

18. Simon Chesterman, *You, the People: The United Nations, Transitional Administration, and State-Building* (Oxford: Oxford University Press, 2004); Michael Doyle and Nicholas Sambanis, *Making War and Building Peace: The United Nations Since the 1990's* (Princeton, NJ: Princeton University Press, 2006).

19. Oliver P. Richmond, "The Problem of Peace: Understanding the 'Liberal Peace,'" *Conflict, Security & Development* 6, no. 3 (2006): 291–314; Michael Barnett and Christoph Zurcher, "The Peacebuilder's Contract: How External Statebuilding Reinforces Weak Statehood," in *The Dilemmas of State-Building: Confronting the Contradictions of Postwar Peace Operations*, ed. Roland Paris and Timothy D. Sisk (London: Routledge, 2009), 23–52; Suhrke, "The Long Decade of State-Building in Afghanistan"; Richmond, "The Problem of Peace."

20. Susan L. Woodward, *The Ideology of Failed States* (Cambridge: Cambridge University Press, 2017), https://doi.org/10.1017/9781316816936; Charles Call, "The Fallacy of the 'Failed State,'" *Third World Quarterly* 29, no. 8 (2008): 1491–1507, https://doi.org/10.1080/01436590802544207.

21. Joel Migdal, "State Building and the Non-nation State," *Journal of International Affairs* 58, no. 1 (1994): 17–46; Douglass C. North, John Joseph Wallis, and Barry R. Weingast, *Violence and Social Orders: A Conceptual Framework for Interpreting Recorded Human History* (Cambridge: Cambridge University Press, 2009), https://doi.org/10.1017/CBO9780511575839; Ariel I. Ahram, *Proxy Warriors: The Rise and Fall of State-Sponsored Militias* (Stanford, CA: Stanford University Press, 2011); Christian Lund, *Twilight Institutions: Public Authority and Local Politics in Africa* (Malden, MA: Blackwell, 2006); Thomas Risse, ed., *Governance Without a State? Policies and Politics in Areas of Limited Statehood* (New York: Columbia University Press, 2011).

22. Volker Boege et al., *On Hybrid Political Orders and Emerging States: State Formation in the Context of "Fragility"* (Berlin: Berghoff Handbook Dialogue, 2008), 8, https://gsdrc.org/document-library/on-hybrid-political-orders-and-emerging-states-state-formation-in-the-context-of-fragility/.

23. Niagalé Bagayoko, "Introduction: Hybrid Security Governance in Africa," *IDS Bulletin* 43, no. 4 (2012): 1–13, https://doi.org/10.1111/j.1759-5436.2012.00330.x; Boege et al., *On Hybrid Political Orders and Emerging States*.

INTRODUCTION 287

24. Renad Mansour and Peter Salisbury, *Between Order and Chaos: A New Approach to Stalled State Transformations in Iraq and Yemen* (London: Royal Institute for International Affairs at Chatham House, 2019), 2.
25. James N. Rosenau and Ernst Otto Czempiel, eds., *Governance Without Government: Order and Change in World Politics* (Cambridge: Cambridge University Press, 1992); Anne L. Clunan and Harold A. Trinkunas, *Ungoverned Spaces: Alternatives to State Authority in an Era of Softened Sovereignty* (Stanford, CA: Stanford Security Studies, 2010); Risse, *Governance Without a State?*; Ahram, *Proxy Warriors*.
26. Robert Malley, "Why the Middle East Is More Combustible Than Ever," *Foreign Affairs*, October 2, 2019, https://www.foreignaffairs.com/articles/middle-east/2019-10-02/unwanted-wars; Michael Crawford and Jami Miscik, "The Rise of the Mezzanine Rulers: The New Frontier for International Law," *Foreign Affairs* 89, no. 6 (2010): 123–132; Volker Boege, Anne M. Brown, and Kevin P. Clements, "Hybrid Political Orders, Not Fragile States," *Peace Review* 21, no. 1 (2009): 13–21, https://doi.org/10.1080/10402650802689997; Vanda Felbab-Brown, Harold A. Trinkunas, and Shadi Hamid, *Militants, Criminals, and Warlords* (Washington, DC: Brookings Institution Press, 2017); Ariel I. Ahram, *War and Conflict in the Middle East and Northern Africa* (Cambridge: Polity Press, 2020); Menkhaus, *Non-state Security Providers and Political Formation in Somalia*.
27. Jennifer Brick Murtazashvili, *Informal Order and the State in Afghanistan* (Cambridge: Cambridge University Press, 2016), https://doi.org/10.1017/CBO9781316286890; Peter Albrecht et al., *Perspectives on Involving Non-state and Customary Actors in Justice and Security Reform* (Rome: International Development Law Organization, 2011); Clunan and Trinkunas, *Ungoverned Spaces*.
28. Timothy Donais and Barbak, Ahmet, "The Rule of Law, the Local Turn, and Rethinking Accountability in Security Sector Reform Processes," *Peacebuilding* 9, no. 2 (2021): 206–221; Mark Sedra, "Adapting Security Sector Reform to Ground-Level Realities: The Transition to a Second-Generation Model," *Journal of Intervention and Statebuilding* 12, no. 1 (January 2, 2018): 48–63, https://doi.org/10.1080/17502977.2018.1426383; Department of Peacekeeping Operations, *Second Generation Disarmament, Demobilization and Reintegration (DDR) Practices in Peace Operations* (New York: United Nations, 2010); Rachel Kleinfeld, *Advancing the Rule of Law Abroad: Next Generation Reform* (Washington, DC: Brookings Institution Press, 2012).
29. Frances Z. Brown, "The U.S. Surge and Afghan Local Governance," United States Institute of Peace, September 12, 2012, https://www.usip.org/publications/2012/09/us-surge-and-afghan-local-governance; Frances Z. Brown, *Dilemmas of Stabilization Assistance: The Case of Syria* (Washington, DC: Carnegie Endowment for International Peace, 2018), https://carnegieendowment.org/2018/10/26/dilemmas-of-stabilization-assistance-case-of-syria-pub-77574; Noah Coburn, *Informal Justice and the International Community in Afghanistan* (Washington, DC: United States Institute of Peace, 2013); Albrecht et al., *Perspectives on Involving Non-state and Customary Actors in Justice and Security Reform*.
30. This sort of rebranding of local mobilization was not uncontested of course—academics and local experts decried U.S. military framing of their tribal mobilization efforts as a

"reification" of tribal traditions, or viewed them as a self-serving way to justify cheap and expedient force mobilization. See, e.g., Sam Vincent, Florian Weigand, and Hameed Hakimi, "The Afghan Local Police—Closing the Security Gap?," *Stability: International Journal of Security and Development* 4, no. 1 (2015), https://doi.org/10.5334/sta.gg; Aziz Hakimi, "Getting Savages to Fight Barbarians: Counterinsurgency and the Remaking of Afghanistan," *Central Asian Survey* 32, no. 3 (2013): 388–405, https://doi.org/10.1080/02634937.2013.843300.

31. Clionadh Raleigh, "Violence Against Civilians: A Disaggregated Analysis," *International Interactions* 38, no. 4 (2012): 462–481, https://doi.org/10.1080/03050629.2012.697049; Alex Alvarez, "Militias and Genocide," *War Crimes, Genocide, and Crimes Against Humanity* 2 (2006): 1–33; Ariel I. Ahram, "Pro-government Militias and the Repertoires of Illicit State Violence," *Studies in Conflict & Terrorism* 39, no. 3 (2016): 207–226, https://doi.org/10.1080/1057610X.2015.1104025; Dara Kay Cohen and Ragnhild Nordås, "Do States Delegate Shameful Violence to Militias? Patterns of Sexual Violence in Recent Armed Conflicts," *Journal of Conflict Resolution* 59, no. 5 (2015): 877–898, https://doi.org/10.1177/0022002715576748; Sara Plana, "'Proxies' and the Public: Testing the Statist Bias in Public Support for Military Aid" (working paper, Massachusetts Institute of Technology, Political Science Department, 2020); Ariel I. Ahram, "Armed Non-state Actors and the Challenge of 21st-Century State Building," *Georgetown Journal of International Affairs* 20, no. 1 (2019): 35–42. State forces may be equally abusive, of course, and may be responsible for even more systematic and widespread levels of violence. Nonetheless, state forces operate under the mantle and legal facade of another sovereign state, somewhat shielding external backers from international opprobrium or legal liability where misconduct arises.

32. U.S. official tracking TMF program, interview by author, Erbil, Iraq, December 7, 2016, interview 154.

33. Brian Glyn Williams, "Fighting with a Double-Edged Sword? Proxy Militias in Iraq, Afghanistan, Bosnia, and Chechnya," in *Making Sense of Proxy Wars: States, Surrogates & the Use of Force*, ed. Michael A. Innes (Washington, DC: Potomac Books, 2012), 61–88; Geraint Hughes, *My Enemy's Enemy: Proxy Warfare in International Politics* (Portland, OR: Sussex Academic Press, 2012), 58–68.

34. Steve Coll, *Ghost Wars: The Secret History of the CIA, Afghanistan, and Bin Laden, from the Soviet Invasion to September 10, 2001* (New York: Penguin Books, 2005); Hillary Rodham Clinton, *Hard Choices* (London: Simon & Schuster, 2014).

35. Corinna Jentzsch, Stathis N. Kalyvas, and Livia Isabella Schubiger, "Militias in Civil Wars," *Journal of Conflict Resolution* 59, no. 5 (2015): 755–769, https://doi.org/10.1177/0022002715576753; Benedetta Berti, "Violent and Criminal Non-state Actors," in *The Oxford Handbook of Governance and Limited Statehood*, ed. Thomas Risse, Anke Draude, and Tanja A. Börzel (Oxford: Oxford University Press, 2018), 1502–1519.

36. Kimberly Marten, *Warlords: Strong-Arm Brokers in Weak States* (Ithaca, NY: Cornell University Press, 2012); Dipali Mukhopadhyay, *Warlords, Strongman Governors, and the State in Afghanistan* (Cambridge: Cambridge University Press, 2014); William Reno, "Persistent Insurgencies and Warlords: Who Is Nasty, Who Is Nice, and Why?," in

Ungoverned Spaces: Alternatives to State Authority in an Era of Softened Sovereignty, ed. Anne L. Clunan and Harold A. Trinkunas (Stanford, CA: Stanford University Press, 2010), 57–76.

37. Thanassis Cambanis et al., *Hybrid Actors: Armed Groups and State Fragmentation in the Middle East* (New York: Century Foundation, 2019); Crawford and Miscik, "The Rise of the Mezzanine Rulers."
38. Huseyn Aliyev, "Strong Militias, Weak States and Armed Violence: Towards a Theory of 'State-Parallel' Paramilitaries," *Security Dialogue* 47, no. 6 (2016): 498–516, https://doi.org/10.1177/0967010616669900; Jentzsch, Kalyvas, and Schubiger, "Militias in Civil Wars."
39. Yezid Sayigh, "Hybridizing Security: Armies, Militias and Constrained Sovereignty," Carnegie Middle East Center, October 30, 2018, https://carnegie-mec.org/2018/10/30/hybridizing-security-armies-militias-and-constrained-sovereignty-pub-77597; Mansour and Salisbury, *Between Order and Chaos*.
40. Erica S. DeBruin, "Preventing Coups d'état: How Counterbalancing Works," *Journal of Conflict Resolution* 62, no. 7 (2017): 1433–1458, https://doi.org/10.1177/0022002717692652; Andrew J. Dowdle, "Civil Wars, International Conflicts and Other Determinants of Paramilitary Strength in Sub-Saharan Africa," *Small Wars & Insurgencies* 18, no. 2 (2007): 161–174, https://doi.org/10.1080/09592310701400796; Sabine C. Carey, Michael P. Colaresi, and Neil J. Mitchell, "Governments, Informal Links to Militias, and Accountability," *Journal of Conflict Resolution* 59, no. 5 (2015): 850–876, https://doi.org/10.1177/0022002715576747; Aliyev, "Strong Militias, Weak States and Armed Violence."
41. Ken Menkhaus, "Governance Without Government in Somalia Spoilers, State Building, and the Politics of Coping," *International Security* 31, no. 3 (2006): 74–106; Ahram, *Proxy Warriors*; Sayigh, "Hybridizing Security."
42. Mumford, *Proxy Warfare*; Tyrone L. Groh, *Proxy War: The Least Bad Option* (Stanford, CA: Stanford University Press, 2019); Idean Salehyan, "The Delegation of War to Rebel Organizations," *Journal of Conflict Resolution* 54, no. 3 (2010): 493–515, https://doi.org/10.1177/0022002709357890; Hughes, *My Enemy's Enemy*.
43. David Galula, *Counterinsurgency Warfare: Theory and Practice* (Westport, CT: Praeger Security International, 2006); Goran Peic, "Civilian Defense Forces, State Capacity, and Government Victory in Counterinsurgency Wars," *Studies in Conflict & Terrorism* 37, no. 2 (2014): 162–184; Govinda Clayton and Andrew Thomson, "Civilianizing Civil Conflict: Civilian Defense Militias and the Logic of Violence in Intrastate Conflict," *International Studies Quarterly* 60, no. 3 (2016): 499–510, https://doi.org/10.1093/isq/sqv011; Stathis N. Kalyvas, *The Logic of Violence in Civil War* (Cambridge: Cambridge University Press, 2006), 107–108.
44. Peic, "Civilian Defense Forces"; Jason Lyall, "Are Coethnics More Effective Counterinsurgents? Evidence from the Second Chechen War," *American Political Science Review* 104, no. 1 (2010): 1–20; Geraint Hughes and Christian Tripodi, "Anatomy of a Surrogate: Historical Precedents and Implications for Contemporary Counter-Insurgency and Counter-Terrorism," *Small Wars & Insurgencies* 20, no. 1 (2009): 1–35, https://doi.org/10.1080/09592310802571552.

45. Austin Long et al., *Locals Rule: Historical Lessons for Creating Local Defense Forces for Afghanistan and Beyond* (Santa Monica, CA: RAND Corporation, 2012), https://www.rand.org/pubs/monographs/MG1232.html.
46. Biddle statement, *Stabilizing Iraq from the Bottom Up*; David Kilcullen, *The Accidental Guerrilla: Fighting Small Wars in the Midst of a Big One* (London: Hurst & Co., 2009); Mark Moyar, *Village Stability Operations and the Afghan Local Police* (Tampa, FL: Joint Special Operations University, 2014).
47. Seth G. Jones and Arturo Muñoz, *Afghanistan's Local War—Building Local Defense Forces* (Santa Monica, CA: RAND Corporation, 2010); Austin Long, "The Anbar Awakening," *Survival* 50, no. 2 (2008): 67–94, https://doi.org/10.1080/00396330802034283.
48. Daniel Byman, "Why Engage in Proxy War? A State's Perspective," *Lawfare*, May 21, 2018, https://www.lawfareblog.com/why-engage-proxy-war-states-perspective#; Geraint Hughes, "Syria and the Perils of Proxy Warfare," *Small Wars & Insurgencies* 25, no. 3 (2014): 522–538, https://doi.org/10.1080/09592318.2014.913542; Austin Long, "Partners or Proxies? U.S. and Host Nation Cooperation in Counterterrorism Operations," *CTC Sentinel* 4, no. 11 (2011): 11–14.
49. Raleigh, "Violence Against Civilians"; Alvarez, "Militias and Genocide"; Ahram, "Pro-Government Militias and the Repertoires of Illicit State Violence"; Cohen and Nordås, "Do States Delegate Shameful Violence to Militias?"; Neil J. Mitchell, Sabine C. Carey, and Christopher K. Butler, "The Impact of Pro-Government Militias on Human Rights Violations," *International Interactions* 40, no. 5 (2014): 812–836, https://doi.org/10.1080/03050629.2014.932783.
50. Clayton and Thomson, "Civilianizing Civil Conflict"; Jentzsch, Kalyvas, and Schubiger, "Militias in Civil Wars," 6; Kalyvas, *The Logic of Violence in Civil War*, 376; Christoph V. Steinert, Janina I. Steinert, and Sabine C. Carey, "Spoilers of Peace: Pro-Government Militias as Risk Factors for Conflict Recurrence," *Journal of Peace Research* 56, no. 2 (2019): 2490263, https://doi.org/10.1177/0022343318800524.
51. Williams, "Fighting with a Double-Edged Sword?"; Hughes, *My Enemy's Enemy*, 58–68.
52. Hughes, "Syria and the Perils of Proxy Warfare"; Thornton, "Problems with the Kurds as Proxies Against Islamic State"; Michael A. Innes, ed., *Making Sense of Proxy Wars: States, Surrogates & the Use of Force* (Washington, DC: Potomac Books, 2012); Daniel Byman, *Deadly Connections: States That Sponsor Terrorism* (Cambridge: Cambridge University Press, 2007).
53. Stephen Biddle, Julia Macdonald, and Ryan Baker, "Small Footprint, Small Payoff: The Military Effectiveness of Security Force Assistance," *Journal of Strategic Studies* 41, nos. 1–2 (2018): 89–142, https://doi.org/10.1080/01402390.2017.1307745; Cochran, "Security Assistance"; Eli Berman and David A. Lake, *Proxy Wars: Suppressing Violence Through Local Agents* (Ithaca, NY: Cornell University Press, 2019); Daniel Byman, "Friends like These: Counterinsurgency and the War on Terrorism," *International Security* 31, no. 2 (2006): 79–115, https://doi.org/10.1162/isec.2006.31.2.79; Walter C. Ladwig III, "Influencing Clients in Counterinsurgency: U.S. Involvement in El Salvador's Civil War, 1979–92," *International Security* 41, no. 1 (2016): 99–146, https://doi.org/10.1162/ISEC_a_00251; Salehyan, "The Delegation of War to Rebel Organizations"; Idean Salehyan, Kristian

Skrede Gleditsch, and David E. Cunningham, "Explaining External Support for Insurgent Groups," *International Organization* 65, no. 4 (2011): 709–744, https://doi.org/10.1017/S0020818311000233; Aliyev, "Strong Militias, Weak States and Armed Violence"; Belgin San-Akca, *States in Disguise: Causes of State Support for Rebel Groups* (Cambridge: Cambridge University, 2016); Daniel Byman and Sarah E. Kreps, "Agents of Destruction? Applying Principal-Agent Analysis to State-Sponsored Terrorism," *International Studies Perspectives* 11, no. 1 (2010): 1–18, https://doi.org/10.1111/j.1528-3585.2009.00389.x.

54. Berman and Lake, *Proxy Wars*; Salehyan, "The Delegation of War to Rebel Organizations"; Idean Salehyan, David Siroky, and Reed M. Wood, "External Rebel Sponsorship and Civilian Abuse: A Principal-Agent Analysis of Wartime Atrocities" 68, no. 3 (2014): 633–661, https://doi.org/10.1017/S002081831400006X; Biddle, Macdonald, and Baker, "Small Footprint, Small Payoff," 100–103.

55. Darren G. Hawkins et al., eds., *Delegation and Agency in International Organizations* (Cambridge: Cambridge University Press, 2006), https://doi.org/10.1017/CBO9780511491368.002; Roderick Kiewiet and Matthew D. McCubbins, *The Logic of Delegation: Congressional Parties and the Appropriations Process* (Chicago: University of Chicago Press, 1991).

56. Byman, "Friends like These"; Biddle, Macdonald, and Baker, "Small Footprint, Small Payoff"; Ladwig, "Influencing Clients in Counterinsurgency"; Carey, Colaresi, and Mitchell, "Governments, Informal Links to Militias, and Accountability"; Salehyan, "The Delegation of War to Rebel Organizations"; Salehyan, Siroky, and Wood, "External Rebel Sponsorship and Civilian Abuse."

57. Graham T. Allison, *Essence of Decision: Explaining the Cuban Missile Crisis* (Boston: Little, Brown and Company, 1971); Chris Alden and Amnon Aran, *Foreign Policy Analysis: New Approaches* (Abingdon, UK: Routledge, 2012); Valerie M. Hudson and Christopher S. Vore, "Foreign Policy Analysis Yesterday, Today, and Tomorrow," *Mershon International Studies Review* 39, no. 2 (1995): 209–238.

58. Alden and Aran, *Foreign Policy Analysis*, 32–33; Graham T. Allison and Morton H. Halperin, "Bureaucratic Politics: A Paradigm and Some Policy Implications," *World Politics* 24, no. S1 (1972): 55–56, https://doi.org/10.2307/2010559; Allison, *Essence of Decision*, 66–71.

59. Richard C. Snyder, H. W. Bruck, and Burton Sapin, *Decision-Making as an Approach to the Study of International Politics* (Princeton, NJ: Princeton University Press, 1954); James N. Rosenau, "Pre-theories and Theories of Foreign Policy-Making," in *Approaches in Comparative and International Politics*, ed. R. B. Farrell (Evanston, IL: Northwestern University Press, 1966), 115–169; Harold Sprout and Margaret Sprout, "Environmental Factors in the Study of International Politics," *Journal of Conflict Resolution* 1, no. 4 (1957): 309–328; Valerie M. Hudson, "Foreign Policy Analysis: Actor-Specific Theory and the Ground of International Relations," *Foreign Policy Analysis* 1, no. 1 (2005): 5–7, https://doi.org/10.1111/j.1743-8594.2005.00001.x.

60. Hudson, "Foreign Policy Analysis"; Alden and Aran, *Foreign Policy Analysis*; Jean A. Garrison, ed., "Foreign Policy Analysis in 20/20: A Symposium," *International Studies Review* 5, no. 2 (2003): 155–202.

61. Allison, *Essence of Decision*.
62. Allison and Halperin, "Bureaucratic Politics"; Morton H. Halperin, "The Decision to Deploy the ABM: Bureaucratic and Domestic Politics in the Johnson Administration," *World Politics* 25, no. 1 (October 1972): 62–95, https://doi.org/10.2307/2010431; Morton H. Halperin, "Why Bureaucrats Play Games," *Foreign Policy*, no. 2 (1971): 70–90.
63. Roger Hilsman, *The Politics of Policymaking in Defense and Foreign Affairs* (Englewood Cliffs, NJ: Prentice-Hall, 1987); Jonathan Bendor and Terry M. Moe, "An Adaptive Model of Bureaucratic Politics," *American Political Science Review* 79, no. 3 (1985): 755–774, https://doi.org/10.2307/1956842.
64. Alden and Aran, *Foreign Policy Analysis*; Garrison, "Foreign Policy Analysis in 20/20"; Hudson and Vore, "Foreign Policy Analysis Yesterday, Today, and Tomorrow."
65. Garrison, "Foreign Policy Analysis in 20/20."
66. Rainer Baumann and Frank A. Stengel, "Foreign Policy Analysis, Globalisation and Non-state Actors: State-Centric After All?," *Journal of International Relations and Development* 17, no. 4 (2013): 489–521, https://doi.org/10.1057/jird.2013.12.
67. Long et al., *Locals Rule*; Seth G. Jones, *The Strategic Logic of Militia* (Washington, DC: RAND Corporation, 2012), https://www.rand.org/pubs/working_papers/WR913.html.
68. Clayton and Thomson, "Civilianizing Civil Conflict," 499. See also Govinda Clayton and Andrew Thomson, "The Enemy of My Enemy Is My Friend . . . The Dynamics of Self-Defense Forces in Irregular War: The Case of the Sons of Iraq," *Studies in Conflict & Terrorism* 37, no. 11 (2014): 920–935, https://doi.org/10.1080/1057610X.2014.952262; Yelena Biberman, "Self-Defense Militias, Death Squads, and State Outsourcing of Violence in India and Turkey," *Journal of Strategic Studies* 41, no. 5 (2017): 751–781, https://doi.org/10.1080/01402390.2016.1202822.
69. Bruce B. Campbell and Arthur D. Brenner, *Death Squads in Global Perspective: Murder with Deniability* (Basingstoke, UK: Macmillan, 2000); Tate, *Counting the Dead*.
70. Dylan Maguire, *A Perfect Proxy? The United States-Syrian Democratic Forces Partnership* (Blacksburg, VA: Proxy Wars Project, Virginia Tech School of Public and International Affairs, 2020), https://doi.org/10.21061/proxy-wars-maguire; Stein, "Partner Operations in Syria"; Thornton, "Problems with the Kurds as Proxies Against Islamic State."
71. Jentzsch, Kalyvas, and Schubiger, "Militias in Civil Wars."
72. The ANA-TF had a different recruitment model from the other three and was closest to being like a regular force. This force is discussed further in chapter 4.
73. Mitchell, Carey, and Butler, "The Impact of Pro-Government Militias on Human Rights Violations."
74. Plana, "'Proxies' and the Public."
75. Rachel Ormston et al., "The Foundations of Qualitative Research," in *Qualitative Research Practice: A Guide for Social Science Students and Researchers*, ed. Jane Ritchie et al. (London: SAGE Publications, 2014), 1–26.
76. Gemma van der Haar, Annelies Heijmans, and Dorothea Hilhorst, "Interactive Research and the Construction of Knowledge in Conflict-Affected Settings," *Disasters* 37, no. 1 (2201): S20–35; Jonathan Goodhand, "Research in Conflict Zones: Ethics and

Accountability," *Migration Review* 8, no. 4 (2000): 12–15; Romain Malejacq and Dipali Mukhopadhyay, "The 'Tribal Politics' of Field Research: A Reflection on Power and Partiality in 21st-Century Warzones," *Perspectives on Politics* 14, no. 4 (2016): 1011–1028, https://doi.org/10.1017/S1537592716002899; Larissa Fast, "A Reflexive Approach to Risk and Intervention for Third-Party Intervenors," *Conflict Resolution Quarterly* 30, no. 4 (2013): 467–489, https://doi.org/10.1002/crq.21075; J. Christopher Kovats-Bernat, "Negotiating Dangerous Fields: Pragmatic Strategies for Fieldwork Amid Violence and Terror," *American Anthropologist* 104, no. 1 (2002): 208–222, https://doi.org/10.1525/AA.2002.104.1.208; Koen Vlassenroot, "War and Social Research: The Limits of Empirical Methodologies in War-Torn Environments," *Civilisations* 54, no. 1 (2006): 191–198.

77. Elisabeth Jean Wood, "The Ethical Challenges of Field Research in Conflict Zones," *Qualitative Sociology* 29, no. 3 (2006): 373–386, https://doi.org/10.1007/S11133-006-9027-8.
78. Vlassenroot, "War and Social Research"; Sultan Barakat et al., "The Composite Approach: Research Design in the Context of War and Armed Conflict," *Third World Quarterly* 23, no. 5 (2002): 991–1003, https://doi.org/10.1080/0143659022000028530; Goodhand, "Research in Conflict Zones."
79. Goodhand, "Research in Conflict Zones," 8.
80. Goodhand, 8.
81. This includes in operations in parts of the Sahel, Libya, and Syria. Dan Sabbagh, "UK and France to Send Further Forces to Syria in Aid of US Withdrawal," *The Guardian*, July 9, 2019, https://www.theguardian.com/world/2019/jul/09/uk-and-france-to-send-further-forces-to-syria-in-aid-of-us-withdrawal; Nathaniel K. Powell, "'Experts in Decolonization?' French Statebuilding and Counterinsurgency in Chad, 1969–1972," *International History Review* 42, no. 2 (2020): 318–335, https://doi.org/10.1080/07075332.2019.1588769; Tarek Megerisi and Andrew Lebovich, "France's Strongman Strategy in the Sahel," European Council on Foreign Relations, March 8, 2019, https://www.ecfr.eu/article/commentary_frances_strongman_strategy_in_the_sahel; Jack Watling and Nick Reynolds, *War by Others' Means: Delivering Effective Partner Force Capacity Building* (London: Routledge, 2020).
82. Tom Ruys, "Of Arms, Funding and 'Non-lethal Assistance'—Issues Surrounding Third-State Intervention in the Syrian Civil War," *Chinese Journal of International Law* 13, no. 1 (2014): 13–53, https://doi.org/10.1093/chinesejil/jmu003; Louisa Loveluck, "What's Non-lethal About Aid to the Syrian Opposition?," *Foreign Policy*, September 20, 2012, https://foreignpolicy.com/2012/09/20/whats-non-lethal-about-aid-to-the-syrian-opposition; Policy and Operations Evaluation Department, *Review of the Monitoring Systems of Three Projects in Syria AJACS, White Helmets and NLA* (The Hague: Netherlands Ministry of Foreign Affairs, 2018).
83. Day, Felbab-Brown, and Haddad, *Hybrid Conflict, Hybrid Peace*; Giustozzi, "Auxiliary Irregular Forces in Afghanistan"; Badi, "Exploring Armed Groups in Libya."
84. Gaston, *Regulating Irregular Actors*.
85. Michael Shurkin and Anelise Bernard, "Ten Things the United States Should Do to Combat Terrorism in the Sahel," *War on the Rocks*, August 30, 2021, https://warontherocks.com/2021/08/ten-things-the-united-states-should-do-to-combat

-terrorism-in-the-sahel/; Saskia Brechenmacher, "Stabilizing Northeast Nigeria After Boko Haram," Carnegie Endowment for International Peace, May 30, 2019, https://carnegieendowment.org/2019/05/03/stabilizing-northeast-nigeria-after-boko-haram-pub-79042; "UNDP Trains Vigilantes and Civilian Joint Task Force Members in Human Rights and Leadership," United Nations Development Programme, July 9, 2019, https://www.undp.org/nigeria/news/undp-trains-vigilantes-and-civilian-joint-task-force-members-human-rights-and-leadership.

86. "Briefing: Sustaining Gains in Somalia's Offensive Against Al-Shabaab," International Crisis Group, March 21, 2023, https://www.crisisgroup.org/africa/horn-africa/somalia/b187-sustaining-gains-somalias-offensive-against-al-shabaab; Andy Pavey, "US Security Assistance to Somalia," Henry L. Stimson Center, March 20, 2023, https://www.stimson.org/2023/us-security-cooperation-with-somalia; Paul Cruickshank, "A View from the CT Foxhole: Harun Maruf, Senior Editor, Voice of America Somali," *CTC Sentinel* 15, no. 11 (2022): 10–20.

87. Ashley Jackson, Afghanistan researcher, interview by author, by WhatsApp, December 10, 2022, interview 219.

88. Gen. (ret.) David Petraeus, interview by author, by telephone, July 30, 2022, interview 208.

89. Gen. (ret.) David Petraeus, interview by author, by telephone, July 30, 2022, interview 208.

90. Groh, *Proxy War*; Mumford, *Proxy Warfare*; Seyom Brown, "Purposes and Pitfalls of War by Proxy: A Systemic Analysis," *Small Wars & Insurgencies* 27, no. 2 (2016): 243–257.

91. Rosenau and Gold, "The Cheapest Insurance in the World?"; The United States and Proxy Warfare;" Yaacov Bar-Siman-Tov, "The Strategy of War by Proxy," *Cooperation and Conflict* 19, no. 4 (1984): 263–273.

92. Lee Hsi-Min and Michael Hunzeker, "The View of Ukraine from Taiwan: Get Real About Territorial Defense," *War on the Rocks*, March 15, 2022, https://warontherocks.com/2022/03/the-view-of-ukraine-from-taiwan-get-real-about-territorial-defense/; Amy Qin and Amy Chang Chien, "Watching the War in Ukraine, Taiwanese Draw Lessons in Self-Reliance," *New York Times*, March 1, 2022; defense contractor, interview by author, by WhatsApp, April 22, 2019, interview 218.

93. Kaldor, *New and Old Wars*; Ahram, *Proxy Warriors*; Boege et al., "On Hybrid Political Orders and Emerging States"; Bagayoko, "Introduction."

94. Arie M. Kacowicz, "Review: Proxy Warriors: The Rise and Fall of State-Sponsored Militias; Ungoverned Spaces: Alternatives to State Authority in an Era of Softened Sovereignty; Strengthening Peace in Post-Civil War States: Transforming Spoilers into Stakeholders," *Perspectives on Politics* 10, no. 2 (2012): 434, https://doi.org/10.1017/S1537592711004968, reviewing Ahram, *Proxy Warriors*; Clunan and Trinkunas, *Ungoverned Spaces*; Matthew Hoddie and Caroline A. Hartzell, eds., *Strengthening Peace in Post–Civil War States: Transforming Spoilers Into Stakeholders* (Chicago: University of Chicago Press, 2010).

95. Michael N. Barnett, "Culture, Strategy and Foreign Policy Change: Israel's Road to Oslo," *European Journal of International Relations* 5, no. 1 (1999): 5–36.

1. THEORETICAL FRAMEWORK

1. Stephen Ross, "The Economic Theory of Agency: The Principal's Problem," *American Economic Review* 63, no. 2 (1973): 134–139, https://doi.org/10.2307/1817064; Michael C. Jensen and William H. Meckling, "Theory of the Firm: Managerial Behavior, Agency Costs, and Ownership Structure," *Journal of Financial Economics* 3, no. 3 (1976): 305–360; Kathleen M. Eisenhardt, "Agency Theory: An Assessment and Review," *Academy of Management Review* 14, no. 1 (1989): 57–74, https://doi.org/10.2307/258191. See also Barry M. Mitnick, "The Theory of Agency: The Policing 'Paradox' and Regulatory Behavior," *Public Choice* 24 (1975): 27–42.
2. Susan P. Shapiro, "Agency Theory," *Annual Review of Sociology* 31 (2005): 270–273; Terry M. Moe, "The New Economics of Organization," *American Journal of Political Science* 28, no. 4 (1984): 739–777; Eisenhardt, "Agency Theory."
3. Kiewiet and McCubbins, *The Logic of Delegation*; Matthew D. McCubbins and Thomas Schwartz, "Congressional Oversight Overlooked: Police Patrols Versus Fire Alarms," *American Journal of Political Science* 28, no. 1 (1984): 165, https://doi.org/10.2307/2110792; John Ferejohn and Charles Shipan, "Congressional Influence on Bureaucracy," *Journal of Law, Economics, & Organization* 6 (1990): 1–20, https://doi.org/10.1093/jleo/6.special_issue.1; Barry R Weingast, "The Congressional-Bureaucratic System: A Principal Agent Perspective (with Applications to the SEC)," *Carnegie Papers on Political Economy* 44, no. 1 (1984): 147–191; Morris P. Fiorina, "Legislative Choice of Regulatory Forms: Legal Process or Administrative Process?," *Public Choice* 39, no. 1 (January 1982): 33–66, https://doi.org/10.1007/BF00242147; Matthew D. McCubbins, Roger G. Noll, and Barry R. Weingast, "Structure and Process, Politics and Policy: Administrative Arrangements and the Political Control of Agencies," *Virginia Law Review* 75, no. 2 (1989): 431–482.
4. Hawkins et al., *Delegation and Agency in International Organizations*; Mark A. Pollack, *The Engines of European Integration: Delegation, Agency, and Agenda Setting in the EU* (Oxford: Oxford University Press, 2003), https://doi.org/10.1093/0199251177.001.0001.
5. Groh, *Proxy War*; Berman and Lake, *Proxy Wars*; Cochran, "Security Assistance"; Amos C. Fox, "Conflict and the Need for a Theory of Proxy Warfare," *Journal of Strategic Security* 12, no. 1 (2019): 44–71, https://doi.org/10.5038/1944-0472.12.1.1701; Byman, *Deadly Connections*; Salehyan, "The Delegation of War to Rebel Organizations."
6. Biddle, Macdonald, and Baker, "Small Footprint, Small Payoff"; Cochran, "Security Assistance"; Berman and Lake, *Proxy Wars*; Byman, "Friends Like These"; Ladwig, "Influencing Clients in Counterinsurgency."
7. Salehyan, "The Delegation of War to Rebel Organizations"; Salehyan, Gleditsch, and Cunningham, "Explaining External Support for Insurgent Groups"; Aliyev, "Strong

Militias, Weak States and Armed Violence"; San-Akca, *States in Disguise*; Byman and Kreps, "Agents of Destruction?"

8. Eisenhardt, "Agency Theory," 58; Jensen and Meckling, "Theory of the Firm."
9. Jensen and Meckling, "Theory of the Firm"; Ross, "The Economic Theory of Agency."
10. Hawkins et al., *Delegation and Agency in International Organizations*, 12–14.
11. Oliver E. Williamson, *The Economic Institutions of Capitalism: Firms, Markets, Relational Contracting* (New York: Free Press, 1985), 30.
12. David A. Lake and Matthew D. McCubbins, "The Logic of Delegation to International Organizations," in Hawkins et al., *Delegation and Agency in International Organizations*, 8, 24; Shapiro, "Agency Theory," 279–280.
13. Eisenhardt, "Agency Theory"; Shapiro, "Agency Theory"; Kenneth J. Arrow, "The Economics of Agency," in *Principals and Agents: The Structure of Business*, ed. John W. Pratt and Richard J. Zeckhauser (Boston: Harvard Business School Press, 1985), 37–51; Jeffrey S. Banks and Barry R. Weingast, "The Political Control of Bureaucracies under Asymmetric Information," *American Journal of Political Science* 36, no. 2 (1992): 509–524, https://doi.org/10.2307/2111488.
14. Lake and McCubbins, "The Logic of Delegation to International Organizations"; Biddle, Macdonald, and Baker, "Small Footprint, Small Payoff," 97.
15. Timothy W. Crawford and Alan J. Kuperman, eds., *Gambling on Humanitarian Intervention: Moral Hazard, Rebellion and Civil War* (Abingdon, UK: Routledge, 2006); Bengt Hölmstrom, "Moral Hazard and Observability," *Bell Journal of Economics* 10, no. 1 (1979): 74–91, https://doi.org/10.2307/3003320.
16. Shapiro, "Agency Theory"; Eisenhardt, "Agency Theory"; Hawkins et al., *Delegation and Agency in International Organizations*, 26–31.
17. Hawkins et al., *Delegation and Agency in International Organizations*; Kiewiet and McCubbins, *The Logic of Delegation*.
18. McCubbins and Schwartz, "Congressional Oversight Overlooked."
19. John Brehm and Scott Gates, "When Supervision Fails to Induce Compliance," *Journal of Theoretical Politics* 6, no. 3 (1994): 323–343; Eli Berman et al., "Introduction: Principals, Agents, and Indirect Foreign Policies," in *Proxy Wars: Suppressing Violence Through Local Agents*, ed. Eli Berman and David A. Lake (Ithaca, NY: Cornell University Press, 2019), 1–27.
20. Darren G. Hawkins and Wade. Jacoby, "How Agents Matter," in Hawkins et al., *Delegation and Agency in International Organizations*, 204, https://doi.org/10.1017/CBO9780511491368.008. See also Hawkins et al., *Delegation and Agency in International Organizations*, 13–14, 21.
21. Kiewiet and McCubbins, *The Logic of Delegation*; McCubbins and Schwartz, "Congressional Oversight Overlooked"; Mark A. Pollack, "Delegation, Agency, and Agenda Setting in the European Community," *International Organization* 51, no. 1 (1997): 99–134; Hawkins et al., *Delegation and Agency in International Organizations*, 24.
22. Kiewiet and McCubbins, *The Logic of Delegation*; Pollack, "Delegation, Agency, and Agenda Setting in the European Community," 108–109.

1. THEORETICAL FRAMEWORK   297

23. Erica R. Gould, "Delegating IMF Conditionality: Understanding Variations in Control and Conformity," in Hawkins et al., *Delegation and Agency in International Organizations*, 290–291, https://doi.org/10.1017/CBO9780511491368.011. See also Kiewiet and McCubbins, *The Logic of Delegation*, 17.
24. Hawkins et al., *Delegation and Agency in International Organizations*, 25; Byman and Kreps, "Agents of Destruction?," 9; Biddle, Macdonald, and Baker, "Small Footprint, Small Payoff," 96.
25. Hawkins et al., *Delegation and Agency in International Organizations*, 13–15.
26. Biddle, Macdonald, and Baker, "Small Footprint, Small Payoff"; Hawkins and Jacoby, "How Agents Matter," 204.
27. Hawkins et al., *Delegation and Agency in International Organizations*, 32; Mona M. Lyne, Daniel L. Nielson, and Michael J. Tierney, "Who Delegates? Alternative Models of Principals in Development Aid," in Hawkins et al., *Delegation and Agency in International Organizations*, 41–76.
28. Salehyan, "The Delegation of War to Rebel Organizations"; Salehyan, Gleditsch, and Cunningham, "Explaining External Support for Insurgent Groups"; Austin Long, "After ISAF: Partners and Proxies in Afghanistan After 2014," *Small Wars & Insurgencies* 27, no. 1 (2016): 22–38, https://doi.org/10.1080/09592318.2016.1122901; Krieg, "Externalizing the Burden of War."
29. Andrew Mumford, "Proxy Warfare and the Future of Conflict," *RUSI Journal* 158, no. 2 (2007): 40–46, https://doi.org/10.1080/03071847.2013.787733; Rosenau and Gold, "The Cheapest Insurance in the World?"; Watling and Reynolds, *War by Others' Means*.
30. Galula, *Counterinsurgency Warfare*, 54; Peic, "Civilian Defense Forces," 65; Rosenau and Gold, "The Cheapest Insurance in the World?"; Salehyan, "The Delegation of War to Rebel Organizations."
31. Kalyvas, *The Logic of Violence in Civil War*, 107–109; Lyall, "Are Coethnics More Effective Counterinsurgents?," 15; Peic, "Civilian Defense Forces"; Clayton and Thomson, "Civilianizing Civil Conflict," 499–510; Salehyan, "The Delegation of War to Rebel Organizations," 504.
32. Salehyan, "The Delegation of War to Rebel Organizations," 504.
33. Thornton, "Problems with the Kurds as Proxies Against Islamic State"; Thomas Waldman, "Vicarious Warfare: The Counterproductive Consequences of Modern American Military Practice," *Contemporary Security Policy* 39, no. 2 (2018): 181–205, https://doi.org/10.1080/13523260.2017.1393201; Krieg, "Externalizing the Burden of War"; Maguire, *A Perfect Proxy?*
34. Ahram, "Pro-Government Militias and the Repertoires of Illicit State Violence"; Clayton and Thomson, "The Enemy of My Enemy Is My Friend"; Jones, "The Strategic Logic of Militia"; Long et al., *Locals Rule*, 161–163.
35. Byman, "Friends Like These"; Biddle, Macdonald, and Baker, "Small Footprint, Small Payoff"; Berman and Lake, *Proxy Wars*; Cochran, "Security Assistance"; Thornton, "Problems with the Kurds as Proxies Against Islamic State"; Hughes, "Syria and the Perils of Proxy Warfare"; Hughes and Tripodi, "Anatomy of a Surrogate"; Walter C.

Ladwig, *The Forgotten Front: Patron-Client Relationships in Counterinsurgency* (Cambridge: Cambridge University Press, 2017), 1–12, https://doi.org/10.1017/9781316756805.001.

36. Nate Rosenblatt and David Kilcullen, *The Tweet of Damocles: Lessons for U.S. Proxy Warfare* (Washington, DC: New America Foundation, 2020), 19–20, https://www.newamerica.org/international-security/reports/tweet-damocles/.

37. Biddle, Macdonald, and Baker, "Small Footprint, Small Payoff," 97. See also Byman, "Friends Like These"; Berman et al., "Introduction"; Cochran, "Security Assistance."

38. Thornton, "Problems with the Kurds as Proxies Against Islamic State"; Hughes, "Syria and the Perils of Proxy Warfare."

39. Michael J. McNerney et al., *Improving Implementation of the Department of Defense Leahy Law* (Santa Monica, CA: RAND Corporation, 2017), https://www.rand.org/pubs/research_reports/RR1737.html; Biddle, Macdonald, and Baker, "Small Footprint, Small Payoff"; Marten, *Warlords*; Entous, "Covert CIA Mission to Arm Syrian Rebels Goes Awry"; Erica Gaston, "Legal Pluralism and Militia Regulation: International, Domestic, and Community Accountability Frameworks for Sub-state Forces in Afghanistan," *Journal of Afghan Legal Studies* 2 (2017), https://papers.ssrn.com/sol3/papers.cfm?abstract_id=3476407; Ahram, *Proxy Warriors*, 90–92.

40. Office of the Inspector General, *(U) Evaluation of Combined Joint Interagency Task Force-Syria Vetting Process for New Syrian Forces (DoDIG-2015-175)* (Washington, DC: U.S. Department of Defense, 2015), https://media.defense.gov/2019/Aug/22/2002174036/-1/-1/1/DODIG-2015-175.PDF; Office of Audits, *Audit of the Department of State Vetting Process for Syrian Non-lethal Assistance* (Washington, DC: Office of the Inspector General, U.S. Department of State, 2016); Office of the Inspector General, *U.S. and Coalition Efforts to Train, Advise, Assist, and Equip Iraqi Sunni Popular Mobilization Forces (DODIG-2016-055)* (Washington, DC: U.S. Department of Defense, 2016).

41. Office of the Inspector General, *(U) Evaluation of Combined Joint Interagency Task Force-Syria Vetting Process for New Syrian Forces*; SIGAR, *Stabilization: Lessons from the U.S. Experience in Afghanistan* (Washington, DC: Special Inspector General for Afghanistan Reconstruction, 2018).

42. SIGAR, *Child Sexual Assault in Afghanistan: Implementation of the Leahy Laws and Reports of Assault by Afghan Security Forces*, SIGAR 17-47-IP (Washington, DC: Special Inspector General for Afghanistan Reconstruction, 2018).

43. Fox, "Conflict and the Need for a Theory of Proxy Warfare"; Salehyan, "The Delegation of War to Rebel Organizations"; Byman, "Friends Like These."

44. Salehyan, "The Delegation of War to Rebel Organizations," 503–504.

45. Hughes, "Syria and the Perils of Proxy Warfare"; Erica Gaston and Douglas Ollivant, *US-Iran Proxy Competition in Iraq* (Washington, DC: New America Foundation and Arizona State University Center for the Future of Warfare, 2020), https://www.newamerica.org/international-security/reports/us-iran-proxy-competition-iraq/; Jeremy Shapiro and Miriam R. Estrin, "The Proxy War Problem in Syria," Brookings Institution, February 4, 2014, https://www.brookings.edu/opinions/the-proxy-war-problem-in-syria/; Alexandra Stark, *The Monarch's Pawns? Gulf State Proxy Warfare*

2011–Today (Washington, DC: New America Foundation and Arizona State University Center on the Future of War, 2020), https://www.newamerica.org/international-security/reports/the-monarchs-pawns/; Kim R. Cragin, "Semi-Proxy Wars and U.S. Counterterrorism Strategy," *Studies in Conflict and Terrorism* 38, no. 5 (2015): 311–327, https://doi.org/10.1080/1057610X.2015.1018024.

46. Mitchell, Carey, and Butler, "The Impact of Pro-Government Militias on Human Rights Violations," 817 See also James D. Morrow, "When Do States Follow the Laws of War?," *American Political Science Review* 101, no. 3 (2007): 559–572; Alvarez, "Militias and Genocide."
47. Mitchell, Carey, and Butler, "The Impact of Pro-Government Militias on Human Rights Violations," 817, citing Arrow, "The Economics of Agency."
48. Berman and Lake, *Proxy Wars*; Biddle, Macdonald, and Baker, "Small Footprint, Small Payoff"; Waldman, "Vicarious Warfare."
49. Snyder, Bruck, and Sapin, *Decision-Making as an Approach to the Study of International Politics*; Rosenau, "Pre-theories and Theories of Foreign Policy-Making"; Sprout and Sprout, "Environmental Factors in the Study of International Politics"; Hudson, "Foreign Policy Analysis," 5–7.
50. Jean A. Garrison, "Introduction: Foreign Policy Analysis in 20/20: A Symposium," *Foreign Policy Analysis in 20/20: A Symposium* 5, no. 2 (2003): 155.
51. Sprout and Sprout, "Environmental Factors in the Study of International Politics."
52. Hudson, "Foreign Policy Analysis"; Alden and Aran, *Foreign Policy Analysis*; Garrison, "Foreign Policy Analysis in 20/20."
53. Sprout and Sprout, "Environmental Factors in the Study of International Politics"; Kal Holsti, "National Role Conceptions in the Study of Foreign Policy," *International Studies Quarterly* 14, no. 3 (1970): 233–309, https://doi.org/10.2307/3013584; Robert Axelrod, ed., *The Structure of Decision: The Cognitive Maps of Political Elites* (Princeton, NJ: Princeton University Press, 1976); Robert Jervis, Richard Ned Lebow, and Janice Gross Stein, eds., *Psychology and Deterrence* (Baltimore: John Hopkins University Press, 1985); Michael Brecher, *The Foreign Policy System of Israel: Setting, Images, Process* (London: Oxford University Press, 1972); Robert Jervis, *Perception and Misperception in International Politics* (Princeton, NJ: Princeton University Press, 1976); Margaret Hermann and Thomas W. Milburn, eds., *Psychological Examination of Political Leaders* (New York: Free Press, 1977).
54. Garrison, "Foreign Policy Analysis in 20/20"; Holsti, "National Role Conceptions in the Study of Foreign Policy"; Alexander L. George, *Presidential Decision Making in Foreign Policy: The Effective Use of Information and Advice* (Boulder, CO: Westview Press, 1980).
55. Barnett, "Culture, Strategy and Foreign Policy Change"; Peter J. Katzenstein, ed., *The Culture of National Security: Norms and Identity in World Politics* (New York: Columbia University Press, 1996). See also Brecher, *The Foreign Policy System of Israel*; Holsti, "National Role Conceptions in the Study of Foreign Policy."
56. Allison, *Essence of Decision*.
57. Graham T. Allison, "Conceptual Models and the Cuban Missile Crisis," *American Political Science Review* 63, no. 3 (1969): 690, https://doi.org/10.1017/S000305540025853X.

58. Allison, *Essence of Decision*, 67–100, 144–184; Morton H. Halperin, Arnold Kanter, and Priscilla Clapp, *Bureaucratic Politics and Foreign Policy* (Washington, DC: Brookings Institution Press, 1974); Allison and Halperin, "Bureaucratic Politics."
59. Allison and Halperin, "Bureaucratic Politics," 42.
60. Allison, *Essence of Decision*, 176.
61. Allison and Halperin, "Bureaucratic Politics," 48–50; Halperin, "Why Bureaucrats Play Games," 74; Allison, "Conceptual Models and the Cuban Missile Crisis," 711; Allison, *Essence of Decision*, 166–176.
62. Allison and Halperin, "Bureaucratic Politics"; Allison, "Conceptual Models and the Cuban Missile Crisis," 707–711.
63. Allison and Halperin, "Bureaucratic Politics," 51–54.
64. Allison and Halperin, 51–54.
65. Steve Smith and Michael Clarke, *Foreign Policy Implementation* (London: G. Allen & Unwin, 1985); Elisabetta Brighi and Christopher Hill, "Implementation and Behaviour," in *Foreign Policy: Theories, Actors, Cases*, ed. Steve Smith, Amelia Hadfield, and Tim Dunne (Cambridge: Cambridge University Press, 2008), 117–135.
66. Ursula C. Schroeder and Cornelius Friesendorf, "State-Building and Organized Crime: Implementing the International Law Enforcement Agenda in Bosnia," *Journal of International Relations and Development* 12, no. 2 (2009): 141, https://doi.org/10.1057/jird.2009.1.
67. Allison and Halperin, "Bureaucratic Politics," 48–49; Halperin, "Why Bureaucrats Play Games," 88.
68. Christopher Hill, *The Changing Politics of Foreign Policy* (London: Palgrave Macmillan, 2002), 88.
69. Allison, "Conceptual Models and the Cuban Missile Crisis," 698; Allison and Halperin, "Bureaucratic Politics," 55–56; Alden and Aran, *Foreign Policy Analysis*, 32–33.
70. Allison, "Conceptual Models and the Cuban Missile Crisis," 700–701.
71. Allison, *Essence of Decision*; Allison, "Conceptual Models and the Cuban Missile Crisis."
72. Halperin, "Why Bureaucrats Play Games."
73. Allison, "Conceptual Models and the Cuban Missile Crisis," 711; Halperin, Kanter, and Clapp, *Bureaucratic Politics and Foreign Policy*, 122; Allison and Halperin, "Bureaucratic Politics," 78.
74. Allison and Halperin, "Bureaucratic Politics," 50.
75. Department of Defense, *Summary of the 2018 National Defense Strategy of the United States of America*; Votel and Keravuori, "The By-With-Through Operational Approach."
76. Sean Naylor, *Relentless Strike: The Secret History of Joint Special Operations Command* (New York: St. Martin's Press, 2015); Charles T. Cleveland and Daniel Egel, *The American Way of Irregular War: An Analytical Memoir* (Washington, DC: RAND Corporation, 2020).
77. Hill, *The Changing Politics of Foreign Policy*, 89–90.
78. Allison, *Essence of Decision*, 91.

79. Hill, *The Changing Politics of Foreign Policy*, 2; Douglas Foyle, "Foreign Policy Analysis and Globalization: Public Opinion, World Opinion, and the Individual, in 'Foreign Policy Analysis in 20/20: A Symposium,'" *International Studies Review* 5, no. 2 (2003): 163–170, https://doi.org/10.1111/1521-9488.5020011.
80. Allison, "Conceptual Models and the Cuban Missile Crisis," 709; Allison and Halperin, "Bureaucratic Politics," 47.
81. Allison and Halperin, "Bureaucratic Politics," 59.
82. Allison and Halperin, 60.
83. Garrison, "Foreign Policy Analysis in 20/20," 181; Eric Stern and Bertjan Verbeek, eds., "Whither the Study of Governmental Politics in Foreign Policymaking? A Symposium," *Mershon International Studies Review* 42 (1998): 206; Baumann and Stengel, "Foreign Policy Analysis"; Robert J. Art, "Bureaucratic Politics and American Foreign Policy: A Critique," *Policy Sciences* 4 (1973): 467–490; Stephen D. Krasner, "Are Bureaucracies Important? (Or Allison Wonderland)," *Foreign Policy* 7, no. 1 (1972): 159–179.
84. Jerel A. Rosati, "Developing a Systematic Decision-Making Framework: Bureaucratic Politics in Perspective," *World Politics* 33, no. 2 (1981): 234–252.
85. Bendor and Moe, "An Adaptive Model of Bureaucratic Politics"; Jonathan Bendor and Thomas H. Hammond, "Rethinking Allison's Models," *American Political Science Review* 86, no. 2 (1992): 301–322, https://doi.org/10.2307/1964222; Hilsman, *The Politics of Policymaking in Defense and Foreign Affairs*.
86. Walter Carlsnaes, Helen Sjursen, and Brian White, eds., *Contemporary European Foreign Policy* (London: Sage Publications, 2004); Henrik Larsen, "A Distinct FPA for Europe? Towards a Comprehensive Framework for Analysing the Foreign Policy of EU Member States," *European Journal of International Relations* 15, no. 3 (2009): 537–566, https://doi.org/10.1177/1354066109388247; Brian White, *Understanding European Foreign Policy* (Basingstoke, UK: Palgrave Macmillan, 2001); Ian Manners and Richard G. Whitman, *The Foreign Policies of European Union Member States* (Manchester: Manchester University Press, 2000).
87. Michael N. Barnett and Martha Finnemore, "The Politics, Power, and Pathologies of International Organizations," *International Organization* 53, no. 4 (1999): 699–732, https://doi.org/10.1162/002081899551048; Michael N. Barnett and Martha Finnemore, *Rules for the World: International Organizations in Global Politics* (Ithaca, NY: Cornell University Press, 2004).
88. Brecher, *The Foreign Policy System of Israel*, 137.
89. Interestingly for the sort of leaders and analysis featured in this book, Hudson gave the example of understanding personal characteristics of group leaders such as Saddam Hussein. Hudson and Vore, "Foreign Policy Analysis Yesterday, Today, and Tomorrow," 211–212.
90. Baumann and Stengel, "Foreign Policy Analysis, Globalisation and Non-state Actors." See also Frank Stengel and Rainer Baumann, "Non-state Actors and Foreign Policy" in *The Oxford Encyclopedia of Foreign Policy Analysis*, ed. Cameron G. Thies (Oxford: Oxford University Press, 2017), https://doi.org/10.1093/acrefore/9780190228637.013.456;

Benedetta Voltolini, "Non-state Actors and Framing Processes in EU Foreign Policy: The Case of EU–Israel Relations," *Journal of European Public Policy* 23, no. 10 (2016): 1502–1519, https://doi.org/10.1080/13501763.2015.1085429.

91. Brighi and Hill, "Implementation and Behaviour"; Smith and Clarke, *Foreign Policy Implementation*.
92. See, e.g., Michael Clarke and Steve Smith, "Perspectives on the Foreign Policy System: Implementation Approaches," in *Understanding Foreign Policy: The Foreign Policy Systems Approach*, ed. Michael Clarke and Brian White (Cheltenham:, UK Edward Elgar, 1989), 163–184; Schroeder and Friesendorf, "State-Building and Organized Crime."
93. Schroeder and Friesendorf, "State-Building and Organized Crime."
94. Allison, "Conceptual Models and the Cuban Missile Crisis"; Allison and Halperin, "Bureaucratic Politics"; Hilsman, *The Politics of Policymaking in Defense and Foreign Affairs*.
95. Bendor and Moe, "An Adaptive Model of Bureaucratic Politics." See also Bendor and Hammond, "Rethinking Allison's Models."
96. Halperin, Kanter, and Clapp, *Bureaucratic Politics and Foreign Policy*, 313–344.
97. McCubbins and Schwartz, "Congressional Oversight Overlooked"; McCubbins, Noll, and Weingast, "Structure and Process, Politics and Policy"; Barry R. Weingast and Mark J. Moran, "Bureaucratic Discretion or Congressional Control? Regulatory Policymaking by the Federal Trade Commission," *Journal of Political Economy* 91, no. 5 (2015): 765–800, https://doi.org/10.1086/261181; Ferejohn and Shipan, "Congressional Influence on Bureaucracy"; Morris S. Ogul, *Congress Oversees the Bureaucracy* (Pittsburgh: University of Pittsburgh Press, 1976); Jason A. MacDonald, "Limitation Riders and Congressional Influence Over Bureaucratic Policy Decisions," *American Political Science Review* 104, no. 4 (2010): 766–782, https://doi.org/10.1017/S0003055410000432.
98. Halperin, Kanter, and Clapp, *Bureaucratic Politics and Foreign Policy*, 313–344.
99. Hilsman, *The Politics of Policymaking in Defense and Foreign Affairs*; Bendor and Moe, "An Adaptive Model of Bureaucratic Politics"; McCubbins and Schwartz, "Congressional Oversight Overlooked"; Kiewiet and McCubbins, *The Logic of Delegation*.
100. Bendor and Moe, "An Adaptive Model of Bureaucratic Politics."
101. Alison Brysk, "From Above and Below: Social Movements, the International System, and Human Rights in Argentina," *Comparative Political Studies* 26, no. 3 (1993): 259–285, https://doi.org/10.1177/0010414093026003001; Daniel C. Thomas, *The Helsinki Effect: International Norms, Human Rights, and the Demise of Communism* (Princeton, NJ: Princeton University Press, 2001); Lisa L. Martin and Kathryn Sikkink, "U.S. Policy and Human Rights in Argentina and Guatemala, 1973–1980," in *Double-Edged Diplomacy: International Bargaining and Domestic Policy*, ed. Peter B Evans, Harold K Jacobson, and Robert D Putnam (Berkeley: University of California Press, 1993), 330–362; Winifred Tate, "Human Rights Law and Military Aid Delivery: A Case Study of the Leahy Law," *Political and Legal Anthropology Review* 34, no. 2 (2011): 337–354; David Forsythe, "Human Rights in American Foreign Policy: From the 1960s to the Soviet Collapse by Joe Renouard (Review)," *Human Rights Quarterly* 38, no. 3 (2016): 841–846, https://doi.org/10.1353/hrq.2016.0044.

102. Thomas Risse-Kappen, "Introduction," in *Bringing Transnational Relations Back In: Non-state Actors, Domestic Structures, and International Institutions*, ed. Thomas Risse-Kappen (Cambridge: Cambridge University Press, 1995), 3–33, https://doi.org/10.1017/CBO9780511598760.
103. Thomas Risse-Kappen, *Cooperation Among Democracies: The European Influence on U.S. Foreign Policy* (Princeton, NJ: Princeton University Press, 1995), 9–10; Robert O. Keohane, "The Big Influence of Small Allies," *Foreign Policy*, no. 2 (Spring 1971): 161–182.
104. Mertus, *Bait and Switch*, 12–15; Keck and Sikkink, *Activists Beyond Borders*, 16–25; Sanjeev Khagram, James V. Riker, and Kathryn Sikkink, eds., *Restructuring World Politics: Transnational Social Movements, Networks, and Norms* (Minneapolis: University of Minnesota Press, 2002); Ann M. Florini and P. J. Simmons, "What the World Needs Now?," in *The Third Force: The Rise of Transnational Civil Society*, ed. Ann M. Florini (Tokyo: Japan Center for International Change; Washington, DC: Carnegie Endowment for International Peace, 1999), 10–11.
105. Thomas Risse, "Transnational Actors and World Politics," in *Handbook of International Relations*, ed. Walter Carlsnaes, Thomas Risse, and Beth Simmons (London: Sage Publications, 2002), 255–274; Brysk, "From Above and Below"; Thomas Risse and Kathryn Sikkink, *The Power of Principles: The Socialization of Human Rights Norms in Domestic Practice* (Cambridge: Cambridge University Press, 1999).
106. Risse-Kappen, "Introduction"; Martha Finnemore and Kathryn Sikkink, "International Norm Dynamics and Political Change" 52, no. 4 (1998): 887–917, https://doi.org/10.1162/002081898550789; Larsen, "A Distinct FPA for Europe?"
107. See, e.g., Aryeh Neier, *The International Human Rights Movement: A History* (Princeton, NJ: Princeton University Press, 2012); Alison Brysk, ed., *Globalization and Human Rights* (Berkeley: University of California Press, 2002); Mertus, *Bait and Switch*.
108. Risse-Kappen, *Cooperation Among Democracies*, 9–10; Keohane, "The Big Influence of Small Allies."
109. Risse-Kappen, *Cooperation Among Democracies*, 4–5.
110. Olivier Schmitt, "More Allies, Weaker Missions? How Junior Partners Contribute to Multinational Military Operations," *Contemporary Security Policy* 40, no. 1 (2019): 70–84, https://doi.org/10.1080/13523260.2018.1501999; Daniel Byman and Matthew Waxman, *The Dynamics of Coercion: American Foreign Policy and the Limits of Military Might* (Cambridge: Cambridge University Press, 2002).
111. Schroeder and Friesendorf, "State-Building and Organized Crime."
112. Carlsnaes, Sjursen, and White, *Contemporary European Foreign Policy*; Larsen, "A Distinct FPA for Europe?"; White, *Understanding European Foreign Policy*; Barnett and Finnemore, *Rules for the World*.
113. Carlsnaes, Sjursen, and White do not suggest that this pooling of sovereignty and multilateral or transnational governance happens across all issue sets or jurisdictions within European Union institutions' mandate, but note that it can vary by field and issue, creating a checkerboard of partially pooled sovereignty in some areas, and others that are still defined by bilateral interests or that might better be analyzed through

conventional comparative analysis. Carlsnaes, Sjursen, and White, *Contemporary European Foreign Policy*.

114. Dominik Zaum, *The Sovereignty Paradox: The Norms and Politics of International Statebuilding* (Oxford: Oxford University Press, 2007), 39, https://doi.org/10.1093/acprof:oso/9780199207435.001.0001; Woodward, *The Ideology of Failed States*; Susan L. Woodward, "Compromised Sovereignty to Create Sovereignty: Is Dayton Bosnia a Futile Exercise or an Emerging Model?," in *Problematic Sovereignty: Contested Rules and Political Possibilities*, ed. Stephen Krasner (New York: Columbia University Press, 2001), 252–300; David Williams, "Aid and Sovereignty: Quasi-States and the International Financial Institutions," *Review of International Studies* 26, no. 4 (2000): 557–573, https://doi.org/10.1017/S026021050000557X; Robert H. Jackson, *Quasi-States: Sovereignty, International Relations and the Third World* (Cambridge: Cambridge University Press, 1991), chap. 5, https://doi.org/10.1017/cbo9780511559020; Astri Suhrke, *When More Is Less: The International Project in Afghanistan* (London: C. Hurst & Co., 2011); Nematullah Bizhan, "Aid and State-Building, Part II: Afghanistan and Iraq," *Third World Quarterly* 39, no. 5 (2018): 1014–1031, https://doi.org/10.1080/01436597.2018.1447369.

115. Clunan and Trinkunas, *Ungoverned Spaces*. See also Felbab-Brown, Trinkunas, and Hamid, *Militants, Criminals, and Warlords*; Brown, "Purposes and Pitfalls of War by Proxy"; Thomas Risse, Anke Draude, and Tanja A. Börzel, eds., *The Oxford Handbook of Governance and Limited Statehood* (Oxford: Oxford University Press, 2018).

2. BARGAINING MOMENTS AND STRUCTURES

1. Over the course of 2005, U.S. troop numbers in Iraq ranged from 138,000 to 160,000. Other coalition members contributed a total of between 23,000 and 25,000 forces over the same period. Michael O'Hanlon and Nina Camp, *Iraq Index* (Washington, DC: Brookings Institution, December 2005), 19. In Afghanistan, in January 2009, there were over 34,000 U.S. forces, across both the counterterrorism mission (approximately 19,000 under Operation Enduring Freedom) and the NATO stabilization mission (approximately 15,000 in ISAF). There were an additional 36,000 international forces from other ISAF countries. Jason Campbell and Jeremy Shapiro, *Afghanistan Index* (Washington, DC: Brookings Institution, January 2009), 9–10.

2. The Sons of Iraq or Awakening forces went by a variety of different names. For consistency, this book will generically refer to them as the *sahwa*, which is the term that most Iraqis use.

3. SIGIR, *Hard Lessons: The Iraq Reconstruction* (Washington, DC: Special Inspector General for Iraq Reconstruction, 2009), 33–36.

4. SIGIR, *Hard Lessons*, 128–134.

5. Bruce R. Pirnie and Edward O'Connell, *Counterinsurgency in Iraq (2003–2006)* (Arlington, VA: RAND Corporation, 2008), 49–52; SIGIR, *Hard Lessons*, 133–134; Thomas E. Ricks, *Fiasco: The American Military Adventure in Iraq* (London: Allen Lane, 2006), 338–341.

2. BARGAINING MOMENTS AND STRUCTURES   305

6. SIGIR, *Hard Lessons*, 134.
7. In 2005, the U.S. command in charge of training troops deemed an exceedingly small number of Iraqi Army or police units "fully capable" of executing counterinsurgency operations (at different points and depending on how these were counted, anywhere from three to just one such unit), and half of the police "incapable" of contributing to counterinsurgency efforts in any way. Jim Fallows, "Why Iraq Has No Army," *The Atlantic*, December 2005, https://www.theatlantic.com/magazine/archive/2005/12/why-iraq-has-no-army/304428/. See also Robert Perito, *Iraq's Interior Ministry: Frustrating Reform* (Washington, DC: United States Institute of Peace, 2008), https://www.usip.org/sites/default/files/PB-Iraq-Interior-5-08.PDF; SIGIR, *Hard Lessons*.
8. James A. Baker et al., *Iraq Study Group Report* (Washington, DC: U.S. Congress, 2006); Ned Parker, "The Conflict in Iraq: A Ministry of Fiefdoms," *Los Angeles Times*, July 30, 2007. Although reports of sectarian violence by those under Ministry of Interior control became even more prominent in 2006, most date the effective takeover of the MoI by sectarian forces, and particularly by the Badr Organization, a Shi'a Islamist group, to 2005. For more, see Toby Dodge, *Iraq: From War to a New Authoritarianism* (Abingdon, UK: Routledge, 2017), 63–69. Perito, *Iraq's Interior Ministry*. He was subsequently replaced with a more neutral Shi'a figure, but these changes among MoI personnel remained.
9. Perito, *Iraq's Interior Ministry*.
10. After a leading Badr figure was appointed to be the minister of interior in 2005, he dismissed many Sunni commanders and policemen, replacing them with Shi'a militiamen. As a result, although sectarian attacks continued, they were now in effect carried out by arms of the state. Historian Toby Dodge notes that "The Badr Brigade's integration into the National Police meant that it became less visible in sectarian killings than the Jaish al-Mahdi, as its militiamen adopted police uniforms to carry out their work." Dodge, *Iraq*, 65. For examples of the ways that Iraqi police facilitated attacks indirectly, see Thomas E. Ricks, *The Gamble : General David Petraeus and the American Military Adventure in Iraq, 2006–2008* (New York: Penguin Press, 2009), 45–46; Baker et al., *Iraq Study Group Report*.
11. These figures, along with those in the subsequent sentence, are derived from an average of the monthly civilian death tolls as recorded by Iraq Body Count and summarized in Anthony Cordesman, *Trends in Iraqi Violence, Casualties and Impact of War: 2003–2015* (Washington, DC: Center for Strategic and International Studies, 2015), 34.
12. Edward Hunt, "Dispatches from Baghdad: Sectarian War in Iraq, 2006–2007," *Middle Eastern Studies* 56, no. 1 (2019): 111n4, https://doi.org/10.1080/00263206.2019.1626726.
13. Robert F. Worth, "Blast at Shiite Shrine Sets Off Sectarian Fury in Iraq," *New York Times*, February 23, 2006.
14. To illustrate the level of violence, Thomas Ricks offers this snapshot of one week in May 2006: on May 7, a car bomb killed 30 in the Shi'a shrine city of Karbala, meanwhile "51 bodies were found, handcuffed, blindfolded and shot" in Baghdad; six days later, a car bomb in the densely packed Shi'a Baghdad neighborhood of Sadr City

resulted in 99 casualties, and on the same day in the Sunni town of Qaim, 40 people were found dead in the street. Ricks, *The Gamble*, 36.
15. Hunt, "Dispatches from Baghdad"; Dodge, *Iraq*, 63–64.
16. Cordesman, *Trends in Iraqi Violence*, 34.
17. Jennifer Pagonis, "Iraq: Rate of Displacement Rising," UNHCR, August 27, 2007, https://www.unhcr.org/en-us/news/briefing/2007/8/46d3f68f4/iraq-rate-displacement-rising.html; International Organization for Migration, *Iraq Displacement 2006 Year in Review* (Geneva: IOM, 2007).
18. This figure is generated based on the average number of IED incidents each month, as reported in Anthony Cordesman, Charles Loi, and Vivek Kocharlakota, *IED Metrics for Iraq: June 2003—September 2010* (Washington, DC: Center for Strategic and International Studies, 2010), 3–5.
19. Clay Wilson, *Improvised Explosive Devices (IEDs) in Iraq and Afghanistan: Effects and Countermeasures* (Washington, DC: Congressional Research Service, Library of Congress, 2007), 1–2.
20. Richard Fontaine, CEO of the Center for New American Security and former chief of staff for Senator John McCain, interview by author, Washington, DC, June 14, 2018, interview 16.
21. Ricks, *The Gamble*, 74–77, 98–99.
22. Ricks, 57–115.
23. Ahmed Hashim, *Insurgency and Counter-Insurgency in Iraq* (Ithaca, NY: Cornell University Press, 2005).
24. Long, "The Anbar Awakening," 78–79.
25. Kimberly Marten, "Warlords," in *The Changing Character of War* (Oxford: Oxford University Press, 2011), 165.
26. Long, "The Anbar Awakening," 80–81; Marten, *Warlords: Strong-Arm Brokers in Weak States* (Ithaca, NY: Cornell University Press, 2012), 166–167. It is worth noting that while MacFarland's initiative is generally credited with kick-starting this wave of bottom-up "reconciliation" and local force mobilization, there had been multiple attempts at tribal outreach prior to this. Stephen Biddle, Jeffrey Friedman, and Jacob N. Shapiro, "Testing the Surge: Why Did Violence Decline in Iraq in 2007?," *International Security* 37, no. 1 (2012): 18–21, https://doi.org/10.1162/ISEC_a_00087; Myriam Benraad, "Iraq's Tribal 'Sahwa': Its Rise and Fall," *Middle East Policy* 18, no. 1 (2011): 121–131, https://doi.org/10.1111/j.1475-4967.2011.00477.x; Long, "The Anbar Awakening," 78–79. In fact, MacFarland partly attributed his willingness to work with Sattar to his prior experience serving under (then) Colonel H. R. McMaster in Tal Afar, in Ninewa Province. However, it is notable that the experience did not spread until the military as a whole had shifted to a community-centric counterinsurgency strategy, with support for these kinds of initiatives encouraged from the top down.
27. Biddle, Friedman, and Shapiro, "Testing the Surge" 26; Nir Rosen, *Aftermath: Following the Bloodshed of America's Wars in the Muslim World* (New York: Nation Books, 2010). After the spate of AQI assassinations against tribal leaders, leaders like Sattar were strongly concerned with concrete demonstrations of security guarantees.

MacFarland stationed a tank in Sattar's front yard, used U.S. resources to fortify other tribal leaders' homes, and created protective details and neighborhood watches in support of those taking part in the police. Carter Malkasian, *Illusions of Victory: The Anbar Awakening and the Rise of the Islamic State* (Oxford: Oxford University Press, 2017), 125, https://doi.org/10.1080/00396330802034283; Ricks, *The Gamble*, 62–64. Despite the high levels of protection, Sattar was assassinated on his farm in Anbar in September 2007, likely by al-Qaeda, although they did not officially claim it. Long, "The Anbar Awakening," 85.

28. Long, "The Anbar Awakening," 80.
29. Biddle, Friedman, and Shapiro, "Testing the Surge" Ricks, *The Gamble*, 69–73.
30. Ricks, *The Gamble*, 67.
31. The U.S. military leadership tended to frame the initiative as a form of "local reconciliation," with Odierno even establishing a "Reconciliation cell" in Baghdad to advise U.S. commanders on how to broker cease-fires with erstwhile insurgents. Ricks, 205. Dodge recounts one senior military adviser to Petraeus framing it as a form of "funky DDR." Dodge, *Iraq*, 101.
32. Ricks, *The Gamble*, 149; Marten, *Warlords*, 149–151, 159.
33. The *sahwa* were initially supported from the Commander's Emergency Response Program (CERP), a slush fund enabling commanders to support local stabilization initiatives. SIGIR, *Commander's Emergency Response Program in Iraq Funds Many Large-Scale Projects* (Washington, DC: Office of the Special Inspector General for Iraq Reconstruction, 2008). The amount of funds spent is limited (typically less than $10,000) and must be registered and accounted for, but these have typically only been lightly scrutinized, even more so in the first few years of the program's inception. SIGIR, *Commander's Emergency Response Program*. Carter Malkasian notes that early on in Anbar, salaries and support came partly through *solatia* payments to families of killed policeman and in the form of projects funded through CERP. Malkasian, *Illusions of Victory*, 121–122.
34. Biddle, Friedman, and Shapiro, "Testing the Surge," 8–10; Department of Defense, *Measuring Stability and Security in Iraq (March 2009)* (Washington, DC: U.S. Department of Defense, 2009).
35. Ricks, *The Gamble*, 202–203. Each *sahwa* member was typically paid $350/month. Dodge, *Iraq*, 97.
36. Robert Kaplan, *The Insurgents: David Petraeus and the Plot to Change the American Way of War* (New York: Simon & Schuster, 2013); Nir Rosen, "The Myth of the Surge," *Rolling Stone*, February 2008, 46–53.
37. Retired U.S. military officer formerly involved in *sahwa* initiative, interview by author, Erbil, Iraq, November 6, 2018, interview 49; former U.S. intelligence officer serving in Iraq and Afghanistan, interview by author, Washington, DC, June 15, 2018, interview 17; Biddle, Friedman, and Shapiro, "Testing the Surge"; Marten, *Warlords*, 140–186.
38. Malkasian, *Illusions of Victory*, 132.
39. Dodge, *Iraq*, 97; Rosen, *Aftermath*, 283; Robinson, *Tell Me How This Ends*, 326–342.

40. Malkasian notes that the Marine commander in charge of military operations in Anbar Province, Major General Richard Zilmer, was worried about abuses by these forces, and issued a letter in late 2006 ordering U.S. forces in Anbar to refrain from working with armed militias, and not to directly pay or arm them. Malkasian, *Illusions of Victory*, 132–133. Given that later accounts do note support going to a wider spread of tribal forces, and the direct arming and paying of such forces via CERP funds, this initial restraint may have been limited to Anbar, or may have been superseded by the rapid pace of the program. Marten, *Warlords*, 160–161.
41. Toby Dodge, professor and Iraq historian, interview by author, by telephone, March 31, 2020, interview 110; former U.S. official overseeing the TMF program, interview by author, by telephone, February 18, 2020, interview 108.
42. Richard Fontaine, CEO of Center for New American Security and former chief of staff for Senator John McCain, interview by author, Washington, DC, June 14, 2018, interview 16.
43. Marten, *Warlords*, 151.
44. Former U.S. intelligence officer serving in Iraq and Afghanistan, interview by author, Washington, DC, June 15, 2018, interview 17. See also Biddle, Friedman, and Shapiro, "Testing the Surge," 24–25n47.
45. Former U.S. military commander, interview by author, Washington, DC, June 13, 2019, interview 95.
46. Dodge, *Iraq*, 97; Marten, *Warlords*, 150–151; Alissa J. Rubin and Damien Cave, "In a Force for Iraqi Calm, Seeds of Future Conflict," *New York Times*, December 23, 2007, https://www.nytimes.com/2007/12/23/world/middleeast/23awakening.html. See also retired U.S. military officer formerly involved in *sahwa* initiative, interview by author, Erbil, Iraq, November 6, 2018, interview 49; former U.S. official overseeing the TMF program, interview by author, by telephone, February 18, 2020, interview 108.
47. Dodge, *Iraq*, 97; Rosen, *Aftermath*, 283; Robinson, *Tell Me How This Ends*, 326–342.
48. Retired U.S. military officer formerly involved in *sahwa* initiative, interview by author, Erbil, Iraq, November 6, 2018, interview 49; former U.S. official overseeing the TMF program, interview by author, by telephone, February 18, 2020, interview 108.
49. Former U.S. intelligence officer serving in Iraq and Afghanistan, interview by author, Washington, DC, June 15, 2018, interview 17; retired U.S. military officer formerly involved in *sahwa* initiative, interview by author, Erbil, Iraq, November 6, 2018, interview 49.
50. Retired U.S. military officer formerly involved in *sahwa* initiative, interview by author, Erbil, Iraq, November 6, 2018, interview 49. See also former congressional staffer, interview by author, Washington, DC, June 14, 2018; Marten, *Warlords*, 150–151.
51. Former U.S. official overseeing the TMF program, interview by author, by telephone, February 18, 2020, interview 108; former senior military official, interview by author, by telephone, July 30, 2022, interview 209.
52. While Iraqi politicians were willing to tolerate U.S. mobilization in Anbar Province, given the more tribal dynamics and limited federal influence there, once the *sahwa* initiative expanded to provinces with mixed populations (like Diyala), and even

2. BARGAINING MOMENTS AND STRUCTURES 309

Baghdad itself, it represented a more potent political challenge. Safa Rasul Al-Sheikh and Emma Sky, "Iraq Since 2003: Perspectives on a Divided Society," *Survival* 53, no. 4 (August 2011): 129, https://doi.org/10.1080/00396338.2011.603565; Marten, *Warlords*, 172–179; Toby Dodge, professor and Iraq historian, interview by author, by telephone, March 31, 2020, interview 110. Petraeus even remembered Maliki enthusiastically going with them and seeking to support the program on early trips, when the program was still concentrated in the Sunni heartland. Gen. (ret.) David Petraeus, interview by author, by telephone, July 30, 2022, interview 208.

53. Safa Rasoul Al-Sheikh, deputy national security adviser for Iraq, interview by author, Baghdad, Iraq, November 5, 2018, interview 47; retired U.S. military officer formerly involved in *sahwa* initiative, interview by author, Erbil, Iraq, November 6, 2018, interview 49; Al-Sheikh and Sky, "Iraq Since 2003"; Priyanka Boghani, "In Their Own Words: Sunnis on Their Treatment in Maliki's Iraq," *PBS Frontline: The Rise of ISIS*, October 28, 2014, https://www.pbs.org/wgbh/frontline/article/in-their-own-words-sunnis-on-their-treatment-in-malikis-iraq/; Marten, *Warlords*, 144–145.
54. Toby Dodge, professor, Iraq historian, and former adviser to General David Petraeus, by telephone, March 31, 2020. A similar account was reflected in the author interview with Safa Rasoul Al-Sheikh, deputy national security adviser for Iraq, interview by author, Baghdad, Iraq, November 5, 2018, interview 47.
55. Ricks, *The Gamble*. See also Al-Sheikh and Sky, "Iraq Since 2003."
56. Toby Dodge, professor, Iraq historian, and former adviser to General David Petraeus, by telephone, March 31, 2020.
57. Ariel I. Ahram and Frederic M. Wehrey, "Harnessing Militia Power: Lessons of the Iraqi National Guard," *Lawfare*, May 27, 2015, https://www.brookings.edu/blog/markaz/2015/05/27/harnessing-militia-power-lessons-of-the-iraqi-national-guard/; Marten, *Warlords*, 178.
58. Berman and Lake, *Proxy Wars*.
59. Safa Rasoul Al-Sheikh, deputy national security adviser for Iraq, interview by author, Baghdad, Iraq, November 5, 2018, interview 47.
60. Safa Rasoul Al-Sheikh, deputy national security adviser for Iraq, interview by author, Baghdad, Iraq, November 5, 2018, interview 47.
61. Boghani, "In Their Own Words.".
62. Retired U.S. military officer formerly involved in *sahwa* initiative, interview by author, Erbil, Iraq, November 6, 2018, interview 49.
63. Retired U.S. military officer formerly involved in *sahwa* initiative, interview by author, Erbil, Iraq, November 6, 2018, interview 49; former U.S. official overseeing the TMF program, interview by author, by telephone, February 18, 2020, interview 108.
64. Retired U.S. military officer formerly involved in *sahwa* initiative, interview by author, Erbil, Iraq, November 6, 2018, interview 49.
65. Department of Defense, *Measuring Stability and Security in Iraq*, v–vi.
66. Dodge, *Iraq*, 100; Frederic M. Wehrey and Ariel I. Ahram, *Taming the Militias: Building National Guards in Fractured Arab States* (Washington, DC: Carnegie Endowment for International Peace, 2015), 7.

67. Rod Nordland and Alissa J. Rubin, "Sunni Militiamen Say Iraq Didn't Keep Promises of Jobs," *New York Times*, March 23, 2009, https://www.nytimes.com/2009/03/24/world/middleeast/24sunni.html; Boghani, "In Their Own Words"; Long et al., *Locals Rule*, 160.
68. Dodge, *Iraq*, 101.
69. Matthieu Aikins, *Contracting the Commanders: Transition and the Political Economy of Afghanistan's Private Security Industry* (New York: Center on International Cooperation, New York University, 2012); Steve Brooking, "Private Security Companies in Afghanistan, 2001–11," Afghanistan Analysts Network, July 2012, https://docplayer.net/17540812-Private-security-companies-in-afghanistan-2001-11.html.
70. U.S. House of Representatives, Committee on Oversight and Government Reform, Subcommittee on National Security and Foreign Affairs, *Warlord, Inc.: Extortion and Corruption Along the U.S. Supply Chain in Afghanistan: Report of the Majority Staff of the Subcommittee on National Security and Foreign Affairs* (Washington, DC: Committee on Oversight and Government Reform, June 2010), https://www.hsdl.org/?abstract&did=23047; Gaston and Clark, *Backgrounder*.
71. There is ample documentation of a range of ISAF country forces—including those of the United States, Britain, the Netherlands, Denmark, Australia, and other countries—developing cooperative relationships with a range of substate or non-state forces in their areas of operations, ranging from hiring militias as auxiliaries to paying off local strongmen who posed a potential threat. See, e.g., Derksen, "Non-state Security Providers and Political Formation in Afghanistan"; Giustozzi, *Auxiliary Irregular Forces in Afghanistan*; Astri Suhrke and Antonio De Lauri, *The CIA's "Army": A Threat to Human Rights and an Obstacle to Peace in Afghanistan* (Providence, RI: Watson Institute of Public and International Affairs, Brown University, 2019); Lizzy Davies and John Hooper, "French Outcry Over Claim Italian Payments Masked Taliban Threat," *The Guardian*, October 16, 2009, https://www.theguardian.com/world/2009/oct/16/france-italy-taliban-afghanistan; Jon Boone, "Top US General Warns on Afghan Self-Defence Plan," *Financial Times*, January 3, 2008, https://www.ft.com/content/f31af380-b95e-11dc-bb66-0000779fd2ac.
72. For greater discussion about liberal peace-building or state-building ambitions in Afghanistan and how these frequently clashed with other power dynamics and agendas, see Jonathan Goodhand and Mark Sedra, "Rethinking Liberal Peacebuilding, Statebuilding and Transition in Afghanistan: An Introduction," *Central Asian Survey* 32, no. 3 (2013): 239–254, https://doi.org/10.1080/02634937.2013.850769; Derksen, "Commanders in Control," 22–29, 72–76; Astri Suhrke, "Statebuilding in Afghanistan: A Contradictory Engagement," *Central Asian Survey* 32, no. 3 (2013): 271–286, https://doi.org/10.1080/02634937.2013.834715; Péter Marton and Nik Hynek, "'Liberal' Statebuilding in Afghanistan," in *Routledge Handbook of International Statebuilding*, ed. David Chandler and Timothy D Sisk (London: Routledge, 2013), 304–314.
73. Suhrke, "The Long Decade of State-Building in Afghanistan."
74. Richard J. Ponzio, *Democratic Peacebuilding: Aiding Afghanistan and Other Fragile States* (Oxford: Oxford University Press, 2011), https://doi.org/10.1093/ACPROF:OSO

/9780199594955.001.0001; Suhrke, "The Long Decade of State-Building in Afghanistan"; Marton and Hynek, "'Liberal' Statebuilding in Afghanistan."
75. Roland Paris, *At War's End: Building Peace After Civil Conflict* (Cambridge: Cambridge University Press, 2007); Roland Paris and Timothy D. Sisk, eds., *The Dilemmas of Statebuilding: Confronting the Contradictions of Postwar Peace Operations* (London: Routledge, 2009); Roger Mac Ginty and Oliver P Richmond, "The Local Turn in Peace Building: A Critical Agenda for Peace," *Third World Quarterly* 34, no. 5 (June 2013): 763–783, https://doi.org/10.1080/01436597.2013.800750; Oliver P. Richmond, ed., *A Post-liberal Peace* (London: Routledge, 2011).
76. Barnett and Zurcher, "The Peacebuilder's Contract"; Suhrke, "The Long Decade of State-Building in Afghanistan"; Brendan Whitty and Hamish Nixon, "The Impact of Counter-Terrorism Objectives on Democratization and Statebuilding in Afghanistan," *Taiwan Journal of Democracy* 5, no. 1 (2009): 187–218.
77. Goodhand and Sedra, "Rethinking Liberal Peacebuilding," 243; Suhrke, "The Long Decade of State-Building in Afghanistan"; Murtazashvili, *Informal Order and the State in Afghanistan*; Coburn, "Informal Justice and the International Community in Afghanistan."
78. The UNAMA human rights unit, which offered regular annual reporting of the ALP, reported 25,277 members by the end of 2013, amounting to under one-third of the estimated 95,000 *sahwa* forces formed in the first year of that program. UNAMA, *Protection of Civilians in Armed Conflict Annual Report 2011* (Kabul: OHCHR, 2012), 6; UNAMA, *Protection of Civilians in Armed Conflict Annual Report 2013* (Kabul: OHCHR, 2014), 50.
79. CFSOCC-A, *Afghan Local Defense Initiative Briefing January 2010* (Kabul: Combined Forces Special Operations Component Command—Afghanistan, 2010) (on file with author).
80. Joshua Partlow and Karen DeYoung, "Gen. Petraeus Runs Into Resistance from Karzai Over Village Defense Forces," *Washington Post*, July 10, 2010, http://www.washingtonpost.com/wp-dyn/content/article/2010/07/09/AR2010070905599.html; Greg Jaffe and Rajiv Chandrasekaran, "U.S. Ambassador Puts Brakes on Plan to Utilize Afghan Militias Against Taliban," *Washington Post*, January 22, 2010, https://www.washingtonpost.com/wp-dyn/content/article/2010/01/21/AR2010012101926.html.
81. Gould, "Delegating IMF Conditionality."
82. Two mid-level U.S. military officials, interview by author, Baghdad, Iraq, March 9, 2019, interview 77; Major General Pat Robertson, interview by author, Baghdad, Iraq, March 10, 2019, interview 78.
83. Rubin, *The Fragmentation of Afghanistan*, 201–225, 258–278; Roy, *Islam and Resistance in Afghanistan*, 12–14; Barfield, *Afghanistan*, 250–254; Giustozzi, "Auxiliary Irregular Forces in Afghanistan."
84. Stanley McChrystal, *COMISAF's Initial Assessment (Unclassified), 30 August 2009* (Kabul: Headquarters International Security Assistance Force, 2009). For additional discussion on differences between the Iraq counterinsurgency strategy and McChrystal's in Afghanistan, including the latter's emphasis on civilian protection, see Carter

Malkasian, *The American War in Afghanistan* (Oxford: Oxford University Press, 2021), 225–234; Romano, Calfano, and Phelps, "Successful and Less Successful Interventions."

85. Stanley McChrystal, "Secretary of Defense Memorandum 26 June 2009, Subject: Initial United States Forces—Afghanistan (USFOR-A) Assessment," June 26, 2009, 6–9, https://static.nzz.ch/files/6/5/4/Afghanistan_Assessment_1.3630654.pdf.

86. Jones, *The Strategic Logic of Militia*, 21, 31–32; McChrystal, "COMISAF's Initial Assessment (Unclassified), 30 August 2009." Many academics and civil society representatives criticized the claims that turning to local tribal forces was more culturally appropriate or legitimate as a "reification" of tribal practices in ways that valorized a "quick fix" solution. Vincent, Weigand, and Hakimi, "The Afghan Local Police"; Hakimi, "Getting Savages to Fight Barbarians"; Reid, *"Just Don't Call It a Militia."*

87. International Crisis Group, *The Future of the Afghan Local Police*, Asia Report No. 268 (New York: International Crisis Group, 2015), 5, https://www.crisisgroup.org/asia/south-asia/afghanistan/future-afghan-local-police; Goodhand and Hakimi, *Counterinsurgency, Local Militias, and Statebuilding in Afghanistan*, 9–10.

88. Moyar, *Village Stability Operations and the Afghan Local Police*, 10–11; Jones, *The Strategic Logic of Militia*, 29–30.

89. On numbers and locations in these pilots, see Matthieu Lefèvre, "The Afghanistan Public Protection Program and the Local Defence Initiatives," in *The Unlearned Lessons of Afghanistan's Decade of Assistance (2001–2011)*, ed. Martine van Bijlert and Sari Kouvo (Kabul: Afghanistan Analysts Network, 2010), https://www.afghanistan-analysts.org/publication/aan-papers/local-defence-in-afghanistan-a-review-of-government-backed-initiatives/; Lisa Saum-Manning, *VSO/ALP: Comparing Past and Current Challenges to Afghan Local Defense*, RAND Working Paper (Washington, DC, December 2012). SOF or other parts of the U.S. military had also experimented with their own tribal or community mobilization and "reconciliation" both prior to and concurrent with these initiatives—including in parts of eastern Afghanistan, in Helmand, and around northern Kunduz Province. However, these other ad hoc initiatives would ultimately have less of an influence on the ALP policy debate and model, and so are not detailed here. Of those given an official name, they included the Critical Infrastructure Protection Program (in northern provinces), the Intermediate Security for Critical Infrastructure (in Helmand), and Community-Based Security Solutions (in eastern Afghanistan). See further details on these in Clark et al., *Ghosts of the Past*; Reid, *"Just Don't Call It a Militia,"* 15–24. Other field accounts from commanders or U.S. officials serving in these areas have identified even more ad hoc efforts that did not go by any particular name or moniker. Jim Gant, *One Tribe at a Time: A Strategy for Success in Afghanistan* (Los Angeles: Nine Sisters Imports, 2009); Malkasian, *The American War in Afghanistan*, 254–256.

90. Jones, *The Strategic Logic of Militia*, 30–32.

91. Clark et al., *Ghosts of the Past*; Jones, *The Strategic Logic of Militia*.

92. Lt. Col. (ret.) Scott Mann, interview by author, by telephone, May 5, 2021, interview 152; Becky Zimmerman, former adviser to ALP initiatives, interview by author, Washington, DC, June 20, 2018, interview 13.

93. US Special Operations officer leading the ALP advisory cell, interview by author, Kabul, Afghanistan, November 12, 2017, interview 166.
94. Andrew Wilder, *Cops or Robbers? The Struggle to Reform the Afghan National Police* (Kabul: Afghanistan Research and Evaluation Unit, 2007); Deedee Derksen, *The Politics of Disarmament and Rearmament in Afghanistan* (Washington, DC: United States Institute of Peace, 2015).
95. Boone, "Top US General Warns on Afghan Self-Defence Plan." On *arbakai*, see Tariq, *Tribal Security System (Arbakai) in Southeast Afghanistan*.
96. Such arguments were later documented in a monograph by one of the chief advisers involved in developing these models, RAND analyst Seth Jones. Jones, *The Strategic Logic of Militia*, 29; Similar arguments are found in Christine C. Fair and Seth G. Jones, *Securing Afghanistan: Getting on Track* (Washington, DC: United States Institute of Peace, 2009), 25, https://www.usip.org/publications/2009/02/securing-afghanistan-getting-track.
97. Department of Defense, "FOIA Release: 220 AR15-6 Inv Credibility Assessment_6—Exhibit_G," U.S. Department of Defense, 2011; Matthieu Lefèvre, *Local Defence in Afghanistan: A Review of Government-Backed Initiatives* (Kabul: Afghanistan Analysts Network, 2010), https://www.afghanistan-analysts.org/publication/aan-papers/local-defence-in-afghanistan-a-review-of-government-backed-initiatives/; Jones, *The Strategic Logic of Militia*.
98. Lefèvre, *Local Defence in Afghanistan*; SIGAR, *Stabilization*, 110; Jones, *The Strategic Logic of Militia*, 30–32.
99. Jon Boone, "US Pours Millions Into Anti-Taliban Militias in Afghanistan," *The Guardian*, November 22, 2009, https://www.theguardian.com/world/2009/nov/22/us-anti-taliban-militias-afghanistan.
100. Moyar, *Village Stability Operations and the Afghan Local Police*, 9–10; Saum-Manning, *VSO/ALP*, 4–7.
101. As Allison wrote in an early article developing BPA, "For players are also people.... The core of the bureaucratic politics mix is personality... each person comes to his position with baggage in tow, including sensitivities to certain issues, commitments to various programs, and personal standing and debts with groups in the society." Allison, "Conceptual Models and the Cuban Missile Crisis," 709.
102. Eikenberry himself later reflected that the classic BPA proposition that "where you stand depends on where you sit," aptly captured both his and other stakeholders' reactions to community defense forces and the ALP in Afghanistan. Ambassador Karl Eikenberry, interview by author, by Zoom, April 28, 2021, interview 150.
103. "White SOF," like Green Berets, identify as specialists in irregular warfare and the sort of local counterinsurgent partner development typified by their work in the Vietnam and El Salvador conflicts. In the period prior to these local defense force experiments, white SOF in Afghanistan had been pulled into counterterrorism-related targeting operations (e.g., nighttime raids and kill-or-capture missions), usually the remit of "black SOF." As one of the advisers to the ALP observed, "Enthusiasm for... [the local defense forces] when it started was not as much for the mission as for the belief... [that

these were] things they should be doing." Becky Zimmerman, former adviser to ALP initiatives, interview by author, Washington, DC, June 20, 2018, interview 13.

104. During the pilot period, SOF had allowed a tribal power broker named Mohammad Arif Khan Noorzai, a Karzai relative and the head of a public highway and tribal support ministry, to nominate members for some of the LDI. Going forward, they proposed that both this tribal support ministry and the Independent Directorate for Local Governance would have a role in the initiative. Karl Eikenberry, "Unconventional Security Forces—What's Out There? [09kabul3661]," leaked U.S. embassy diplomatic cable, Wikileaks, November 12, 2009, paras. 19–20, https://wikileaks.org/plusd/cables/09KABUL3661_a.html; Lefèvre, *Local Defence in Afghanistan*, 19–20; Boone, "US Pours Millions Into Anti-Taliban Militias in Afghanistan." Goodhand and Hakimi offer a further breakdown of different interests and positions among international actors and national and provincial elites. Goodhand and Hakimi, *Counterinsurgency, Local Militias, and Statebuilding in Afghanistan*, 12–13, 16.
105. Lefèvre, *Local Defence in Afghanistan*, 19.
106. Goodhand and Hakimi, *Counterinsurgency, Local Militias, and Statebuilding in Afghanistan*, 11; Lefèvre, *Local Defence in Afghanistan*, 19.
107. Goodhand and Hakimi, *Counterinsurgency, Local Militias, and Statebuilding in Afghanistan*, 9–13; Lefèvre, *The Afghanistan Public Protection Program and the Local Defence Initiatives*, 13–19.
108. Ambassador Karl Eikenberry, interview by author, by Zoom, April 28, 2021, interview 150.
109. Malkasian, *The American War in Afghanistan*, 91.
110. Ambassador Karl Eikenberry, interview by author, by Zoom, April 28, 2021, interview 150.
111. Eikenberry, "Unconventional Security Forces," para. 3.
112. Eikenberry, para. 18.
113. Eikenberry, para. 21.
114. Jaffe and Chandrasekaran, "U.S. Ambassador Puts Brakes on Plan to Utilize Afghan Militias Against Taliban."
115. Partlow and DeYoung, "Gen. Petraeus Runs Into Resistance from Karzai Over Village Defense Forces"; Rajiv Chandrasekaran, "US Forces Training Afghan Villagers to Watch for Taliban," *Washington Post*, May 2, 2010, http://archive.boston.com/news/world/middleeast/articles/2010/05/02/us_forces_training_afghan_villagers_to_watch_for_taliban/; Jaffe and Chandrasekaran, "U.S. Ambassador Puts Brakes on Plan to Utilize Afghan Militias Against Taliban."
116. Reid, *"Just Don't Call It a Militia"*; SIGAR, *Stabilization*; Boone, "US Pours Millions Into Anti-Taliban Militias in Afghanistan"; Alissa J. Rubin and Richard A. Oppel, "U.S. and Afghanistan Debate More Village Forces," *New York Times*, July 12, 2010, https://www.nytimes.com/2010/07/13/world/asia/13afghan.html?_r=2&ref=world.
117. Greg Bruno, "A Tribal Strategy for Afghanistan," Council on Foreign Relations, November 5, 2008, https://www.cfr.org/backgrounder/tribal-strategy-afghanistan.

2. BARGAINING MOMENTS AND STRUCTURES   315

118. One UN official who had worked with Afghan institutions through much of the early decade of international engagement attributed Karzai and Atmar's negative reaction to the same patronage-building games that had roiled other ANSF recruitment, disarmament, and other institution-building processes. Reflecting the consensus view of several analysts and observers interviewed, he saw Karzai and Atmar's stiff opposition, and their demands for institutionalization, as a reflection of their desire to appoint those loyal to them in these positions. Former UNAMA adviser, interview by author, by Skype, May 28, 2020, interview 132. For further discussion, see Gaston, "Afghanistan Case Study"; Goodhand and Hakimi, *Counterinsurgency, Local Militias, and Statebuilding in Afghanistan.*
119. Former President Hamid Karzai, interview by author, by Whatsapp, February 15, 2024, interview 227.
120. Partlow and DeYoung, "Gen. Petraeus Runs Into Resistance from Karzai Over Village Defense Forces"; see also former Afghan official and adviser to President Hamid Karzai, interview by author, Washington, DC, September 2, 2017, interview 164. Accounts describe the negotiations between Karzai and Petraeus as intense, with Karzai "storming out" of their first meeting (again see Partlow and DeYoung, "Gen. Petraeus Runs Into Resistance from Karzai Over Village Defense Forces").
121. Former Afghan official and adviser to President Hamid Karzai, interview by author, Washington, DC, September 2, 2017, interview 164.
122. Former President Hamid Karzai, interview by author, by Whatsapp, February 15, 2024, interview 330.
123. Clark et al., *Ghosts of the Past.*
124. Former adviser to General Petraeus in Iraq and Afghanistan, interview by author, Washington, DC, November 14, 2019, interview 102.
125. Moyar, *Village Stability Operations and the Afghan Local Police*, 17, 89.
126. Clark et al., *Ghosts of the Past*; Gaston, "Afghanistan Case Study."
127. CFSOCC-A, *Afghan Local Defense Initiative Briefing January 2010*, 6.
128. Partlow and DeYoung, "Gen. Petraeus Runs Into Resistance from Karzai Over Village Defense Forces."
129. Former UNAMA adviser, interview by author, by Skype, May 28, 2020, interview 132.
130. Partlow and DeYoung, "Gen. Petraeus Runs Into Resistance from Karzai Over Village Defense Forces."
131. The insertion of language explicitly prohibiting the program from recruiting Taliban insurgents is surprising given that many of the leading U.S. military sponsors of the program were inspired by their experience "flipping" insurgent affiliates in Iraq, and that many of the leading Afghan advocates saw it as a way to support local reconciliation and reintegration with Taliban fighters. Jonathan Goodhand and Aziz Hakimi, *Counterinsurgency, Local Militias, and Statebuilding in Afghanistan* (Washington, DC: United States Institute of Peace, 2013), 16, https://www.usip.org/publications/2013/12/counterinsurgency-local-militias-and-statebuilding-afghanistan; Rachel Reid, *"Just Don't Call It a Militia": Impunity, Militias, and the "Afghan Local Police"* (New York: Human Rights Watch, 2011), 88–91. There is insufficient evidence in the public record

132. Becky Zimmerman, former adviser to ALP initiatives, interview by author, Washington, DC, June 20, 2018, interview 13. See also Saum-Manning, *VSO/ALP*.

or in interviewees' recollections on this point to fully satisfy how or why this restriction was inserted. However, given that the overall U.S. position was largely against open talks with or reconciliation with the Taliban until 2017, it might be presumed that this was inserted to respond to those concerns. John F. Sopko, *What We Need to Learn: Lessons from 20 Years of Afghan Reconstruction* (Washington, DC: Special Inspector General for Afghanistan Reconstruction, 2021).

133. U.S. adviser on ANA-TF development, interview by author, by telephone, June 10, 2019, interview 94; Mark Jacobson, former deputy political adviser at the NATO mission in Afghanistan, interview by author, by Zoom, April 24, 2020, interview 130; former senior adviser to U.S. commanders in Iraq and Afghanistan from 2004 until 2009, interview by author, Washington, DC, June 15, 2018, interview 14; Gen. (ret.) David Petraeus, interview by author, by telephone, July 30, 2022, interview 208; senior DoD policy official with prior deployments in Iraq and Afghanistan, interview with author, Washington, DC, June 19, 2018, interview 15.

134. Senior DoD policy official with prior deployments in Iraq and Afghanistan, interview with author, Washington, DC, June 19, 2018, interview 15; Mark Jacobson, former deputy political adviser at the NATO mission in Afghanistan, interview by author, by Zoom, April 24, 2020, interview 130.

135. Larry Lewis and Sarah Holewinski, "Changing of the Guard: Civilian Protection for an Evolving Military," *Prism* 4, no. 2 (2013): 57–66; human rights advocate, interview by author, Washington, DC, July 13, 2019, interview 30; human rights advocate, interview by author, by WhatsApp, May 12, 2020, interview 13; UN human rights investigator, interview by author, by telephone, March 9, 2019, interview 75.

136. Suhrke, *When More Is Less*, 130–132; Ashraf Ghani, Clare Lockhart, and Michael Carnahan, *Closing the Sovereignty Gap: An Approach to State-Building* (London: Overseas Development Institute, 2005).

137. William Maley, "Surviving in a War Zone: The Problem of Civilian Casualties in Afghanistan," in *Protecting Civilians During Violent Conflict: Theoretical and Practical Issues for the 21st Century*, ed. Igor Primoratz and David W. Lovell (Aldershot, UK: Ashgate., 2012), 231–250; Joseph H. Felter and Jacob N. Shapiro, "Limiting Civilian Casualties as Part of a Winning Strategy: The Case of Courageous Restraint," *Daedalus* 146, no. 1 (2017): 44–58; Malkasian, *The American War in Afghanistan*.

138. Mark Jacobson, former deputy political adviser at the NATO mission in Afghanistan, interview by author, by Zoom, April 24, 2020, interview 130.

139. Mark Jacobson, former deputy political adviser at the NATO mission in Afghanistan, interview by author, by Zoom, April 24, 2020, interview 130.

140. Mark Jacobson, former deputy political adviser at the NATO mission in Afghanistan, interview by author, by Zoom, April 24, 2020, interview 130; human rights advocate, interview by author, Washington, DC, July 13, 2019, interview 30; human rights advocate, interview by author, by WhatsApp, May 12, 2020, interview 31.

2. BARGAINING MOMENTS AND STRUCTURES 317

141. CFSOCC-A, *Afghan Local Defense Initiative Briefing January 2010*, 4.
142. Human rights advocate, interview by author, Washington, DC, July 13, 2019, interview 30; human rights advocate, interview by author, by WhatsApp, May 12, 2020, interview 31.
143. Allison, "Conceptual Models and the Cuban Missile Crisis," 711; Halperin, Kanter, and Clapp, *Bureaucratic Politics and Foreign Policy*, 122.
144. Allison and Halperin, "Bureaucratic Politics," 78.
145. Lt. Col. (ret.) Scott Mann, senior U.S. Special Forces commander involved in VSO/ALP development and early mobilization, interview by author, by telephone, May 5, 2021, interview 152.
146. Former UNAMA adviser, interview by author, by Skype, May 28, 2020, interview 132.
147. Human rights advocate, interview by author, Washington, DC, July 13, 2019, interview 30; human rights advocate, interview by author, by WhatsApp, May 12, 2020, interview 31.
148. Ambassador Karl Eikenberry, interview by author, by Zoom, April 28, 2021, interview 150.
149. Ambassador Karl Eikenberry, interview by author, by Zoom, April 28, 2021, interview 150.
150. O'Hanlon and Camp, *Iraq Index*; Campbell and Shapiro, *Afghanistan Index*.
151. Former senior military official, interview by author, by telephone July 30, 2022, interview 209.
152. Ricks, *The Gamble*, 138–139, 261–262. Petraeus's level of authority was so great that he did not even ask Bush for permission to pay and arm the *sahwa*, nor was it ever raised to him that he should have. Ricks, 202.
153. Toby Dodge, professor and Iraq historian, interview by author, by telephone, March 31, 2020, interview 110.
154. Senior DoD policy official with prior deployments in Iraq and Afghanistan, interview with author, Washington, DC, June 19, 2018, interview 15.
155. Safa Rasoul Al-Sheikh, deputy national security adviser for Iraq, interview by author, Baghdad, Iraq, November 5, 2018, interview 47.
156. Ian S. Livingston, Heather L. Messera, and Michael O'Hanlon, *Afghanistan Index* (Washington, DC: Brookings Institution, February 2010), 10.
157. Rosa Brooks, "Obama vs. the Generals," *Politico Magazine*, November 2013, https://www.politico.com/magazine/story/2013/11/obama-vs-the-generals-099379/.
158. Lt. Col. (ret.) Scott Mann, senior U.S. Special Forces commander involved in VSO/ALP development and early mobilization, interview by author, by telephone, May 5, 2021, interview 152; Becky Zimmerman, former adviser to ALP initiatives, interview by author, Washington, DC, June 20, 2018, interview 13. This view of the local defense forces as not just an immediate security fix, but part of a broader-based, community-development initiative was certainly not universal. Some of the ad hoc piloting of local defense forces or tribal outreach led by other U.S. forces seemed much more premised on immediate security or intelligence gains. However, the SOF cell and military

advisers involved in developing the core proposal for local defense forces—the one that would lead to the creation of the ALP—were focused on this more community-based model. As such, this is the model that is more significant with respect to understanding bargaining preferences.

3. SEARCHING FOR UNICORNS

1. Mona Yacoubian, "Critical Junctures in United States Policy Toward Syria: An Assessment of the Counterfactuals," Simon-Skjodt Center for the Prevention of Genocide, Occasional Papers No. 3 (August 2017): 20–21, https://www.ushmm.org/m/pdfs/Yacoubian-Critical-Junctures-US-Policy-Syria.pdf.
2. Christopher M. Blanchard, "Syria and U.S. Policy," *In Focus*, Congressional Research Service, April 19, 2022, https://crsreports.congress.gov/product/pdf/IF/IF11930#:~:text=The; Office of Audits, *Audit of the Department of State Vetting Process for Syrian Non-lethal Assistance* (Washington, DC: Office of Inspector general, U.S. Department of State, November 2016), 1, https://www.oversight.gov/sites/default/files/oig-reports/aud-mero-17-01.pdf. Separate from this, humanitarian aid to Syria accounted for $14 billion in U.S. support from 2012 to 2022. Blanchard, "Syria and U.S. Policy."
3. Julian Borger and Nick Hopkins, "West Training Syrian Rebels in Jordan," *The Guardian*, March 8, 2013, https://www.theguardian.com/world/2013/mar/08/west-training-syrian-rebels-jordan; Ewan MacAskill, "UK to Send 75 Military Trainers to Help Moderate Syrian Rebels," *The Guardian*, March 26, 2015, https://www.theguardian.com/uk-news/2015/mar/26/uk-military-trainers-help-syrian-rebels; Sabbagh, "UK and France to Send Further Forces to Syria in Aid of US Withdrawal"; Ari Khalidi, "Turkish State Media Exposes French Troop Locations in Syria," *Kurdistan24*, March 30, 2018, https://www.kurdistan24.net/en/news/cce35809-b1c8-4e77-afbc-172e26769bfe.
4. Nonlethal assistance most commonly involved food, humanitarian, or medical supplies, but could also include tactical equipment such as trucks and other vehicles, body armor, night vision goggles, generators, protection kits against chemical weapons, and radio and communications equipment. Loveluck, "What's Non-lethal About Aid to the Syrian Opposition?"; "US and UK Suspend Non-lethal Aid for Syria Rebels," *BBC News*, December 11, 2013, https://www.bbc.com/news/world-middle-east-25331241. In the course of Syria assistance, each donor country adopted its own interpretation of what type of assistance might be seen as a sovereign violation, with some willing to provide "nonlethal" but not lethal assistance, or willing to support unarmed police but not armed opposition.
5. Policy and Operations Evaluation Department, *Review of the Monitoring Systems of Three Projects in Syria*; Holger Stark and Matthias Gebauer, "Deutschland Liefert Schusswesten an Assad-Gegner," *Der Spiegel*, May 26, 2013, http://www.spiegel.de/politik/ausland/syrien-deutschland-liefert-schusswesten-an-assad-gegner-a-901956.html; Ruys, "Of Arms, Funding and 'Non-lethal Assistance.'"

6. Former senior Obama administration official, interview by author, by telephone, May 29, 2019, interview 86.
7. Julian Borger, "Austria Says UK Push to Arm Syrian Rebels Would Violate International Law," *The Guardian*, May 14, 2013, https://www.theguardian.com/world/julian-borger-global-security-blog/2013/may/14/austria-eu-syria-arms-embargo; Republic of Austria, "The Austrian Position on Arms Embargo in Syria," *The Guardian*, May 15, 2013, https://www.theguardian.com/world/julian-borger-global-security-blog/interactive/2013/may/15/austria-eu-syria-arms-embargo-pdf.
8. Since 2001 the United States has consistently justified unilateral intervention absent UN mandates as part of its right to collective and sovereign self-defense, particularly where it deems the sovereign territorial holder in question to be "unwilling or unable" to deal with the threats in question. Gareth D. Williams, "Piercing the Shield of Sovereignty: An Assessment of the Legal Status of the 'Unwilling or Unable' Test," *University of New South Wales Law Journal* 36, no. 2 (2013): 619; Erica Gaston, "War Powers Far from a Hot Battlefield: Checks and Balances on Presidential War-Making Through Individual and Unit Self-Defense," *Harvard National Security Journal* 10 (2019): 195–258. Not all states share this legal interpretation, but it is so entrenched as the U.S. legal position that it helped alleviate internal bureaucratic discomfort with intervention when it came to arming anti-ISIL groups.
9. Ruys, "Of Arms, Funding and 'Non-lethal Assistance' "; Loveluck, "What's Non-lethal About Aid to the Syrian Opposition?"
10. Former USAID official involved in U.S. Syria assistance, interview by author, Washington, DC, September 18, 2019, interview 98; former State Department officer, interview by author, Washington, DC, November 20, 2019, interview 105; State Department officer working on Iraq and Syria anti-ISIL policy and programming, interview by author, by WhatsApp, June 4, 2019, interview 90.
11. 18 U.S.C. §§2339A and 2339B. The provision has been interpreted so broadly that it might result in felony imprisonment even if the support was not given with the intent of furthering terrorism or the organization in question. Charles Doyle, *Terrorist Material Support: An Overview of 18 U.S.C. §2339A and §2339B* (Washington, DC: Congressional Research Service, 2016), https://fas.org/sgp/crs/natsec/R41333.pdf; Holder v. Humanitarian Law Project, 130 S. Ct. 2705 (2010). As such, if any U.S. material support was inadvertently provided to groups with terrorist affiliations (now or in the future), or later transferred by the recipient group to DTOs, it might create personal liability for U.S. officials or organizations involved.
12. The group later renamed itself Hayat Tahrir ash-Sham. However, it often continued to be known as Jabhat al-Nusra after this name change. Because of this, and to avoid potential confusion generated by using different names, this book will refer to the group as Jabhat al-Nusra across all time periods.
13. European diplomat involved in assistance to Syrian opposition, interview by author, Istanbul, May 8, 2018, interview 10.
14. Clinton, *Hard Choices*, 463.

15. As will be discussed in the relevant case studies, it was designed to apply to forces of a foreign state, not those opposed to them. It was also generally inapplicable to the types of funding in question.
16. 18 U.S. Code § 2442; Michael A. Weber, "Child Soldiers Prevention Act of 2008: Security Assistance Restrictions," *In Focus*, Congressional Research Service, July 10, 2019, https://fas.org/sgp/crs/misc/IF10901.pdf.
17. As journalist Mark Landler noted, "In a White House where many of the top officials, including the president, had law degrees, the lawyers played an important, underappreciated role"—particularly when it came to limits on Syrian assistance. Mark Landler, *Alter Egos: Obama's Legacy, Hillary's Promise and the Struggle over American Power* (London: W. H. Allen, 2016), 223.
18. Former senior State Department official, interview by author, London, March 29, 2018, interview 4.
19. Former State Department adviser, interview by author, March 24, 2018, London, interview 2.
20. The group of Kurdish and Arab forces whom the United States supported in northeastern Syria did not officially rebrand themselves as the Syrian Democratic Forces until October 2015. There was some U.S. support to the group before it adopted this name. However, to avoid the use of multiple names, this chapter will generally use the "SDF" abbreviation to refer to the Kurdish-Arab fighting coalition in northeastern Syria, with the exception of some specific references to their pre-October 2015 iteration.
21. The start date for this case study could arguably be one of several points. As early as the summer of 2012, the CIA was providing advice and working to channel the funding and arms provided by other regional partners to certain FSA groups. Journalist Mark Landler (and other reporting by the *New York Times*) dates the presidential authorization for the program to April 2013, although most other records suggest that little in the way of planning or decision making around it had happened before July 2013, when the intelligence committees agreed. U.S. covert assistance did not reach the FSA until later in the fall of 2013 according to news reports. Since bargaining is crucial for the present discussion, this case study begins with the White House debate over covert assistance in September 2012. Landler, *Alter Egos*, 217–219; C. J. Chivers and Eric Schmitt, "Arms Airlift to Syrian Rebels Expands, with C.I.A. Aid," *New York Times*, April 12, 2013, https://www.nytimes.com/2013/03/25/world/middleeast/arms-airlift-to-syrian-rebels-expands-with-cia-aid.html; Eric Schmitt, "C.I.A. Said to Aid in Steering Arms to Syrian Rebels," *New York Times*, June 21, 2012, https://www.nytimes.com/2012/06/21/world/middleeast/cia-said-to-aid-in-steering-arms-to-syrian-rebels.html. The end date coincides with the effective end of assistance in early 2017. President Trump froze the program upon coming into office, and a few months later he ended it. David E. Sanger, Eric Schmitt, and Ben Hubbard, "Trump Ends Covert Aid to Syrian Rebels Trying to Topple Assad," *New York Times*, July 19, 2017, https://www.nytimes.com/2017/07/19/world/middleeast/cia-arming-syrian-rebels.html.
22. Charles Lister, *The Free Syrian Army: A Decentralized Insurgent Brand* (Washington, DC: Brookings Institution, April 2016), 405.

23. "The Extent of Conflict-Related Deaths in the Syrian Arab Republic—Background Note," OHCHR, September 24, 2021, https://www.ohchr.org/en/documents/status-and-update-reports/oral-update-extent-conflict-related-deaths-syrian-arab-republic; "The Facts: What You Need to Know About the Syria Crisis," Mercy Corps, March 12, 2021, https://www.mercycorps.org/blog/facts-syria-crisis#:~:text=In%20July%202012%2C.
24. Landler, *Alter Egos*, 211–212.
25. Former senior State Department official, interview by author, London, March 29, 2018, interview 4; former State Department adviser, interview by author, March 24, 2018, London, interview 2; State Department officer working on Iraq and Syria anti-ISIL policy and programming, interview by author, by WhatsApp, June 4, 2019, interview 90.
26. Iraqi tribal representatives, interview by author, Washington, DC, June 7, 2018, interview 12.
27. "U.S. Sets Aside $25 Million for Non-lethal Aid to Syria Rebels," Reuters, August 1, 2012, https://www.reuters.com/article/us-syria-crisis-usa-idUSBRE8701DU20120801; Clinton, *Hard Choices*, 461–462; Landler, *Alter Egos*, 215–218. In her memoirs, former secretary of state Hillary Clinton observed that the vetoed February 2012 Security Council resolution was taken as a sign that diplomacy was not moving forward. Clinton, *Hard Choices*, 461. Others date the sense of a diplomatic dead end to the collapse of Annan-led talks in summer 2012. Yacoubian, "Critical Junctures in United States Policy Toward Syria."
28. Yacoubian, "Critical Junctures in United States Policy Toward Syria," 10.
29. Yacoubian, 8.
30. Max Boot, "The Pentagon's Cold Feet on Syria Should Not Decide the Matter," *Washington Post*, March 14, 2012; Leon E. Panetta and Jim Newton, *Worthy Fights: A Memoir of Leadership in War and Peace* (New York: Penguin Press, 2014); Josh Rogin, "McCain to Call for Air Strikes on Syria," *Foreign Policy*, March 5, 2012, https://foreignpolicy.com/2012/03/05/mccain-to-call-for-air-strikes-on-syria/.
31. Ben Norton, "Leaked Hillary Clinton Emails Show U.S. Allies Saudi Arabia and Qatar Supported ISIS," *Salon*, October 11, 2016, https://www.salon.com/2016/10/11/leaked-hillary-clinton-emails-show-u-s-allies-saudi-arabia-and-qatar-supported-isis/; Chivers and Schmitt, "Arms Airlift to Syrian Rebels Expands."
32. Landler, *Alter Egos*, 217–219; Chivers and Schmitt, "Arms Airlift to Syrian Rebels Expands"; Schmitt, "C.I.A. Said to Aid in Steering Arms to Syrian Rebels."
33. Clinton, *Hard Choices*, 461; Karen DeYoung, "Congressional Panels Approve Arms Aid to Syrian Opposition," *Washington Post*, July 22, 2013, https://www.washingtonpost.com/world/national-security/congressional-panels-approve-arms-aid-to-syrian-opposition/2013/07/22/393035ce-f31a-11e2-8505-bf6f231e77b4_story.html?utm_term=.da03e1b2d207.
34. Steven Lee Myers, "U.S. Joins Effort to Equip and Pay Rebels in Syria," *New York Times*, April 1, 2012, https://www.nytimes.com/2012/04/02/world/middleeast/us-and-other-countries-move-to-increase-assistance-to-syrian-rebels.html.
35. Public reports that surfaced in August 2012 suggested that $25 million had at that point been designated for nonlethal assistance to opposition forces (including

communications equipment) and was already in use. Reuters, "U.S. Sets Aside $25 Million for Non-lethal Aid to Syria Rebels."

36. Landler, *Alter Egos*, 216; Yacoubian, "Critical Junctures in United States Policy Toward Syria."

37. Clinton, *Hard Choices*, 464.

38. Erika Solomon, "The Rise and Fall of a US-Backed Rebel Commander in Syria," *Financial Times*, February 9, 2017, https://www.ft.com/content/791ad3bc-ecfc-11e6-930f-061b01e23655; Youssef Sadaki, "The MOC's Role in the Collapse of the Southern Opposition," *Syria Source* (blog), Atlantic Council, September 23, 2016, https://www.atlanticcouncil.org/blogs/syriasource/the-moc-s-role-in-the-collapse-of-the-southern-opposition; International Crisis Group, *New Approach in Southern Syria* (Brussels: International Crisis Group, 2015), 9, https://www.crisisgroup.org/middle-east-north-africa/eastern-mediterranean/syria/new-approach-southern-syria.

39. Solomon, "The Rise and Fall of a US-Backed Rebel Commander in Syria"; Sadaki, "The MOC's Role in the Collapse of the Southern Opposition"; International Crisis Group, *New Approach in Southern Syria*, 9.

40. Andru E. Wall, "Demystifying the Title 10-Title 50 Debate: Distinguishing Military Operations, Intelligence Activities & Covert Action," *Harvard National Security Journal* 3 (2011): 85–142; Mazzetti, *The Way of the Knife*, 76–79.

41. Former FSA spokesman and coordinator, interview by author, Istanbul, May 8, 2018, interview 9; political leader with U.S.-supported FSA group, interview by author, Gaziantep, Turkey, September 24, 2018, interview 40. See also Entous, "Covert CIA Mission to Arm Syrian Rebels Goes Awry."

42. Entous, "Covert CIA Mission to Arm Syrian Rebels Goes Awry."

43. Hasan Mustafa, "The Moderate Rebels: A Growing List of Vetted Groups Fielding BGM-71 TOW Anti-tank Guided Missiles," *Hasan Mustafa* (blog), April 12, 2015, https://hasanmustafas.wordpress.com/2015/05/08/the-moderate-rebels-a-complete-and-growing-list-of-vetted-groups-fielding-tow-missiles/; Lister, "The Free Syrian Army"; Entous, "Covert CIA Mission to Arm Syrian Rebels Goes Awry."

44. Former FSA communications and training coordinator, interview by author, Istanbul, September 22, 2018, interview 37; political leader with U.S.-supported FSA group, interview by author, Gaziantep, Turkey, September 24, 2018, interview 40; commander formerly with the al-Zenki group, interview by author, by telephone, September 24, 2018, interview 41; Entous, "U.S. Readies 'Plan B' to Arm Syria Rebels."

45. The full name of the group was Harakat Nour ad-Din az-Zenki, or the Nour al-Din al-Zenki Movement, named after a historical twelfth-century figure Nour ad-Din az-Zenki. The degree to which the battalion was considered an independent force varied as the group tried to or successfully merged with several others from 2014 to 2017. The name of the group changed in response to these various mergers, but it tended to still be known within U.S. policy circles as the al-Zenki group.

46. Sam Heller, "Commentary: In Syrian Proxy War, America Can Keep Its Hands Clean or It Can Get Things Done," Century Foundation, August 17, 2016, https://tcf.org/content/commentary/syrian-proxy-war-america-can-keep-hands-clean-can-get

-things-done/. Former senior State Department official, interview by author, London, March 29, 2018, interview 4.
47. Political leader with U.S.-supported FSA group, interview by author, Gaziantep, Turkey, September 24, 2018, interview 40.
48. Liz Sly, "The Rise and Ugly Fall of a Moderate Syrian Rebel Offers Lessons for the West," *Washington Post*, January 5, 2015, https://www.washingtonpost.com/world/middle_east/the-rise-and-ugly-fall-of-a-moderate-syrian-rebel-offers-lessons-for-the-west/2015/01/04/3889db38-80da-4974-b1ef-1886f4183624_story.html?utm_term=.2b73d78c4d9c.
49. Nick Heras, Syria analyst, interview by author, by telephone, June 20, 2018, interview 22.
50. Former intelligence agency analyst, interview by author, Washington, DC, July 15, 2022, interview 207; former senior military official, interview by author, by telephone, July 30, 2022, interview 209.
51. Former intelligence agency analyst, interview by author, Washington, DC, July 15, 2022, interview 207; Nancy A. Youssef, "Syrian Rebels Describe U.S.-Backed Training in Qatar," *PBS Frontline*, May 26, 2014, https://www.pbs.org/wgbh/frontline/article/syrian-rebels-describe-u-s-backed-training-in-qatar/.
52. Greg Miller and Karen DeYoung, "Secret CIA Effort in Syria Faces Large Funding Cut," *Washington Post*, December 6, 2015, https://www.washingtonpost.com/world/national-security/lawmakers-move-to-curb-1-billion-cia-program-to-train-syrian-rebels/2015/06/12/b0f45a9e-1114-11e5-adec-e82f8395c032_story.html.
53. Solomon, "The Rise and Fall of a US-Backed Rebel Commander in Syria"; Lister, "The Free Syrian Army"; Nicholas A. Heras, *From the Bottom, Up: A Strategy for U.S. Military Support to Syria's Armed Opposition* (Washington, DC: Center for a New American Security, 2016), https://www.cnas.org/publications/reports/from-the-bottom-up-a-strategy-for-u-s-military-support-to-syrias-armed-opposition; Entous, "Covert CIA Mission to Arm Syrian Rebels Goes Awry."
54. Yacoubian, "Critical Junctures in United States Policy Toward Syria," 17.
55. Entous, "Covert CIA Mission to Arm Syrian Rebels Goes Awry."
56. Former FSA spokesman and coordinator, interview by author, Istanbul, May 8, 2018, interview 9; political leader with U.S.-supported FSA group, interview by author, Gaziantep, Turkey, September 24, 2018, interview 40.
57. Yacoubian, "Critical Junctures in United States Policy toward Syria," 17.
58. Former senior military official, interview by author, by telephone July 30, 2022, interview 209.
59. Nick Heras, Syria analyst, interview by author, by telephone, June 20, 2018, interview 22; Charles Lister, Syria specialist, interview by author, Washington, DC, May 23, 2019, interview 84.
60. Charles Lister, Syria specialist, interview by author, Washington, DC, May 23, 2019, interview 84.
61. Former senior Obama administration official, interview by author, by telephone, May 29, 2019, interview 86.

62. Former non-U.S. political adviser involved in the MOC, interview by author, London, May 30, 2018, interview 6.
63. Former non-U.S. political adviser involved in the MOC, interview by author, London, May 30, 2018, interview 6.
64. Halperin, "Why Bureaucrats Play Games," 70–90; Allison, "Conceptual Models and the Cuban Missile Crisis"; Graham T. Allison and Philip Zelikow, *Essence of Decision: Explaining the Cuban Missile Crisis* (New York: Longman, 1999).
65. Allison and Halperin, "Bureaucratic Politics," 50.
66. Landler, *Alter Egos*, 211–218; Reuters, "U.S. Sets Aside $25 Million for Non-lethal Aid to Syria Rebels"; Clinton, *Hard Choices*.
67. Former intelligence agency analyst, interview by author, Washington, DC, July 15, 2022, interview 207. For greater background on the CIA's reengagement in paramilitary operations after the September 11 attacks, see Mazzetti, *The Way of the Knife*; L. Britt Snider, *The Agency and the Hill: The CIA's Relationship with Congress (1946–2004)* (Scotts Valley, CA: CreateSpace, 2008).
68. Landler, *Alter Egos*, 215.
69. Landler, 215.
70. Clinton, *Hard Choices*, 461.
71. Clinton, 462.
72. Clinton, 461–463; Landler, *Alter Egos*, 216–218.
73. Mark Mazzetti, "C.I.A. Study of Covert Aid Fueled Skepticism About Helping Syrian Rebels," *New York Times*, October 14, 2014, https://www.nytimes.com/2014/10/15/us/politics/cia-study-says-arming-rebels-seldom-works.html.
74. Mazzetti, "C.I.A. Study of Covert Aid."
75. Clinton, *Hard Choices*, 461–463; Landler, *Alter Egos*, 216–218.
76. Clinton, *Hard Choices*, 463.
77. Clinton, 461.
78. Landler, *Alter Egos*, 210.
79. Landler, 210.
80. Landler, 217–219.
81. Landler, 221.
82. Landler, 219–221.
83. Mazzetti, "C.I.A. Study of Covert Aid"; Panetta and Newton, *Worthy Fights*, 450; Clinton, *Hard Choices*, 465.
84. DeYoung, "Congressional Panels Approve Arms Aid to Syrian Opposition."
85. Jeremy M. Sharp and Christopher M. Blanchard, *Armed Conflict in Syria: Background and U.S. Response*, RL33487 (Washington, DC: Congressional Research Service, September 2013), 8, https://www.globalsecurity.org/military/library/report/crs/rl33487_130906.pdf; DeYoung, "Congressional Panels Approve Arms Aid to Syrian Opposition"; Mark Hosenball and Phil Stewart, "Exclusive: Congress Delaying U.S. Aid to Syrian Rebels," Reuters, July 8, 2013, https://www.reuters.com/article/us-usa-syria-arms/exclusive-congress-delaying-u-s-aid-to-syrian-rebels-sources-idUSBRE96713N20130708.

86. DeYoung, "Congressional Panels Approve Arms Aid to Syrian Opposition."
87. Former intelligence agency analyst, interview by author, Washington, DC, July 15, 2022, interview 207; former senior military official, interview by author, by telephone, July 30, 2022, interview 209.
88. Former senior Obama administration official, interview by author, by telephone, May 29, 2019, interview 86; former intelligence agency analyst, interview by author, Washington, DC, July 15, 2022, interview 207; former senior military official, interview by author, by telephone July 30, 2022, interview 209.
89. Entous, "Covert CIA Mission to Arm Syrian Rebels Goes Awry."
90. Mazzetti, *The Way of the Knife*, 225.
91. Former senior military official, interview by author, by telephone, July 30, 2022, interview 209.
92. Former senior military official, interview by author, by telephone, July 30, 2022, interview 209.
93. The United States committed to provide greater nonlethal assistance, including to the FSA, at an April 2012 Friends of Syria conference, but the public announcement to actually deliver on that promise, and evidence of FSA assistance, only came in February 2013. Anne Gearan and Karen DeYoung, "U.S. Announces Expanded Battlefield Aid to Syrian Rebels, but Not Arms," *Washington Post*, February 28, 2013, https://www.washingtonpost.com/world/middle_east/us-announces-expanded-battlefield-aid-to-syrian-rebels/2013/02/28/f0a32414-819b-11e2-b99e-6baf4ebe42df_story.html?utm_term=.05197e3243d9. The start date for this case study begins with the internal deliberations within the State Department, which began generally for all nonlethal assistance in the summer of 2012, and by the fall of 2012 had progressed to the question of expanding support to armed opposition, according to interviewees. On the end date for this case study, State Department nonlethal assistance, including limited support to armed opposition groups, continued beyond the end of 2014, but CSO involvement in it ceased. In early 2015, CSO handed over all of its Syria nonlethal assistance programs to the NEA. Office of Audits, *Audit of the Department of State Vetting Process for Syrian Non-lethal Assistance*. NEA based its procedures on CSO's vetting protocols and risk-mitigation measures, but also adopted its own interpretations. Office of Audits, 6. This case study will keep to the period of CSO management.
94. Allison and Halperin, "Bureaucratic Politics," 51–54.
95. Smith and Clarke, *Foreign Policy Implementation*; Brighi and Hill, "Implementation and Behaviour."
96. Allison and Halperin, "Bureaucratic Politics," 51–54; Alden and Aran, *Foreign Policy Analysis*, 32–33; Halperin, "Why Bureaucrats Play Games," 72–74.
97. State Department staff member involved in anti-ISIL policy coordination, interview by author, by telephone, April 26, 2020, interview 131.
98. State department staff with past experience in Syria and Iraq anti-ISIL policies and programs, interview by author, Washington, DC, November 18, 2019, interview 103; former DRL officer involved in Leahy vetting, interview by author, Washington, DC, May 14, 2019, interview 83. See also Landler, *Alter Egos*\, 224.

99. State Department staff with past experience in Syria and Iraq anti-ISIL policies and programs, interview by author, Washington, DC, November 18, 2019, interview 103; State Department officer working on Syria programming, interview by author, Washington, DC, June 23, 2018, interview 20.
100. Office of Audits, *Audit of the Department of State Vetting Process for Syrian Non-lethal Assistance*, 33; Office of Audits, *Audit of Department of State Management and Oversight of Non-lethal Assistance Provided for the Syrian Crisis* (Washington, DC: Office of the Inspector General, U.S. Department of State, 2015).
101. Sharp and Blanchard, *Armed Conflict in Syria*, 20–22; Christopher M. Blanchard, Carla E. Humud, and Mary Beth D. Nikitin, *Armed Conflict in Syria: Overview and U.S. Response*, RL33487 (Washington, DC: Congressional Research Service, April 2014), https://www.refworld.org/docid/5375df914.html.
102. Sharp and Blanchard, *Armed Conflict in Syria*, 20–22; "U.S. Security Assistance and Human Rights," Brookings Institution, December 12, 2016, https://www.brookings.edu/events/u-s-security-assistance-and-human-rights/.
103. Although mundane in nature, several officials flagged the issue of the Leahy Law database struggling to identify known perpetrators simply because of name misspellings, particularly given the many different possible transliterations of non-Roman script. GAO, *Additional Guidance, Monitoring, and Training Could Improve Implementation of the Leahy Laws*, GAO-13-866 (Washington, DC: United States Government Accountability Office, 2013); McNerney et al., *Improving Implementation of the Department of Defense Leahy Law*; Dan Mahanty, "The 'Leahy Law' Prohibiting US Assistance to Human Rights Abusers: Pulling Back the Curtain," *Just Security*, June 27, 2017, https://www.justsecurity.org/42578/leahy-law-prohibiting-assistance-human-rights-abusers-pulling-curtain/.
104. Former State Department officer working on Syria nonlethal assistance programming, interview by author, by telephone, July 6, 2018, interview 24; former senior State Department official, interview by author, London, March 29, 2018, interview 4.
105. Former State Department officer working on Syria nonlethal assistance programming, interview by author, by telephone, July 6, 2018, interview 24.
106. Former State Department officer working on Syria nonlethal assistance programming, interview by author, by telephone, July 6, 2018, interview 24.
107. Former State Department officer working on Syria nonlethal assistance programming, interview by author, by telephone, July 6, 2018, interview 24.
108. Former State Department officer working on Syria nonlethal assistance programming, interview by author, by telephone, July 6, 2018, interview 24; former senior State Department official, interview by author, London, March 29, 2018, interview 4.
109. The thresholds for when a program is subject to congressional notification are not uniform, and may vary based on the specific legislation or because of country-specific restrictions. In general, these were much more common on all of the Syria assistance, both because of the high levels of attention toward Syria policy in general, and because of other preexisting designations on Syria (i.e., its status even prior to 2011 as a state sponsor of terrorism). All State Department officials engaged in implementing

nonlethal assistance in Syria mentioned frequent special notification processes and a more regular degree of oversight and informal question and answers on Syria program than is standard across all portfolios. Former senior State Department official, interview by author, London, March 29, 2018, interview 4; State Department officer working on Syria programming, interview by author, Washington, DC, June 23, 2018, interview 20; State Department staff member involved in anti-ISIL policy coordination, interview by author, by telephone, April 26, 2020, interview 131.

110. State Department staff with past experience in Syria and Iraq anti-ISIL policies and programs, interview by author, Washington, DC, November 18, 2019, interview 103; State Department staff member involved in anti-ISIL policy coordination, interview by author, by telephone, April 26, 2020, interview 131.

111. Former State Department officer working on Syria nonlethal assistance programming, interview by author, by telephone, July 6, 2018, interview 24; former senior State Department official, interview by author, London, March 29, 2018, interview 4; State Department staff with past experience in Syria and Iraq anti-ISIL policies and programs, interview by author, Washington, DC, November 18, 2019, interview 103; former State Department officer, interview by author, Washington, DC, November 20, 2019, interview 105.

112. Former State Department adviser, interview by author, March 24, 2018, London, interview 2; former State Department officer, interview by author, Washington, DC, November 20, 2019, interview 105.

113. State Department staff with past experience in Syria and Iraq anti-ISIL policies and programs, interview by author, Washington, DC, November 18, 2019, interview 103; former State Department officer, interview by author, Washington, DC, November 20, 2019, interview 105.

114. Former State Department officer working on Syria nonlethal assistance programming, interview by author, by telephone, July 6, 2018, interview 24; former senior State Department official, interview by author, London, March 29, 2018, interview 4. Although the fact that sanctions were frequently applied is supported by multiple interviews, there was also a counterview among some U.S. officials that based on the supposed standards and redlines, even more should have been cut. One former official argued that there was a sort of bureaucratic "pathology" and attachment to the Syrian cause within the State Department that led to groups being funded even when they had clearly transgressed redlines. Former State Department officer, interview by author, London, March 30, 2018, interview 5. Another argued that because of this attachment to the Syrian cause, "There was [a] climate of not tolerating criticism of the opposition," which led to a much lower enforcement of sanctions than should have been the case. Former State Department officer working on Iraq and Syria anti-ISIL policy and programming, by WhatsApp, June 4, 2019, interview 90.

115. Former State Department officer working on Syria nonlethal assistance programming, interview by author, by telephone, July 6, 2018, interview 24; former senior State Department official, interview by author, London, March 29, 2018, interview 4.

116. Former State Department adviser, interview by author, March 24, 2018, London, interview 2.

117. Former State Department officer working on Syria nonlethal assistance programming, interview by author, by telephone, July 6, 2018, interview 24; former senior State Department official, interview by author, London, March 29, 2018, interview 4.
118. Former senior State Department official, interview by author, London, March 29, 2018, interview 4.
119. Former State Department adviser, interview by author, March 24, 2018, London, interview 2. Landler's reporting reflects similar fears. He describes one internal State Department meeting in which the department's lawyers told those planning to transport aid across the Syrian border that they would "go to jail." Landler, *Alter Egos*, 224.
120. Former senior State Department official, interview by author, London, March 29, 2018, interview 4.
121. Jonathan Weisman, "House Votes to Authorize Aid to Syrian Rebels in ISIS Fight," *New York Times*, September 17, 2014, https://www.nytimes.com/2014/09/18/us/politics/house-vote-isis.html.
122. Austin Wright, "Price Tag for Syrian Rebels: $4 Million Each," *Politico*, April 12, 2015, https://www.politico.eu/article/isil-isis-islmaic-state-price-tag-for-syrian-rebels-4-million-each-middle-east-conflict-fighters/; Christopher M. Blanchard, Carla E. Humud, and Mary Beth D. Nikitin, *Armed Conflict in Syria: Overview and U.S. Response*, RL33487 (Washington, DC: Congressional Research Service, October 2015), https://www.refworld.org/docid/566694264.html.
123. Jabhat al-Nusra and other more powerful opposition groups attacked the new trainees upon their reentry into Syria and appropriated the U.S.-provided weapons and equipment. Blanchard, Humud, and Nikitin, *Armed Conflict in Syria* [October 2015], 22–23; Wright, "Price Tag for Syrian Rebels."
124. Spencer Ackerman, "US Has Trained Only 'Four or Five' Syrian Fighters Against Isis, Top General Testifies," *The Guardian*, April 12, 2015, http://www.theguardian.com/us-news/2015/sep/16/us-military-syrian-isis-fighters; Blanchard, Humud, and Nikitin, *Armed Conflict in Syria* [October 2015], 23.
125. Former State Department officer, interview by author, London, March 30, 2018, interview 5.
126. This change in conflict dynamics also shifted the overarching legal framework issue. While the United States was cautious about intervening in Syria against Assad (due to nonintervention principles), it had no scruples about military intervention against ISIL, which it justified under the U.S. interpretation of collective and sovereign self-defense. In the U.S. view, consent is not required to counter terrorist threats on another state's territory where the government in question is either "unable or unwilling" to counter them itself. Ashley S. Deeks, "'Unwilling or Unable': Toward a Normative Framework for Extraterritorial Self-Defense," *Virginia Journal of International Law* 52, no. 3 (2012): 483–550.
127. Christopher M. Blanchard and Amy Belasco, *Train and Equip Program for Syria: Authorities, Funding, and Issues for Congress* (Washington, DC: Congressional Research Service, June 2015), 2–3, https://apps.dtic.mil/dtic/tr/fulltext/u2/a622754.pdf.

128. Lt. Gen. (ret.) Mike Nagata, interview by author, by telephone, October 12, 2020, interview 135.
129. Former DRL officer involved in Leahy vetting, interview by author, Washington DC, May 14, 2019, interview 83.
130. Lt. Gen. (ret.) Mike Nagata, interview by author, by telephone, October 12, 2020, interview 135; Austin Wright and Philip Ewing, "Carter's Unwelcome News: Only 60 Syrian Rebels Fit for Training," *Politico*, July 7, 2015, https://www.politico.com/story/2015/07/ash-carter-syrian-rebel-training-119812; Missy Ryan and Greg Miller, "U.S. Prepares to Send First Group of Syrian Fighters Back onto Battlefield," *Washington Post*, July 2, 2015, https://www.washingtonpost.com/world/national-security/us-prepares-to-send-first-group-of-syrian-fighters-back-onto-battlefield/2015/07/02/6540be30-20dc-11e5-bf41-c23f5d3face1_story.html; Office of the Inspector General, *(U) Evaluation of Combined Joint Interagency Task Force-Syria Vetting Process for New Syrian Forces (DoDIG-2015-175)*.
131. Wright and Ewing, "Carter's Unwelcome News."
132. Lt. Gen. (ret.) Mike Nagata, interview by author, by telephone, October 12, 2020, interview 135.
133. Lt. Gen. (ret.) Mike Nagata, interview by author, by telephone, October 12, 2020, interview 135.
134. Lt. Gen. (ret.) Mike Nagata, interview by author, by telephone, October 12, 2020, interview 135.
135. Weisman, "House Votes to Authorize Aid to Syrian Rebels in ISIS Fight."
136. *U.S. Policy Towards Iraq and Syria and the Threat Posed by the Islamic State of Iraq and the Levant (ISIL): Hearing Before the Armed Services Committee*, 113th Cong., 2d Sess. (September 16, 2014), 9, https://www.armed-services.senate.gov/imo/media/doc/14-66%20-%209-16-14.pdf.
137. Senate Armed Services Committee, *U.S. Policy Towards Iraq and Syria and the Threat Posed by the Islamic State of Iraq and the Levant*, 32–33.
138. NDAA FY2015, Carl Levin and Howard P. "Buck" McKeon National Defense Authorization Act for Fiscal Year 2015, Pub. L. No. 113-291, 128 Stat. 3292 (2014), sec. 1209(e)(1). Henceforth cited as "NDAA FY2015."
139. NDAA FY2015, sec. 1209(e)(2).
140. Weisman, "House Votes to Authorize Aid to Syrian Rebels in ISIS Fight"; Senate Armed Services Committee, *U.S. Policy Towards Iraq and Syria and the Threat Posed by the Islamic State of Iraq and the Levant*; Ed O'Keefe and Paul Kane, "House Approves Obama's Iraq-Syria Military Strategy Amid Skepticism," *Washington Post*, September 17, 2014, https://www.washingtonpost.com/politics/congress-poised-to-approve-obamas-iraq-syria-military-strategy-amid-skepticism/2014/09/17/c2494df2-3e85-11e4-b0ea-8141703bbf6f_story.html.
141. O'Keefe and Kane, "House Approves Obama's Iraq-Syria Military Strategy Amid Skepticism."
142. Blanchard and Belasco, *Train and Equip Program for Syria*, 2.

143. Blanchard and Belasco, 3. There were also other provisions designed to exercise control over the strategic objectives that the funds were used for. For example, Congress also mandated annual reporting on the strategic dividends of the Train and Equip efforts, as well as on these efforts' progress and any shortfalls. Two Senate Armed Services Committee staff, interview by author, Washington, DC, June 13, 2018, interview 21; Senate Armed Services Committee staff, interview by author, Washington, DC, May 31, 2018, interview 89; Senate Armed Services Committee staff, interview by author, Washington, DC, June 6, 2019, interview 92; Weisman, "House Votes to Authorize Aid to Syrian Rebels in ISIS Fight."
144. Ryan and Miller, "U.S. Prepares to Send First Group of Syrian Fighters Back Onto Battlefield"; Office of the Inspector General, *(U) Evaluation of Combined Joint Interagency Task Force-Syria Vetting Process for New Syrian Forces (DoDIG-2015-175)*, 20–21.
145. Office of the Inspector General, *(U) Evaluation of Combined Joint Interagency Task Force-Syria Vetting Process for New Syrian Forces (DoDIG-2015-175)*, 20–21.
146. Former State Department officer, interview by author, London, March 30, 2018, interview 5; former non-U.S. political adviser involved in the MOC, interview by author, London, May 30, 2018, interview 6; Charles Lister, Syria specialist, interview by author, Washington, DC, May 23, 2019, interview 84.
147. Wright and Ewing, "Carter's Unwelcome News"; Missy Ryan, Karen DeYoung, and Craig Whitlock, "Pentagon Plans Major Shift in Effort to Counter the Islamic State in Syria," *Washington Post*, October 9, 2015, https://www.washingtonpost.com/world/national-security/pentagon-plans-sharp-scaledown-in-efforts-to-train-syrian-rebels/2015/10/09/78a2553c-6e80-11e5-9bfe-e59f5e244f92_story.html?itid=lk_inline_manual_13.
148. Senate Armed Services Committee staff, interview by author, Washington, DC, June 6, 2019, interview 92.
149. Former senior Obama administration official, interview by author, by telephone, May 29, 2019, interview 86.
150. Jeff Martini, analyst, RAND Corporation, interview by author, Washington, DC, June 20, 2018, interview 23.
151. Former State Department officer, interview by author, Washington, DC, November 20, 2019, interview 105.
152. Michael D. Shear, Helene Cooper, and Eric Schmitt, "Obama Administration Ends Effort to Train Syrians to Combat ISIS," *New York Times*, October 10, 2015, https://www.nytimes.com/2015/10/10/world/middleeast/pentagon-program-islamic-state-syria.html; Blanchard and Belasco, *Train and Equip Program for Syria*; Ryan, DeYoung, and Whitlock, "Pentagon Plans Major Shift in Effort to Counter the Islamic State in Syria."
153. The Train and Equip funding was also used to support Syrian forces in other parts of the country, in particular Syrian tribal fighters operating in areas around the Al-Tanf base, on the Syria-Iraq border in southeastern Syria. This case study, however, only focuses on the forces that the United States attempted to support jointly with Turkey.
154. Former senior Obama administration official, interview by author, by telephone, May 29, 2019, interview 86; State Department officer working on Iraq and Syria

anti-ISIL policy and programming, interview by author, by WhatsApp, June 4, 2019, interview 90; former State Department officer, interview by author, Washington, DC, November 20, 2019, interview 105.

155. Mehmed Cavid Barkcin, "First Group of FSA Soldiers Trained by US, Turkey Enters Syria," *Daily Sabah*, July 15, 2015, https://www.dailysabah.com/politics/2015/07/15/first-group-of-fsa-soldiers-trained-by-us-turkey-enters-syria.

156. Adam Entous, "U.S., Turkey Narrow Differences on Islamic State Fight," *Wall Street Journal*, December 1, 2014, https://www.wsj.com/articles/u-s-turkey-move-closer-in-talks-involving-bases-air-zones-1417414812.

157. Christopher Phillips, *Into the Quagmire: Turkey's Frustrated Syria Policy* (London: Royal Institute of International Affairs at Chatham House, 2012); Aaron Stein, "The Origins of Turkey's Buffer Zone in Syria," *War on the Rocks*, December 11, 2014, https://warontherocks.com/2014/12/the-origins-of-turkeys-buffer-zone-in-syria/.

158. "Kobane: Air Strikes Help Syria Town Curb IS," *BBC News*, October 4, 2014, https://www.bbc.co.uk/news/world-middle-east-29526783; Constanze Letsch, "US Drops Weapons and Ammunition to Help Kurdish Fighters in Kobani," *The Guardian*, October 20, 2013, https://www.theguardian.com/world/2014/oct/20/turkey-iraqi-kurds-kobani-isis-fighters-us-air-drops-arms.

159. Karen DeYoung, "Administration Searches for New Approach to Aiding Rebels in Syria," *Washington Post*, September 16, 2015, https://www.washingtonpost.com/world/national-security/administration-searches-for-new-approach-to-aiding-rebels-in-syria/2015/09/16/938fd336-5c9e-11e5-8e9e-dce8a2a2a679_story.html; Ryan, DeYoung, and Whitlock, "Pentagon Plans Major Shift in Effort to Counter the Islamic State in Syria."

160. Former State Department officer, interview by author, London, March 30, 2018, interview 5; FSA commander, interview by author, Gaziantep, Turkey, September 25, 2018, interview 38; State Department officer working on Iraq and Syria anti-ISIL policy and programming, interview by author, by WhatsApp, June 4, 2019, interview 90.

161. NDAA FY2015, sec. 1209(e)(2).

162. Former State Department officer, interview by author, London, March 30, 2018, interview 5; former senior U.S. government official based in Afghanistan, interview by author, Washington, DC, November 24, 2020, interview 136; Stein, *Partner Operations in Syria*; Ryan, DeYoung, and Whitlock, "Pentagon Plans Major Shift in Effort to Counter the Islamic State in Syria." U.S. forces reportedly took part in the training in Turkey, as did other coalition partners, but it is unclear how much direct training was provided. Missy Ryan, "In Syrian Border Battle, Pentagon Touts Role of Fighters from Troubled Train-and-Equip Program," *Washington Post*, August 24, 2016, https://www.washingtonpost.com/news/checkpoint/wp/2016/08/24/in-syrian-border-battle-pentagon-touts-role-of-fighters-from-troubled-train-and-equip-program/.

163. FSA commander, interview by author, Gaziantep, Turkey, September 25, 2018, interview 38.

164. This is not to suggest the existence of a formalized or written vetting and screening process, similar to the U.S. approach. FSA commander, interview by author,

Gaziantep, Turkey, September 25, 2018, interview 38; former State Department officer working on Syria nonlethal assistance programming, interview by author, by telephone, July 6, 2018, interview 24. There were also some measures taken to check and hold to account misconduct by supported forces, according to one Turkish official involved in oversight, although he did not enumerate the standards in question. Senior Turkish official, interview by author, by WhatsApp, July 6, 2023, interview 224.

165. Former State Department officer, interview by author, London, March 30, 2018, interview 5.
166. Senior Turkish official, interview by author, by WhatsApp, July 6, 2023, interview 224.
167. Former State Department officer, interview by author, London, March 30, 2018, interview 5. Further support for this evaluation also features in Aaron Stein, "Reconciling U.S.-Turkish Interests in Northern Syria," Council on Foreign Relations, February 13, 2017, https://www.cfr.org/report/reconciling-us-turkish-interests-northern-syria.
168. Former senior Obama administration official, interview by author, by telephone, May 29, 2019, interview 86.
169. Former State Department officer, interview by author, Washington, DC, November 20, 2019, interview 105.
170. FSA commander, interview by author, Gaziantep, Turkey, September 25, 2018, interview 38.
171. Stein, *Partner Operations in Syria*, 10–11, 21.
172. Stein, *Partner Operations in Syria*; Ryan, "In Syrian Border Battle, Pentagon Touts Role of Fighters from Troubled Train-and-Equip Program."
173. Support to the forces that came to be known as the SDF began with the battle for Kobane in October 2014, which is taken as the start date for this case study. It increased in level and kind with the deployment of U.S. Special Forces officers to assist Kurdish-linked forces in taking the town of Manbij in the summer of 2016. From that point on the SDF might be considered the main recipient of U.S. Train and Equip funding, and the main focal point of the anti-ISIL campaign in Syria. The end point of this case study is the end of 2019 given that the field research had largely concluded by this point, and this is also when then president Donald Trump announced that the United States would begin withdrawing U.S. support from the SDF. Nonetheless, some assistance continued as this book went to press.
174. As one U.S. official observed, reflecting the comments of other officials and military commanders interviewed, "By the time we got to the SDF, we had exhausted all other options." State Department staff with past experience in Syria and Iraq anti-ISIL policies and programs, interview by author, Washington, DC, November 18, 2019, interview 103. See also former senior Obama administration official, interview by author, by telephone, May 29, 2019, interview 86; former State Department officer, interview by author, London, March 30, 2018, interview 5.
175. Former State Department officer, interview by author, Washington, DC, November 20, 2019, interview 105.

176. Former senior Obama administration official, interview by author, by telephone, May 29, 2019, interview 86.
177. This link was acknowledged publicly by U.S. officials, including then secretary of defense Ashton Carter. Ashton Carter, testimony before the U.S. Senate Armed Services Committee, *Counter-ISIL (Islamic State of Iraq and the Levant) Operations and Middle East Strategy*, 114th Cong., 2d Sess. (April 28, 2016), https://www.armed-services.senate.gov/imo/media/doc/16-51_04-28-16.pdf.
178. Former senior Obama administration official, interview by author, by telephone, May 29, 2019, interview 86.
179. Former State Department officer, interview by author, London, March 30, 2018, interview 5; former senior Obama administration official, interview by author, by telephone, May 29, 2019, interview 86; former State Department officer, interview by author, Washington, DC, November 20, 2019, interview 105.
180. Former U.S. military intelligence officer and DoD policy adviser, interview by author, Washington, DC, May 29, 2019, interview 87; former State Department officer, interview by author, London, March 30, 2018, interview 5.
181. Allison, "Conceptual Models and the Cuban Missile Crisis," 709.
182. State Department officer working on Iraq and Syria anti-ISIL policy and programming, interview by author, by WhatsApp, June 4, 2019, interview 90.
183. Former State Department officer, interview by author, London, March 30, 2018, interview 5.
184. Former State Department officer, interview by author, London, March 30, 2018, interview 5.
185. One U.S. official later observed to analyst Dylan Maguire that taking Raqqa instead might have required "tens of thousands of American troops." Maguire, *A Perfect Proxy?*, 7.
186. Stein, *Partner Operations in Syria*; former senior Obama administration official, interview by author, by telephone, May 29, 2019, interview 86; former U.S. military intelligence officer and DoD policy adviser, interview by author, Washington, DC, May 29, 2019, interview 87.
187. Former senior Obama administration official, interview by author, by telephone, May 29, 2019, interview 86; and Senior Turkish official, interview by author, New York, November 28, 2023.
188. Reuters, "U.S. General Told Syria's YPG."
189. Serwan Derwish, spokesman of the Manbij Military Council, interview by author, Kobane, Syria, November 9, 2018, interview 61.
190. Senior adviser to the SDF, interview by author, Qamishli, Syria, November 8, 2018, interview 59; senior Trump administration security official, interview by author, by telephone, May 6, 2021, interview 220.
191. Senior adviser to the SDF, interview by author, Qamishli, Syria, November 8, 2018, interview 59. Similar accounts of equipment tracking were provided in other interviews with SDF officials or commanders. See, for example, Serwan Derwish, spokesman of the Manbij Military Council, interview by author, Kobane, Syria, November 9, 2018, interview 61.

192. Former senior Obama administration official, interview by author, by telephone, May 29, 2019, interview 86.
193. Congressional Research Service, *Armed Conflict in Syria: Overview and U.S. Response*, RL33487 (Washington, DC: Congressional Research Service, February 2018), 18, https://www.everycrsreport.com/files/20180227_RL33487_1ba69865eb893e71e089d6021ca0a17c026e1579.pdf.
194. Serwan Derwish, spokesman of the Manbij Military Council, interview by author, Kobane, Syria, November 9, 2018, interview 61; former media center employee, interview by author, Qamishli, Syria, November 11, 2018, interview 64.
195. NDAA FY2015, sec. 1209 (e)(1).
196. Serwan Derwish, spokesman of the Manbij Military Council, interview by author, Kobane, Syria, November 9, 2018, interview 61; former media center employee, interview by author, Qamishli, Syria, November 11, 2018, interview 64.
197. Manbij, and particularly U.S. support in holding it, continued to be a flash point between the United States and Turkey. The SDF occupation of Manbij in the summer of 2016 was a contributing factor for Turkey launching its own military intervention in northern Syria, Operation Euphrates Shield, which led to a partial Turkish occupation of northern Syria. For further background, see Stein, *Reconciling U.S.-Turkish Interests in Northern Syria*.
198. Former senior Obama administration official, interview by author, by telephone, May 29, 2019, interview 86; former DoD policy adviser, interview by author, by telephone, May 3, 2021, interview 151; Maguire, *A Perfect Proxy?*
199. Senior Turkish official, interview by author, by WhatsApp, July 6, 2023, interview 224.
200. Senior Turkish official, interview by author, by WhatsApp, July 6, 2023, interview 224.
201. "Syria: US Ally's Razing of Villages Amounts to War Crimes," Amnesty International, October 13, 2015, https://www.amnesty.org/en/latest/news/2015/10/syria-us-allys-razing-of-villages-amounts-to-war-crimes/.
202. Senior adviser to the SDF, interview by author, Qamishli, Syria, November 8, 2018, interview 59; former media center employee, interview by author, Qamishli, Syria, November 11, 2018, interview 64; Serwan Derwish, spokesman of the Manbij Military Council, interview by author, Kobane, Syria, November 9, 2018, interview 61.
203. Gabriel Kino, SDF spokesman, interview by author, Qamishli, Syria, November 12, 2018, interview 70; senior U.S. military officer, interview by author, Baghdad, March 11, 2019, interview 221.
204. Former senior Obama administration official, interview by author, by telephone, May 29, 2019, interview 86.
205. Representative of political party, interview by author, Qamishli, Syria, November 10, 2018, interview 63; Gabriel Kino, SDF spokesman, interview by author, Qamishli, Syria, November 12, 2018, interview 70; security adviser based in Qamishli, Syria, interview by author, by telephone, October 20, 2018, interview 57.
206. "Press Release: Syria: Kurdish Forces Violating Child Soldier Ban," Human Rights Watch, July 15, 2015, https://www.hrw.org/news/2015/07/10/syria-kurdish-forces-violating-child-soldier-ban-0.

207. Child Soldiers Prevention Act, Title IV of Pub. L. No. 110-457.
208. Former senior Obama administration official, interview by author, by telephone, May 29, 2019, interview 86; Serwan Derwish, spokesman of the Manbij Military Council, interview by author, Kobane, Syria, November 9, 2018, interview 61; Gabriel Kino, SDF spokesman, interview by author, Qamishli, Syria, November 12, 2018, interview 70.
209. Jared Szuma, "ISIS's 'Caliphate' Was Crushed. Now Syria's Kurd-Led Alliance Faces Bigger Battles," *Defense Post*, March 29, 2019, https://www.thedefensepost.com/2019/03/29/syria-sdf-kurds-face-bigger-battles-isis/.
210. Szuma, "ISIS's 'Caliphate' Was Crushed."
211. Elizabeth Tsurkov and Esam Al-Hassan, "Kurdish-Arab Power Struggle in Northeastern Syria," Carnegie Endowment for International Peace, July 24, 2019, https://carnegieendowment.org/sada/79542.
212. Gabriel Kino, SDF spokesman, interview by author, Qamishli, Syria, November 12, 2018, interview 70; local researcher, interview by author, Qamishli, Syria, November 12, 2018, interview 60; NGO representative engaging with SDF, interview by author, by WhatsApp, October 16, 2018, interview 55; Bedir Mulla Rashid, *Military and Security Structures in the Autonomous Administration of Syria* (Istanbul: Omran Center for Strategic Studies, 2018).
213. Noah Bonsey, International Crisis Group Syria analyst, interview by author, by WhatsApp, August 1, 2018, interview 27.
214. State Department officer working on Iraq and Syria anti-ISIL policy and programming, interview by author, by WhatsApp, June 4, 2019, interview 90; senior U.S. military officer, interview by author, Baghdad, March 11, 2019, interview 221; former USAID official involved in U.S. Syria assistance, interview by author, Washington, DC, September 18, 2019, interview 98.
215. Noah Bonsey, International Crisis Group Syria analyst, interview by author, by WhatsApp, August 1, 2018, interview 27.
216. Senior U.S. military officer, interview by author, Baghdad, March 11, 2019, interview 221; political adviser to Combined Joint Task Force operations, interview by author, Baghdad, March 15, 2019, interview 80; State Department officer working on Iraq and Syria anti-ISIL policy and programming, interview by author, by WhatsApp, June 4, 2019, interview 90.
217. Former State Department officer, interview by author, Washington, DC, November 20, 2019, interview 105.
218. Former State Department officer, interview by author, Washington, DC, November 20, 2019, interview 105.
219. Former State Department officer, interview by author, London, March 30, 2018, interview 5.
220. Former State Department officer, interview by author, London, March 30, 2018, interview 5.
221. Former State Department officer, interview by author, London, March 30, 2018, interview 5.

222. Former State Department adviser, interview by author, March 24, 2018, London, interview 2.

4. STANDARD OPERATING PROCEDURES AND EXCEPTIONS TO THE RULE

1. Alden and Aran, *Foreign Policy Analysis*, 33; Halperin, "Why Bureaucrats Play Games."
2. Hudson, "Foreign Policy Analysis," 8.
3. Alden and Aran, *Foreign Policy Analysis*, 32–33; Halperin, Kanter, and Clapp, *Bureaucratic Politics and Foreign Policy*, 311; Rosati, "Developing a Systematic Decision-Making Framework"; Allison, "Conceptual Models and the Cuban Missile Crisis," 699.
4. Allison, "Conceptual Models and the Cuban Missile Crisis," 700–701.
5. Mahanty, "The 'Leahy Law' Prohibiting US Assistance to Human Rights Abusers."
6. Former State Department officer working on Syria nonlethal assistance programming, interview by author, by telephone, July 6, 2018, interview 24; U.S. State Department contractor involved in Syria assistance, interview by author, Istanbul, September 21, 2018, interview 36; State Department officer working on Syria programming, interview by author, Washington, DC, June 23, 2018, interview 20.
7. Christopher Woody, "'A Fighting War with the Main Enemy': How the CIA Helped Land a Mortal Blow to the Soviets in Afghanistan 32 Years Ago," *Business Insider*, October 2, 2018, https://www.businessinsider.com/32-year-anniversary-of-first-stinger-missile-use-in-afghanistan-2018-9?r=US&IR=T; Molly Moore, "CIA Falters in Recovery of Missiles," *Washington Post*, March 7, 1994, https://www.washingtonpost.com/archive/politics/1994/03/07/cia-falters-in-recovery-of-missiles/73a9a4d7-2952-4077-9746-46bd2e5b81ca/.
8. The way that the norms embedded in the Leahy Law might have been ingested in the CIA, despite the fact that they were not fully applicable to it, is taken up in greater depth in chapter 5.
9. Johan P. Olsen and James G. March, "The Logic of Appropriateness," in *The Oxford Handbook of Public Policy*, ed. Robert Goodin, Michael Moran, and Martin Rein (Oxford: Oxford University Press, 2008), 689–708, https://doi.org/10.1093/oxfordhb/9780199548453.003.0034.
10. State Department officer working on Syria programming, interview by author, Washington, DC, June 23, 2018, interview 20.
11. State Department officer working on Syria programming, interview by author, Washington, DC, June 23, 2018, interview 20.
12. Former State Department officer working on Syria nonlethal assistance programming, interview by author, by telephone, July 6, 2018, interview 24.
13. In responding to tough congressional questions about the risks of training and equipping Syrian rebels in anticipation of the first Train and Equip program, General Dempsey responded by pointing explicitly to the experience of controls, information,

and vetting in the nonlethal assistance program. *U.S. Policy Towards Iraq and Syria and the Threat Posed by the Islamic State of Iraq and the Levant (ISIL)*, 32–33.
14. Landler, *Alter Egos*, 216–217.
15. *U.S. Policy Towards Iraq and Syria and the Threat Posed by the Islamic State of Iraq and the Levant (ISIL)*, 32–33.
16. The most common term applied to the post-2014 Sunni tribal forces, by both Iraqi citizens and U.S. officials, was Hashd ash-Shairi, which translates to "tribal Hashd" or "tribal PMF," denoting that the force was (for most of its existence) a subsidiary of the larger Shi'a-dominated PMF, or Hashd ash-Shaabi. Some U.S. documents also referred to them as the "Sunni Popular Mobilization Forces." However, there were also other Sunni PMF not supported by the United States—some were mobilized and controlled by Shi'a PMF groups. As a result, this book will employ an alternate term used by some U.S. officials, the Tribal Mobilization Force, to distinguish U.S.-supported tribal forces.
17. The Shi'a militias that formed the core of the PMF had long been acting in concert with Maliki's administration and were more closely linked to some of the most serious sectarian abuses and retaliation. Maliki justified their mobilization against ISIL initially by promulgating an executive decree. This was not legally sufficient—they would still have constituted illegal armed groups under the constitution until formally legalized by the parliament in 2016. For further background see Renad Mansour and Faleh Jabar, *The Popular Mobilization Forces and Iraq's Future* (Washington, DC: Carnegie Endowment for International Peace, 2017).
18. The Peshmerga are generally considered to be a state force. They were officially recognized under the 2005 Iraqi Constitution (article 117) and are managed under the Ministry of Peshmerga, a KRG ministry supported through the Iraqi state budget. However, while the so-called Regional Guard Brigades do operate under the supervision of the MoP, in conformity with regular professional forces, the strongest forces within the Peshmerga are kept under the personal and party control of the two main KRG political parties and their respective political families. Wladimir Van Wilgenburg and Mario Fumertonn, *Kurdistan's Political Armies: The Challenge of Unifying the Peshmerga Forces* (Beirut: Carnegie Middle East Center, 2015). They much more closely match definitions of militias or, alternately, of hybrid forces. U.S. and foreign donor support frequently went to these more partisan forces, even if attempts were made to only support the more state-like forces. Gaston, *Regulating Irregular Actors*; Cambanis et al., *Hybrid Actors*.
19. Maj. Gen. Pat Robertson, interview by author, Baghdad, March 10, 2019, interview 78; U.S. senior military commander, interview by author, Baghdad, March 9, 2019, interview 76; former U.S. official overseeing the TMF program, interview by author, by telephone, February 18, 2020, interview 108. The *sahwa* had not formally ceased to exist by this point. There was still a roster of *sahwa*, paid monthly by the Iraqi government, but most appeared to exist on paper only. Mohammed Salmān, adviser to the Iraqi prime minister on reconciliation, interview by author, Baghdad, November 18, 2018, interview 54; Norman Cigar, *Tribal Militias: An Effective Tool to Counter al-Qaeda and Its Affiliates?* (Carlisle, PA: United States Army War College Press, 2014).

338   4. SOPs AND EXCEPTIONS TO THE RULE

20. Michael R. Gordon and Eric Schmitt, "Saudi Arabia Will Grant U.S. Request for Anti-ISIS Training Program," *New York Times*, September 10, 2014, https://www.nytimes.com/2014/09/11/world/middleeast/saudi-arabia-isis.html?_r=0.
21. Former State Department official working with the TMF initiative, interview by author, by telephone, April 21, 2020, interview 129.
22. Renad Mansour, *Iraq After the Fall of ISIS: The Struggle for the State* (London: Chatham House, 2017), https://www.chathamhouse.org/sites/default/files/publications/research/2017-07-04-iraq-after-isis-mansour-final.pdf; Erica Gaston and András Derzsi-Horváth, *Iraq After ISIL: Sub-state Actors, Local Forces, and the Micro-Politics of Control* (Berlin: Global Public Policy Institute, April 6, 2018), http://www.gppi.net/publications/peace-security/article/iraq-after-isil-sub-state-actors-local-forces-and-the-micro-politics-of-control/; Gaston and Ollivant, *US-Iran Proxy Competition in Iraq*, 13–17.
23. "Iraqi Parliament Passes Contested Law on Shi'ite Paramilitaries," Reuters, November 26, 2016, https://www.reuters.com/article/us-mideast-crisis-iraq-military-idUSKBN13L0IE; Mansour and Jabar, *The Popular Mobilization Forces and Iraq's Future*, 6–7.
24. For more information on the estimated numbers of the PMF over time, see Gaston and Ollivant, *US-Iran Proxy Competition in Iraq*, 11, 43–44n37.
25. In 2009, the United States designated Kata'ib Hezbollah (and specifically its leader, Abu Mahdi "al-Muhandis") a global terrorists. The United States would also subsequently designate several additional PMF groups and leaders terrorists between 2018 and 2020. For more, see Gaston and Ollivant, *US-Iran Proxy Competition in Iraq*, 11, 43–44n39.
26. Gaston and Ollivant, *US-Iran Proxy Competition in Iraq*; Erica Gaston, "Sunni Tribal Forces," Project on Local, Hybrid and Substate Actors in Iraq, Global Public Policy Institute, August 30, 2017, https://www.gppi.net/2017/08/30/sunni-tribal-forces.
27. One U.S. official who managed the program in 2015 and 2016 estimated that well over 60,000 TMF were registered by mid-2016, the vast majority in Anbar Province and with a substantial portion of those acting on a volunteer or part-time basis. As the operations shifted more to Ninewa Province in early 2017, the number of officially salaried forces in both provinces was capped at 32,000, a number that declined steadily over 2018 and 2019. Former State Department official working with the TMF initiative, interview by author, by telephone, April 21, 2020, interview 129; U.S. official tracking TMF program, interview by author, Erbil, Iraq, December 7, 2016, interview 154; U.S. official tracking TMF program, interview by author, Erbil, Iraq, February 28, 2017, interview 155.
28. NDAA FY2015, sec. 1236 (e)(1)(2).
29. U.S. official tracking TMF program, interview by author, Erbil, Iraq, February 28, 2017, interview 155.
30. Armed groups operating "outside the framework of the armed forces" are prohibited under article 9 of the Iraqi Constitution, so presumably before the November 2016 legalization of the PMF (which would then include the TMF), the TMF forces would have constituted illegal armed groups. The United States hoped to resolve this legal status

4. SOPs AND EXCEPTIONS TO THE RULE   339

by having the TMF formally instituted as an Iraqi national guard, but the national guard bill proposed in the Iraqi parliament in the fall of 2014 never gained momentum. Wehrey and Ahram, *Taming the Militias*, 8; Office of the Inspector General, *U.S. and Coalition Efforts to Train, Advise, Assist, and Equip Iraqi Sunni Popular Mobilization Forces (DODIG-2016-055)*.

31. Office of the Inspector General, *U.S. and Coalition Efforts to Train, Advise, Assist, and Equip Iraqi Sunni Popular Mobilization Forces (DODIG-2016-055)*.
32. Office of the Inspector General, *Operation Inherent Resolve: Report to the United States Congress (April 1, 2016—June 30, 2016)* (Washington, DC: U.S. Department of Defense, June 2016), 5.
33. U.S. official tracking TMF program, interview by author, Erbil, Iraq, February 28, 2017, interview 155.
34. Former UK officer within ISAF command, interview by author, London, December 17, 2017, interview 29. See also Office of the Inspector General, *U.S. and Coalition Efforts to Train, Advise, Assist, and Equip Iraqi Sunni Popular Mobilization Forces (DODIG-2016-055)*, 3.
35. Former State Department official working with the TMF initiative, interview by author, by telephone, April 21, 2020, interview 129.
36. Office of the Inspector General, *Operation Inherent Resolve: Report to the United States Congress (April 1, 2016—June 30, 2016)*, 24; U.S. official tracking TMF program, interview by author, Erbil, Iraq, February 28, 2017, interview 155. Due primarily to the limited availability of trainers, training was not mandatory. In May 2017, for example, only one-third of the TMF in Ninewa received training before being deployed, according to U.S. tracking data. Gaston, "Sunni Tribal Forces." U.S. officials noted an even lower provision of training in the first year of the Anbar TMF. Former State Department official working with the TMF initiative, interview by author, by telephone, April 21, 2020, interview 129; former U.S. official overseeing the TMF program, interview by author, by telephone, February 18, 2020, interview 108; Danish stabilization adviser, interview by author, Istanbul, May 7, 2018, interview 223.
37. Some of the TMF forces or affiliated groups mentioned suggested a fixed limit of no more than three hundred units, and this appeared to be the reality based on a list of TMF units (and the number of forces attached to each). However, this formal limit was not mentioned by any U.S. or Iraqi officials and did not appear in any other program documentation.
38. Former State Department official working with the TMF initiative, interview by author, by telephone, April 21, 2020, interview 129; U.S. official tracking TMF program, interview by author, by Skype, July 3, 2017, interview 156.
39. General Ahmed Rafad, Federal Police commander for southern Ninewa, interview by author, Qayarra, Iraq, March 6, 2017, interview 201; district manager (mayor) of Qayarra, interview by author, Qayarra, Iraq, February 21, 2017, interview 197.
40. Deputy chief of police, interview by author, Qayarra, Iraq, February 20, 2017, interview 194; head of local council, interview by author, Qayarra, Iraq, February 20, 2017, interview 196.

41. U.S. monitoring appeared to serve two functions—to track the conduct of the TMF units, and to determine whether the TMF were being adequately supported. For example, U.S. personnel might raise TMF leaders' complaints that they were not being provided the equipment and salaries allotted to them with Iraqi authorities.
42. For example, some units purportedly failed the vetting process because of evidence that their force was engaged in recruiting or using child soldiers. In terms of the overall nature of oversight, U.S. officials regularly monitored which units were commissioned, which received training, where TMF were deployed, and any complaints that arose about particular units, as well as complaints by TMF units about the Iraqi government (for example, lack of provisioning or pay). U.S. official tracking TMF program, interview by author, Erbil, Iraq, February 28, 2017, interview 155; former State Department official working with the TMF initiative, interview by author, by telephone, April 21, 2020, interview 129; former U.S. official overseeing the TMF program, interview by author, by telephone, February 18, 2020, interview 108.
43. U.S. official tracking TMF program, interview by author, Erbil, Iraq, February 28, 2017, interview 155; tribal militia force leader in southern Ninewa, interview by author, December 6, 2016, Erbil, Iraq, interview 188.
44. Retired U.S. military officer formerly involved in *sahwa* initiative, interview by author, Erbil, Iraq, November 6, 2018, interview 49; U.S. senior military commander, interview by author, Baghdad, March 9, 2019, interview 76; former State Department official working with the TMF initiative, interview by author, by telephone, April 21, 2020, interview 129; Oliver Holmes et al., "U.S. Scouts for Sunni Allies on the Ground in Iraq," Reuters, September 16, 2014, https://www.reuters.com/article/us-iraq-crisis-sunnis-insight/u-s-scouts-for-sunni-allies-on-the-ground-in-iraq-idUSKBN0HB0BD20140916; Paul McCleary and Lara Jakes, "U.S. Works to Bring More Sunni Tribal Fighters Into Islamic State War," *Foreign Policy*, June 19, 2015, https://foreignpolicy.com/2015/06/10/more-u-s-advisers-in-iraq-to-train-sunni-tribes/; statement of Deputy Assistant Secretary Brett McGurk, *Al-Qaeda's Resurgence in Iraq: A Threat to U.S. Interests: Hearing Before the Committee on Foreign Affairs*, 113th Cong., 2d Sess. (February 5, 2014), https://www.govinfo.gov/content/pkg/CHRG-113hhrg86588/pdf/CHRG-113hhrg86588.pdf.
45. Safa Rasoul Al-Sheikh, deputy national security adviser for Iraq, interview by author, Baghdad, November 5, 2018, interview 47. Even the Iraqi government "reconciliation" office, which was formally responsible for managing the *sahwa*, still existed, even though the *sahwa* constituted only rosters on paper by the time the ISIL threat broke out. Mohammed Salmān, adviser to the Iraqi prime minister on reconciliation, interview by author, Baghdad, November 18, 2018, interview 54.
46. Safa Rasoul Al-Sheikh, deputy national security adviser for Iraq, interview by author, Baghdad, November 5, 2018, interview 47.
47. Al-Sheikh and Sky, "Iraq Since 2003," 129; Marten, *Warlords*, 16–179; Safa Rasoul Al-Sheikh, deputy national security adviser for Iraq, Baghdad, November 5, 2018.
48. Gaston, "Sunni Tribal Forces"; Michael Knights, Hamdi Malik, and Aymenn Jawad Al-Tamimi, *Honored, Not Contained: The Future of Iraq's Popular Mobilization Forces* (Washington, DC: Washington Institute for Near East Policy, 2020), 39.

4. SOPs AND EXCEPTIONS TO THE RULE   341

49. Congressional debate leading up to and during the ISIL crisis codified such sentiments. In one such debate, one congressional representative called for a "reconciliation process that reverses his [Maliki's] attempts to marginalize Sunnis," while others focused on inclusion in the Iraqi government as a safeguard against future ISIL recruitment. Another summarized the strategy as follows: "if a new government forms in Iraq that is much more inclusive, the Sunnis within Iraq become much more open to not supporting ISIL." "Testimony of Deputy Assistant Secretary Brett McGurk, House Foreign Affairs Committee," 4–5. The Obama administration's response to such calls reflected a similar tone, as seen in the testimony of then assistant secretary Brett McGurk: "the Iraqi Government must take a page out of our play book from the Iraq war and enlist moderate Sunni tribes in the fight. I understand that Vice President Biden recently discussed this issue with Prime Minister Maliki, encouraging him to incorporate tribal militias fighting ISIS into the Iraqi security forces." "Testimony of Deputy Assistant Secretary Brett McGurk, House Foreign Affairs Committee," 4.
50. Senior DoD policy official with prior deployments in Iraq and Afghanistan, interview with author, Washington, DC, June 19, 2018, interview 15; U.S. official tracking TMF program, interview by author, Erbil, Iraq, February 28, 2017, interview 155.
51. Former State Department official working with the TMF initiative, interview by author, by telephone, April 21, 2020, interview 129. This view was not universally held, the same State Department official said, and other U.S. officials and forces internally objected to PMF consultation.
52. Gaston and Ollivant, *US-Iran Proxy Competition in Iraq*, 55–56; Knights, Malik, and Al-Tamimi, *Honored, Not Contained*, 39.
53. *U.S. Policy Towards Iraq and Syria and the Threat Posed by the Islamic State of Iraq and the Levant (ISIL)*, 26–27; *Terrorist March in Iraq: The U.S. Response: Hearing Before the Committee on Foreign Affairs*, 113th Cong., 2d Sess. (July 23, 2014), 40, 43, https://www.govinfo.gov/app/details/CHRG-113hhrg88829/context.
54. NDAA FY2015, secs. 1236 (e) and 1208 (e)(1).
55. Two members of the Senate Armed Services Committee staff, interview by author, Washington, DC, June 13, 2018, interview 21.
56. Former State Department official working with the TMF initiative, interview by author, by telephone, April 21, 2020, interview 129; U.S. official tracking TMF program, interview by author, by Skype, July 3, 2017, interview 156; former U.S. official overseeing the TMF program, interview by author, by telephone, February 18, 2020, interview 108.
57. U.S. senior military commander, interview by author, Baghdad, March 9, 2019, interview 76; senior U.S. military officer, interview by author, Baghdad, March 11, 2019, interview 221; senior DoD policy official, interview with author, Washington, DC, June 19, 2018, interview 15; U.S. official tracking TMF program, interview by author, Erbil, Iraq, December 7, 2016, interview 154.
58. Senior DoD policy adviser, interview with author, Washington, DC, June 19, 2018, interview 15.
59. Mujib Mashal, "U.S. Plan for New Afghan Force Revives Fears of Militia Abuses," *New York Times*, September 15, 2017, https://www.nytimes.com/2017/09/15/world/asia/afghan

-local-police.html; SIGAR, *Quarterly Report to the United States Congress July 2018* (Washington, DC: Special Inspector General for Afghanistan Reconstruction, 2018), 99; Brad Townsend, "The Development and Creation of the Afghanistan National Army Territorial Forces," *Military Review*, March 2019, 74–81.
60. The U.S. military at one point estimated that ANA-TF companies would cost 45 percent less than regular ANA companies. SIGAR, *Quarterly Report to the United States Congress July 2018*, 99.
61. Clark et al., *Ghosts of the Past*, 42–47.
62. For further details and sources on the numbers of ALP over time, see Clark et al., 75n3.
63. Clark et al., 27–34.
64. Consultant previously conducting stabilization evaluations in Afghanistan, interview by author, by Skype, January 11, 2018, interview 106; former U.S. military commander, interview by author, Washington, DC, June 13, 2019, interview 95; interview with senior U.S. military adviser, June 13, 2019, Washington, DC; Vanda Felbab-Brown, "Hurray for Militias? Not So Fast: Lessons from the Afghan Local Police Experience," *Small Wars & Insurgencies* 27, no. 2 (2016): 258–281, https://doi.org/10.1080/09592318.2015.1129169.
65. Karl Eikenberry et al., "Case Study: Afghanistan," in *Elite Capture and Corruption of the Security Sector* (Washington, DC: United States Institute of Peace, n.d.), 35–59.
66. Kate Clark, *Afghanistan's Newest Local Defence Force: Were 'All the Mistakes of the ALP' Turned Into ANA-TF Safeguards* (Kabul: Afghanistan Analysts Network, August 2020).
67. For example, site selection and recruitment processes appeared to be almost wholly decided by Afghan inter-ministerial processes, rather than by community input. In addition, rather than deliberately trying to recruit "local sons," who might be of a more irregular force element, the ANA-TF strongly tried to recruit former ANA or ANP local to an area. Many local community members or members of previous local defense forces (the ALP or another local force initiative known as the "Uprising Forces") did not meet the ANA-TF criteria.
68. For example, the ANA-TF site locations were selected according to a much stricter set of location criteria and surrounding process discussions. The initial site selection took place only after months of deliberation, during which the number of sites deemed acceptable were whittled down from forty to nine. Clark et al., *Ghosts of the Past*, 63–71; former Afghan MoD official, interview by author, location not disclosed, November 29, 2018, interview 74.
69. U.S. adviser on ANA-TF development, interview by author, by telephone, June 10, 2019, interview 94.
70. Townsend, "The Development and Creation of the Afghanistan National Army Territorial Forces," 80–81; Clark et al., *Ghosts of the Past*, 65.
71. U.S. military official supporting the ANA-TF, Kabul, July 27, 2019.
72. Former Afghan MoD official, interview by author, location not disclosed, November 29, 2018, interview 74; special adviser with Afghanistan's National Security Council,

interview by author, Kabul, November 14, 2017, interview 174; Kate Clark, "Disbanding the ALP—an Update: Major Transition of Security Forces Achieved During Wartime, but at a Cost," Afghanistan Analysts Network, April 15, 2021, https://www.afghanistan-analysts.org/en/reports/war-and-peace/disbanding-the-alp-an-update-major-transition-of-security-forces-achieved-during-wartime-but-at-a-cost/.

73. Clark et al., *Ghosts of the Past*, 66.
74. Mashal, "U.S. Plan for New Afghan Force Revives Fears of Militia Abuses"; Kate Clark, "More Militias? Part 1: Déjà Vu Double Plus with the Proposed 'Afghan Territorial Army,'" Afghanistan Analysts Network, September 21, 2017, https://www.afghanistan-analysts.org/more-militias-part-1-deja-vu-double-plus-with-the-proposed-afghan-territorial-army/.
75. UNAMA political officer, interview by author, Kabul, July 26, 2019, interview 128.
76. DoD official based at U.S. embassy in Kabul, interview by author, Kabul, November 16, 2017, interview 178.
77. CFSOCC-A, *Afghan Local Defense Initiative Briefing January 2010*; CFSOCC-A, *Ministry of Interior Afghan Local Police Fact Sheet CFSOCC-A PAO 031911* (Kabul: Combined Forces Special Operations Component Command—Afghanistan, 2011) (on file with author); Saum-Manning, *VSO/ALP*.
78. For example, over the same period, the Trump administration loosened the rules of engagement for U.S. forces in Afghanistan in ways that many argued would increase the risk of civilian casualties. Doyle McManus, "Column: Trump's Brand of War Is Killing More Civilians than Before," *Los Angeles Times*, September 8, 2019.
79. U.S. adviser on ANA-TF development, interview by author, by telephone, June 10, 2019, interview 94.
80. Long, "After ISAF"; Mujib Mashal, "C.I.A.'s Afghan Forces Leave a Trail of Abuse and Anger," *New York Times*, December 31, 2018, https://www.nytimes.com/2018/12/31/world/asia/cia-afghanistan-strike-force.html?action=click&module=Top%20Stories&pgtype=Homepage; Suhrke and De Lauri, The CIA's 'Army.'"
81. Naylor, *Relentless Strike*, 353–368; Bob Woodward, *Obama's Wars* (New York: Simon & Schuster, 2010), 8.
82. Julius Cavendish, "CIA Trains Covert Units of Afghans to Continue the Fight Against Taliban," *The Independent*, October 23, 2011, https://www.independent.co.uk/news/world/asia/cia-trains-covert-units-afghans-continue-fight-against-taliban-2317182.html; Naylor, *Relentless Strike*, 353–365.
83. Yaroslav Trofimov, "After Afghan Raid, Focus on Captors," *Wall Street Journal*, March 11, 2013, http://www.wsj.com/articles/SB10001424127887323826704578354563161104832; Cavendish, "CIA Trains Covert Units of Afghans to Continue the Fight Against Taliban"; Naylor, *Relentless Strike*.
84. For example, the Kandahar Strike Force was based at Camp Gecko, a CIA and Special Operations base in Kandahar Province. Trofimov, "After Afghan Raid, Focus on Captors"; Cavendish, "CIA Trains Covert Units of Afghans to Continue the Fight Against Taliban"; Naylor, *Relentless Strike*.

344 4. SOPs AND EXCEPTIONS TO THE RULE

85. Rod Nordland, "After Airstrike, Afghan Points to C.I.A. and Secret Militias," *New York Times*, April 13, 2013, https://www.nytimes.com/2013/04/19/world/asia/after-airstrike-afghan-points-to-cia-and-secret-militias.html?pagewanted=all&_r=0; Emma Graham-Harrison, "Hamid Karzai Seeks to Curb CIA Operations in Afghanistan," *The Guardian*, April 19, 2013, https://www.theguardian.com/world/2013/apr/19/hamid-karzai-curb-cia-afghanistan-operations.

86. Andrew Quilty, "The CIA's Afghan Death Squads," *The Intercept*, December 18, 2020, https://theintercept.com/2020/12/18/afghanistan-cia-militia-01-strike-force/; NDS provincial director, interview by author, Kabul, July 20, 2019, interview 114; security analyst focused on eastern Afghanistan, interview by author, Kabul, July 23, 2019, interview 124; senior Afghan government official, interview by author, Kabul, July 21, 2019, interview 116.

87. Quilty, "The CIA's Afghan Death Squads"; Jessica Purkiss, Abigail Fielding-Smith, and Emran Feroz, "CIA-Backed Afghan Unit Accused of Atrocities Is Able to Call in Air Strikes," Bureau of Investigative Journalism, February 8, 2019, https://www.thebureauinvestigates.com/stories/2019-02-08/cia-backed-afghan-unit-atrocities.

88. Sudarsan Raghavan, "CIA Runs Shadow War with Afghan Militia Implicated in Civilian Killings," *Washington Post*, December 13, 2015, https://www.washingtonpost.com/world/cia-backed-afghan-militias-fight-a-shadow-war/2015/12/02/fe5a0526-913f-11e5-befa-99ceebcbb272_story.html; David Jolly, "Civilian Deaths Raise Questions About CIA-Trained Forces in Afghanistan," *Washington Post*, December 3, 2015, http://www.nytimes.com/2015/12/04/world/asia/afghanistan-civilian-casualty-khost.html; Gaston and Clark, *Backgrounder*; UNAMA, *Update on the Treatment of Conflict-Related Detainees in Afghan Custody: Accountability and Implementation of Presidential Decree 129* (Kabul: United Nations Office of the High Commissioner for Human Rights, 2015); Matthieu Aikins, "The A-Team Killings," *Rolling Stone*, November 2013, https://www.rollingstone.com/interactive/feature-a-team-killings-afghanistan-special-forces/.

89. Patricia Gossman, *"They've Shot Many Like This": Abusive Night Raids by CIA-Backed Afghan Strike Forces* (New York: Human Rights Watch, 2019); Bill van Auken, "CIA Death Squads Responsible for Spike in Afghan Civilian Casualties," *Wall Street Journal*, November 2, 2019, https://www.wsws.org/en/articles/2019/11/02/afgh-n02.html; Purkiss, Fielding-Smith, and Feroz, "CIA-Backed Afghan Unit Accused of Atrocities Is Able to Call in Air Strikes"; Quilty, "The CIA's Afghan Death Squads."

90. UN human rights investigator, interview by author, by telephone, March 9, 2019, interview 75.

91. Mitchell, Carey, and Butler, "The Impact of Pro-Government Militias on Human Rights Violations."

92. U.S. military officer monitoring the TMF and other tribal engagement, interview by author, by telephone, September 14, 2018, interview 34; U.S. military officer monitoring tribal engagement, interview by author, Erbil, Iraq, October 10, 2018, interview 45; former U.S. official overseeing the TMF program, interview by author, by telephone, February 18, 2020, interview 108.

4. SOPs AND EXCEPTIONS TO THE RULE 345

93. Former U.S. official overseeing the TMF program, interview by author, by telephone, February 18, 2020, interview 108; U.S. military officer monitoring the TMF and other tribal engagement, interview by author, by telephone, September 14, 2018, interview 34.
94. Former U.S. official overseeing the TMF program, interview by author, by telephone, February 18, 2020, interview 108; Danish stabilization adviser, interview by author, Istanbul, May 7, 2018, interview 223. This may have been because Danish forces appeared to have more permissive caveats and force restrictions, which allowed their special forces to operate across the border in Syria.
95. Former U.S. official overseeing the TMF program, interview by author, by telephone, February 18, 2020, interview 108.
96. Senate Armed Services Committee staff, interview by author, Washington, DC, May 31, 2018, interview 89; House staffer involved in foreign operations oversight and accountability issues, interview by author, Washington, DC, June 6, 2019, interview 93. There is no public reporting on where the 127e funding is used annually, and congressional staff members and executive branch officials privy to such information are not permitted by law to confirm whether 127e funds were used in a given country or for a given force.
97. For example, there were substantial allegations that U.S. SOF's main and long-standing partner, the Iraqi Counter Terrorism Service, engaged in torture and mistreatment of suspected ISIL detainees, among other potential legal violations. If U.S. Special Forces were unwilling or unable to constrain the abuses of their closest partners—and, moreover, those with a level of command and control that might have made disciplinary responses possible—it seems unlikely that they would demand higher conduct standards from irregular tribal partners.
98. House staffer involved in foreign operations oversight and accountability issues, interview by author, Washington, DC, June 6, 2019, interview 93. The 127e fund does not lack oversight or control. For example, SOF are supposed to give a fifteen-day notification to the relevant congressional committee before initiating use of the fund, and there is also informal oversight in the form of monthly meetings and back-and-forth questioning about ongoing missions. Senate Armed Services Committee staff, interview by author, Washington, DC, May 31, 2018, interview 89.
99. William M. (Mac) Thornberry National Defense Authorization Act for Fiscal Year 2021, Pub. L. No 116-283 (2020), sec. 1051, https://www.govtrack.us/congress/bills/116/hr6395/text. Henceforth cited as "NDAA FY2021."
100. Mitchell, Carey, and Butler, "The Impact of Pro-Government Militias on Human Rights Violations"; Carey, Colaresi, and Mitchell, "Governments, Informal Links to Militias, and Accountability"; Ahram, *Proxy Warriors*, 14–15.
101. Groh, *Proxy War*, 44–45; Marshall, "From Civil War to Proxy War."
102. This would not be true in all cases. For example, there was evidence of Karzai pushing back against some of the CIA and "Other Government Agencies" forces in Afghanistan. In 2012 he appeared to force the disbandment of several such forces, at least temporarily. Trofimov, "After Afghan Raid, Focus on Captors.."

103. U.S. official tracking TMF program, interview by author, by Skype, July 3, 2017, interview 156.
104. Statement of General Raymond A. Thomas III, *Three Decades Later*.
105. Mazzetti, *The Way of the Knife*; Mark Mazzetti, Jeffrey Gettleman, and Eric Schmitt, "In Somalia, U.S. Escalates a Shadow War," *New York Times*, October 16, 2016, https://www.nytimes.com/2016/10/16/world/africa/obama-somalia-secret-war.html; Rukmini Callimachi et al., "'An Endless War': Why 4 U.S. Soldiers Died in a Remote African Desert," *New York Times*, February 20, 2018, https://www.nytimes.com/interactive/2018/02/17/world/africa/niger-ambush-american-soldiers.html; Kyle Rempfer, "Special Operations Launches 'Secret Surrogate' Missions in New Counter-Terrorism Strategy," *Military Times*, February 8, 2018, https://www.militarytimes.com/news/your-army/2019/02/08/fighting-terrorism-may-rely-on-secret-surrogate-forces-going-forward/.
106. Philip Carter and Andrew Swick, "Why Were US Soldiers Even in Niger? America's Shadow Wars in Africa, Explained," *Vox*, October 26, 2017, https://www.vox.com/world/2017/10/26/16547528/us-soldiers-niger-johnson-widow-africa-trump; Callimachi et al., "An Endless War."
107. Senate Armed Services Committee staff, interview by author, Washington, DC, June 6, 2019, interview 92.
108. Senate Armed Services Committee staff, interview by author, Washington, DC, June 6, 2019, interview 92.
109. Senate Armed Services Committee staff, interview by author, Washington, DC, June 6, 2019, interview 92.
110. Fabrice Balanche, "The End of the CIA Program in Syria," *Foreign Affairs*, August 2, 2017, https://www.foreignaffairs.com/articles/syria/2017-08-02/end-cia-program-syria.
111. Lt. Gen. (ret.) Mike Nagata, interview by author, by telephone, October 12, 2020, interview 135.
112. Entous, "Covert CIA Mission to Arm Syrian Rebels Goes Awry"; Heller, "Commentary"; Jeff Stein, "Inside the CIA's Syrian Rebels Vetting Machine," *Newsweek*, November 10, 2014, http://www.newsweek.com/2014/11/21/moderate-rebels-please-raise-your-hands-283449.html.
113. Blanchard, Humud, and Nikitin, *Armed Conflict in Syria*, 9.
114. Heller, "Commentary."
115. DeYoung, "Congressional Panels Approve Arms Aid to Syrian Opposition."
116. Such statements are not intended as an endorsement of these legal positions or patterns of unrestrained global operations, which have been controversial. Gaston, "War Powers Far from a Hot Battlefield." The point here is that each operation would not necessarily trigger an authorization moment or require specific authorization because such operations are assumed to already be covered by these domestic and international bases.
117. For example, the 127e fund requires a fifteen-day notification. However, the threshold for when such congressional notification is required is undefined, so it might not be activated by each partner operation.

118. Senate Armed Services Committee staff, interview by author, Washington, DC, June 6, 2019, interview 92.
119. NDAA FY2021, sec. 1051.

5. CHANGE OVER TIME

1. Alden and Aran, *Foreign Policy Analysis*, 96–100.
2. Keck and Sikkink, *Activists Beyond Borders*; Richard Price, "Transnational Civil Society and Advocacy in World Politics," *World Politics* 55, no. 4 (July 2003): 579–606, https://doi.org/10.1353/wp.2003.0024; Finnemore and Sikkink, "International Norm Dynamics and Political Change."
3. Mertus, *Bait and Switch*, 13–16; Florini, *The Third Force*, 583–584; Keck and Sikkink, *Activists Beyond Borders*, 25–26; Finnemore and Sikkink, "International Norm Dynamics and Political Change."
4. Winifred Tate defines a "policy assemblage" as "the collection of heterogeneous, often incommensurate elements that come together for a period of time, sometimes quite fleeting, to produce a policy construct." Tate, "Human Rights Law and Military Aid Delivery," 339, citing Susan Greenhalgh, *Just One Child: Science and Policy in Deng's China* (Berkeley: University of California Press, 2008), 13.
5. Many of the other controls—for example, controls on site selection and on community vetting and scrutiny (which SOF initially argued were the most important for controlling adverse behavior) lapsed almost as soon as the program devolved. Gaston, "Regulating Irregular Actors"; Clark et al., *Ghosts of the Past*.
6. Keck and Sikkink, *Activists Beyond Borders*, 18–25. In his summary of the findings of the literature on transnational civil society and normative change, scholar Richard Price offers a similar list of tactics, including identifying a concern and documenting or evidencing it, developing solutions and recommending policy change, building coalitions of allies, and employing tactics of pressure and persuasion to change practices or encourage compliance with norms. Richard Price, "Transnational Civil Society and Advocacy in World Politics," *World Politics* 55, no. 4 (2003): 584.
7. Keck and Sikkink describe a strategy of trying to nudge governments toward better compliance through this accountability politics: "Once a government has publicly committed itself to a principle—for example, in favor of human rights or democracy—networks can use those positions, and their command of information, to expose the distance between discourse and practice." Keck and Sikkink, *Activists Beyond Borders*, 24. For other discussions of accountability practices or "naming and shaming," see Khagram, Riker, and Sikkink, *Restructuring World Politics*, 24; Emilie M. Hafner-Burton, "Sticks and Stones: Naming and Shaming the Human Rights Enforcement Problem," *International Organization* 62, no. 4 (2008): 689–716, https://doi.org/10.1017/S0020818308080247; James C. Franklin, "Human Rights Naming and Shaming: International and Domestic Processes," in *The Politics of Leverage in International*

Relations, ed. H. Richard Friman (London: Palgrave Macmillan, 2015), 43–60, https://doi.org/10.1057/9781137439338_3.

8. Keck and Sikkink, *Activists Beyond Borders*, 23–24.
9. Florini, *The Third Force*, 214.
10. Risse, "Transnational Actors and World Politics." For a similar analysis of the "boomerang effect" and interactions between local and transnational or international advocacy spaces, see, e.g., Keck and Sikkink, *Activists Beyond Borders*, 12–13; Brysk, "From Above and Below"; Thomas Risse, Stephen C. Ropp, and Kathryn Sikkink, eds., *The Power of Human Rights: International Norms and Domestic Change* (Cambridge: Cambridge University Press, 1999).
11. This is not to suggest that international organizations were the sole drivers behind civilian casualties rising to the level of a strategic issue. As historian Carter Malkasian observes, civilian casualties, as well as other often associated practices such as night raids or other dragnet detention operations, were not a "Taliban ruse" or a "Karzai-manufactured complaint," but a very serious and significant source of outrage for the Afghan population. Malkasian, *The American War in Afghanistan*, 225. Civilian protest, often highlighted and brought to greater public attention by Karzai, was also a significant factor for why these had risen to a strategic level, and then further amplified and given policy traction through NGO documentation, advocacy, and spotlighting. For further discussion, see, e.g., Maley, "Surviving in a War Zone," 240; Antonio Giustozzi and Niamatullah Ibrahimi, *Thirty Years of Conflict: Drivers of Anti-government Mobilisation in Afghanistan, 1978–2011* (London: Afghanistan Research and Evaluation Unit, 2012), 47–48.
12. Some of these would result in published reports, while other documentation efforts (such as those by the International Committee of the Red Cross) were used solely in private meetings and engagement. For a sample of published reports, see, e.g., Reid, "'Just Don't Call It a Militia' "; Afghanistan Independent Human Rights Commission, *From Arbaki to Local Police* (Kabul: Afghanistan Independent Human Rights Commission, 2012); UNAMA, *Protection of Civilians in Armed Conflict Annual Report 2010* (Kabul: UN Office of the High Commissioner for Human Rights, 2011), 40–45.
13. For one documented example of the advocacy methods deployed, see, e.g., Afghanistan Working Group on Conflict-Related Detentions, *Afghan Local Police Recommendations, October 19, 2010* (Kabul: Afghanistan Working Group on Conflict-Related Detainees, 2010, on file with author).
14. Examples of riskier operating patterns or duties that human rights advocates argued against included ALP involvement in detention and offensive operations. These recommendations for controls as a policy response were made in a largely private persuasion mode during the initial authorization debate, but they are evidenced in the later public reporting and report recommendations. See, e.g., Reid, "'Just Don't Call It a Militia' "; UNAMA, *Protection of Civilians in Armed Conflict Annual Report 2010*, 40–45.
15. Keck and Sikkink, *Activists Beyond Borders*, 25; Price, "Transnational Civil Society and Advocacy in World Politics," 584; Mertus, *Bait and Switch*, 12–15.

16. Thomas Risse and Stephen C. Ropp, "International Human Rights Norms and Domestic Change: Conclusions," in *The Power of Human Rights: International Human Rights Norms and Domestic Change*, ed. Thomas Risse, Stephen C. Ropp, and Kathryn Sikkink (Cambridge: Cambridge University Press, 1999), 276. See also Finnemore and Sikkink, "International Norm Dynamics and Political Change."
17. Finnemore and Sikkink, "International Norm Dynamics and Political Change," 902.
18. Finnemore and Sikkink, 902.
19. Richard Price, "Reversing the Gun Sights: Transnational Civil Society Targets Land Mines," *International Organization* 52, no. 3 (1998): 621.
20. Keck and Sikkink, *Activists Beyond Borders*, 35.
21. The literature on this is extensive. A select sample from a range of authors would include the following: UNAMA, *Protection of Civilians in Armed Conflict Annual Report 2012* (Kabul: Office of the High Commission for Human Rights, 2013); UNAMA, *Protection of Civilians in Armed Conflict Annual Report 2013*; UNAMA, *Protection of Civilians in Armed Conflict Annual Report 2015* (Kabul: Office of the High Commission for Human Rights, 2016); UNAMA, *Protection of Civilians in Armed Conflict Annual Report 2014* (Kabul: United Nations Office of the High Commissioner for Human Rights, 2015); Reid, " 'Just Don't Call It a Militia' "; International Crisis Group, *The Future of the Afghan Local Police*; SIGAR, *Child Sexual Assault in Afghanistan*; Clark et al., *Ghosts of the Past*.
22. Human rights advocate, interview by author, Washington, DC, July 13, 2019, interview 30; Senate Armed Services Committee staff, interview by author, Washington, DC, September 24, 2019, interview 99.
23. Senate Armed Services Committee staff, interview by author, Washington, DC, September 24, 2019, interview 99. Continued NGO advocacy and media coverage of ALP abuses also foreclosed other avenues for funding, as parliamentarians in the capitals of other NATO countries foreswore any cooperation or support for it. "Aufbau der afghanischen Polizei, Einbindung von Milizen und die Auswirkungen auf den Schutz von Menschenrechten und die Verbesserung der Sicherheitslage in Afghanistan, Anhörung vor der 17. Wahlperiode, Drucksache 17/8039, November 29, 2011," Deutscher Bundestag, 2011; Deutscher Bundestag, *Zum Tod Des KSK-Elite-Soldaten in Afghanistan, Anhörung Vor Der 17. Wahlperiode, Drucksache 17/13980, December 16, 2013 (Antwort Der Bundesregierung Auf Die Kleine Anfrage Der Abgeordneten Heike Hänsel, Wolfgang Gehrcke, Christine Buchholz, Weiterer Abgeo)* (Berlin: Deutscher Bundestag, 2013).
24. Reid, " 'Just Don't Call It a Militia.' "
25. Senior DoD policy adviser, interview with author, Washington, DC, June 19, 2018, interview 15; human rights advocate, interview by author, by WhatsApp, May 12, 2020, interview 31. Some of the DoD investigation was subsequently released in a series of FOIA releases. See, e.g., Department of Defense, "FOIA Release: 228 AR15-6 Inv Credibility Assessment_6—Exhibit_O," U.S. Department of Defense, 2011; Department of Defense, "FOIA Release: 220 AR15-6 Inv Credibility Assessment_6—Exhibit_G."
26. Members of UNAMA directly attributed this re-vetting to public pressure and documentation of issues with the ALP, based on their conversations with ISAF and MoI

officials at the time. UNAMA, *Protection of Civilians in Armed Conflict Annual Report 2012*, 43.
27. Senior DoD policy adviser, interview with author, Washington, DC, June 19, 2018, interview 15; Saum-Manning, *VSO/ALP*, 18n54.
28. Department of Defense, *Report on Progress Toward Security and Stability in Afghanistan* (Washington, DC: U.S. Department of Defense, 2014), 59.
29. UNAMA, *Protection of Civilians in Armed Conflict Annual Report 2012*, 9.
30. UNAMA, 9.
31. See, e.g., UNAMA, 44; UNAMA, *Protection of Civilians in Armed Conflict Annual Report 2013*, 10; UNAMA, *Protection of Civilians in Armed Conflict Annual Report 2015*, 67; UNAMA, *Protection of Civilians in Armed Conflict Annual Report 2016* (Kabul: United Nations Assistance Mission in Afghanistan Human Rights Unit, 2017), 49, 97.
32. Clark et al., *Ghosts of the Past*.
33. Nina M. Serafino et al., *"Leahy Law" Human Rights Provisions and Security Assistance* (Washington, DC: Congressional Research Service, 2014).
34. "Leahy Fact Sheet," Bureau of Democracy, Rights, and Labor, U.S. Department of State, March 9, 2018, https://2017-2021.state.gov/leahy-fact-sheet/.
35. State Department officials have a duty to inform the foreign government which individuals are blocked under the Leahy Law, in order to give an opportunity for remediation. This is also intended as a forcing mechanism within U.S. policy so that U.S. diplomats raise these issues and perhaps spur a larger accountability discussion.
36. John Sifton, "Afghanistan's U.S.-Funded Torturers and Murderers," Human Rights Watch, March 6, 2015, https://www.hrw.org/news/2015/03/06/afghanistans-us-funded-torturers-and-murderers; Reid, "'Just Don't Call It a Militia'" 100; Human Rights Watch, *Today We Shall All Die*.
37. SIGAR, *Child Sexual Assault in Afghanistan: Implementation of the Leahy Laws and Reports of Assault by Afghan Security Forces*, 46–55.
38. GAO, *Additional Guidance, Monitoring, and Training Could Improve Implementation of the Leahy Laws*; GAO, *Security Assistance: Lapses in Human Rights Screening in North African Countries Indicate Need for Further Oversight*, GAO-06-850 (Washington, DC: U.S. Government Accountability Office, 2006), https://www.gao.gov/cgi-bin/getrpt?GAO-06-850; GAO, *Better Human Rights Reviews and Strategic Planning Needed for U.S. Assistance to Foreign Security Forces*, GAO-05-793 (Washington, DC: U.S. Government Accountability Office, 2005), https://www.gao.gov/cgi-bin/getrpt?GAO-05-793.
39. McNerney et al., *Improving Implementation of the Department of Defense Leahy Law*.
40. Serafino et al., *"Leahy Law" Human Rights Provisions and Security Assistance*. See also statement of Lauren Ploch Blanchard, specialist in African affairs, Congressional Research Service, *Human Rights Vetting: Nigeria and Beyond: Hearing Before the Committee on Foreign Affairs*, 113th Cong., 2d Sess. (July 10, 2014), https://www.govinfo.gov/content/pkg/CHRG-113hhrg88627/html/CHRG-113hhrg88627.htm.
41. Mahanty, "The 'Leahy Law' Prohibiting US Assistance to Human Rights Abusers"; Serafino et al., *"Leahy Law" Human Rights Provisions and Security Assistance*.
42. Tate, "Human Rights Law and Military Aid Delivery."

43. Mertus, *Bait and Switch*, 29; Serafino et al., *"Leahy Law" Human Rights Provisions and Security Assistance*.
44. Tate, "Human Rights Law and Military Aid Delivery." See also Mertus, *Bait and Switch*, 28–38; Halperin, Kanter, and Clapp, *Bureaucratic Politics and Foreign Policy*, 314–334.
45. The director of the Washington, DC, office of Human Rights Watch, Tom Malinowski, was appointed to lead DRL. The then director of the Washington, DC, office of Open Society Foundations, Stephen Rickard, was seconded to DRL for a year to work on Leahy Law development, among other duties.
46. See, e.g., Pattricia Gossman, "How US-Funded Abuses Led to Failure in Afghanistan," Human Rights Watch, July 6, 2021, https://www.hrw.org/news/2021/07/06/how-us-funded-abuses-led-failure-afghanistan; "Human Rights Watch Testimony at House Foreign Affairs Subcommittee on Africa, Global Health, Global Human Rights, and International Organizations," Human Rights Watch, July 11, 2014, https://www.hrw.org/news/2014/07/11/human-rights-watch-testimony-house-foreign-affairs-subcommittee-africa-global-health.
47. McNerney et al., *Improving Implementation of the Department of Defense Leahy Law*.
48. Human rights advocate focusing on accountability in U.S. security assistance, interview by author, Washington, DC, August 29, 2016, interview 183; Senate staff member, interview by author, Washington, DC, May 28, 2019, interview 85.
49. Human rights advocate focusing on accountability in U.S. security assistance, interview by author, Washington, DC, August 29, 2016, interview 183; human rights advocate, interview by author, by WhatsApp, May 12, 2020, interview 31; Aikins, "Our Man in Kandahar."
50. Former Pentagon desk officer, interview by author, by telephone, February 19, 2017, interview 177.
51. This might be construed as part of an inter-branch bargaining process. The decision to apply it more proactively in Afghanistan was concurrent with congressional decisions—over some DoD hesitation—to expand the Leahy Law's application. In addition, DoD were willing to adopt this more proactive system in part because Congress created a loophole for it, such that Afghan partners whom the secretary of defense deemed critical for security could be exempted from the Leahy Law's application. Erica Gaston, "The Leahy Law and Human Rights Accountability in Afghanistan," Afghanistan Analysts Network, March 6, 2017, https://www.afghanistan-analysts.org/the-leahy-law-and-human-rights-accountability-in-afghanistan-too-little-too-late-or-a-model-for-the-future/.
52. It is important to note that U.S. troop withdrawals and the country's exit from major combat operations in 2014 meant that from that year onward—effectively about the time this new system was in effect—U.S. troops were no longer regularly co-deployed and based with Afghan forces in the field. One U.S. Special Forces officer assigned to the ALP monitoring cell in 2017 observed that 2013 was the "high-water mark" in terms of SOF ability to monitor the ALP on the ground. After that, he said, we no longer had "touch points at the tactical level," leading to only an ad hoc level of oversight and

monitoring of any issues. U.S. Special Operations officer leading the ALP advisory cell, interview by author, Kabul, November 12, 2017, interview 166.

53. DoD official charged with dealing with Leahy Law issues, interview by author, Washington, DC, September 1, 2016, interview 161; former Pentagon desk officer in charge of Leahy Law application in Afghanistan, interview by author, by telephone, August 10, 2017, interview 163.
54. State Department officials involved in Leahy Law issues, interview by author, Washington DC, August 29, 2016, interview 160.
55. McCubbins and Schwartz, "Congressional Oversight Overlooked."
56. State Department officials involved in Leahy Law issues, interview by author, Washington DC, August 29, 2016, interview 160. The officials involved did not specify which remediation approaches were adopted in Afghanistan, but noted generally that it was easier to manage these processes with the MoD and its military justice system than through the MoI, which has a weaker reputation for accountability. See also "U.S. Security Assistance and Human Rights," Brookings Institution, December 12, 2016, https://www.brookings.edu/events/u-s-security-assistance-and-human-rights/.
57. Charles Tilly initially coined the idea of a repertoire of contention to describe a regular set of practices or routines that are recognized as a way for competing groups or individuals to make claims upon/against each other. Charles Tilly, *Big Structures, Large Processes, Huge Comparisons* (New York: Russell Sage, 1985); Charles Tilly, "War Making and State Making as Organized Crime," in *Bringing the State Back In*, ed. Peter B. Evans, Dietrich Rueschemeyer, and Theda Skocpol (Cambridge: Cambridge University Press, 2010), 169–191, https://doi.org/10.1017/cbo9780511628283.008; Doug McAdam, Sidney Tarrow, and Charles Tilly, *Dynamics of Contention* (Cambridge: Cambridge University Press, 2001). The repertoire analogy has frequently been applied in conflict studies to discuss violent practices that recur within an armed conflict context or among certain armed groups, or within the literature on protest movement to describe patterns or practices that become accepted as legitimate means of contention. Ahram, "Pro-Government Militias and the Repertoires of Illicit State Violence"; Ariel I. Ahram, "The Role of State-Sponsored Militias in Genocide," *Terrorism and Political Violence* 26, no. 3 (2014): 488–503, https://doi.org/10.1080/09546553.2012.734875; Elisabeth Jean Wood, "The Social Processes of Civil War: The Wartime Transformation of Social Networks," *Annual Review of Political Science* 11 (2008): 539–561, https://doi.org/10.1146/annurev.polisci.8.082103.104832. For a look at protests or social movements, see Sidney Tarrow, *Power in Movement: Social Movements, Collective Action and Politics* (Cambridge: Cambridge University Press, 1998); Bertrand M. Roehner and Tony Syme, *Pattern and Repertoire in History* (Cambridge, MA: Harvard University Press, 2013), https://doi.org/10.4159/harvard.9780674418479.
58. NDAA FY2014; SIGAR, *Afghan Local Police: A Critical Rural Security Initiative Lacks Adequate Logistics Support, Oversight, and Direction*, SIGAR 16-3-AR (Washington, DC: Special Inspector General for Afghanistan Reconstruction, 2015); Gaston, "The Leahy Law and Human Rights Accountability in Afghanistan."

59. Interview with former Afghan minister of interior Ali Jalali, interview by author, by telephone, April 13, 2021, interview 146.
60. Former U.S. military commander, interview by author, Washington, DC, June 13, 2019, interview 95.
61. Tate, "Human Rights Law and Military Aid Delivery," 349.
62. Tate, 349.
63. Former senior military official, interview by author, by telephone, July 30, 2022, interview 209.
64. Former senior military official, interview by author, by telephone, July 30, 2022, interview 209; former senior U.S. adviser, interview by author, by Zoom, April 28, 2021, interview 211.
65. Former senior military official, interview by author, by telephone, July 30, 2022, interview 209.
66. Allison, "Conceptual Models and the Cuban Missile Crisis," 699.
67. Allison, 700.
68. Alden and Aran, *Foreign Policy Analysis*, 96–100.
69. For example, some of these databases are referenced in U.S. and other partner states' audits of the vetting processes applied to Syrian groups. Office of Audits, *Audit of the Department of State Vetting Process for Syrian Non-lethal Assistance*; Policy and Operations Evaluation Department, *Review of the Monitoring Systems of Three Projects in Syria*.
70. Other literature examining norm entrepreneurship across institutionalized policy spaces has found similar trajectories over time. See, e.g., Jutta Joachim, "Framing Issues and Seizing Opportunities: The UN, NGOs, and Women's Rights," *International Studies Quarterly* 47, no. 2 (2003): 247–274. https://doi.org/10.1111/1468-2478.4702005.

6. FOREIGN PLAYERS IN THE MIX

1. See, e.g., Allison and Halperin, "Bureaucratic Politics," 59–60.
2. Thomas Risse-Kappen, ed., *Bringing Transnational Relations Back In: Non-state Actors, Domestic Structures and International Institutions* (Cambridge: Cambridge University Press, 1995), https://doi.org/10.1017/cbo9780511598760.
3. Human rights advocate, interview by author, by WhatsApp, May 12, 2020, interview 31; human rights advocate, interview by author, Washington, DC, July 13, 2019, interview 30.
4. NGOs, civil society, and other external actors shaped how control mechanisms were applied through information gathering and direct or public advocacy. Those U.S. officials interviewed on Syria policy frequently referenced the overall atmosphere of media pressure and fear of public exposure in discussing the motivation for many of the controls and safeguards adopted. Heller, "Commentary"; Amnesty International, *"Torture Was My Punishment": Abductions, Torture and Summary Killings Under Armed*

Group Rule in Aleppo and Idleb, Syria (London: Amnesty International, 2015), https://www.amnesty.org/en/documents/mde24/4227/2016/en/.

5. Those observing this sort of personal advocacy noted it not only from foreign allies but also in the ways that diplomats within the State Department sometimes appeared to take on a personal advocacy role within their own bureaucracy, working jointly with outside groups or actors. See, e.g., Landler, *Alter Egos*; Clinton, *Hard Choices*. See also senior diplomat, interview by author, Istanbul, May 8, 2018, interview 8.
6. Risse-Kappen, *Cooperation Among Democracies*, 9–10; Keohane, "The Big Influence of Small Allies."
7. Keohane, "The Big Influence of Small Allies."
8. For example, accounts of the internal debate on FSA lethal assistance frequently mention the pressure of foreign allies to get more involved by directly supporting the FSA. Clinton, *Hard Choices*, 461–464; Landler, *Alter Egos*, 217–222. France was one of the countries that was most vocal about supporting the Syrian opposition and favoring more aggressive intervention positions, including a no-fly zone over areas of Syria. For examples, see John Irish, "France's Hollande Says Assad No Ally in Fight Against Islamic State," Reuters, August 28, 2014, https://www.reuters.com/article/idUSKBN0GS0LL/; Samuel Ramani, "Why France Is So Deeply Entangled in Syria," *Washington Post*, November 19, 2015, https://www.washingtonpost.com/news/monkey-cage/wp/2015/11/19/why-france-is-so-deeply-entangled-in-syria/.
9. For example, although U.S. support to Kurdish forces affiliated with the KRG was not a main case study focus (and such forces certainly have a different legal status from the other groups examined), there were some analogous patterns to the other LHSF case studies. U.S. officials frequently pointed to strong ties between certain parties within the KRG and the policy community in DC (including in Congress) to explain continued U.S. funding for Kurdish forces, despite issues in implementing control mechanisms and ensuring fiscal accountability. DoD official managing security sector assistance, interview by author, Erbil, Iraq, November 17, 2019, interview 52.
10. U.S. officials cited examples of congressional representatives exerting pressure to protect funding for certain TMF units (predominantly Christian militias) despite evidence of violations of U.S. rules (e.g., use of child soldiers). U.S. official tracking TMF program, interview by author, Erbil, Iraq, February 28, 2017, interview 155.
11. Risse-Kappen, *Cooperation Among Democracies*, 4–5.
12. Schmitt, "More Allies, Weaker Missions?"; Byman and Waxman, *The Dynamics of Coercion*.
13. Schmitt, "More Allies, Weaker Missions?"; Patrick A. Mello, "Afghanistan: Unconditional Support but Selective Engagement?," in *Democratic Participation in Armed Conflict* (Basingstoke, UK: Palgrave Macmillan, 2014), 100; Patrick A. Mello and Stephen M. Saideman, "The Politics of Multinational Military Operations," *Contemporary Security Policy* 40, no. 1 (2019): 30–37, https://doi.org/10.1080/13523260.2018.1522737.
14. Heller, "Commentary"; Lister, "The Free Syrian Army"; International Crisis Group, *New Approach in Southern Syria*, 9.

15. Southern FSA commander, interview by author, by telephone, September 30, 2018, interview 43; commander formerly with the al-Zenki group, interview by author, by telephone, September 24, 2018, interview 41; Entous, "U.S. Readies 'Plan B' to Arm Syria Rebels."
16. Former non-U.S. political adviser involved in the MOC, interview by author, London, May 30, 2018, interview 6.
17. Former FSA spokesman and coordinator, interview by author, Istanbul, May 8, 2018, interview 9.
18. Risse-Kappen, *Cooperation Among Democracies*; Schmitt, "More Allies, Weaker Missions?"; Byman and Waxman, *The Dynamics of Coercion*.
19. Former non-U.S. political adviser involved in the MOC, interview by author, London, May 30, 2018, interview 6; Charles Lister, Syria specialist, interview by author, Washington, DC, May 23, 2019, interview 84; former USAID official involved in U.S. Syria assistance, interview by author, Washington, DC, September 18, 2019, interview 98; International Crisis Group, *New Approach in Southern Syria*, 3.
20. Brighi and Hill, "Implementation and Behaviour"; Clarke and Smith, "Perspectives on the Foreign Policy System"; Schroeder and Friesendorf, "State-Building and Organized Crime."
21. Schroeder and Friesendorf, "State-Building and Organized Crime."
22. Schroeder and Friesendorf, 141.
23. Although the focus of this chapter is the role and influence of other government partners, in the case of U.S. support to the FSA (both covert support and nonlethal assistance), there would also be an implementation role for other nongovernmental actors. Other contracting agents, NGOs, or nongovernment proxies provided the information that might determine when and to whom aid was provided. Those who played a role in delivering material or otherwise facilitating implementation inside Syria might also affect foreign policy outputs.
24. Policy and Operations Evaluation Department, *Review of the Monitoring Systems of Three Projects in Syria*; State Department contractor involved in Syria assistance, interview by author, Istanbul, September 21, 2018, interview 36; manager for contracting organization implementing Syria nonlethal assistance, interview by author, Istanbul, September 27, 2018, interview 42; European diplomat involved in nonlethal assistance to Syrian opposition, interview by author, Istanbul, May 4, 2018, interview 7; European diplomat involved in assistance to Syrian opposition, interview by author, Istanbul, May 8, 2018, interview 10; State Department officer working on governance in northeastern Syria, interview by author, Washington, DC, June 6, 2019, interview 91.
25. Former State Department officer working on Syria nonlethal assistance programming, interview by author, by telephone, July 6, 2018, interview 24; State Department contractor involved in Syria assistance, interview by author, Istanbul, September 21, 2018, interview 36.
26. This more oppositional form of bargaining might be seen in game theory modeling of competing negotiating points and influences or liberal institutional theories of

cooperation. Robert Powell, "Bargaining Theory and International Conflict," *Annual Review of Political Science* 5 (2002): 1–30; Robert O. Keohane and Joseph Nye, *Power and Interdependence* (Boston: Longman, 2012); Gerald Schneider, "Capacity and Concessions: Bargaining Power in Multilateral Negotiations," *Millenium: Journal of International Studies* 33, no. 3 (2005): 665–689; Robert D. Putnam, "Diplomacy and Domestic Politics: The Logic of Two-Level Games," *International Organization* 42, no. 3 (1988): 427–460; Risse-Kappen, *Cooperation Among Democracies*.

27. Allison and Halperin, "Bureaucratic Politics," 57.
28. Carlsnaes, Sjursen, and White, *Contemporary European Foreign Policy*; Larsen, "A Distinct FPA for Europe?"; White, *Understanding European Foreign Policy*; Manners and Whitman, *The Foreign Policies of European Union Member States*.
29. Barnett and Finnemore, *Rules for the World*, iix–x, 1–3.
30. Zaum, *The Sovereignty Paradox*; Robert Walker, "State Sovereignty and the Articulation of Political Space/Time," *Millenium* 20, no. 3 (1991): 445–461, https://doi.org/10.1177/03058298910200030201; Woodward, *The Ideology of Failed States*; Thomas Risse, "Governance Under Limited Sovereignty," in *Back to Basics: State Power in a Contemporary World*, ed. Martha Finnemore and Judith Goldstein (Oxford: Oxford University Press, 2013), 78–104, https://doi.org/10.1093/acprof:oso/9780199970087.003.0005; Stephen D. Krasner, "Sharing Sovereignty: New Institutions for Collapsed and Failing States," *International Security* 29, no. 2 (2004): 85–120, https://doi.org/10.1162/0162288042879940; Stephen Krasner, ed., *Problematic Sovereignty: Contested Rules and Political Possibilities* (New York: Columbia University Press, 2001), https://doi-org.ezp.lib.cam.ac.uk/10.7312/kras12178; Risse, Draude, and Börzel, *The Oxford Handbook of Governance and Limited Statehood*; Woodward, "Compromised Sovereignty to Create Sovereignty"; Williams, "Aid and Sovereignty"; Jackson, *Quasi-states*.
31. Krasner, *Problematic Sovereignty*, 11, 14; Krasner, "Sharing Sovereignty," 98–99; Zaum, *The Sovereignty Paradox*, 39; Williams, "Aid and Sovereignty"; Jackson, *Quasi-states*, chap. 5.
32. Zaum, *The Sovereignty Paradox*, 39; Woodward, *The Ideology of Failed States*.
33. Toby Dodge, "Iraq: The Contradictions of Exogenous State-Building in Historical Perspective," *Third World Quarterly* 27, no. 1 (2006): 190–191, https://doi.org/10.1080/01436590500370061; Toby Dodge, "Can Iraq Be Saved?," *Survival* 56, no. 5 (2014): 10–11, https://doi-org.ezp.lib.cam.ac.uk/10.1080/00396338.2014.962795; Michael Mann, "The Autonomous Power of the State: Its Origins, Mechanisms and Results," *European Journal of Sociology* 25, no. 2 (1984): 185–213; Joel Migdal, *Strong Societies and Weak States: State-Society Relations and State Capabilities in the Third World* (Princeton, NJ: Princeton University Press, 1988), https://doi.org/10.2307/1963229; Tilly, "War Making and State Making as Organized Crime"; Francis Fukuyama, "What Is Governance?," *Governance* 26, no. 3 (2013): 347–368, https://doi.org/10.1111/gove.12035; Krasner, *Problematic Sovereignty*.
34. In Iraq, between May 2003 and late 2008, there were some 150,000 to 180,000 forces, of which 130,000 to 150,000 were American. By contrast, there were roughly 350,000 Iraqi forces in mid-2007. Ian S. Livingston and Michael O'Hanlon, *Afghanistan Index"*

(Washington, DC: Brookings Institution, September 2012), 3–4; Michael O'Hanlon and Jason H. Campbell, *Iraq Index* (Washington, DC: Brookings Institution, September 2008), 26–27, 34. In Afghanistan in 2010, there were approximately 140,000 international forces, 100,000 of which were American, compared with 260,000 in the same period. Livingston and O'Hanlon, *Afghanistan Index*, 3, 4; Suhrke, *When More Is Less*, 1, 6.

35. O'Hanlon and Campbell, *Iraq Index*, 34; SIGIR, *Hard Lessons*, 133, 359–363; Fallows, "Why Iraq Has No Army"; Antonio Giustozzi and Mohammed Isaqzadeh, *Afghanistan's Paramilitary Policing in Context* (Kabul: Afghanistan Analysts Network, 2011); International Crisis Group, *A Force in Fragments*.
36. Suhrke, *When More Is Less*, 81, 129.
37. Suhrke, "Statebuilding in Afghanistan"; Suhrke, *When More Is Less*; Bizhan, "Aid and State-Building, Part II."
38. Suhrke, "Statebuilding in Afghanistan," 277–278.
39. Suhrke, *When More Is Less*, 137–138.
40. Eric Herring and Glen Rangwala, *Iraq in Fragments: The Occupation and Its Legacy* (London: Hurst & Co., 2006), 86.
41. Dodge, *Iraq*; Lionel Beehner, "U.S. Intervention in Iraqi Politics," Council on Foreign Relations, March 6, 2006, https://www.cfr.org/backgrounder/us-intervention-iraqi-politics.
42. Baker et al., *Iraq Study Group Report*, 23.
43. World Bank, *Rebuilding Iraq: Economic Reform and Transition* (Washington, DC: Middle East and Norther Africa Region, the World Bank, 2006); James D. Savage, *Reconstructing Iraq's Budgetary Institutions: Coalition Statebuilding After Saddam* (Cambridge: Cambridge University Press, 2013); Robert Looney, "The IMF's Return to Iraq," *Challenge* 49, no. 3 (2006): 26–47.
44. Alessandro Monsuttie, "Fuzzy Sovereignty: Rural Reconstruction in Afghanistan, Between Democracy Promotion and Power Games," *Comparative Studies in Society and History* 54, no. 3 (2012): 563–591.
45. Suhrke, *When More Is Less*, 1, 130–132. See also Bizhan, "Aid and State-Building, Part II," 1019–1020; Ghani, Lockhart, and Carnahan, *Closing the Sovereignty Gap*.
46. Former senior U.S. official on Afghanistan policy, interview by author, by Zoom, April 28, 2021, interview 210.
47. SIGIR, *Lessons Learned on the Department of Defense's Commander's Emergency Response Program in Iraq (13-005)* (Washington, DC: Office of the Special Inspector General for Iraq Reconstruction, 2013); Curt Tarnoff, *Iraq: Reconstruction Assistance*, RL31833 (Washington, DC: Congressional Research Service, August 2009), 18, https://crsreports.congress.gov/product/pdf/RL/RL31833/40.
48. Former senior military official, interview by author, by telephone, July 30, 2022, interview 209.
49. Suhrke, *When More Is Less*; SIGIR, *Hard Lessons*; David Witty, *The Iraqi Counter Terrorism Service* (Washington, DC: Brookings Institution, 2016); Dodge, *Iraq*.

50. On the concept of "symbolic power" and its function within conceptions of sovereignty, see, e.g., Dodge, "Can Iraq Be Saved?," 10–11; Steven Loyal, "Bourdieu's Theory of the State," in *Bourdieu's Theory of the State*, ed. Steven Loyal (New York: Palgrave Macmillan, 2017), 67–82, https://doi.org/10.1057/978-1-137-58350-5_4.
51. Suhrke, *When More Is Less*, 139.
52. In this analogy, the two most influential principals on the Afghan side would have been Atmar and the presidential adviser Massoom Stanekzai, who saw the proposal as a means of advancing lower-level reconciliation. Goodhand and Hakimi, *Counterinsurgency, Local Militias, and Statebuilding in Afghanistan*, 16.
53. Allison and Halperin, "Bureaucratic Politics," 57.
54. Clunan and Trinkunas, *Ungoverned Spaces*. See also Felbab-Brown, Trinkunas, and Hamid, *Militants, Criminals, and Warlords*; Brown, "Purposes and Pitfalls of War by Proxy"; Risse, Draude, and Börzel, *The Oxford Handbook of Governance and Limited Statehood*.
55. Between 900 and 2,000 U.S. military forces were deployed in Syria (predominantly northeastern Syria) at any given time between late 2015 and 2022. These were complemented by what is estimated to be 300 to 400 private military contractors and a handful of U.S. civilian officials, several of whom were interviewed for this book. This was not a substantial enough number of staff to be directly involved in implementation in the same way that U.S. officials had in other contexts. Jack Detsch, "Pentagon Acknowledges US Contractor Presence in Syria for First Time," *Al-Monitor*, April 13, 2018, https://www.al-monitor.com/originals/2018/04/pentagon-acknowledge-us-contractor-presence-syria-iraq.html; "A Timeline of the US Involvement in Syria's Conflict," Associated Press, January 11, 2019, https://apnews.com/article/96701a254c5a448cb253f14ab697419b.
56. Maj. Gen. Pat Robertson, interview by author, Baghdad, March 10, 2019, interview 78; political adviser to Combined Joint Task Force operations, interview by author, Baghdad, March 15, 2019, interview 80; State Department officer working on Iraq and Syria anti-ISIL policy and programming, interview by author, by WhatsApp, June 4, 2019, interview 90.

CONCLUSION

1. Former senior State Department official, interview by author, London, March 29, 2018, interview 4.
2. Former State Department adviser, interview by author, March 24, 2018, London, interview 2.
3. Former State Department officer, interview by author, Washington, DC, November 20, 2019, interview 105.
4. NDAA FY2015, secs. 1208(e)(2), 1236 (e)(2).
5. State Department officer working on Iraq and Syria anti-ISIL policy and programming, interview by author, by WhatsApp, June 4, 2019, interview 90.

6. Former State Department officer, interview by author, Washington, DC, November 20, 2019, interview 105.
7. Former State Department officer, interview by author, London, March 30, 2018, interview 5.
8. Former State Department officer, interview by author, London, March 30, 2018, interview 5.
9. Former State Department officer, interview by author, London, March 30, 2018, interview 5.
10. Garrison, "Introduction," 155.
11. Alex De Waal, "Mission Without End? Peacekeeping in the African Political Marketplace," *International Affairs* 85, no. 1 (2009): 99–113, https://doi.org/10.1111/j.1468-2346.2009.00783.x; Ken Menkhaus, "Governance Without Government in Somalia: Spoilers, State Building, and the Politics of Coping," *International Security* 31, no. 3 (December 2006): 74–106, https://doi.org/10.1162/ISEC.2007.31.3.74; Antonio Giustozzi and Dominique Orsini, "Centre–Periphery Relations in Afghanistan: Badakhshan Between Patrimonialism and Institution-Building," *Central Asian Survey* 28, no. 1 (March 2009): 1–16, https://doi.org/10.1080/02634930902771466.
12. The case study evidence in this book has so far not illustrated substantial German engagement with non-state armed groups, even at the level of nonlethal assistance (as the Netherlands and the United Kingdom provided to the FSA in Syria). However, Germany has increasingly faced the challenge of whether and how to engage with non-state security actors in countries where it provides stabilization assistance or other forms of support, including in Afghanistan, Somalia, Mali, and other parts of West and Central Africa. For this reason, as of 2023, the German Foreign Ministry was deliberating the establishment of a SOP or framework for how to deal with non-state security actors, including how to approach or mitigate risks that arose in the course of this engagement. Virtual workshop on security sector assistance and non-state armed groups, December 14, 2023.
13. One Turkish official noted that when they worked with Syrian armed groups, they tried to keep them to certain standards, including giving them verbal warnings and referring them to Syrian justice mechanisms (informal in opposition-controlled areas), when they "violated international law." He did not elaborate on whether certain conduct standards were provided in training, nor did he give any greater detail on oversight and enforcement mechanisms. Senior Turkish official, interview by author, by WhatsApp, July 6, 2023, interview 224.
14. Steven R. Ward, "The Continuing Evolution of Iran's Military Doctrine," *Middle East Journal* 59, no. 4 (2005): 559–576, https://doi.org/10.3751/59.4.12.
15. Tim Arango et al., "The Iran Cables: Secret Documents Show How Tehran Wields Power in Iraq," *New York Times*, November 19, 2019, https://www.nytimes.com/interactive/2019/11/18/world/middleeast/iran-iraq-spy-cables.html; Seth G. Jones, *War by Proxy: Iran's Growing Footprint in the Middle East* (Washington, DC: Center for Strategic and International Studies, 2019), https://www.csis.org/analysis/war-proxy-irans-growing-footprint-middle-east-0; Brian Katz, "What the U.S. Can Learn from

the Iranian Qods Force," *The Atlantic*, October 19, 2019, https://www.theatlantic.com/politics/archive/2019/10/what-us-can-learn-iranian-warfare/600082/.

16. Candace Rondeaux and David Sterman, *Twenty-First Century Proxy Warfare: Confronting Strategic Innovation in a Multipolar World Since the 2011* (Washington, DC: New America Foundation and Arizona State University's Center on the Future of War, 2019), 12, https://www.newamerica.org/international-security/reports/twenty-first-century-proxy-warfare-confronting-strategic-innovation-multipolar-world/; Assaf Moghadam and Michel Wyss, "The Political Power of Proxies: Why Nonstate Actors Use Local Surrogates," *International Security* 44, no. 4 (2020): 128, https://doi.org/10.1080/09592318.

17. Benedetta Voltolini, "Non-state Actors and Framing Processes in EU Foreign Policy: The Case of EU–Israel Relations," *Journal of European Public Policy* 23, no. 10 (2016): 1502–1519, https://doi.org/10.1080/13501763.2015.1085429; Knud Jørgensen and Gunther Hellmann. *Theorizing Foreign Policy in a Globalized World* (Basingstoke, UK: Palgrave Macmillan, 2015).

18. Lt. Col. (ret.) Scott Mann, senior U.S. Special Forces commander involved in VSO/ALP development, interview by author, by telephone, May 5, 2021, interview 152; former senior U.S. Special Operations commander, interview by author, by telephone, June 26, 2019, interview 97.

19. Mazzetti, "C.I.A. Study of Covert Aid Fueled Skepticism About Helping Syrian Rebels."

20. Lt. Col. (ret.) Scott Mann, senior U.S. Special Forces commander involved in VSO/ALP development and early mobilization, interview by author, by telephone, May 5, 2021, interview 152; former senior U.S. defense official, interview by author, by Zoom, May 19, 2021, interview 212; former senior U.S. official on Afghanistan policy, interview by author, May 11, 2021, by telephone, interview 217.

21. There were similar observations documented in International Crisis Group, *The Future of the Afghan Local Police*.

22. Lt. Gen. (ret.) Mike Nagata, interview by author, by telephone, October 12, 2020, interview 135; former senior U.S. Special Operations commander, interview by author, by telephone, June 26, 2019, interview 97.

23. Former senior U.S. Special Operations commander, interview by author, by telephone, June 26, 2019, interview 97.

24. Lt. Col. (ret.) Scott Mann, senior U.S. Special Forces commander involved in VSO/ALP development, interview by author, by telephone, May 5, 2021, interview 152; Becky Zimmerman, former adviser to ALP initiatives, interview by author, Washington, DC, June 20, 2018, interview 13.

25. With the ALP and the question of whether it might advance governance or community-development gains, the emphasis tended to be on the time commitment and political support, rather than on the degree of international engagement and mentorship with the force. In fact, one survey of the ALP experience found that the best examples of locally owned and protective forces came out of areas where local communities were allowed to select and manage their own ALP units, as compared with those that were

CONCLUSION 361

26. Lt. Col. (ret.) Scott Mann, senior U.S. Special Forces commander involved in VSO/ALP development, interview by author, by telephone, May 5, 2021, interview 152.

hand-picked by international or national Afghan forces. For more on these points, see Clark et al., *Ghosts of the Past*, 31, 52–53, 72–73; Gaston, "Afghanistan Case Study."

27. Former senior military official, interview by author, by telephone July 30, 2022, interview 209; former senior U.S. official on Afghanistan policy, interview by author, by Zoom, April 28, 2021, interview 210; Ali Jalali, former Afghan minister of interior, interview by author, by telephone, April 13, 2021, interview 146.

28. Dr. Omer, cochair of foreign affairs for the SDC, interview by author, Qamishli, Syria, November 8, 2018, interview 58; Amjed Osman, member of the SDC, interview by author, Qamishli, Syria, November 10, 2018, interview 62; Muhammad Abo Adel, military leader of Manbij Military Council, interview by author, by WhatsApp, November 12, 2018, interview 71; senior adviser to the SDF, interview by author, Qamishli, Syria, November 8, 2018, interview 59. Over the course of the research for the case study, the U.S. administration at several points threatened or announced a withdrawal of military support, although this was later walked back.

29. See, e.g., McGurk statement, *Al-Qaeda's Resurgence in Iraq*, 4–5.

30. For discussions of the overall political dynamics and competition at this time, see Gaston and Ollivant, *US-Iran Proxy Competition in Iraq*; Gaston and Derzsi-Horváth, *Iraq After ISIL*.

31. This perspective was voiced in a range of interviews: Lt. Gen. (ret.) Charlie Cleveland, former commander of U.S. Army Special Operations Command, interview by author, by telephone, June 18, 2019, interview 96; former U.S. military commander, interview by author, Washington, DC, June 13, 2019, interview 95; State Department officer working on governance in northeastern Syria, interview by author, Washington, DC, June 6, 2019, interview 91; security adviser formerly involved with LHSFs in Afghanistan and Syria, Istanbul, September 20, 2018, interview 35; senior Turkish official, interview by author, by WhatsApp, July 6, 2023, interview 224.

32. Iraqi analyst, interview by author, Sulaimani, Iraq, October 7, 2018, interview 44; Rian Kaldani, leader of Christian PMF group, interview by author, Baghdad, March 14, 2019, interview 81. For more, see Gaston and Ollivant, *US-Iran Proxy Competition in Iraq*.

33. Iraqi political commentator, interview by author, by Skype, July 17, 2017, interview 175.

34. Three advisers to KDP political officials, interview by author, Erbil, Iraq, November 17, 2019, interview 265; Iraqi analyst, interview by author, Sulaimani, Iraq, October 7, 2018, interview 44.

35. Safa Rasoul Al-Sheikh, deputy national security adviser for Iraq, interview by author, Baghdad, November 5, 2018, interview 47. Notably, Al-Sheikh offered that U.S. unreliability was due not only to changes in administration and political preferences, but also the fact that U.S. security assistance was governed by an elaborate range of technical rules of conditions—the sort of technical control embodied by control mechanisms—which could create bureaucratic blocks to assistance at any point.

36. Former senior U.S. Special Operations commander, interview by author, by telephone, June 26, 2019, interview 97; Lt. Gen. (ret.) Charlie Cleveland, former commander of U.S. Army Special Operations Command, interview by author, by telephone, June 18, 2019, interview 96.
37. Lt. Gen. (ret.) Mike Nagata, interview by author, by telephone, October 12, 2020, interview 135; former senior U.S. Special Operations commander, interview by author, by telephone, June 26, 2019, interview 97; Maj. Gen. Pat Robertson, interview by author, Baghdad, March 10, 2019, interview 78.
38. Former senior U.S. Special Operations commander, interview by author, by telephone, June 26, 2019, interview 97.
39. For example, one FSA commander who received some form of lethal or nonlethal assistance across the State Department, DoD, and CIA initiatives for Syrian armed groups observed that, particularly with DoD assistance, it was important to "have a clear CV"—both in terms of the human rights record and in terms of affiliation with banned groups. FSA commander, interview by author, Gaziantep, Turkey, September 25, 2018, interview 38.
40. This proposition was supported by multiple interview accounts and in the broader literature on militia conduct. On the latter, see, e.g., Mitchell, Carey, and Butler, "The Impact of Pro-Government Militias on Human Rights Violations."
41. Former DRL officer involved in Leahy vetting, interview by author, Washington, DC, May 14, 2019, interview 83.
42. Former DRL officer involved in Leahy vetting, interview by author, Washington, DC, May 14, 2019, interview 83.
43. Gaston, "The Leahy Law and Human Rights Accountability in Afghanistan"; SIGAR, *Child Sexual Assault in Afghanistan*.
44. Senior Afghan government security official, interview by author, by WhatsApp, April 16, 2021, interview 148.
45. U.S. senior military commander, interview by author, Baghdad, March 9, 2019, interview 76.
46. U.S. senior military commander, interview by author, Baghdad, March 9, 2019, interview 76.
47. Former DRL officer involved in Leahy vetting, interview by author, Washington, DC, May 14, 2019, interview 83.
48. Former senior U.S. adviser, interview by author, by Zoom, April 28, 2021, interview 211.
49. Former senior U.S. adviser, interview by author, by Zoom, April 28, 2021, interview 211.
50. Former senior military official, interview by author, by telephone July 30, 2022, interview 209.
51. "Taliban Restrictions on Women's Rights Deepen Afghanistan's Crisis," International Crisis Group, February 23, 2023, https://www.crisisgroup.org/asia/south-asia/afghanistan/329-taliban-restrictions-womens-rights-deepen-afghanistans-crisis; Kate Clark, "From Land-grabbing to Haircuts: The decrees and edicts of the Taleban supreme leader," Afghanistan Analysts Network, July 15, 2023, https://www.afghanistan-analysts

.org/en/reports/rights-freedom/from-land-grabbing-to-haircuts-the-decrees-and-edicts-of-the-taleban-supreme-leader/.
52. As of January 31, 2023, the UNHCR was reporting that 1,618,816 Afghans had recently become refugees to neighboring countries since August 2021. See "Afghanistan Situation," United Nations High Commissioner for Refugees, Operations Data Portal, accessed November 30, 2023, https://data.unhcr.org/en/situations/afghanistan. This statistic did not appear to include the estimated several hundred thousand Afghans who fled to other countries beyond the region.
53. Human rights monitor, interview by author, Kabul, June 15, 2023, interview 225. See also UNAMA, *Human Rights in Afghanistan: 15 August 2021–15 June 2022* (Kabul: OHCHR, 2022).
54. The Uppsala Conflict Data Program is an academic database that tracks levels of violence globally. In 2022, its tracking suggested that levels of violence in Afghanistan no longer met the intensity thresholds that it associates with armed conflict. For more, see "Afghanistan," Uppsala Conflict Data Program, accessed November 30, 2023, https://ucdp.uu.se/country/700. Additionally, the UN mission's human rights team observed a drop in civilian casualties from 7,400 in the eight months leading up to the takeover, to 2,106 in the ten months following it. UNAMA, *Human Rights in Afghanistan*, 9–10.
55. Afghan medical officer, interview by author, Bamiyan Province, Afghanistan, August 26, 2023, interview 226.
56. Four Afghan women, interview by author, Kandahar, August 22, 2023, interview 227.
57. Senior Turkish official, interview by author, by WhatsApp, July 6, 2023, interview 224.

BIBLIOGRAPHY

Ackerman, Spencer. "US Has Trained Only 'Four or Five' Syrian Fighters Against Isis, Top General Testifies." *The Guardian*, April 12, 2015. http://www.theguardian.com/us-news/2015/sep/16/us-military-syrian-isis-fighters.
Afghanistan Justice Project. *Casting Shadows: War Crimes and Crimes Against Humanity: 1978–2001*. N.p.: Afghanistan Justice Project, 2005. https://www.opensocietyfoundations.org/publications/casting-shadows-war-crimes-and-crimes-against-humanity-1978-2001.
Afghanistan Working Group on Conflict-Related Detentions. *Afghan Local Police Recommendations, October 19, 2010*. Kabul: Afghanistan Working Group on Conflict-Related Detainees, 2010. On file with author.
Ahram, Ariel I. "Armed Non-state Actors and the Challenge of 21st-Century State Building." *Georgetown Journal of International Affairs* 20, no. 1 (2019): 35–42.
——. "Pro-Government Militias and the Repertoires of Illicit State Violence." *Studies in Conflict & Terrorism* 39, no. 3 (2016): 207–226. https://doi.org/10.1080/1057610X.2015.1104025.
——. *Proxy Warriors: The Rise and Fall of State-Sponsored Militias*. Stanford, CA: Stanford University Press, 2011.
——. "The Role of State-Sponsored Militias in Genocide." *Terrorism and Political Violence* 26, no. 3 (2014): 488–503. https://doi.org/10.1080/09546553.2012.734875.
——. *War and Conflict in the Middle East and Northern Africa*. Cambridge: Polity Press, 2020.
Ahram, Ariel I., and Frederic M. Wehrey. "Harnessing Militia Power: Lessons of the Iraqi National Guard." *Lawfare*, May 27, 2015. https://www.brookings.edu/blog/markaz/2015/05/27/harnessing-militia-power-lessons-of-the-iraqi-national-guard/.
AIHRC (Afghanistan Independent Human Rights Commission). *From Arbaki to Local Police*. Kabul: Afghanistan Independent Human Rights Commission, 2012.
Aikins, Matthieu. "The A-Team Killings." *Rolling Stone*, November 2013. https://www.rollingstone.com/interactive/feature-a-team-killings-afghanistan-special-forces/.

———. *Contracting the Commanders: Transition and the Political Economy of Afghanistan's Private Security Industry*. New York: Center on International Cooperation, New York University, 2012. https://ciaotest.cc.columbia.edu/wps/cic/0026826/f_0026826_21916.pdf.

———. "Our Man in Kandahar." *The Atlantic*, November 2011. https://www.theatlantic.com/magazine/archive/2011/11/our-man-in-kandahar/308653/.

Albrecht, Peter, Helene Maria Kyed, Deborah Isser, and Erica Harper. *Perspectives on Involving Non-state and Customary Actors in Justice and Security Reform*. Rome: International Development Law Organization, 2011.

Alden, Chris, and Amnon Aran. *Foreign Policy Analysis: New Approaches*. Abingdon, UK: Routledge, 2012.

Aliyev, Huseyn. "Strong Militias, Weak States and Armed Violence: Towards a Theory of 'State-Parallel' Paramilitaries." *Security Dialogue* 47, no. 6 (2016): 498–516. https://doi.org/10.1177/0967010616669900.

Allison, Graham T. "Conceptual Models and the Cuban Missile Crisis." *American Political Science Review* 63, no. 3 (1969): 689–718. https://doi.org/10.1017/S000305540025853X.

———. *Essence of Decision: Explaining the Cuban Missile Crisis*. Boston: Little, Brown and Company, 1971.

Allison, Graham T., and Morton H. Halperin. "Bureaucratic Politics: A Paradigm and Some Policy Implications." *World Politics* 24, S1 (1972): 40–79. https://doi.org/10.2307/2010559.

Allison, Graham T., and Philip Zelikow. *Essence of Decision: Explaining the Cuban Missile Crisis*. New York: Longman, 1999.

Alvarez, Alex. "Militias and Genocide." *War Crimes, Genocide, and Crimes Against Humanity* 2 (2006): 1–33.

Amnesty International. *"Torture Was My Punishment": Abductions, Torture and Summary Killings Under Armed Group Rule in Aleppo and Idleb, Syria*. London: Amnesty International, 2015. https://www.amnesty.org/en/documents/mde24/4227/2016/en/.

Andres, Richard B., Craig Wills, and Thomas E. Griffith. "Winning with Allies: The Strategic Value of the Afghan Model." *International Security* 30, no. 3 (2005): 124–160. https://doi.org/10.1162/016228805775969591.

Arango, Tim, James Risen, Farnaz Fassihi, Ronen Bergman, and Murtaza Hussain. "The Iran Cables: Secret Documents Show How Tehran Wields Power in Iraq." *New York Times*, November 19, 2019. https://www.nytimes.com/interactive/2019/11/18/world/middleeast/iran-iraq-spy-cables.html.

Arrow, Kenneth J. "The Economics of Agency." In *Principals and Agents: The Structure of Business*, edited by John W. Pratt and Richard J. Zeckhauser, 37–51. Boston: Harvard Business School Press, 1985.

Art, Robert J. "Bureaucratic Politics and American Foreign Policy: A Critique." *Policy Sciences* 4, no. 4 (1973): 467–490.

"Aufbau der afghanischen Polizei, Einbindung von Milizen und die Auswirkungen auf den Schutz von Menschenrechten und die Verbesserung der Sicherheitslage in Afghanistan, Anhörung vor der 17. Wahlperiode, Drucksache 17/8039, November 29, 2011." Deutscher Bundestag, 2011.

Auken, Bill van. "CIA Death Squads Responsible for Spike in Afghan Civilian Casualties." *Wall Street Journal*, November 2, 2019. https://www.wsws.org/en/articles/2019/11/02/afgh-n02.html.

Axelrod, Alan. "Mercenaries of the Air (1861–Present)." In *Mercenaries: A Guide to Private Armies and Private Military Companies*, 123–148. Thousand Oaks, CA: CQ Press, 2014.

Axelrod, Robert, ed. *The Structure of Decision: The Cognitive Maps of Political Elites*. Princeton, NJ: Princeton University Press, 1976.

Badi, Emadeddin. *Exploring Armed Groups in Libya: Perspectives on Security Sector Reform in a Hybrid Environment*. Geneva: Geneva Centre for Security Sector Governance, 2020. https://www.dcaf.ch/exploring-armed-groups-libya-perspectives-ssr-hybrid-environment.

Bagayoko, Niagalé. "Introduction: Hybrid Security Governance in Africa." *IDS Bulletin* 43, no. 4 (2012): 1–13. https://doi.org/10.1111/j.1759-5436.2012.00330.x.

Baker, James A., Lee H. Hamilton, Lawrence S. Eagleburger, Vernon E. Jordan, Edwin Meese, Sandra Day O'Connor, Leon E. Panetta, William J. Perry, Charles S. Robb, and Alan K. Simpson. *Iraq Study Group Report*. Washington, DC: U.S. Congress, 2006.

Balanche, Fabrice. "The End of the CIA Program in Syria." *Foreign Affairs*, August 2, 2017. https://www.foreignaffairs.com/articles/syria/2017-08-02/end-cia-program-syria.

Banks, Jeffrey S., and Barry R. Weingast. "The Political Control of Bureaucracies Under Asymmetric Information." *American Journal of Political Science* 36, no. 2 (1992): 509–524. https://doi.org/10.2307/2111488.

Barakat, Sultan, Margaret Chard, Tim Jacoby, and William Lume. "The Composite Approach: Research Design in the Context of War and Armed Conflict." *Third World Quarterly* 23, no. 5 (2002): 991–1003. https://doi.org/10.1080/0143659022000028530.

Barfield, Thomas. *Afghanistan: A Cultural and Political History*. Princeton, NJ: Princeton University Press, 2010.

Barkcin, Mehmed Cavid. "First Group of FSA Soldiers Trained by US, Turkey Enters Syria." *Daily Sabah*, July 15, 2015. https://www.dailysabah.com/politics/2015/07/15/first-group-of-fsa-soldiers-trained-by-us-turkey-enters-syria.

Barnett, Michael N. "Culture, Strategy and Foreign Policy Change: Israel's Road to Oslo." *European Journal of International Relations* 5, no. 1 (1999): 5–36.

Barnett, Michael N., and Martha Finnemore. "The Politics, Power, and Pathologies of International Organizations." *International Organization* 53, no. 4 (1999): 699–732. https://doi.org/10.1162/002081899551048.

———. *Rules for the World: International Organizations in Global Politics*. Ithaca, NY: Cornell University Press, 2004.

Barnett, Michael, and Christoph Zurcher. "The Peacebuilder's Contract: How External Statebuilding Reinforces Weak Statehood." In *The Dilemmas of State-Building: Confronting the Contradictions of Postwar Peace Operations*, edited by Roland Paris Timothy D. Sisk, 23–52. London: Routledge, 2009.

Bar-Siman-Tov, Yaacov. "The Strategy of War by Proxy." *Cooperation and Conflict* 19, no. 4 (1984): 263–273.

Baumann, Rainer, and Frank A. Stengel. "Foreign Policy Analysis, Globalisation and Non-state Actors: State-Centric After All?" *Journal of International Relations and Development* 17, no. 4 (2013): 489–521. https://doi.org/10.1057/jird.2013.12.

Beehner, Lionel. "U.S. Intervention in Iraqi Politics." Council on Foreign Relations, March 6, 2006. https://www.cfr.org/backgrounder/us-intervention-iraqi-politics.

Bendor, Jonathan, and Thomas H. Hammond. "Rethinking Allison's Models." *American Political Science Review* 86, no. 2 (1992): 301–322. https://doi.org/10.2307/1964222.

Bendor, Jonathan, and Terry M. Moe. "An Adaptive Model of Bureaucratic Politics." *American Political Science Review* 79, no. 3 (1985): 755–774. https://doi.org/10.2307/1956842.

Benraad, Myriam. "Iraq's Tribal 'Sahwa:' Its Rise and Fall." *Middle East Policy*, 18, no. 1 (2011): 121–131. https://doi.org/10.1111/j.1475-4967.2011.00477.x.

Berman, Eli, and David A. Lake, eds. *Proxy Wars: Suppressing Violence Through Local Agents*. Ithaca, NY: Cornell University Press, 2019.

Berman, Eli, David A. Lake, Gerard Padró i Miquel, and Pierre Yared. "Introduction: Principals, Agents, and Indirect Foreign Policies." In *Proxy Wars: Suppressing Violence Through Local Agents*, edited by Eli Berman and David A. Lake, 1–27. Ithaca, NY: Cornell University Press, 2019.

Berti, Benedetta. "Violent and Criminal Non-state Actors." In *The Oxford Handbook of Governance and Limited Statehood*, edited by Thomas Risse, Anke Draude, and Tanja A. Börzel, 1502–1519. Oxford: Oxford University Press, 2018.

Biberman, Yelena. "Self-Defense Militias, Death Squads, and State Outsourcing of Violence in India and Turkey." *Journal of Strategic Studies* 41, no. 5 (2017): 751–781. https://doi.org/10.1080/01402390.2016.1202822.

Biddle, Stephen. "Allies, Airpower, and Modern Warfare: The Afghan Model in Afghanistan and Iraq." *International Security* 30, no. 3 (2005): 161–176. https://doi.org/10.1162/016228805775969555.

Biddle, Stephen, Jeffrey Friedman, and Jacob N. Shapiro. "Testing the Surge: Why Did Violence Decline in Iraq in 2007?" *International Security* 37, no. 1 (2012): 7–40. https://doi.org/10.1162/ISEC_a_00087.

Biddle, Stephen, Julia Macdonald, and Ryan Baker. "Small Footprint, Small Payoff: The Military Effectiveness of Security Force Assistance." *Journal of Strategic Studies* 41, nos. 1–2 (2018): 89–142. https://doi.org/10.1080/01402390.2017.1307745.

Bizhan, Nematullah. "Aid and State-Building, Part II: Afghanistan and Iraq." *Third World Quarterly* 39, no. 5 (2018): 1014–1031. https://doi.org/10.1080/01436597.2018.1447369.

Blanchard, Christopher M. "Syria and U.S. Policy." *In Focus*, Congressional Research Service, April 19, 2022. https://crsreports.congress.gov/product/pdf/IF/IF11930#:~:text=The.

Blanchard, Christopher M., and Amy Belasco. *Train and Equip Program for Syria: Authorities, Funding, and Issues for Congress*, R43727. Washington, DC: Congressional Research Service, June 2015. https://reliefweb.int/report/syrian-arab-republic/armed-conflict-syria-overview-and-us-response.

Blanchard, Christopher M., Carla E. Humud, and Mary Beth D. Nikitin. *Armed Conflict in Syria: Overview and U.S. Response*, RL33487. Washington, DC: Congressional Research Service, April 2014. https://www.refworld.org/docid/5375df914.html.

———. *Armed Conflict in Syria: Overview and U.S. Response*, RL33487. Washington, DC: Congressional Research Service, October 2015. https://www.refworld.org/docid/566694264.html.

Blum, William. *Killing Hope: US Military and CIA Interventions Since World War II*. London: Zed Books, 2014.

Boege, Volker, Anne Brown, Kevin Clements, and Anna Nolan. *On Hybrid Political Orders and Emerging States: State Formation in the Context of "Fragility."* Berlin: Berghoff Handbook Dialogue, 2008. https://berghof-foundation.org/library/on-hybrid-political-orders-and-emerging-states-state-formation-in-the-context-of-fragility.

Boege, Volker, M. Anne Brown, and Kevin P. Clements. "Hybrid Political Orders, Not Fragile States." *Peace Review* 21, no. 1 (2009): 13–21. https://doi.org/10.1080/10402650802689997.

Boghani, Priyanka. "In Their Own Words: Sunnis on Their Treatment in Maliki's Iraq." *PBS Frontline*, October 28, 2014. https://www.pbs.org/wgbh/frontline/article/in-their-own-words-sunnis-on-their-treatment-in-malikis-iraq/.

Boone, Jon. "Top US General Warns on Afghan Self-Defence Plan." *Financial Times*, January 3, 2008. https://www.ft.com/content/f31af380-b95e-11dc-bb66-0000779fd2ac.

———. "US Pours Millions Into Anti-Taliban Militias in Afghanistan." *The Guardian*, November 22, 2009. https://www.theguardian.com/world/2009/nov/22/us-anti-taliban-militias-afghanistan.

Boot, Max. "The Pentagon's Cold Feet on Syria Should Not Decide the Matter." *Washington Post*, March 14, 2012. https://www.washingtonpost.com/opinions/the-pentagons-cold-feet-on-syria-should-not-decide-the-matter/2012/03/14/gIQAVMloES_story.html.

———. *The Savage Wars of Peace: Small Wars and the Rise of American Power*. New York: Basic Books, 2014.

Borger, Julian. "Austria Says UK Push to Arm Syrian Rebels Would Violate International Law." *The Guardian*, May 14, 2013. https://www.theguardian.com/world/julian-borger-global-security-blog/2013/may/14/austria-eu-syria-arms-embargo.

Borger, Julian, and Nick Hopkins. "West Training Syrian Rebels in Jordan." *The Guardian*, March 8, 2013. https://www.theguardian.com/world/2013/mar/08/west-training-syrian-rebels-jordan.

Brechenmacher, Saskia. "Stabilizing Northeast Nigeria After Boko Haram." Carnegie Endowment for International Peace, May 30, 2019. https://carnegieendowment.org/2019/05/03/stabilizing-northeast-nigeria-after-boko-haram-pub-79042.

Brecher, Michael. *The Foreign Policy System of Israel: Setting, Images, Process*. London: Oxford University Press, 1972.

Brehm, John, and Scott Gates. "When Supervision Fails to Induce Compliance." *Journal of Theoretical Politics* 6, no. 3 (1994): 323–343.

Brighi, Elisabetta, and Christopher Hill. "Implementation and Behaviour." In *Foreign Policy: Theories, Actors, Cases*, edited by Steve Smith, Amelia Hadfield, and Tim Dunne, 117–135. Cambridge: Cambridge University Press, 2008.

Brooking, Steve. "Private Security Companies in Afghanistan, 2001–11." Afghanistan Analysts Network, July 2012. https://docplayer.net/17540812-Private-security-companies-in-afghanistan-2001-11.html.

Brown, Frances Z. *Dilemmas of Stabilization Assistance: The Case of Syria.* Washington, DC: Carnegie Endowment for International Peace, 2018. https://carnegieendowment.org/2018/10/26/dilemmas-of-stabilization-assistance-case-of-syria-pub-77574.

———. "The U.S. Surge and Afghan Local Governance." United States Institute of Peace, September 12, 2012. https://www.usip.org/publications/2012/09/us-surge-and-afghan-local-governance.

Brown, Seyom. "Purposes and Pitfalls of War by Proxy: A Systemic Analysis." *Small Wars & Insurgencies* 27, no. 2 (2016): 243–257.

Bruno, Greg. "A Tribal Strategy for Afghanistan." Council on Foreign Relations, November 5, 2008. https://www.cfr.org/backgrounder/tribal-strategy-afghanistan.

Brysk, Alison. "From Above and Below: Social Movements, the International System, and Human Rights in Argentina." *Comparative Political Studies* 26, no. 3 (1993): 259–285. https://doi.org/10.1177/0010414093026003001.

———, ed. *Globalization and Human Rights.* Berkeley: University of California Press, 2002.

Byman, Daniel. *Deadly Connections: States That Sponsor Terrorism.* Cambridge: Cambridge University Press, 2007.

———. "Friends Like These: Counterinsurgency and the War on Terrorism." *International Security* 31, no. 2 (2006): 79–115. https://doi.org/10.1162/isec.2006.31.2.79.

———. "Why Engage in Proxy War? A State's Perspective." *Lawfare*, May 21, 2018. https://www.lawfareblog.com/why-engage-proxy-war-states-perspective#.

Byman, Daniel, and Sarah E. Kreps. "Agents of Destruction? Applying Principal-Agent Analysis to State-Sponsored Terrorism." *International Studies Perspectives* 11, no. 1 (2010): 1–18. https://doi.org/10.1111/j.1528-3585.2009.00389.x.

Byman, Daniel, and Matthew Waxman. *The Dynamics of Coercion: American Foreign Policy and the Limits of Military Might.* Cambridge: Cambridge University Press, 2002.

Call, Charles. "The Fallacy of the 'Failed State.'" *Third World Quarterly* 29, no. 8 (2008): 1491–1507. https://doi.org/10.1080/01436590802544207.

Callimachi, Rukmini, Helene Cooper, Eric Schmitt, Alan Blinder, and Thomas Gibbons-Neff. "'An Endless War': Why 4 U.S. Soldiers Died in a Remote African Desert." *New York Times*, February 20, 2018. https://www.nytimes.com/interactive/2018/02/17/world/africa/niger-ambush-american-soldiers.html.

Cambanis, Thanassis, Dina Esfandiary, Ghaddar Sima, Michael Wahid Hanna, Aron Lund, and Renad Mansour. *Hybrid Actors: Armed Groups and State Fragmentation in the Middle East.* New York: Century Foundation, 2019.

Campbell, Bruce B., and Arthur D. Brenner. *Death Squads in Global Perspective: Murder with Deniability.* Basingstoke, UK: Macmillan, 2000.

Campbell, Jason, and Jeremy Shapiro. *Afghanistan Index.* Washington, DC: Brookings Institution, January 2009.

Carey, Sabine C., Michael P. Colaresi, and Neil J. Mitchell. "Governments, Informal Links to Militias, and Accountability." *Journal of Conflict Resolution* 59, no. 5 (2015): 850–876. https://doi.org/10.1177/0022002715576747.

Carlsnaes, Walter, Helen Sjursen, and Brian White, eds. *Contemporary European Foreign Policy.* London: SAGE Publications, 2004.

Carter, Philip, and Andrew Swick. "Why Were US Soldiers Even in Niger? America's Shadow Wars in Africa, Explained." *Vox*, October 26, 2017. https://www.vox.com/world/2017/10/26/16547528/us-soldiers-niger-johnson-widow-africa-trump.

Cavendish, Julius. "CIA Trains Covert Units of Afghans to Continue the Fight Against Taliban." *The Independent*, October 23, 2011. https://www.independent.co.uk/news/world/asia/cia-trains-covert-units-afghans-continue-fight-against-taliban-2317182.html.

CFSOCC-A (Combined Forces Special Operations Component Command—Afghanistan). "Afghan Local Defense Initiative Briefing January 2010." Kabul: Combined Forces Special Operations Component Command—Afghanistan, 2010. On file with author.

———. "Ministry of Interior Afghan Local Police Fact Sheet CFSOCC-A PAO 031911." Kabul: Combined Forces Special Operations Component Command—Afghanistan, 2011. On file with author.

Chandrasekaran, Rajiv. "US Forces Training Afghan Villagers to Watch for Taliban." *Washington Post*, May 2, 2010. http://archive.boston.com/news/world/middleeast/articles/2010/05/02/us_forces_training_afghan_villagers_to_watch_for_taliban/.

Chesterman, Simon. *You, the People: The United Nations, Transitional Administration, and State-Building*. Oxford: Oxford University Press, 2004.

Chivers, C. J., and Eric Schmitt. "Arms Airlift to Syrian Rebels Expands, with C.I.A. Aid." *New York Times*, April 12, 2013. https://www.nytimes.com/2013/03/25/world/middleeast/arms-airlift-to-syrian-rebels-expands-with-cia-aid.html.

Cigar, Norman. *Tribal Militias: An Effective Tool to Counter al-Qaeda and Its Affiliates?* Carlisle, PA: United States Army War College Press, 2014.

Clark, Kate. *Afghanistan's Newest Local Defence Force: Were "All the Mistakes of the ALP" Turned Into ANA-TF Safeguards?* Kabul: Afghanistan Analysts Network, August 2020.

———. "Disbanding the ALP—An Update: Major Transition of Security Forces Achieved During Wartime, But at a Cost." Afghanistan Analysts Network, April 15, 2021. https://www.afghanistan-analysts.org/en/reports/war-and-peace/disbanding-the-alp-an-update-major-transition-of-security-forces-achieved-during-wartime-but-at-a-cost/.

———. "From Land-Grabbing to Haircuts: The Decrees and Edicts of the Taleban Supreme Leader." Afghanistan Analysts Network, July 15, 2023, sec. Rights and Freedoms. https://www.afghanistan-analysts.org/en/reports/rights-freedom/from-land-grabbing-to-haircuts-the-decrees-and-edicts-of-the-taleban-supreme-leader/.

———. "More Militias? Part 1: Déjà Vu Double Plus with the Proposed 'Afghan Territorial Army.'" Afghanistan Analysts Network, September 21, 2017. https://www.afghanistan-analysts.org/more-militias-part-1-deja-vu-double-plus-with-the-proposed-afghan-territorial-army/.

Clark, Kate, Erica Gaston, Borhan Osman, Ali Mohammad Sabawoon, and Fazal Muzhary. *Ghosts of the Past: Lessons from Local Force Mobilisation in Afghanistan and Prospects for the Future*. Kabul: Afghanistan Analysts Network; Berlin: Global Public Policy Institute, 2020.

Clarke, Michael, and Steve Smith. "Perspectives on the Foreign Policy System: Implementation Approaches." In *Understanding Foreign Policy: The Foreign Policy Systems Approach*, edited by Michael Clarke and Brian White, 163–184. Cheltenham, UK: Edward Elgar, 1989.

Clayton, Govinda, and Andrew Thomson. "Civilianizing Civil Conflict: Civilian Defense Militias and the Logic of Violence in Intrastate Conflict." *International Studies Quarterly* 60, no. 3 (2016): 499–510. https://doi.org/10.1093/isq/sqv011.

——. "The Enemy of My Enemy Is My Friend ... The Dynamics of Self-Defense Forces in Irregular War: The Case of the Sons of Iraq." *Studies in Conflict & Terrorism* 37, no. 11 (2014): 920–935. https://doi.org/10.1080/1057610X.2014.952262.

Cleveland, Charles T., and Daniel Egel. *The American Way of Irregular War: An Analytical Memoir*. Washington, DC: RAND Corporation, 2020.

Clinton, Hillary Rodham. *Hard Choices*. London: Simon and Schuster, 2014.

Clunan, Anne L., and Harold A. Trinkunas. *Ungoverned Spaces: Alternatives to State Authority in an Era of Softened Sovereignty*. Stanford, CA: Stanford Security Studies, 2010.

Coburn, Noah. *Informal Justice and the International Community in Afghanistan*. Washington, DC: United States Institute of Peace, 2013.

Cochran, Shawn T. "Security Assistance, Surrogate Armies, and the Pursuit of US Interests in Sub-Saharan Africa." *Strategic Studies Quarterly* 4, no. 1 (2010): 111–152.

Cohen, Dara Kay, and Ragnhild Nordås. "Do States Delegate Shameful Violence to Militias? Patterns of Sexual Violence in Recent Armed Conflicts." *Journal of Conflict Resolution* 59, no. 5 (2015): 877–898. https://doi.org/10.1177/0022002715576748.

Colás, Alejandro, and Bryan Mabee, eds. *Mercenaries, Pirates, Bandits and Empires: Private Violence in Historical Context*. New York: Columbia University Press, 2010.

Coll, Steve. *Ghost Wars: The Secret History of the CIA, Afghanistan, and Bin Laden, from the Soviet Invasion to September 10, 2001*. New York: Penguin Books, 2005.

Cordesman, Anthony. *Trends in Iraqi Violence, Casualties and Impact of War: 2003–2015*. Washington, DC: Center for Strategic and International Studies, 2015.

Cordesman, Anthony, Charles Loi, and Vivek Kocharlakota. *IED Metrics for Iraq: June 2003–September 2010*. Washington, DC: Center for Strategic and International Studies, 2010.

Cragin, Kim R. "Semi-proxy Wars and U.S. Counterterrorism Strategy." *Studies in Conflict and Terrorism* 38, no. 5 (2015): 311–327. https://doi.org/10.1080/1057610X.2015.1018024.

Crawford, Michael, and Jami Miscik. "The Rise of the Mezzanine Rulers: The New Frontier for International Law." *Foreign Affairs* 89, no. 6 (2010): 123–132.

Crawford, Timothy W., and Alan J. Kuperman, eds. *Gambling on Humanitarian Intervention: Moral Hazard, Rebellion and Civil War*. Abingdon, UK: Routledge, 2006.

Cruickshank, Paul. "A View from the CT Foxhole: Harun Maruf, Senior Editor, Voice of America Somali." *CTC Sentinel* 15, no. 11 (2022): 10–20.

Davies, Lizzy, and John Hooper. "French Outcry Over Claim Italian Payments Masked Taliban Threat." *The Guardian*, October 16, 2009. https://www.theguardian.com/world/2009/oct/16/france-italy-taliban-afghanistan.

Day, Adam, Vanda Felbab-Brown, and Fanar Haddad. *Hybrid Conflict, Hybrid Peace: How Militias and Paramilitary Groups Shape Post-Conflict Transitions*. New York: United Nations University Centre for Policy Research, 2020.

DeBruin, Erica S. "Preventing Coups d'état: How Counterbalancing Works." *Journal of Conflict Resolution* 62, no. 7 (2017): 1433–1458. https://doi.org/10.1177/0022002717692652.

Deeks, Ashley S. "'Unwilling or Unable': Toward a Normative Framework for Extraterritorial Self-Defense." *Virginia Journal of International Law* 52, no. 3 (2012): 483–550.

Department of Defense. "FOIA Release: 220 AR15-6 Inv Credibility Assessment_6—Exhibit_G." U.S. Department of Defense, 2011. On file with author.

———. "FOIA Release: 228 AR15-6 Inv Credibility Assessment_6—Exhibit_O." U.S. Department of Defense, 2011. On file with author.

———. *Measuring Stability and Security in Iraq (March 2009)*. Washington, DC: U.S. Department of Defense, 2009.

———. *Report on Progress Toward Security and Stability in Afghanistan*. Washington, DC: U.S. Department of Defense, 2014.

———. *Summary of the 2018 National Defense Strategy of the United States of America*. Washington, DC: U.S. Department of Defense, 2018.

Department of Peacekeeping Operations. *Second Generation Disarmament, Demobilization and Reintegration (DDR) Practices in Peace Operations*. New York: United Nations, 2010.

Derksen, Deedee. "Commanders in Control: Disarmament, Demobilization and Reintegration in Afghanistan Under the Karzai Administration." PhD diss., King's College London, 2016. https://kclpure.kcl.ac.uk/portal/files/74662477/2017_Derksen_Linde_Dorien_0946805_ethesis.pdf.

———. *Non-state Security Providers and Political Formation in Afghanistan*. Waterloo, ON: Centre for Security Governance, 2016. https://reliefweb.int/report/afghanistan/non-state-security-providers-and-political-formation-afghanistan.

———. *The Politics of Disarmament and Rearmament in Afghanistan*. Washington, DC: United States Institute of Peace, 2015.

Detsch, Jack. "Pentagon Acknowledges US Contractor Presence in Syria for First Time." *Al-Monitor*, April 13, 2018. https://www.al-monitor.com/originals/2018/04/pentagon-acknowledge-us-contractor-presence-syria-iraq.html.

Deutsch, Karl W. "External Involvement in Internal War." In *Internal War*, edited by Harry Eckstein, 98–110. New York: Free Press of Glencoe, 1964.

Deutscher Bundestag. *Zum Tod Des KSK-Elite-Soldaten in Afghanistan, Anhörung Vor Der 17. Wahlperiode, Drucksache 17/13980, December 16, 2013 (Antwort Der Bundesregierung Auf Die Kleine Anfrage Der Abgeordneten Heike Hänsel, Wolfgang Gehrcke, Christine Buchholz, Weiterer Abgeo)*. Berlin: Deutscher Bundestag, 2013.

Developments in Afghanistan: Hearing Before the Committee on Armed Services. 112th Cong., 1st Sess. (March 16, 2011). https://www.govinfo.gov/content/pkg/CHRG-112hhrg65591/html/CHRG-112hhrg65591.htm.

De Waal, Alex. "Mission Without End? Peacekeeping in the African Political Marketplace." *International Affairs* 85, no. 1 (2009): 99–113. https://doi.org/10.1111/j.1468-2346.2009.00783.x.

DeYoung, Karen. "Administration Searches for New Approach to Aiding Rebels in Syria." *Washington Post*, September 16, 2015. https://www.washingtonpost.com/world/national-security/administration-searches-for-new-approach-to-aiding-rebels-in-syria/2015/09/16/938fd336-5c9e-11e5-8e9e-dce8a2a2a679_story.html.

———. "Congressional Panels Approve Arms Aid to Syrian Opposition." *Washington Post*, July 22, 2013. https://www.washingtonpost.com/world/national-security/congressional-panels-approve-arms-aid-to-syrian-opposition/2013/07/22/393035ce-f31a-11e2-8505-bf6f231e77b4_story.html?utm_term=.da03e1b2d207.

Dodge, Toby. "Can Iraq Be Saved?" *Survival* 56, no. 5 (2014): 7–20. https://doi-org.ezp.lib.cam.ac.uk/10.1080/00396338.2014.962795.

———. "Iraq: The Contradictions of Exogenous State-Building in Historical Perspective." *Third World Quarterly* 27, no. 1 (2006): 187–200. https://doi.org/10.1080/01436590500370061.

———. *Iraq: From War to a New Authoritarianism*. Abingdon, UK: Routledge, 2017.

Donais, Timothy, and Barbak, Ahmet. "The Rule of Law, the Local Turn, and Re-thinking Accountability in Security Sector Reform Processes." *Peacebuilding* 9, no. 2 (2021): 206–221.

Dörmann, Knut, and Jose Serralvo. "Common Article 1 to the Geneva Conventions and the Obligation to Prevent International Humanitarian Law Violations." *International Review of the Red Cross* 96, nos. 895–896 (2014): 707–736. https://doi.org/10.1017/S181638311400037X.

Dowdle, Andrew J. "Civil Wars, International Conflicts and Other Determinants of Paramilitary Strength in Sub-Saharan Africa." *Small Wars & Insurgencies* 18, no. 2 (2007): 161–174. https://doi.org/10.1080/09592310701400796.

Doyle, Charles. *Terrorist Material Support: An Overview of 18 U.S.C. §2339A and §2339B*. Washington, DC: Congressional Research Service, 2016. https://fas.org/sgp/crs/natsec/R41333.pdf.

Doyle, Michael, and Nicholas Sambanis. *Making War and Building Peace: The United Nations Since the 1990's*. Princeton, NJ: Princeton University Press, 2006.

Eikenberry, Karl. "Unconventional Security Forces—What's Out There? [09kabul3661]." Leaked U.S. embassy diplomatic cable, Wikileaks, November 12, 2009. https://wikileaks.org/plusd/cables/09KABUL3661_a.html.

Eikenberry, Karl, Anne Patterson, William Taylor, and Dawn Liberi. "Case Study: Afghanistan." In *Elite Capture and Corruption of the Security Sector*, edited by Karl Eikenberry, Anne Patterson, William Taylor, and Dawn Liberi, 35–59. Washington, DC: United States Institute of Peace, n.d.

Eisenhardt, Kathleen M. "Agency Theory: An Assessment and Review." *Academy of Management Review* 14, no. 1 (1989): 57–74. https://doi.org/10.2307/258191.

Entous, Adam. "Covert CIA Mission to Arm Syrian Rebels Goes Awry." *Wall Street Journal*, April 12, 2015.

———. "U.S. Readies 'Plan B' to Arm Syria Rebels." *Wall Street Journal*, April 12, 2016. https://www.wsj.com/articles/u-s-readies-plan-b-to-arm-syria-rebels-1460509400.

———. "U.S., Turkey Narrow Differences on Islamic State Fight." *Wall Street Journal*, December 1, 2014. https://www.wsj.com/articles/u-s-turkey-move-closer-in-talks-involving-bases-air-zones-1417414812.

"The Extent of Conflict-Related Deaths in the Syrian Arab Republic—Background Note." Office of the United Nations High Commissioner for Human Rights, September 24, 2021. https://www.ohchr.org/en/documents/status-and-update-reports/oral-update-extent-conflict-related-deaths-syrian-arab-republic.

Fair, Christine C., and Seth G. Jones. *Securing Afghanistan: Getting on Track*. Washington, DC: United States Institute of Peace, 2009. https://www.usip.org/publications/2009/02/securing-afghanistan-getting-track.

Fallows, Jim. "Why Iraq Has No Army." *The Atlantic*, December 2005. https://www.theatlantic.com/magazine/archive/2005/12/why-iraq-has-no-army/304428/.

Fast, Larissa. "A Reflexive Approach to Risk and Intervention for Third-Party Intervenors." *Conflict Resolution Quarterly* 30, no. 4 (2013): 467–489. https://doi.org/10.1002/crq.21075.

Felbab-Brown, Vanda. "Hurray for Militias? Not So Fast: Lessons from the Afghan Local Police Experience." *Small Wars & Insurgencies* 27, no. 2 (2016): 258–281. https://doi.org/10.1080/09592318.2015.1129169.

Felbab-Brown, Vanda, Harold A Trinkunas, and Shadi Hamid. *Militants, Criminals, and Warlords*. Washington, DC: Brookings Institution Press, 2017.

Felter, Joseph H., and Jacob N. Shapiro. "Limiting Civilian Casualties as Part of a Winning Strategy: The Case of Courageous Restraint." *Daedalus* 146, no. 1 (2017): 44–58.

Ferejohn, John, and Charles Shipan. "Congressional Influence on Bureaucracy." *Journal of Law, Economics, & Organization* 6 (1990): 1–20. https://doi.org/10.1093/jleo/6.special_issue.1.

Finnemore, Martha, and Kathryn Sikkink. "International Norm Dynamics and Political Change." *International Organization* 52, no. 4 (1998): 887–917. https://doi.org/10.1162/002081898550789.

Fiorina, Morris P. "Legislative Choice of Regulatory Forms: Legal Process or Administrative Process?" *Public Choice* 39, no. 1 (1982): 33–66. https://doi.org/10.1007/BF00242147.

Florini, Ann, ed. *The Third Force: The Rise of Transnational Civil Society*. Tokyo: Japan Center for International Change; Washington, DC: Carnegie Endowment for International Peace, 1999. https://doi.org/10.1353/wp.2003.0024.

Forsberg, Carl, and Tim Sullivan. "Criminal Patronage Networks and the Struggle to Rebuild the Afghan State." *Prism: A Journal of the Center for Complex Operations* 4, no. 4 (2013): 157–173.

Forsythe, David. "Human Rights in American Foreign Policy; from the 1960s to the Soviet Collapse by Joe Renouard (Review)." *Human Rights Quarterly* 38, no. 3 (2016): 841–846. https://doi.org/10.1353/hrq.2016.0044.

Fox, Amos C. "Conflict and the Need for a Theory of Proxy Warfare." *Journal of Strategic Security* 12, no. 1 (2019): 44–71. https://doi.org/10.5038/1944-0472.12.1.1701.

Foyle, Douglas. "Foreign Policy Analysis and Globalization: Public Opinion, World Opinion, and the Individual, in 'Foreign Policy Analysis in 20/20: A Symposium.'" *International Studies Review* 5, no. 2 (2003): 163–170. https://doi.org/10.1111/1521-9488.5020011.

Franklin, James C. "Human Rights Naming and Shaming: International and Domestic Processes." In *The Politics of Leverage in International Relations*, edited by H. Richard Friman, 43–60. London: Palgrave Macmillan, 2015. https://doi.org/10.1057/9781137439338_3.

Fukuyama, Francis. *State-Building: Governance and World Order in the 21st Century*. Ithaca, NY: Cornell University Press, 2004.

———. "What Is Governance?" *Governance* 26, no. 3 (2013): 347–368. https://doi.org/10.1111/gove.12035.

Galula, David. *Counterinsurgency Warfare: Theory and Practice.* Westport, CT: Praeger Security International, 2006.

Gant, Jim. *One Tribe at a Time: A Strategy for Success in Afghanistan.* Los Angeles: Nine Sisters Imports, 2009.

GAO (U.S. Government Accountability Office). *Additional Guidance, Monitoring, and Training Could Improve Implementation of the Leahy Laws,* GAO-13-866. Washington, DC: U.S. Government Accountability Office, 2013.

———. *Better Human Rights Reviews and Strategic Planning Needed for U.S. Assistance to Foreign Security Forces,* GAO-05-793. Washington, DC: U.S. Government Accountability Office, 2005. https://www.gao.gov/cgi-bin/getrpt?GAO-05-793.

———. *Security Assistance: Lapses in Human Rights Screening in North African Countries Indicate Need for Further Oversight,* GAO-06-850. Washington, DC: U.S. Government Accountability Office, 2006. https://www.gao.gov/cgi-bin/getrpt?GAO-06-850.

Garrison, Jean A. "Introduction: Foreign Policy Analysis in 20/20: A Symposium." *International Studies Review* 5, no. 2 (2003): 155–202.

Gaston, Erica. "Afghanistan Case Study." In *Elite Capture in US Security Assistance.* Washington, DC: United States Institute of Peace, 2022.

———. "Legal Pluralism and Militia Regulation: International, Domestic, and Community Accountability Frameworks for Sub-state Forces in Afghanistan." *Journal of Afghan Legal Studies* 2 (2017). https://papers.ssrn.com/sol3/papers.cfm?abstract_id=3476407.

———. "The Leahy Law and Human Rights Accountability in Afghanistan." Afghanistan Analysts Network, March 6, 2017. https://www.afghanistan-analysts.org/the-leahy-law-and-human-rights-accountability-in-afghanistan-too-little-too-late-or-a-model-for-the-future/.

———. *Regulating Irregular Actors: Can Due Diligence Checks Mitigate the Risks of Working with Non-state and Substate forces?* London: Overseas Development Institute; Berlin: Global Public Policy Institute, 2021. https://gppi.net/2021/06/02/regulating-irregular-actors.

———. "Sunni Tribal Forces." Project on Local, Hybrid and Substate Actors in Iraq, Global Public Policy Institute, August 30, 2017. https://www.gppi.net/2017/08/30/sunni-tribal-forces.

———. "War Powers Far from a Hot Battlefield: Checks and Balances on Presidential War-Making Through Individual and Unit Self-Defense." *Harvard National Security Journal* 10 (2019): 195–258.

Gaston, Erica, and Kate Clark. *Backgrounder: Literature Review of Local, Community or Sub-state Forces in Afghanistan.* Berlin: Global Public Policy Institute, 2017.

Gaston, Erica, and Jonathan Horowitz. *The Cost of Kill/Capture: Impact of the Night Raid Surge on Afghan Civilians.* New York: Open Society Foundations, 2011.

Gaston, Erica, and András Derzsi-Horváth. *Iraq After ISIL: Sub-state Actors, Local Forces, and the Micro-Politics of Control.* Berlin: Global Public Policy Institute, April 2018. http://www.gppi.net/publications/peace-security/article/iraq-after-isil-sub-state-actors-local-forces-and-the-micro-politics-of-control/.

Gaston, Erica, and Douglas Ollivant. *US-Iran Proxy Competition in Iraq.* Washington, DC: New America Foundation and Arizona State University Center for the Future of Warfare, 2020.

https://www.newamerica.org/international-security/reports/us-iran-proxy-competition-iraq/.

Gearan, Anne, and Karen DeYoung. "U.S. Announces Expanded Battlefield Aid to Syrian Rebels, but Not Arms." *Washington Post*, February 28, 2013. https://www.washingtonpost.com/world/middle_east/us-announces-expanded-battlefield-aid-to-syrian-rebels/2013/02/28/f0a32414-819b-11e2-b99e-6baf4ebe42df_story.html?utm_term=.05197e3243d9.

George, Alexander L. *Presidential Decision Making in Foreign Policy: The Effective Use of Information and Advice.* Boulder, CO: Westview Press, 1980.

Ghani, Ashraf, Clare Lockhart, and Michael Carnahan. *Closing the Sovereignty Gap: An Approach to State-Building.* London: Overseas Development Institute, 2005.

Giustozzi, Antonio. "Auxiliary Irregular Forces in Afghanistan: 1978–2008." In *Making Sense of Proxy Wars: States, Surrogates & the Use of Force*, edited by Michael A. Innes, 89–108. Washington, DC: Potomac Books, 2012.

———. "Bureaucratic Façade and Political Realities of Disarmament and Demobilisation in Afghanistan." *Conflict, Security & Development* 8, no. 2 (2008): 169–192. https://doi.org/10.1080/14678800802095369.

Giustozzi, Antonio, and Niamatullah Ibrahimi. *Thirty Years of Conflict: Drivers of Antigovernment Mobilisation in Afghanistan, 1978–2011.* London: Afghanistan Research and Evaluation Unit, 2012.

Giustozzi, Antonio, and Mohammed Isaqzadeh. *Afghanistan's Paramilitary Policing in Context.* Kabul: Afghanistan Analysts Network, 2011.

Giustozzi, Antonio, and Dominique Orsini. "Centre-Periphery Relations in Afghanistan: Badakhshan Between Patrimonialism and Institution-Building." *Central Asian Survey* 28, no. 1 (March 2009): 1–16. https://doi.org/10.1080/02634930902771466.

Goodhand, Jonathan. "Research in Conflict Zones: Ethics and Accountability." *Migration Review* 8, no. 4 (2000): 12–15.

Goodhand, Jonathan, and Aziz Hakimi. *Counterinsurgency, Local Militias, and Statebuilding in Afghanistan.* Washington, DC: United States Institute of Peace, 2013. https://www.usip.org/publications/2013/12/counterinsurgency-local-militias-and-statebuilding-afghanistan.

Goodhand, Jonathan, and Mark Sedra. "Rethinking Liberal Peacebuilding, Statebuilding and Transition in Afghanistan: An Introduction." *Central Asian Survey* 32, no. 3 (2013): 239–254. https://doi.org/10.1080/02634937.2013.850769.

Gordon, Michael R., and Eric Schmitt. "Saudi Arabia Will Grant U.S. Request for Anti-ISIS Training Program." *New York Times*, September 10, 2014. https://www.nytimes.com/2014/09/11/world/middleeast/saudi-arabia-isis.html?_r=0.

Gossman, Patricia. *"They've Shot Many Like This": Abusive Night Raids by CIA-Backed Afghan Strike Forces.* New York: Human Rights Watch, 2019.

———. "How US-Funded Abuses Led to Failure in Afghanistan." Human Rights Watch, July 6, 2021. https://www.hrw.org/news/2021/07/06/how-us-funded-abuses-led-failure-afghanistan.

Gould, Erica R. "Delegating IMF Conditionality: Understanding Variations in Control and Conformity." In *Delegation and Agency in International Organizations*, edited by Darren G.

Hawkins, David A. Lake, Daniel L. Nielson, and Michael J. Tierney, 281–311. Cambridge: Cambridge University Press, 2006. https://doi.org/10.1017/CBO9780511491368.011.

Graham-Harrison, Emma. "Hamid Karzai Seeks to Curb CIA Operations in Afghanistan." *The Guardian*, April 19, 2013. https://www.theguardian.com/world/2013/apr/19/hamid-karzai-curb-cia-afghanistan-operations.

Greenhalgh, Susan. *Just One Child: Science and Policy in Deng's China*. Berkeley: University of California Press, 2008.

Groh, Tyrone L. *Proxy War: The Least Bad Option*. Stanford, CA: Stanford University Press, 2019.

Haar, Gemma van der, Annelies Heijmans, and Dorothea Hilhorst. "Interactive Research and the Construction of Knowledge in Conflict-Affected Settings." *Disasters* 37, no. 1 (2201): S20–S35.

Hafner-Burton, Emilie M. "Sticks and Stones: Naming and Shaming the Human Rights Enforcement Problem." *International Organization* 62, no. 4 (2008): 689–716. https://doi.org/10.1017/S0020818308080247.

Hakimi, Aziz. "Getting Savages to Fight Barbarians: Counterinsurgency and the Remaking of Afghanistan." *Central Asian Survey* 32, no. 3 (2013): 388–405. https://doi.org/10.1080/02634937.2013.843300.

Halperin, Morton H. "The Decision to Deploy the ABM: Bureaucratic and Domestic Politics in the Johnson Administration." *World Politics* 25, no. 1 (October 1972): 62–95. https://doi.org/10.2307/2010431.

———. "Why Bureaucrats Play Games." *Foreign Policy*, no. 2 (1971): 70–90.

Halperin, Morton H., Arnold Kanter, and Priscilla Clapp. *Bureaucratic Politics and Foreign Policy*. Washington, DC: Brookings Institution Press, 1974.

Hashim, Ahmed. *Insurgency and Counter-Insurgency in Iraq*. Ithaca, NY: Cornell University Press, 2005.

Hawkins, Darren G., and Wade Jacoby. "How Agents Matter." In *Delegation and Agency in International Organizations*, edited by Darren G. Hawkins, David A. Lake, Daniel L. Nielson, and Michael J. Tierney, 199–228. Cambridge: Cambridge University Press, 2006. https://doi.org/10.1017/CBO9780511491368.008.

Hawkins, Darren G., David A. Lake, Daniel L. Nielson, and Michael J. Tierney, eds. *Delegation and Agency in International Organizations*. Cambridge: Cambridge University Press, 2006. https://doi.org/10.1017/CBO9780511491368.002.

Heller, Sam. "Commentary: In Syrian Proxy War, America Can Keep Its Hands Clean or It Can Get Things Done." Century Foundation, August 17, 2016. https://tcf.org/content/commentary/syrian-proxy-war-america-can-keep-hands-clean-can-get-things-done/.

Heras, Nicholas A. *From the Bottom, Up: A Strategy for U.S. Military Support to Syria's Armed Opposition*. Washington, DC: Center for a New American Security, 2016. https://www.cnas.org/publications/reports/from-the-bottom-up-a-strategy-for-u-s-military-support-to-syrias-armed-opposition.

Hermann, Margaret, and Thomas W. Milburn, eds. *Psychological Examination of Political Leaders*. New York: Free Press, 1977.

Herring, Eric, and Glen Rangwala. *Iraq in Fragments: The Occupation and Its Legacy*. London: Hurst and Co., 2006.
Hill, Christopher. *The Changing Politics of Foreign Policy*. London: Palgrave Macmillan, 2002.
Hilsman, Roger. *The Politics of Policymaking in Defense and Foreign Affairs*. Englewood Cliffs, NJ: Prentice-Hall, 1987.
Hoddie, Matthew, and Caroline A. Hartzell, eds. *Strengthening Peace in Post–Civil War States: Transforming Spoilers Into Stakeholders*. Chicago: University of Chicago Press, 2010.
Holmes, Oliver, Suleiman Al-Khalidi, Jason Szep, and Ned Parker. "U.S. Scouts for Sunni Allies on the Ground in Iraq." Reuters, September 16, 2014. https://www.reuters.com/article/us-iraq-crisis-sunnis-insight/u-s-scouts-for-sunni-allies-on-the-ground-in-iraq-idUSKBN0HB0BD20140916.
Hölmstrom, Bengt. "Moral Hazard and Observability." *Bell Journal of Economics* 10, no. 1 (1979): 74–91. https://doi.org/10.2307/3003320.
Holsti, Kal. "National Role Conceptions in the Study of Foreign Policy." *International Studies Quarterly* 14, no. 3 (1970): 233–309. https://doi.org/10.2307/3013584.
Hosenball, Mark, and Phil Stewart. "Exclusive: Congress Delaying U.S. Aid to Syrian Rebels." Reuters, July 8, 2013. https://www.reuters.com/article/us-usa-syria-arms/exclusive-congress-delaying-u-s-aid-to-syrian-rebels-sources-idUSBRE96713N20130708.
Hsi-Min, Lee, and Michael Hunzeker. "The View of Ukraine from Taiwan: Get Real About Territorial Defense." *War on the Rocks*, March 15, 2022. https://warontherocks.com/2022/03/the-view-of-ukraine-from-taiwan-get-real-about-territorial-defense/.
Hudson, Valerie M. "Foreign Policy Analysis: Actor-Specific Theory and the Ground of International Relations." *Foreign Policy Analysis* 1, no. 1 (2005): 1–30. https://doi.org/10.1111/j.1743-8594.2005.00001.x.
Hudson, Valerie M., and Christopher S. Vore. "Foreign Policy Analysis Yesterday, Today, and Tomorrow." *Mershon International Studies Review* 39, no. 2 (1995): 209–238.
Hughes, Geraint. *My Enemy's Enemy: Proxy Warfare in International Politics*. Portland, OR: Sussex Academic Press, 2012.
———. "Syria and the Perils of Proxy Warfare." *Small Wars & Insurgencies* 25, no. 3 (2014): 522–538. https://doi.org/10.1080/09592318.2014.913542.
Hughes, Geraint, and Christian Tripodi. "Anatomy of a Surrogate: Historical Precedents and Implications for Contemporary Counter-Insurgency and Counter-Terrorism." *Small Wars & Insurgencies* 20, no. 1 (2009): 1–35. https://doi.org/10.1080/09592310802571552.
Human Rights Vetting: Nigeria and Beyond: Hearing Before the Committee on Foreign Affairs. 113th Cong., 2d Sess. (July 10, 2014). https://www.govinfo.gov/content/pkg/CHRG-113hhrg88627/html/CHRG-113hhrg88627.htm.
Human Rights Watch. *Today We Shall All Die: Afghanistan's Strongmen and the Legacy of Impunity*. New York: Human Rights Watch, 2015.
"Human Rights Watch Testimony at House Foreign Affairs Subcommittee on Africa, Global Health, Global Human Rights, and International Organizations." Human Rights Watch, July 11, 2014. https://www.hrw.org/news/2014/07/11/human-rights-watch-testimony-house-foreign-affairs-subcommittee-africa-global-health.

Hunt, Edward. "Dispatches from Baghdad: Sectarian War in Iraq, 2006–2007." *Middle Eastern Studies* 56, no. 1 (2019): 100–115. https://doi.org/10.1080/00263206.2019.1626726.

Innes, Michael A., ed. *Making Sense of Proxy Wars: States, Surrogates & the Use of Force*. Washington, DC: Potomac Books, 2012.

International Committee of the Red Cross. *Allies, Partners, and Proxies: Managing Support Relationships in Armed Conflict to Reduce the Human Cost of War*. Geneva: International Committee of the Red Cross, 2021.

———. "Rule 149. Responsibility for Violations of International Humanitarian Law." Customary IHL Database, accessed December 7, 2023. https://ihl-databases.icrc.org/customary-ihl/eng/docs/v1_rul_rule149.

International Crisis Group. *A Force in Fragments: Reconstituting the Afghan National Army*. Asia Report No. 190. Brussels: International Crisis Group, 2010.

———. "The Future of the Afghan Local Police." *Asia Report No. 268* (June 4, 2015). https://icg-prod.s3.amazonaws.com/268-the-future-of-the-afghan-local-police.pdf.

———. "New Approach in Southern Syria." *Middle East Report No. 163* (September 2, 2015). https://icg-prod.s3.amazonaws.com/163-new-approach-in-southern-syria.pdf.

———. "Sustaining Gains in Somalia's Offensive Against Al-Shabaab." *Crisis Group Africa Briefing No. 187* (March 21, 2023). https://icg-prod.s3.amazonaws.com/s3fs-public/2023-03/b187-somalias-offensive-against-al-shabaab_0.pdf.

———. "Taliban Restrictions on Women's Rights Deepen Afghanistan's Crisis." *Asia Report No. 329* (February 23, 2023). https://icg-prod.s3.amazonaws.com/s3fs-public/2023-02/329-afghanistan-womens-rights.pdf.

International Organization for Migration. *Iraq Displacement 2006 Year in Review*. Geneva, 2007.

"Iraqi Parliament Passes Contested Law on Shi'ite Paramilitaries." Reuters, November 26, 2016. https://www.reuters.com/article/us-mideast-crisis-iraq-military-idUSKBN13L0IE.

Irish, John. "France's Hollande Says Assad No Ally in Fight Against Islamic State." Reuters, September 28, 2016. https://www.reuters.com/article/idUSKBN0GSoLL/.

Jackson, Ashley. *Politics and Governance in Afghanistan: The Case of Nangarhar Province*. Kabul: Afghanistan Research and Evaluation Unit, 2014.

Jackson, Robert H. *Quasi-States: Sovereignty, International Relations and the Third World*. Cambridge: Cambridge University Press, 1991. https://doi.org/10.1017/cbo9780511559020.

Jaffe, Greg, and Rajiv Chandrasekaran. "U.S. Ambassador Puts Brakes on Plan to Utilize Afghan Militias against Taliban." *Washington Post*, January 22, 2010. https://www.washingtonpost.com/wp-dyn/content/article/2010/01/21/AR2010012101926.html.

Jensen, Michael C., and William H. Meckling. "Theory of the Firm: Managerial Behavior, Agency Costs, and Ownership Structure." *Journal of Financial Economics* 3, no. 4 (1976): 305–360.

Jentzsch, Corinna, Stathis N. Kalyvas, and Livia Isabella Schubiger. "Militias in Civil Wars." *Journal of Conflict Resolution* 59, no. 5 (2015): 755–769. https://doi.org/10.1177/0022002715576753.

Jervis, Robert. *Perception and Misperception in International Politics*. Princeton, NJ: Princeton University Press, 1976.

Jervis, Robert, Richard Ned Lebow, and Janice Gross Stein, eds. *Psychology and Deterrence.* Baltimore: John Hopkins University Press, 1985.

Jeursen, Thijs, and Chris van der Borgh. "Security Provision After Regime Change: Local Militias and Political Entities in Post-Qaddafi Tripoli." *Journal of Intervention and Statebuilding* 8, nos. 2–3 (2014): 173–191. https://doi.org/10.1080/17502977.2014.925249.

Jolly, David. "Civilian Deaths Raise Questions About CIA-Trained Forces in Afghanistan." *New York Times*, December 3, 2015. http://www.nytimes.com/2015/12/04/world/asia/afghanistan-civilian-casualty-khost.html.

Jones, Seth G. *The Strategic Logic of Militia.* Washington, DC: RAND Corporation, 2012. https://www.rand.org/pubs/working_papers/WR913.html.

———. *War by Proxy: Iran's Growing Footprint in the Middle East.* Washington, DC: Center for Strategic and International Studies, 2019. https://www.csis.org/analysis/war-proxy-irans-growing-footprint-middle-east-0.

Jones, Seth G., and Arturo Muñoz. *Afghanistan's Local War—Building Local Defense Forces.* Santa Monica, CA: RAND Corporation, 2010.

Kacowicz, Arie M. "Review: Proxy Warriors: The Rise and Fall of State-Sponsored Militias; Ungoverned Spaces: Alternatives to State Authority in an Era of Softened Sovereignty; Strengthening Peace in Post–Civil War States: Transforming Spoilers into Stakeholders." *Perspectives on Politics* 10, no. 2 (2012): 433–434. https://doi.org/10.1017/S1537592711004968.

Kaldor, Mary. *New and Old Wars: Organised Violence in a Global Era.* Stanford, CA: Stanford University Press, 2010.

Kalyvas, Stathis N. *The Logic of Violence in Civil War.* Cambridge: Cambridge University Press, 2006.

Kaplan, Robert. *The Insurgents: David Petraeus and the Plot to Change the American Way of War.* New York: Simon and Schuster, 2013.

Katz, Brian. "What the U.S. Can Learn from the Iranian Qods Force." *The Atlantic*, October 19, 2019. https://www.theatlantic.com/politics/archive/2019/10/what-us-can-learn-iranian-warfare/600082/.

Katzenstein, Peter J., ed. *The Culture of National Security: Norms and Identity in World Politics.* New York: Columbia University Press, 1996.

Keck, Margaret E., and Kathryn Sikkink. *Activists Beyond Borders: Advocacy Networks in International Politics.* Ithaca, NY: Cornell University Press, 2014.

Keen, David. *Complex Emergencies.* Cambridge: Polity Press, 2008.

Keohane, Robert O. "The Big Influence of Small Allies." *Foreign Policy*, no. 2 (Spring 1971): 161–182.

Keohane, Robert O., and Joseph Nye. *Power and Interdependence.* Boston: Longman, 2012.

Khagram, Sanjeev, James V. Riker, and Kathryn Sikkink, eds. *Restructuring World Politics: Transnational Social Movements, Networks, and Norms.* Minneapolis: University of Minnesota Press, 2002.

Khalidi, Ari. "Turkish State Media Exposes French Troop Locations in Syria." *Kurdistan24*, March 30, 2018. https://www.kurdistan24.net/en/news/cce35809-b1c8-4e77-afbc-172e26769bfe.

Kiewiet, Roderick, and Matthew D. McCubbins. *The Logic of Delegation: Congressional Parties and the Appropriations Process.* Chicago: University of Chicago Press, 1991.

Kilcullen, David. *The Accidental Guerrilla: Fighting Small Wars in the Midst of a Big One.* London: Hurst and Co., 2009.

Kleinfeld, Rachel. *Advancing the Rule of Law Abroad: Next Generation Reform.* Washington, DC: Brookings Institution Press, 2012.

Knights, Michael, Hamdi Malik, and Aymenn Jawad Al-Tamimi. *Honored, Not Contained: The Future of Iraq's Popular Mobilization Forces.* Washington, DC: Washington Institute for Near East Policy, 2020.

"Kobane: Air Strikes Help Syria Town Curb IS." *BBC News*, October 4, 2014. https://www.bbc.co.uk/news/world-middle-east-29526783.

Kovats-Bernat, J. Christopher. "Negotiating Dangerous Fields: Pragmatic Strategies for Fieldwork amid Violence and Terror." *American Anthropologist* 104, no. 1 (2002): 208–222. https://doi.org/10.1525/AA.2002.104.1.208.

Krasner, Stephen D. "Are Bureaucracies Important? (Or Allison Wonderland)." *Foreign Policy* 7, no. 1 (1972): 159–179.

———, ed. *Problematic Sovereignty: Contested Rules and Political Possibilities.* New York: Columbia University Press, 2001. https://doi-org.ezp.lib.cam.ac.uk/10.7312/kras12178.

———. "Sharing Sovereignty: New Institutions for Collapsed and Failing States." *International Security* 29, no. 2 (2004): 85–120. https://doi.org/10.1162/0162288042879940.

Krasner, Stephen D., and Carlos Pascual. "Addressing State Failure." *Foreign Affairs* 84, no. 4 (2005): 153–163.

Krieg, Andreas. "Externalizing the Burden of War: The Obama Doctrine and US Foreign Policy in the Middle East." *International Affairs* 92, no. 1 (2016): 97–113. https://doi.org/10.1111/1468-2346.12506.

Ladwig, Walter C. *The Forgotten Front: Patron-Client Relationships in Counterinsurgency.* Cambridge: Cambridge University Press, 2017. https://doi.org/10.1017/9781316756805.001.

———. "Influencing Clients in Counterinsurgency: U.S. Involvement in El Salvador's Civil War, 1979–92." *International Security* 41, no. 1 (2016): 99–146. https://doi.org/10.1162/ISEC_a_00251.

Lake, David A., and Matthew D. McCubbins. "The Logic of Delegation to International Organizations." In *Delegation and Agency in International Organizations*, edited by Darren G. Hawkins, David A. Lake, Daniel L. Nielson, and Michael J. Tierney, 341–368. Cambridge: Cambridge University Press, 2006. https://doi.org/10.1017/CBO9780511491368.

Landler, Mark. *Alter Egos: Obama's Legacy, Hillary's Promise and the Struggle Over American Power.* London: W. H. Allen, 2016.

Larsen, Henrik. "A Distinct FPA for Europe? Towards a Comprehensive Framework for Analysing the Foreign Policy of EU Member States." *European Journal of International Relations* 15, no. 3 (2009): 537–566. https://doi.org/10.1177/1354066109388247.

"Leahy Fact Sheet." Bureau of Democracy, Rights, and Labor, U.S. Department of State, March 9, 2018. https://2017-2021.state.gov/leahy-fact-sheet/.

Lefèvre, Matthieu. "The Afghanistan Public Protection Program and the Local Defence Initiatives." In *The Unlearned Lessons of Afghanistan's Decade of Assistance (2001–2011)*, edited by Martine van Bijlert and Sari Kouvo. Kabul: Afghanistan Analysts Network, 2010. https://www.afghanistan-analysts.org/publication/aan-papers/local-defence-in-afghanistan-a-review-of-government-backed-initiatives/.

———. *Local Defence in Afghanistan: A Review of Government-Backed Initiatives.* Kabul: Afghanistan Analysts Network, 2010. https://www.afghanistan-analysts.org/publication/aan-papers/local-defence-in-afghanistan-a-review-of-government-backed-initiatives/.

Letsch, Constanze. "US Drops Weapons and Ammunition to Help Kurdish Fighters in Kobani." *The Guardian*, October 20, 2013. https://www.theguardian.com/world/2014/oct/20/turkey-iraqi-kurds-kobani-isis-fighters-us-air-drops-arms.

Lewis, Larry, and Sarah Holewinski. "Changing of the Guard: Civilian Protection for an Evolving Military." *Prism* 4, no. 2 (2013): 57–66.

Lister, Charles. *The Free Syrian Army: A Decentralized Insurgent Brand.* Washington, DC: Brookings Institution, April 2016.

Livingston, Ian S., Heather L. Messera, and Michael O'Hanlon. *Afghanistan Index.* Washington, DC: Brookings Institution, February 2010.

Livingston, Ian S., and Michael O'Hanlon. *Afghanistan Index.* Washington, DC: Brookings Institution, September 2012.

Long, Austin. "After ISAF: Partners and Proxies in Afghanistan After 2014." *Small Wars & Insurgencies* 27, no. 1 (2016): 22–38. https://doi.org/10.1080/09592318.2016.1122901.

———. "The Anbar Awakening." *Survival* 50, no. 2 (2008): 67–94. https://doi.org/10.1080/00396330802034283.

———. "Partners or Proxies? U.S. and Host Nation Cooperation in Counterterrorism Operations." *CTC Sentinel* 4, no. 11 (2011): 11–14.

Long, Austin, Stephanie Pezard, Bryce Loidolt, and Todd C. Helmus. *Locals Rule: Historical Lessons for Creating Local Defense Forces for Afghanistan and Beyond.* Santa Monica, CA: RAND Corporation, 2012. https://www.rand.org/pubs/monographs/MG1232.html.

Looney, Robert. "The IMF's Return to Iraq." *Challenge* 49, no. 3 (2006): 26–47.

Loveluck, Louisa. "What's Non-lethal About Aid to the Syrian Opposition?" *Foreign Policy*, September 20, 2012. https://foreignpolicy.com/2012/09/20/whats-non-lethal-about-aid-to-the-syrian-opposition.

Loyal, Steven. "Bourdieu's Theory of the State." In *Bourdieu's Theory of the State*, edited by Steven Loyal, 67–82. New York: Palgrave Macmillan, 2017. https://doi.org/10.1057/978-1-137-58350-5_4.

Lund, Christian. *Twilight Institutions: Public Authority and Local Politics in Africa.* Malden, MA: Blackwell, 2006.

Lyall, Jason. "Are Coethnics More Effective Counterinsurgents? Evidence from the Second Chechen War." *American Political Science Review* 104, no. 1 (2010): 1–20.

Lyne, Mona M., Daniel L. Nielson, and Michael J. Tierney. "Who Delegates? Alternative Models of Principals in Development Aid." In *Delegation and Agency in International Organizations*, edited by Darren G. Hawkins, David A. Lake, Daniel L. Nielson, and Michael J. Tierney, 41–76. Cambridge: Cambridge University Press, 2006. https://doi.org/10.1017/CBO9780511491368.003.

MacAskill, Ewan. "UK to Send 75 Military Trainers to Help Moderate Syrian Rebels." *The Guardian*, March 26, 2015. https://www.theguardian.com/uk-news/2015/mar/26/uk-military-trainers-help-syrian-rebels.

MacDonald, Jason A. "Limitation Riders and Congressional Influence Over Bureaucratic Policy Decisions." *American Political Science Review* 104, no. 4 (2010): 766–782. https://doi.org/10.1017/S0003055410000432.

Mac Ginty, Roger. "Warlords and the Liberal Peace: State-Building in Afghanistan." *Conflict, Security & Development* 10, no. 4 (2010): 577–598. https://doi.org/10.1080/14678802.2010.500548.

Mac Ginty, Roger, and Oliver P Richmond. "The Local Turn in Peace Building: A Critical Agenda for Peace." *Third World Quarterly* 34, no. 5 (2013): 763–783. https://doi.org/10.1080/01436597.2013.800750.

Maguire, Dylan. *A Perfect Proxy? The United States-Syrian Democratic Forces Partnership*. Blacksburg, VA: Proxy Wars Project, Virginia Tech School of Public and International Affairs, 2020. https://doi.org/10.21061/proxy-wars-maguire.

Mahanty, Dan. "The 'Leahy Law' Prohibiting US Assistance to Human Rights Abusers: Pulling Back the Curtain." *Just Security*, June 27, 2017. https://www.justsecurity.org/42578/leahy-law-prohibiting-assistance-human-rights-abusers-pulling-curtain/.

Malejacq, Romain, and Dipali Mukhopadhyay. "The 'Tribal Politics' of Field Research: A Reflection on Power and Partiality in 21st-Century Warzones." *Perspectives on Politics* 14, no. 4 (2016): 1011–1028. https://doi.org/10.1017/S1537592716002899.

Maley, William. "Statebuilding in Afghanistan: Challenges and Pathologies." *Central Asian Survey* 32, no. 3 (2013): 255–270. https://doi.org/10.1080/02634937.2013.834719.

———. "Surviving in a War Zone: The Problem of Civilian Casualties in Afghanistan." In *Protecting Civilians During Violent Conflict: Theoretical and Practical Issues for the 21st Century*, edited by Igor Primoratz and David W. Lovell, 231–250. Aldershot, UK: Ashgate, 2012.

Malkasian, Carter. *The American War in Afghanistan*. Oxford: Oxford University Press, 2021.

———. *Illusions of Victory: The Anbar Awakening and the Rise of the Islamic State*. Oxford: Oxford University Press, 2017. https://doi.org/10.1080/00396330802034283.

Malley, Robert. "Why the Middle East Is More Combustible Than Ever." *Foreign Affairs*, October 2, 2019. https://www.foreignaffairs.com/articles/middle-east/2019-10-02/unwanted-wars.

Mann, Michael. "The Autonomous Power of the State: Its Origins, Mechanisms and Results." *European Journal of Sociology* 25, no. 2 (1984): 185–213.

Manners, Ian, and Richard G. Whitman. *The Foreign Policies of European Union Member States*. Manchester: Manchester University Press, 2000.

Mansour, Renad. *Iraq After the Fall of ISIS: The Struggle for the State*. London: Chatham House, 2017. https://www.chathamhouse.org/sites/default/files/publications/research/2017-07-04-iraq-after-isis-mansour-final.pdf.

Mansour, Renad, and Faleh Jabar. *The Popular Mobilization Forces and Iraq's Future*. Washington, DC: Carnegie Endowment for International Peace, 2017.

Mansour, Renad, and Peter Salisbury. *Between Order and Chaos: A New Approach to Stalled State Transformations in Iraq and Yemen*. London: Royal Institute for International Affairs at Chatham House, 2019.

Marshall, Alex. "From Civil War to Proxy War: Past History and Current Dilemmas." *Small Wars & Insurgencies* 27, no. 2 (2016): 183–195. https://doi.org/10.1080/09592318.2015.1129172.

Marten, Kimberly. "Warlords." In *The Changing Character of War*, edited by Hew Strachan and Sibylle Scheipers, 302–314. Oxford: Oxford University Press, 2011.

———. *Warlords: Strong-Arm Brokers in Weak States*. Ithaca, NY: Cornell University Press, 2012.

Martin, Lisa L., and Kathryn Sikkink. "U.S. Policy and Human Rights in Argentina and Guatemala, 1973–1980." In *Double-Edged Diplomacy: International Bargaining and Domestic Policy*, edited by Peter B. Evans, Harold K. Jacobson, and Robert D. Putnam, 330–362. Berkeley: California University Press, 1993.

Marton, Péter, and Nik Hynek. "'Liberal' Statebuilding in Afghanistan." In *Routledge Handbook of International Statebuilding*, edited by David Chandler and Timothy D Sisk, 304–314. London: Routledge, 2013.

Mashal, Mujib. "C.I.A.'s Afghan Forces Leave a Trail of Abuse and Anger." *New York Times*, December 31, 2018. https://www.nytimes.com/2018/12/31/world/asia/cia-afghanistan-strike-force.html?action=click&module=Top%20Stories&pgtype=Homepage.

———. "U.S. Plan for New Afghan Force Revives Fears of Militia Abuses." *New York Times*, September 15, 2017. https://www.nytimes.com/2017/09/15/world/asia/afghan-local-police.html.

Mazzetti, Mark. "C.I.A. Study of Covert Aid Fueled Skepticism About Helping Syrian Rebels." *New York Times*, October 14, 2014. https://www.nytimes.com/2014/10/15/us/politics/cia-study-says-arming-rebels-seldom-works.html.

———. *The Way of the Knife: The CIA, a Secret Army, and a War at the Ends of the Earth*. New York: Penguin Books, 2014.

Mazzetti, Mark, Jeffrey Gettleman, and Eric Schmitt. "In Somalia, U.S. Escalates a Shadow War." *New York Times*, October 16, 2016. https://www.nytimes.com/2016/10/16/world/africa/obama-somalia-secret-war.html.

McAdam, Doug, Sidney Tarrow, and Charles Tilly. *Dynamics of Contention*. Cambridge: Cambridge University Press, 2001.

McChrystal, Stanley. *COMISAF's Initial Assessment (Unclassified), 30 August 2009*. Kabul: Headquarters International Security Assistance Force, 2009.

———. "Secretary of Defense Memorandum 26 June 2009, Subject: Initial United States Forces—Afghanistan (USFOR-A) Assessment." June 26, 2009. https://static.nzz.ch/files/6/5/4/Afghanistan_Assessment_1.3630654.pdf.

McCleary, Paul, and Lara Jakes. "U.S. Works to Bring More Sunni Tribal Fighters Into Islamic State War." *Foreign Policy*, June 19, 2015. https://foreignpolicy.com/2015/06/10/more-u-s-advisers-in-iraq-to-train-sunni-tribes/.

McClintock, Michael. *Instruments of Statecraft: U.S. Guerrilla Warfare, Counter-Insurgency, and Counter-Terrorism, 1940–1990*. New York: Pantheon Books, 1992.

McCubbins, Matthew D., Roger G. Noll, and Barry R. Weingast. "Structure and Process, Politics and Policy: Administrative Arrangements and the Political Control of Agencies." *Virginia Law Review* 75, no. 2 (1989): 431–482.

McCubbins, Matthew D., and Thomas Schwartz. "Congressional Oversight Overlooked: Police Patrols Versus Fire Alarms." *American Journal of Political Science* 28, no. 1 (1984): 165–179. https://doi.org/10.2307/2110792.

McManus, Doyle. "Column: Trump's Brand of War Is Killing More Civilians Than Before." *Los Angeles Times*, September 8, 2019. https://www.latimes.com/politics/story/2019-09-07/trumps-shameful-rules-of-engagement-are-killing-civilians.

McNerney, Michael J., Jonah Blank, Becca Wasser, Jeremy Boback, and Alexander Stephenson. *Improving Implementation of the Department of Defense Leahy Law*. Santa Monica, CA: RAND Corporation, 2017. https://www.rand.org/pubs/research_reports/RR1737.html.

Megerisi, Tarek, and Andrew Lebovich. "France's Strongman Strategy in the Sahel." European Council on Foreign Relations, March 8, 2019. https://www.ecfr.eu/article/commentary_frances_strongman_strategy_in_the_sahel.

Mello, Patrick A. "Afghanistan: Unconditional Support but Selective Engagement?" In *Democratic Participation in Armed Conflict*. Basingstoke, UK: Palgrave Macmillan, 2014.

Mello, Patrick A., and Stephen M. Saideman. "The Politics of Multinational Military Operations." *Contemporary Security Policy* 40, no. 1 (2019): 30–37. https://doi.org/10.1080/13523260.2018.1522737.

Menkhaus, Ken. "Governance Without Government in Somalia: Spoilers, State Building, and the Politics of Coping." *International Security* 31, no. 3 (2006): 74–106. https://doi.org/10.1162/ISEC.2007.31.3.74.

———. *Non-state Security Providers and Political Formation in Somalia*. Geneva: Center for Security Governance, 2016.

"The Facts: What You Need to Know About the Syria Crisis." Mercy Corps, March 12, 2021. https://www.mercycorps.org/blog/quick-facts-syria-crisis#:~:text=In July 2012%2C.

Mertus, Julie A. *Bait and Switch: Human Rights and U.S. Foreign Policy*. New York: Routledge, 2008.

Migdal, Joel. "State Building and the Non-nation State." *Journal of International Affairs* 58, no. 1 (1994): 17–46.

———. *Strong Societies and Weak States: State-Society Relations and State Capabilities in the Third World*. Princeton, NJ: Princeton University Press, 1988. https://doi.org/10.2307/1963229.

Miller, Greg, and Karen DeYoung. "Secret CIA Effort in Syria Faces Large Funding Cut." *Washington Post*, December 6, 2015. https://www.washingtonpost.com/world/national-security/lawmakers-move-to-curb-1-billion-cia-program-to-train-syrian-rebels/2015/06/12/b0f45a9e-1114-11e5-adec-e82f8395c032_story.html.

Mitchell, Neil J., Sabine C. Carey, and Christopher K. Butler. "The Impact of Pro-Government Militias on Human Rights Violations." *International Interactions* 40, no. 5 (2014): 812–836. https://doi.org/10.1080/03050629.2014.932783.

Mitnick, Barry M. "The Theory of Agency: The Policing 'Paradox' and Regulatory Behavior." *Public Choice* 24 (1975): 27–42.

Moe, Terry M. "The New Economics of Organization." *American Journal of Political Science* 28, no. 4 (1984): 739–777.

Moghadam, Assaf, and Michel Wyss. "The Political Power of Proxies: Why Nonstate Actors Use Local Surrogates." *International Security* 44, no. 4 (2020): 119–157. https://doi.org/10.1080/09592318.

Monsuttie, Alessandro. "Fuzzy Sovereignty: Rural Reconstruction in Afghanistan, Between Democracy Promotion and Power Games." *Comparative Studies in Society and History* 54, no. 3 (2012): 563–591.

Moore, Molly. "CIA Falters in Recovery of Missiles." *Washington Post*, March 7, 1994. https://www.washingtonpost.com/archive/politics/1994/03/07/cia-falters-in-recovery-of-missiles/73a9a4d7-2952-4077-9746-46bd2e5b81ca/.

Morgan, Wesley. "Behind the Secret U.S. War in Africa." *Politico*, July 2, 2018. https://www.politico.com/story/2018/07/02/secret-war-africa-pentagon-664005.

Morrow, James D. "When Do States Follow the Laws of War?" *American Political Science Review* 101, no. 3 (2007): 559–572.

Moyar, Mark. *Village Stability Operations and the Afghan Local Police*. Tampa, FL: Joint Special Operations University, 2014.

Mukhopadhyay, Dipali. *Warlords, Strongman Governors, and the State in Afghanistan*. Cambridge: Cambridge University Press, 2014.

Mumford, Andrew. *Proxy Warfare*. Cambridge: Polity Press, 2013.

———. "Proxy Warfare and the Future of Conflict." *RUSI Journal* 158, no. 2 (2007): 40–46. https://doi.org/10.1080/03071847.2013.787733.

Munkler, Herfried. *The New Wars*. Cambridge: Polity Press, 2004.

Murtazashvili, Jennifer Brick. *Informal Order and the State in Afghanistan*. Cambridge: Cambridge University Press, 2016. https://doi.org/10.1017/CBO9781316286890.

Mustafa, Hasan. "The Moderate Rebels: A Growing List of Vetted Groups Fielding BGM-71 TOW Anti-tank Guided Missiles." *Hasan Mustafa* (blog), April 12, 2015. https://hasanmustafas.wordpress.com/2015/05/08/the-moderate-rebels-a-complete-and-growing-list-of-vetted-groups-fielding-tow-missiles/.

Myers, Steven Lee. "U.S. Joins Effort to Equip and Pay Rebels in Syria." *New York Times*, April 1, 2012. https://www.nytimes.com/2012/04/02/world/middleeast/us-and-other-countries-move-to-increase-assistance-to-syrian-rebels.html.

Naylor, Sean. *Relentless Strike: The Secret History of Joint Special Operations Command*. New York: St. Martin's Press, 2015.

Neier, Aryeh. *The International Human Rights Movement: A History*. Princeton, NJ: Princeton University Press, 2012.

Nordland, Rod. "After Airstrike, Afghan Points to C.I.A. and Secret Militias." *New York Times*, April 13, 2013. https://www.nytimes.com/2013/04/19/world/asia/after-airstrike-afghan-points-to-cia-and-secret-militias.html?pagewanted=all&_r=0.

Nordland, Rod, and Alissa J. Rubin. "Sunni Militiamen Say Iraq Didn't Keep Promises of Jobs." *New York Times*, March 23, 2009. https://www.nytimes.com/2009/03/24/world/middleeast/24sunni.html.

North, Douglass C., John Joseph Wallis, and Barry R. Weingast. *Violence and Social Orders: A Conceptual Framework for Interpreting Recorded Human History*. Cambridge: Cambridge University Press, 2009. https://doi.org/10.1017/CBO9780511575839.

Norton, Ben. "Leaked Hillary Clinton Emails Show U.S. Allies Saudi Arabia and Qatar Supported ISIS." *Salon*, October 11, 2016. https://www.salon.com/2016/10/11/leaked-hillary-clinton-emails-show-u-s-allies-saudi-arabia-and-qatar-supported-isis/.

Office of Audits. *Audit of Department of State Management and Oversight of Non-lethal Assistance Provided for the Syrian Crisis*. Washington, DC: Office of the Inspector General, U.S. Department of State, 2015.

———. *Audit of the Department of State Vetting Process for Syrian Non-lethal Assistance*. Washington, DC: Office of the Inspector General, U.S. Department of State, 2016.

Office of the Inspector General. *Operation Inherent Resolve: Report to the United States Congress (April 1, 2016—June 30, 2016)*. Washington, DC: U.S. Department of Defense, June 2016.

———. *(U) Evaluation of Combined Joint Interagency Task Force-Syria Vetting Process for New Syrian Forces (DoDIG-2015-175)*[redacted]. Washington, DC: U.S. Department of Defense, 2015. https://media.defense.gov/2019/Aug/22/2002174036/-1/-1/1/DODIG-2015-175.PDF.

———. *U.S. and Coalition Efforts to Train, Advise, Assist, and Equip Iraqi Sunni Popular Mobilization Forces (DODIG-2016-055)*. Washington, DC: U.S. Department of Defense, 2016.

Ogul, Morris S. *Congress Oversees the Bureaucracy*. Pittsburgh, PA: University of Pittsburgh Press, 1976.

O'Hanlon, Michael, and Nina Camp. *Iraq Index*. Washington, DC: Brookings Institution, December 2005.

O'Hanlon, Michael, and Jason H. Campbell. *Iraq Index*. Washington, DC: Brookings Institution, September 2008.

O'Keefe, Ed, and Paul Kane. "House Approves Obama's Iraq-Syria Military Strategy Amid Skepticism." *Washington Post*, September 17, 2014. https://www.washingtonpost.com/politics/congress-poised-to-approve-obamas-iraq-syria-military-strategy-amid-skepticism/2014/09/17/c2494df2-3e85-11e4-b0ea-8141703bbf6f_story.html.

Olsen, Johan P., and James G. March. "The Logic of Appropriateness." *ARENA Working Papers*, no. 9 (2004). https://www.sv.uio.no/arena/english/research/publications/arena-working-papers/2001-2010/2004/wp04_9.pdf.

Ormston, Rachel, Liz Spencer, Matt Barnard, and Dawn Snape. "The Foundations of Qualitative Research." In *Qualitative Research Practice: A Guide for Social Science Students and Researchers*, edited by Jane Ritchie, Jane Lewis, Carol McNaughton Nicholls, and Rachel Ormston, 1–26. London: SAGE Publications, 2014.

Pagonis, Jennifer. "Iraq: Rate of Displacement Rising." UNHCR, August 27, 2007. https://www.unhcr.org/en-us/news/briefing/2007/8/46d3f68f4/iraq-rate-displacement-rising.html.

Panetta, Leon E., and Jim Newton. *Worthy Fights: A Memoir of Leadership in War and Peace*. New York: Penguin Press, 2014.

Paris, Roland. *At War's End: Building Peace After Civil Conflict*. Cambridge: Cambridge University Press, 2007.

Paris, Roland, and Timothy D. Sisk, eds. *The Dilemmas of Statebuilding: Confronting the Contradictions of Postwar Peace Operations*. London: Routledge, 2009.

Parker, Ned. "The Conflict in Iraq: A Ministry of Fiefdoms." *Los Angeles Times*, July 30, 2007.

Partlow, Joshua, and Karen DeYoung. "Gen. Petraeus Runs Into Resistance from Karzai Over Village Defense Forces." *Washington Post*, July 10, 2010. http://www.washingtonpost.com/wp-dyn/content/article/2010/07/09/AR2010070905599.html.

Pavey, Andy. "US Security Assistance to Somalia." Stimson Center, March 20, 2023. https://www.stimson.org/2023/us-security-cooperation-with-somalia.

Peceny, Mark, and Yury Bosin. "Winning with Warlords in Afghanistan." *Small Wars & Insurgencies* 22, no. 4 (2011): 603–618. https://doi.org/10.1080/09592318.2011.599166.

Peic, Goran. "Civilian Defense Forces, State Capacity, and Government Victory in Counterinsurgency Wars." *Studies in Conflict & Terrorism* 37, no. 2 (2014): 162–184.

Perito, Robert. *Iraq's Interior Ministry: Frustrating Reform*. Washington, DC: United States Institute of Peace, 2008. https://www.usip.org/sites/default/files/PB-Iraq-Interior-5-08.PDF.

Phillips, Christopher. *Into the Quagmire: Turkey's Frustrated Syria Policy*. London: Royal Institute of International Affairs at Chatham House, 2012.

Phillips, Jonathan. "Mercenaries, Private Military Contractors, and Non-traditional Forces." In *Blackwell Companions to American History: A Companion to American Military History*, edited by James C. Bradford, 507–516. Oxford: Blackwell, 2010.

Pirnie, Bruce R., and Edward O'Connell. *Counterinsurgency in Iraq (2003–2006)*. Arlington, VA: RAND Corporation, 2008.

Plana, Sara. *"Proxies" and the Public: Testing the Statist Bias in Public Support for Military Aid*. Cambridge, MA: Massachusetts Institute of Technology, Political Science Department, 2020.

Policy and Operations Evaluation Department. *Review of the Monitoring Systems of Three Projects in Syria AJACS, White Helmets and NLA*. The Hague: Netherlands Ministry of Foreign Affairs, 2018.

Pollack, Mark A. "Delegation, Agency, and Agenda Setting in the European Community." *International Organization* 51, no. 1 (1997): 99–134.

———. *The Engines of European Integration: Delegation, Agency, and Agenda Setting in the EU*. Oxford: Oxford University Press, 2003. https://doi.org/10.1093/0199251177.001.0001.

Ponzio, Richard J. *Democratic Peacebuilding: Aiding Afghanistan and Other Fragile States*. Oxford: Oxford University Press, 2011. https://doi.org/10.1093/ACPROF:OSO/9780199594955.001.0001.

Powell, Nathaniel K. "'Experts in Decolonization?' French Statebuilding and Counterinsurgency in Chad, 1969–1972." *International History Review* 42, no. 2 (2020): 318–335. https://doi.org/10.1080/07075332.2019.1588769.

Powell, Robert. "Bargaining Theory and International Conflict." *Annual Review of Political Science* 5 (2002): 1–30.

Price, Richard. "Reversing the Gun Sights: Transnational Civil Society Targets Land Mines." *International Organization* 52, no. 3 (1998): 613–644.

———. "Transnational Civil Society and Advocacy in World Politics." *World Politics* 55, no. 4 (July 2003): 579–606. https://doi.org/10.1353/wp.2003.0024.

Purkiss, Jessica, Abigail Fielding-Smith, and Emran Feroz. "CIA-Backed Afghan Unit Accused of Atrocities Is Able to Call in Air Strikes." Bureau of Investigative Journalism, February 8, 2019. https://www.thebureauinvestigates.com/stories/2019-02-08/cia-backed-afghan-unit-atrocities.

Putnam, Robert D. "Diplomacy and Domestic Politics: The Logic of Two-Level Games." *International Organization* 42, no. 3 (1988): 427–460.

Qin, Amy, and Amy Chang Chien. "Watching the War in Ukraine, Taiwanese Draw Lessons in Self-Reliance." *New York Times*, March 1, 2022. https://www.nytimes.com/2022/03/01/world/asia/ukraine-taiwan-china-russia.html.

Quilty, Andrew. "The CIA's Afghan Death Squads." *The Intercept*, December 18, 2020. https://theintercept.com/2020/12/18/afghanistan-cia-militia-01-strike-force/.

Raghavan, Sudarsan. "CIA Runs Shadow War with Afghan Militia Implicated in Civilian Killings." *Washington Post*, December 13, 2015. https://www.washingtonpost.com/world/cia-backed-afghan-militias-fight-a-shadow-war/2015/12/02/fe5a0526-913f-11e5-befa-99ceebcbb272_story.html.

Raleigh, Clionadh. "Violence Against Civilians: A Disaggregated Analysis." *International Interactions* 38, no. 4 (2012): 462–481. https://doi.org/10.1080/03050629.2012.697049.

Ramani, Samuel. "Why France Is So Deeply Entangled in Syria." *Washington Post*, November 19, 2015.

Rashid, Bedir Mulla. *Military and Security Structures in the Autonomous Administration of Syria*. Istanbul: Omran Center for Strategic Studies, 2018.

Reid, Rachel. *"Just Don't Call It a Militia": Impunity, Militias, and the "Afghan Local Police."* New York: Human Rights Watch, 2011.

Rempfer, Kyle. "Special Operations Launches 'Secret Surrogate' Missions in New Counter-Terrorism Strategy." *Military Times*, February 8, 2018. https://www.militarytimes.com/news/your-army/2019/02/08/fighting-terrorism-may-rely-on-secret-surrogate-forces-going-forward/.

Reno, William. "Persistent Insurgencies and Warlords: Who Is Nasty, Who Is Nice, and Why?" In *Ungoverned Spaces: Alternatives to State Authority in an Era of Softened Sovereignty*, edited by Anne L. Clunan and Harold A. Trinkunas, 57–76. Stanford, CA: Stanford University Press, 2010.

Republic of Austria. "The Austrian Position on Arms Embargo in Syria." *The Guardian*, May 15, 2013. https://www.theguardian.com/world/julian-borger-global-security-blog/interactive/2013/may/15/austria-eu-syria-arms-embargo-pdf

Richmond, Oliver P., ed. *A Post-Liberal Peace*. London: Routledge, 2011.

———. "The Problem of Peace: Understanding the 'Liberal Peace.'" *Conflict, Security & Development* 6, no. 3 (2006): 291–314.

Ricks, Thomas E. *Fiasco: The American Military Adventure in Iraq*. London: Allen Lane, 2006.

———. *The Gamble: General David Petraeus and the American Military Adventure in Iraq, 2006–2008*. New York: Penguin Press, 2009.

Risse, Thomas. "Governance Under Limited Sovereignty." In *Back to Basics: State Power in a Contemporary World*, edited by Martha Finnemore and Judith Goldstein, 78–104. Oxford: Oxford University Press, 2013. https://doi.org/10.1093/acprof:oso/9780199970087.003.0005.

———, ed. *Governance Without a State? Policies and Politics in Areas of Limited Statehood*. New York: Columbia University Press, 2011.

———. "Transnational Actors and World Politics." In *Handbook of International Relations*, edited by Walter Carlsnaes, Thomas Risse, and Beth Simmons, 255–274. London: SAGE Publications, 2002.

Risse, Thomas, Anke Draude, and Tanja A. Börzel, eds. *The Oxford Handbook of Governance and Limited Statehood*. Oxford: Oxford University Press, 2018.

Risse, Thomas, and Stephen C. Ropp. "International Human Rights Norms and Domestic Change: Conclusions." In *The Power of Human Rights: International Human Rights Norms and Domestic Change*, edited by Thomas Risse, Stephen C. Ropp, and Kathryn Sikkink, 234–278. Cambridge: Cambridge University Press, 1999.

Risse, Thomas, Stephen C. Ropp, and Kathryn Sikkink, eds. *The Power of Human Rights: International Norms and Domestic Change*. Cambridge: Cambridge University Press, 1999.

Risse, Thomas, and Kathryn Sikkink. *The Power of Principles: The Socialization of Human Rights Norms in Domestic Practice*. Cambridge; New York: Cambridge University Press, 1999.

Risse-Kappen, Thomas, ed. *Bringing Transnational Relations Back In: Non-state Actors, Domestic Structures and International Institutions*. Cambridge University Press, 1995. https://doi.org/10.1017/cbo9780511598760.

———. *Cooperation Among Democracies: The European Influence on U.S. Foreign Policy*. Princeton, NJ: Princeton University Press, 1995.

———. "Introduction." In *Bringing Transnational Relations Back In: Non-state Actors, Domestic Structures, and International Institutions*, edited by Thomas Risse-Kappen, 3–33. Cambridge: Cambridge University Press, 1995. https://doi.org/10.1017/CBO9780511598760.

Robinson, Linda. *Tell Me How This Ends: General David Petraeus and the Search for a Way out of Iraq*. Washington, DC: PublicAffairs, 2008.

Roehner, Bertrand M., and Tony Syme. *Pattern and Repertoire in History*. Cambridge, MA: Harvard University Press, 2013. https://doi.org/10.4159/harvard.9780674418479.

Rogin, Josh. "McCain to Call for Air Strikes on Syria." *Foreign Policy*, March 5, 2012. https://foreignpolicy.com/2012/03/05/mccain-to-call-for-air-strikes-on-syria/.

Romano, David, Brian Calfano, and Robert Phelps. "Successful and Less Successful Interventions: Stabilizing Iraq and Afghanistan." *International Studies Perspectives* 16, no. 4 (2015): 388–405.

Rondeaux, Candace, and David Sterman. *Twenty-First Century Proxy Warfare: Confronting Strategic Innovation in a Multipolar World Since the 2011*. Washington, DC: New America Foundation and Arizona State University's Center on the Future of War, 2019. https://www.newamerica.org/international-security/reports/twenty-first-century-proxy-warfare-confronting-strategic-innovation-multipolar-world/.

Rosati, Jerel A. "Developing a Systematic Decision-Making Framework: Bureaucratic Politics in Perspective." *World Politics* 33, no. 2 (1981): 234–252.

Rosen, Nir. *Aftermath: Following the Bloodshed of America's Wars in the Muslim World*. New York: Nation Books, 2010.

———. "The Myth of the Surge." *Rolling Stone*, February 2008, 46–53.

Rosenau, James N. "Pre-theories and Theories of Foreign Policy-Making." In *Approaches in Comparative and International Politics*, edited by R. B. Farrell, 115–169. Evanston, IL: Northwestern University Press, 1966.

Rosenau, James N., and Ernst Otto Czempiel, eds. *Governance Without Government: Order and Change in World Politics*. Cambridge: Cambridge University Press, 1992.

Rosenau, William, and Zack Gold. *The Cheapest Insurance in the World? The United States and Proxy Warfare*. Washington, DC: Center for Naval Affairs, 2019.

Rosenblatt, Nate, and David Kilcullen. *The Tweet of Damocles: Lessons for U.S. Proxy Warfare*. Washington, DC: New America Foundation, 2020. https://www.newamerica.org/international-security/reports/tweet-damocles/.

Ross, Stephen. "The Economic Theory of Agency: The Principal's Problem." *American Economic Review* 63, no. 2 (1973): 134–139. https://doi.org/10.2307/1817064.

Rotberg, Robert I. *State Failure and State Weakness in a Time of Terror*. Washington, DC: Brookings Institution Press, 2003.

———. *When States Fail: Causes and Consequences*. Princeton, NJ: Princeton University Press, 2010.

Roy, Olivier. *Islam and Resistance in Afghanistan*. Cambridge: Cambridge University Press, 1986.

Rubin, Alissa J., and Damien Cave. "In a Force for Iraqi Calm, Seeds of Future Conflict." *New York Times*, December 23, 2007. https://www.nytimes.com/2007/12/23/world/middleeast/23awakening.html.

Rubin, Alissa J., and Richard A. Oppel. "U.S. and Afghanistan Debate More Village Forces." *New York Times*, July 12, 2010. https://www.nytimes.com/2010/07/13/world/asia/13afghan.html?_r=2&ref=world.

Rubin, Barnett R. *The Fragmentation of Afghanistan*. New Haven, CT: Yale University Press, 2002.

Ruys, Tom. "Of Arms, Funding and 'Non-lethal Assistance'—Issues Surrounding Third-State Intervention in the Syrian Civil War." *Chinese Journal of International Law* 13, no. 1 (2014): 13–53. https://doi.org/10.1093/chinesejil/jmu003.

Ryan, Missy. "In Syrian Border Battle, Pentagon Touts Role of Fighters from Troubled Train-and-Equip Program." *Washington Post*, August 24, 2016. https://www.washingtonpost.com/news/checkpoint/wp/2016/08/24/in-syrian-border-battle-pentagon-touts-role-of-fighters-from-troubled-train-and-equip-program/.

Ryan, Missy, Karen DeYoung, and Craig Whitlock. "Pentagon Plans Major Shift in Effort to Counter the Islamic State in Syria." *Washington Post*, October 9, 2015. https://www.washingtonpost.com/world/national-security/pentagon-plans-sharp-scaledown-in-efforts-to-train-syrian-rebels/2015/10/09/78a2553c-6e80-11e5-9bfe-e59f5e244f92_story.html?itid=lk_inline_manual_13.

Ryan, Missy, and Greg Miller. "U.S. Prepares to Send First Group of Syrian Fighters Back Onto Battlefield." *Washington Post*, July 2, 2015. https://www.washingtonpost.com/world/national-security/us-prepares-to-send-first-group-of-syrian-fighters-back-onto-battlefield/2015/07/02/6540be30-20dc-11e5-bf41-c23f5d3face1_story.html.

Sabbagh, Dan. "UK and France to Send Further Forces to Syria in Aid of US Withdrawal." *The Guardian*, July 9, 2019. https://www.theguardian.com/world/2019/jul/09/uk-and-france-to-send-further-forces-to-syria-in-aid-of-us-withdrawal.

Sadaki, Youssef. "The MOC's Role in the Collapse of the Southern Opposition." *Syria Source* (blog), Atlantic Council, September 23, 2016. https://www.atlanticcouncil.org/blogs/syriasource/the-moc-s-role-in-the-collapse-of-the-southern-opposition.

Salehyan, Idean. "The Delegation of War to Rebel Organizations." *Journal of Conflict Resolution* 54, no. 3 (2010): 493–515. https://doi.org/10.1177/0022002709357890.

Salehyan, Idean, Kristian Skrede Gleditsch, and David E. Cunningham. "Explaining External Support for Insurgent Groups." *International Organization* 65, no. 4 (2011): 709–744. https://doi.org/10.1017/S0020818311000233.

Salehyan, Idean, David Siroky, and Reed M. Wood. "External Rebel Sponsorship and Civilian Abuse: A Principal-Agent Analysis of Wartime Atrocities" 68, no. 3 (2014): 633–661. https://doi.org/10.1017/S002081831400006X.

San-Akca, Belgin. *States in Disguise: Causes of State Support for Rebel Groups*. Cambridge: Cambridge University, 2016.

Sanger, David E., Eric Schmitt, and Ben Hubbard. "Trump Ends Covert Aid to Syrian Rebels Trying to Topple Assad." *New York Times*, July 19, 2017. https://www.nytimes.com/2017/07/19/world/middleeast/cia-arming-syrian-rebels.html.

Saum-Manning, Lisa. *VSO/ALP: Comparing Past and Current Challenges to Afghan Local Defense*. RAND Working Paper. Washington, DC: RAND Corporation, December 2012.

Savage, James D. *Reconstructing Iraq's Budgetary Institutions: Coalition Statebuilding After Saddam*. Cambridge: Cambridge University Press, 2013.

Sayigh, Yezid. "Hybridizing Security: Armies, Militias and Constrained Sovereignty." Carnegie Middle East Center, October 30, 2018. https://carnegie-mec.org/2018/10/30/hybridizing-security-armies-militias-and-constrained-sovereignty-pub-77597.

Schmitt, Eric. "C.I.A. Said to Aid in Steering Arms to Syrian Rebels." *New York Times*, June 21, 2012. https://www.nytimes.com/2012/06/21/world/middleeast/cia-said-to-aid-in-steering-arms-to-syrian-rebels.html.

Schmitt, Olivier. "More Allies, Weaker Missions? How Junior Partners Contribute to Multinational Military Operations." *Contemporary Security Policy* 40, no. 1 (2019): 70–84. https://doi.org/10.1080/13523260.2018.1501999.

Schneider, Gerald. "Capacity and Concessions: Bargaining Power in Multilateral Negotiations." *Millenium: Journal of International Studies* 33 (2005): 665–689.

Schroeder, Ursula C., and Cornelius Friesendorf. "State-Building and Organized Crime: Implementing the International Law Enforcement Agenda in Bosnia." *Journal of International Relations and Development* 12, no. 2 (2009): 137–167. https://doi.org/10.1057/jird.2009.1.

Sedra, Mark. "Adapting Security Sector Reform to Ground-Level Realities: The Transition to a Second-Generation Model." *Journal of Intervention and Statebuilding* 12, no. 1 (2018): 48–63. https://doi.org/10.1080/17502977.2018.1426383.

Serafino, Nina M., June S. Beittel, Lauren Ploch Blanchard, and Liana Rosen. *"Leahy Law" Human Rights Provisions and Security Assistance.* Washington, DC: Congressional Research Service, 2014.

Shapiro, Jeremy, and Miriam R. Estrin. "The Proxy War Problem in Syria." Brookings Institution, February 4, 2014. https://www.brookings.edu/opinions/the-proxy-war-problem-in-syria/.

Shapiro, Susan P. "Agency Theory." *Annual Review of Sociology* 31 (2005): 263–284.

Sharp, Jeremy M., and Christopher M. Blanchard. *Armed Conflict in Syria: Background and U.S. Response*, RL33487. Washington, DC: Congressional Research Service, September 2013. https://www.globalsecurity.org/military/library/report/crs/rl33487_130906.pdf.

Shear, Michael D., Helene Cooper, and Eric Schmitt. "Obama Administration Ends Effort to Train Syrians to Combat ISIS." *New York Times*, October 10, 2015. https://www.nytimes.com/2015/10/10/world/middleeast/pentagon-program-islamic-state-syria.html.

Sheikh, Safa Rasul al-, and Emma Sky. "Iraq Since 2003: Perspectives on a Divided Society." *Survival* 53, no. 4 (August 2011): 119–142. https://doi.org/10.1080/00396338.2011.603565.

Shurkin, Michael, and Bernard, Anelise. "Ten Things the United States Should Do to Combat Terrorism in the Sahel." *War on the Rocks*, August 30, 2021. https://warontherocks.com/2021/08/ten-things-the-united-states-should-do-to-combat-terrorism-in-the-sahel/.

Sifton, John. "Afghanistan's U.S.-Funded Torturers and Murderers." Human Rights Watch, March 6, 2015. https://www.hrw.org/news/2015/03/06/afghanistans-us-funded-torturers-and-murderers.

SIGAR (Special Inspector General for Afghanistan Reconstruction). *Afghan Local Police: A Critical Rural Security Initiative Lacks Adequate Logistics Support, Oversight, and Direction*, SIGAR 16-3-AR. Washington, DC: Special Inspector General for Afghanistan Reconstruction, 2015.

——. *Child Sexual Assault in Afghanistan: Implementation of the Leahy Laws and Reports of Assault by Afghan Security Forces*, SIGAR 17-47-IP. Washington, DC: Special Inspector General for Afghanistan Reconstruction, 2018.

——. *Quarterly Report to the United States Congress July 2018*. Washington, DC: Special Inspector General for Afghanistan Reconstruction, 2018.

——. *Stabilization: Lessons from the U.S. Experience in Afghanistan*. Washington, DC: Special Inspector General for Afghanistan Reconstruction, 2018.

SIGIR (Office of the Special Inspector General for Iraq Reconstruction). *Commander's Emergency Response Program in Iraq Funds Many Large-Scale Projects*. Washington, DC: Office of the Special Inspector General for Iraq Reconstruction, 2008.

——. *Hard Lessons: The Iraq Reconstruction*. Washington, DC: Special Inspector General for Iraq Reconstruction, 2009.

——. *Lessons Learned on the Department of Defense's Commander's Emergency Response Program in Iraq (13-005)*. Washington, DC: Office of the Special Inspector General for Iraq Reconstruction, 2013.

Sly, Liz. "The Rise and Ugly Fall of a Moderate Syrian Rebel Offers Lessons for the West." *Washington Post*, January 5, 2015. https://www.washingtonpost.com/world/middle_east

/the-rise-and-ugly-fall-of-a-moderate-syrian-rebel-offers-lessons-for-the-west/2015/01/04/3889db38-80da-4974-b1ef-1886f4183624_story.html?utm_term=.2b73d78c4d9c.
Smith, Steve, and Michael Clarke. *Foreign Policy Implementation*. London: G. Allen and Unwin, 1985.
Snider, L. Britt. *The Agency and the Hill: The CIA's Relationship with Congress (1946–2004)*. Scotts Valley, CA: CreateSpace, 2008.
Snyder, Richard C., H. W. Bruck, and Burton Sapin. *Decision-Making as an Approach to the Study of International Politics*. Princeton, NJ: Princeton University Press, 1954.
Solomon, Erika. "The Rise and Fall of a US-Backed Rebel Commander in Syria." *Financial Times*, February 9, 2017. https://www.ft.com/content/791ad3bc-ecfc-11e6-930f-061b01e23655.
Sopko, John F. *What We Need to Learn: Lessons from 20 Years of Afghan Reconstruction*. Washington, DC: Special Inspector General for Afghanistan Reconstruction, 2021.
Sprout, Harold, and Margaret Sprout. "Environmental Factors in the Study of International Politics." *Journal of Conflict Resolution* 1, no. 4 (1957): 309–328.
Stabilizing Iraq from the Bottom Up: Testimony Before the Committee on Foreign Relations, 110th Cong., 2d Sess. (April 2, 2008). https://www.govinfo.gov/content/pkg/CHRG-110shrg47921/pdf/CHRG-110shrg47921.pdf.
Stark, Alexandra. *The Monarch's Pawns? Gulf State Proxy Warfare 2011–Today*. Washington, DC: New America Foundation and Arizona State University's Center on the Future of War, 2020. https://www.newamerica.org/international-security/reports/the-monarchs-pawns/.
Stark, Holger, and Matthias Gebauer. "Deutschland Liefert Schusswesten an Assad-Gegner." *Der Spiegel*, May 26, 2013. http://www.spiegel.de/politik/ausland/syrien-deutschland-liefert-schusswesten-an-assad-gegner-a-901956.html.
"Statement of General Raymond A. Thomas, III, U.S. Army Commander United States Special Operations Command Before the House Armed Services Committee Subcommittee on Emerging Threats and Capabilities." U.S. House of Representatives, May 2, 2017. https://docs.house.gov/meetings/AS/AS26/20170502/105926/HHRG-115-AS26-Wstate-ThomasR-20170502.PDF.
Stein, Aaron. *Partner Operations in Syria: Lessons Learned and the Way Forward*. Washington, DC: Atlantic Council, 2017.
——. "Reconciling U.S.-Turkish Interests in Northern Syria." Council of Foreign Relations, February 13, 2017. https://www.cfr.org/report/reconciling-us-turkish-interests-northern-syria.
——. "The Origins of Turkey's Buffer Zone in Syria." *War on the Rocks*, December 11, 2014. https://warontherocks.com/2014/12/the-origins-of-turkeys-buffer-zone-in-syria/.
Stein, Jeff. "Inside the CIA's Syrian Rebels Vetting Machine." *Newsweek*, November 10, 2014. http://www.newsweek.com/2014/11/21/moderate-rebels-please-raise-your-hands-283449.html.
Steinert, Christoph V., Janina I. Steinert, and Sabine C. Carey. "Spoilers of Peace: Pro-Government Militias as Risk Factors for Conflict Recurrence." *Journal of Peace Research* 56, no. 2 (2019): 2490263. https://doi.org/10.1177/0022343318800524.

Stengel, Frank A., and Rainer Baumann. "Non-state Actors and Foreign Policy." In *The Oxford Encyclopedia of Foreign Policy Analysis*, edited by Cameron G. Thies. Oxford: Oxford University Press, 2017. https://doi.org/10.1093/acrefore/9780190228637.013.456.

Stern, Eric, and Bertjan Verbeek, eds. "Whither the Study of Governmental Politics in Foreign Policymaking? A Symposium." *Mershon International Studies Review* 42 (1998): 205–255.

Suhrke, Astri. "The Long Decade of State-Building in Afghanistan." In *Managing Conflict in a World Adrift*, edited by Chester A. Crocker, Fen Osler Hampson, and Pamela Aall, 555–570. Washington, DC: United States Institute of Peace, 2015.

——. "Statebuilding in Afghanistan: A Contradictory Engagement." *Central Asian Survey* 32, no. 3 (2013): 271–286. https://doi.org/10.1080/02634937.2013.834715.

——. *When More Is Less: The International Project in Afghanistan*. London: C. Hurst and Co., 2011.

Suhrke, Astri, and Antonio De Lauri. *The CIA's "Army": A Threat to Human Rights and an Obstacle to Peace in Afghanistan*. Providence, RI: Watson Institute of Public and International Affairs, Brown University, 2019.

"Syria: Kurdish Forces Violating Child Soldier Ban." Human Rights Watch, July 15, 2015. https://www.hrw.org/news/2015/07/10/syria-kurdish-forces-violating-child-soldier-ban-0.

"Syria: US Ally's Razing of Villages Amounts to War Crimes." Amnesty International, October 13, 2015. https://www.amnesty.org/en/latest/news/2015/10/syria-us-allys-razing-of-villages-amounts-to-war-crimes/.

Szuma, Jared. "ISIS's 'Caliphate' Was Crushed. Now Syria's Kurd-Led Alliance Faces Bigger Battles." *Defense Post*, March 29, 2019. https://www.thedefensepost.com/2019/03/29/syria-sdf-kurds-face-bigger-battles-isis/.

Tariq, Mohammed Osman. *Tribal Security System (Arbakai) in Southeast Afghanistan*. London: Crisis States Research Center, London School of Economics, 2008.

Tarnoff, Curt. *Iraq: Reconstruction Assistance*, RL31833. Washington, DC: Congressional Research Service, August 2009. https://crsreports.congress.gov/product/pdf/RL/RL31833/40.

Tarrow, Sidney. *Power in Movement: Social Movements, Collective Action and Politics*. Cambridge: Cambridge University Press, 1998.

Tate, Winifred. *Counting the Dead: The Culture and Politics of Human Rights Activism in Colombia*. Berkeley: University of California Press, 2007.

——. "Human Rights Law and Military Aid Delivery: A Case Study of the Leahy Law." *Political and Legal Anthropology Review* 34, no. 2 (2011): 337–354.

Terrorist March in Iraq: The U.S. Response: Hearing Before the Committee on Foreign Affairs. 113th Cong., 2d Sess. (July 23, 2014). https://www.govinfo.gov/app/details/CHRG-113hhrg88829/context.

Terse, Nick. *The Changing Face of Empire: Special Ops, Drones, Spies, Proxy Fighters, Secret Bases and Cyber Warfare*. Chicago: Haymarket, 2012.

——. "Special Operations Forces Continue to Expand Across the World—Without Congressional Oversight." *The Nation*, July 17, 2018. https://www.thenation.com/article/archive

/special-operations-forces-continue-expand-across-world-without-congressional-oversight/.

"Testimony of Deputy Assistant Secretary Brett McGurk, House Foreign Affairs Committee Hearing: Iraq." U.S. House of Representatives, February 5, 2014. http://docs.house.gov/meetings/FA/FA00/20140205/101716/HHRG-113-FA00-Wstate-McGurkB-20140205.pdf

The Authorization of the Use of Force in Syria: Hearings Before the Committee on Foreign Relations, 113th Cong., 1st Sess. (September 3, 2013). https://www.foreign.senate.gov/imo/media/doc/090313_Transcript_The Authorization of the Use of Force in Syria.pdf.

Thomas, Daniel C. *The Helsinki Effect: International Norms, Human Rights, and the Demise of Communism*. Princeton, NJ: Princeton University Press, 2001.

Thornton, Rod. "Problems with the Kurds as Proxies Against Islamic State: Insights from the Siege of Kobane." *Small Wars & Insurgencies* 26, no. 6 (2015): 865–885. https://doi.org/10.1080/09592318.2015.1095844.

Tilly, Charles. *Big Structures, Large Processes, Huge Comparisons*. New York: Russell Sage, 1985.

———. "War Making and State Making as Organized Crime." In *Bringing the State Back In*, edited by Peter B. Evans, Dietrich Rueschemeyer, and Theda Skocpol, 169–191. Cambridge: Cambridge University Press, 2010. https://doi.org/10.1017/cbo9780511628283.008.

"A Timeline of the US Involvement in Syria's Conflict." Associated Press, January 11, 2019. https://apnews.com/article/96701a254c5a448cb253f14ab697419b.

Townsend, Brad. "The Development and Creation of the Afghanistan National Army Territorial Forces." *Military Review*, March 2019, 74–81.

Trofimov, Yaroslav. "After Afghan Raid, Focus on Captors." *Wall Street Journal*, March 11, 2013. http://www.wsj.com/articles/SB10001424127887323826704578354563161104832.

Tsurkov, Elizabeth, and Esam Al-Hassan. "Kurdish-Arab Power Struggle in Northeastern Syria." Carnegie Endowment for International Peace, July 24, 2019. https://carnegieendowment.org/sada/79542.

UNAMA (United Nations Assistance Mission in Afghanistan). *Human Rights in Afghanistan: 15 August 2021–15 June 2022*. Kabul: Office of the High Commissioner for Human Rights, 2022.

———. *Protection of Civilians in Armed Conflict Annual Report 2010*. Kabul: Office of the High Commissioner for Human Rights, 2011.

———. *Protection of Civilians in Armed Conflict Annual Report 2011*. Kabul: Office of the High Commissioner for Human Rights, 2012.

———. *Protection of Civilians in Armed Conflict Annual Report 2012*. Kabul: Office of the High Commissioner for Human Rights, 2013.

———. *Protection of Civilians in Armed Conflict Annual Report 2013*. Kabul: Office of the High Commissioner for Human Rights, 2014.

———. *Protection of Civilians in Armed Conflict Annual Report 2014*. Kabul: Office of the High Commissioner for Human Rights, 2015.

———. *Protection of Civilians in Armed Conflict Annual Report 2015*. Kabul: Office of the High Commissioner for Human Rights, 2016.

———. *Protection of Civilians in Armed Conflict Annual Report 2016*. Kabul: United Nations Assistance Mission in Afghanistan Human Rights Unit, 2017.

———. *Update on the Treatment of Conflict-Related Detainees in Afghan Custody: Accountability and Implementation of Presidential Decree 129.* Kabul: Office of the High Commissioner for Human Rights, 2015.

"UNDP Trains Vigilantes and Civilian Joint Task Force Members in Human Rights and Leadership." United Nations Development Programme, July 9, 2019. https://www.undp.org/nigeria/news/undp-trains-vigilantes-and-civilian-joint-task-force-members-human-rights-and-leadership.

"US and UK Suspend Non-lethal Aid for Syria Rebels." *BBC News*, December 11, 2013. https://www.bbc.com/news/world-middle-east-25331241.

"U.S. General Told Syria's YPG: 'You Have Got to Change Your Brand.'" Reuters, April 12, 2017. https://www.reuters.com/article/us-mideast-crisis-usa-ypg/u-s-general-told-syrias-ypg-you-have-got-to-change-your-brand-idUSKBN1A62SS.

U.S. House of Representatives, Committee on Oversight and Government Reform, Subcommittee on National Security and Foreign Affairs. *Warlord, Inc.: Extortion and Corruption Along the U.S. Supply Chain in Afghanistan: Report of the Majority Staff of the Subcommittee on National Security and Foreign Affairs.* Washington, DC: Committee on Oversight and Government Reform, June 2010. https://www.hsdl.org/?abstract&did=23047.

U.S. Policy Towards Iraq and Syria and the Threat Posed by the Islamic State of Iraq and the Levant (ISIL): Hearing Before the Armed Services Committee. 113th Cong., 2d Sess. (September 16, 2014). https://www.govinfo.gov/content/pkg/CHRG-113shrg93641/html/CHRG-113shrg93641.htm.

"U.S. Security Assistance and Human Rights." Brookings Institution, December 12, 2016. https://www.brookings.edu/events/u-s-security-assistance-and-human-rights/.

"U.S. Sets Aside $25 Million for Non-lethal Aid to Syria Rebels." Reuters, August 1, 2012. https://www.reuters.com/article/us-syria-crisis-usa-idUSBRE8701DU20120801.

Van Wilgenburg, Wladimir, and Mario Fumertonn. *Kurdistan's Political Armies: The Challenge of Unifying the Peshmerga Forces.* Beirut: Carnegie Middle East Center, 2015.

Vincent, Sam, Florian Weigand, and Hameed Hakimi. "The Afghan Local Police—Closing the Security Gap?" *Stability: International Journal of Security and Development* 4, no. 1 (2015). https://doi.org/10.5334/sta.gg.

Vlassenroot, Koen. "War and Social Research: The Limits of Empirical Methodologies in War-Torn Environments." *Civilisations* 54, no. 1 (2006): 191–198.

Votel, Joseph L., and Eero R. Keravuori. "The By-With-Through Operational Approach." *Joint Force Quarterly* 89, no. 2 (2018): 40–47.

Waldman, Thomas. "Strategic Narratives and US Surrogate Warfare." *Survival* 61, no. 1 (2019): 161–178. https://doi.org/10.1080/00396338.2019.1568049.

———. "Vicarious Warfare: The Counterproductive Consequences of Modern American Military Practice." *Contemporary Security Policy* 39, no. 2 (2018): 181–205. https://doi.org/10.1080/13523260.2017.1393201.

Walker, Robert. "State Sovereignty and the Articulation of Political Space/Time." *Millenium* 20, no. 3 (1991): 445–461. https://doi.org/10.1177/03058298910200030201.

Wall, Andru E. "Demystifying the Title 10-Title 50 Debate: Distinguishing Military Operations, Intelligence Activities & Covert Action." *Harvard National Security Journal* 3 (2011): 85–142.

Ward, Steven R. "The Continuing Evolution of Iran's Military Doctrine." *Middle East Journal* 59, no. 4 (2005): 559–576. https://doi.org/10.3751/59.4.12.

Watling, Jack, and Nick Reynolds. *War by Others' Means: Delivering Effective Partner Force Capacity Building.* London: Routledge, 2020.

Weber, Michael A. "Child Soldiers Prevention Act of 2008: Security Assistance Restrictions." *In Focus*, Congressional Research Service, July 10, 2019. https://fas.org/sgp/crs/misc/IF10901.pdf.

Wehrey, Frederic M., and Ariel I. Ahram. *Taming the Militias: Building National Guards in Fractured Arab States.* Washington, DC: Carnegie Endowment for International Peace, 2015.

Weingast, Barry R. "The Congressional-Bureaucratic System: A Principal Agent Perspective (with Applications to the SEC)." *Carnegie Papers on Political Economy* 44, no. 1 (1984): 147–191.

Weingast, Barry R., and Mark J. Moran. "Bureaucratic Discretion or Congressional Control? Regulatory Policymaking by the Federal Trade Commission." *Journal of Political Economy* 91, no. 5 (2015): 765–800. https://doi.org/10.1086/261181.

Weisman, Jonathan. "House Votes to Authorize Aid to Syrian Rebels in ISIS Fight." *New York Times*, September 17, 2014. https://www.nytimes.com/2014/09/18/us/politics/house-vote-isis.html.

White, Brian. *Understanding European Foreign Policy.* Basingstoke, UK: Palgrave, 2001.

Whitlock, Craig. "U.S. Intensifies Its Proxy Fight against al-Shabab in Somalia." *Washington Post*, November 24, 2011. https://www.washingtonpost.com/world/national-security/us-intensifies-its-proxy-fight-against-al-shabab-in-somalia/2011/11/21/gIQAVLyNtN_story.html.

Whitty, Brendan, and Hamish Nixon. "The Impact of Counter-Terrorism Objectives on Democratization and Statebuilding in Afghanistan." *Taiwan Journal of Democracy* 5, no. 1 (2009): 187–218.

Wilder, Andrew. *Cops or Robbers? The Struggle to Reform the Afghan National Police.* Kabul: Afghanistan Research and Evaluation Unit, 2007.

Williams, Brian Glyn. "Fighting with a Double-Edged Sword? Proxy Militias in Iraq, Afghanistan, Bosnia, and Chechnya." In *Making Sense of Proxy Wars: States, Surrogates & the Use of Force*, edited by Michael A. Innes, 61–88. Washington, DC: Potomac Books, 2012.

Williams, David. "Aid and Sovereignty: Quasi-States and the International Financial Institutions." *Review of International Studies* 26, no. 4 (2000): 557–573. https://doi.org/10.1017/S026021050000557X.

Williams, Gareth D. "Piercing the Shield of Sovereignty: An Assessment of the Legal Status of the 'Unwilling or Unable' Test." *University of New South Wales Law Journal* 36, no. 2 (2013): 619–641.

Williamson, Oliver E. *The Economic Institutions of Capitalism: Firms, Markets, Relational Contracting.* New York: Free Press, 1985.

Wilson, Clay. *Improvised Explosive Devices (IEDs) in Iraq and Afghanistan: Effects and Countermeasures.* Washington, DC: Congressional Research Service, Library of Congress, 2007.

Witty, David. *The Iraqi Counter Terrorism Service.* Washington, DC: Brookings Institution, 2016.

Wood, Elisabeth Jean. "The Ethical Challenges of Field Research in Conflict Zones." *Qualitative Sociology* 29, no. 3 (2006): 373–386. https://doi.org/10.1007/S11133-006-9027-8.

———. "The Social Processes of Civil War: The Wartime Transformation of Social Networks." *Annual Review of Political Science* 11 (2008): 539–561. https://doi.org/10.1146/annurev.polisci.8.082103.104832.

Woodward, Bob. *Obama's Wars*. New York: Simon and Schuster, 2010.

Woodward, Susan L. "Compromised Sovereignty to Create Sovereignty: Is Dayton Bosnia a Futile Exercise or an Emerging Model?" In *Problematic Sovereignty: Contested Rules and Political Possibilities*, edited by Stephen Krasner, 252–300. New York: Columbia University Press, 2001.

———. *The Ideology of Failed States*. Cambridge: Cambridge University Press, 2017. https://doi.org/10.1017/9781316816936.

Woody, Christopher. "'A Fighting War with the Main Enemy': How the CIA Helped Land a Mortal Blow to the Soviets in Afghanistan 32 Years Ago." *Business Insider*, October 2, 2018. https://www.businessinsider.com/32-year-anniversary-of-first-stinger-missile-use-in-afghanistan-2018-9?r=US&IR=T.

World Bank. *Rebuilding Iraq: Economic Reform and Transition*. Washington, DC: Middle East and North Africa Region, World Bank, 2006.

Worth, Robert F. "Blast at Shiite Shrine Sets Off Sectarian Fury in Iraq." *New York Times*, February 23, 2006.

Wright, Austin. "Price Tag for Syrian Rebels: $4 Million Each." *Politico*, April 12, 2015. https://www.politico.eu/article/isil-isis-islmaic-state-price-tag-for-syrian-rebels-4-million-each-middle-east-conflict-fighters/.

Wright, Austin, and Philip Ewing. "Carter's Unwelcome News: Only 60 Syrian Rebels Fit for Training." *Politico*, July 7, 2015. https://www.politico.com/story/2015/07/ash-carter-syrian-rebel-training-119812.

Yacoubian, Mona. "Critical Junctures in United States Policy Toward Syria: An Assessment of the Counterfactuals." Simon-Skjodt Center for the Prevention of Genocide, Occasional Papers No. 3 (August 2017). https://www.ushmm.org/m/pdfs/Yacoubian-Critical-Junctures-US-Policy-Syria.pdf.

Youssef, Nancy A. "Syrian Rebels Describe U.S.-Backed Training in Qatar." *PBS Frontline*, May 26, 2014. https://www.pbs.org/wgbh/frontline/article/syrian-rebels-describe-u-s-backed-training-in-qatar/.

Zaum, Dominik. *The Sovereignty Paradox: The Norms and Politics of International Statebuilding*. Oxford: Oxford University Press, 2007. https://doi.org/10.1093/acprof:oso/9780199207435.001.0001.

INDEX

"01" and "02" forces (Afghanistan), 181–182, 184
127e fund, 3, 183–184, 188–189, 191, 248, 381–382
Abadi, Haider al-, 163, 168
Afghan Local Police (ALP), 3, 17, 19–20; Leahy Law application in, 201, 203–205, 210–212, 215; Monitoring and Investigation unit, 202–203; number of forces, 175, 347; summary chart of control mechanisms, 92–93
Afghan National Army Territorial Force (ANA-TF), 17–19, 174–180, 378; reflecting standard or "common approach" to controls, 192–193, 205, 252
Afghan National Auxiliary Police (ANAP), 82, 89
Afghan Public Protection Program (AP3), 81, 84
al Qaeda in Iraq (AQI), 68, 70–71, 74, 129, 162, 171, 173, 342
Allison, Graham: BPA theorization and writing, 12–13, 51–55, 91–94, 215; core versus ad hoc players, 57, 59, 218
Amnesty International, 145

Amri, Hadi al-, 166, 170
Anbar province, Iraq, 68, 72, 163; *sahwa* or "Awakening" forces, 68, 70, 342–344; TMF, 165–167, 169, 183, 374–375
anti-ballistic missile (ABM), 57
arbakai (Afghan tribal forces), viii, 82, 317
armed group typologies, 8–10, 17–19, 22–23
Assad, Bashar al-, 2, 102; chemical weapons use, 102, 118; regime/government of, 18, 108–110, 131, 134, 241
Atmar, Hanif, 84–86, 96, 226, 351, 394

Biden, Joe, 117, 274, 377
Bureau of Conflict and Stabilization Operations (CSO), U.S. State Department, 122–127, 156, 159, 160, 361
Bureau of Democracy, Rights, and Labor (DRL), U.S. State Department, 122–125, 204–209, 387
Bureau of Near Eastern Affairs (NEA), U.S. State Department, 122, 141, 361
bureaucratic policy analysis (BPA), 11–12, 51–52; change over time, theory of, 15, 33, 195–217, 258–259; Congress or legislative

bureaucratic policy analysis (BPA) (*continued*)
actors, role within, 12, 42, 56–60;
expanding BPA framework, 13, 30–33, 64, 218–238, 249–251, 258–259; future research directions, 260–264; organizational process or organizational theory within, 11–12, 32, 38, 53, 55, 64, 154, 156, 246–247, 255, 259; "stand-sit" positions, 52, 54, 83–84, 121–122, 141, 177, 226–227, 233
"by, with, and through" paradigm, 2–3, 54, 187, 256, 268

"campaign forces," in Afghanistan, 23, 181
Child Soldiers Prevention Act, 106, 146, 158
child soldiers: in Iraq, 167–168, 376, 390; regulatory controls regarding, 173, 246, 376, 390; in Syria, 104, 129, 146, 236
civilian deaths or civilian casualties: in Afghanistan, 79–80, 90, 182, 379, 384, 399; in Iraq, 67–68, 341; risk of, associated with LHSFs or irregular forces, 6, 10, 20–21, 49, 79–80, 111–112, 324; in Syria, 102, 108–109
Clinton, Hillary, 105, 109, 111, 116–117, 357
Commander's Emergency Response Program (CERP), 69, 343–344
compromised or shared sovereignty, 33–34, 62, 219, 228; Afghanistan and Iraq, 226–230, 237; BPA bargaining amidst, 62, 227, 228, 233, 234–235, 250, 263
control mechanisms: definitions and expectations for, 10, 43–45, 48–51; ALP, created for, 78, 81–82, 88–93; ANA-TF, created for, 176–178; evolution of common or standard controls for LHSFs, 32–33, 155, 161, 173–174, 192–194, 248; "fire alarms" versus "police patrols," 43–44, 48, 210, 212; in FSA covert assistance, 111–112; information asymmetries, 10, 42–44, 47–49, 50, 241–242, 274; in State Department nonlethal assistance, 122–126; in Syria Train and Equip initiatives, 129–132, 137–138, 142–144; TMF, created for, 165–168

counterinsurgency strategy or COIN, 2, 6, 173, 232, 342; in Afghanistan, viii, xi, 75, 77, 79–81, 87, 89, 347; in Iraq, 3, 68–70, 172, 347; local, community-based, or "hold" forces, relation to, 6, 9, 17, 36, 172–173, 189–191, 247
counterterrorism auxiliary forces, 17–21, 180–192
Counterterrorism Pursuit Teams, in Afghanistan, 23, 181, 184

death squads, 18, 23, 70, 182, 185
Designated Terrorist Organizations (DTOs), 105, 141, 157, 355; "material support" standard, 140, 143, 216, 355
disarmament initiatives, ix, x, 79, 86, 99, 351
drones or Unmanned Aerial Vehicles (UAVs), 2, 13; strikes by, 2, 166

Eikenberry, Karl: bargaining over ALP authorization, 27, 83–85, 90, 94- 99, 219; "stand-sit" positions, 349
ethics of research in conflict zones, 28–30

foreign policy analysis (FPA), 11–12, 38–39, 51–52, 58, 60, 62, 227, 258
foreign policy implementation, 33, 52, 58, 61–62, 121, 219, 222–223, 237, 262
France: Afghanistan, engagement in, 99; Special Forces operations worldwide, 35; Syrian forces support, 35, 103–104, 109, 111, 222, 390
Free Syrian Army (FSA), 18, 103–104; CIA lethal assistance to, 115–121, 188; "marbling" within, 26, 104, 146–147; "moderate" opposition,105–106, 110, 116, 127, 133; nonlethal assistance via State Department, 121–127; redlines, enforcement of, 7, 106, 112, 114, 125, 137, 222, 224, 242, 269, 363
Free Syrian Police, 224–225
Friends of Syria, 110, 122, 220, 361

Ghani, Ashraf, 174, 274

Halperin, Morton: BPA theorization and writing, 12–13, 52, 54, 91, 94, 115, 218; on congressional role in BPA, 54, 59
human rights advocates and NGOs, 197, 199, 211, 217; ALP controls and accountability, role in advocating, 196, 202, 205, 271; ALP debate, 89–90, 92, 94, 97, 244
human rights training and standards for LHSFs, x, 11, 78, 92, 166–167, 173, 176, 178, 184, 241, 252, 269
Human Rights Watch (HRW), x, 146, 199, 201, 205, 207
hybrid political orders or environments, 4–5, 8–9, 14–15; research implications for, 35–37, 251, 257–264

improvised explosive devices (IEDs), 67
International Committee of the Red Cross (ICRC), 199–200, 384
international humanitarian law (IHL) / Laws of Armed Conflict: due diligence obligations, xii; LHSF training on, x, 6, 79, 92, 105, 106, 158, 166–167, 173, 176, 178, 203, 246, 269; pledge for New Syrian Forces, based upon, 131–132, 137, 145, 252, 269
International Security Assistance Force (ISAF), 77, 86, 89–90, 95, 99–100, 201–202, 205, 221, 340
Iraqi National Guard, 73, 375
Islamic State in Khorasan (ISK), 175, 181
Islamic State of Iraq and the Levant (ISIL), xi, 2–3, 18; in Iraq, 163–164, 169, 171, 173; in Syria, 105, 122, 128, 130, 136, 140–141, 145–146, 236

Jabhat al-Nusra (the Nusra Front), 105, 110, 116, 118, 122, 130, 355, 364
Jordan, supporting role in Syria LHSF initiatives, 103, 111–112, 127, 222–223

Karzai, Hamid: in ALP authorization debate, 85–87, 96–97; as a bargaining player, analysis of, 218, 226, 231, 233–237, 244, 250, 351; civilian casualties, public advocacy on, 90, 384
Kobane, battle of, 136, 140–142, 368
Kurdish Regional Government (KRG), 163, 166–167, 170, 373, 390

Leahy Law, 33, 106, 122–124, 157–159, 176–177, 179–183, 201, 203–217, 249, 270–273, 362, 387; Afghanistan loopholes, 205, 270; ALP, as applied to, 201, 203–205, 210–212, 215; challenges to effective implementation, 123, 206, 209, 212, 269–273; CIA support, relevance to, 111, 120, 214, 372; database for, 123–124, 157, 204, 206, 208–209, 362; "gross violations of human rights" standard, 106, 123, 157, 168, 176, 179, 204, 208, 210–211; "Leahy Law–like" standards in Syria, 120, 123–125, 129, 133, 137, 145, 157–160, 183–184, 269; TMF, as applied to, 165, 167–168
legacy effects, 32, 101, 154, 162, 171, 174, 178–180, 192–193, 247
Libya: international intervention in, 109; militias or auxiliary forces within, 2–3, 35, 109, 260, 329
Local Defense Initiative (LDI) in Afghanistan, 81, 83–84, 86, 93, 350
local, tribal, or community-based forces, 1, 3, 8, 17–18, 22–23, 191; in Afghanistan, 1, 3, 9, 17–18, 76, 354; in Iraq, 1, 3, 9, 17–18; rationales for reliance on, 5, 9; risks associated with, 9–10; in the Sahel, 36; in Somalia, 36; in northern Syria, 18, 146–147
logic of appropriateness, 159, 173, 179

Maliki, Nouri al-, 72–75, 96–97, 100–101, 144, 162, 168, 187, 244, 267, 373, 377; player in transnational bargaining, 218, 226, 233–237, 250; sectarian policies and affiliations, 67, 373, 377

McChrystal, Stanley, 77, 79, 80, 83, 86, 99, 233, 347
McGurk, Brett, 141, 377
McMaster, H.R., 27, 342
Military Operation Center (MOC), 111–114, 222–224
Miller, "Scottie," vii, x, 90, 175
moral hazards, and control mechanisms, 43, 151, 153, 274
Muhandis, Abu Mehdi al-, 166, 170
mujahideen (Afghan), viii, 6, 105, 158
Müşterek Operasyon Merkezi (MOM), 111–113, 222–224

Nagata, Mike, 129, 130, 158
New Syrian Forces, 127–135; train-and-equip funding for, 128–129, 131; pledge of conduct, 131–132, 137, 145, 252, 269; selection against "anti-Assad" motivations, 131–133, 244
nighttime or counterterrorism raids, viii, 180–182, 349, 384
nonintervention, principle of, 104, 364
nonlethal assistance in Syria, 102–104, 110; European countries' provision of, 35, 103, 222, 225, 395; Free Syrian Police and related assistance, 224–225; types of, 104, 354; standard-setting and legacy effects of, 129, 133, 156–157, 160–161; State Department provision of, 117, 121–127, 156–159, 242, 357–358, 361, 363
North Atlantic Treaty Organization (NATO), 1, 35, 201; in Afghanistan, 1, 82, 89, 91, 94, 232, 340; consultative norms within, 61–62, 221

Partîya Karkerên Kurdistanê (PKK) (Kurdistan Workers' Party), 103, 106, 136, 140, 142, 163, 255
People's Protection Units (Yekîneyên Parastina Gel, or YPG), 136, 142, 144
Peshmerga (Kurdish), 163, 373
Petraeus, David, 27, 36, 77, 98–99; ALP, viii, 86–87; CIA covert support to FSA, 116–117;

Field Manual, 3–24 / COIN theory, 68; future of local force initiatives, 27; *sahwa* or Sons of Iraq, 69–72, 187, 233, 345
policy assemblage, in social movement theory, 196, 206–208, 211, 217, 383
Popular Mobilization Forces (PMF) or Hashd ash-Shaabi, 163–164, 373; designated terrorist organizations or individuals, link with, 374; legal status, 165, 374–375; number of forces, 164, 374; TMF control mechanisms, role in, 166, 167, 169–171, 267, 377
principal-agent theory, 8–10, 42–45; adverse selection, 43–48, 50, 241; agent slack, 10, 42–50; comparative application, Afghanistan versus Iraq, 77–80, 95–96; complex principal, 45, 49, 133; explanatory value for controls, conclusions regarding, 240–246; delegation of security tasks, 42, 46–47, 64, 185; future research directions, 257–259, 262; *sahwa* case study, application to, 72–75; Syria control mechanisms, alignment with, 106–107, 114, 126, 149
Provincial Reconstruction Teams (PRTs), in Afghanistan, 76, 99–100, 230
proxy relationships or proxies, 1–3; case study examples of, 22–23, 35, 138, 139, 391; Iranian use of, 261–262; theoretical assumptions surrounding, xii, 10, 46, 261–263; Turkey's use of, 138–139; United States' use of, 2–3, 13, 262, 265–267, 321
proxy warfare, 9, 36–37; principal-agent theory, linkage with, 42, 258; theory and assumptions of, 10, 14, 30, 36–38, 260–262; United States' approach to, 2–3, 13, 261, 265–267

Qatar, role in Syria LHSF initiatives, 103, 110–111, 113, 222, 261

Resolute Support (RS) mission, Afghanistan, 174–175, 177–178, 181
Rishawi, Abu Satar al-, 68–70, 343

INDEX   405

sahwa forces or Sons of Iraq, 3, 17, 19, 66–75, 245; control mechanisms, 70–74; creation of, 68–69; dissolution, 74, 169; legacy effects, 101, 162–164, 168–175, 192, 247; number of forces, 69, 347

Samarra, al-Askari Mosque bombing, 67

Saudi Arabia, in relation to Syrian armed group support, 103, 111, 222, 261

sectarian violence or abuses in Iraq, 66–67, 169, 341; Iraqi forces implicated in, 67, 162, 169, 341, 373

security assistance (U.S.), 21, 39, 61, 263, 397; principal-agent theories, association with, 10, 30, 46–49, 240; standard protocols and practices within, 111, 124, 129–131, 147, 157–159, 207–209, 216, 246, 263, 397; Syria, 111, 124, 129–131

state-building, 4–5; Afghanistan, ix, 16–17, 76, 86, 221–222, 224, 346; "bottom-up," 5–6, 76, 79, 264; in Iraq, 16–17; liberal peace model, critiques of, 4–5, 346; local forces, link with, 190–191, 222, 252–253; neo-Weberian expectations of, ix, 4, 78, 228

Syrian Democratic Forces (SDF), 18–19, 105–106, 139–148, 254–255, 356, 368; as bargaining player or co-participant, 147–148, 234–238, 250; child soldier allegations, regarding, 146, 236; DTO and "material support" risks, 140–143; external support (non-U.S.), 35; ISIL affiliation, scrutiny for, 236; renaming or rebranding of, 20, 140, 356; "self-defense" units within, 18, 146–147; Syrian Democratic Council (SDC), 235

TOW (tube-launched, optically tracked, wireless-guided) missiles, xi, 111–113, 158, 253

Turkey: player in bargaining, 222–223, 234–238, 243, 250; proxy forces, 139, 261–262; SDF, opposition to, 105–106, 139–148, 151–152, 222–223, 254–255, 266;

Syria policies and armed group support, 22, 34, 110, 139, 220, 370; U.S.-led LHSF initiatives, support to, 103, 110–112, 127–128, 135–139, 157

transnational advocacy actors and networks: ALP and human rights controls, involvement in, 89–91, 198–204; as bargaining players, 89–91, 94–95, 211–212, 217, 219–220, 225, 249; foreign policy, role in, 60–61, 195–196, 198, 259; Leahy Law revision and implementation, 204–214; Syria policy, 220–221

Tribal Mobilization Forces (TMF), 17–19, 162–180, 251–252, 264, 266–267; congressional support for, 171–172, 377; control mechanisms within TMF, 165–168, 375–376; counterterrorism auxiliaries, overlap with, 182–183; Leahy Law applicability within, 165, 167–168, 270, 374–375; numbers within, 165, 374; training by international forces, 35, 166–167, 183, 375

troop withdrawal (U.S.): from Afghanistan, 16, 36, 181, 209, 271, 274, 387; from Iraq, 73, 97, 162, 169; Syria, announcement of, 142, 397

Trump Administration, 174, 180, 248, 379

Trump, Donald: CIA lethal assistance, ending of, 356; SDF assistance, reducing, 142, 368

U.S. Special Forces or Special Operations Forces (SOF), 2–4, 13, 32; ALP and other Afghan community forces, vii–x, 78, 81–92, 94, 100, 201–203, 233, 348, 350, 353–354, 383, 387; Iraq, 18, 163, 176, 381; irregular auxiliary or proxy forces, partnering with, 2–4, 18, 155, 180–193, 265, 266; scope of operations worldwide, 2–4, 187; Syria, 265, 368; White SOF, 54, 83, 349

UNAMA, 89, 100, 178, 199–200, 202, 205, 347

United Arab Emirates, support to Syria LHSF initiatives, 111, 222

United Kingdom: Afghan tribal forces, support for, 35, 82; Special Forces or intelligence operatives worldwide, 35; Syrian forces support, 35, 103–104, 109, 111, 222–223, 395

United Nations due diligence policy, 35, 261

vetting standards for LHSFs, xi-xiii; community-based, in Afghanistan, x, 81–82; Counterterrorism or "CT" 165, 172, 179–180, 216–217; double or triple vetting (in Syria), 26, 125; human rights or conduct-based, x, 94, 119, 171, 179, 182–183, 193, 202–205; for "Islamist" ideologies (in Syria), 113, 129, 138, 140, 147, 242; in NDAA legislation (Iraq and Syria), 131, 137, 143, 165, 167; Principal-Agent theory expectations, 48–50

Village Stability Operations, 83

war crimes or human rights abuses: Afghan militias or LHSFs, concerns regarding, viii-x, 75–76, 79–80, 86, 182; counter-terrorism auxiliary forces, association with, 181–185; redlines and funding cuts due to, 7, 106, 112, 114, 126–127, 211; risks of, with regard to LHSFs, 6, 9–10, 224, 254, 269–270; in Syria, risks of, 104, 116, 122, 186, 224, 265

Yekîneyên Parastina Gel (People's Protection Units)(YPG), 136–137, 140, 142, 144, 152

Zenki group or al-Zenki group, 112, 358

Printed and bound by CPI Group (UK) Ltd, Croydon, CR0 4YY
11/07/2024